The Sociology of Childhood and Youth in Canada

The Sociology of Childhood and Youth in Canada

Edited by Xiaobei Chen, Rebecca Raby, and Patrizia Albanese

CANADIAN
SCHOLARS

Toronto | Vancouver

The Sociology of Childhood and Youth in Canada
Edited by Xiaobei Chen, Rebecca Raby, and Patrizia Albanese

First published in 2017 by
Canadian Scholars
425 Adelaide Street West, Suite 200
Toronto, Ontario
M5V 3C1

www.canadianscholars.ca

Library and Archives Canada Cataloguing in Publication

The sociology of childhood and youth in Canada / edited by Xiaobei Chen, Rebecca Raby, and Patrizia Albanese.

Includes bibliographical references.
Issued in print and electronic formats.
ISBN 978-1-77338-018-6 (softcover).--ISBN 978-1-77338-019-3 (PDF).--
ISBN 978-1-77338-020-9 (EPUB)

1. Children--Canada--Social conditions. I. Chen, Xiaobei, 1969-, editor II. Raby, Rebecca, 1968-, editor III. Albanese, Patrizia, editor

HQ767.9.C3S63 2017   305.230971   C2017-906829-6
                                                C2017-906830-X

Text and cover design by Elisabeth Springate
Cover image by Elizabeth Lei Chen-Baker (age 10), *Our World* (2017)

17 18 19 20 21   5 4 3 2 1

Printed and bound in Canada by Webcom.

MIX
Paper from
responsible sources
FSC® C004071

CONTENTS

Section III—Inequalities and Intersections in Experiences of Childhood and Youth

Section IV—Citizenship, Rights, and Social Engagement

CONTRIBUTORS

Jihan Abbas holds a PhD in sociology (Carleton University). She was an inaugural Vanier Canada Graduate scholar. Her research interests include disability policy, activism, and inclusion. Jihan has been involved in the disability movement for several years in both a personal and professional capacity.

Patrizia Albanese is a Professor of Sociology at Ryerson University and a past president of the Canadian Sociological Association. She is currently Chair of the Research Ethics Board at Ryerson University. Her research interests are in the area of Canadian policies affecting children, youth, and families, with a recent focus on adolescents in Canadian Armed Forces families and child care in Canada.

Nicole Andrejek is a doctoral student in sociology at McMaster University. She is interested in the intersections of youth, gender, and sexuality. Her dissertation explores young adult women's experiences with love and dating in a digital age. She is also interested in how social and sexual norms were communicated in classic children's literature.

Nathalie Bélanger is a Full Professor at the University of Ottawa (Faculty of Education) and University Chair of Education and Francophonie. Her research interests are on the issues of inclusion/exclusion and marginalization experienced by children and youth and their families, and also include minority and Francophone studies. She is a member of the Laboratoire de recherche interdisciplinaire sur les droits de l'enfant/Interdisciplinary Research Laboratory on the Rights of the Child (LRIDE-IRLRC) and member of the Laboratoire international sur l'inclusion scolaire (LISIS).

Rachel Berman is currently an Associate Professor and the Graduate Program Director in the School of Early Childhood Studies at Ryerson University. She is the editor of *Corridor Talk: Canadian Feminist Scholars Share Stories of Research Partnerships*, published by Inanna Publications in 2014.

Xiaobei Chen is an Associate Professor and the Graduate Coordinator for Sociology in the Department of Sociology and Anthropology at Carleton University. Her research examines the governance of child-centred problems in their articulation with citizenship, neoliberalism, race, colonialism, and postcoloniality. Her work includes *Tending the Gardens of Citizenship: Child Saving in Toronto, 1880s–1920s* (2005).

Natalie Coulter is currently an Assistant Professor in Communication Studies at York University. Her book *Tweening the Girl: The Crystallization of the Tween Market* was published in Peter Lang's Mediated Youth series in 2014. She has published in the *Canadian Journal of Communication, Journal of Children and Media*, and *Jeunesse*. She is a founding member of ARCYP (Association for Research on the Cultures of Young People).

Adam Davies is a PhD Student in the Department of Curriculum, Teaching and Learning at the Ontario Institute for Studies in Education (OISE) of the University of Toronto. His doctoral research explores the ways queer politics are imagined within the newly reformed sexual health curriculum and within sexual education in elementary and secondary schools. His recent publications in the *Canadian Journal of Human Sexuality* and *Canadian Journal of Action Research* explore the implementation of sexuality education in early childhood, and the experiences of trans youth in gendered washrooms.

Diane Farmer is an Associate Professor in the Department of Social Justice Education and member of the Centre de recherche en education franco-ontarienne at the Ontario Institute for Studies in Education (OISE) of the University of Toronto. She is interested in how children make sense of the(ir) world(s). She integrates creative visual methods in doing school ethnographies.

Marnina Gonick is a Professor of Education and Women's Studies and Canada Research Chair at Mount Saint Vincent University. Her current research interests are in the areas of girl studies, identity, visual culture, feminist cultural studies, gender and schooling, feminist pedagogies, feminist poststructural theory, and feminist qualitative research.

Christine Goodwin-DeFaria is a PhD candidate in the Policy Studies program at Ryerson University. She completed her master's and bachelor's degrees in Child and Youth Studies at Brock University. Christine's PhD research examines the experiences of accused Aboriginal youth at various courthouses in the Greater Toronto Area, including Canada's first and only Aboriginal Youth Court. Christine previously worked as a youth diversion coordinator and also as a residential counsellor in a youth custody facility.

Cameron Greensmith is currently an Assistant Professor in the Department of Social Work and Human Services at Kennesaw State University. His research explores the various and complex ways queer politics are embedded within the larger colonial structure in North America. Paying particular attention to queer and trans youth activism, his most recent scholarship addresses how Gay-Straight Alliances (GSAs) might reinforce and reproduce normativity as they attempt to work against heterosexist and cis-sexist oppression that young people face. He is currently working on a manuscript titled *Unsettling Queer Complicity: Whiteness and Settler Colonialism in the Queer Service Sector.*

Nathan Innocente is an Assistant Professor (Teaching) in the Department of Sociology at the University of Toronto Mississauga. His research on youth punishment explores the role of local structures and cultures on the implementation of youth justice legislation, and uses youth sanctions to study the role of the community in criminal justice. In addition, he is engaged in ongoing research on fraud and organizations that brings together elements of institutionalism, identity crime, and strain to explain the perpetration of mortgage fraud and the ways in which fraud is used to achieve home ownership.

Noah Kenneally is a contract lecturer at Ryerson University's School of Early Childhood Studies and a doctoral candidate in the Department of Humanities, Social Sciences and Social Justice Education at the Ontario Institute for Studies in Education (OISE) of the University of Toronto. His research focuses on children's perspectives of their social worlds.

Jacqueline Kennelly is an Associate Professor in the Department of Sociology and Anthropology at Carleton University. She is the author of numerous publications, including *Olympic Exclusions: Youth, Poverty, and Social Legacies* (2016) and *Citizen Youth: Culture, Activism, and Agency in a Neoliberal Era* (2011).

Kate MacDonald, MA in Social Justice and Equity Studies, BA in Child and Youth Studies, is a social activist focusing on children's agency and promoting community engagement for young people as a way of addressing systemic inequalities. Kate's research explores children's experiences in outdoor learning environments.

Maggie MacNevin completed her BA in Child and Youth Studies at Mount Saint Vincent University in Halifax, Nova Scotia, and has worked as an Early Childhood Educator (ECE) since 2008. She has worked in preschool education, family resources, and most recently as a toddler teacher. She earned her MA in Early Childhood Studies at Ryerson University in 2014.

Voula Marinos is an Associate Professor at the Department of Child and Youth Studies, Brock University. Her research includes youth criminal justice diversion, court processes, and sentencing; plea bargaining practices for both adults and youth; and court adaptations for persons with intellectual disabilities.

L. Alison Molina-Girón is an Assistant Professor in the Faculty of Education at the University of Regina, where she teaches courses on social justice education. Her current SSHRC research program investigates the civic and political engagement of Canadian youth. Alison is a member of the Saskatchewan Citizenship Education Advisory Committee responsible for the province's new K–12 citizenship education program.

Shauna Pomerantz is an Associate Professor in the Department of Child and Youth Studies at Brock University. Her research focuses on girls' negotiations of identity through the lenses of feminist poststructuralism and new materialism. She is author of *Girls, Style, and School Identities: Dressing the Part* and co-author of *'Girl Power': Girls Reinventing Girlhood*. Her latest book (with Rebecca Raby) is entitled *Smart Girls: Success, School, and the Myth of Post-Feminism*.

Rebecca Raby is a sociologist and a Professor in the Department of Child and Youth Studies at Brock University. Her research and publications address regulation, resistance, and inequality in young people's lives. She has authored *School Rules: Obedience, Discipline, and Elusive Democracy* (UTP) and S*mart Girls: Success, School, and the Myth of Post-Feminism* (University of California Press) (with Shauna Pomerantz), and co-edited the textbook *Power and Everyday Practices* (Nelson) (with Debi Brock and Mark Thomas).

Lynette Schick is a recent graduate of the Master of Social Work program at Carleton University. Lynette has front-line and research experience working within homeless, substance-using, and sex-worker communities across Canada. Lynette is committed to anti-poverty and anti-colonial practices as well as to the principles of harm reduction.

Cornelia Schneider is an Associate Professor at Mount Saint Vincent University in Halifax, Nova Scotia. Her main research interests focus on children and youth with disabilities and inclusive education. Originally from Germany, she completed her PhD at the University of Paris Descartes (Sorbonne), studying peer relationships of children with and without disabilities.

Erwin Dimitri Selimos is an instructor of sociology at Lansing Community College in Michigan, US. His research focuses on the sociology of childhood and youth and the sociology of migration.

Raven Sinclair, BA, CISW, BISW, MSW, PhD, is a Cree/Assiniboine/Saulteaux adoptee from Gordon First Nation in Treaty 4 territory located in southern Saskatchewan. Raven is presently an Associate Professor at the University of Regina, Faculty of Social Work in Saskatoon, a founding editorial member of the *Journal of Indigenous Voices in Social Work* (University of Hawaii), and a regional editor for *AlterNative: An International Journal of Indigenous Peoples*. Raven's academic and research interests include traditional and contemporary healing theories and modalities, Indigenous cultural identity issues, adoption, colonial and decolonization theories, and mental health and wellness.

Dale C. Spencer, BA, MA, PhD, is a criminologist and socio-legal studies scholar and an Assistant Professor in the Department of Law and Legal Studies at the Carleton University. His main interests are violence, victimization, policing, and the criminalization of marginalized populations, with a specific focus on youth and homeless people.

Anuppiriya Sriskandarajah teaches in the Pauline Jewett Institute of Women's and Gender Studies at Carleton University. Her research interests include citizenship, gender, youth social movements, racialization and space, and youth claims to the city.

Valerie Stam is a PhD candidate in the Department of Sociology and Anthropology at Carleton University. Her research focuses on the intersection of Islamophobia and racism, comparing the impact of municipal policies in Ottawa and The Hague. Valerie co-edited *Generation NGO*, a collection of essays by Canadian youth working in International Development.

Cheryl Williams is a PhD candidate in the Communication and Culture program at York University. Her chapter in *Girls' Economies* (Forman-Brunell and Anselmo-Sequeira [Eds.]) undertakes a critical analysis of girls' mobile apps and connected toys to generate awareness of how companies are mobilizing children's immaterial labour in the digital age. Prior to graduate school, Cheryl spent 12 years working in digital and social media marketing in Canada's technology sector, and this experience continues to uniquely flavour her academic research.

Introduction: Taking Stock and Claiming Space for the Sociology of Childhood and Youth in Canada

Xiaobei Chen, Rebecca Raby, and Patrizia Albanese

LEARNING OBJECTIVES

- To situate the sociology of childhood and youth in Canada within international and Canadian scholarship on and with young people
- To frame childhood and youth studies around four key themes: engaging children and youth in research; conceptualizing childhood and youth as social constructs; keeping sight of social inequalities and their intersections; and highlighting children's citizenship, rights, and social engagement
- To highlight key topics in the sociology of child and youth studies in Canada, from children's innovative, art-based research strategies to experiences of poverty and racism

THE CURRENT STATE OF RESEARCH AND THEORIZING IN THE SOCIOLOGY OF CHILDHOOD AND YOUTH IN CANADA

Canada's poverty "report card" recently delivered the bleak news that child poverty rates are on the rise and are disproportionately high among **Indigenous** children (Kohut, 2015). We are often reminded of child poverty during the many toy drives in the holiday season, but in December 2015, some of those stories were overshadowed by the marketing campaign for "Elf on the Shelf." This pre-holiday phenomenon has an elf toy (purchased by parents) hiding in a new location each day (with a parent's help), spying on children and reporting to Santa each night on the children's behaviour. Elf on the Shelf provoked questions about whether it perpetuates intensive parenting (Henwood and Coltart, 2012), extreme marketing to children, and/or the normalization of surveillance in children's lives (Buck, 2015; John, 2015). Yet others mounted a staunch defence of the Elf on the Shelf, seeing it as a growing, fun family tradition (Schoepflin, 2015). Children too have opinions about toys, and many other aspects of their lives. For instance, in 2014, seven-year-old Charlotte sparked debate about the gendering of toys when she wrote a letter to Lego regarding the lack of female characters, especially those who "go on adventure, work, save people, and have jobs, even swim with sharks" (Bowman, 2014). Many people were impressed with her intervention, and some agreed that toys are overly gendered.

In part, these debates are about what **childhood** is or what it should look like. Similar concerns arise around **youth**. Who should be included under the category of youth, what is unique about this group, and should we be concerned about them? Are they fine as they are? **At risk?** Trouble-makers in need of more discipline? In November 2015, in response to a spate of vandalism, the community of La Ronge, Saskatchewan, dusted off an old curfew for anyone under 18, keeping them at home between 11 p.m. and 6 a.m. (Allen, 2015), thus suggesting that teenagers are a problem in need of greater control. Yet teens are also responsible, valuable participants in Canadian society. We see this in the actions of Nekiiyaa Noakes, a young Anishnaabe woman and a grade 11 student at Manitoulin Secondary School, who spoke out on Facebook against her school staff's anti-Indigenous attitudes. Noakes's actions alerted the public's attention to racism against Indigenous students that did not end with the closure of residential schools (Neigh, 2015). Many other youth are busy fighting for environmental and other issues (e.g. Macgregor, 2015), volunteering many hours of their time (e.g. see Molina-Girón's chapter 19), as well as going to school, participating in extracurricular activities, and working part-time.

These wide-ranging stories suggest that there are many dimensions to childhood and youth in Canada, both in terms of the meaning we give to these concepts and how they are lived by a diversity of young people. It is these kinds of stories that inspire the work of those studying the **sociology of childhood** and youth. What beliefs do Canadians hold about children and youth? What are young people's lives like in Canada? How do we know when something is fun or valuable, or when it becomes harmful or troublesome? When are actions needed to protect young people, and why is it that such actions are so often inseparable from control? When should young people have a say, and how can we better value and hear them when they speak out?

It is widely recognized that childhood and youth studies are multidisciplinary and interdisciplinary (Alanen, Brooker, & Mayall, 2015; Corsaro, Qvortrup, & Honig, 2009; Prout, 2011); childhood and youth research has increasingly appeared across a range of disciplines, including history, sociology, anthropology, geography, education, and social work. The expanding institutionalization of childhood and youth studies through interdisciplinary degree programs and research centres testifies to the widespread interest in the field, as well as to the rich work it has produced. That said, in this collection, we take a specifically sociological approach in which we focus on how the seemingly private experiences of children and youth are connected to large-scale societal processes and social structures. This sociological approach is taken up in this collection by contributors whose academic homes lie both inside and outside of traditional sociology departments, reminding us that it is an approach that can also inform a diversity of disciplines and related professions.

Children and youth navigate between adult authority, mutual dependency, and individual autonomy, as well as hierarchies among themselves. A focus on this interplay has underpinned child and youth studies in sociology since the 1980s, a field of study that surged out of countries such as the United Kingdom, Finland, and Australia. Prior to this, within sociology, children were primarily treated as passive recipients of **care** and socialization in the family and other social institutions because mainstream sociology had, with some notable exceptions, been interested in adulthood (Mayall, 2015). Youth, in contrast, were scrutinized largely through the lenses of risk, potential delinquency, and associated youth subcultures (Widdicombe & Wooffitt, 1995). Only recently, with the new sociology of childhood, has the lens really widened to encapsulate a broad diversity of aspects of young people's lives, and shifted towards conceptualizing children and youth as social actors and subjects in their own right (Alanen et al., 2015; Prout, 2011). Furthermore, only recently has childhood been treated as a structural dimension of significance similar to other dimensions such as class, gender, and race.

In Canada, until the 1990s, the bulk of research about children and youth took place within developmental psychology, education, anthropology, or history. Within sociology itself, concern with children was most commonly covered through education, family, and criminological studies. We are now seeing an exciting increase in Canadian research and publishing in the sociology of childhood and youth as a field in itself. This research and theorizing—a key focus in this book—is largely informed by a premise that children and youth should be studied in their own right, using a broadly constructionist orientation that prioritizes context, with attention to noting and addressing intersecting inequalities, and a commitment to respecting and understanding young people's **agency**—or the capacity to act in a given context in order to respond to and shape the world around them. Within this framework, Canadian scholarship reflects a breadth of theorizing including critical theory, feminist theory, phenomenology, poststructuralism, de-colonial and postcolonial theory, citizenship studies, **queer** theory, and critical disability studies, as demonstrated by various chapters in this anthology.

A collection highlighting some recent Canadian developments in this area is certainly overdue, and responds to a need for greater attention to the sociology of childhood and youth in Canada. This anthology evolved out of the Children, Childhood and Youth Research Cluster's sessions at the Canadian Sociological Association meeting in June 2015. Contributors include many who presented their work at those sessions and others who are doing interesting and important research in this area and were able to take part in our project. Highlighting Canadian sociological work on a wide range of topics related to childhood and youth, this collection is concerned with foregrounding four key analytical themes and associated concepts, all of which are united by an interest in social justice: research on and with children and youth; childhood and youth as social constructs; inequalities and intersections in the experiences of childhood and youth; and child and youth **citizenship**, **rights**, and engagement.

RESEARCH ON AND WITH CHILDREN AND YOUTH

Imagine if we did research on women by only asking men's opinions and insights? Or research on men, only asking women? Most of us would discount that work as invalid, anecdotal, nonsensical, or biased. But we have, to date, had no problem when the lives of young people are studied from the point of view of adults.

Looking back historically, children, for the most part, have been ignored as objects of study in the social sciences. While more attention has been paid to children and childhood in some disciplines and in recent years, children themselves seldom have been the subjects of research, and to this day, are rarely asked to provide insight into their own lives. Youth, while somewhat more likely to be consulted directly, have been either treated as adults, or research on them has taken a problem-centred approach, compartmentalizing young people's lives into discrete "youth issues," often resulting in inaccurately and narrowly defining "youth as problem" (Wyn and White, 1998). Overall, much of what we have known about the lives of young people has come from adults, either reflecting upon their own experiences growing up, or reporting on the experiences of young people for whom they have responsibility. While this "adult-focused" research may be valuable, and at times necessary, it also limits or filters our understanding of children, childhood, and youth (Mahon, Glendinning, Clarke, & Craig, 1996).

Excluding young people from the research process has happened, in part, because as a society we continue to view children and youth as variably innocent, naïve, vulnerable, special, incapable, or as risk. Orellana (2001) noted that the exclusion of young people from the research process points to our belief that they are incomplete adults or adults in the making (see also Grover, 2004). Some have noted that children have not participated in research because of **power** differences between them and adult researchers, and for fear that they will be intimidated or coerced in their diminished social position. Young people's participation in research can be daunting, as power differences between the "expert" or researcher and the young person can and do reflect well-established hierarchies and cultural differences between young people and adults (Christensen, 2004). However, excluding them from research simply reinforces their powerlessness and acts to further marginalize them.

As we will see in various chapters in this collection, greater efforts are now being made to involve young people, as subjects, contributors, and participants in—rather than objects of—the research process. Some, like Farmer, in chapter 2, are including young people as reliable informants on their own experiences—as co-constructors of meaning and understanding (Mason & Danby, 2011; Tay-Lim & Lim, 2013). But often, when researchers begin conceptualizing research with children and youth, they encounter colleagues, ethics boards, or organizations responsible for young people, such as school boards or community organizations, with questions about young people's ability to know, understand, and talk about social phenomena. Many are especially questioned about younger children's ability to understand notions like "consent," "confidentiality," and the importance of the voluntary nature of participating (or not) in research. Yet some pioneers in this evolving area of inquiry have shown us that young people, including younger children, are concerned with and aware of the importance of privacy in research (Christensen, 2004; Hill, 2006). Similarly, research by Covell, Howe, and McNeil (2008) notes that young children can and do understand their rights and responsibilities in real, applied, and meaningful ways. Christensen (2004) reminds us that children are aware of the possible exploitation or misuse of their personal information, and of the importance of confidentiality, because this is already part of children's worlds. This is especially true today, given how notions of privacy have gained prominence with the ubiquitous presence of the Internet in young people's lives. While their understanding may vary greatly depending on their individual experiences, even very young children are increasingly aware of whom they should and should not speak to, whom to trust and confide in, and what to report to adult authority figures.

Over a decade ago, Danby and Farrell (2004) challenged us to overcome some of our stereotypical and normative assumptions that young people are incompetent, that adults know best, and that adults are always out to protect the interests of young people. Authors in this collection recognize that young people are similar to adults in some ways, but that they also possess different competencies, identities, social locations, and sets of experiences. This insight challenges us to develop new and wide-ranging innovative research tools and techniques, using pictures, diaries, sentence completion, iPads, photo elicitation, dolls, or props (Mason and Danby, 2011; Pyle, 2013; Rowsell & Harwood, 2015; Shaw, Brady, & Davey, 2011; Teachman & Gibson, 2013), or, as we will see in chapter 2 by Farmer and chapter 4 by Gonick, creative visual methods and art-based methodologies, such as digital narratives, collages, painting, and drama, to provide young people's "insider accounts" of their sociocultural knowledge and experiences. Authors like Kennelly, Stam, and Schick, in chapter 5, challenge us to explore the complicated research relationships between academics and nonacademics in the spaces, groups, and organizations that young people inhabit (see chapter 3 by MacDonald). These more child- and youth-centred orientations and methods force us as researchers to explore, to reflect upon, and to understand young people's social locations, as we simultaneously critically assess our own assumptions about ourselves as researchers and about the children and youth we include in research and seek to understand. Chapter 1 by Berman and MacNevin and chapter 5 by Kennelly, Stam, and Schick also remind us of the importance of identifying institutional barriers, negotiating access to spaces occupied by children and youth, and reconceptualizing our own social position as researchers in relation to our young research participants. While this is indeed challenging, if we succeed at doing this effectively, we may find that there is a great deal to learn about young people and, more importantly, from them.

CHILDHOOD AND YOUTH AS SOCIAL CONSTRUCTS

For many scholars doing research on and with children and youth, childhood and youth are understood to be social constructs. Social construction is one of the most influential concepts of the past few decades in the social sciences. It is also controversial and often misunderstood; and to add to the confusion, some scholars who take a constructionist approach do not necessarily apply the label to their work. Prominent Canadian philosopher Ian Hacking offered helpful clarifications when he famously asked, "the social construction of what?" (1999). Hacking explained that when we talk about the social construction of something, it really refers to the social construction of the *idea* of that something. We agree. In this collection, we too are referring to the social construction of ideas about childhood and youth. While the life cycle—maturing from young to old—is a naturally occurring phenomenon, when childhood and youth begin and end, what meaning we give them, and what constitutes the "content" of these categories, including ideas about how lives should be lived during childhood and youth, have varied historically, geographically, socially, and culturally, and are always contested.

Ideas arise in particular social settings. To scholars who adopt a social constructionist perspective, one crucial aspect of analysis is to explore the ideas of childhood and youth within their associated social settings. This means understanding how the social meanings and statuses of childhood and youth are influenced by forces that transcend a specific individual or family, to include industrialization, colonialism, racism, patriarchal dominance, regulation of sexuality, class inequalities, nationalism, technological transformation, war, and so on. Many scholars consider these forces by examining **discourses**, or logics, about a topic that powerfully define how we think and talk about it, as well as by studying relationships, networks, and **materiality**, or the material components of social life, including nature, bodies, devices, artifacts, or architectural structures (Prout, 2011). Ideas about childhood and youth, and the practices informed by them, in turn shape society's institutions, social relations, and norms (James, Jenks, & Prout, 1998; James & Prout, 1997; Jenks, 1982, 1990; Stephens, 1995). Social constructionism thus directs scholars to be skeptical and critical about notions that have been taken for granted. It reminds us that, for instance, the notion of the **"best interests of the child"** and its meanings are not fixed and self-evident across settings, but rather that this idea is a product of particular changing historical and ideological conditions (Stephens, 1995; Woodhead, 2005). For example, in Canada since the mid-nineteenth century, "growing up" has come to be understood primarily as the process of becoming a good citizen and a capable worker. The discourse of young people as "future citizens" thus powerfully shaped Canadian society through the institutionalization of education and child protection—processes that have, in turn, reinforced this focus on children as "developing" or "becoming" (see Gleason 2001; Chen, 2005; Osborne, 2000; Stanbridge, 2007; Wotherspoon, 2006) and have raised debates about whether public institutions really perpetuate or challenge inequality. Bélanger (chapter 7) focuses on some of these challenges in education when she examines children's engagement with processes of inclusion and exclusion in three urban French-language schools in Ontario. The fraught nature of educational processes is also evident in Raby and Pomerantz's chapter 15 on student protests against dress codes.

Relationality is another important element of constructionist analysis. This means that the terms *childhood*, *youth*, and *adulthood* are best understood with regard to their interrelatedness. As early as the 1980s, Jens Qvortrup (1985) argued for the importance of studying childhood in connection to adulthood. Alanen and colleagues' (2015) work similarly considers the central role of generational relations in defining childhood. Some scholars extend their concern with relationality further, asking how categories of childhood, youth, and adulthood are formed hierarchically and in relation to each other, and examining such constructions' concrete consequences. One example can be found in the discourses on "victimized children" that have dominated recent public policy agendas. In poor households often headed by single women, mothers tend to be seen, problematically, as perpetrators of neglect, and children as their victims, when really these are families who together experience the challenge of poverty (Chen, 2008; Little, 2012; Little & Morrison, 1999; Swift, 1995). In another example, the theme of relationality is taken up by Abbas (chapter 6), who critically assesses the dominant social construction of sibling relationships that assumes the presence of a disabled child as disrupting the family and preventing the siblings from having a "normal childhood."

In constructionist analysis, it is also important to consider the processes involved in **subject formation**, or, more precisely, in how individuals are made social (Gonick & Gannon, 2014), come to think about themselves in certain ways, and internalize dominant ideas such as "children should go to school" or "girls should wear their hair long." A social constructionist approach aims to reveal the exercise of power in this process of producing individuals as subjects, and to unsettle such power. In this volume, Chen (chapter 9) questions the tendency multicultural children's books have to cast white children as tolerating subjects and **racialized** ethnic minority children as passive heirs of cultural traditions, and neither as agents with a critical awareness of, and political interest in, contesting racism. In a similar vein, Andrejek (chapter 8) analyzes the role of Western classic fairy tales in forming values in girls regarding innocence, propriety, and sexual morality. Williams and Coulter (chapter 10) address the **market segmentation** of babies, preschoolers, and tweens as niche consumers and its implications for how childhood and youth are thought about and experienced.

Related to the concern with the exercise of power, a social constructionist analysis questions the assumed inevitability of present practices and ways of thinking, seeing these as historical, shifting, and commonly reflecting dominant interests. Consequently, some scholars are interested in identifying ways that children and youth disrupt and manipulate the categories that are applied to them. For instance, Byrd Clark's research (2008) explores how Italian Canadian youth problematize hegemonic social categories of "Italian Canadian," "multilingual," and "multicultural" through their lived social and linguistic practices, such as claiming varied identities ("Italian here and Canadian everywhere else," "Canadian of Italian origin," etc.). Young people's lives are profoundly affected by powerful discourses and structural inequalities, but they also respond to and shape the social spaces they inhabit.

INEQUALITIES AND INTERSECTIONS IN EXPERIENCES OF CHILDHOOD AND YOUTH

In December of 2015, police arrested a suspect in the murder of 15-year-old Tina Fontaine, an Indigenous girl whose body was found in the Red River on August 17, 2014, after being reported missing a few weeks before. Her body had been wrapped in a duvet cover. When Tina Fontaine had gone missing, she had been in the care of Manitoba's Child and Family Services and she had only been in Winnipeg for a month. She had been living in a downtown hotel because there were not enough places available in foster care, and she was spending a lot of time on the streets of Winnipeg. Tina Fontaine's death led to an outcry of concern about young people in provincial care and about the many similar deaths and disappearances of Indigenous women and girls in Canada that remain unsolved. These gravely disproportionate incidences of deaths and disappearances have their historical and social roots in the colonial—and many would argue continuing—regulation and devastation of Indigenous communities (Lawrence, 2004).

In addition to a constructionist perspective, underpinning chapters in this collection is the recognition that Canadian children and youth's lives are deeply shaped by material and **symbolic inequalities** arising from significant intersecting social divisions like gender, race, class, sexuality, disability, and, of course, generation and age. It is crucial for sociological studies of childhood and youth not to focus on the categories of "children" and "youth" in isolation, but instead to consider them in terms of social divisions, diversity of experiences, and social inequalities (James et al., 1998). Inequalities are structurally embedded in Canadian society, and inequalities in the lives of children and youth both mirror overall broader social patterns and have some unique features of their own. Some inequalities are easily identified. Others take more subtle but enduring forms—notions about "normal" childhood and youth fall into the second category. These norms reflect dominating groups' ideas about how childhood and youth should be experienced, ideas that inform and are in turn reproduced through discourses and institutions. Assumptions about what childhood *should* look like are often embedded in middle-class ideals, for instance (Lareau, 2003). As such, children and youth in dominating groups experience privileges, even though they may not be aware of it— perpetuating patterns of inequality into the next generation.

One most significant and persistent dimension of inequality is economic. Class inequalities affect all Canadian young people: there are children who grow up in significant poverty and others whose families are just a paycheque away, creating insecurity and stress; others are comfortably middle class and able to access the advantages that economic security brings, including peer acceptance, the latest fashions, extracurricular activities, tutoring if needed, and vacations. Some live in families that are very wealthy. Available family finances have a significant impact on young people's chances of injury (Morton, 2012), on their physical and psychological health (Elgar et al., 2013), and on their life satisfaction (Levin et al., 2011). As we will see in chapter 11 by Albanese, rising social inequalities increase the consequent disparities in the lives of children and youth, with particularly difficult consequences for children living in poverty. Howe and Covell (2003) remind us that by ratifying the **UN Convention on the Rights of the Child** in 1991, Canada was obligated to advance the basic economic security rights of children. Instead, policies and services targeting children and youth in economic need remain underfunded or marginalized (Gharabaghi & Stuart, 2010).

Economic inequalities in Canada hinder certain groups of young people more than others. Here we begin to see how inequalities intersect with one another. Indigenous peoples in Canada, for example, have faced historical and ongoing racism and discrimination, and the erosion of Indigenous cultures through the implementation of the Indian Act and residential schools are at the root of much of the poverty that many Indigenous families must deal with today. Recent research reveals that 40 percent of Indigenous children live in poverty and many Indigenous communities are without facilities that most other Canadians take for granted, such as well-funded schools, safe drinking water, and sufficient housing (Macdonald & Wilson, 2013).

Another group of young people facing high rates of poverty, as well as other challenges, are **immigrant** and **refugee** children and youth. A United Nations (2011) report ranked Canada seventh in the world in the number of immigrants it receives. Refugee and immigrant children are at a greater risk of poverty because of barriers faced by their parents due to a lack of recognition of foreign credentials, language differences, labour market inequalities, and migration's negative impact on family stability, either as a result of immigration policy (e.g. restrictions on the rights of live-in caregivers) or disruptions associated with migration (Livingstone & Weinfeld, 2015). Future research will likely reveal similar challenges faced by Syrian refugee children, youth, and families arriving in Canadian cities in 2015 and 2016. Studies have shown that contrary to the belief that it is easy for young newcomers to integrate into Canadian society, many are instead faced with unique difficulties (Wilkinson, Yan, Tsang, Sin, & Lauer, 2012). Some of these challenges are evident in young immigrants' stories presented by Selimos in chapter 14.

Racialized inequalities affect young people's lives in numerous other ways as well. Prolific cultural critic Henry Giroux argues that youth have been marginalized, disenfranchised, and demonized in a commodified American society that is preoccupied with terrorism. In this context, meaningful education has been eroded, and young people are being increasingly criminalized in what Giroux has termed a "war" on youth (2013). These shifts do not affect all young people equally—those who are poor and those who are not white are much more vulnerable to these processes. In Canada, we also see such racialized inequalities embedded within the criminal justice system. Black youth are far more likely to be stopped and searched by police (Wortley & Tanner, 2005), for example, and the number of Black young men in Ontario jails is four times higher than for other young men; for Indigenous young men, the rate is five times higher (Rankin & Ng, 2013). This issue caught international attention and concern when the United Nations asked Canada to urgently address the situation (Rankin & Ng, 2013). Marinos, Innocente, and Goodwin-DeFaria (chapter 13) draw on the voices of Indigenous youth to specifically consider inconsistencies in the use of **diversion** measures that are available through the **Youth Criminal Justice Act**. Youth growing up in marginalized neighbourhoods similarly negotiate issues of support, belonging, and citizenship, a topic that is taken up by Sriskandarajah (chapter 20).

Inequalities arising around gender and sexuality in the lives of young Canadians are also of concern to sociologists. Violence against women remains a deeply disturbing issue in Canada, for example, from the levels of harassment reported by girls in Ontario schools (Safe Schools Action Team, 2008) to the missing and murdered Indigenous women and girls across Canada that were the focus of numerous demands for a public inquiry (Walker, 2015). Future inequalities in the job market continue to await young women upon graduation (Williams, 2010), and most can expect to experience the "double day" that disproportionately saddles women with paid work outside the home alongside an unequal level of responsibility for housework and child care when they get home (Statistics Canada, 2011). In the meantime, while there are certainly more supports available for **LGBTQ+** young people than in the past, and some LGBTQ+ youth are thriving, many face peer bullying, isolation, and rejection from parents within a broader society that assumes that everyone is (and wants to be) heterosexual (Taylor & Peter, 2011). Peer-based homophobic harassment is well documented in Canada, and particularly in the North, with devastating effects in terms of young people dropping out of school and even ending their own lives (Peter, Taylor, & Chamberland, 2015). These incredibly pressing issues are outlined by Greensmith and Davies in chapter 16, who also discuss how in some schools, students have initiated Gay-Straight Alliances as one step in making schools more supportive environments for LGBTQ+ youth.

The idea that there is one way to be "normal" within society and that anyone else is somehow a "problem" or in need of correction similarly haunts many children and youth with disabilities, who are frequently unheard and excluded from decision-making about their lives. In this collection, Abbas (chapter 6) has shown that because of her brother's intellectual disability, his childhood, like those of other children with disabilities, is frequently seen as problematic when compared to a "normal childhood." Canadian scholar LeFrancois (2008) is concerned with young Canadians' encounters with mental health services, and advocates that their concerns need to be heard. Schneider (chapter 18) draws on a children's rights framework to examine such exclusion and to advocate that we need to hear the views of children with disabilities. Both LeFrancois (2008) and Schneider note the importance of seeing and understanding how children and youth themselves define and experience equality and inclusion. These studies remind us that across families, support services, schools, and other alternative systems of care, we need to better balance adult responsibilities towards children with children's rights to self-expression and self-determination.

Disadvantages caused by inequalities often occur simultaneously and in intersecting ways, as the tragic death of Tina Fontaine, a young Indigenous woman with few economic and social resources, shows. Sociologists who study intersectionality are also interested in examining how one form of hierarchy operates to justify and cement another—for example, how Euro-centric and derogatory stereotypes about Muslim women and girls fuel Islamophobia in the post-9/11 era of securitization, or the dominance of national security as the paramount logic. Recognizing intersecting patterns of oppression means noting that young people variously experience oppressions and privileges when they are located at different cross-points of social divisions and social inequalities. Given the different ways that gender, race, class, age, physical/mental disability, sexuality, and so on intersect and mutually constitute each other, we need a plurality of knowledge from multiple standpoints. This means that it is important to understand children's and youth's perspectives on what inequality, inclusion, and justice mean to them. Children and youth have an important role to play in addressing social inequalities, whether facilitating inclusion of peers with communication impairment (Eilertsen, 2014), participating in a First Nations youth mentoring program (Zinga, 2012), or taking action for justice in the classroom (Johnson, 2013; Stanley, 2011). This connects with the fourth analytical theme of this collection: young people's participation.

CITIZENSHIP, RIGHTS, AND SOCIAL ENGAGEMENT

Should children be considered citizens, with the same rights and responsibilities as adults? What kind of say should children and youth have in decisions that affect their lives? How do we at the same time ensure their protection? How should we think about young people as participants in producing our social world? Many concepts and debates that revolve around the question of young people's involvement in their communities and beyond currently preoccupy scholars within the field of sociology of children and youth. This interest is largely driven by a desire for children's rights to be respected, and for young people to be heard, influence decisions, and be recognized as participants in shaping culture. It also engages with key concepts such as citizenship, rights, participation, and agency.

Citizenship defines someone as holding certain rights, duties, and protections within a social body, thus it distinguishes who is included and excluded from these rights, duties, and protections. The idea of citizenship has tended to exclude young people (Lister, 2007;

Wyness, Harrison, & Buchanan, 2004), as it has been tied to reaching an age of majority and, historically, has been premised on economic independence and even property ownership. Children have instead been considered under the purview of the family (Roche, 1999; Such & Walker, 2005; Wyness et al., 2004). Rather than children being considered as citizens in the present, they tend to be seen as in the process of *becoming* citizens (Lister, 2007), as we see in much citizenship education in Canada, for example (Kennelly, 2011). Some have been interested in redefining the relationship between children and citizenship in order to prioritize young people's participation in the present. For instance, Roche (1999) favours children's "partial citizenship" and Larkins (2014) redefines citizenship to include socially interdependent practices in order to recognize children's involvement as social actors. These approaches seek to highlight children's citizenship actions that occur well before they reach an age of majority, from their participation in family decision-making to their contributions through chores and paid work. For example, L. Alison Molina-Girón, in chapter 19 of this collection, demonstrates the important role played by young people's involvement in civic/public life through volunteering.

Canadian scholars Richard Mitchell and Shannon Moore (2012) argue that we need to embrace a more critical citizenship education, starting with the 1989 UN Convention of the Rights of the Child (CRC), underscoring the significant interrelationship between citizenship and rights. Children's rights outlined in the CRC can be categorized as protection, provision, and participation rights. Rights to protection include protection from sexual exploitation and dangerous work, for example, while provision rights recognize that children have the right to go to school and to access health care. Participation rights assert that children have a right to free expression and should be involved in decision-making about their lives, guided by their "evolving capacities" (OHCCHR, 1989). Researchers have investigated participation rights in such broad areas as family decision-making, research on/with children, provision of child welfare services, schooling, and more. Participation rights can sometimes come into conflict with protection and provision rights, however, as we see in Schneider's chapter (18), when practitioners exclude young people with disabilities from participation in the name of their protection. Participation and protection rights can also complement each other, for example, when children speak up in order to garner their own protection (Stasiulis, 2002). In this volume, Kenneally (chapter 17) provides a detailed discussion of the CRC and re-imagines articles of the CRC based on a shift away from rights as something that can be held or taken away, towards a focus on rights as relational social processes.

Canada has signed the CRC and we have several centres focused on children's rights, including the Children's Rights Centre at Cape Breton University, the Landon Pearson Centre for the Study of Childhood at Carleton University, and the Canadian Coalition for the Rights of Children. But despite the existence of these centres and the important work that comes out of them, Canadians have generally remained unaware of children's rights (Howe & Covell, 2007). This book seeks to address this shortcoming by providing some examples of what has been (and should further be) explored in this area.

Beyond citizenship and rights, the sociology of childhood and youth includes a strong interest in young people's broader forms of participation, including as consumers (e.g. Pugh, 2009), workers (e.g. Wyness, 2013), students (e.g. Raby, 2012), and activists (e.g. Kennelly, 2011), as well as online (e.g. Reich, Black, & Korobkova, 2014), in institutions (e.g. LeFrancois, 2008), and in families (e.g. Holland & O'Neill, 2006). Across this breadth of scholarship, we see a myriad of examples of young people as active, interested, involved, opinionated, concerned, and invested. We see this in Greensmith and Davies's chapter (16) on Gay-Straight Alliances, in Selimos's chapter (14) on how young new immigrants to Canada construct a sense of belonging through negotiating peer relations, and in Raby and Pomerantz's chapter (15) on girls' increasing public objections to dress code regulations in high schools. Many would argue that these are all examples of young people's agency.

Agency can be understood as the ability to make change in the world around us, and it is a concept undergirding much of this scholarship on participation. It is also a concept that is contentious. Some emphasize that agency is something that we can foster in children, encouraging them to participate and to speak out (Mitra, 2004), while others prioritize considering children as agentic beings already, intentionally shaping their worlds from a very young age (Kehily, 2004). More theoretically, many writing on young people's participation assume that agency is something that resides in each of us, including children, as choice-making individuals. Others have questioned this position, recognizing that our "choices" are often made within narrow, structural, or discursive conditions and that individuals are enmeshed within collectivities that significantly shape them, challenging the idea of the independent, decision-making individual (e.g. see Kennelly, 2011; Laws & Davies, 2000).

The wide body of work on children's citizenship, rights, participation, and agency includes other critical engagement as well. Some are uncomfortable with the idea of children having rights or being encouraged in their participation, believing that children's innocence, vulnerability, and gradual development are incompatible with participation (see Lansdown, 2010; Wyness et al., 2004). From an entirely different angle, citizenship, rights-based, and participatory discourses have been criticized for being tokenistic (Lansdown, 2010), overly Euro-centric as they define children primarily through a Western lens (Reynaert, Bouverne-de Bie, & Vandevelde, 2009), and **neoliberal** in their focus on individual (rather than collective) rights (Rutherford, 2009). Programs fostering participation have been found to favour those with privilege, such as middle-class children (Black, 2011), to emphasize spoken, rather than material (e.g. work), contributions (Wyness, 2013), and to prioritize individual autonomy and responsibility over context (Reynaert et al., 2009). Projects intent on bolstering young people's participation, in schools for instance, have similarly led scholars to ask whether children are learning to govern themselves along lines that benefit established, dominant society rather than encouraging young people to question and challenge (Kennelly, 2011; Reynaert et al., 2009).

USING THIS BOOK

Sociological studies of children, childhood, and youth cover a wide and exciting range of topics and questions. In this volume we draw together some of the current, cutting-edge work that is being done in this field. This is not an exhaustively comprehensive volume, covering every possible topic or drawing on all relevant child and youth studies scholars in Canada, as this text is, of course, only a beginning. While we touch on a wide range of topics in the growing field of the sociology of childhood and youth in Canada, there are many others, including areas such as employment, health, recreation, and play. The lives of Canadian children and youth are also significantly shaped by where they are located across this nation. Variations in provincial governance affect many facets of young people's lives, from what is covered in sex education curriculum, to what age someone can start working for money, to what kinds of services are available for youth living on the streets. We need to pay more attention to how differences in service provision, provincial politics, culture, and geography importantly shape the diversity of young people's experiences. Echoing the ongoing, problematic dominance of Central Canada in much of Canadian life, many of our chapters focus on Ontario. Future publications must more successfully challenge this central pull. We must also attend more fully, in research, writing, and publishing, to the lives of rural children and youth. Finally, while we are very pleased to include Spencer and Sinclair's chapter (12) on the "Sixties Scoop," and information about the Aboriginal Youth Court in Toronto, there are numerous aspects of Indigenous young people's lives that need attention in texts such as this one, including research that focuses on strength, resilience, and resistance.

Across our four themes, contributors engage with a range of key concepts including power, agency, subject formation, relationality, inequality, materiality, and bodies. Many chapter authors also include the voices of children and youth, and consciously bring out the materiality of childhood and youth through description, illustrations of artifacts, and consideration of technology in children's and youth's lives. While these chapters by no means capture the full breadth of important topics, concepts, and themes now emerging in Canadian research on children, this collection highlights some very recent Canadian sociological work in this field. We hope that these chapters inspire new students and scholars to reach further and to challenge existing perceptions, misconceptions, and limitations in the Canadian sociology of childhood and youth; and we hope that this volume will be joined by many more related publications to come.

To conclude this chapter, we provide you with a road map to help you navigate this anthology. We have included a number of features that we hope will help you make the best use of this collection as a whole. To start, the book is divided into four parts, reflecting our key themes: (1) research on and with children and youth; (2) childhood and youth as social constructs; (3) inequalities and intersections in the experiences of childhood and youth; and (4) citizenship, rights, and engagement.

Each of these parts has a section introduction that highlights the central ideas featured in the chapters that populate the section. As you read through each chapter, you will also see links and references to other chapters in the collection.

Each chapter opens with a list of key learning objectives and then ends with a point-form chapter summary, which returns to and highlights some of the key points in the chapter. As with this introductory chapter, within each chapter you will also find a series of key terms in bold at first use that are then defined in the collection's glossary. Following each chapter, you will find study questions and research assignments to guide your thinking and help you engage with the main concepts covered in each chapter. We also have included suggested films/video clips and links to websites to help guide discussions and further research you might wish to do in the area. We hope that each of these features will bring you closer to independently contributing to the development of this important and growing field in Canadian sociology and to better understanding and engaging with children and youth in all aspects of your life and career.

REFERENCES

Alanen, L., Brooker, L., and Mayall, B. (Eds.). (2015). *Childhood with Bourdieu*. New York & Basingstoke: Palgrave Macmillan.

Allen, B. (2015, November 26). Police can fine parents under curfew aimed at stopping teen vandals. *CBC News Saskatchewan*. Retrieved from www.cbc.ca/news/canada/saskatchewan/la-ronge-sask-curfew-bylaw-polices-parents-1.3335805

Black, R. (2011). Student participation and disadvantage: Limitations in policy and practice. *Journal of Youth Studies, 14*(4), 463–474.

Bowman, J. (2014). Girl's letter to Lego sparks gender debate. *CBC*. Retrieved from www.cbc.ca/newsblogs/yourcommunity/2014/02/girls-letter-to-lego-sparks-gender-debate.html

Buck, N. (2015). Elves on Shelves, destroyers of Christmas magic. *The Globe and Mail*. Retrieved from www.theglobeandmail.com/globe-debate/the-elves-on-the-shelves-are-ruining-christmas/article27607352/

Byrd Clark, J. (2008). *Journeys of integration in Canada's pluralistic society: Italian Canadian youth and the symbolic investments in French as official language*. Unpublished doctoral dissertation, Ontario Institute for Studies in Education of the University of Toronto.

Chen, X. (2005). *Tending the gardens of citizenship: Child saving in Toronto, 1880s–1920s*. Toronto: University of Toronto Press.

Chen, X. (2008). The child-citizen and the biopolitics of recasting citizenship. In E. F. Isin (Ed.), *Recasting the social in citizenship*. Toronto: University of Toronto Press.

Christensen, P. H. (2004). Children's participation in ethnographic research: Issues of power and representation. *Children & Society, 18*, 165–176.

Corsaro, W. A., Qvortrup, J., & Honig, M. S. (2009). *The Palgrave handbook of childhood studies*. New York: Palgrave Macmillan.

Covell, K., Howe, B., & McNeil, J. (2008). "If there's a dead rat, don't leave it." Young children's understanding of their citizenship rights and responsibilities. *Cambridge Journal of Education, 38*(3), 321–339.

Danby, S., & Farrell, A. (2004). Accounting for young people's competence in educational research: New perspectives on research ethics. *Australian Educational Researcher, 31*(3), 35–49.

Eilertsen, L.-J. (2014). Maintaining intersubjectivity when communication is challenging: Hearing impairment and complex needs. *Research on Language and Social Interaction, 47*(4), 353–379.

Elgar, F. J., Pickett, K. E., Pickett, W., Craig, W., Molcho, M., Hurrelmann, K., & Lenzi, M. (2013). School bullying, homicide and income inequality: A cross-national pooled time series analysis. *International Journal of Public Health, 58*(2), 237–245.

Gharabaghi, K., & Stuart, C. (2010). Voices from the periphery: Prospects and challenges for the homeless youth service sector. *Children & Youth Services Review, 32*(12), 1683–1689.

Giroux, H. (2013). *America's education deficit and the war on youth.* New York: Monthly Review Press.

Gleason, M. (2001). Disciplining the student body: Schooling and the construction of Canadian children's bodies, 1930–1960. *History of Education Quarterly, 41*(2), 189–215.

Gonick, M., & Gannon, S. (Eds.). (2014). *Becoming girl: Collective biography and the production of girlhood.* Toronto: Women's Press.

Grover, S. (2004). Why won't they listen to us? On giving power and voice to children participating in social research. *Childhood, 11*(1), 81–93.

Hacking, I. (1999). *The social construction of what?* Cambridge: Harvard University Press.

Henwood, K., & Coltart, C. (2012). Meeting the challenges of intensive parenting culture: Gender, risk management and the moral parent. *Sociology, 46*(1), 25–40.

Hill, M. (2006). Children's voices on ways of having a voice: Children's and young people's perspectives on methods used in research and consultation. *Childhood, 13*(1), 69–89.

Holland, S., & O'Neill, S. (2006). "We had to be here to make sure it was what we wanted": Enabling children's participation in family decision-making through the family group conference. *Childhood, 13*(1), 91–111.

Howe, B., & Covell, K. (2003). Child poverty in Canada and the rights of the child. *Human Rights Quarterly, 25*(4), 1067–1087.

Howe, B., & Covell, K. (Eds.). (2007). *A question of commitment: Children's rights in Canada.* Waterloo: Wilfrid Laurier University Press.

James, A., Jenks, C., & Prout, A. (1998). *Theorizing childhood.* Cambridge: Polity Press.

James, A., & Prout, A. (Eds.). (1997). *Constructing and reconstructing childhood: Contemporary issues in the sociological study of childhood.* London: Falmer Press.

Jenks, C. (Ed.). (1982). *The sociology of childhood: Essential readings.* London: Batsford.

Jenks, C. (1990). *Childhood.* London: Routledge.

John. (2015). Christmas as social control, featuring Elf on the Shelf. *Sociological Images.* Retrieved from thesocietypages.org/socimages/2015/12/22/christmas-as-social-control-featuring-elf-on-the-shelf/

Johnson, L. (2013). Segregation or "thinking black"?: Community activism and the development of black-focused schools in Toronto and London, 1968–2008. *Teachers College Record, 115*(11), 1–25.

Kehily, M. J. (2004). Understanding childhood: An introduction to some key themes and issues. In M. J. Kehily (Ed.), *An introduction to childhood studies* (pp. 1–21). Maidenhead: Open University Press/ McGraw Hill.

Kennelly, J. (2011). *Citizen youth: Culture, activism, and agency in a neoliberal era.* Palgrave McMillan: New York.

Kohut, T. (2015). Nearly 1 in 5 Canadian children living in poverty: Report. *Global News.* Retrieved from globalnews.ca/news/2360311/nearly-1-in-5-canadian-children-living-in-poverty-report/

Lansdown, G. (2010). The realization of children's participation rights: Critical reflections. In B. Percy-Smith & N. Thomas (Eds.), *A Handbook of children and young people's participation: Perspectives from theory and practice* (pp. 11–23). New York: Routledge.

Lareau, A. (2003). *Unequal childhoods: Class, race and family life.* Berkeley: University of California Press.

Larkins, C. (2014). Enacting children's citizenship: Developing understandings of how children enact themselves as citizens through actions and acts of citizenship. *Childhood, 21*(1), 7–21.

Lawrence, B. (2004). *"Real" Indians and others: Mixed blood Native Peoples and Indigenous nationhood.* Lincoln: University of Nebraska Press.

Laws, C., & Davies, B. (2000). Poststructuralist theory in practice: Working with "behaviourally disturbed" children. *International Journal of Qualitative Studies in Education, 13*(3), 205–221.

LeFrancois, B. (2008). "It's like mental torture": Participation and mental health services. *International Journal of Children's Rights, 16*, 211–227.

Levin, K. A., Torsheim, T., Vollebergh, W., Richter, M., Davies, C. A., Schnohr, C.W., & Due, P. (2011). National income and income inequality, family affluence and life satisfaction among 13 year old boys and girls: A multilevel study in 35 countries. *Social Indicators Research, 104*(2), 179–194.

Lister, R. (2007). Why citizenship? Where, when and how children? *Theoretical Inquiries in Law, 8*(2), 693–718.

Little, M. H. (2012). Poverty, regulation & social justice: Readings on the criminalization of poverty. *Labour/Le Travail, 70*, 286–288.

Little, M. H., & Morrison, I. (1999). The Pecker Detectors are back: Regulation of the family form in Ontario welfare policy. *Journal of Canadian Studies, 34*(2), 110–124.

Livingstone, A. M., & Weinfeld, M. (2015). Black families and socio-economic inequality in Canada. *Canadian Ethnic Studies, 47*(3), 1–23.

Macdonald, D., & Wilson, D. (2013). *Poverty or prosperity: Indigenous children in Canada.* Ottawa: Save The Children and Canadian Centre for Policy Alternatives.

Macgregor, R. (2015, Nov. 27). Ontario teen activist takes on the bottled water industry. *The Globe and Mail.* Retrieved from www.theglobeandmail.com/news/national/ontario-teen-activist-takes-on-the-bottled-water-industry/article27518523/

Mahon, A., Glendinning, C., Clarke, K., & Craig, G. (1996). Researching children: Methods and ethics. *Children & Society, 10*, 145–154.

Mason, J., & Danby, S. (2011). Children as experts in their lives: Child inclusive research. *Child Indicators Research, 4*(2), 185–189.

Mayall, B. (2015). Understanding inter-generational relations: The case of health maintenance by children. *Sociology of Health & Illness, 37*(2), 312–324.

Mitchell, R., & Moore, S. (2012). Transdisciplinary approaches to young people's citizenship: From bystanders to action. In R. Mitchell & S. Moore (Eds.), *Politics, participation & power relations* (pp. 183–205). Rotterdam, Boston: Sense Publishers.

Mitra, D. L. (2004). The significance of students: Can increasing "student voice" in schools lead to gains in youth development? *Teachers College Record, 106*(4), 651–688.

Morton, T. R. (2012). *Neighbourhood correlates of childhood injury: A case study of Toronto, Canada.* PhD dissertation, Factor-Inwentash Faculty of Social Work, University of Toronto.

Neigh, S. (2015). Anti-First Nations racism in a Manitoulin Island high school. *Sudbury Working Group Media Co-op.* Retrieved from sudbury.mediacoop.ca/story/anti-first-nations-racism-manitoulin-island-high-s/33091

Orellana, M. F. (2001). The work kids do: Mexican and Central American immigrant children's contributions to households and schools in California. *Harvard Educational Review, 71*(3), 366–389.

Osborne, K. (2000). Public schooling and citizenship education in Canada. *Canadian Ethnic Studies, 32*(1), 8–37.

Peter, T., Taylor, C., & Chamberland, L. (2015). A queer day in Canada: Examining Canadian high school students' experiences with school-based homophobia in two large-scale studies. *Journal of Homosexuality, 62,* 186–206.

Prout, A. (2011). Taking a step away from modernity: Reconsidering the new sociology of childhood. *Global Studies of Childhood, 1*(1), 4–14.

Pugh, A. (2009). *Longing and belonging: Parents, children, and consumer culture.* Berkeley: University of California Press.

Pyle, A. (2013). Engaging young children in research through photo elicitation. *Early Child Development & Care, 183*(11), 1544–1558.

Qvortrup, J. (1985). Placing children in the division of labour. In P. Close & R. Collins (Eds.), *Family and economy in modern society* (pp. 129–145). London: Macmillan.

Raby, R. (2012). *School rules: Obedience, discipline and elusive democracy.* Toronto: University of Toronto Press.

Rankin, J. W., & Ng, P. H. (2013, March 1). Race data obtained under freedom of information paints a disturbing picture of Black and Aboriginal overrepresentation in Ontario youth and adult jails. *The Toronto Star.* Retrieved from www.thestar.com/news/insight/2013/03/01/unequal_justice_aboriginal_and_black_inmates_disproportionately_fill_ontario_jails.html

Reich, S. M., Black, R. W., & Korobkova, K. (2014). Connections and communities in virtual worlds designed for children. *Journal of Community Psychology, 42*(3), 255–267.

Reynaert, D., Bouverne-de Bie, M., & Vandevelde, S. (2009). A review of children's rights literature since the adoption of the United Nations Convention on the Rights of the Child. *Childhood, 16*(4), 518–534.

Roche, J. (1999). Children: Rights, participation and citizenship. *Childhood, 6*(4), 475–493.

Rowsell, J., & Harwood, D. (2015). "Let it go": Exploring the image of the child as a producer, consumer, and inventor. *Theory Into Practice, 54*(2), 136–146.

Rutherford, M. B. (2009). Children's autonomy and responsibility: An analysis of childrearing advice. *Qualitative Sociology, 32,* 337–353.

Safe Schools Action Team. (2008). *Shaping a culture of respect in our schools: Promoting safe and healthy relationships.* Ministry of Education, Ontario. Toronto: Queen's Printer for Ontario.

Schoepflin, T. (2015). *The Elf on the Shelf: An endorsement.* Retrieved from creativesociology.blogspot.ca/2015/11/the-elf-on-shelf-endorsement.html

Shaw, C., Brady, L. M., & Davey, C. (2011). *Guidelines for research with children and young people*. London: National Children's Bureau Research Centre. Retrieved from www.nfer.ac.uk/nfer/schools/developing-young-researchers/ncbguidelines.pdf

Stanbridge, K. (2007). Framing children in the Newfoundland Confederation debate, 1948. *Canadian Journal of Sociology, 32*(2), 177–201.

Stanley, T. J. (2011). *Contesting white supremacy: School segregation, anti-racism, and the making of Chinese Canadians*. Vancouver: UBC Press.

Stasiulis, D. (2002). The active child citizen: Lessons from Canadian policy and the children's movement. *Citizenship Studies, 6*(4), 507–538.

Statistics Canada. (2011). Women in Canada: A gender based statistical report. Ottawa: Minister of Industry.

Stephens, S. (1995). *Children and the politics of culture*. Princeton, NJ: Princeton University Press.

Such, E., & Walker, R. (2005). Young citizens or policy objects? Children in the "rights and responsibilities" debate. *Journal of Social Policy, 34*(1), 39–57.

Swift, K. (1995). *Manufacturing "bad mothers": A critical perspective on child neglect*. Toronto: University of Toronto Press.

Tay-Lim, J., & Lim, S. (2013). Privileging younger children's voices in research: Use of drawings and a co-construction process. *International Journal of Qualitative Methods, 12*(1), 65–84.

Taylor, C., & Peter, T. (2011). *Every class in every school: Final report on the first national climate survey on homophobia, biphobia and transphobia in Canadian schools*. Toronto: Egale Canada Human Rights Trust.

Teachman, G., & Gibson, B. (2013). Children and youth with disabilities: Innovative methods for single qualitative interviews. *Qualitative Health Research, 23*(2), 264–274.

United Nations, Department of Economic and Social Affairs, Population Division. (2011). *International migration report 2009: A global assessment* (United Nations, ST/ESA/SER.A/316). New York: United Nations.

United Nations, Human Rights Office of the High Commissioner (OHCCHR). (1989). *Convention on the Rights of the Child*. Geneva: Office of the United Nations High Commissioner for Human Rights (OHCHR). Retrieved from www.ohchr.org/Documents/ProfessionalInterest/crc.pdf

Walker, C. (2015, December 8). 22 cases added to CBC's missing and murdered indigenous women database. *CBC News*. Retrieved from www.cbc.ca/news/aboriginal/22-cases-added-to-cbc-s-missing-and-murdered-indigenous-women-database-1.3355012

Widdicombe, S., & Wooffitt, R. (1995). *The language of youth subcultures: Social identity in action*. New York: Harvester Wheatsheaf.

Wilkinson, L., Yan, M. C., Tsang, A. K. T., Sin, R., & Lauer, S. (2012). The school-to-work transitions of newcomer youth in Canada. *Canadian Ethnic Studies, 44*(3), 29–44.

Williams, C. (2010). *Economic well-being*. Ottawa: Statistics Canada.

Woodhead, M. (2005). Early childhood development: A question of rights. *International Journal of Early Childhood, 37*(3), 79.

Wortley, S., & Tanner, J. (2005). Inflammatory rhetoric? Baseless accusations? A response to Gabor's critique of racial profiling research in Canada. *Canadian Journal of Criminology and Criminal Justice, 47*(3), 581–609.

Wotherspoon, T. (2006). Teachers' work in Canadian Aboriginal communities. *Comparative Education Review, 50*(4), 672–694.

Wyn, J., & White, R. (1998). Young people, social problems and Australian youth studies. *Journal of Youth Studies, 1*(1), 23–38.

Wyness, M. (2013). Global standards and deficit childhoods: The contested meaning of children's participation. *Children's Geographies, 11*(3), 340–353.

Wyness, M., Harrison, L., & Buchanan, I. (2004). Childhood, politics and ambiguity: Towards an agenda for children's political inclusion. *Sociology, 38*(1), 81–99.

Zinga, R. D. (2012). Journeying with youth: Re-centering indigeneity in child and youth care. *Child and Youth Services, 33*, 258–280.

SECTION I

RESEARCH ON AND WITH CHILDREN AND YOUTH

Many of us approach the idea of doing research with apprehension, disinterest, or dislike; however, understanding and doing research is extremely important, and can be insightful, empowering, and creative. Many of us "trust the experts" unquestioningly, or accept research results because they involve numbers, but not all research involves numbers and not all numbers are valid and informative (Albanese, 2016). *Quantitative research* involves the numerical representation and manipulation of observations for the purpose of describing and explaining social phenomena. Increasingly, though, we are seeing and accepting the value of *qualitative research*, which involves non-numerical examination and interpretation of observations for the purpose of discovering underlying meanings, patterns, and relationships. Qualitative research is especially important when doing research with children, as it provides an opportunity to better understand the richness and complexity of children's lives, environments, activities, choices, and thoughts. Until recently, most research did not bother to involve children at all.

It was not that long ago that medical research and drug testing involved mostly male research participants. It was assumed that a body is a body, and that women and children were vulnerable populations that needed "protecting." Researchers quickly learned that bodies react differently to procedures and drugs, depending on body size, genetic and hormonal composition, and so on, and that women and children needed to be the focus of research in their own right, because "protection" often really meant paternalistic exclusion.

With time, we saw the development of feminist ontologies and epistemological approaches that not only "added" women to research but developed distinct methods that showed that what is known and the ways in which this knowledge can be known is subject to the position, situation, and perspective of the knower. While we have come to accept the value of including (some) women's voices in research, we have, for the most part, yet to do the same for children and youth. Many continue to believe that the experiences and opinions of young people are less competent and less believable than those of adults. We often call upon parents and teachers—"persons most knowledgeable" (PMKs)—to "inform" us about the lives of children.

Youth are not treated much better. While youth are believed to be competent "enough" to be consulted, they have often been framed as "problems" or "risks." As a result, much of what we know about children and youth is the product of research done by adults, for adults, using adult participants. The result has been that children and youth are studied not in their own right, but as a group subsidiary to the larger family structure or deviating from the norms of the adult world, for purposes that are in the interests of adults, and often not those of young people. The chapters that follow—and the entire collection, for that matter—go to great lengths to involve young people as contributors or participants, to ensure that the voices of children and youth are part of the story that they tell. The chapters in this opening section begin by outlining the importance of having children participate in the research process. They exemplify some of the unique approaches that can and have been used to engage young people in research. While such approaches can sometimes be challenging, these chapters illustrate how they can also be deeply rewarding.

Chapter 1, titled "Adults Researching with Children," by Rachel Berman and Maggie MacNevin, sets the stage by identifying key differences between research *on* children and research *with* children. Berman and MacNevin begin by framing their chapter in terms of key high-level issues that arise in research with children, and also focusing on the importance of reflexivity in qualitative research, particularly as it relates to researcher positionality. They write convincingly about the value of understanding "gatekeeper" issues and ethical ways of seeking children's participation in research. As such, Berman and MacNevin set the stage for the chapters that follow, where authors challenge or critically engage with traditional methodological approaches, while showcasing their craft and sharing insights into their distinctive and creative child-focused methods and approaches.

Chapter 2, entitled "'You Even Wrote Down Our Homework!': Ethnography and Creative Visual Methods in Doing Research Along with Children and Young People," by Diane Farmer, points to the value of working "in the field," in spaces inhabited by children and youth. Farmer opens chapter 2 with a discussion that builds on that of Berman and MacNevin in chapter 1 by outlining the importance of doing research along with children, and then tackles the deeper question of what might foster meaningful participation for young people, through her focus on two research initiatives, both ethnographic studies that she conducted over the last decade in Ontario's French-language schools. Using these two projects as examples, she combines observations, interviews, and creative visual research tools to illustrate the complexities of life in school. Her second study provides especially vivid insight through young peoples' use of digital language portraits and photography as biographical tools. What emerge are rich depictions that capture young lives that shape and are shaped by social class, race, gender, culture, language, migration experiences, and "minority" status.

Kate MacDonald's chapter 3, "'We Can Play Whatever We Want': Exploring Children's Voices in Education and in Research," provides another example of the importance of doing research with children for the purpose of social change. It underscores the importance of doing research in spaces that children inhabit—in their own worlds and through their eyes and experiences. Her research shows how the social construction of childhood influences our current understanding of learning and of children's capacities, and how this comes to shape the public education system. Her research on an outdoor classroom and inquiry-based learning underscores the importance and value of treating children as experts on their own lives, and of treating the voices of children as valuable.

Marnina Gonick's chapter 4, *"About Us, By Us* and Other Stories of Arts-Based Research and Marginalized Girls," focuses on two examples of arts-based approaches that help amplify the voices of, and shed light on, the rich and multifaceted experiences of marginalized girls. One of these voices is that of Amerah, who challenges us to "think about it," as the 13-year-old Palestinian girl from Saudi Arabia decisively shares her story of wearing the hijab in Halifax. Beyond sharing insights into her craft and the young women's stories, like other chapters in this section, Gonick grapples with key issues that arise through the research process, including the complex relationships between research and social change.

To conclude this section, in chapter 5, Kennelly, Stam, and Schick exemplify the value of doing community-engaged and participatory action research (PAR). They use fieldwork vignettes to illustrate the benefits and complications of community-based and participatory action research methodologies, and, like Berman and MacNevin in chapter 1, work deeply to examine the ethics and power relations embedded in their research. Kennelly et al. are especially committed to unpacking the tensions and contradictions that arise when working across "fields," and between academics and social service providers. They use Bourdieu's concepts of *field*, *doxa*, and *habitus* to analytically reflect on the ways these concepts help explain their own experiences as researchers.

Taken together, the five chapters in this section challenge us, as Amerah does, to "think about it"—to think about how we as researchers, authors, students, practitioners, teachers, parents, and allies can work with children to craft opportunities and spaces that help celebrate, amplify, and empower all manner of voices.

REFERENCE

Albanese, P. (2016). *Children in Canada today* (2nd ed.). Toronto: Oxford University Press.

1 Adults Researching with Children

Rachel Berman and Maggie MacNevin

LEARNING OBJECTIVES

- To consider the issues of reflexivity, positionality, and power in research with children
- To identify the differences between research *on* versus research *with* children
- To understand gatekeeper issues and ethical ways of seeking children's participation in research
- To explore a variety of ways of generating data with children
- To engage with an example of ethics-in-practice

There are many children and many childhoods, each constructed by our understandings of childhood and what children are and should be.

—Dahlberg, Moss, & Pence, 2007, p. 43

INTRODUCTION

Since the 1980s, in conjunction with and spurred on by the rise of the global children's rights movement, the new **sociology of childhood** has driven a growing body of research with children on a variety of topics, particularly in the United Kingdom, Australia, and New Zealand. However, this has happened to a lesser degree in North America. In 2009, Canadian sociologist Patrizia Albanese observed that

> Sociology in Canada has been relatively and comparatively slow to jump to action when it comes to its own distinct contributions to childhood studies.... Canadian sociology has seemingly "given up" children as social subjects, worthy of study in their own right, to developmental psychologists, instead focusing on socialization and the intergenerational transmission of culture and roles. For the most part, Canadian sociologists treat children as objects that are being acted upon by parents and society. In mainstream Canadian sociology, children remain undefined, a homogenous lump to be sculpted and acted upon, either virtually invisible or in need of protection. (p. 138)

Although this state of inaction is slowly changing (as the existence of this book signifies) the dominant approach in sociological research in this country remains research *on* rather than *with* children. This is the case for many reasons, including what research gets funded, and what research gets approved by Research Ethics Boards, bodies that are also impacted by and participate in the perpetuation of prevailing cultural norms about children and childhood. What is encouraging for the state of research with children in Canada is that the latest version of the *Tri-Council Policy Statement: Ethical Conduct for Research Involving Humans-2* (CIHR, NSERC, & SSHRC, 2014), a policy of the funding body of the Social Sciences and Humanities Research Council of Canada (SSHRC), has recently shifted greatly in its conceptualization of children. Since its previous edition (CIHR, NSERC, & SSHRC, 2010), it has moved away from an age-based, developmentalist approach to consent towards ideas regarding children's maturity, decision-making capacity, and the importance of context.

The focus of this chapter is on research with younger children, and on what Corsaro (2005) describes as micro-level approaches to data generation, such as interviews, focus groups, and **ethnography**, as well as creative methods, paying particular attention to the role(s) of the researcher and conceptualizations of children in the process (for a discussion of reflexivity in research with youth, see Raby, 2007). More specifically, we begin the chapter with a discussion of reflexivity in **qualitative research**, particularly as it relates to researcher positionality, and then move to examine how children are conceptualized in research, paying particular attention to research *on* children and research *with* children. We next consider issues connected to gaining access to child participants, as well as what is involved in seeking participation from children themselves in research. The researcher's role is then discussed, as are issues of **power** in the research process. A dilemma faced by a research team is presented prior to the conclusion of the chapter.

RESEARCHERS AS INSIDERS? RESEARCHERS AS OUTSIDERS?

Reflexivity is a key feature of qualitative research. It involves being explicit about our process of doing research and considering issues of power and authority (Berman, 2014). Davis, Watson, and Cunningham-Burley (2008) explain that reflexivity involves self-scrutiny and political awareness during the research process and propose that it involves both academic knowledge and the personal culture or perceptions of the researcher. Day (2012) proposes three questions that are important to consider when discussing reflexivity and qualitative research:

> First, in our representations of the social world, what are our underlying assumptions about the production of knowledge—how do we know, and who can claim to know? What is considered legitimate knowledge, and what role does power, identity and positionality play in this process? Finally, how does one put into practice the reflexive techniques and address methodological issues in a way that results in valid, good-quality social research? (p. 61)

With regard to "who can claim to know" and "the role of power, identity and positionality," traditionally, qualitative researchers have described a researcher's social location or positionality as being either inside or outside, with the insider researcher defined as someone who can say "I hold prior knowledge and understandings of the group I wish to study, and am also a member of that group" (Greene, 2014, p. 2). As Bhopal (2010) points out, however, "who and what we choose to study is based on our appreciation of *difference*" (p. 193); in other words, even a researcher located deeply inside a particular group may feel there are things she or he does not know about the community, and would like to find out. As well, Gregory and Ruby (2011) argue, although a researcher may consider her/himself to be an insider, participants may actually feel otherwise. They also contend that one cannot be both an insider and an outsider at the same time, while Gair (2012) maintains that our common humanity renders us all insiders with some ability to understand and empathize with one another. Benefits and risks may be connected to both positions.

Other researchers, particularly those working within critical, feminist, and postmodernist approaches, argue that our identities are not fixed, but rather fluid and shifting, and therefore resist easy categorization (Merriam et al., 2001). We are positioned on a continuum and are always, to some degree, both inside and outside (Merriam et al., 2001; Ochieng, 2010). How so? Being an insider or an outsider is a relative position that shifts in relation to others participating in the research and as the research unfolds. To describe one's positionality in research is clearly more complex than simply identifying oneself as either an insider or an outsider.

In research with children, reflexivity may involve considerations of "our own positionality, what brings us to the project and what we really think of children" (Nutbrown, 2010, p. 11). In regard to our own positionality, when we think about research with children, we may believe that we are automatically insiders—after all, we've all been children at one time! However, we are also outsiders; firstly, we are no longer children; secondly, children and childhoods are diverse; and thirdly, children today exist in a different historical context than we did.

WHAT DO WE REALLY THINK OF CHILDREN/ "THE CHILD"/CHILDHOOD?

Research *on* Children

If you adhere to the idea that children, by virtue of their age and stage, are cognitively, emotionally, and socially fundamentally different from adults, that there are universal patterns of development that unfold predictably, and that children are unreliable research informants, you are taking up a psychological, or more specifically a developmentalist, approach to children. Chances are your research questions likely centre on growth and developmental norms that you seek to measure, you seek consent (only) from parents or guardians before conducting your research, and your chosen methods encompass research *on* children by carrying out nonparticipant observations that take place in a laboratory and/or by conducting interviews or surveys with parents and/or teachers about children. Your explanation of the data is informed by this approach as well. If interviews or focus groups are conducted with children, questions are modified to suit developmental stages, and topics that are deemed unsuitable for a child's developmental stage are avoided, for example, topics that involve sexuality or race.

Research *with* Children

In contrast, if you take up a new sociology of childhood approach, your research is informed by very different assumptions. Sociologists working within this paradigm assert that childhood is not a natural state; rather it is a social construct (Honig, 2009) and a social institution (Prout & James, 1997). Conceptualizations of childhood are said to vary according to cultural, social, economic, historical, and geographical context, among other dimensions. Children in this framework are viewed as social actors, active agents, not merely passive subjects of social structures and socialization processes (Prout & James, 1997). Alanen (2009) explains that **agency** involves how "those positioned as children ... influence, organize, coordinate and control events taking place in their social worlds (p. 170).

Sociologists working within this framework assert that researchers need to focus on children's lives in the here and now, on the idea of children as beings, rather than becomings (although see Uprichard, 2008, for a discussion of children as beings *and* becomings). These sociologists want to know what children can tell us about their lives, and see children as competent and capable, and able to share their views with researchers (Prout & James, 1997; Thorne, 1993/2005). Moreover, there are researchers working within the new sociology of childhood who argue that children are a marginalized group in society akin to other minority groups, and assert that it is the generational order, or children as a generational category, that requires the attention of researchers seeking to understand childhood. In other words, what knowledge do children have of their social position in society, of the status of being a child, and of adult/child relations (Alanen & Mayall, 2001; Mayall, 2002, 2008)? Generally, researchers working within the framework of the new sociology of childhood take a qualitative approach to research and utilize ethnography as a method, although this is by no means always the case, as will become apparent later in this chapter.

Research *on* children versus research *with* children is not necessarily a strict dichotomy. Mayall (2008), for instance, locates herself somewhere between these two sites. Prout and James (1997) assert that it would be absurd not to pay attention to children's biological commonalities. It is also important to emphasize that children (like adults) are not a monolithic group, and there is no such thing as the child. Children vary by social class, ability/disability, gender and gender identity, ethnicity, immigration status, "race," and, of course, age. Ajodhia-Andrews's (2016) work provides an example of the importance of considering intersectionality in research with children. In her Canadian study about children's school life and their experiences of inclusion and exclusion, she "co-researched" with children with disabilities from ethnoculturally diverse backgrounds via **participatory** and narrative approaches. In the next section we will see that dominant conceptualizations of children and childhood play a key role in gaining access and seeking children's participation in research.

GAINING ACCESS AND SEEKING CHILDREN'S PARTICIPATION

Before conducting a research project, approval must be given by an ethics committee. In the context of the university, this is the institution's Research Ethics Board (REB) (although there may be exceptions for undergraduate student researchers who may seek ethical approval from an instructor). For researchers seeking to recruit children as participants, issues of access are influenced primarily by the need for parental consent. Indeed, in some places, children cannot legally agree to participate in research without the prior consent of their parent or guardian; in other places this is not a requirement. In Canada, this legal requirement varies from province to province (Mishna, Antle, &

Regehr, 2004); however, it would be highly unusual for an institutional review board not to require parental consent, regardless of the legal context. While the need for parental consent is intended to protect children, it also restricts children's autonomy and participation rights (Hill, 2005). Moreover, oftentimes once parental consent is provided, researchers do not seek the **informed consent** or **assent** of a child participant. More is said about the issue of seeking children's informed consent or assent shortly.

When REB approval is received, researchers must then navigate a system of **gatekeepers,** such as school administrators, child care (daycare/preschool) managers, and/or classroom teachers in order to connect with the parents or guardians of potential child participants. In Toronto, for example, the Toronto District School Board (TDSB) has an External Research Review Board. If a project is given approval from that body, the principal at the designated research site/school must still provide approval for research to take place. In contrast to gatekeepers within adult social communities, these gatekeepers have more definitive authority to restrict access and often have a protectionist stance towards the children in their care (Corsaro & Molinari, 2008).

If and when access to participants is granted, Powell, Fitzgerald, Taylor, and Graham (2012) note that children may be wary of refusing to participate in research, or of dropping out once a study has begun. This is particularly likely if the researcher plays another authoritative role in the participants' lives, such as teacher or therapist, or if the research is conducted in an educational or therapeutic setting in which children are conditioned to submit to the authority of adults (Fargas-Malet, McSherry, Larkin, & Robinson, 2010; Powell et al., 2012).

Institutional settings such as child care centres, schools, hospitals, or other clinical settings are not the only places research with children is conducted. Depending on the focus of the research, other sites may be preferable, such as homes and/or community spaces, although all sites have their own gatekeeping challenges and ethical concerns. For example, Bushin (2007) discusses benefits and concerns regarding researching with children in their homes; she notes the flexibility involved in using the child's home as a research site, as opposed to trying to set up a rushed interview in a school setting. She reports parental gatekeeping requires discussion and negotiation, as she expected. However, she notes her concerns that children may have been told to participate and not given a choice, that an interview could be potentially overheard, and/or that even if an arranged time may have been convenient for the parent, it may not be so from the child's point of view.

Barnikis (2015) also used children's homes as a site for **research conversations** with five- and six-year-old children, where they compared their child care experiences to their current experiences in elementary school in Ontario. When she showed up at their homes to carry out the interview, most of the children had an idea that she was coming to do research. However, one child appeared to have no idea that she was coming, leaving her wondering how much choice that child had to participate (personal communication, August 2014). In an effort to respect their rights, the children were given a choice about whether their parent would remain present during the interview, and one of the five children she interviewed made this request (Barnikis volunteered in the child care centre where the children had attended and so was familiar to both the children and their parents). She also sought assent from each child before beginning the study and maintained vigilance with regard to their willingness, verbally and nonverbally, to continue throughout the time she was with them (Barnikis, 2014). While Australian researchers Dockett and Perry (2011) advocate for the use of assent with young children (ages two to six years), the REB affiliated with the Canadian university Barnikis was connected with did not require assent from children younger than seven at the time she submitted her ethics protocol. The practice of this REB has changed since 2014 and is in keeping with the directions in the publication of the latest Tri-Council policy (2014) discussed at the outset of this chapter.

There is a growing body of literature on ethics in research with children, with a large amount of space devoted to debates around informed consent and assent (see Alderson & Morrow, 2011, and Powell, 2012, for further discussion). Not surprisingly, these debates are linked to how children are conceptualized. As well as varying by academic discipline or paradigm, it is important to note that how children are conceptualized also varies by culture. This variation speaks to the need for researchers—particularly researchers from the dominant culture—to be respectful and attentive to such differing conceptualizations of children, as this will (and should) impact the way research is approached. See Ball (2005) for a discussion of research partnerships with non-Indigenous researchers and **Indigenous** communities and their children.

CRAFTING THE RESEARCHER'S ROLE

As we have illustrated above, conceptualizations of children impact the very possibility that children may partake in research, and the ways we attempt to seek their participation in order to generate meaningful data. Christensen (2004) recommends that, in addition to reflecting on conceptualizations of child/children, what it means to be an adult needs consideration given that adults and children have different cultural experiences based on generation and social/group membership. Such constructions will also impact how power is negotiated throughout the study and how data is generated (Christensen, 2004).

In her study with children at school, Christensen (2004) describes herself as adopting the role of "an unusual type of adult" (p. 174), an adult who does not intervene in children's conflicts or direct children's activities as she observes. In her research conversations with children, Mayall (2008) presents herself as an outsider, a "familiar adult," who has forgotten much about childhood and acknowledges that childhood has changed over the years and is therefore seeking knowledge about contemporary childhood from those who are most knowledgeable about the topic. Other researchers have sought to share insider status by adopting a "least-adult role," a concept introduced by Mandel (1988) in her ethnographic study with children. In ethnographic research, the researcher spends an extended period at a site in an effort to become a member of the group he or she is studying. The goal is to see the world from the point of view of the participants (Hadly Gold, 2007). Given the nature of ethnographic research, negotiating the researcher's role becomes particularly important.

In taking on the least-adult role, a researcher seeks to "blend … into the social world of the children, not siding with adults, operating physically and metaphorically on the children's level in their social worlds" (Mayall, 2008, p. 110). Mandel (1988) spent time in the playgrounds, classrooms, hallways, bathrooms, and lunchrooms of two childcare centres. Between 1976 and 1978 she was at a centre in Boston, Massachusetts, for 15 months, and between 1978 and 1979 she spent 10 months at a centre in Hamilton, Ontario. She focused her time with the two- to four-year-old children. Most of the time that she spent in the least-adult role was during children's "free play" time. She explained that she did not direct or correct children's actions. She initially assumed the role of learner and over time became an active participant, spending great lengths of time with the children in their sandpit play. Her attempt at the least-adult role was not without problems, which she discusses.

In Corsaro and Molinari's (2008) longitudinal ethnographic research in a classroom in Italy, the researchers spent hundreds of hours with a group of children, following them from preschool to elementary school in order to understand how children made meaning of group life and daily transitions over time. The researchers found that Corsaro's identity as a cultural outsider, an American and an Anglophone with limited ability to speak Italian, was helpful in that it positioned him as "an atypical, less powerful adult" (p. 240). The children teased the researcher for his lack of understanding, positioning the children as more competent, and helping the researcher to empathize with the generally lower social status of children. As Seele (2012) points out, researchers cannot simply choose a role to play and expect it be so; rather, it develops in relation to the participants. Further, she argues that children, like adults, construct and reconstruct their identities in interactions with other people; this "involves aspects of belonging and connectedness as well as distancing and drawing boundaries" (p. 323). Ultimately "Big Bill" (Corsaro) was not seen as a peer, but rather as an "adult friend" (Corsaro & Molinari, 2005, p. 10), similar in many ways to the least-adult role.

The pros and cons of the least-adult role are debated in the literature. Buchbinder, Longhofer, Barrett, Lawson, and Floersch (2006) assert the significant physical size difference immediately marks adults as different from, and more powerful than, children. However, in Warming's (2011) ethnographic study, she argues that rather than take on the role of "other adult" or "detached observer," in her study with children in child care in Denmark, she took up the "least-adult role" with success. She also took up other participant roles, including performing childlike positions and paying attention to her body or "embodied knowing." She explains that as she analyzed and reanalyzed her field notes and engaged in reflexivity, paying attention to power and embodied knowing enabled her to gain a sense of "**critical sociological empathy**" (p. 7), which in turn served as a source of insight, especially into interpreting the nonverbal actions of some of the children. She argues that such an approach provides a sound and ethical way to interpret the perspectives of children.

In addition to the critique regarding physical size difference, the least-adult role prevents the researcher from intervening, which may send the message that he or she condones particular behaviour. Birbeck and Drummond (2005) argue that because there is a societal expectation that adults protect children from harm, a researcher assuming the least-adult role and failing to intervene when a child's emotional or physical safety is at risk is not only behaving unethically but is also creating an artificial social environment. They advocate for adopting the role of "caring participant observer." A further critique of the least-adult role is that it is deceptive; that is, the researcher hopes that children will (mistakenly) regard him or her as a peer, and forget that they are under observation (Una Qualitative Methods Working Group, 2010).

WHO'S GOT THE POWER?

Whether or not you accept the position that children are a minority group, adult control over children's lives is a central feature of most children's experience, be it explicitly or implicitly (Mayall, 2008). This has important implications for researchers working with children, as we have seen in the previous discussions regarding access and participation and the researcher's role. Connolly (2008), however, notes that child participants can and do resist, and even subvert, the power of adult researchers, thereby demonstrating their agency. For example, in his year-long ethnographic research on South Asian girls in a London, UK, school, Connolly (2000, 2008) found that some very young participants introduced explicitly sexualized, gendered, and racist language to research conversations. Instead of interpreting this as a problem to be corrected, he interpreted this as an attempt to undermine the researcher's power and authority, as well as perhaps to impress him, as they recognized the high social status he enjoyed as a white male. He clarifies that he did not introduce the concepts of race or racism into the study with the five- and six-year-old participants, but in an effort not to appear to condone racist statements expressed in the interviews, he relays that he would always ask the children to justify what they said and ask them such questions as whether they felt that what they said was a "nice" thing to say (2000, p. 506). As he explains, such an approach allowed him to understand the "complex and contradictory" nature of their perspectives and the justificatory frameworks they used while also sending the message that he did not agree with or approve of what they said.

Warming (2011), writing from a poststructuralist perspective, argues that "power relations are not fixed once and for all. On the contrary, they are continually reconstructed, negotiated and altered through verbal and non-verbal (mis-)reiterating performance and interaction in the complex and contested discursive space of sense-making

(Butler, 1993). Power relations between adults and children are thus shaped through the different ways in which adults and children perform their roles" (p. 5). In box 1.1, an adult sociologist is positioned by one of the child participants in her study as "seen but not heard."

Box 1.1: Seen But Not Heard, Brenda Gladstone, PhD

During my ethnographic study of a peer support group for school-aged children in Toronto, I was first confronted by the question of who I was in the study setting and how I should explain my role to the participants I was observing. Methods texts advised me on ways to help the children become more at ease with my presence in their classrooms, clinical care settings, and neighbourhoods. Much of this guidance was simply pragmatic, but it also raised questions about the power and privilege of the adult researcher working in childhood settings. Recognizing this created tensions that were not easy to resolve. I was reluctant to embrace suggestions to take the least-adult role in order to align myself with my young participants. My ongoing ambivalence about this issue is illustrated in the following reflections from my observational field notes:

> I sat as unobtrusively as possible near the discussion and the action, so that I could observe and take notes without disrupting the routine set by the [adult] facilitators and children. Sometimes I was asked to participate in activities, and I did so when it would have drawn too much attention to me to refuse. I also participated in those activities where appropriate, meaning that they were not associated with having a parent with a mental illness, such as competing in a liquorice eating contest, just for fun. I chose to work more as observer than participant because the formal, didactic teaching style used by the facilitators afforded such a role. This made recording written notes quite unobtrusive, meaning that it did not interrupt the action or make the research too obvious, at least as far as I was aware. As neither a child participant, nor facilitator I didn't want the children to see me as they saw the other adults. I wanted them to feel that they could talk with me about the program more easily as an outsider. I found it amusing in one of the later sessions when a child named me "Seen But Not Heard" as she named each of us, indicating where we were to sit, having been given a rare opportunity to do so by the facilitators. I also played a cat-and-mouse game with one of the boys who liked to "pretend" he was trying to read my notes. He seemed to be teasing me, and to have fun, but I also wondered whether he or others were curious about what I was writing. Another boy seemed incredulous that I would "write all this stuff down."

Continued

Observations of these interactions with the children implied that they were also interested in who I was and what I was doing and why. But they did not ask this directly. Instead, they challenged me, albeit indirectly, and with humour, naming me "Seen But Not Heard." By reversing the way this English idiom is usually interpreted, I was censured by the children for my silence and refusal to claim my status within the group. This understanding is not unlike other instances in the study when children used humour to reduce tensions and to build rapport among peers and deal with complex emotions in a group context, without explicitly challenging those in positions of power to do so.

ADULTS AS INSIDERS RESEARCHING WITH CHILDREN?

The least-adult role is an attempt to become part of children's social world by being more like a child, but people are not only categorized as adults or children, as noted earlier. They are **racialized**, gendered, and so forth. It is possible that a child may orient to the adult interviewer as insider based on one or more of these other dimensions. Kurban and Tobin (2009) note, "[t]hings are said in certain contexts, to particular people with whom the speaker shares, to a greater or lesser extent, language, assumptions and a point of view" (p. 27). Notably, a review of research concerning race and ethnicity and young children found that few studies described in detail the race, ethnicity, and social class demographics of the participants, the community, and the researchers themselves, suggesting that increased reflexivity is needed (Una Qualitative Methods Working Group, 2010).

Can we talk about race? Confronting Colour Blindness in Early Childhood Settings is a research project underway in Toronto (Berman et al., 2016; MacNevin & Berman, 2016). One of the research questions includes "what **discourses** about 'race' and racial identities are employed by children in this early learning setting?" Twenty-one children were each asked to draw herself/himself and a friend as a way of engaging in conversations about "race" and identity with an interviewer. The team is made up of a diverse group of racialized bodies, including the authors of this chapter, and we have spent some time reflecting on how this might impact our data gathering. Preliminary analysis of interviews with the children suggests that participants as young as two-and-a-half years were aware of similarities and differences between their own and the interviewers' skin colours. For example, a South Asian participant who was two-and-a-half years old began to draw a picture of the white interviewer, and then rejected the brown paper he had been using for his self-portrait, stating, "This is too dark." A four-year-old white child being interviewed by the same researcher identified his skin colour as "white, like yours." When asked later in the interview if there were any skin colours he would not like to have, the same participant can be seen orienting to the interviewer once again, and marking them both as a certain type of insider: "Maybe all of the other skins than white, and there would just be white-skinned people like you and me. I think maybe I just want white and tan."

In their analysis of an interview with two young Turkish girls in Germany, Kurban and Tobin (2009) interpret the girls' utterances in relation to the researcher's and participants' gender, race, social class, and age, the physical setting of the interview, the geographical location, the language of communication, and other contextual factors. For example, they infer that the researcher's identity as a non-German-speaking Turkish woman evoked a heightened awareness in the girls of their own ethnic identities and, consequently, elicited interview responses that highlighted Turkishness.

A particular social location may work to make an adult researcher feel like an insider in some way. For example, in Thorne's (1993/2005) ethnographic study, in which she examined how, when, and why gender makes a difference or not in everyday interactions in two US schools, she noted that she felt closer to the girl participants, given her own familiarity with their gender-typed interactions. She also noted that, paradoxically, she was able to see the boys' interactions and activities more "clearly" than those of the girls' (p. 26). Social location(s) beyond age require consideration when "adults" are researching with "children."

ADDITIONAL METHODS OF DATA GENERATION IN RESEARCH WITH CHILDREN

Griffin, Lahman, and Opitz (2016) highlight the potential for thoughtfully chosen data collection methods to reduce the power imbalance between adult researchers and child participants. In addition to participant observation, interviews, and focus groups, creative approaches are also utilized both within and outside of ethnographic research. Mayall (2008) asserts that children generate and make meaning of their knowledge through discussing, comparing, and debating with other children, and as such advocates for the use of what she calls the "research conversation." In his study, Connolly (2008) used a similar method, interviewing children in friend groupings, thereby promoting a sense of ease and rapport, and generating rich informal conversations among children. Likewise, Kurban and Tobin (2009) found the conversation between their two young participants, with little input from the researcher, to be a rich source of data.

In Di Santo and Berman's (2012) study exploring children's views about their impending transition to kindergarten in Toronto, Ontario, focus groups incorporating a puppet were used. Thirty-three focus groups were conducted over a period of two months in 2005. Mauthner (1997) suggests that three children for small group discussions with five- and six-year-olds is the optimal size for a focus group; the average number of children per focus group in the Di Santo and Berman (2012) study was three, with the smallest being two and the largest consisting of nine participants. These group sizes were reflective of the challenges of recruitment, such as withdrawal from the research and absenteeism on the day the focus group was conducted. For example, five children were interviewed individually because they were the only participants from their program. If a child did not want to participate even after giving assent, his or her wishes were respected and the child had the option to re-join the group later. This approach reflects an ongoing or fluid approach to consent (Flewitt, 2005). It is worth noting that our study differs from the previous studies with groups of children discussed in this chapter, in that the University Research Ethics Board that approved this study required researchers to adhere to a very strict script; thus, engaging in **research conversations** was not possible.

Griffin, Lahman, and Opitz (2016) contend that group conversations are not always the best method, arguing that one-on-one interviews can facilitate sharing about certain topics, and allow for interpretation of data that is unaffected by group interpretation. In her research on how young people solve personal problems, however, Punch (2002a) employed both group and one-on-one interviews, and on feedback forms, some participants indicated they preferred individual interviews because they were less embarrassing, while others preferred group interviews for the same reason. Griffin et al. (2016) describe several alternatives to the traditional one-on-one interview technique. In shoulder-to-shoulder interviews, the researcher sits beside the child, perhaps on the floor, creating a sense of comfort and intimacy without the formality of direct eye contact. In walk-around interviews, the researcher converses with the child as he or she moves about freely; the child goes about his or her routine and thus retains some power and control over the interview.

Underwood, Chan, Koller, and Valeo (2015) discuss the use and efficacy of particular types of interview questions and techniques in their use of participatory play-based interview methods with children with disabilities. They used content analysis to examine the types of questions posed by the researchers; these included direct questions, routine-based questions, rapport-building questions/comments, steering questions/comments, and play-based questions/comments. They also considered the types of responses that were generated. Underwood and colleagues (2015) report that a combination of question types, in no particular order, was critical for yielding a range of responses. Rapport-building activities, however, were found to be crucial, and the authors recommend that 15 to 20 minutes of play time be built into all interviews. They explain that "the interviewers followed the children's lead, which included stepping back when children did not want their play to be interrupted and giving children time to transition to the next activity. These actions were intended to give children control and develop rapport" (p. 15).

Punch (2002b) depicts the use of visual and written methods of data collection as a means of reducing the power imbalance between adults and children, as children may feel less pressure to produce the "correct" answer than they do in a one-on-one interview. Veal (2005) outlines what she calls creative methods: methods or tools that may be more participatory or transformative than traditional methods, depending on how they are used and the context of study. They include drawings, social mapping, story games, and drama. Clarke and Moss (2001), working within the field of education, introduced the "mosaic approach," in which visual and kinesthetic (physical) modes of communication are valued alongside verbal modes. Such methods include book-making, photography by children, drawing, child-led tours, map-making, and interviews underpinned by participant observation. Clarke (2011) describes this approach as a multimodal and participatory form of ethnography in which meaning is co-constructed with children. As noted earlier, Di Santo and Berman (2012) incorporated puppetry as way of engaging child participants, as have others.

Punch (2002b) cautions against perceiving children as a unified group for whom certain "child-friendly" research methods are always appropriate (she notes that many adults would benefit from and may prefer the use of more innovative techniques, which she terms "person-friendly" rather than "child-friendly," p. 337). Similarly, Barnikis (2014) cautions that we should not assume that all children like to engage in creative activities, for example, drawing. A child in her study was very clear that he did not want to partake in drawing, but was happy to engage in a research conversation with her. However, all 21 children in the Can we talk about race? project seemed happy to draw themselves and a friend as they talked about the colour of their eyes, hair, lips, nose, and skin. Researchers working with children continue to grapple with issues such as what makes for **participatory research** with children, how best to represent children's voice(s), as well as how to interpret their silence(s), among other issues (Bucknall, 2014; Pascal & Bertram, 2009; Spyrou, 2015; Warming, 2011).

RESEARCH FOR CHILDREN

Lundy and McEvoy (2012) make a distinction between those researchers working within a "new sociology of children" framework and those working within a "children's rights" paradigm. Although both seek to employ participatory methods and emphasize children as capable and competent agents, the later approach also explicitly makes the connection between children's rights in research and children's rights as recognized in the **United Nations Convention on the Rights of the Child (UNCRC)**. The focus in their discussion is on matters that affect children, not insight into children's lived experiences. They advocate for taking up a children's rights approach to research whereby adults provide children with support and guidance so as to enable them to form a view on all matters affecting them. This approach has been referred to as research for children.

CHILDREN LEADING THE RESEARCH

Roberts-Holmes (2014) makes a point that should be very clear from your reading of this chapter so far when he asserts that "the power dynamics between adults and children are perhaps the major difficulty that faces researchers. Such power dynamics can be a barrier to the collection of high-quality evidence from young children." Rather than adults trying to negotiate outsider status or insider status, or engaging as co-researchers, he asserts that a "possible way to overcome this difficulty is to invite other children to be researchers themselves" (p. 142). Although still somewhat unusual, there are a growing number of studies in which adults take a back seat and the research is led by children and young people of different ages and abilities (see e.g. Alderson, 2008; Bucknall, 2010; Burke, 2005; Brownlie, Anderson, & Ormston, 2006; Kim, 2016; Levy & Thompson, 2015). For a discussion about involving children and young people in analysis of data, see Coad and Evans (2008). Whatever approach is taken in the research, strategies for disseminating results with children also require consideration and action (Tisdall, 2009).

A POINT OF CONSIDERATION FOR RESEARCHERS AND REBS: ETHICS-IN-PRACTICE

Ethics-in-practice refers to grappling with decisions regarding unanticipated issues that arise as a project unfolds (Guilemin & Guillan, cited in Dorner, 2015). We provide one such example that arose in our Can we talk about race? project connected to issues of confidentiality and conceptualizations of children. When discussing confidentiality in research, Hill (2005) explains that public confidentiality involves not identifying research participants in research reports, presentations, and so forth. One widely used way of attempting to protect public confidentiality is anonymizing data during transcription (however, he also notes how it is difficult to make drawings anonymous; Levin, 1995, as cited in Hill, 2005). When it comes to research with children, Thomas and O'Kane (1998) point out that "[c]onfidentiality is complicated by the fact that adults may expect to be told about the private lives or thoughts of children for whom they are responsible" (p. 337). They were discussing a study in which children were in the care of the state/social workers; however, this expectation could also be shared by parents or guardians of the children. Indeed, Bushin (2007), who interviewed parents and children separately in their home, was asked directly by the child and the parent what the other said. When she explained (again) that everything told to her was in confidence, some of the parents persisted, so she told them whether a topic had not been discussed (if it had not) and whether it had. She also asked them to raise their concerns directly with the child. She noted that this potentially put the child in a difficult position, as the child may have been confronted post-interview by the parent about the content of the interview. She added that she was not sure what the solution is to this dilemma. Our research team was confronted with a similar dilemma, in that a parent noted on her signed consent form that she wanted access to her child's audio-taped interview.

As Thomas and O'Kane (1998) point out, how you handle ethical issues in research with children depends on your conceptualization of children. Thus, this request from the parent was not straightforward, given our orientation in the study to view children as having the right to privacy and confidentiality. The *Tri-Council Policy Statement: Ethical Conduct for Research Involving Humans-2* (2014), a policy of the Social Sciences and

Humanities Research Council of Canada (SSHRC), which provided funding for the study, contains a section on privacy and confidentiality. However, it provides no advice on this issue, other than to note that child abuse must be reported if legally required. We looked to the literature to see what was said on this topic. On the one hand, Johnson, Hart, and Colwell (2014) appear to have no problem with passing data along to parents, although their brief discussion is framed as future information for the child participant; they write "[t]ranscriptions of interviews can even be left with parents or guardians so that children can have a record of them later." (p. 29). Similarly, Cuskelly (2005) is clear that she will grant a parent's request for a copy of raw video data. Sargeant and Harcourt (2012), assert, however, that such a route is not to be taken lightly.

> The children should be fully informed prior to the project beginning about exactly who will have access to the information they provide, in what form; individual transcript/responses, or aggregated data with any identifying information removed. The children should be informed whether their teachers, parents or other adults with authority will know, hear or see what each person has to say. It is then of critical ethical importance that the researcher ensures that *only* those who have been nominated in the informing process are able to access the information. (Sargeant & Harcourt, 2012, p. 56)

Hill (2005) takes another position entirely and discusses a type of confidentiality he calls social network confidentiality, which he describes as not passing on information to family members, friends, or others known to the child, including teachers. Alderson (2014) makes no such distinctions between various types of confidentiality and explains "privacy involves ensuring no one except the primary research team sees identifiable data or personal records and all reports are anonymised. Confidentiality means that each person's responses and identifiable data will not be discussed with anyone else in the study, including parents or teachers, but only among the research team" (p. 94). In the end, in the Can we talk about race? project, we put a letter for the parent in the child's cubby explaining our position, and noting that we would be sharing the final results of the study with the families. We did not hear back from this parent and did not proceed with the interview with this child.

CONCLUSION: REFLEXIVITY AGAIN

Powell et al. (2012) discuss how reflexivity can highlight the situated, contextual nature of children's voices in research. Employing reflexivity, the researcher can interpret how social context influenced the data and why, and what that says about the participants and their knowledge. Reflexivity can also heighten awareness of the diversity that exists within the social group "children" (Christensen & James,

2008). Reflexivity can highlight the complex power relationships that exist between researchers and participants and among children (Connolly, 2008) and make explicit how and why researchers arrived at particular interpretations of children's utterances, which may not always be readily understood (Kurban & Tobin, 2009; Warming, 2011). Reflexive analysis openly acknowledges the researcher's subjectivity, a position that challenges the long-held belief, particularly in developmentalist research, that researchers can be objective and neutral observers of children. Thus, researchers working within the "new" sociology of childhood must unpack dominant conceptualizations and assumptions of the child and children both within and beyond the research process in order to reconsider the role of children within sociology and more broadly within Canadian society itself.

CHAPTER SUMMARY

Together, in this chapter, we

- Considered the issues of reflexivity, positionality, and power in research with children.
- Identified the differences between research *on* versus research *with* children.
- Sought to understand gatekeeper issues and ethical ways of seeking children's participation in research.
- Explored a variety of ways of generating data with children.
- Engaged with an example of ethics-in-practice.

STUDY QUESTIONS

1. Why is researcher reflexivity important to consider throughout the research process?
2. What are some criticisms of the "least-adult role" in ethnographic research with children?
3. If you were going to conduct a research project with children, what is a research conversation you would like to have? Is there a topic you wish a researcher might have asked you about when you were a young child?
4. What challenges do you think you might encounter in doing research **with** children? What are some of the benefits of conducting research **with** children?
5. What do you think of the way the researchers handled the dilemma regarding the parent's request to access their child's raw data? Do you think this might have been handled differently? Why or why not? What can you take from this example that could assist you with any future research you might do with children?

SUGGESTED RESEARCH ASSIGNMENT

Locate a peer-reviewed article in which the approach is research *on* children. Then, find a peer-reviewed article in which research *with* children is the approach. Compare and contrast the two articles. Consider the research questions, data generation methods, findings, discussion, and so on. Be sure to discuss the assumptions about children and/or childhood the authors make in each of the articles.

SUGGESTED FILMS/VIDEO CLIPS

Ethical Research Involving Children
www.youtube.com/watch?v=eLckZKue5Bo
In this video, Associate Professor Nicola Taylor, Director of the Children's Issues Centre at the University of Otago in New Zealand, speaks briefly about ethical research involving children.

Young Children's Rights
www.youtube.com/watch?v=sgwA8US7_ik
In this video, Professor Emerita Priscilla Alderson, Childhood Studies, Social Science Research Unit, Institute of Education, University of London, discusses her work in the area of children's rights, particularly in relation to informed consent.

SUGGESTED WEBSITES

International Ethical Research Involving Children Project
childethics.com
This is the website for the international Ethical Research Involving Children (ERIC) project. "ERIC aims to assist researchers and the research community to understand, plan and conduct ethical research involving children and young people in any geographical, social, cultural or methodological context." This site contains numerous resources.

Children's Research Centre
www.open.ac.uk/researchprojects/childrens-research-centre/
This is the website for the Children's Research Centre, which is affiliated with the Open University in the United Kingdom. The Centre "draws upon a range of disciplinary perspectives and theoretical approaches to evaluate whether and how children and young people can benefit from designing, implementing and sharing findings from their own research into areas that interest them." The site contains links to research projects by children and young people, links to publications by adult researchers affiliated with the Centre, and descriptions of various ongoing projects.

REFERENCES

Ajodhia-Andrews, A. (2016). Reflexively conducting research with ethnically diverse children with disabilities. *Qualitative Report, 21*(2), 252–287. Retrieved from www.nsuworks.nova.edu/tqr/vol21/iss2/6

Alanen, L. (2009). Generational order. In J. Qvortrup, W. Corsaro, & M. Honig (Eds.), *The Palgrave handbook of childhood studies* (pp. 159–174). New York: Palgrave MacMillian.

Alanen, L., & Mayall, B. (Eds.). (2001). *Conceptualizing child-adult relations.* London: RoutledgeFalmer.

Albanese, P. (2009). The missing child in Canadian sociology, is it time for change? *Jeunesse: Young People, Texts, Cultures, 1*(2), 136–146.

Alderson, P. (2008). Children as researchers: Participation rights and research methods. In P. Christensen & A. James (Eds.), *Research with children: Perspectives and practices* (2nd ed.) (pp. 276–290). London: Routledge.

Alderson, P. (2014). Ethics. In A. Clarke, R. Flewitt, M. Hammersley, & M. Robb (Eds.), *Understanding research with children and young people* (pp. 85–102). Los Angeles: Sage.

Alderson, P., & Morrow, V. (2011). *The ethics of research with children and young people.* London: Sage.

Ball, J. (2005). "Nothing about us without us": Restorative research partnerships involving Indigenous children and communities in Canada. In A. Farrell (Ed.), *Ethical research with children* (pp. 81–96). Berkshire, UK: Open University Press.

Barnikis, T. (2014). *"This is how I learn": Children's perceptions of their experiences in two different learning environments.* (Unpublished Major Research Paper). Ryerson University: Toronto, ON.

Barnikis, T. (2015). Children's perceptions of their experiences in early learning environments: An exploration of power and hierarchy. *Global Studies of Childhood, 5,* 291–304. doi:10.1177/2043610615597148

Berman, R. (2014). Introduction. In R. Berman (Ed.), *Corridor talk: Canadian feminist scholars share their stories of research partnerships* (pp. 1–6). Toronto: Inanna Publications.

Berman, R., Daniel, B. J., Butler, A., MacNevin, M., Quadri, R., & Royer, N. (2016). *"Can we talk about race?" Confronting colour-blindness in early childhood education settings.* Paper presented at the Anti-Black Racism Conference, Ryerson University, Toronto, Ontario, February 19, 2016.

Bhopal, K. (2010). Gender, identity and experience: Researching marginalised groups. *Women's Studies International Forum, 33,* 188–195. doi:10.1016/j.wsif.2009.12.005

Birbeck, D., & Drummond, M. (2005). Interviewing, and listening to the voices of, very young children on body image and perceptions of self. *Early Childhood Development and Care, 176*(6), 579–596. doi:10.1080/03004430500131379

Brownlie, J., Anderson, S., & Ormston, R. (2006). *Children as Researchers.* Edinburgh: Scottish Executive. Retrieved from www.scotland.gov.uk/insight/

Buchbinder, M., Longhofer, J., Barrett, T., Lawson, P., & Floersch, J. (2006). Ethnographic approaches to child care research: A review of the literature. *Journal of Early Childhood Research, 4*(1), 45–63. doi:10.1177/1476718X06059789

Bucknall, S. (2010). *Children as researchers in English primary schools: Developing a model for good practice.* Paper presented at the British Education Research Association Annual conference, University of Warwick, Coventry, UK, September 2010. Retrieved from www.leeds.ac.uk/educol/documents/193279.pdf

Bucknall, S. (2014). Doing qualitative research with children and young people. In A. Clark, R. Flewitt, & M. Hammersley (Eds.), *Understanding research with children and young people* (pp. 69–84). Los Angeles: Sage.

Burke, C. (2005). "Play in focus": Children researching their own spaces and places for play. *Children, Youth and Environments, 15*(1), 27–53.

Bushin, N. (2007). Interviewing children in their homes: Putting ethical principles into practice and developing flexible techniques. *Children's Geographies, 5*(3), 235–251.

Butler J. (1993). *Bodies that matter: On the discursive limits of "sex."* New York: Routldege.

Canadian Institutes of Health Research (CIHR), Natural Sciences and Engineering Research Council of Canada (NSERC), & Social Sciences and Humanities Research Council of Canada (SSHRC). (2010). *Tri-Council policy statement: Ethical conduct for research involving humans.*

Canadian Institutes of Health Research (CIHR), Natural Sciences and Engineering Research Council of Canada (NSERC), & Social Sciences and Humanities Research Council of Canada (SSHRC) . (2014). *Tri-Council policy statement: Ethical conduct for research involving humans.*

Christensen, P. (2004) Children's participation in ethnographic research: Issues of power and representation. *Children and Society, 18*, 165–176.

Christensen, P., & James, A. (2008). *Research with children: perspectives and practices* (2nd ed.). London: Routledge.

Clarke, A. (2011). Multimodal map making with young children: Exploring ethnographic and participatory methods. *Qualitative Research, 11*(3), 311–330.

Clarke, A., & Moss, P. (2001). *Listening to young children: The MOSAIC approach.* London: National Children's Bureau.

Coad, J., & Evans, R. (2008). Reflections on practical approaches to involving children and young people in the data analysis process. *Children & Society, 22*(1), 31–52.

Connolly, P. (2000). Racism and young girls' peer-group relations: The experiences of South Asian girls. *Sociology, 3*(3), 499–519.

Connolly, P. (2008). Race, gender and critical reflexivity in research with young children. In P. Christensen & A. James (Eds.), *Research with children: Perspectives and practices* (2nd ed.) (pp. 173–188). London: Routledge.

Corsaro, W. A. (2005). *Sociology of childhood* (2nd ed.). Newbury Park, CA: Pine Forge Press.

Corsaro, W. A., & Molinari, L. (2005). *I Compagni: Understanding children's transition from preschool to elementary school.* New York: Teachers' College Press.

Corsaro, W. A., & Molinari, L. (2008). Entering and observing in children's worlds: A reflection on a longitudinal ethnography of early childhood in Italy. In P. Christensen & A. James (Eds.), *Research with children: Perspectives and practices* (2nd ed.) (pp. 239–259). London: Routledge.

Cuskelly, M. M. (2005). Ethical inclusion of children with disabilities in research. In A. Farrell (Ed.), *Ethical research with children* (pp. 97–111). Berkshire, UK: Open University Press.

Dahlberg, G., Moss, P., & Pence, A. R. (2007). *Beyond quality in early childhood education and care: Languages of evaluation* (2nd ed.). London: Routledge.

Davis, J., Watson, N., & Cunningham-Burley, S. (2008). Learning the lives of disabled children: developing a reflexive approach. In P. Christensen & A. James (Eds.), *Research with children: Perspectives and practices* (2nd ed.) (pp. 220–238). London: Routledge.

Day, S. (2012). A reflexive lens: Exploring dilemmas of qualitative methodology through the concept of reflexivity. *Qualitative Sociology Review, 8*(1), 60–84.

Di Santo, A., & Berman, R. (2012). Beyond the preschool years: Children's perceptions about starting kindergarten. *Children & Society*, *26*(6), 469–479.

Dockett, S., & Perry, B. (2011). Research with young children: Seeking assent. *Child Indicators Research*, *4*(2), 231–247.

Dorner, L. (2015). From relating to (re)presenting: Challenges and lessons learned from an ethnographic study with young children. *Qualitative Inquiry*, *21*(4), 354–365. doi:10.1177/1077800414557824

Fargas-Malet M., McSherry, D., Larkin, E., & Robinson, C. (2010). Research with children: Methodological issues and innovative techniques. *Journal of Early Childhood Research*, *8*(2), 175–192.

Flewitt, R. (2005). Conducting research with young children: Some ethical considerations. *Early Child Development and Care*, *175*(6), 553–563.

Gair, S. (2012). Feeling their stories: Contemplating empathy, insider/outsider positionings, and enriching qualitative research. *Qualitative Health Research*, *22*(1), 134–143. doi:10.1177/1049732311420580

Greene, M. J. (2014). On the inside looking in: Methodological insights and challenges in conducting qualitative insider research. *The Qualitative Report*, *19*, 1–13.

Gregory, E., & Ruby, M. (2011). The "insider/outsider" dilemma of ethnography: Working with young children and their families in cross-cultural contexts. *Journal of Early Childhood Research*, *9*(2), 162–174. doi:10.1177/1476718X10387899

Griffin, K. M., Lahman, M. K. E., & Opitz, M. F. (2016). Shoulder-to-shoulder research *with* children: Methodological and ethical considerations. *Journal of Early Childhood Research*, *14*(1), 18–27.

Hadly Gold, K. (2007). Will the least adult please stand up? Life as "older sister Katy" in a Taiwanese elementary school. In A. Best (Ed.), *Representing youth: Methodological issues in critical youth studies* (pp. 157–181). New York: NYU Press.

Hill, M. (2005). Ethical considerations in researching children's experiences. In S. Greene & D. Hogan (Eds.), *Researching children's experience* (pp. 61–86). London: Sage.

Honig, M. (2009). How is the child constituted in childhood studies? In J. Qvortrup, W. Corsaro, & M. Honig (Eds.), *The Palgrave handbook of childhood studies* (pp. 62–77). New York: Palgrave Macmillan.

Johnson, V., Hart, R., & Colwell, J. (2014). *Steps to engaging young children in research, Vol. 1*. Retrieved from www.bernardvanleer.org/steps-to-engaging-young-children-in-research

Kim, C.-Y. (2016). Participation or pedagogy? Ambiguities and tensions surrounding the facilitation of children as researchers. *Childhood*, *24*(1), 84–98. doi:10.1177/0907568216643146

Kurban, F., & Tobin, J. (2009). "They don't like us": Reflections of Turkish children in a German preschool. *Contemporary Issues in Early Childhood*, *10*(1), 24–34.

Levy, R., & Thompson, P. (2015). Creating "buddy partnerships" with 5- and 11-year old-boys: A methodological approach to conducting participatory research with young children. *Journal of Early Childhood Research*, *13*(2), 137–149.

Lundy, L., & McEvoy, L. (2012). Children's rights and research processes: Assisting children to (in)formed views. *Childhood*, *19*(1), 116–129.

MacNevin, M., & Berman, R. (2016). The Black baby doll doesn't fit: The disconnect between early childhood "diversity" policy, early childhood educator practices, and children's play. *Early Child Development and Care*, *187*(5/6), 827–839. doi:10.1080/03004430.2016.1223065

Mandel, N. (1988). The least-adult role in studying children. *The Journal of Contemporary Ethnography*, *16*(4), 433–467.

Mauthner, M. (1997). Methodological aspects of collecting data from children: Lessons from three research projects. *Children & Society, 11*, 16–28.

Mayall, B. (2002). *Towards a sociology for childhood: Thinking from children's lives.* Buckingham: Open University Press.

Mayall, B. (2008). Conversations with children: Working with generational issues. In P. Christensen & A. James (Eds.), *Research with children: Perspectives and practices* (2nd ed.) (pp. 109–124). London: Routledge.

Merriam, S. B., Johnson-Bailey, J., Lee, M., Kee, Y., Ntseane, G., & Muhamad, M. (2001). Power and positionality: Negotiating insider/outsider status within and across cultures. *International Journal of Lifelong Education, 20*(5), 405–416. doi:10.1080/02601370110059537

Mishna, F., Antle, B. J., & Regehr, C. (2004). Tapping the perspectives of children: Emerging ethical issues in qualitative research. *Qualitative Social Work, 3*(4), 449–468.

Nutbrown, C. (2010). Naked by the pool? Blurring the image? Ethical issues in the portrayal of young children in arts-based educational research. *Qualitative Inquiry, 17*, 3–14.

Ochieng, B. M. N. (2010). "You know what I mean": The ethical and methodological dilemmas and challenges for Black researchers interviewing Black families. *Qualitative Health Research, 20*(12), 1725–1735. doi:10.1177/1049732310381085

Pascal, C., & Bertram, T. (2009). Listening to young citizens: The struggle to make a real participatory paradigm in research with young children. *European Early Childhood Education Research Journal, 17*(2), 249–262.

Powell, M. A., Fitzgerald, R. M., Taylor, N., & Graham, A. (2012). *International literature review: Ethical issues in undertaking research with children and young people* (Literature review for the Childwatch International Research Network). Lismore: Southern Cross University, Centre for Children and Young People / Dunedin, NZ: University of Otago, Centre for Research on Children and Families. Retrieved from www.epubs.scu.edu.au/cgi/viewcontent.cgi?article=1041&context=ccyp_pubs

Prout, A., & James, A. (1997). A new paradigm for the sociology of childhood? Provenance, promise and problems. In A. James & A. Prout (Eds.), *Constructing and reconstructing childhood: Contemporary issues in the sociological study of childhood* (2nd ed.) (pp. 7–32). London: RoutledgeFalmer.

Punch, S. (2002a). Interview strategies with young people: The "secret box," stimulus material and task-based activities. *Children & Society, 16*, 45–56.

Punch, S. (2002b). Research with children: The same or different from research with adults? *Childhood, 9*(3), 321–341.

Raby, R. (2007). Across a great gulf? Conducting research with adolescents. In A. Best (Ed.), *Representing youth: Methodological issues in critical youth studies* (pp. 39–59). New York: NYU Press.

Roberts-Holmes, G. (2014). *Doing your early years research project: A step-by-step guide* (3rd ed.). London: Sage.

Sargeant, J., & Harcourt, D. (2012). *Doing ethical research with children.* Berkshire, UK: Open University Press.

Seele, C. (2012). Ethnicity and early childhood: An ethnographic approach to children's ethnifying practices in peer interactions at preschool. *International Journal of Early Childhood, 44*(3), 307–325. doi:10.1007/s13158-012-0070-1

Spyrou, S. (2015). The limits of children's voices: From authenticity to critical reflexive representation. *Childhood, 18*(2), 151–165.

Thomas, N., & O'Kane, C. (1998). The ethics of participatory research with children. *Children & Society*, *12*, 336–348.

Thorne, B. (2005). *Gender play: Girls and boys at school*. New Brunswick, NJ: Rutgers University Press (Original work published 1993)

Tisdall, E. K. M. (2009). Dissemination—or engagement? In E. K. M. Tisdall, J. M. Davis, & M. Gallagher (Eds.), *Research with children & young people: Research design, methods and analysis* (pp. 194–220). London: Sage.

Una Qualitative Methods Working Group. (2010). *Researching "race" and ethnicity with children in the field: A critical appraisal of qualitative research approaches, methods and techniques*. Retrieved from www.unaglobal. org/documents/unaworkingpaper3.pdf

Underwood, K., Chan, C., Koller, D., & Valeo, A. (2015). Understanding young children's capabilities: Approaches to interviews with young children experiencing disability. *Child Care in Practice*, *21*(3), 220–237. doi:10.1080/13575279.2015.1037249

Uprichard, E. (2008). Children as beings and becomings. *Children & Society*, *22*(4), 303–313.

Veal, A. (2005). Creative methodologies in participatory research with children. In S. Green & D. Hogan (Eds.), *Researching children's experience: Approaches and methods* (pp. 253–272). New York: Sage.

Warming, H. (2011). Getting under their skins? Accessing young children's perspectives through ethnographic fieldwork. *Childhood*, *18*(1), 39–53. doi:10.1177/0907568210364666

2

"You Even Wrote Down Our Homework!": Ethnography and Creative Visual Methods in Doing Research Along with Children and Young People

Diane Farmer

LEARNING OBJECTIVES

- To discuss a crucial methodological shift in which researchers are moving away from studies undertaken *on* children and embracing methods that offer insights *from* children's lives
- To explore some of the strengths, challenges, and evolving tools in conducting ethnographic studies along with Canadian students
- To hear from children on what schooling is like by adapting observation and interview techniques
- To consider some examples of children's autobiography in how they make use of creative visual methods to explore experience and meaning on their own terms

---

Leon[1]: These are pictures of my friends that came over that night when I got the camera. That's Kim, walking away. And this is her doing a cartwheel.

Interviewer: Is she in this school as well?

Leon: No.

Cody: What is the name of this category (of pictures taken)?

Leon: Friends. And this is a picture of her again with her hair messed up.... And this is her again, we were having pizza that night.

(Interview on pictures taken at home by students. Leon and Cody are in a grade 5/6 class. Interview transcript with a group of four students, *École du Monde.*)

INTRODUCTION

What changes when doing research *along with* children and youth? O'Kane's account of seminal scholarship describes a methodological shift, one in which researchers are moving away from studies undertaken *on* children conceived as "objects of concern," and embracing methods that offer opportunities for children and youth to engage more actively in the research process (O'Kane, 2008). With this shifting focus, scholars have been asking questions such as Who is the research for? or What can we ask young people, and to what end (Tilleczek, 2011)?

While researchers agree on the centrality of young people's perspective, methodological debates are abundant in view of finding ways to accomplish this, as seen in chapter 1 in this collection, by Berman and MacNevin (see also Farmer & Cepin, 2015). **Power** imbalance is presented as the biggest challenge in research involving children and young people (Coad & Evans, 2008; O'Kane, 2008). This chapter discusses how exploring research techniques in new ways and through various mediums may help reduce gaps in the power imbalance between adult researchers and young participants while offering a better-informed perspective on social phenomena. In the short exchange presented above, the researcher takes on a more discreet position, asking clarification of context (Is she in this school as well?), a student spontaneously takes on the role of the interviewer (What is the name of this category?), while the author of the pictures, Leon, decides to introduce the theme of movement, introduced by the researcher, through a cherished **friendship** (That's Kim, walking away. And this is her doing a cartwheel…. And this is a picture of her again with her hair messed up). Children, in particular, have long been excluded from research. It was assumed that they lacked the maturity, competence, and understanding to be seriously included as legitimate participants in a study. This raises two issues: first, the need to recognize children as capable of introspection and as co-constructors of meaning in research situations, and second, the need to recognize that research design and tools, developed with adult participants in mind, need be reexamined. Including young participants requires acknowledging their status as valuable social actors, uniquely located and therefore capable of offering valuable insights along with (and in interaction with) other social actors on the complexity of the social world. It also demands that, as researchers, we critically examine our ways of engaging with research and offer young people the appropriate tools for a meaningful engagement into research. I have conducted several ethnographic studies in Ontario's French-language schools since the early 2000s. Knowledge gained in these ethnographic encounters will serve as the contextual backdrop in developing this theme. I will focus on two research initiatives: first, a project undertaken in collaboration with my colleague, Nathalie Bélanger[2], between 2003 and 2006, and second, a study I conducted as sole investigator[3] between 2009 and 2012.

In offering a retrospective view on the methodologies experimented with in these projects I will start by presenting how, in the first case, classical techniques of school ethnographies were adapted so that children's worlds and perspectives on schooling would emerge. This initial exploration led to a deeper questioning of what might foster meaningful participation for young people. The second example further emphasizes the need to develop enabling tools in studies conducted with children and youth. I will illustrate how creative visual techniques may enrich classical school ethnographies as a reflexive methodological approach to inquiry. The chapter starts with brief descriptions of the context and ethnographies undertaken in French-language minority schools in Ontario. I will then present the methodologies that were developed in each of the projects and discuss how young participants responded to the research situation. Lessons learned from these initiatives will offer insights, as a way of concluding, on new ways of knowing in doing research along with children and youth.

DESCRIPTION OF CONTEXT AND OF STUDIES

Ethnography as a research method is often used when a holistic approach to understanding a question is sought. It is useful in exploring emerging phenomena in everyday life and in questioning often taken-for-granted beliefs. It also serves as a means to restitute marginalized voices (Beaud & Weber, 1997), that is, voices that are often discussed "on behalf of," such as the child in institutional **discourses**, and the student, in particular, when it comes to education (as seen in this collection in Raby and Pomerantz's chapter on girls pushing back on school dress codes). I have used ethnography with the intent of restituting children's perspectives within their educational world.

Early work undertaken by Qvortrup (1994) posits childhood as a minority, exposed to similar societal constraints affecting adulthood, although in a particular way. An ethnographic approach may help in rendering accounts of children's views while unveiling, as well, the context in which such views are being generated. Conceptualizing childhood as a minority doesn't entail, though, that the notion of childhood be understood in isolation. It is worth noting that comparative and cross-cultural analysis reveals a variety of childhoods (as seen in the historical and class-based variation explored by Andrejek in chapter 8 in this collection; Alanen, 2001; Bluebond-Langner & Korbin, 2007; Fass, 2007; James, 2007; James, Jenks, & Prout, 1998; Mayall, 2002; Qvortrup, 2008; Sirota, 1998, 2006). In doing research along with children, one needs to integrate the study of childhood with other defining variables such as class, race, gender, ethnicity, ability, and language (see chapter 6 by Abbas, chapter 9 by Chen, and chapter 18 by Schneider, in this collection). Furthermore, scholars in childhood studies view the social positions of adult and child as inherently **relational**, meaning that one cannot exist without the other (Alanen, 2001; Christensen & Prout, 2002; Mayall, 2000, 2002; Qvortrup, 2008). These considerations have methodological implications.

Participants in the ethnographic studies presented in this chapter were students in Ontario French-language minority schools (for research conducted in Canadian French-language minority schools, see also chapter 7 by Bélanger in this collection).

Historically, French-language schools have been instituted to protect and promote the minority's identity through the curricula and extracurricular activities (Ministère de l'Éducation de l'Ontario, 2004). Given that Ontario Francophones were relegated to a minority status through educational restrictions prescribed during the early establishment of Ontario's public education system (Gervais 1995, 1996; Orfali 2016), education remains a very important site for the community's sense of identity and belonging. While this serves to inform my analysis, my interest lies in opening up the space of schooling in view of gaining a better understanding of students' experiences in everyday life. French-language schools are approached, as well, as microcosms of a particular kind, of the broader educational system in Ontario. In that sense, children and youth who participated in these studies offer insights on experiences that are at once specific to their location, to the school they are attending, and to the community, as well as shared, in a broader sense, with other youth in Canada. I will begin by introducing two multi-year ethnographic studies, the first carried out between 2003 and 2006, on the experience of being a student in a split-level classroom and the second, carried out between 2009 and 2012, on students' exposure to global movements.

Study 1: *Métier d'élève* and Peer Socialization in Split-Level Classes (2003–2006)

The focus of the first study is on the idea of a ***métier d'élève*** (understood as "the art of being a student"), a notion introduced by Perrenoud (1995) to illustrate the complexities of life in school. The notion refers to how a student constructs meaning around her/his sense of "being in school" and of scholarly work, the particular learning contexts in which s/he navigates, and the multiple, and often conflicting, pressures within the particular system in which s/he is located. It also unveils a dual network of socialization (consisting of teacher-student communications as well as through peer interactions) by which a student's experience is shaped and transformed. It positions students as pivotal in the intersection of school, family, and peer relations. Perrenoud's notion of *métier d'élève* inspired numerous studies in Europe in the late 1990s (see, for instance, Bélanger & Farmer, 2004; Dubet & Martuccelli, 1996; Felouzi, 1993; Gayet, 1998; Montandon, 1997, 1999; Sirota, 1993, 1998, 2006; Vasquez-Bronfmann & Martinez, 1992, 1996). These scholars focused on the interplay between (school) normativity and student **agency** (Perrenoud, 1995; Duru-Bellat & van Zanten, 1992) as a distinct lens in the analysis of inequalities in education. In juggling the competing expectations, deadlines, and inner logics within the everyday life of schooling, children construct meaning, progressively and in differentiated ways (Dubet & Martuccelli, 1996). In doing so, they develop representations of who they are as learners, their role as students, the extent to which school is "for them" (Bourdieu & Champagne, 1999; Bourdieu & Passeron, 1979), and ultimately, what to hope from education.

Our particular project on *métier d'élève* examined what happens in contexts of split-level classes, a classroom setting that combines two or more grades under the responsibility of one teacher. The study aimed at understanding the extent to which this specific setting could provide insights on how students view their *métier d'élève*, a concept that hadn't been explored in Canadian sociology. We aimed to unveil, more broadly, processes of inclusion and exclusion at play within the dual network of socialization (teacher-student and student-student interactions) that are generated within this particular type of learning environment (Farmer & Bélanger, 2007; Bélanger & Farmer, 2012). Fieldwork was done over a three-year period in four elementary schools in Ontario, with students who were between 9 and 12 years old, teachers, school administrators, professionals in education, and parents (81 participants, including 40 students). Three of these schools are French-language minority schools frequented by families of socioeconomic status ranging from middle to upper class, in a school located in an affluent suburb of the Greater Toronto Area, to lower to middle class in two other settings, one labelled as "inner-city" in southern Ontario and the other located in a northern Ontario rural community (for more on "priority neighbourhoods," see chapter 20 by Sriskandarajah in this collection). Conventional school ethnographic fieldwork methods were put to work with the added particularity of providing a lens on students as a central focus, which we sought to understand in relation to their teachers and peers (see also Albanese, 2016).

Study 2: New Mobilities and Transnationalism: Children and Youth Mobile Stories (2009–2012)

This study examined students' experiences of migration, their understanding of a global world, and how schools were adjusting to today's increased diversity and high levels of geographic movement in the context of Ontario's French-language schools. I sought to explore this important shift through a three-year research project that focused on children and young participants' life stories. Rather than having the school as my unit of analysis, I paid attention to how children and young people move through school. I focused on children's journeys as my ethnographic lens. The study explored how students make sense of their diverse pathways at the heart of an expanding culture of mobility.

I conducted this second study, which I will be reporting on, in four classes of students ranging from grade 3 to grade 6, and a fifth class of grade 10 students. The study was undertaken in three schools in central and southwestern Ontario characterized by distinct socioeconomic backgrounds, including a French international private school (junior kindergarten to grade 12); a French elementary school, labelled as inner-city (junior kindergarten to grade 6); and a pilot study conducted in a French immersion elementary school, attended by low- to middle-income families (junior kindergarten to grade 8). Some 125 participants took part in the study, including students, teachers, school administrators, professionals in education, and parents (71 students from the two French language schools and 20 students from the pilot study).

The project combined observations and interviews with exploratory creative visual research tools. The intent was for students to express themselves and reflect on their lives by drawing on enabling methodologies (see, for instance, Christensen & James, 2008; Freeman & Mathison, 2009; Gauntlett & Holzwarth, 2006 ; Heath, Brooks, Cleaver, & Ireland, 2009; Kingsley, 2009). I used drawing and digital photography to support a biographical and reflexive inquiry (Farmer & Cepin, 2015; Farmer & Prasad, 2014). The project was designed as a multi-year, intra-site, and multi-site ethnographic study (Milnes & Huberman, 2003).

EVOLVING METHODS IN "DOING ETHNOGRAPHY" *ALONG WITH* CHILDREN AND YOUNG PEOPLE

Observations

Prolonged observations and interviews are typical techniques deployed in ethnographic studies. I will start with an account of the methodological strengths and challenges in applying these techniques with children in the project on *métier d'élève*, using excerpts from field notes and interview transcripts. In negotiating entry as a researcher into the classroom, the teacher's preferences greatly influenced how observations were carried out. In the first school, observations were made from a distance, as the teacher had asked that the research team have no contact with students. Our direct communications with students occurred during interviews. In the two remaining schools, we circulated and interacted with students and therefore engaged with students during individual and group working sessions. While this illustrates that adults—teachers in this case (and parents, as well, who gave formal consent, or not, for their child to participate in the study)—serve as **gatekeepers** in research that involves children. From a methodological perspective, this didn't prevent observations from taking place; it only meant that these would be executed either from a distance or in close proximity to young participants. What was most important was to keep the student and her/his peers at the forefront of the observations. This is illustrated in the following example of an ethnographic scene from the first school.

It is through recording such mundane situations, repeatedly, that it becomes possible to capture the complexity of classroom interactions. In this short example, we first see how the teacher sets the stage for the interaction, dividing the class into two groups, reading out loud with one group and having the other group do independent work. This is one way of managing a split-level class but other models exist as well, which would also change the classroom dynamic. Looking at what grade 6 students were actually doing during this independent work reveals a world that is rich and that is partly hidden from the teacher. Students do all kinds of things with "their time": gazing, writing, reading, coding, and, if the observation sequence were longer, other types of interactions would occur such as quiet talks and discreet movements. The latter part of the observation reveals the human aspect of class interactions, as illustrated by the use of humour by both the teacher and a student, and the teacher maintaining the flow of communication (Goffman, 1959) by saying, "Another answer?" As discussed earlier, adult and child cannot exist without the other, from a **childhood studies** perspective. In this setting, teaching and learning are inherently relational. This perspective allows us to envision students and teachers as both possessing agency.

Box 2.1: Example of an Ethnographic Scene in a Grade 5/6 Classroom

École Sainte-Sophie[4] (Grade 5/6)

11:05 on a warm day of June 2004

The teacher, Madame Claire, is finishing a lesson on time zones with her group of grade 5 students. She asks students to set aside their school agenda, which they were using to consult a graph on time zones. She instructs them to open their notebooks and take turns reading a short text out loud. She then indicates important information that students are to highlight in coded colours. The reading is on the Canada-US Free Trade Accord. Meanwhile, grade 6 students do independent work.

Grade 6 students:

Neville looks up absentmindedly.

Matt moves in his chair, looks at his exercise sheets.

Kim is writing.

Chris is reading.

Neville has resumed reading.

Philip highlights information in green.

Nan is flipping pages.

Jim is reading as he leans his head on his hand.

11:30

(Author's transcription of own field notes)

Group reading continues with the grade 5 students. At that time, Aïcha is reading out loud. Madame Claire makes a little joke about cross-border shopping in the US. She indicates that she has been planning to do so for the past three weekends, unsuccessfully, and then asks the group to define the meaning of "Douanes/Customs."

Peter: "Quand on fouille dans ta voiture."/When your car is being searched.

Madame Claire: "Autre réponse ?"/Another answer?

(Karine explains that it is what divides two countries.)

Madame Claire: "Bonne réponse."/Good answer. (*Field notes, École Sainte-Sophie*)

During school visits, young participants became increasingly curious about the research and the process of note-taking. They would often come to me and ask why I wrote "so much" or what could I "possibly be writing" in my notebook. "You even wrote down our home-work!" was a common reaction. I used this opening to get to know the students, provided examples of notes taken that could be shared, such as sketches I had made of the classroom and where they sat, and discussed their role as research participants in this project.

Observations served as a useful tool in bringing to the surface a rich world of inter-actions between students. However, opportunities to interact with young participants were fairly limited within the structure of a school day. As a research strategy, while considering the overall classroom activities, paying closer attention to specific moments of interaction, such as formal presentations, small group activities, and moments of tran-sition between activities, was key (Farmer & Bélanger, 2007; Perrenoud, 1995). In one of the schools, for instance, upon arrival on my first day, the teacher asked students to introduce themselves by saying something unique about themselves. They responded as follows: *"J'ai neuf ans. Ma mère est de Russie, mon père est du Rwanda." "Je suis Syrienne, je parle plusieurs langues." "Je suis musulmane, je viens du Liban, j'aime aider"* (Farmer, 2008, p. 126)./"I am nine years old. My mother is from Russia, my father is from Rwanda." "I am Syrian, I speak many languages." "I am Muslim, I come from Lebanon, I like to help" (see also Farmer, 2008, p. 115). Such poignant moments emerged at what I would call *research interstices* and raised the question of how we might develop biographical tools that would better capture the richness of children's life experience.

Interviews

Interviews with students were conducted in small groups (three or four students), grouping networks of close friends. In selecting the groups, I was guided by my ob-servations about who interacted with whom in class and resisted the teachers' well-intended attempt to organize students into groups *for me*. This was a deliberate strategy agreed upon within our research team prior to engaging in site visits. Having group in-terviews and ensuring that such groups were composed of mutual friends were intended to alleviate power dynamics between the adult researcher and the young participants, as well as power struggles at play within peer groups. We felt that individual interviews with the adult researcher might be intimidating for the children. However, this was not necessarily the case for every student, as some students preferred individual interviews. Paying close(r) attention to contexts and specific requests thus became an important ethical consideration.

Group interview techniques generated mixed results. Student standpoints comple-mented and at times challenged views of parents and teachers. In these exchanges, it became clear, for instance, that age was a definite marker of status among youth and that embodying this status was exacerbated in this type of learning environment.

> ## Box 2.2: Group Interview with Samantha (Grade 6), Nan (Grade 6), and Aïcha (Grade 5)
>
> ### École Sainte-Sophie
> This interview occurred in June 2004. The research team had been to the class periodically over the previous three months. As a research team, we asked students how they had been selected for a split-level class. They attended a large school where they could also have been placed in a classroom that wasn't split.
>
> *Aïcha:* Je pense qu'on est dans une classe double parce que, comme, je pense qu'ils regardent nos bulletins puis ceux qui sont plus avancés vont dans une classe double, je pense. / I think we are in a split-level class because, like, I think they look at our report cards and those who are ahead are placed in a split class, I think.
>
> *Samantha:* C'est comme Aïcha a dit mais aussi, comme, ceux qui sont plus, comme, indépendants. / It's like Aïcha just said but also, like, those (students) that are more, like, independent. (*Interview transcript, École Sainte-Sophie*)

While parents preferred their child to be in the lower grade (grade 5) of a split class, as this provided an opportunity, in their view, for the child to get ahead, and conversely were reluctant to have their older child (in grade 6) placed with a lower grade, students within *both* grades, instead, shared a common understanding of positive and distinct features that qualified them as "good students" as exemplified by Samantha (grade 6) and Aïcha (grade 5). For the children, being selected for these classes afforded a special standing in relation to peers of the same age.

At times children's statements appeared somewhat reactive rather than being open to the many possibilities for self-inquiry. In the school where we had limited communication with students, for example, a student asked for clarifications regarding the relevance of the interview, stating, "You were there (in the classroom); didn't you see?" The student was reacting to a discipline strategy used by the teacher where girls and boys were assigned alternate seats in the classroom, something I hadn't noticed (field notes). Thus, a question arose about how to increase possibilities for dialogue in ways that would generate a positive space for inquiry. Also, the absence of elements, "obvious" to students, from my account as a researcher, points to the limitation of adult observation techniques on children's worlds. The outcome of this project underlined the importance of expanding methods for researching *with* children and youth. The next step involved developing tools that would not only help in documenting children's complex life stories but support young participants in making sense of their reality and schooling experience.

EXPLORING CREATIVE AND REFLEXIVE VISUAL METHODS

In exploring visual methods, the idea was to expand the parameters for interaction with children and youth in research situations and to encourage students to express themselves and reflect on their experience through tools most familiar to them. The intent was to develop enabling methods in researching *with* children and youth. In using creative research methods with young participants, researchers often employ mixed or multiple media such as digital photography, dramatic performance, drawing, and mapping (see Heath & Walker, 2012). These techniques usually consort with some form of narrative expression (Rose, 2014). Making available several methods gives participants more opportunities to choose as well as some control "about how to contribute and what to say" (Darbyshire, MacDougall, & Schiller, 2005, p. 242).

The use of **creative visual methods** in research does not seek to dismiss traditional ethnographic techniques but rather to combine them with new approaches (see, as well, chapter 1 by Berman and MacNevin in this collection). It is important to underline, as well, that in any research, methodological tools are specifically crafted in light of the nature of the inquiry. Creative methods are no exception and need to be transformed into workable research tools. Used within an ethnographic approach, these tools were allowed to evolve, given that ethnographic work generally requires researchers to reflect on fieldwork activities as they evolve, and adapt research strategies and techniques accordingly. In the second study, I used the drawing of digital **language portraits** and photography as biographical tools. Students took part in the research while in class, as well as outside of class time, during school hours. They conducted additional activities on their own time, at home and in their communities. Teachers were present for the discussions held in class and supported the activities at home and in the community by facilitating the sharing of technology (such as digital cameras).

Language Self-Portraits as Biographic Tools

Students were asked to use the silhouette of a body map to support their reflection on languages, cultures, and movements through life, a tool described as **language portrait as body mapping**. Sociolinguists such as Busch (2010), Krumm (2008), and Castellotti and Moore (2009) developed what are described as language portraits to study the use of languages, power dynamics, and identity. Busch (2010) and her participants co-constructed rich language biographies through the representation of the body as a metaphor (see also Busch, Jardine, & Tjoutuku, 2006; Krumm, 2008).

I was inspired by Busch's technique of drawing and adapted it in the second ethnographic study (2009–2012) discussed in this chapter. In order to capture young people's understanding of their connectedness to the global world, students in my study were invited to respond to the following prompt in French and English: "Je dessine sur ma

Figure 2.1: Manon (Age 16)

Source: Drawing collected in the context of research project entitled Mobilités et transnationalisme: Histoires d'enfants et de jeunes dans la redefinition de l'espace scolaire de langue française de l'Ontario. Funded by the Social Sciences and Humanities Research Council of Canada, 2009–2012 (Farmer, D., Principal Investigator).

silhouette les langues et les cultures qui m'habitent."/"I draw on my silhouette languages and cultures that connect me." To further clarify the scope of the statement, I added, "*des cultures avec lesquelles tu as développé un lien au courant de ta vie*"/"cultures with which you have developed ties throughout your life." Students were also instructed to use a colour legend, as in Busch's studies, to capture the embodied experiences of mobility. They were asked to choose their own legend and apply the colours associated with specific languages and cultures on their body map in whatever places they saw as meaningful. Busch used a "cookie cutter style" of mapping with adults or invited adults to draw their own silhouette. In conducting my pilot study, and through experimenting with digital technologies, a generic drawing of silhouettes was progressively replaced by a digital representation of the student's actual silhouette (Farmer & Prasad, 2014). This had a significant impact on students who understood the biographical work in progress as a unique and individualized metaphor to chart their own body/life experience (Farmer & Cepin, 2015).

Over the course of the study, some 60 students drew themselves. Whether from local or migrant families, every participant presented in his/her portrait broader influences of languages and cultures, many emerging from classroom day-to-day contacts and knowledge of children and teachers' particular stories of migration. The narrative presented students' stories in relation to the overarching theme on mobility. It also presented stories of families and mapped these globally. This is illustrated in a selection of excerpts from interviews conducted with Manon, a grade 10 student at the École Internationale, and Zakia, a grade 6 student in a grade 5/6 class at the École du Monde.

Manon is a grade 10 student enrolled in a French private school in Ontario. Affluent transnational and local upper- to middle-class families attend the school.

> *Manon:* Okay, for mine [my self-portrait], I only speak ... well I speak English and French I would say fluently and uh ... Spanish is a language I've just started learning, it's my third year I would say learning Spanish at [name of school]. And so uh ... what I did, was I divided my body in two. On the right is the English. It's slightly bigger than the French side because I speak English more than French. I would say I speak French with my mom at home, French at school, and I speak English everywhere else. Mostly with my friends I'd say I speak English and outside when I go out, well it's English with everyone else. And I didn't colour my body in ... in ... pink or blue or any colour, because I would say a language is just a part of me so it's not ... the language isn't what represents me. What I wanted to do initially was draw a Canadian flag on me because I am Canadian ... you know, that's really what defines me ... but I didn't know how to draw the leaf. So instead I put Canada on the bottom to show that I am born in Canada, that I am grounded here, this is where I started off. And I put Spanish as a kind of superficial kind of covering on my body [a yellow contour], meaning that I've just started learning it, I haven't really incorporated it completely so I'm really defined by French and English and I've just started in Spanish [laughs].
>
> *Interviewer:* That's great. What about your choice of colours?
>
> *Manon:* I wanted to put two opposing colours but at the same time that looked good together. 'Cause French and English are so different but at the same time in this school, they come into contact so well ... so I thought they went well together like that. (Interview transcript, École Internationale)

Zakia left Algeria two years ago and has been attending a French-language public school in Ontario. She is in grade 6 of a grade 5/6 class. I asked Zakia to comment on her self-portrait, discussing the legend she had created, the categories she constructed, choices of colours, and arrangement on her body:

Figure 2.2: Zakia (Age 11)

Source: Drawing collected in the context of research project entitled Mobilités et transnationalisme: Histoires d'enfants et de jeunes dans la redefinition de l'espace scolaire de langue française de l'Ontario. Funded by the Social Sciences and Humanities Research Council of Canada, 2009–2012 (Farmer, D., Principal Investigator).

Zakia: J'ai choisi le vert pour l'Algérie car à chaque fois que l'équipe de mon pays joue au soccer, ils [les joueurs] portent toujours le vert, parce que c'est une couleur qui a beaucoup de sens dans mon pays, et c'est parce que la liberté c'est vert pour nous, parce que dans les années passées, c'était une guerre et quand on a gagné, on a choisi la couleur verte. J'ai choisi l'orange pour l'arabe, j'ai mis l'orange ici [sur mon foulard] car je suis arabe et si je n'étais pas arabe, je ne le mettrais pas, j'ai choisi le rouge pour le Canada pour la feuille d'érable et pour le rose, je n'ai pas trouvé une couleur et j'ai juste choisi le français et le bleu pour l'anglais./I chose green for Algeria because every time my country's team plays soccer, they [the players] wear a green uniform, because this is a colour that has a lot of meaning for my country, and it's because freedom is represented in green for us, because in past years there was a war and when we won, we choose the colour green. I chose orange for Arabic, I have put it here (on my hijab) because I am Arabic[5] and if I were not I wouldn't be wearing it. I choose red for Canada for the maple leaf and for pink, I did not have a colour and I just choose it for French and blue for English. (*Interview transcript, École du Monde*)

Drawing their self-portrait enabled students to define themselves on their own terms and express themselves using rich and colourful metaphors. Allusion to one's roots consistently came up in discussions and was often associated with the heart and feet. Hands often expressed what they "did" and in using which language. Their narrative included their stories and those of their family and friends. It alluded to life situations and political contexts in which children had been exposed, the bilingual landscape that Manon navigates or the understanding of Algeria's independence in Zakia's narrative and recent migration to Canada. Creative visual methods supported young participants in exploring the many possibilities for self-inquiry, bringing to the forefront a broader perspective on children and young people's lives.[6]

Mobility Mapping through Digital Photography

In this second project, photography was used in school as a way to ease into the project and as a means of training students for the next phase, which consisted of documenting and reflecting on their mobile lives. Digital photography was then used at home and in young participants' neighbourhoods. Students were told the following: *"Avec cet appareil, je prends en photo des endroits, des personnes et des objets qui me branchent."*/"With this camera, I take pictures of places, people, and things that connect me." As an opening statement to the many ways of making sense of personal mobility, the following prompts were included: How do I move? What moves me? Who moves (with) me? The photos were subsequently used in the context of an interview to unpack the subjective meanings of the image. The use of photography as a data collection tool has been referred to as photo-elicitation interviewing (Cappello, 2005), participatory photo interviewing (Jorgensen & Sullivan, 2010), and auto-photography (Clark, 1999). I was drawn to this method because their photographs would allow us to see students' representations of mobility in relation to their home space, local community, and connections worldwide while doing so on their own terms and through their guidance (Farmer & Cepin, 2015). Among other things, we found that objects that families transported throughout their travel held symbolic value. Andréa, a grade 10 student, exemplifies this in the following excerpt, where she discusses pictures taken at home. Andréa attends the same school as Manon, and has been there for several years. Her family has moved often, from one country to another, every four to five years. When asked to discuss the pictures she had taken, she commented on a painting the family has preciously carried with them while migrating from one country to another.

Figure 2.3: "The City Where I Was Born"

Source: Photograph collected in the context of research project entitled Mobilités et transnationa-lisme: Histoires d'enfants et de jeunes dans la redefinition de l'espace scolaire de langue française de l'Ontario. Funded by the Social Sciences and Humanities Research Council of Canada, 2009–2012 (Farmer, D., Principal Investigator).

> *Andréa:* J'ai pris la photo de … d'un … d'un tableau parce que ç'est un paysage de [nom de la ville], ma ville natale d'une église … oui c'est une église je suppose. Ah je ne sais pas en français … une … oui on va dire une église, un couvent./I took this picture of a painting because it is a landscape of [name of city], where I was born, a church … yes it is church I suppose. Ah, I don't remember in French … a … yes a church let's say, a convent. (*Interview transcript, École Internationale*)

Using photography complemented self-portraits by moving from personal narratives about young people's mobile journeys to discussing broader questions of concern about friendship, closeness with family members, poverty, and war (Farmer & Prasad, 2014; Leitch, 2008).[7] In the example above, a sense of belonging and of family roots is nurtured through the experience of movement. Young participants' response to the research activities and group interviews support other studies that have documented that such techniques allow students to engage in research on many levels, including narrative, emotional, expressive, consensual, and conflicting (Busch, 2010; Busch et al. 2006; Castellotti & Moore, 2009; Leavy, 2009).

NEW WAYS OF KNOWING

Conducting ethnographic studies with children and youth has been a learning process for both researchers and participants. It started initially in the *métier d'élève* project by envisioning students as the protagonists of school ethnographic scenes and seizing opportunities to make explicit the purpose of the research and the legitimate role of young participants. Group interviews were meant to empower young participants. These evolved in the project on "new mobilities," going beyond the experience of being interviewed with friends to engaging in a creative reflexive process.

Developments such as these have led researchers to conclude that in "**doing**" youth studies the knowledge gained needs to be useful to young people. Thus, there is a transformative aspect *for the young* in knowledge produced *along with* young people. Attention to the dialogical relationship between researchers and young participants then becomes highly significant as a building block for transformation (Tilleczek, 2011). While enabling methods are crucial to the meaningful participation of young people in research, young people also need to be trained into becoming researchers. Just as research tools are specifically crafted for an intended purpose, knowing how to use these tools takes time. In the case of the studies presented here, it meant discussing concepts (*métier d'élève* and mobility) as they featured in the everyday occurrences of site visits. In the second study, I also used photography in school in preparation for students' research task anticipated at home. Also, through repeated exposure to the interview process in the new mobilities project, students were given opportunities to develop their own skills in the art of interviewing.

As in all research activity, dissemination is an important aspect. In doing research with children and youth it became important to imagine a way of reporting that would be meaningful to young participants. Influenced by Cummins's (2006) notion of identity, text findings from the second project discussed in this chapter were disseminated as a visual research report.[8] Students' drawings, pictures, and words were used as the foundation of the report along with a short presentation on the purpose of the study and emerging themes. These visual reports were specific to the school (for more on these booklets, see Farmer & Prasad, 2013; Farmer & Cepin, 2015). While research methodologies vary greatly, the studies discussed in this chapter offer some insights on new ways of knowing when research is understood as dialogical and reflexive. Such insights and the broader methodological shift in researching *along with* children and young people may support recent trends in Canadian educational systems towards infusing student **inquiry-based learning** in the curriculum (see www.edugains.ca/newsite/studentVoice/).

Understanding one's identity and location by making things and reflecting on the material representation of complex identities may serve as powerful tools in personal and collective transformation, for both young people and adults, as illustrated in the work of Gauntlett (see davidgauntlett.com/research-practice/research-methods-as-a-site-of-dynamic-innovation/). The studies on *métier d'élève* (2003–2006) and on new mobilities (2009–2012) highlighted the use of a combination of tools, from conventional ethnography to visual methods, that require our creative thinking. Allowing time for exploration and offering space to share ideas holds tremendous possibilities in deepening stories and in co-constructing new ones in the collective endeavour we share of theorizing childhood in Canadian society.

CHAPTER SUMMARY

Together, in this chapter, we

- Examined, through discussion and ethnographic studies undertaken with young students in Ontario's French-language schools, what a methodological shift may bring when embracing methods that offer insights *from* children's lives.
- Explored, by cueing on how children and young people responded to research activities held in the context of multi-year ethnographic studies, the strengths and challenges involved in crafting enabling research tools in research involving young participants.
- Sought to gain insights on what schooling and peer relations may look like from students' perspectives using the notion of *métier d'élève*.
- Saw examples of children's visual autobiography and the unbounded rich narratives this approach may reveal, when used by asking, from an ethical perspective, what the research is for and what we can ask young people.
- Saw how giving consideration to the need for young participants to experience and learn how to grow into their role as researchers is crucial in doing research along with children.

STUDY QUESTIONS

1. What would be relevant topics in doing research along with children and youth? To whom would these topics be relevant and in what ways? Reflect on the methodological choices, interactions between researchers and young people, and the various phases in research activities.
2. In what ways do creative visual methods counteract the imbalances of power that exist between adults and youth? Reflect on examples.

3. Have you ever experienced a significant difference between what you value or how you understand particular social issues and what you have read in the media and in scholarly work? In reflecting on enabling approaches when engaging with youth, what else do you see as developing in terms of new ways of knowing?

4. In your view, what does it take in order to create a positive space for self-inquiry in research which children and youth? How could this be done in infusing student inquiry-based learning in school curriculum?

5. In what ways do prevailing cultural assumptions disadvantage young people's status as agents of ability and power? What would be ways for you to challenge such assumptions in your scholarship, at work, and in public discourses?

SUGGESTED RESEARCH ASSIGNMENT

Undertake a review of the literature on a topic that relates to young people. Compare studies undertaken *on children* conceived as "objects of concern" and studies undertaken *along with* children. In questioning what can be asked of young people, and to what end (Tilleczek, 2011), determine the circumstances in which it is suitable to include children. Consider the research design and methods used in studies reviewed, the benefits and challenges researchers faced in their methodological choices, and the assumptions they may hold as adults—in studies both *with* as well as *on* young participants—on how they understand young people's status as agents of ability and power.

SUGGESTED FILMS/VIDEO CLIPS

Artsmethods Manchester. Using Visual Methods with Su Corcoran
www.youtube.com/watch?v=2IsxRWtK_7Y
This video clip discusses the purpose of visual methods in contemporary humanities research and introduces ideas on how to proceed.

Teach Cambodia NGO. Sampour Primary School Visual Ethnography
www.youtube.com/watch?v=svP4n089ZrU
This video clip offers a montage of a visual ethnography project that focused on bringing students' schooling and home experiences closer. Elementary students told stories, drew, and selected an image to create a school mural of village life.

David Gauntlett. Representing Identities (Part 1 and 2: Methods)
www.youtube.com/watch?v=LtS24Iqluq0
In this video clip, researcher David Gauntlett offers a short introduction into research where participants are invited to make things as part of the research process and to build

metaphors using creative visual tools such as drawing or collage. In this presentation, Gauntlett focuses on a study on identities using Lego blocks. Legos were used by participants to reflect on their worlds and lives.

SUGGESTED WEBSITES

EduGains, SpeakUp: You Are the Student Voice
www.edugains.ca/newsite/studentVoice/
This website is designed for Ontario students interested in sharing their ideas and projects undertaken on student engagement. Materials, videos, and animation tools are made available to students and schools to support students in their roles as inquirers, leaders, and advisors. References are also made available for additional reading. Edu-Gains is a website that brings together resources developed by the province of Ontario.

Open University Children Research Centre, Empowering Children as Researchers
www.open.ac.uk/research/main/impact/reports/empowering-children-researchers
This website presents research activities and publications from the Open University Children Research Centre. The Research Centre was established in 2004.

Australian Government. Australian Institute of Family Studies, What Is PAR
   (Participatory Action Research)?
aifs.gov.au/cfca/publications/participatory-action-research
This website offers basic information, workshop material, and references to studies on participatory action research. It discusses when PAR should be used. Although the focus is on the adult population, some of PAR's foundational principles may be of mutual interest to young people and adult participants.

NOTES

1.   Pseudonyms were used for schools and for all participants in the studies discussed throughout the chapter. An earlier paper version, on our evolving methodologies in doing research along with children, was presented by Farmer and Prasad (2013) at the conference Language and Superdiversity: Explorations and Interrogations, University of Jyväskylä, Finland. The paper focused on language and diversity and included a third project undertaken by Prasad in the context of her doctoral dissertation on plurilingual children and pluriliteracies. See Prasad (2015).

2.   Bélanger, N., & Farmer, D. (2003–2006). *Classes à niveaux multiples: Socialisation et exercice du métier d'élève dans les écoles françaises et anglaises de l'Ontario.* SSHRC Standard Grant.

3.   Farmer, D. (2009–2012). *Mobilités et transnationalisme: Histoires d'enfants et de jeunes dans la redefinition de l'espace scolaire de langue française de l'Ontario.* SSHRC Standard Grant. I

would like to acknowledge the invaluable contribution of my colleague, Nathalie Bélanger, as we undertook the first study together. I wish to express my gratitude to the students and adults who participated in these studies, to graduate students who served as research assistants, and to editing comments made by anonymous reviewers. Finally, I would like to express my gratitude to the Social Sciences and Humanities Research Councils of Canada for their generous contribution in both studies discussed in this chapter.

4.   As indicated earlier, pseudonyms were used for schools and for all participants in the studies discussed throughout the chapter. I have used italics to indicate texts that were selected from field notes, as well as from participants, verbatim.

5.   Referring here to the practice of her faith as a young Muslim woman, rather than referring to her cultural identity, and having chosen to wear the hijab.

6.   For additional presentations of language self-portraits see Farmer, 2012; Farmer and Prasad, 2014; Farmer, 2015; Farmer and Cepin, 2015; Farmer, Cepin, and Breton-Carbonneau, 2015.

7.   For more illustrations of young participants' interviews on the photos that they took in the project on "new mobilities," refer to Farmer and Cepin, 2015.

8.   I would like to extend my gratitude to Alissa Adair, research assistant on the project, whose help was invaluable in designing the booklets.

REFERENCES

Alanen, L. (2001). Explorations in generational analysis. In L. Alanen and B. Mayall (Eds.), *Conceptualizing child-adult relations* (pp. 11–22). London: Routledge Falmer.

Albanese, P. (2016). *Children in Canada today* (2nd ed.). Toronto: Oxford University Press.

Beaud, S., & Weber, F. (1997). *Guide de l'enquête de terrain. Produire et analyser des données ethnographiques.* Paris: La Découverte.

Bélanger, N., & Farmer, D. (2004). L'exercice du métier d'élève, processus de socialisation et sociologie de l'enfance. *McGill Journal of Education/La revue des sciences de l'éducation de McGill, 39*(1), 45–67.

Bélanger, N., & Farmer, D. (2012). L'autonomie de l'enfant dans sa construction de soi: Trois études de cas comparées. *Revue Éducation et Sociétés, 29*, 173–191.

Bluebond-Langner, M., & Korbin, J. E. (2007). Challenges and opportunities in the anthropology of childhoods: An introduction to "Children, childhoods, and childhood studies." *American Anthropologist, 109*(2), 241–246.

Bourdieu, P., & Champagne, P. (1999). Outcasts on the inside. In P. Bourdieu et al., *The Weight of the world: Social suffering in contemporary society* (pp. 421–426). Stanford: Stanford University Press.

Bourdieu, P., & Passeron, J. C. (1979). *The inheritors. French students and their relation to culture* (R. Nice, Trans.). Chicago and London: University of Chicago Press.

Busch, B. (2010). School language profiles: Valorizing linguistic resources in heteroglossic situations in South Africa. *Language and Education, 24*(4), 283–294.

Busch, B., Jardine, A., & Tjoutuku, A. (Eds). (2006). *Language biographies for multilingual learning.* Cape Town: PRAESA.

Cappello, M. (2005). Photo interviews: Eliciting data through conversations with children. *Field Methods*, *17*(2), 170–182.

Castellotti, V., & Moore, D. (2009). Dessins d'enfants et constructions plurilingues Territoires imagés et parcours imaginés. In M. Molinié (Ed.), *Le dessin réflexif. Élément pour une herméneutique du sujet plurilingue* (pp. 45–85). Paris: Centre de Recherche Text Francophonies (CRTF)—Encrages, Belles Lettres.

Christensen, P., & James, A. (Eds.). (2008). *Research with children: Perspectives and practices* (2nd ed.). Routledge.

Christensen, P., & Prout, A. (2002). Working with ethical symmetry in social research with children. *Childhood*, *9*(4), 477–497.

Clark, C. D. (1999). The autodriven interview: A photographic viewfinder into children's experience. *Visual Studies*, *14*(1), 39–50.

Coad, J., & Evans, R. (2008). Reflections on practical approaches to involving children and young people in the data analysis process. *Children and Society*, *22*(1), 41–52.

Cummins, J. (2006). Identity texts: The imaginative construction of self through multiliteracies pedagogy. In O. Garcia, T. Skutnabb-Kangas, & M. E. Torrs-Guzman (Eds.), *Imagining multilingual schools: Language in education and globalization* (pp. 51–68). Toronto: Multilingual Matters.

Darbyshire, P., MacDougall, C., & Schiller, W. (2005). Multiple methods in qualitative research with children: More insight or just more? *Qualitative Research*, *5*(4), 417–436.

Dubet, F., & Martuccelli, D. (1996). *À l'école. Sociologie de l'expérience scolaire*. Paris: Seuil.

Duru-Bellat, M., & van Zanten, A. (1992). *Sociologie de l'école*. Paris: Armand Colin.

Farmer, D. (2008). "Ma mère est de Russie, mon père est du Rwanda": Les familles immigrantes dans leurs rapports avec l'école en contexte francophone minoritaire. / "My mother is from Russia, my father is from Rwanda": The relationship between immigrant families and the school system in francophone minority communities. *Canadian Themes/Thèmes canadiens*, (Spring), 124–127 / 113–115.

Farmer, D. (2012). Portraits de jeunes migrants dans une école diversifiée au Canada. *Revue internationale de l'éducation familiale*, *31*, 73–94.

Farmer, D. (2015). Children and youth's mobile journeys: Making sense and connections within global contexts. In C. Ní Laoire, A. White, & T. Skelton (Eds.), *Geographies of children and young people, vol. 6: Movement, Mobilities and Journeys*. New Delhi: Springer.

Farmer, D., & Bélanger, N. (2007). Le métier d'élève dans la classe à niveaux multiples: Regards d'élèves dans une école de langue française en milieu minoritaire. In Y. Herry & C. Mougeot (Eds.), *Recherche en éducation en milieu minoritaire francophone* (pp. 259–266). Ottawa: University of Ottawa Press.

Farmer, D., & Cepin, J. (2015). Creative visual methods in research with children and young people. In L. Holt, R. Evans, & T. Skelton (Eds.), *Geographies of children and young people, vol. 2: Methodological approaches*. New Delhi: Springer.

Farmer, D., Cepin, J., & Breton-Carbonneau, G. (2015). Students' pathways across local, national and supranational borders: Representations of a globalized world in a Francophone minority school in Ontario, Canada. *Journal of Social Sciences Education*, *14*(3), 75–83.

Farmer, D., & Prasad, G. (2013). *Co-Researching and co-producing knowledge with plurilingual students: Reflecting on research collaboration with children and youth across Ontario schools in Canada*. Paper presented at Language and Superdiversity: Explorations and Interrogations conference, University of Jyväskylä, Finland, June 5–7.

Farmer, D., & Prasad, G. (2014). Mise en récit de la mobilité chez les élèves plurilingues: Des portraits de langues qui engagent les jeunes dans une démarche réflexive. *Glottopol. Revue de sociolinguistique en ligne, 24*, 80–98.

Fass, P. A. (2007). *Children of a new world.* New York: New York University Press.

Felouzi, G. (1993). Interactions en classes et réussite scolaire. *Revue française de sociologie, 34*, 199–222.

Freeman, M., & Mathison, S. (2009). *Researching children's experiences.* New York: Guilford.

Gauntlett, D., & Holzwarth, P. (2006). Creative and visual methods for exploring identities. *Visual Studies, 21*(1), 82–91.

Gayet, D. (1998). *École et socialisation. Le profil social des écoliers de 8 à 12 ans.* Paris: L'Harmattan.

Gervais, G. (1995). L'historiographie franco-ontarienne: À l'image de l'Ontario français. In J. Cotnam, Y. Frenette, & A. Whitfield (Eds.), *La francophonie ontarienne: Bilan et perspectives de recherche* (pp. 123–134). Ottawa: Le Nordir.

Gervais, G. (1996). Le Règlement XVII (1912–1927). *Revue du Nouvel Ontario, 18*, 49–125.

Goffman, E. (1959). *The presentation of self in everyday life.* Garden City, NY: Anchor.

Heath, S., Brooks, R., Cleaver, E., & Ireland, J. (2009). *Researching young people's lives.* London: Sage.

Heath, S., & Walker, C. (2012). Innovations in young people research: An introduction. In S. Heath & C. Walker (Eds.), *Innovations in young people research.* New York: Palgrave Macmillan.

James, A. (2007). Giving voice to children's voices: Practices and problems, pitfalls and potentials. *American Anthropologist, 109*(2), 261–272.

James, A., Jenks, C., & Prout, A. (1998). *Theorizing childhood.* Cambridge: Polity Press.

Jorgensen, R., & Sullivan, P. (2010). *Scholastic heritage and success in school mathematics.* Melbourne: Monash University Publishing.

Kingsley, J. (2009). Visual methodology in classroom inquiry: Enhancing complementary qualitative research designs. *Alberta Journal of Educational Research, 55*(4), 534–548.

Krumm, H. J. (2008). Plurilinguisme et subjectivité: Portraits de langues par les enfants plurilingues. In G. Zarate, D. Lévy, & C. Kramsch (Eds.), *Précis du plurilinguisme et du pluriculturalisme* (pp. 109–112). Paris: Éditions des archives contemporaines.

Leavy, P. (2009). *Method meets art: Arts-based research practice.* New York: Guilford.

Leitch, R. (2008). Creatively researching children's narratives through images and drawings. In P. Thompson (Ed.), *Visual research with children and young people* (pp. 37–58). New York: Taylor and Francis.

Mayall, B. (2000). Conversations with children. In P. Christensen & A. James (Eds.), *Research with children: Perspectives and practices* (pp. 109–124). London: Falmer Press.

Mayall, B. (2002). *Towards a sociology for childhood: Thinking from children's lives.* Philadelphia: Open University Press.

Milnes, M., & Huberman, A. (2003). *Analyse des données qualitatives.* Bruxelles: De Boeck.

Ministère de l'Éducation de l'Ontario. (2004). *L'aménagement linguistique—Une politique au service des écoles et de la communauté de langue française de l'Ontario.* Retrieved from www.edu.gov.ca/fre/document/policy/linguistique/guide/index.html

Montandon, C. (1997). *L'éducation du point de vue des enfants: Un peu blessé au fond du cœur.* Paris: L'Harmattan.

Montandon, C. (1999). La sociologie de l'enfance: L'essor des travaux de langue anglaise. *Éducation et sociétés, 2,* 91–118.

O'Kane, C. (2008). The development of participatory techniques: Facilitating children's views about decisions which affect them. In P. Christensen & A. James (Eds.), *Research with children: Perspectives and practices* (pp. 125–155). Adingdon: Routledge.

Orfali, P. (2016, February 23). Kathleen Wynne présente des excuses officielles aux Franco-ontariens. *Le Devoir.* Retrieved from www.ledevoir.com/politique/canada/463649/ontario-kathleen-wynne-presentera-des-excuses-officielles-aux-franco-ontariens

Perrenoud, P. (1995). *Métier d'élève et sens du travail scolaire* (2nd ed.). Paris: ESF.

Prasad, G. (2015). *The prism of children's plurilingualism: A multi-site inquiry with children as co-researchers across English and French schools in Toronto and Montpellier.* A thesis submitted in conformity with the requirements for the degree of Doctor of Philosophy. Toronto: OISE of the University of Toronto.

Qvortrup, J. (1994). Childhood matters: An introduction. In J. Qvortrup, M. Bardy, G. Sgritta, & H. Wintersberger (Eds.), *Childhood matters: Social theory, practice and politics* (pp. 1–24). Aldershot: Avebury.

Qvortrup, J. (2008). Macroanalysis of childhood. In P. Christensen & A. James (Eds.), *Research with children: Perspectives and practices* (pp. 66–86). New York: Routledge.

Rose, G. (2014). On the relation between "visual research methods" and contemporary visual culture. *The Sociological Review, 62*(1), 24–46.

Sirota, R. (1993). Le métier d'élève. *Revue française de pédagogie, 104,* 85–108.

Sirota, R. (1998). L'émergence d'une sociologie de l'enfance: Évolution de l'objet, évolution du regard. *Éducation et société, 2,* 9–34.

Sirota, R. (2006). *Éléments pour une sociologie de l'enfance.* Rennes: Presses Universitaires de Rennes.

Tilleczek, K. (2011). *Approaching youth studies: Being, becoming, and belonging.* Toronto: Oxford University Press Canada.

Vasquez-Bronfmann, A., & Martinez, I. (1992). Paris-Barcelona: Invisible interactions in the classroom. *Anthropology and Education Quarterly, 23*(4), 291–312.

Vasquez-Bronfmann, A., & Martinez, I. (1996). *La socialization à l'école.* Paris: PUF.

3

"We Can Play Whatever We Want": Exploring Children's Voices in Education and in Research

Kate MacDonald

LEARNING OBJECTIVES

- To think critically about how current ideologies of children and childhood impact young people's daily lives
- To read about an example of young children as research participants and experts in their own lives
- To reflect on the disconnect between young people today and the outdoors, and question the boundaries of both indoor and outdoor learning environments
- To think critically about the ways that "natural" spaces are constructed
- To explore the impact that culture and the environment play on individual learning experiences, and to consider the ways that diverse populations may experience the public education system differently
- To question the roles that teachers play in classroom learning and consider models of education and pedagogies that provide alternatives to the current dominant public education system

INTRODUCTION

With the bulk of public education today occurring in formalized, standardized, indoor settings, students have become accustomed to learning within the four walls of their traditionally structured classrooms. In many areas of Ontario, particularly in urban and suburban communities, students' exposure to the outdoors is often limited to the time spent in their schoolyards, spaces that are often flat and barren, with the odd metal play structure, sandpit, running track, or soccer field, and little biodiversity (Samborski, 2010). Not only are schoolyards noted to have an absence of natural aesthetic and sensory aspects, these outdoor spaces are typically designed and constructed by adults. The dominance of adults over young peoples' spaces, such as their classrooms, highlights the structural inequalities faced by children and youth in their daily lives.

Like most environments that are made for children, the design of classrooms and schoolyards is based on common conceptions about childhood that frame young people as incomplete and in the process of becoming adults (Mason & Hood, 2011; Matthews, 2007; Moss & Petrie, 2002; Palaiologou, 2014). A specific social construction of childhood has informed the Ontario public education system, leading to classroom learning that is grounded in behaviourist and developmental approaches in which students are seen as passive recipients of knowledge that is handed down to them by their teachers (Hein, 1995; Roberts, 2009). In this setting, students are typically instructed and assessed by teachers through the reiteration of particular predetermined facts and ideas that make up the public curriculum (Gordon, 2009; Pyle & DeLuca, 2013).

Not only is this school system designed by adults, it is designed to reflect the interests of the dominant social groups. Through standardization, the public education system further **marginalizes** young people who do not fit the hegemonic ideals of a white, capitalist patriarchy. Social constructionists acknowledge that experiences vary depending on social and historical context; however, within this model of education everything from the design of learning spaces to the content that is learned and the way learning is approached is typically determined based on the assumptions that adults have about students' needs. According to Palaiologou (2014, p. 699), "typically adults are the ones who pose what is and what should be for children; they are the decision-makers and the planners in the eyes of the children and, as adults, hold different levels of **power**." In this system, young people are disempowered, as greater value is being placed on children's rights to protection than on participation in the decisions that directly affect their lives.

BEYOND TRADITIONAL EDUCATION

Noting that formalized learning in schools typically relies on the rote transmission of predetermined information from teachers to their students, critical educational scholars have described traditional education as being largely decontextualized and as failing to actively engage students in their education (Dewey, 1938; Giroux, 2014; Scribner & Cole, 1973; Subramaniam, 2002). Recognizing the way that knowledge is constructed based on the social and cultural contexts of a learning environment, these educators have critiqued the traditional behaviourist model of education that views knowledge as absolute and applied across contexts (Desmond, Grieshop, & Subramaniam, 2002; Dewey, 1938; Freire, 1970; Montessori, 1967; Roberts, 2009; Subramaniam, 2002).

Conversely, these educators approach education through constructivist learning theories that acknowledge individuals as active participants in their learning, and support learners in the construction of meaning as they reflect on their experiences (Gordon,

2009; Roberts, 2009). In contrast to traditional behaviourist approaches to education, which promote the reiteration of particular facts and experiences as the ultimate indication of successful learning (Gordon, 2009; Roberts, 2009), constructivist educators employ hands-on learning techniques in student-centred environments using a philosophy referred to as experiential education (Itin, 1999).

Experiential learning can take on many forms, and includes models such as service learning, problem-based learning, adventure education, and **inquiry-based learning**, to name a few (Breunig, 2013; Fenwick, 2001; Gordon, 2009; Roberts, 2009). Inquiry-based learning—one form of experiential education—involves pursuing certain lessons in the classroom based on a student's inquiries and is "focused on questioning, critical thinking, and problem solving" (Savery, 2006, p. 16). In viewing children as possessing knowledge and being capable of critical engagement in their lives, inquiry-based learning places a focus on children's questions, observations, and interpretations of the world around them as a primary method of instruction (Fielding, 2012; Scardamalia, 2002; Savery, 2006). In this learning setting, students have a chance to discuss and reflect on their explorations, and are encouraged to participate in social and collaborative learning. Throughout this collaboration and reflection, students have an opportunity to test theories and grow as learners in a way that makes information more interesting and relevant to their lives. Experiential educators emphasize that praxis, or the connection between theory and practice (Breunig, 2005), can only be achieved through the active process of critical thinking, exchanging ideas, and articulating problems (Gordon, 2009).

As an alternative to traditional, formalized learning environments, experiential learning can take place in a variety of settings and often occurs outdoors (Blair, 2009; Dyment, 2005; Roberts, 2009; Subramaniam, 2002). Outdoor learning spaces provide an arena for spontaneous interaction with inquiry, and therefore a platform for young students to become more actively engaged in their education. There are numerous benefits of learning in outdoor, student-centred environments, including the impact that being outdoors can have on one's achievement of the curricular goals (Blair, 2009; Ghent, Trauth-Nare, Dell, & Haines, 2014; Samborski, 2010), the opportunity that outdoors provides for symbolic or make-believe play (Samborski, 2010), and the level of personal and social development that can occur (Blair, 2009; Dyment, 2005; Jacobi-Vessels, 2013; Kiewra, Reeble, & Rosenow, 2011; Samborski, 2010). Beyond these benefits, outdoor learning environments provide spontaneous opportunities for children's interactions with their surroundings, sparking the students' queries and their desire to engage and explore.

THE STUDY

As children are increasingly being seen as having **agency** in their own lives rather than simply being treated as vulnerable, innocent, and naïve, this chapter incorporates the voices of young people involved in experiential, child-centred education. Specifically,

Figure 3.1: The Outdoor Classroom

Source: MacDonald, K., research project: Back to the *Garten*: Inquiry-Based Learning in an Outdoor Kindergarten Classroom, 2015–2016.

the data explore the experiences of kindergarten students in an outdoor, inquiry-based classroom in Fonthill, Ontario. In inquiry-based settings, students have an opportunity to discover their surroundings and acquire curricular goals in a way that is guided by their interests, rather than through a teacher's dictation (Michalopoulou, 2014).

In an effort to highlight children's voices, I conducted one-on-one interviews with the kindergarteners and asked the students to guide me on a tour of their **outdoor classroom** and tell me about how they like to spend their time in the space. The outdoor classroom tours added a visual element to the interviews, where the students could move around the space and interact with the different parts of the outdoor classroom, for instance running around, climbing on the rocks, digging, or jumping in snow.

The data was supported by subsequent interviews with the kindergarteners' teachers, which provided more context for the kindergarteners' responses and raised additional themes for consideration. The study makes use of phenomenographic methodology, a **qualitative** methodology that values participants' descriptions of their own lived experiences, and presents an account of the kindergarteners' experiences as described by the children themselves. This discussion describes both individual and collective experiences; however, it is intended to raise questions for future research regarding outdoor, inquiry-based learning and should not be generalized beyond the population at hand.

The Outdoor Classroom

I interviewed the kindergarten students and teachers from a public elementary school in Fonthill, a small town in the Niagara Region in southern Ontario. With recent developments placing the community in a high socioeconomic demographic (Town of Pelham, 2014), and the landscape somewhere in between suburban and rural (Environmental Defence, 2013), the school in this study is located in a largely white, affluent area. This school is unique in that it is a part of the public school system, where informal learning spaces are less common.

At the time of this study, the outdoor classroom at the school had just recently been constructed, and was still referred to as being in the process of development by the teachers and students involved. The outdoor classroom spanned a small section of the schoolyard and was made up of mulch pathways with willow arches for entrances. Around the pathways were garden beds with newly planted native plant species and in between the pathways were some older maple trees and some newly planted oaks. At one end of the outdoor classroom, there were rows of large rocks situated as if they were the basis of a classroom structure.

The outdoor classroom was designed by a small group of volunteers from the community and was constructed with the help and support of teachers, school administrators, students, parents, and community members. The outdoor classroom was regularly used by the three kindergarten classes, typically on a daily basis. This was weather dependent, and throughout my interviews I found that the classes used the space for much shorter periods of time, or not at all, on the colder winter days.

The Kindergarteners

I conducted semi-structured interviews with twelve kindergarteners, four students from each of the three classes, as well as with the three kindergarten teachers at the school. In order to make sure that the kindergarteners were fully informed about the research and were interested in participating, I explained to them that I was a student and that I would be writing a story for my school about their outdoor classroom. I asked each child if they wanted to tell me about the outdoor classroom and quickly noticed that while some were eager to show me around, others were less interactive.

Although all of the students who had parental consent to participate also verbally agreed prior to the interviews, there were two cases where kindergarteners who had initially agreed to participate didn't show much interest in doing the interviews. I reminded them that it was okay to stop participating by asking them questions like "Do you still want to talk to me, or would you rather go back and play with your friends?" In these cases, the two children chose to withdraw from the study and return to their classmates. All 15 interviews were conducted in the morning, between the months of January and March in 2015.

Tours of the Outdoor Classroom

I asked each kindergartener to guide me on a tour of their outdoor classroom space and to tell me about how they spent their time outside. The research design and methodology in this study are sensitive to the needs of the young participants and work to minimize the position of power between adult researcher and child. Towards this end, when conducting the interviews, I introduced myself to the kindergarteners by my first name and wore my snow pants in order to be able to sit with the children in the snow and interact with them on equal ground.

The questions that I asked the children were open-ended, and I encouraged them to expand on whatever they felt was most important to talk about. Prompted by the kindergarteners, I often found myself asking additional questions that were not written in my original interview guide. For example, Brandon (a pseudonym) was quiet at first and when I asked what kinds of games he played in the outdoor classroom, he replied saying he didn't know. He mentioned, however, that he liked to run, so I asked him to show me where. Here is how our conversation unfolded:

> *Me:* So what do you guys do out here? What do you spend most of your time doing in the outdoor classroom?
> *Brandon:* Just running and playing.
> *Me:* Running and playing? What kinds of games do you play?
> *Brandon:* I don't know.
> *Me:* Any ideas, like do you remember any games you guys play?
> *Brandon:* Tag.
> *Me:* Tag, yeah, anything else?
> *Brandon:* [Silent]
> *Me:* Anything else you guys do, like other than play games?
> *Brandon:* Run.
> *Me:* You run? And how do you, where do you run, can you show me? Can you show me around?
> *Brandon:* [Gets up and runs around pathways and through arches] We go all the way. [Jumps in sandbox]
> *Me:* You go to the sandbox? Cool, what do you guys do out here?
> *Brandon:* Just dig. [Starts digging in frozen sand with a stick]

Brandon later revealed that he mostly spent time alone in the outdoor classroom. He talked about digging and building in the sandbox, leading to a discussion about the different kinds of things that Brandon would like to build for the outdoor classroom if he had the chance. Even though Brandon was reserved at first, by allow-ing his interests to guide the discussion I was able to learn more about his experiences in the outdoor classroom.

Researcher Responsibility

Putting a focus on what is important to the participants in a research study is one way to use what Nairn and Clarke (2012) call an *ethical radar*. The authors describe this as an essential part of conducting research with young people since, as Kirk (2007, p. 1252) explains, "the unequal power relations that exist between children and adults are duplicated in the research process." In order to more accurately reflect the voices of participants in descriptive research, phenomenographers advocate for a process called researcher reflexivity, during which researchers attempt to recognize their subjectiv-ities and allow their **discourses**, emotions, and identities to inform their investiga-tions (Bednall, 2006; Lippke & Tanggaard, 2014). By consciously acknowledging a researcher's subjectivities, the discussion of her personal worldview can work to en-hance the rigour of a research study and can lead to improved validity and reliability of the results (Sin, 2010).

EXPERIENCES IN THE OUTDOOR CLASSROOM

Throughout my discussions with kindergarteners and their teachers, it was commonly indicated that the outdoor classroom acted as an arena for spontaneous engagement with inquiry. Children's inquiries in the outdoor classroom were described as being sparked by the students' surroundings, as well as through interactions with their peers and through play.

Student-Led Experiences in the Outdoor Classroom

The children described how they spent their time in the outdoor classroom and ex-plained the activities that they liked to engage in while showing me the different areas where they liked to spend their time. These activities were often guided by the students' interests. For example, Brandon described playing tag, running, and digging in the sandbox. When I asked Robert how he spent most of his time in the outdoor space he eagerly explained "we can play whatever we want," and Chelsea talked about exploring the space, stating, "Well me and my friend, um just like, like look around in the outdoor classroom. We just like go look around in the, in the arches."

For the most part the kindergarteners described the activities that they liked to participate in as being "play;" however, it became clear throughout the interviews that through play the students were also participating in learning experiences. For example,

Shane incorporated math concepts when looking at the trees from different perspectives, stating, "um like, those [trees] are a little bit smaller, and how far you are from the tree [shows how big the trees are with his hands] ... if you go farther, the, the, it's almost taller than the other one [walks backwards to sit on the next farthest row of rocks]. He also discussed temperature, stating, "It's really cold but it has this [tree collar] so the, and that part doesn't get cold at all."

Similarly, Anneka demonstrated her learning when she explained, "we know that some of the trees are maple leaf trees because we found a lot of maple leaves in the fall." She also hypothesized about the snow when she said, "I found out that in the winter time when it's like deep snow like this you can go in the arch and the snow is sha ... it's, it's not so deep ... because maybe the, the branches are so strong that the snow, they keep the snow out."

Anneka also explained, "I see the bean plant; this is the bean plant [points up to one of the arches] I could tell because of the vines." Here, despite demonstrating their learning to me, most of the kindergarteners reported that they had not been learning in the outdoor classroom, indicating that they did not recognize their activities as learning activities.

My interviews with the teachers reiterated the autonomy of the kindergarteners in the outdoor space as they described the outdoor classroom as an "open-ended," "natural" arena for inquiry. When I asked Mrs. Teather what the students spent their time doing in the outdoor classroom, she replied, "whatever their imagination is doing that day." One example of this use of imagination was when Anneka described the outdoor classroom, stating, "sometimes we pretend that this is a jungle ... and once, sometimes we pretend that the rocks are cars and busses and stuff like that." Rose explained, "sometimes we ask questions, and sometimes we do animal jokes, like we make little tiny animals, and sometimes we run around." When I asked her what they made animals out of, she clarified "um our bodies," and demonstrated: "like this [gets on hands and knees] that's a little doggie, and if you wanna be a cheetah you just [runs on hands and knees and jumps in the snow]. I'm okay." She went on to explain that they would take turns raising their hand and asking questions to guess each animal.

The students were engaging with the space in a way that promoted their own personal and interpersonal development, as in previous research on informal outdoor learning spaces (Childs, 2011; Jacobi-Vessels, 2013; Kiewra et al., 2011; Samborski, 2010). The way the kindergarteners were involved in dictating how their time was spent in the outdoor classroom promoted intrapersonal learning, including encouraging them to recognize their likes and dislikes and embrace their personal learning styles. By incorporating one's actions, feelings, and thoughts into learning, Novak (2010, p. 23) notes that one can gain "a sense of ownership and control" over his or her knowledge. In having the opportunity to be involved in guiding their own learning experiences in the outdoor classroom, the kindergarteners were thus a part of the process of the **democratization of education** (Roberts, 2009), in which their autonomy was recognized.

Additionally, learning in the outdoor classroom was demonstrated as often being collaborative, where kindergarteners were practising skills such as problem-solving, co-operation, and teamwork. In my interviews with the kindergarten teachers, collaborative learning was emphasized when Mrs. Gall described an instance when a group of kindergarteners collaborated to fix one of the broken willow arches in the outdoor classroom, and explained that they quickly learned that they would need to cooperate in order to achieve their goal. This collaborative learning allowed for constructive growth among students, rather than competition. Similarly, Mrs. Teather talked about the way that the students would effectively negotiate the rules to a game, and Mrs. Corey explained that conflict resolution, including negotiating who was using which parts of the space, happened more fluidly outdoors than in the indoor classroom.

One kindergartener, Anneka, described negotiating the space with her peers when she explained, "sometimes in the winter time a lot of people like to go down there [points down the hill to the field] and, because it's so big and, and there's, and it's a good way for you to be doing stuff like acting around a lot and doing stuff like running around because there's not very much room in the outdoor classroom." Similarly, Shane mentioned "sometimes in the spring a lot, all of the people come out to the outdoor classroom." When I asked him what they did when everyone came out he said, "like we, we just have it be a road and when all the people are right here we make it their road." These findings resonate with Dyment (2005), who describes the social and interpersonal benefits of outdoor learning spaces, as they offer safer, more inclusive, and less hostile social environments among students. Dyment suggests that developing an enhanced sense of empathy, responsibility to others, and communication can lead to more engaged **citizenship** among young people. Thus, collaborative, student-led learning is one way for young people to become empowered to express their voices.

Adult Intervention in the Outdoor Classroom

Although outdoor learning spaces are seen as child-centred and therefore as being more "natural" areas for kindergarteners to engage with inquiry, decisions regarding the design and construction of outdoor classrooms are still ultimately made by adults (Wake, 2008). In this way, the experiences of the students in informal learning settings are still largely constructed by their teachers as well as by the context of their learning space. In this study, while the kindergarteners were initially consulted in designing the outdoor classroom, as well as involved in the initial construction of the space, the students are generally relying on their teachers or other adults to make decisions regarding its further development.

This reliance on adults to make decisions regarding the outdoor classroom was depicted in my interview with Chelsea when she explained, "um, we have a special friend, and um she decided what, if, she decided that we planted the arches and the peppers so she's the, in the summer she's usually, um, she usually tells us if we can plant some stuff or if we don't plant stuff." The friend that Chelsea referred to here is an adult volunteer from the community who was highly involved in the original design and construction of the outdoor classroom. When I asked another kindergartener, Becky, if the students would do any more planting in the spring, she emphasized the importance of the teachers in the outdoor classroom, replying, "yeah, probably, but I don't know yet."

Additionally, both the kindergarteners and the teachers in this study discussed the future growth of the outdoor classroom, describing what it might look like and changes that they would like to see. Further growth of the outdoor classroom was generally discussed as being advantageous to the kindergarteners' inquiries. For instance, when I asked Becky if she thought anything was missing from the outdoor classroom she said that she would like to have a playground right beside the outdoor classroom, stating, "there's a playground over there but I want another one over here," and when I asked Chelsea if she wanted anything else in the outdoor classroom space she said, "Um we want some raspberries too." Brandon told me that he wanted to build a treehouse and to get a telescope to look at the trees.

The teachers in this study similarly discussed the physical elements of the classroom as helping to facilitate learning for the students. For example, Mrs. Teather discussed adding an art easel or a place for the students to record their observations in the outdoor classroom, and Mrs. Corey discussed her desire for more of a natural playground for students' physical use. While further development and growth of the outdoor classroom was discussed as being beneficial to the students' learning in this study, this also reiterates the continued impact that adults have on children's learning spaces. In a discussion about balancing the needs of adults with the needs of children in children-centred spaces, Wake (2008, pp. 424–425) points to a "tendency for adult agendas to dominate the design of children's gardens" and "the prioritization of adults' views over children's needs."

Teachers' involvement in the creation of the outdoor learning environment was highlighted by Mrs. Teather, who expressed that changes in the outdoor space would impact the students' learning experiences, explaining, "we have some beds and some trees and [we will] just make sure that they're maturing and we're still creating that space that's for the students." Similarly, when discussing further development of the outdoor classroom, Mrs. Corey described her role as becoming more intentional, stating, "once I see what's out there I can be a bit more intentional with my questioning and where I'm leading them [the kindergarteners]." The way the teachers discuss their roles here is resonant with the findings of Wake (2008, p. 430), who describes typical outdoor learning spaces as being fundamentally "designed on behalf of children" and "influenced by adult expectations and politics, which determines the expression and use of the garden."

Furthermore, when I asked the students what they learned in the outdoor classroom, they reported learning rules about safety and about caring for the outdoor classroom space. The kindergarteners indicated that they learn to integrate rules that they have been taught in other learning settings, such as rules about safety and care for their surroundings. For example, when I asked Becky what she had learned in the outdoor classroom, she explained, "um, we learned not to touch them [the willow arches], and we learned um, we learned not to pull them out … that there's some things that you can't touch, like you can't touch the string [tied to the arches] and pull them off because it [the willow arch] will fall on somebody in the outdoor classroom and that's all I know." Similarly, Jenny discussed safety when she said that she and her peers liked doing cartwheels in the summer but couldn't do them in the winter in case it was icy. When I asked Jenny if she had learned anything in the outdoor classroom she stated, "Um, yes. I think we've learned not to jump on the rocks." This learning supports the findings of Rose and Paisley (2012, p. 144), who state that "many pedagogical traditions of experiential education also confer privilege to the educator. For instance, just as class bells, assigned seats, and rows of desks are indicative of traditional education settings, experiential education often incorporates similarly universalized mechanisms of control."

Each teacher described their role in the outdoor classroom as that of a facilitator or a provocateur. Mrs. Corey explained, "we've never done direct instruction.… I try and kind of stand back and just see what's happening out there, which I try to do in the classroom as well but … because of the environment of the outdoor classroom it's a lot easier to do that out there." She followed up, saying, "I definitely feel more just like kind of a facilitator there, or a supervisor." Mrs. Teather echoed this, stating, "we try to encourage if they are showing an interest in nature like a bug or stick they found or a leaf or a rock, we try to really bring other students into that learning to see what we can do with it and how we can further that discovery or that investigation." Here, **provocation** is described as an essential element of inquiry-based learning in which the teachers are not seen as instructors but as facilitators involved in the co-creation of meaning with their students (Breunig, 2005; Itin, 1999; Roberts, 2009). A teacher's intervention in this way impacts the meaningfulness of a student's learning by encouraging thoughtful and purposeful reflection on the significance of his or her experiences.

With provocation being an essential part of inquiry-based learning, the teachers' roles as facilitators in the outdoor classroom can also have an impact on students' experiences. While the impact of the teachers' influences can be mitigated in part by the use of student-centred techniques, as demonstrated in the above findings, "the teacher is part of the experiential education process, and that teacher necessarily brings along her or his own values and experiences" (Rose & Paisley, 2012, p. 143). While this study demonstrated the kindergarteners as having input and autonomy in decisions regarding the outdoor classroom, inquiry-based learning "necessarily involves the use of a teacher (instructor, facilitator, or similar leadership position) regardless of calls for decreasing or eliminating the distance between these two entities" (Rose & Paisley, 2012, p. 143).

In this study, the teachers influenced the learning experiences of the kindergarteners in the outdoor classroom through their leadership in the design, construction, and continued maintenance of the space, as well as in their roles as facilitators and their interactions with the students while in the outdoor classroom. This involvement from teachers had an impact on the way that students interacted with and comprehended their learning experiences, in that, as Goulart and Roth contend, "even the most ardent constructivist educators prescribe the tasks and materials" (2006, p. 681).

This discussion raises questions about the involvement of teacher intervention in the outdoor classroom environment, both in the roles that they play in students' inquiries and in the design of the outdoor classroom space. While inquiry-based learning recognizes the need for facilitation, and students are engaging with the physical, constructed elements of the outdoor classroom, the influence of adult intervention in the outdoor classroom spaces demonstrates that students' experiences are inherently connected to the social and cultural aspects of any learning environment. Here I turn to Wake (2008, p. 425), who cautions about the use of outdoor classrooms as spaces in which teachers' intentions "manifest as design, management, and education decisions within gardens, which in turn influence children's experiences."

CONTEXT OF LEARNING SPACES

Even when young people are involved in the democratization of education, or are included in the process of creating learning spaces, learning is inevitably shaped by the social and cultural context in which it is experienced. As Roberts (2009), in his discussion on the historical and theoretical development of the experiential education field, states, "experiential education is not, in fact, 'neutral' nor more resistant than any other pedagogy to the influence of the cultural milieu around it." The context in which inquiry-based learning is employed is therefore highly influential to students' learning experiences.

It is important to reiterate here that while the demographics of the participants, such as race and class, were not collected for this study, the data presented comes from a school in a suburban area of southern Ontario that is primarily white and middle class. Therefore, the sample of participants referred to here does not aim to be representative of diverse groups or generalizable beyond the population at hand. In presenting descriptions of the experiences of the participants in this study, I aim to bring to light potential uses of outdoor, inquiry-based learning and to raise discussions for further research on the topic.

In Ontario, informal and outdoor learning spaces are increasingly being instituted in mainstream public education. As a part of its Capacity Building Series, implemented as one effort to improve instructional methods in Ontario schools, the Ontario Ministry of Education has developed a document intended to act as a guide for implementing inquiry-based techniques into public school classrooms. As of 2014, inquiry-based learning serves as the new standard model for kindergarten within this system (Ontario Ministry of Education, 2013). Similarly, outdoor classrooms and schoolyard garden projects are increasingly emerging at schools throughout the public education system, but these projects often require initiation and significant commitment from members of the school and community.

With the increase in informal learning in the public education system, it is important to recognize that there are social divisions reflected in how outdoor inquiry-based learning has been accepted and implemented in Ontario. For example, children most subject to teacher-led drills, tests, and standard assessment are often in low-income communities, while informal or alternative learning is made most available at schools that reside in predominantly white, affluent areas such as the school in this study. Therefore, while the data presented here does not reflect the experiences of minoritized groups in outdoor, inquiry-based learning, it supports previous research, which indicates that there is an underrepresentation of the experiences of diverse groups in experiential education (Rose & Paisley, 2012).

That being said, it is important not to assume that minoritized groups would benefit from experiential learning and not to imply that their involvement in this model of learning would necessarily be linked to social justice. Rather than simply promoting the inclusion of diverse groups in outdoor experiential learning, Rose and Paisley (2012, p. 142) attest that "we need to examine … the often unquestioned systems of privilege that support and reproduce these conditions of uneven access and underrepresentation." It is therefore vital to further address students' experiences of outdoor learning in public school settings with diverse populations and, as Rose and Paisley (2012) assert, to "trouble educational practices, including those that take place in experiential or outdoor settings," as even these spaces "remain sites of power, privilege, and oppression" (p. 142).

CONCLUSION

All too often adults make decisions on behalf of children. From the design of children's play and learning spaces to the way their time is spent, young people have the right to participate in the decisions that directly effect their lives. By allowing young people the opportunity to explore and experiment, make mistakes and overcome their challenges, it is more likely that students will be able to exercise their autonomy and become engaged, self-directed, motivated, and self-fulfilled learners. Conducting child-centred research and using child-centred classroom pedagogies are both valuable in ensuring that young people are taken seriously when it comes to applying their agency and expressing their voices.

CHAPTER SUMMARY

Together, in this chapter, we

- Saw how the social construction of childhood influences current understandings of learning and of children's capacities, and shapes the public education system.
- Treated children as experts on their own lives, and their voices as valuable and significant.
- Uncovered that most "natural" outdoor learning spaces are still constructed by and/or highly controlled by adults.
- Explored how students' learning experiences are influenced by factors within their learning context as well as by their previous life experiences, and therefore learning experiences differed for every student.
- Recognized that outdoor, inquiry-based learning can be an emancipatory, democratic practice, inspiring young people with the desire to learn, and encouraging learning for social and environmental justice.

STUDY QUESTIONS

1. Imagine a research study that you would like to conduct with young people as your participants. Describe what method(s) you might use to conduct your research, what ethical considerations you might make, and any potential challenges that you might come across in conducting the research.

2. There are currently trends to "naturalize" learning and play spaces, both in Ontario and around the world. Consider the concept of "nature-based learning"; what does it mean to "naturalize" a schoolyard? Are these spaces really natural?

3. Consider your own experiences as a student. How might children's experiences with outdoor inquiry-based learning differ based on their social context? In what ways could a classroom become more a democratic space?

4. There are ethical concerns to take into consideration when working with young people. While being critical of current ideologies about children and childhood, describe some steps that could be taken by a researcher or professional working with young people to help alleviate the power imbalances.

5. Much of the learning that young people do is through play; theorize and explain why the kindergarteners in this study describe their experiences in the outdoor classroom solely as play, despite demonstrating that they had been learning in the space.

SUGGESTED ASSIGNMENTS

1. Design the ideal outdoor classroom space, keeping in mind curriculum goals as well as the goals of inquiry-based learning, such as children's' agency, participation, play, exploration, and imagination. Refer to relevant research on outdoor classroom design.
2. Consider the different ways that children could be involved in the design of an outdoor classroom space. Have a child (preferably kindergarten age) review your outdoor classroom design and collaborate to decide how you would make the best use of the space with the child's interests in mind.

SUGGESTED FILMS/VIDEO CLIPS

Nature Kindergarten
www.youtube.com/watch?time_continue=600&v=MOngsiy67YY

Lecture by Frances Krusekopf, who discusses children's disconnection from nature and the engaging experiences of students in a nature kindergarten. Krusekopf describes sensory experiences had by the kindergarteners and the way the students learned to take risks and develop connections to their learning environment in the nature classroom.

CTV News Clip on Nature Kindergarten in Calgary
www.ctvnews.ca/video?playlistId=1.1333744

A look at Calgary's first public Nature Kindergarten class including testimonies from both the students and the teachers in the program.

Changing School Paradigms: Ken Robinson
www.ted.com/talks/ken_robinson_changing_education_paradigms

In this animated Ted Talk, Ken Robinson discusses the need to change current systems of public education away from models based on conformity and standardization, towards systems where students are stimulated by learning and engaged in their education. Robinson presents a critical discussion on how learning happens and on our conceptions of young peoples' capacities for learning.

Kids Gone Wild: Denmark's Forest Kindergartens
www.sbs.com.au/news/dateline/story/kids-gone-wild

Provides an international context for outdoor learning. Takes a look at outdoor "forest school" kindergarten classes in Denmark, and demonstrates how the social construction of childhood differs based on cultural contexts and influences education.

Neoliberalism, Youth, and Social Justice

www.youtube.com/watch?v=KW5FRuMkQ6g

Educational theorist Henry Giroux discusses the way neoliberalism has contributed to the disinvestment in young people, and to what he calls the *war on youth*. He talks about the loss of the public sphere and critiques public institutions, such as schools, for supporting ideologies of punishment and self-interest over social responsibility. He also discusses changing cultural conceptions of childhood and learning, and reclaiming democratic education.

SUGGESTED WEBSITES

How Does Learning Happen? Ontario's Pedagogy for the Early Years

www.edu.gov.on.ca/childcare/pedagogy.html

A professional learning resource for those working in child care and child and family programs. It supports pedagogy and program development in early years settings that is shaped by views about children, the role of educators and families, and the relationships among them. It builds on foundational knowledge about children and is grounded in new research and leading-edge practice from around the world.

Association for Experiential Education

www.aee.org/what-is-ee

The Association for Experiential Education (AEE) exists to connect a global community of educators and practitioners and expand their capacity to enrich lives through Experiential Education. Website provides resources, networking, and further reading.

Nature Kindergarten: Learning Outside the Box

naturekindergarten.sd62.bc.ca/proposal/

This website provides a proposal for a Nature Kindergarten in Victoria, BC, and supporting documents as well as further reading.

Forest Schools: When Every Day Is a Field Trip Day

www.todaysparent.com/family/parenting/forest-schools-when-every-day-is-a-field-trip-day/

This article in *Today's Parent* outlines the benefits of outdoor learning and incorporates many of the key discussions and debates surrounding this type of education, including exercise and curricular benefits, the roles of nature and technology in development, learning through play, the benefits of sensory experiences, and practising self-regulation in a learning environment.

The Outdoor Classroom Project

outdoorclassroomproject.org/about/the-outdoor-classroom/

Website for the Outdoor Classroom Project, an initiative of the Child Educational Center in California, which advocates for increasing the quantity, quality, and benefit of outdoor experiences for children in early care and education programs through providing educational and consulting services on the value and design of engaging outdoor learning environments to teachers, administrators, and parents.

REFERENCES

Bednall, J. (2006). Epoche and bracketing within the phenomenological paradigm. *Issues in Educational Research, 16*(2), 123–138.

Blair, D. (2009). The child in the garden: An evaluative review of the benefits of school gardening. *Journal of Environmental Education, 40*(2), 15–38.

Breunig, M. (2005). Turning experiential education and critical pedagogy theory into praxis. *Journal of Experiential Education, 28*(2), 106–122.

Breunig, M. (2013). Environmental sustainability and environmental justice: From buzzwords to emancipatory pro-environmental behaviour change. *Journal of Sustainability Education, 5.*

Childs, E. A. (2011). *Impact of school gardens on student attitudes and beliefs.* (Graduate Theses and Dissertations, Iowa State University), Digital Repository.

Desmond, D., Grieshop, J., & Subramaniam, A. (2002). Revisiting garden based learning in basic education: Philosophical roots, historical foundations, best practices and products, impacts, outcomes, and future directions. *Food and Agriculture Organization, 59.*

Dewey, J. (1938). *Education and experience.* New York: Kappa Delta Pi.

Dyment, J. (2005). Green school grounds as sites for outdoor learning: Barriers and opportunities. *International Research in Geographical and Environmental Education, 14*(1), 28–45.

Environmental Defence Canada. (2013). *The high costs of sprawl: Why building more sustainable communities will save us time and money.* Toronto: Environmental Defence Canada.

Fenwick, T. (2001). Experiential learning: A theoretical critique from five perspectives. Information Series No. 385. *ERIC Clearing house on Adult, Career, and Vocational Education.*

Fielding, M. (2012). Beyond student voice: Patterns of partnership and the demands of deep democracy. *Revista de Educación, 359,* 45–65.

Freire, P. (1970). *Pedagogy of the oppressed.* New York: Bloomsbury Publishing.

Ghent, C., Trauth-Nare, A., Dell, K., & Haines, S. (2014). The influence of a statewide green school initiative on student achievement in K–12 classrooms. *Applied Environmental Education & Communication, 13*(4), 250–260.

Giroux, H. A. (2014). Public intellectuals against the neoliberal university. *Qualitative Inquiry Outside the Academy, 9,* 35.

Gordon, M. (2009). Toward a pragmatic discourse of constructivism: Reflections on lessons from practice. *Educational Studies, 45*(1), 39–58.

Goulart, M. I., & Roth, W. M. (2006). Margin|centre: Toward a dialectic view of participation. *Journal of Curriculum Studies, 38*(6), 679–700.

Hein, G. (1995). The constructivist museum. *Journal for Education in Museums, 16*, 21–23.

Itin, C. (1999). Reasserting the philosophy of experiential education as a vehicle for change in the 21st century. *Journal of Experiential Education, 22*(2), 91–98.

Jacobi-Vessels, J. L. (2013). Discovering nature: The benefits of teaching outside of the classroom. *Dimensions of Early Childhood, 41*(3).

Kiewra, C., Reeble, T., & Rosenow, N. (2011). *Growing with nature: Supporting whole-child learning in outdoor classrooms.* Lincoln, NE: Dimensions Educational Research Foundation.

Kirk, S. (2007). Methodological and ethical issues in conducting qualitative research with children and young people: A literature review. *International Journal of Nursing Studies, 44*(7), 1250–1260.

Lippke, L., & Tanggaard, L. (2014). Leaning in to "muddy" interviews. *Qualitative Inquiry, 20*(2), 136–143.

Mason, J., & Hood, S. (2011). Exploring issues of children as actors in social research. *Children and Youth Services Review, 33*(4), 490–495.

Matthews, S. H. (2007). A window on the "new" sociology of childhood. *Social Compass, 1*(1), 322–334.

Michalopoulou, A. (2014). Inquiry-based learning through the creative thinking and expression in early years education. *Creative Education, 5*, 377–385.

Montessori, M. (1967). *The discovery of the child.* Notre Dame, IN: Fides Publishers.

Moss, P., & Petrie, P. (2002). The need for some theory. In *From children's services to children's spaces: Public policy, children and childhood* (pp. 17–54).

Nairn, A., & Clarke, B. (2012). Researching children: Are we getting it right? *International Journal of Market Research, 54*(2), 177–198.

Novak, J. (2010). *Learning, creating, and using knowledge: Concept maps as facilitative tools in schools and corporations.* New York: Routledge.

Ontario Ministry of Education. (2013). Inquiry-based learning. *Capacity Building Series, 32*.

Palaiologou, I. (2014). "Do we hear what children want to say?" Ethical praxis when choosing research tools with children under five. *Early Child Development and Care, 184*(5), 689–705.

Pyle, A., & DeLuca, C. (2013). Assessment in the kindergarten classroom: An empirical study of teachers' assessment approaches. *Early Childhood Education Journal, 41*(5), 373–380.

Roberts, J. (2009). *Beyond learning by doing: Theoretical currents of experience in education.* (Doctoral Dissertation, Miami University), Ohio: Oxford.

Rose, J., & Paisley, K. (2012). White privilege in experiential education: A critical reflection. *Leisure Sciences, 34*(2), 136–154.

Samborski, S. (2010). Biodiverse or barren school grounds: Their effects on children. *Children, Youth and Environments, 20*(2), 67–115.

Savery, J. (2006). Overview of problem-based learning: Definitions and distinctions. *Interdisciplinary Journal of Problem-based Learning, 1*(1), 9–20.

Scardamalia, M. (2002). Collective cognitive responsibility for the advancement of knowledge. In B. Smith (Ed.), *Liberal education in a knowledge society, 97* (pp. 67–98).

Scribner, S., & Cole, M. (1973). Cognitive consequences of formal and informal education. *Science, 182*(4112), 553–559.

Sin, S. (2010). Considerations of quality in phenomenographic research. *International Journal of Qualitative Methods, 9*(4), 305–319.

Subramaniam, A. (2002). *Garden-based learning in basic education: A historical review.* Monograph, Centre for Youth Development, University of California.

Town of Pelham. (2014). *Economic development.* Retrieved from www.pelham.ca/en/services/Economic-Development.aspx

Wake, S. (2008). In the best interests of the child: Juggling the geography of children's gardens (between adult agendas and children's needs). *Children's Geographies, 6*(4), 423–435.

4 About Us, By Us and Other Stories of Arts-Based Research and Marginalized Girls

Marnina Gonick

LEARNING OBJECTIVES

- To learn about arts-based research methods
- To understand the contexts in which arts-based approaches may be useful in working with marginalized girls
- To consider some examples of projects using arts-based methods
- To understand how to work with "data" produced through arts-based approaches
- To consider the relationships between research and social change

---

"Is everyone ready? Okay, places everyone!" LeLy[1] shouts. "Come on people! We haven't got all day!" "Oh my god, that thing is heavy," Fanny complains, not for the first time today, as she picks up the video camera. "If this were a real movie, I wouldn't have to hold this the whole time. We'd have one of those things for the camera to go on."

"Cheap, this school is so cheap, man." Mai slowly gets up, removes the last vestiges of our lunch break from the table that will now form the centre of the video set and leaves Maria peering at her image in the monitor. Staring back at her is Crystal, the character she plays. Maria makes some adjustments to her makeup and hair and then adjusts the adjustments. LeLy and Mai roll their eyes at each other. This is not the first time they have been kept waiting by the exigencies of Maria's hair and lipstick. Maria looks up. "Okay, okay!" She is enjoying herself. "I'm ready." "Ready? AAAAnd action!" LeLy calls out.

We have spent months together developing the characters whose stories make up the video—working out the intricate details of plot, scenes, dialogue, wardrobe, and props necessary to represent girls' lives. The girls are participants in a school–community research project and we are in the final stages of filming the stories of five fictional girl characters that they have written over the school year.

INTRODUCTION

In this chapter I present three different research projects that, like the one described above, use arts-based methodologies in working with **marginalized** girls. I explore the possibilities, potentials, and practicalities of using arts-based research methodologies with and about marginalized girls. These methodologies have been a presence in child and youth research for some time; however, recently they have expanded from a fairly fringe position to one that is being taken up in an increasing number of contexts and by a range of researchers (de Lange, Moletsane, & Mitchell, 2015). The availability of new and relatively inexpensive technologies such as cellphones, video cameras, and disposable cameras have contributed to the increased interest in this way of working with young people. However, it is mainly because of their emphasis on voice, **agency**, and participatory agendas that these methodologies are finding their way into the work of researchers interested in the lives of marginalized children and youth and questions of inequality, social justice, subjectivity, and **power**. Researchers drawing on these approaches often use feminist, critical race, **queer**, disability, **Indigenous**, and/or poststructural theory as their analytical frameworks.

Arts-based research methodologies, like other participatory methodologies interested in social justice, often make a shift in the dynamic between investigators and young people, from one where research is conducted *on* or *about* to one where research is *with* participants (see also chapter 1 by Berman and MacNevin). As the introduction to this section of the book suggests, children and young people's perspectives on their own lives have been insufficiently featured in research about them. In contrast, arts-based research projects are often designed, organized, and implemented by research participants who shape the content, form, and approaches taken. Participants may also be involved with or in control of the dissemination or display of the products created in the course of the project (see chapter 2 by Farmer in this collection). Often presentations of the work take place in the home communities in which the research took place, and/or for policy makers in the hopes of creating a dialogue leading to further discussion and negotiations for social change. In this way, a certain **reciprocity** emerges in the relationships between researchers and those researched—researchers are not merely going into a community and extracting the information or data they need for their own purposes. Participants also gain something, beyond the skills that may be learned or the intrinsic pleasure of creating art with others— sometimes what is gained is framed as empowerment, voice, and/or agency. However, even with this shift in the research dynamic, it is important not to romanticize relations between researchers and researched. As feminist researchers have argued for decades, there are always unequal power relations shaped by differences such as age, race, gender, class, disability, sexuality, etc., and these need to be engaged with, acknowledged, and theorized by researchers (Alcoff, 1995; Bannerji, 1991; Behar & Gordon, 1995).

Marginalized young people are often members of communities who have endured trauma, loss, and forms of **structural violence** such as racism, homophobia, classism, or sexism. For example, Mythili Rajiva (2014) has coined the term *ordinary trauma* to characterize the pervasiveness of sexual violence in girls' everyday lives. She suggests that there is an embodied awareness for girls that their lives are shaped by both societal **discourses** of fear and risk, as well as the very real existence of danger, exemplified in the wealth of feminist research on violence against women (Rajiva, 2014, p. 138). But how is this awareness of trauma and other nameless losses articulated? What if there are no words, no language with which to do so? Depending on the age of participants, even nontraumatic experiences and/or named losses may be difficult to convey in language, if, for example, the participants have had no experience of sharing personal stories, have no habit of self-reflexivity, or are not fully conscious of the forces at work shaping their lives. For these reasons, an arts-based approach may offer access to ways of knowing and routes to knowledge that include, but are not limited by, rationality and existing language. They offer what Pink, Hubbard, O'Neill, and Radley (2010) have called multisensory ways of knowing of everyday contexts. They engage the senses—vision, touch, audio, and emotion—in ways that situate knowing and meaning where language may hesitate, falter, and collapse. Whereas much of research language and analysis demands an orderly hierarchy of coherence, linearity, and causality, including answering questions with long paragraphs of speech, children and young people do not necessarily communicate in this way. Arts-based approaches make room for what Lecercle (2002, p. 53) has called the "unholy mixture"—expressions of uncertainty, contradiction, ambivalence, and that which may not yet be known or sayable.

An arts-based approach draws on the power of imagination, the sense that there could be "something and somewhere else" (Walkerdine, 2016, p. 3). For example, in collecting data and producing analyses, social scientists often depend on and make use of existing social categories such as youth, child, or girl (see also Raby & Pomeranz in this collection). These reflect the way the world is usually organized, the categories that are used to order and make sense of social organization and patterns. Using these categories is useful and probably necessary for delineating the boundaries of a research project, for generating inclusions and exclusions of research subjects and themes, and for communicating results to practitioners and policy makers. However, in making use of these categories, researchers are not only reflecting the social world that currently exists, they are also (re)creating it. These categories emerge from social institutions such as the family, the education system, and religious institutions and allow us to see, understand, and be in the world in certain ways over others.

Art, however, often has a very different raison d'être. It is meant to provoke, to make us re-evaluate what we think we know, and to show us how we might look at the world differently and how we might create new ways of being in the world and relating to others. Thus, not only does the use of art allow for the expression of young people's subjugated knowledge, and to reorient adult-child conversations—to focus less on the assumptions, preconceptions, and concerns of adults and more on those of young people—it also offers the opportunity to imagine alternatives to what currently exists. As de Leeuw and Rydin (2007) suggest, arts practice offers young people the possibility of placing themselves in imaginative cultural identities—what one could be, even if just for a moment. It engages with the complex affective pathways that need to be engaged to think about the possibility of change—not simply at the individual level, but in the wider social context—and to imagine what those changes might entail. We might envision the process as one that provokes a creative flow of potentiality where new thought and meanings may emerge in unpredictable ways. As Wendy Luttrell (2010) writes, arts projects open up opportunities to unsettle, fragment, or dislodge others' gazes, where young people can see themselves and be seen by others in alternative ways to those that have framed them and the communities they come from—for example, as creative, thoughtful, engaged, and articulate.

In what follows I illustrate how these principles of arts-based methodologies may be made concrete through presenting some specific research projects in which I have used this approach in working with marginalized girls. In outlining this methodology, my interest is not to propose an orthodoxy for arts-based research. On the contrary, my goal is to incite the doing of research that multiplies the settings, approaches, and potentialities of these approaches. What any such project might look like will depend on a range of factors such as the goals of the research, the experience of the researchers and participants, the available materials, the context of the research, and the funding (Mitchell, 2011).

Since there is a multiplicity of forms, purposes, and goals that an arts-based project might engender, I draw on three different projects, each of which allows me to foreground some of the various features of arts-based approaches and their relationship to youth research that I outlined above. Two of these projects can be characterized as girl-made media (Kearney, 2006). As Kearney outlines, this connotes an active engagement by girls with forms of creative expression and communication that open up opportunities for exploration, resistance, opposition, and subversion of the cultural representations and practices that often marginalize girls' voices and experiences (2006, p. 95). The two projects realize these aims in different ways, as I will elaborate further in the next section of this chapter. The first is the video project *About Us, By Us*, highlighted in this chapter's opening, where the girls worked collaboratively on the invention of fictional characters to explore a range of issues of concern to them. The second project involved **digital narratives** created by individual girls and worked directly with their own lived experience. The third arts-based project takes a very different approach. It is a video installation entitled *Voices in Longitude and Latitude* that I collaborated on with a professional filmmaker/artist,[2] combining art with **ethnography**.

What unites the three projects is that they each involve marginalized girls, whose voices and images are often excluded from considerations of what it means to be young in Canada today. They all take an intersectional approach, exploring the multiple forms gendered femininities may take, showing how there is no one meaning, but rather that femininities' meanings only emerge in relation to other social identities such as race, class, age, sexuality, ability, etc. As Nina Lykke (2010) notes, intersectionality means not simply adding gender, class, ethnicity, race, sexuality, and so on, but rather analyzing them all as interwoven, entangled, and mutual.

In discussing these projects, I consider a number of questions relating to arts-based methodologies and youth research: How might these methodologies assist in the reorientation of conversations between adults (including researchers) and youth? How might they engender dialogue about enduring social inequalities? How might they be useful for assisting young people in the expression and understanding of their and others' multiple and intersecting identities? How might they enable young people to place themselves in imaginative cultural identities and/or alternatives to the ones made available to them by socially dominant forces?

ABOUT US, BY US: VIDEO STORIES FROM AN INNER-CITY TORONTO SCHOOL[3]

About Us, By Us is a video that tells the stories of five fictional girl characters, each negotiating an issue or problem encountered by young people. The video was created by a group of middle-school girls attending a school in Toronto's west end whose population reflects the area's largely **immigrant, refugee**, and working-class residents. The ethnic makeup of the community is in constant flux, but at the time the video was made the students' families were mainly from Portuguese, Asian, South Asian, and Caribbean backgrounds.

The school principal and some of the teachers were concerned that the girls in the school were disengaged and uninterested in participating in the extracurricular programs on offer. As a researcher of youth cultures, I was invited into the school to work with the girls and to come up with a project that would interest them. And thus, Crystal, Tori, Sang, Charlene, and Kathy were brought to life through weekly lunchtime meetings that culminated in June, the end of the school year, with the shooting of the video. The video group's numbers swelled and shrank over the course of the year, with a core of about 10 girls who consistently took part. These were the girls who considered themselves socially and academically marginalized in the school, not popular, not considered smart by their teachers, but also not in any kind of trouble. Their reasons for participating were varied. For some, there was the anticipation of heightened visibility and positive recognition in the school; for others it was the video project itself that held the appeal; and for still others it was just something to do over their lunch hours since they, unlike others in the school, ate their lunch at school and not at home.

From a research perspective, my focus was on questions of gendered identity more so than on questions of girls' participation in school programs, though the two are not entirely unrelated. I was interested in the discourses of femininity the girls drew on to construct their characters and how they might imagine alternative versions of girlhood for their characters. The questions I asked were, What are the kinds of stories that girls turn life into, the kinds of lives that girls turn stories into? How do these stories connect with ideas about gender, race, sexuality, age, and ethnicity? What are the conditions under which new storylines will break the bounds of the old, creating the possibility for "something else to be" (Morrison, 1992, p. 52)?

The stories the girls created for their characters included that of Crystal, a Portuguese immigrant who was dating a Black guy without her parents' knowledge and against their wishes; Tori, who is considered a nerd within the context of her school and wants to be popular; Kathy, who is smart but is concerned this will work against her in the world of teen heterosexual romance; Sang, who has recently arrived to Canada as a refugee from Vietnam and is struggling over what it means to be a Canadian girl; and Charlene, who is questioning her sexual identity, eventually coming out as a lesbian. Our lunchtime meetings had us working on how each of the characters' stories would unfold, writing dialogue, and planning wardrobe and sets. There were certain hurdles to solve; for example, Crystal's story not only involved a boy, and there were no boys in the group, but also a kiss, which was seen as quite risqué by the girls. Here we are discussing the issue:

> *Marnina:* Let's try to think of a scene where we are going to see some of these issues.
> *LeLy:* Okay, probably her parents walk by the park and see her with that guy making out or something like that.
> *Fanny:* Kissing—pretend.
> *Mai:* Where are we going to find a guy to kiss her? No. I'm talking about lots of guys would want to kiss you, but would you let them kiss you? And where are we going to find a guy?
> *Fanny:* I don't think so! A guy would kiss Maria! (Maria plays Crystal)
> *Mai:* Lots of guys would kiss Maria! But, would Maria let them kiss?

To resolve this dilemma, the girls decided that Crystal's story would take the form of a diary. What would be seen on screen would be Crystal writing and narrating her predicament—which was summarized by one of the girls as "she doesn't know how to be good, without being bad." That is, she is struggling with the competing definitions of both good and bad as they relate to heterosexuality, being a good daughter, her identity as a member of the Portuguese community, and the contradictory demands that these entail. This positioning of Crystal also served as a means for the girls to investigate their own struggles and competing desires—discussions of the characters' dilemmas often slipped into a discussion of their own.

> *Marnina:* Is part of what her parents want her to be good about, about being a good Portuguese girl?
> *Maria:* Exactly. They want me to marry a Portuguese guy and I don't want to marry a Portuguese guy. Cause, please, I don't need that attitude from him like I get from my father!

Through critical and collaborative work a form of conversation evolved among us as a group that allowed us to engage in what Macpherson and Fine call "collective consciousness work" as a form of feminist methodology (1995, p. 201). Using such an approach, they argue, participants may engage in interpreting their own experiences in ways that reveal how these experiences have been shaped and influenced within and by social, cultural, political, and economic spheres of society. Making the video was a process that allowed the girls to become cultural producers, a position that contrasts significantly with the ways that girls' relation to culture is usually theorized by cultural critics as being one of mere consumer (Kearney, 2006). Part of our work as a group was to create a space in which the girls could express their own experiential knowledge through their characters. Such a space may not only serve the purpose of struggling over what counts as legitimate knowledge, but is also an opportunity to engage with girls' experiences in a practice that is both affirmative and critical.

However, as important as taking a critical perspective may be, there are certain risks in asking marginalized girls to critique the (gendered) dynamics of their own experiences, families, and/or communities. As I have argued in more detail elsewhere (Gonick, 2007), there are moral and ethical considerations of such a task. This kind of critique may entail having to publically scrutinize their own families' lives or pleasures, which dominant cultures have pathologized and/or ridiculed. In focusing on fictional characters, this arts-based project was able to offer the girls some distance from having to use their own and their families' experience as a site of critique in instances when it may have been too painful or conflictual to do so.

In engaging the imaginary world of their characters, the girls were able to temporarily "try on" identities that were not their own. This allows for an opportunity to juxtapose various possibilities and to examine the contradictions within and between them. Emerging from the process may be new ways of viewing old situations and hence new possibilities for action and change.

SO THINK ABOUT IT: DIGITAL NARRATIVES AND WEARING THE HIJAB IN HALIFAX

The second project I want to highlight takes place in Halifax, Nova Scotia, with a group of **newcomer** girls whose families have recently arrived in Canada from Syria, Saudi Arabia, Ethiopia, and the Czech Republic. In this instance, I collaborated with the local YMCA, which runs a series of after-school programs for newcomer youth from across the city. The group of approximately 12 girls explored the issue of structural violence (racism, sexism, classism, homophobia, etc.) in their lives through the creation of digital narratives.[4] These are relatively short stories (less than eight minutes) that are created using new digital tools, photographs, music, voiceover, graphics, and animation. Each of the girls chose to create their own individual narrative, taking photos with digital

cameras, drawing pictures, writing and recording the accompanying voiceover, selecting music, and working on the computer to put it all together. Their stories covered a
range of personal experiences including their first day at a Canadian school, feeling left
out or bullied by classmates, dealing with unfair and sexist attitudes at home, and the
experience of wearing the hijab in Halifax, a city with very few other hijab-wearing
Muslims. Some of the group members knew each other from attending the programs at
the YMCA (there were also two sisters and two cousins), but others were more recent
arrivals to the program. Although by the end of our time together they had developed
a strong sense of **friendship** and community, this did not necessarily exist when we
started. Because of the differing issues particular girls wanted to work on, the group dynamics, and the time limits on our work together, creating individual digital narratives
rather than producing one collaboratively seemed better suited to this project.

The story I want to focus on here was created by Amerah, a 13-year-old Palestinian
girl whose family immigrated to Canada from Saudi Arabia, where her father worked
as a medical engineer. Although she only began participating in our group towards the
very end of our sessions, she focused immediately on the issue she wanted to engage,
even as some of the girls who had been attending longer struggled to identify their topics. She worked quickly and decisively on her narrative of wearing the hijab in Halifax.
As Jarmakani (2012, p. 159) outlines, the hijab, or head scarf, is both a cultural and
religious form of dress. In the contemporary context, it is generally worn by women and
girls as an article of religious belonging, signifying both modesty and piety. Halifax,
on the east coast of Canada, has only very recently seen a rise of Muslim immigrants.
Moreover, although the city is surrounded by many Indigenous Mi'kmaq and African-
Canadian communities, visible signs of difference are all too uncommon.

"It all started in Saudi Arabia," Amerah narrates. "When I found out I was moving
to Canada, I started to wonder what people would think about me wearing a head scarf.
I decided not to worry about it." Soft music with a slow, rhythmic beat plays behind
Amerah's deep, accented voice. The narrative begins with a photograph of a drawing she
has made with the title of her story, "So Think about It," spelled out with colourful pipe
cleaners and feathers on a pink sheet of construction paper, covered in polka dots and a
smiley face for the O. A quick series of photos she has found on the Internet follow—a
woman in a dark head scarf, the Canadian and Saudi Arabian flags flying side-by-side,
a view of the Halifax skyline. "Then when I got to Halifax, I noticed people were staring
at me," she continues, with another Internet image of a line of people with eyes wide
open, glaring, suspicious, and curious. She lists a series of questions she is constantly
asked: "Why do you wear that? Are you bald? Ugh, who'd want to wear that! Are you
forced to wear it? Will they kill you if you take it off?" "I am so tired and bored of all
these questions and the teasing at school," she sighs as a photograph she has staged with
some of the other girls in the group crosses the screen. She appears in her hijab surrounded by other girls who are pointing and jeering at her. "I explain that it is because of
my religion and that I want to wear it. Canada is freedom. Here I can go out shopping

if I want. In Saudi Arabia I only stay inside; I can't go anywhere. So why are they telling me in Canada what I should and shouldn't wear? Everyone should be able to wear what they want. I will never care. All people are different. I've thought about it. I'd like others to think about it. So please think about it." Her handmade poster, "So Think about It," reappears and the digital narrative ends with her name crossing the screen.

Public conversations about the hijab have been loud, confused, and contentious in Western countries, including Canada. Rarely are the voices of young girls who wear the hijab heard in these debates. In France, for example, a law passed in 2004 prohibits the wearing of the hijab by girls attending public schools. A similar ban has been discussed in the province of Quebec. Often these heated discussions circulate around the idea of personal freedom. As Jarmakani (2012) suggests, the liberal democratic framework privileges the notion of individual rights, and assumes that the hijab is a cultural-patriarchal imposition that violates the individual rights of Muslim women and girls. She suggests that women and girls who wear the hijab are often cast into one of two dichotomous positions: that of the subjugated female needing to be rescued and/or pitied and that of the suspicious and threatening figure.

Figure 4.1: "So Think about It"

Source: "Amerah," participant in the research project "Promoting Health Through Collaborative Engagement with Youth in Canada." Funded by the Canadian Institute for Health Research, 2012–2017.

Amerah's digital narrative refuses both of these positions and instead insists on a "third space" (Khan, 1998) that works to dislodge the binaries that position Muslim girls who wear the hijab as either in need of rescue or suspicion. She uses the Western logic of personal freedom and turns it on itself to disrupt the overdetermined meanings the hijab takes on in the West. She insists that in wearing the hijab she is actually wearing what she wants and thus partaking in the freedoms that Canada offers. The narrative answers back to the underlying assumptions of all the questions and teasing she has experienced, claims entitlement to belonging, and points out the contradictions of juxtaposing the ideals of personal freedom with (in her case) erroneous assumptions about what wearing the hijab means. She turns the tables on her interrogators, telling them/us to "please think about it."

In creating the digital narrative, Amerah exemplifies how marginalized girls may challenge and defy dominant stereotypes of girlhood in culturally specific ways. Her narrative suggests a need to reconsider the relations between girlhood, power, agency, and resistance to be able to portray the complexities of girls' wants, wishes, and desires (Gonick, Renold, Ringrose, & Weems, 2009). The medium of the digital narrative allows Amerah and the other girls in the group to become producers, interpreters, circulators, exhibitors, and social analysts of their own lives.

VOICES IN LONGITUDE AND LATITUDE: GIRLHOOD AT THE INTERSECTION OF ART AND ETHNOGRAPHY

The third and final example of using an arts-based approach in research about/with marginalized girls is a video installation entitled *Voices in Longitude and Latitude* that I collaborated on with a professional filmmaker, designed for exhibition in an art gallery setting. The piece was exhibited at the Mount Saint Vincent Art Gallery in 2014. *Voices in Longitude and Latitude* is an experiment in thinking, situated at the intersection of research and art, and aims to provoke questions about common sense understandings of girls and girlhood. The piece was conceptualized as a way of entering into a dialogue with the very dominant discourse about girls circulating at the time, which can be encapsulated by the concept of "girl power." Elsewhere I have written about "girl power" as a multi-stranded discourse with a complex genealogy (Gonick, 2006), and showed the progressive narrowing of the term's meaning. That is, "girl power" has become shorthand for articulating a shift in gender relations from an established subordination to an era where girls are seen not only to have the same opportunities as boys, but to compete and outscore them in spheres such as education. Widespread as this discourse is, in many ways it is also very problematic. Most significantly, it supports a **neoliberal** ideology that has made public recognition of ongoing issues of systemic inequalities such as sexism, racism, and homophobia difficult to address (Brodie, 2008) and threatens democratic institutions and goals (Brown, 2015). While acknowledging that some girls are indeed thriving, *Voices* seeks to disrupt the notion that *all* girls are doing so, by representing a diversity of experiences and images of girlhood. We shot in four Canadian locations and regions with girls (aged 13 to 23) from different communities— Inuit in Kugluktuk, Nunavut, **transgender** in Halifax, Nova Scotia, Jewish in Toronto, Ontario, and immigrants from different African countries (Congo, Rwanda, Ethiopia, Sudan) in Winnipeg, Manitoba. The video is an 18-minute loop, drawing on 80 hours of footage of landscape/cityscape representing the various regional Canadian geographies; girls going about their daily activities such as playing soccer, walking through their neighbourhoods, ice fishing, playing musical instruments; images of inside and outside their houses; and a series of ethnographic interviews with the girls that were shot on professionally designed sets. The audio consists of the girls' voices with snippets of their interviews woven together, ambient landscape sounds (the whirr of a snow mobile in Nunavut, the lapping of waves against rocks at Peggy's Cove, Nova Scotia, the walk signal at a busy Toronto intersection, children running through a sprinkler in Winnipeg), and the music of Glenn Gould playing Bach's *Goldberg Variations*.

Voices is quite a different kind of arts-based project from the two previously outlined, with a different set of intentions and perspectives. It is a hybrid methodological space that aims to suggest or invite routes through embodied multisensory ways of knowing. In the gallery, the viewer enters a dark room and is confronted with two floor-to-ceiling screens projecting both on the front and back, and two smaller screens set against opposing walls. There are two large speakers on the outside of the architectural space of the screens. It is impossible to watch all four screens at the same time; standing in the middle of the screens, the viewer is immersed in what my brother/collaborator calls video sculpture. There is no preconceived route through the material. Rather, the possible narrative paths viewers may take are constantly shifting, depending on at what point in the 18-minute loop they enter the gallery, which screens draw their attention, and which speaker they are standing close to. The piece allows viewers to explore connections between multiple locales and girls' stories simultaneously on different screens. As Kohn (2013, p. 554) suggests, multi-screen video installations may give conceptual form to some of ethnography's pressing interests, how to render complex representations of others' lives, how to employ multi-vocality and multi-perspectivity. In other words, *Voices* sets out to disrupt the prevailing notion of what it means to be a Canadian girl by not only including the experiences of girls whose stories are usually marginalized or left out altogether, but by also creating the conditions for viewers to pose questions about how these experiences come to materialize in such different ways.

It does so through the design of the interplay of the girls' narratives with the images moving across the screens. The narratives are not linear or singular; rather they are treated like a form of textile: threaded together in very short segments and interwoven into a textured, subtle soundscape. The voices are ephemeral, in transition, opening and unfolding such that meaning emerges not through the individual voice, but in the relations between voices, bodies, and images. We hear the Toronto girls enthusiastically list the numerous vacation destinations they have visited, while one of the Inuit girls speaks wistfully of her desire to go to Paris one day. The Winnipeg girls speak of the national trauma of their countries of origin while one of the Halifax participants talks about experiences of familial abuse and homelessness. While some of the girls speak of their imagined future families, others speak of the children they already have or the children their families have lost due to illness or the conditions wrought by national violence. Aspirations of becoming doctors, lawyers, and celebrities are juxtaposed with others who hope to be able to graduate from high school. The structure of the stories, images, and landscape threads means that the narratives from the different regions and communities are encountered as always in relation to another's story, another place, rather than an individualized account of a singular story or location. The indeterminacy of meaning-making is suggested. Not only are notions of girlhood and what it means to be a girl challenged, but so are neoliberal conceptions of the isolated, rational, self-inventing subject (Davies & Bansel, 2007; Gonick, 2006). What slowly emerges in between the gaps and interstices of voice and image, body and landscape is the flow of potentiality, the subtle and open processes that link subjects, their social, physical, and structural milieus together. How do bodies and geographies define and shape one another? What is the relationship between girls and the places they inhabit? How does landscape work as a cultural practice shaping privilege, inequalities, and diverse experiences of girlhood? What kinds of girlhoods currently exist and what kinds are possible?

Voices is an art project that asks sociological questions. However, because it is an art project it is not limited to only representing what currently exists. In juxtaposing the strange relations among voices, bodies, geographies, and sound it also unsettles the orderly relationships between words and world, knowledge and girlhood, experience and image. It connects and opens, stumbling towards new ways of being and understanding girls' lives.

CONCLUSION

The three projects outlined in this chapter demonstrate how arts-based approaches to research may be considered to be not only a mode of inquiry into the lives of marginalized girls, but also a mode of representation and a mode of dissemination. In the first two projects, girls themselves were involved in creating representations of their own or imagined lives. We saw the ways in which this shifts researcher-researched relations such that the researched become protagonists and agents of their own lives and more than just sociological categories recorded by the researcher. The girls each had copies of the video and digital narratives they made and could disseminate them as they wished. In the video installation *Voices*, questions of representation and dissemination are also relevant. Here dominant representations of the lives of Canadian girls are questioned and broadened to suggest other meanings girlhood might hold. The dissemination of the project in an art gallery setting also expands the idea of the forms, contexts, and settings that sociological questions might take and in which they might be asked.

I suggest that arts-based research offers new insights into a range of questions that are central to childhood and youth studies. Among others, these include questions about identity, how inequality shapes young people's experience, and the relationship between research, social change, and activism.

CHAPTER SUMMARY

Together, in this chapter, we

- Learned about arts-based approaches to working with marginalized girls.
- Sought to understand how these approaches engage girls' voices.
- Considered the possibility that social forms other than the ones that currently exist are possible and that these may be brought into existence through the creative imaginings of young people.
- Thought through how social science questions can be explored through art.
- Considered how arts-based research methodologies are particularly interesting in circumstances in which there is no language with which to describe certain experiences, including traumatic ones.

STUDY QUESTIONS

1. What contexts or kinds of research projects are best suited for using arts-based methodologies? Do you see any limitations of using these methodologies? What are they?
2. What does the concept of marginalization allow us to consider about the lives of young people? In what ways does it make you rethink your own experiences or what you consider to be the story of young people in Canada today?
3. In looking around you at the narratives and images of girls/young people currently in the media, in movies, and in the news, do you see your own experiences represented? What stories are missing? How do you account for which stories get told and which do not?
4. You have been asked into a school/community centre because administrators are concerned about youth disengagement. No matter how many programs are offered to them, the girls, especially, are not interested in participating. How would you proceed in developing a program that would engage these young people?
5. Imagine your own life story as a digital narrative. What would be included? How would you tell the story? What are the images you would use? What would you leave out and why?

SUGGESTED RESEARCH ASSIGNMENT

Research three artists whose work engages with sociological questions about children and/or youth. What kinds of sociological questions about youth does the artist focus on? In what ways is this work similar to a social science approach? What is accomplished by it that would not be possible with an academic approach? What engages you about the work of these artists?

SUGGESTED FILMS/VIDEO CLIPS

Voices in Longitude and Latitude
www.bing.com/videos/search?q=noam+gonick+vimeo&view=detail&mid=
   245AF74FB3BAC2B486F6245AF74FB3BAC2B486F6&FORM=VIRE
This film, by Marnina and Noam Gonick, is the one referred to in this chapter.

A Red Girl's Reasoning
A short film (10 minutes) by Indigenous filmmaker Elle-Maija Tailfeathers, which tells the story of a young Indigenous woman. After the justice system fails the survivor of a brutal, racially driven sexual assault, she becomes a motorcycle-riding, ass-kicking vigilante who takes on the attackers of other young women who've suffered the same fate.

Practice-Based Research in the Arts
www.youtube.com/watch?v=hpoCf851uNg&list=PLC2ijZ2U-avgWfn_
   OrhQJUZyimFD53tUY
Nine short videos that outline arts-based research, including definitions of research, specific kinds of arts projects, and lectures by practitioners in different fields.

Viva Other Ways of Knowing: Decolonizing Education Through Participatory
   Arts-Based Research
www.youtube.com/watch?v=1rSeNff2wn0
This is a two-hour video of a lecture delivered by Dr. Deborah Barndt, Professor Emeritus, York University, in July 2016 at Lakehead University. Dr. Barndt has used arts-based methodologies in her research since the 1970s. She looks back at some of her early research using this methodology in South America, as well as her current projects.

SUGGESTED WEBSITES

Kyla Mallett
www.kylamallett.com

Kyla Mallett is a Vancouver-based artist whose work is often focused on youth and youth resistance. For example, in her *Notes* series, she photographs notes that were created by high school girls and passed to each other in class. In her *Marginalia* series, she photographs the margin notes written in books borrowed from the Vancouver Public Library, many of which are about youth-focused issues.

The Art Hives Network
www.arthives.org

The Art Hives Network is based at Concordia University in Montreal, Quebec. The network connects small and regenerative community arts studios together in order to build solidarity across geographic distances. This effort seeks to strengthen and promote the benefits of these inclusive, welcoming spaces across Canada and throughout the world. Also known as "public homeplaces," these third spaces create multiple opportunities for dialogue, skill-sharing, and art-making between people of differing socioeconomic backgrounds, ages, cultures, and abilities.

Voices against Violence
www.voicesagainstviolence.ca/project.html

This is the website for one of the projects discussed in this chapter that uses an arts-based approach to examine the subtle and explicit ways in which structural violence is woven into the everyday lives of young people in Canada, how it influences their health, and strategies that can be used by youth to overcome and resist violence. *Voices against Violence* is based at Western University and works in partnership with youth using a participatory action approach. This means youth help to shape and develop the design and activities of the project. Their ideas and perspectives guide the project.

Girls Action Foundation
girlsactionfoundation.ca/en

Girls Action Foundation is a nonprofit organization based in Montreal, Quebec, that works with girls as agents of social change. Through a network of organizations across Canada, the organization leads, develops, and implements transformative programs that are adapted and relevant to the changing realities of girls' and young women's lives.

Native Youth Sexual Health Network
nativeyouthsexualhealth.com/

The Native Youth Sexual Health Network (NYSHN) is an organization by and for Indigenous youth that works across issues of sexual and reproductive health, rights, and justice throughout the United States and Canada.

NOTES

1.   All names have been changed to protect the identity of research participants.
2.   The filmmaker is Winnipeg-based Noam Gonick, my brother.
3.   The full accounting of this research can be found in Gonick, 2003, *Between Femininities: Identity, Ambivalence and the Education of Girls*, Albany: SUNY Press.
4.   This was part of a national research project funded by the Canadian Institute for Health Research.

REFERENCES

Alcoff, L. (1995). The problem of speaking for others. In J. Roof & R. Wiegman (Eds.), *Who can speak? Authority and cultural identity* (pp. 97–119). Urbana: University of Illinois Press.

Bannerji, H. (1991). But who speaks for us? Experience and agency in conventional feminist paradigms. In H. Bannerji, L. Carty, K. Dehli, S. Heald, & K. McKenna (Eds.), *Unsettling relations: The university as a site of feminist struggles* (pp. 67–108). Toronto: Women's Press.

Behar, R., & Gordon, D. A. (Eds). (1995). *Women writing culture*. Berkeley: University of California Press.

Brodie, J. (2008). We are all equal now: Contemporary gender politics in Canada. *Feminist Theory, 9*(2), 145–164.

Brown, W. (2015). *Undoing the demos: Neoliberalism's stealth revolution*. New York: Zone Books.

Davies, B., & Bansel, P. (2007). Neoliberalism and education. *International Journal of Qualitative Studies in Education, 20*(3), 247–259.

De Lange, N., Moletsane, R., & Mitchell, C. (2015). See how it works: A Visual essay about critical and transformative research in education. *Perspectives in Education, 33*(4), 151–175.

De Leeuw, S., & Rydin, I. (2007). Migrant children's digital stories: Identity formation and self-representation through media production. *European Journal of Cultural Studies, 10*(4), 447–464.

Gonick, M. (2003). *Between femininities: Identity, ambivalence and the education of girls*. Albany: SUNY Press.

Gonick, M. (2006). Between girl power and reviving Ophelia: Constituting the neo-liberal girl subject. *NWSA Journal, 18*(2), 1–23.

Gonick, M. (2007). Girl number twenty revisited: Feminist literacies for new hard times. *Gender and Education, 19*(4), 433–454.

Gonick, M., Renold, E., Ringrose, J., & Weems, L. (2009). Rethinking agency and resistance: What comes after girlpower? *Girlhood Studies: An Interdisciplinary Journal, 2*(2), 1–9.

Jarmakani, A. (2012). Hijab. In N. Lesko & S. Talburt (Eds.), *Keywords in youth studies: Tracing affects, movements, knowledges* (pp. 158–163). New York: Routledge.

Kearney, M. C. (2006). *Girls make media*. New York: Routledge.

Khan, S. (1998). Muslim women: Negotiations in the third space. *Signs: Journal of Women in Culture and Society, 23*(2), 463–494.

Kohn, S. (2013). Organizing complexities: The potential of multi-screen video installations for ethnographic practice and representation. *Critical Arts: A South-North Journal of Cultural and Media Studies, 27*(5), 553–568.

Lecercle, J. J. (2002). *Deleuze and language.* Basingstoke: Palgrave Macmillan.

Luttrell, W. (2010). A camera is a big responsibility: A lens for analysing children's visual voices. *Visual Studies, 25*(3), 224–237.

Lykke, N. (2010). *Feminist studies: A guide to intersectional theory, methodology and writing.* New York: Routledge.

Macpherson, P., & Fine, M. (1995). Hungry for an us: Adolescent girls and adult women negotiating territories of race, gender, class and difference. *Feminism and Psychology, 5*(2), 181–200.

Mitchell, C. (2011). *Doing visual research.* Los Angeles: Sage.

Morrison, T. (1992). *Playing in the dark: Whiteness and the literary imagination.* Cambridge: Harvard University Press.

Pink, S., Hubbard, P., O'Neill, M., & Radley, A. (2010). Walking across disciplines: From ethnography to arts practice. *Visual Studies, 25*(1), 1–15.

Rajiva, M. (2014). Trauma and the girl. In M. Gonick & S. Gannon (Eds.), *Becoming girl: Collective biography and the production of girlhood* (pp. 137–158). Toronto: Women's Press.

Walkerdine, V. (2016). Coming to know. *Rhizomes, 27*, 1–13.

5

"Breaking with Inside Experience": Navigating Practical and Scholarly Knowledge in Research with Young People

Jacqueline Kennelly, Valerie Stam, and Lynette Schick

LEARNING OBJECTIVES

- To expose students to recent trends and debates in youth-related research, participatory action research (PAR) methodology, and community-engaged research
- To illustrate with fieldwork vignettes the benefits and complications of community-based and participatory action research methodologies, including an examination of ethics and power
- To explore tensions and contradictions that arise when working across "fields," especially between those of the academy and the social services sector
- To connect theory to practice using Bourdieu's concepts of *field*, *doxa*, and *habitus*, and to analytically reflect on the ways these concepts help explain the authors' actual research experience

---

I was broadly familiar with the norms and language of these [social services] sectors from my work in Vancouver, where I had coordinated a youth mental health promotion program and also spent many years on the board of directors of a youth-driven community activism organization. But I had also spent many years as an academic, and this had shifted my perceptions and understandings of the world in ways I often did not recognize or realize until facing the differences. (*Excerpt from Jackie's vignette*)

I felt that my experience working in the non-profit community would be an asset and would help open doors to us as academics. I came to realize that this was not always the case. (*Excerpt from Valerie's vignette*)

[Introducing myself to the youth], I chose to emphasize my shelter-work experience, saying in present-tense that "I work at St. Frank's,"[1] which is the colloquial name for the St. Francis House adult homeless shelter in town ... I could tell by their facial expressions that they both knew of St. Frank's and thought it was a rough place. Strangely, I think this was the reaction I was hoping for; working at a place like St. Frank's seemed to gain me some credibility in their eyes. (*Excerpt from Lynette's vignette*)

INTRODUCTION

This chapter explores both theoretical and pragmatic issues related to doing academic research with homeless youth in the context of **social services** organizations. As the opening excerpts illustrate, we each have experience in the social services sector and sought to use this knowledge to navigate our relationships in the context of the research. In this chapter, we analyze the complex research relationship between academics, social service providers, and youth. Navigating these relationships made us critically question our social position as researchers in relation to the youth we were working with and the social service providers who were **institutional gatekeepers**. Being critically aware of our social position enabled us to better address some of the **power** differences at play between us, as perceived "experts," and the young people who we approached in this project as experts of their own lives.

Drawing on an ongoing **qualitative** and **participatory action research** project with homeless and street-involved youth in Ottawa, Ontario, we theorize moments when our *practical* **knowledge** of the social services sector overlapped, competed, and sometimes clashed with our *scholarly* knowledge and academic goals. We do so with the help of Bourdieu's conceptual corpus, including his concepts of **habitus, doxa,** and **field.** Methodologically, we draw on fieldwork "vignettes," which we each wrote in order to engage in reflexive consideration of the moments in our research when we have felt the worlds of academia and community social services brushing up against each other, not always comfortably.

Attempting to gain enough analytical distance from our own experience, in order to provide an adequate theoretical account of it, is no easy task. The title of the chapter reflects this tension, and is drawn from Bourdieu's English introduction to *Homo Academicus*. The complete quotation reads:

In choosing to study the social world in which we are *involved*, we are obliged to confront, in *dramatized* form as it were, a certain number of fundamental epistemological problems, all related to the question of the difference between practical knowledge and scholarly knowledge, and particularly to the special difficulties involved first in breaking with inside experience and then in reconstituting the knowledge which has been obtained by means of this break. (Bourdieu, 1990, p. 1, emphasis his)

The difficulties of our task here are very much reflected in Bourdieu's words above. We are seeking to analytically separate our *practical* knowledge from our *scholarly* knowledge, understand how the one influences the other, and take into account the manner in which our practical knowledge and scholarly knowledge do not always sit easily together. As sometime insiders to both the community worlds in which we are researching and the academic worlds in which we are each currently positioned, we are seeking to "break" with that insider experience that informs our actions in both, and step back in order to see more clearly where the fault lines and fissures lie between these two related but also separate worlds.

What we are endeavouring to do here, then, is twofold: first of all, we aim to address the question of the difference between practical knowledge—particularly as it pertains to our embodied and experiential appreciations of the community sector with which we are doing our research—and scholarly knowledge. Second, we seek to theorize both our practical knowledge and academic knowledge as elements of what Bourdieu would identify as distinct *fields* and *doxas* that shape the research relationship in specific ways. We are thus hoping to "break with inside experience," both in the sense of trying to provide some reflective distance between our own respective experiences of the social services sector within which we have all worked, and in attempting to understand the manner in which the *doxa* of academia differs from, and sometimes contradicts, that of the community organizations with which we are working.

MARGINALIZED YOUTH AND PARTICIPATORY RESEARCH: TOWARDS CRITICAL AND ETHICAL ENGAGEMENT

Our research contributes to a broader shift occurring in relation to work with marginalized youth, towards more person-centred (rather than category-based) approaches across a variety of methodologies (Varney & van Vliet, 2008). At one level this is reflected in the changing language used to describe youth experiencing homelessness, with a decided shift away from earlier criminological labels like *delinquency* that focused on the supposed deficits of street-entrenched youth. Much research today describes marginalized youth in terms of "**risk**" (e.g. "**at-risk** youth") (Foster & Spencer, 2011), especially in epidemiological studies like those of Brownell et al. (2010). These mostly longitudinal, population-based studies identify "risk markers," or factors associated with future negative outcomes for youth. However, we align ourselves with other critical researchers who question the categories of *risk*, *delinquency*, and even terms such as *homeless* or *marginalized*, believing that these labels, when applied to people, can be quite disempowering. Instead, we lean towards grounded, collaborative approaches that elicit youth's own perspectives about their current and future lives (Foster & Spencer, 2011).

Our research is also aligned with the work of other justice-oriented approaches that explore the structural and systemic causes of youth homelessness. This body of literature considers the socio-spatial politics of homelessness, including the gendered and **racialized** experiences of young people who are street-involved (Klodawsky, Aubry, & Farrell, 2006). Other studies look at the criminalization and stigmatization of homeless youth in Canada through policies like the Safe Streets Act. Under the pretense of increasing community safety, the act in fact penalizes visible poverty, giving police the ability to fine, arrest, or relocate squeegee kids and panhandlers who are occupying public spaces (O'Grady, Gaetz, & Buccieri, 2011; Parnaby, 2003). Some researchers illustrate state-led and municipal "cleanup" efforts that target visible poverty and homeless youth (Kennelly, 2015). Still others interrogate notions of **citizenship** in a neoliberal era, and its governance role in the lives of marginalized young people (Butler & Benoit, 2015; Kennelly, 2011). The focus on citizenship is particularly relevant to our larger project (though we do not discuss it in detail here), as we are interested in the civic engagement practices of homeless youth, and how to work with youth to represent the issues of greatest importance to them through an advocacy project.

Importantly, researchers working directly in the field of youth homelessness recognize the heterogeneity of these young people, including the multiple pathways into homelessness (Varney & van Vliet, 2008). While there are diverse experiences among this population, it is also true that **LGBTQ+** and Indigenous young people are overrepresented, as are Black youth in Toronto (Gaetz, 2014b). Researchers also increasingly understand that what is true of adults experiencing homelessness is not necessarily true of young people (Gaetz, 2014a). For this reason, making research relevant for youth, and linking it to policy and programming, is an important justice component of contemporary youth studies like ours. To this end, we have sought to design a project that is participatory, relevant, engaging, and of use to the youth and the wider communities within which we work.

In these efforts, we are not alone. Studies with children and youth have increasingly moved away from talking *about* youth to talking *with* youth (Christensen, 2004; Fine, 2008; Kellett, 2005). Benefits of participatory research include creating space for marginalized voices, accessing a rich source of data, and more effectively implementing results (Bialeschki & Conn, 2011; McCartan, Schubotz, & Murphy, 2012; Sanders, Munford, Liebenberg, & Henaghan, 2014). Community-based participatory research (CBPR) and **participatory action research** (PAR) are two research frameworks that place emphasis on collaboration and participation. Drawing on work rooted in these two approaches, we situate our chapter within conversations around methods, representation, and ethics.

A host of factors come into play when determining the level and type of participation youth may have in a given project. In their review of the literature on youth engagement, Jacquez, Vaughn, and Wagner (2013) found that youth participation in research described as "participatory" varies significantly from project to project. Some research projects are structured so that youth sit on advisory bodies, formulate research questions, are involved in data collection, and help analyze and disseminate research results (Dentith, Measor, & O'Malley, 2012; Rodriguez & Brown, 2009; Sanchez, 2009). Others engage youth in participatory activities such as focus groups (Merryweather, 2010), **visual methods** like photovoice, creative writing, film, board games (Kagan & Duggan, 2011), and social media (Mallan, Singh, & Giardina, 2010). Kagan and Duggan (2011) argue for an emphasis on methods that are accessible, generate new relationships in safe contexts, and develop the skills of participants. They particularly highlight the importance of fun, saying, "[W]e need to pay more serious attention to the fun element of engagement and partnership if we want and expect those who will freely be giving up their time to work meaningfully with us" (p. 402). Street-involved youth have a lot going on in their lives; in order to make our research engaging, we utilized focus groups, photography, film, visual mapping, and walking interviews. These methods resonated with different youth depending on their interests and availability. We also honoured their participation by providing honoraria, a practice that is common in research with marginalized youth.

A priority in participatory research projects is giving prominence to marginalized voices, particularly those who are most fundamentally affected by adverse circumstances (Dentith, Measor, & O'Malley, 2012). Participatory research aims to foreground youth voices and, in so doing, provide a platform for youth to influence policy, public debate, and systems change (Iwaski, Springett, Dashora, Mclaughlin, & McHugh, 2014). However, the reality of incorporating youth voices and affecting structural change is not so straightforward. As we demonstrate in our vignettes around clothing and word choice, negotiating power relations between youth (insiders) and researchers (often outsiders) can be fraught (McNess, Arthur, & Crossely, 2015; Rodriguez & Brown, 2009). McCartan, Schubotz, and Murphy (2012) argue for an intentional and self-conscious working out of power relations, particularly at the beginning of a participatory project, to help level the playing field. There is also increasing recognition that Western assumptions of individuality may not accurately reflect youth's **relational** situated-ness. Their "**agency** and voices—their choices, dreams, and interpretations—must be considered as intimately intertwined and conditioned by the very social worlds in which they live" (Meloni, Vanthuyne, & Rousseau, 2015, p. 119). This means youth's voices must be contextualized in the relationships and structures within which they live their lives. It also means that navigating access to the social worlds within which young people live is part of the research process. As we explore in the remainder of the paper, this is not always as straightforward as it may seem.

BOURDIEU'S THEORETICAL CORPUS DEFINED: FIELD, DOXA, HABITUS

Bourdieu uses *field* to specify a particular "social space" where people interact, such as institutions, community groups, and workplaces (Bourdieu & Wacquant, 1992). For instance, as a student, you are immersed in the field of university or college. That broad field is cross-cut by smaller fields, such as your particular discipline and its culture (e.g. a sociology department that values political activism), sports teams and their particular norms and practices (e.g. a men's football team that reinforces hegemonic masculinity), or student clubs and their values (e.g. a Young Liberals club that sees voting as important). The field is not necessarily a physical space, though it may be delimited as such in certain situations. It is, rather, the social arena within which certain norms and common sense assumptions are dominant—these norms and assumptions make up the *doxa* of the field. They are what is thinkable and sayable; the set of behaviours and thoughts that are taken for granted in any given field. When you started university or college, you had to learn what the expectations were in terms of attendance and assignments. Now you take these expectations for granted; these form part of the doxa of higher education. When a person enters a particular field, their *habitus* comes into play. The habitus consists of the embodied beliefs, dispositions, and habits that constitute a person's capacity to act and make choices within certain situations. Everyone is socialized to behave and think in certain ways. These behaviours and thoughts become second nature, thus forming, in the words of Bourdieu, your habitus: how society is embodied in you. For example, you (generally) don't wear your pyjamas to class. This is because it is a societal expectation that you dress a certain way when leaving your house. Knowing what clothes are appropriate for different situations is a social skill you have learned. If an individual is situated within a field that carries a doxa that is consistent with their own habitus, they will be at ease within that field and be able to conduct themselves in a manner that others within the field recognize as normal. For instance, if you are familiar with and comfortable on sports teams, you will know how to dress, act, and talk in a way that others on that team find recognizable and understandable. However, if an individual's habitus does not match the doxa of the field, then they may be at a loss as to the language or behaviour that is considered acceptable within that field. For example, if you have never been part of a sports team, and you show up wearing high heel shoes and a cocktail dress when everyone else is in track suits and running shoes, you will feel extremely uncomfortable (Bourdieu, 1997/2000; Bourdieu, 1972/1977; Bourdieu & Wacquant, 1992).

Bourdieu's description of the academic field, found with particular detail in *Homo Academicus*, informs our analysis here. As Bourdieu (1990, p. 40) notes, "The structure of the university field reflects the structure of the field of power, while its own activity of selection and indoctrination contributes to the reproduction of that structure." With a focus on French academic culture in the 1960s and 1970s, his study demonstrates the manner in which the university both belongs to, and attempts to set itself apart from, the rest of the social and cultural world. Its belonging to the wider social world is marked by the way in which the dominant structures of hegemonic power tend to get reproduced within its walls: specifically, those with the most cultural, social, and economic capital from within their families of origin tend to become those with the most academic capital within the university.[2] But it is also *apart* from the rest of the social world, in the sense that university professors are "holders of an institutionalized form of cultural capital, which guarantees them a bureaucratic career and a regular income" (1990, p. 36). This distinguishes them from those who work in sectors that are less institutionalized and often more marginalized; Bourdieu refers specifically here to artists and freelance writers, but we would suggest that those employed by social service organizations are similarly marginalized, in the sense of being relatively poorly paid and often precariously employed or underemployed. The gap is even greater between academics and the youth with whom we are ultimately working. And of course there also exist tensions and power differentials between the three authors, of whom one is a tenured university professor, another is a doctoral student, and the third is a master's student.

In what follows, we explore three themes, influenced by Bourdieu's concepts, in order to theorize the complex relationship between our academic worlds and those of the social service organizations with which we are conducting research. The first theme is entitled "practical knowledge": here, we explore the forms of practical knowledge that we brought to bear in navigating these two worlds, drawing on our respective intuitive "feel for the game" that comes from our own years of experience in the social services sector. The second theme explores the moments of apparent conflict between academic doxa and social services doxa, and how we responded in those moments. The third and final theme discusses our "presentations of self" (Goffman, 1959), or the ways in which we strategically worked to appear as though we comfortably belonged across a range of diverse settings. In order to explore these themes, we draw on our respective field note vignettes as the data for the paper. We each wrote a two- to three-page vignette with the overarching theme of the paper in mind (i.e. the tensions, overlaps, and contradictions of working between academia and social service organizations). The first author then coded each for the sub-themes that we explore below, and organized the themes into an initial draft. The second and third authors subsequently reviewed the draft paper, adding their own insights and analyses to the final product.

THEME 1: PRACTICAL KNOWLEDGE

Bourdieu often describes the manner in which individuals acquire a habitus that matches the doxa of a particular field as having a "feel for the game" (Bourdieu, 1997/2000, p. 151). In other words, he describes how one comes to feel like a "fish in water," where what happens within the specified field seems like what is natural, generating no sense of discomfort or unease. When one does not have the habitus that goes with a specific field, then the feeling can be the opposite—of a fish out of water, without a feel for the game. This can produce discomfort, unease, embarrassment, or a sort of cognitive dissonance, to name a few of the likely emotions.

We each brought a "feel for the game" about the norms and expectations of community organizations that came from our respective years of work in the social services sector. One shared knowledge that we brought was understanding the importance of building trust with the community organizations with which we sought to work, and establishing that our research was relevant and useful to their own aims and goals:

> Coming into the research, I knew that I needed to establish credibility within the community, so as to build trust and be able to negotiate access to homeless young people for a fairly time- and labour-intensive research project. (Jackie)

> I feel like my previous workplace connections help build trust because there is a history there that people can refer to, and that I can also draw on in my interactions with others. My previous work holds the possibility of helping to smooth out academic-practitioner relationships. (Valerie)

However, our social services doxa, which gave us a "feel for the game" in working with community organizations, did not always translate directly across different players within this field. Specifically, we recognized, or came to re-notice, that there were hierarchies and subfields within the social services sector that influenced the manner in which we were read and how we could position ourselves:

> I was mindful that most of my work with homeless communities has been adult-oriented, and that my experience with homeless youth has, in contrast, been wildly unsuccessful at times and thus short lived. For these reasons I wondered—and even worried—about how the youth would read me and my various identity markers. (Lynette)

> Our first meeting was at a supportive housing centre for young Indigenous women. Jackie introduced herself as a professor at Carleton, and introduced me as her research assistant. Later in the conversation, I mentioned that I also had housing experience, having worked at Ottawa Community Housing (OCH). This was awkward. It felt like I was trying to create a connection that was not there. I am not sure why this was. Perhaps it is because the differences between OCH and this centre are enormous; OCH is one of the largest housing providers in Canada, and this centre for Indigenous women is a small, culturally-specific space. OCH also has a negative reputation in some circles. I wondered if these things were working against me. (Valerie)

As a consequence of our respective attunement to the norms of the social services sector, we designed a research project that was participatory and involved a lot of stakeholder feedback, including ongoing contact with the community organizations and the youth with whom we were intending to work, and culminating in an advocacy project that drew on participatory action research (PAR) methodology. This made sense within the context of the community organizations with which we wished to work.

> Each of the community organizations we met with commented that the project was very well-designed and would be of interest to the youth they worked with. They often seemed pleasantly surprised by this, leading me to wonder what other kinds of research they had been exposed to before. (Jackie)

This research design, drawn from our "feel for the game" within the social services sector, clashed with certain subsets of academic doxa, as revealed by comments from the Research Ethics Board (REB) on our initial submission of the project for ethics approval. Referring specifically to the advocacy project, the REB questioned the research value of this task, and whether it might be coercive towards the youth involved. With subsequent explanation and reference to participatory action research literature, the project as designed was passed by the REB. This experience highlights another important theme for our exploration here: namely, the tension between the doxa of the social services sector and the doxa of academia.

THEME 2: CONFLICT BETWEEN ACADEMIC AND SOCIAL SERVICES DOXA

The doxa of a field, as described by Bourdieu, is typically unspoken, and is often only noticed by those who are part of that field when the norms have been broken. In this way, it is sometimes easier for those unfamiliar with the field to discern its doxa. As a tenured professor with more than a decade of enculturation in the field of academia, Jackie was less attuned to the ways in which academic norms might seem foreign or irrational to those in the social services sector; Valerie, on the other hand, had spent the last decade working within the field of community organizations, and had only recently returned to academia. She was thus more sensitive to the points at which academic assumptions might not match the doxa of the community organizations with which we were trying to build relationships. Indeed, Valerie was finding the transition to academia challenging, in part because of the shifting norms and practices associated with the respective sectors:

> In March, I attended the Ottawa Youth Justice Network's learning day. I was hoping it would be a good chance to network, as well as connect with former colleagues and partners. I had been feeling disconnected from my former peers and missing

the connections and vitality of the social services sector in Ottawa. PhD work is very isolating. I was coming from a workplace where I regularly had three to four meetings a day in different parts of the city. Now I am working by myself most of the time. Needless to say, this has been a hard transition. (Valerie)

Valerie's attunement to the social services sector meant that she was particularly attentive to establishing that the research we were conducting was relevant to the community organizations, and that we were committed to their well-being. In reflecting on a conversation at the Ottawa Youth Justice Network learning day with a representative from a prominent funder in the city and the executive director of one of the organizations we were working with, Valerie notes the following:

Having Dan[3] introduce me using my former workplace connections, I believe, reassured Jenny that I not only knew the sector, but that I was a respected worker in the social services world. It gave me some credibility. I also felt reassured, personally, that people knew I was not some random academic coming into their space, but that I had connections to that world and also cared about it. (Valerie)

As a fish who is still slightly out of water in academia, Valerie finds herself trying to translate the value of academic research to the community organizations—and also to herself, at times. At ease with the doxa of the social services sector, and also having many connections and contacts in that world, by returning for the day to the Ottawa Youth Justice Network, Valerie's equilibrium was momentarily restored. Jackie, on the other hand, who has spent more years absorbing the doxa of academia and has not been a full-time worker in the community services sector for 12 years, struggles in different ways with the relation between academic research and the goals of the community organizations:

The community partner with which we ultimately worked was keen to see the youth engaged in an ongoing project such as this one, comparing our project to a video project the youth had recently done, that many of them had found very inspirational. I am glad our research can fill this niche, but it also makes me uneasy because, in the end, we are going to be working with the youth for a relatively short period and we are also seeking to understand their worlds, not necessarily to give them skills or opportunities that will help them do better in the world—at least not in the short run. While I do feel that research is an important part of the picture for changing social conditions for the better, and while I do think participating in our research can be helpful to the youth in the sense that they are exposed to new things, our ultimate goal is writing up and presenting our findings, not helping these young people find the housing or employment that they need. So there is a fundamental disconnect, in some ways, between research and the social services sector we have worked our way into. (Jackie)

Lynette also included, in her vignette, reflections on the differences between the doxa of the social services sector and that of academia:

> Admittedly I felt some trepidation in the days leading up to our first focus group session. Though I have been employed for many years in homeless and substance using communities, I was technically on an unpaid leave-of-absence for the previous 8 months while I began the Masters of Social work program. Because this return-to-academia was a marked departure from the grittiness of shelter work, I wondered if I still had the "realness" necessary to work with people experiencing homelessness. (Lynette)

Reflected here is another tension between social services doxa and that of academia: namely, the perceived difference between "real world" experiences, and particularly the "grittiness" that is associated with living as a homeless or substance-using person, versus the perception of academia as being detached from the "real world," and locked in the euphemistic "ivory tower."

In order to bridge the gap between differing doxas in academia and the social services sector, all three of us worked to "translate" between these two worlds, often through the use of different language depending on the context in which we were working. Jackie reflects on her struggles to accurately describe the research we are doing to the community partners:

> I am also conscious of the language I use; I typically frame the research project as being about "**youth civic engagement**" with the community partners, though I actually intensely dislike the language of "civic engagement," co-opted as it has been to be about becoming the well-behaved, self-regulating neoliberal citizen (see Kennelly & Llewellyn 2011 for a critique of the related language of "active citizenship" in Canadian curricula). (Jackie)
> [Note that Jackie is so immured in the *doxa* of academia that she even cites her own research in her vignette!]

Lynette worked to make herself decipherable to the youth with whom we were working by changing the language she used to describe herself:

> As I introduced myself I remember intentionally downplaying my academic credentials, believing that university specific words like "graduate student" or even "research assistant" may not have meaning for many of the youth there. (Lynette)

She also sought to establish connections with the youth through the use of shared language, though in hindsight she wondered whether such efforts were unwittingly deceptive—less in what she said and more in what she failed to say:

Also in my introduction to the group I remember decidedly saying that I was a Carleton student but also did paid work at the school and that Jackie was my "boss." I said this strategically because I felt like dichotomous words like "boss" versus "worker" would resonate for these youth, likely familiar with only the most precarious employment, where power and hierarchy are highly visible. I also recognize in hindsight that by self-identifying as a worker (in contrast to a "boss") I was actively minimizing the ways I hold power in the world, in an effort to make myself further relatable to the youth. In essence I was trying to say that though I have a job I don't get to be the boss. By obscuring the ways my work history has been enormously different than theirs, I was subtly, though problematically overemphasizing our similarities rather than our differences. (Lynette)

As the three of us worked to navigate across various, often dissimilar, fields for this research project, we strategically worked to employ the doxa we assumed most appropriate to each field. Of course our assumptions about which doxa was required for a particular field were informed by our own unique habitus, which came from our past experiences and individual social locations. With each of us coming from different places, the precise ways we displayed doxa was also distinct to each of us. We each made choices—consciously or otherwise—about the language we would use in particular settings, as these excerpts have demonstrated. As with most social encounters, however, the complexity of the exchange makes it impossible to know how effective we were in our attempts to translate across the different doxas.

THEME 3: PRESENTATION OF SELF

Our efforts to represent ourselves and the research through language are related to the third theme that emerged in our respective vignettes, that of self-presentation. Bourdieu marks an interesting relationship between one's habitus and one's appearance, specifically clothing, when he describes habitus as being that which a subject knows "in a sense, too well, without objectifying distance, and takes it for granted, precisely because he is caught up in it, bound up with it; he inhabits it like a garment [*un habit*], or a familiar habitat" (Bourdieu, 1997/2000, p. 143). He notes the manner in which our habitus is incorporated bodily, and often represented externally through clothing, as well as through ways of "walking, talking, looking, sitting, etc." (Bourdieu, 1997/2000, p. 141). The **presentation of self** is in some ways chosen, though always constrained by the habitus, field, and doxa that have shaped us over our lifetimes and that shape the manner in which we move through the world. However, to the extent that we are attentive to the differential doxas that exist across differing fields, we are able to adjust our presentations of self to reflect our incorporation of this knowledge and to attempt to mark ourselves as belonging, or as "in the know." These efforts emerged through our reflective vignettes:

I was conscious of my appearance and demeanour at every meeting. For meetings with the gatekeepers (generally youth workers at the organizations), I would dress "formal casual," trying to look professional but not too officious. This typically took the form of jeans with a more formal jacket. Once we started working with the youth, I would tone it down a notch, opting for jeans and a t-shirt and leaving the jacket behind. I am youthful looking as it is, and I think this works in my favour in the research I do, but I also find myself balancing that apparent youthfulness with an effort to establish that I am, indeed, a university professor and that this research is worthwhile and leading somewhere. (Jackie)

Understanding that others' perceptions of me are based largely on my ability to re-veal and alternately curtain versions of myself, I thought about the characteristics I wanted to highlight and/or minimize. My efforts to overtly self-manage therefore began on the morning of that first focus group, even before I got dressed for the day. I needed something to wear that would speak to the audience about who I was, or at least reflected the version of me most appropriate for the occasion. Typically during that period I was required to wear business casual for my practicum placement with the government. In strategic contrast to that stale routine, I opted for something hopefully more relatable to the youth participants: skinny jeans, Bluntstones, a leop-ard print shirt, hoop earrings. Donning my metaphorical power-suit, I hoped the participants would read me as youthful, current, and maybe even stylish. (Lynette)

Each of these vignettes captures efforts we were making to be "read" in a certain way: for Jackie, she expressed concern that she be seen as relatable, yet also preserve the perception of her professionalism and thus capacity to successfully complete the task at hand. Lynette strove to connect to the youth through clothing choices that she hoped they would recognize and appreciate, and perhaps even admire. As Lynette notes, we each recognized that we had a capacity to "reveal and alternately curtain" aspects of ourselves, and we used this strategically throughout the research process. At times we felt like we had successfully passed—when youth complimented our clothing, for in-stance—yet other times these strategic presentations felt uncomfortable, particularly when juggling different meetings in different spaces all in one day—like conducting walking interviews with youth downtown in the morning, and attending an adminis-trative meeting at the university in the afternoon.

CONCLUSION

Through the use of self-reflective field note "vignettes," we have sought to explore the tensions, contradictions, and confluences between the worlds of academia and the so-cial services sector, when researching across the two. Bourdieu's theoretical concepts, specifically *field, habitus,* and *doxa,* provide a useful framework for our analysis. In considering the themes of practical knowledge, conflict between academic and social services doxa, and presentations of self, we have sought to illustrate the manner in which all three of us worked to negotiate our various identities as they manifested in relationship to the research project. These negotiations are ongoing. As we continually reflect and "break" with insider experience we seek to develop a research practice that is ethically responsive to the academic and social services sectors with which we engage. Being critically aware of presentations of self and one's own practical knowledge may also be useful for students, scholars, and practitioners as they reflect on power differentials in their research and work. Research Ethics Boards may find that a deeper understanding of the conflict between academic and social services doxas can help them to make more informed decisions regarding ethics processes for research with marginalized communities. As we demonstrate through our vignettes, we worked to address and minimize power dynamics and inequality during the research process by, strategically at times, demonstrating particular ways of dressing and speaking that we thought most appropriate to those "fields." There is power embedded in those assumptions, however, which must be acknowledged at the fore. No matter how we might try to alter our appearance or language in order to be relatable to the youth and social service workers, there was no way to compensate for the structural inequalities that meant we had (for instance) more economic power than the people we worked with, and privileges associated with being white, educated, and holding Canadian citizenship (to name a few of our structural advantages).

For us, intentionally situating ourselves in a participatory research framework also necessitates critical reflection on categories such as "at-risk" or "marginalized" youth. Additionally, it means privileging youth perspectives in a social context that often devalues their societal contributions and potential. As our work continues to unfold, we seek to provide platforms through which homeless young people have the opportunity to share their perspectives on the social world more directly, specifically in the form of participatory videos that we developed in the final months of this project (see www. jacquelinekennelly.ca/encountering-democracy). As this chapter has sought to demonstrate, privileging the voices of homeless youth is not a straightforward process, shot through as it is with dynamics that emerge due to the differing doxas of academia and social services as well as the differences between researchers and youth themselves. Nonetheless, as researchers we take seriously the ethical imperative to work towards securing a public sphere that, according to the words of Pierre Bourdieu's student Loic Wacquant, undertakes "a never-ending effort to make social relations *less* arbitrary, institutions *less* unjust, distributions of resources and options *less* imbalanced, recognition *less* scarce" (Wacquant, 2005, p. 21).

CHAPTER SUMMARY

Together, in this chapter, we

- Read about past and ongoing trends and debates in youth studies scholarship, participatory action research methodology, and community-engaged research.
- Glimpsed the behind-the-scenes perspectives of researchers as they engaged in a participatory action research (PAR) project with homeless youth. Here we saw how fieldwork vignettes were a useful way for researchers to capture and better reflect on their own experiences in the field.
- Heard about some of the difficulties and tensions that might arise in collaborative, community-based research projects where the experiences and expectations of academic researchers and social service workers are not always the same.
- Learned about Bourdieu and his important theoretical contributions, especially his concepts of *field*, *doxa*, and *habitus*. We studied the definition of these terms and saw how they could be applied to the actual lives of real people.

STUDY QUESTIONS

1. In what ways did the authors navigate between academic and social service worlds (i.e. practical knowledge and scholarly knowledge)? Were these approaches effective? Why or why not?

2. In the second section, the authors discuss the differing doxas in academia and the social services sector. How do the authors translate between these two contexts? Can you think of other ways academics and practitioners could relate?

3. In the section "Presentation of Self" the authors talk about how they presented themselves in order to be "read" in a certain way by different audiences. Think of a time when you presented yourself in a certain way in order to relate to your audience. Were you successful? Why or why not?

4. Applying Bourdieu's theoretical concepts to your life, what fields do you navigate? When does your habitus fit with the doxa of the field? (i.e. when do you have a "feel for the game"?) When does your habitus clash with the doxa of the field? (i.e. when do you feel like a "fish out of water"?)

5. The authors describe various inequalities between themselves and the people and organizations they are researching with. Name three of these inequalities. In what ways can research practice level the playing field? In what ways can it reinforce inequality?

SUGGESTED RESEARCH ASSIGNMENT

1. Journal Reflection: The next time you are at work, university, or another "field" that you operate in, pay attention to how you present yourself. What are you wearing? How are you talking? Is there a protocol for emails or texts or phone calls? Do you adopt a particular demeanour in this setting? Think about how others are presenting themselves. Write a journal entry with these three questions in mind: How do I present myself in this field? What is the doxa of this field (the norms and common sense assumptions)? How does my presentation of self reflect my habitus (how I have been habituated—or not—to be able to function and make decisions in this field)?

2. Informational interview: Talk to an acquaintance, friend, colleague, or family member about how they present themselves in different environments. How do they decide what to wear, how to talk, how to write emails? What things do they have to think about? What things come naturally? Have they ever experienced a time when they felt like "a fish out of water"? Ask them to describe that moment and why it occurred. Write a summary of your conversation, using Bourdieu's concepts of field, doxa, and habitus to describe and analyze what was discussed.

SUGGESTED FILMS/VIDEO CLIPS

These three videos emerged from the research process described in this chapter.

"Encountering Democracy" Youth and Policing
www.youtube.com/watch?v=24KfQX_nGs0
Part of a three-phased research project exploring homeless youth's concepts of democracy and citizenship, this video considers youth/police relations as understood by the youth themselves.

"Encountering Democracy" Criminalization of Marijuana
www.youtube.com/watch?v=CBjP2kghz1k
Part of a three-phased research project exploring homeless youth's concepts of democracy and citizenship, this video considers (de)criminalization of marijuana as understood by the youth themselves.

"Encountering Democracy" Transitioning Out of Homelessness
www.youtube.com/watch?v=SLpHYULkxjk
Part of a three-phased research project exploring homeless youth's concepts of democracy and citizenship, this video considers the difficulties of exiting out of homelessness as understood by the youth themselves.

SUGGESTED WEBSITES

Alliance to End Homelessness, Ottawa

endhomelessnessottawa.ca/

A nonpartisan, provincially incorporated nonprofit, the Alliance to End Homelessness is a local umbrella organization connected to a larger, international movement aimed at ending homelessness. The organization brings together local stakeholders to share knowledge, set priorities, and measure progress.

The Homeless Hub

homelesshub.ca/content/about-us

Launched in 2007, the Homeless Hub is an electronic research library and information centre. It is a place where government departments, researchers, and service providers can share stories and best practices related to homelessness in Canada. Importantly, the Homeless Hub believes that research should be practical and contribute meaningful solutions to ending homelessness.

NOTES

1. A pseudonym.
2. The concept of capital is another important piece of Bourdieu's conceptual corpus. He delineates different types of capital, most commonly referencing cultural capital, social capital, and economic capital. Economic capital is the most straightforward of these, referring as it does to the economic resources at an individual's disposal. Cultural capital refers to the degree to which an individual is recognized (or not) as "in the know" within specific fields—Bourdieu sees academics as having a high degree of cultural capital, while not necessarily having as ready access to economic capital as others in powerful positions within hegemonic social structures. Academic capital is a sub-form of cultural capital that is specific to the academic field; those within this field will recognize it as being, for instance, number of publications, number of awards and scholarships, degree of external recognition, number and prestige of research grants, etc.
3. All names used in the paper are pseudonyms.

REFERENCES

Bialeschki, M. D., & Conn, M. (2011). Welcome to our world: Bridging youth development research in nonprofit and academic communities. *Journal of Research on Adolescence, 21*(1), 300–306.

Bourdieu, P. (1977). *Outline of a theory of practice.* (R. Nice, Trans.). Cambridge, New York, & Melbourne: Cambridge University Press. (Original work published 1972)

Bourdieu, P. (1990). *Homo academicus.* Stanford: Stanford University Press.

Bourdieu, P. (2000). *Pascalian meditations.* (R. Nice, Trans.). Stanford: Stanford University Press. (Original work published 1997)

Bourdieu, P., & Wacquant, L. J. D. (1992). *An invitation to reflexive sociology.* Chicago: University of Chicago Press.

Brownell, M. D., Roos, N. P., MacWilliam, L., Leclair, L., Ekuma, O., & Fransoo, R. (2010). Academic and social outcomes for high-risk youths in Manitoba. *Canadian Journal of Education, 33*(4), 804–836.

Butler, K., & Benoit, C. (2015). Citizenship practices among youth who have experienced government care. *Canadian Journal of Sociology, 40*(1), 25–50.

Christensen, P. H. (2004). Children's participation in ethnographic research: Issues of power and representation in the recognition of children's social agency and active participation. *Children and Society, 18,* 165–181.

Dentith, A., Measor, L., & O'Malley, M. P. (2012). The research imagination amid dilemmas of engaging young people in critical participatory work. *Forum Qualitative Sozialforschung/Forum: Qualitative Social Research, 13*(1).

Fine, M. (2008). An epilogue, of sorts. In J. Cammarota & M. Fine (Eds.), *Revolutionizing education: Youth participatory action research in motion* (pp. 213–234). New York: Routledge.

Foster, K. R., & Spencer, D. (2011). At risk of what? Possibilities over probabilities in the study of young lives. *Journal of Youth Studies, 14*(1), 125–143.

Gaetz, S. (2014a). *A safe and decent place to live: Towards a housing first framework for youth. Executive summary.* Toronto: The Homeless Hub Press. Retrieved from homelesshub.ca/resource/safe-and-decent-place-live-towards-housing-first-framework-youth#sthash.SumRCfx5.dpuf

Gaetz, S. (2014b). *Coming of age: Reimagining the response to youth homelessness in Canada.* Toronto: The Canadian Homelessness Research Network Press.

Goffman, E. (1959). *The presentation of self in everyday life.* New York: Anchor.

Iwaski, Y., Springett, J., Dashora, P., Mclaughlin, A-M., & McHugh, T. L. (2014). Youth-guided youth engagement: Participatory action research (PAR) with high-risk, marginalized youth. *Child and Youth Services, 35*(4), 316–342.

Jacquez, F., Vaughn, L. M., & Wagner, E. (2013). Youth as partners, participants or passive recipients: A review of children and adolescents in community-based participatory research (CBPR). *American Journal of Community Psychology, 51*(1–2), 176–189.

Kagan, C., & Duggan, K. (2011). Creating community cohesion: The power of using innovative methods to facilitate engagement and genuine partnership. *Social Policy and Society, 10*(3), 393–404.

Kellett, M. (2005). *Developing children as researchers.* London: Paul Chapman.

Kennelly, J. (2011). Policing young people as citizens-in-waiting: Legitimacy, spatiality and governance. *British Journal of Criminology, 51,* 336–354.

Kennelly, J. (2015). "You're making our city look bad": Olympic security, neoliberal urbanization, and homeless youth. *Ethnography, 16*(1), 3–24.

Kennelly, J., & Llewellyn, K. (2011). Educating for active compliance: Discursive constructions in citizenship education. *Citizenship Studies, 15*(6–7), 897–914.

Klodawsky, F., Aubry, T., & Farrell, S. (2006). Care and the lives of homeless youth in neoliberal times in Canada. *Gender, Place and Culture, 13*(4), 419–436.

Mallan, K. M., Singh, P., & Giardina, N. (2010). The challenges of participatory research with "tech-savvy" youth. *Journal of Youth Studies, 13*(2), 255–272.

McCartan, C., Schubotz, D., & Murphy, J. (2012). The self-conscious researcher—Post-modern perspectives of participatory research with young people. *Forum Qualitative Sozialforschung/Forum: Qualitative Social Research, 13*(1).

McNess, E., Arthur, L., & Crossely, M. (2015). "Ethnographic dazzle" and the construction of the "other": Revisiting dimensions of insider and outsider research for international and comparative education. *Compare: A Journal of Comparative and International Education, 45*(2), 295–316.

Meloni, F., Vanthuyne, K., & Rousseau, C. (2015). Towards a relational ethics: Rethinking ethics, agency and dependency in research with children and youth. *Anthropological Theory, 15*(1), 106–123.

Merryweather, D. (2010). Using focus group research in exploring the relationships between youth, risk and social position. *Sociological Research Online, 15*(1). doi:10.5153/sro.2086

O'Grady, B., Gaetz, S., & Buccieri, K., (2011). *Can I see your ID? The policing of youth homelessness in Toronto.* Toronto: JFCY & Homeless Hub. Retrieved from homelesshub.ca/caniseeyourID#sthash.rX1ckyzY.dpuf

Parnaby, P. (2003). Disaster through dirty windshields: Law, order and Toronto's squeegee kids. *Canadian Journal of Sociology, 28*(3), 281–307.

Rodriguez, L. F., & Brown, T. M. (2009). From voice to agency: Guiding principles for participatory action research with youth. *New Directions for Youth Development, 123*, 19 –34.

Sanchez, P. (2009). Chicana feminist strategies in a participatory action research project with transnational Latina youth. *New Directions for Youth Development, 123*, 83–97.

Sanders, J., Munford, R., Liebenberg, L., & Henaghan, M. (2014). Show some emotion? Emotional dilemmas in undertaking research with vulnerable youth. *Field Methods, 26*(3), 239–251.

Varney, D., & van Vliet, W. (2008). Homelessness, children, and youth: Research in the United States and Canada. *American Behavioral Scientist, 51*(6), 715–720.

Wacquant, L. (2005). Pointers on Pierre Bourdieu and democratic politics. In L. Wacquant (Ed.), *Pierre Bourdieu and Democratic Politics* (pp. 10–28). Malden, MA: Polity Press.

SECTION II

SOCIAL CONSTRUCTION OF CHILDHOOD AND YOUTH

As presented in the Introduction, a social constructionist approach examines the ideas we hold about childhood and youth, including what these ideas are, why some are so powerful, and what their consequences are. Of central importance is that certain ideas emerge and hold authority within specific contexts. Sociologists of childhood and youth are especially interested in understanding how the categories, meanings, statuses, and experiences of childhood and youth are influenced by larger, structural forces that transcend an individual or a family, forces that tend to reflect and reproduce significant inequalities. These ideas are powerful in their impact. Consider the example of the Sixties Scoop—the Canadian state's practice of removing an estimated 20,000 Indigenous children from their homes and placing them with non-Indigenous families in the decades from the 1960s to the late 1980s (for an extensive discussion, see chapter 12 by Spencer and Sinclair in section III). This atrocity happened partly because the Canadian child welfare system is dominated by white, middle-class ideas about "normal" childhood and, in keeping with a colonial mentality, it dismisses Indigenous notions about what is important to Indigenous children and communities (Mas, 2016).

In this section we have assembled a group of papers that share a social constructionist approach as they frame their questions, analyses, and arguments. While each has a different emphasis, uses different research methods, and takes a distinct direction in the analysis, each one engages with the production of certain kinds of childhood. The chapters explore how relationality reproduces but also complicates dominant framings of childhood and the process of subject formation; how stories that we tell our children participate in creating certain kinds of gendered and racialized childhoods; and how seemingly benign categories of childhood can be manufactured and deployed, e.g. in order to sell things. In chapter 6, "Perceptions of Our Childhood: Confronting Social Constructions of Care, Disability, and Childhood,"

Abbas draws on the daily experiences of her brother, who lives with an intellectual disability, and her own memories, reflections, and experiences as his sibling. She effectively uses auto-ethnographic methods, reflexivity, and children's voices to analyze how children's lives are shaped by prevailing assumptions about having a "normal" childhood, and about disability, care, and sibling relationships in health care institutions, social services, and schools. She reflects on and is critical of popular assumptions about how her and her brother's lives are marked by dependency, burden, and lost childhoods—and how these assumptions in turn construct limited and problematic ideas about childhood.

Bélanger's chapter 7, "Studying Friendship among Children at School from a Sociological Approach to Childhood," challenges us to explore friendship as an aspect of childhood and youth that is of central importance to young people but which has so far been understudied and much less understood from sociological perspectives. Specifically, she studies how individuals form, negotiate, and understand friendships and child-to-child socialization in specific sociocultural contexts such as schools. She further examines how practices of friendship take on forms and meanings within the broader social relations of migration, racialization, class stratification, and gender. Bélanger does this through the use of ethnographic research strategies, including inviting children to draw and talk about a "social constellation." Her chapter shows us how the school environment in three urban French-language schools in Ontario, in mixed neighbourhoods that include low-income housing, impact on children's school experiences and friendships. She demonstrates that friendships are key mechanisms for children to make meaning of school norms and at times question, resist, or circumvent rules. In other words, friendship relationships play a role in children's negotiation and construction of their social worlds.

Chapters by Andrejek (chapter 8), Chen (chapter 9), and Williams and Coulter (chapter 10) each utilize interpretivist, qualitative analyses of texts (both narrative and visual) and artifacts that are central to childhood to reveal that childhood is constructed through intersecting categories of inequality, including between girls and boys, racialized minorities and the white majority, and teens, tweens and adults. The role of children's literature as a form of material culture and as an institution of socialization is explored in both Andrejek's and Chen's chapters, while consumer products targeted at young people is the empirical focus in the chapter by Williams and Coulter. Across these chapters we see the productive force of media.

Constructs of gender have implications in children's lives as they shape how children understand themselves and what they feel they are able to do and be. In this way, gender structures and limits possibilities for children's subjectivities and social relations. Andrejek, in chapter 8, "Pedagogy and Propriety: A Gendered Analysis of Children's Fairy Tales," argues that Western classic children's fairy tales tenaciously reproduce and disseminate patriarchal morals and social norms—norms that continue into today. Through entertaining stories, these fairy tales seek to cultivate values in girls regarding innocence, propriety, and sexual morality. Also looking at stories for children, Chen's chapter 9, "Racism, Culture, and Power in Children's Books," examines how racialized minority children are alternatively excluded or represented in ways that reflect dominant ideological assumptions about race and culture. With the premise that children's books constitute a process through which individuals are made social, Chen develops a critique about how they tend to have the effect of casting white children as tolerating subjects and racialized ethnic minority children as passive heirs of cultural traditions—and neither one as agents with a critical awareness of, and political interest in, contesting racism.

Opening with a social history of Lego's transformation from being a simple children's toy to becoming a transmedia franchise, Williams and Coulter's contribution, chapter 10, "From Babies to Teens: Children Are a Marketer's Dream," shows how material culture, specifically consumerist production of toys, has played an increasingly powerful role in defining children and youth and, conversely, how young people and their consumer culture are central to the evolution of capitalism. For example, the category of "toddler" became part of everyday understanding about childhood as a result of marketing strategies. Importantly, the authors also explore young people's agency in engaging with consumer culture, negotiating, for example, the gendered categories that are applied to them.

Collectively, these five chapters actively illustrate the social construction of certain forms of childhood and youth. What we hope you will gain from these chapters is a better understanding of how social forces influence young people's experiences, such as their relationships with siblings and friends, but also how various understandings and consequent experiences of childhood and youth are produced. These chapters also illustrate how these productions are not benign: they hierarchically position some children as normal and some children as not, they gender and racialize children, and they segment children into subcategories for the purpose of selling products. Through these chapters, you are thus able to see connections between what happens to young people in their everyday lives and their location in wider social productions and positionings. We hope these chapters will equip you with analytical tools to ask questions about how children and youth become specific kinds of social selves through various social processes.

REFERENCE

Mas, Susana. (2016, August 16). Indigenous leaders call on Justin Trudeau for redress on Sixties Scoop. *CBC News*. Retrieved from ww.cbc.ca/news/politics/indigenous-leaders-justin-trudeau-sixties-scoop-apology-1.3722807

6

Perceptions of Our Childhood: Confronting Social Constructions of Care, Disability, and Childhood

Jihan Abbas

LEARNING OBJECTIVES

- To critically reflect on the problematic ways disability, care, sibling relationships, and childhoods have been socially constructed through dominant literature
- To challenge notions of a "normal childhood" as it relates to the presence of disabled family members
- To explore the concept of interdependence and apply this lens to children and family dynamics, rather than notions of dependence and independence
- To understand how critical disability studies can play a role in creating a new space for exploring the experiences of disabled children in childhood studies

My brother was born in 1979. At the time, little was known about Down syndrome. According to prevailing medical knowledge, he would never have a "normal" or fulfilling life. One nurse even advised my mother to "give him up" before she fell in love. In the last 36 years, despite persistent barriers, my brother has defied these initial expectations.

From a very young age, I was an important part of my brother's support system. I sat in on development sessions to learn how to better support his fine and gross motor development, address his "problematic behaviours," and respond to his communication needs. Once a "plan" was put in place by a professional (e.g. behaviour modification, speech language therapist, etc.), every member of our family was tasked with carrying it out.

Before my brother's hearing issues were resolved, we all learned some sign language so we could communicate around activities of daily living (e.g. meal time, play time, etc.). Also, based on the advice of the speech-language pathologist, we stopped communicating in Arabic in our home, as she felt this would confuse his development. Incidentally, despite this, my brother picked up Arabic through spending time with our grandparents and by learning to accommodate for their communication needs.

When my brother had difficulty developing his gross motor skills, my parents had a small play structure built, and our living room was rearranged to accommodate this and various other tunnels and tents that helped facilitate crawling, standing, walking, and running.

The popularity of normalization and behaviour modification in the 1980s also meant that my sister and I were often instructed to help "correct" unwanted behaviours. For example, because of my brother's protruding tongue (a common trait with Down syndrome) "specialists" advised we all "flick" his tongue anytime we noticed it was protruding. If this didn't work, my parents were advised shock treatment was always an option for more persistent and difficult cases. Like other fad interventions, the specialists' obsession with my brother's tongue thankfully passed.

INTRODUCTION

I open this chapter with this vignette as a means of situating myself as an active participant in narratives of childhood and disability and to draw attention to how support and interventions were arranged for my brother and how these helped shape our childhood.[1] Grounded in aspects of **relationality** and with a focus on the family unit, disability, and sibling dynamics, this chapter will explore how dominant constructions of these ideas influence how disability and childhood are often understood. This chapter is critical of dominant social constructions of disability and sibling relationships that reinforce notions that disabled individuals negatively impact the family unit, and instead argues for a more complex understanding of these relationships and the unique and valued contributions of each member of the family unit. I argue throughout this chapter that the social construction of **care**, disability, childhood, and our roles as siblings play an important role in shaping our childhood experiences. Indeed, how we theorize disabled children and their place within the family does matter, as this impacts policies and programs that regulate childhoods (Curran & Runswick-Cole, 2014). From a very early age my brother's place and role in our family was dictated through a myriad of professionals, supports, and services all aimed at "normalizing" his body. While some of these interventions were welcome and helpful (I don't know any other children who grew up with a play structure in their living room), the majority of these were intrusive, harmful, and problematic. I write about these sibling experiences as an adult because I believe they provide insight into the many ways theories of care and disability perpetuate negative stereotypes that assume our childhood was undesirable because of the presence of his disability. My interest in disability and sibling relationships is thus deeply rooted in our experiences as a family and my own identity.

The space I occupy situates me uniquely, as in addition to being a sibling of a disabled person, I am also a person with a learning disability. Yet the invisible nature of my own disability has meant that my presence within our family has not been read in the same way as my brother's. While there is something to be said for the very real differences we faced in terms of inclusion and barriers, for me this is also illustrative of how powerful the social construction of intellectual disability and the family experience can be. For the purpose of this chapter, I will position myself primarily as a sibling of a man with an intellectual disability and will engage strands within the care, disability, and childhood literature that seek to explore our childhood identities and related, negative assumptions that others make about our childhood experiences. In this chapter I will touch on literature that speaks to the ways disability, care, sibling relationships, and childhood are socially constructed in an effort to problematize dominant understandings that assume my own experiences of childhood were not reflective of a "normal childhood." I will begin with a brief exploration of care literature and related disability critiques, through which I argue that care, as a concept, is an important tool in how disabled bodies are socially constructed and intervened upon. I will also explore how the concept of **interdependence** is helpful in understanding the capacities and contributions of disabled bodies and thus moving away from notions of dependency and burden that are typically applied to our childhoods. Finally, I will explore the role of critical disability studies in influencing **childhood studies** in ways that create important spaces to better understand the value and complexities of our childhood. I argue that the literature on care, disability studies, and childhood all include problematic aspects and gaps that have yet to be fully addressed, and will touch on emerging literature that may be helpful in countering notions of dependency and burden while also creating an important space to explore narratives of disability in childhood. Throughout this chapter I will share my own experiences and insights as a means of countering dominant social constructions that shape collective understandings of disabled bodies, families, and children. I situate my own stories within interdisciplinary literature encompassing childhood studies, critical disability studies, and theories of interdependence, in an attempt to counter misconceptions about the quality of our childhoods, better understand our childhoods, and bring visibility to disabled bodies, their **agency**, and the importance and value of their presence within the family.

THEORIES OF CARE AND THE CONSTRUCTION OF DISABLED BODIES

> Care—whether it refers to people giving paid or unpaid help—does not mean to "care about" someone, in the sense of loving them. Rather it means to "care for" someone, in the sense of taking responsibility for them, taking charge of them. (Morris, 1994, p. 26)

Care is an important concept that has been instrumental in shaping policy responses and support for disabled persons. While care theory is broad and complex, my interest here is to engage with aspects within this well-developed body of literature that help illustrate how care is instrumental to understanding the conception of disabled bodies in dominant **discourse**. I argue that the narrow and able-centred way care is conceptualized frames disabled bodies as passive and dependent recipients of the care labour of others. Thus, where disability is concerned, *how* we understand care is central as it is linked to assumptions around dependency and burden that powerfully shape collective understandings of disabled bodies and their place within the family. The interest within care literature in carving out an identity for "caregivers" based on the presence of disabled family members has often meant that the needs of disabled bodies are secondary to the needs of the caregiver (Keith & Morris, 1995). This is an important aspect that needs to be highlighted, as I believe a focus on the presence of disability and its perceived impacts on nondisabled family members extends beyond theories of care and also shapes understandings of childhood. Indeed, there are strong parallels between how policy makers frame and understand both childhood and disability that should be acknowledged, as notions around dependency, incompetent actors, minority groups, and so on strongly relate to how disabled bodies have historically been read and categorized (Tisdall, 2012).

While I will return to the place of disability in childhood studies later, it is important to understand how discourse about the well-being of the family unit and its able-bodied members has shaped disability policy and related supports, which further influence how our childhoods are understood. Historically, the perceived health and well-being of the family unit was a driving force in policies aimed at disabled bodies, including the growth in institutionalization, which was often rationalized as a means "to give the rest of the family a normal, healthy life" (Castles, 2004, p. 362). It was believed that segregation was the only way to protect families and nondisabled siblings (Castles, 2004). Discourse around protecting families and providing "normal" childhoods for nondisabled siblings represents powerful beliefs that still influence how we understand dynamics within families where disability is visible.

Of specific interest to me as a sibling are strands within the care literature devoted to the care labour provided by children that frame us as "young carers." In the literature, "young carers" are defined as children who help care for disabled family members (O'Dell, Crafter, de Abreu, & Cline, 2010). At the heart of the debate around the role and needs of "young carers" are conflicting notions about the burden of care for child family members and the individual rights of disabled persons. Lois Keith and Jenny Morris (1995) caution that within this debate, nondisabled academics have constructed a dichotomy within the family between those who provide care and those who receive care that has in turn silenced the experiences of disabled bodies. They call to task founding ideas within the care literature, including Hilary Graham's (1983) notion of "taking charge of," within the caring relationship. For Keith and Morris (1995), the focus within the care literature on "informal care" has obscured broader debates about rights and disabled persons. Conversely, within the "young carers" literature, disability rights advocates have been accused of ignoring the care labour of children (Olsen & Parker, 1997).

Yet disability rights advocates maintain that the issue of "young carers" is problematic because of the negative way it frames disability and because it is seen to divert resources away from the real issue at hand—a lack of comprehensive **disability supports**. For Morris (1997), the issue is not whether some children take on more responsibility and care labour but rather the general lack of support for disabled people. From a disability rights perspective, then, addressing the lack of support and services within the home would address the needs of disabled individuals and these "young carers."

Keith and Morris (1995) also argue that "young carers" have been constructed through this literature in particular ways to support the development of government policies for addressing the perceived negative impact of disabled family members on nondisabled youth. Yet conceptualizing the nondisabled youth's role exclusively as a caregiver and through the lens of burden led to policy and support responses that were not supportive of our needs as a family, but rather aimed at removing the perceived disruptive presence of my brother. For example, workers were tasked with getting my brother out of the home (and away from us), and there was support for special and seg-regated day and summer camps that supported his development but were also framed as opportunities to provide our family with respite. Yet looking back, what my brother needed was not more time away from his family and community (his childhood was already heavily marked by isolation and segregation), but instead support that enabled him greater participation in the community, like the ability to attend the same neigh-bourhood school as his siblings (this was never an option for him).

The classification of "young carers" and associated narratives that construct our identities based on the presence of disability are thus problematic for a number of rea-sons. First, the underlying assumption that for "young carers" the responsibility of caring for a family member with a disability is a negative situation that interferes with a child's ability to have a "normal" childhood promotes an idealized notion of a "universal child-hood" (O'Dell et al., 2010). Of note are parallels within childhood studies, in which "the dominance of accounts of 'normal' development and 'normal' childhoods, by main-stream childhood studies researchers, individualises all children's needs in ways that erase the social contexts that produce them" (Curran & Runswick-Cole, 2014, p. 1620). What we need is to develop approaches to care and childhood studies that reject notions of normality of childhood and family experiences, and that seek to better understand the value and diversity in individual lived experiences.

It is also problematic to treat nondisabled children as a discrete category at the ex-pense of their disabled counterparts. Indeed, those who provide informal care often note that they receive "considerable validation for 'caring'" (Beckett, 2007, p. 364). Yet there is also danger in "valorising the role of the family in disabled children's lives" (Curran & Runswick-Cole, 2014). In my own experience, my role in my brother's life is exclusively read as a caregiver, even though this overlooks the reciprocal aspects of our relationship and erases my brother's important role within the family. The powerful notion of depen-dency that hangs over our family relationships reinforces conceptualizations that give nondisabled family members identities and place value on "our" role at the expense of disabled persons (Beckett, 2007). While many are too quick to assume that everything I did with and for my brother in our childhood was a reflection of his "dependency," there was a parallel tendency to minimize his labour and contributions. For example, while my brother may have gotten someone else a snack or completed a chore, those outside of our family rarely read this as a form of "care." Rather, because someone with an intellectual disability carried it out, his actions were often seen by outsiders as token gestures or mimicked activity, as if the presence of an intellectual disability precluded him from having the capacity to "care for" in these same ways.

Finally, embedded within the "young carers" discourse is the notion that the unique responsibilities of nondisabled siblings lead to their resentment of disabled family members, yet this has not been my experience or the experience of other siblings I know. In my own experience as a sibling I have found that the presence of my brother's disability frames our relationship to the outside world as one in which I provide care and my brother passively receives it—this is how our relationship is known to many friends, extended family, and neighbours. My time with my brother has often been read as a kind of respite for my parents or an opportunity for him to develop socially in the community. Rarely has our time together been read as a brother and sister spending time together because that's what siblings do.

As an adult I am often asked to speak to parent groups about disability and sibling dynamics. I often hesitate, as these invitations are typically framed as supporting the needs of nondisabled siblings because of the perceived negative impact of a disabled child. Parents often want to speak to me about burden and resentment and frequently cite the negative research about our childhoods. At one recent meeting, a mother confided in me that while she tries to arrange special activities for her daughters during their disabled sibling's in-home therapy, they insist on being home and a part of these therapy sessions. As a mother, she struggled to understand why they felt the need to attend and worried that this was a reflection of the burden of care on them as children. Yet, as a sibling, and reflecting on my participation in my brother's therapy, I suggested that respecting their wishes was important, as being a part of this may be desirable for them. While I do not know with certainty their motivation for wanting to be a part of their sibling's therapy, I know that as a child it was important for me to be a part of these sessions because I wanted to support my brother and, more importantly, I wanted to ensure that those supporting him understood him and did not harm him. A lot of the therapeutic interventions used when he was younger (and many of the interventions still used today) were harmful and abusive, and even as a child I felt the need to be there to protect him (the obsession with my brother's tongue by professionals and their invasive corrections stand out as a strong motivating factor for this participation).

Yet in literature concerned with the "young carers" and related policy and support interventions, there is no space for these considerations, nor the reciprocal and ever-changing nature of our relationship or the value of my brother's experiences, capacities, and contributions. For me, these absences illustrate how the literature on "young carers" misses important aspects of the experiences of people with disabilities and their siblings. There is uniqueness to our shared experiences that deserves a space within the literature. These experiences do not fit an independent/dependent dichotomy, nor do they indicate that informal care labour interferes with our ability to have positive and meaningful childhoods. To be certain, if anything is negative about having a disabled brother or sister, it is how quickly one learns how little some of our loved ones matter within broader society. Although there may be some unique responsibilities involved in supporting a disabled family member, in my experience these are linked to inadequate disability supports, persistent barriers, and invasive therapies. Memories of my childhood are not dominated by what I might have to have done to support my brother. My happiest memories involve his welcome presence. My worst memories involve how horribly others often treated him because he has Down syndrome. When there are assumptions that the presence of disability within a family is negative because of the informal care certain bodies require, there are also powerful and problematic statements about the place and meaning of disability.

CARE AS A FORM OF INTERDEPENDENCE

While disabled individuals are often understood through an independent/dependent dichotomy, interdependence, a space that allows for the growth and the contributions of each individual, is a better reflection of the care process and dynamics within the family and among siblings.

While there is much in the care literature that is problematic when examined against our own experiences, there are elements within the care literature that better reflect informal care, shifting dynamics, and the value, contributions, and agency of disabled bodies. Indeed, while the "carer" and "cared for" dichotomy often used to explain the disabled/nondisabled dynamic may be dominant, it is false and completely fails to appreciate relational aspects and forms of interdependence that better illustrate our experiences. In part, this reflects the "dual meaning" of care within the literature and the difference between "'caring *for* someone' (carrying out caring work) and 'caring *about* someone' (having caring feelings)" (Thomas, 1993, p. 649; Graham, 1983), and the reality that care is "both an activity and a feeling state" (Thomas, 1993, p. 652). There are emotional aspects within the caring process that are important to acknowledge, specifically for me as a sibling, as they speak to more complex conceptualizations of the relationship between my brother and me that also capture the love, affection, and positive impacts we have on each other. Building on this insight, Fiona Robinson's work confronts the idea that there is an autonomy/dependency dichotomy and instead argues, "the nature and extent of dependence and independence in social, political, and economic life are constantly shifting and evolving, with different kinds of costs and benefits for different actors" (2011, p. 99). These insights

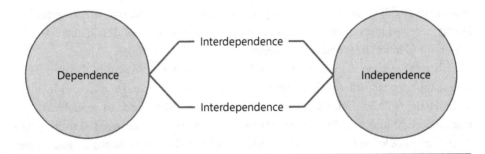

Figure 6.1: Interdependence

While disabled individuals are often understood through an independent/dependent dichotomy, interdependence, a space that allows for the growth and the contributions of each individual, is a better reflection of the care process and dynamics within the family and among siblings.

further align with important strands within care theory as they highlight how social, political, and economic forces shape these relationships. Here, then, care is not a static activity that only specific bodies need, but rather this suggests that "relations of care are the basis of all social life" (Robinson, 2011, p. 163). From my own experiences, I would argue that care is a highly complex activity wherein individual recipients of care are more than "dependent"; rather, they exist in interdependent relations with their carers and they are also agentic subjects with contributions and capacities that need to be more fully recognized.

Paula Pinto's work on reconstituting care suggests that looking at care offers us an opportunity "to look at both sides of the relationship, the carer and the cared for, and to address the complexities that emerge when these two roles become entwined" (2008, p. 120). There is a need, then, for more layered analyses of care relationships that are inclusive of disability rights and value disabled identities. In keeping with this vein, Pinto reminds us that feminist philosophers, including Eva Kittay, have argued, "interdependence is a better concept to describe the relational nature of care than the usual binary of dependence/independence" (Pinto, 2008, p. 124). Theories of interdependence have the potential to reframe how our experiences are understood in important ways that acknowledge the individual experiences and contributions of each family member, including disabled children. Indeed, many discussions of care that are centred on either the needs of the provider or the recipient ignore the more complex and reciprocal nature of our relationships. Thus, "to be caring or cared for are not positions, attributes or roles that are necessarily dualistic in practice, but are part of the weave of social in any social relationship" (Beckett, 2007, p. 356). For example, "I may make tea for my partner because I care about them. If that partner becomes disabled so that I *have* to make tea, do I then become a carer for them?" (Beckett, 2007, p. 365). From within the context of the family, and as a sibling, it is important to critically question these distinctions, as much of what has historically been read as "care" and "burden" is simply the reality of being a part of an interdependent family unit. Indeed, the assumption that my role as a sibling was dominated by a one-sided relationship in which I provided informal care and my brother received it completely erases important elements of our childhood and erases his important identity, role, and contributions to our family.

These observations are in keeping with other interpretations within the care literature that understand these relationships as more complex, layered, and shaped by social and material realities. Indeed, not only do family relationships need to be understood as more reciprocal in nature, but these relationships must also be understood as shifting over time. For example, with respect to informal care within the context of the family, Andrea Doucet's (2013) work examining fathering, embodiment, and care provides additional insight into embodied care and how conceptualizations that include multiple actors open up space for new understandings. Care here is conceptualized as a process "encompassing skills, feelings, dispositions, activities, and practices that are deeply rooted in social relationships of interdependence which change constantly across time and space" (Doucet, 2013, p. 289). This idea that care changes across time and space is important with respect to disability, as I believe failure to acknowledge shifting aspects of interdependence is in part what renders disabled bodies and their contributions invisible. Seeing care as fluid and changing, rather than a constant and unchanging state, allows us to better accept dualities and changing roles. Doucet argues these shifts occur "within complex webs of social and institutional relationships" (2013, p. 291). As such, we are in a constant state of "becoming" that sees us as dynamic, layered, and changing through shifting forms of agency (2013). Reflecting on my own experiences of childhood, our roles and needs changed overtime. While there were times that I provided care, there were also times that my brother used his knowledge and experiences to support and care for me. For example, when I was afraid before my first minor day-surgery procedure, my mother encouraged me to talk to my brother about my fears. By this time, my brother had already undergone several invasive surgical procedures and endured long hospital stays, including open-heart surgery. When I confided in my brother how afraid I was of having surgery, my brother, always the comedian, responded with a devilish grin and "You should be!" before providing comfort and guidance. After the surgery, my brother took it upon himself to entertain me and care for me throughout my recovery.

There are clear benefits to conceptualizing care in ways that frame this process as reciprocal and create spaces in which actors are not static in their roles, but rather grow and change over time. For me these elements of interdependence better capture our childhood experiences, as they move us away from narratives of pity, burden, and dependency.

CRITICAL DISABILITY STUDIES AND DISABLED CHILDHOOD STUDIES

Care as a concept is instrumental in terms of the social construction of disabled bodies, yet there is an obvious **power** imbalance when care is conceptualized in ways that erase the place, agency, and contributions of disabled bodies. When discussions around care tend to rest on the problematic notion that an implicit link exists between disability and care that is disempowering, a very specific "model" of disability is promoted (Beckett, 2007). Focusing on "a situation in which one party to a relationship has a clear identity as a carer while the other is clearly cared for can only represent one type of caring relationship—and may, in fact, not be the most common" (Morris, 1991, p. 38). If the focus instead shifts to also include the other party in the relationship, "we may find that in some situations the roles are blurred, or shifting" (Morris, 1991, p. 38). It is here that I argue that there are opportunities for critical disability studies and childhood studies to counter the ways dominant understandings of care have socially constructed disabled bodies, and the influence this has had on collective understandings around sibling relationships and childhood. Disability studies theorists have illustrated how dominant social constructions of disability place the disabled body as a deviation from the norm and have worked to illustrate that disability is in fact a valued part of the human condition. Yet it should also be noted that while the social model has been extremely important in understanding the social construction of disability, it has largely failed to include the experiences of disabled children (Connors & Stalker, 2007).

Where childhood is concerned, Andrea Doucet notes that while children are seen as creating care labour for parents, they are rarely seen "as actors within this relational process" (2013, p. 299). Extending this understanding to disabled children and seeing these bodies as actors within a relational process opens up a space in which their actions are visible. Read through this lens, disabled individuals, including children, are not passive recipients, but instead an integral and active part of this shifting landscape.

Within childhood studies there has been important recent work that serves as a reminder that childhood itself is socially constructed (James & Prout, 2015), illustrating that attempts to define a normal and/or natural childhood are problematic. Indeed, in the past two decades, sociology and anthropology have informed childhood studies in ways that now call for an understanding of how childhood is socially constructed rather than a set of normalized developments (Tisdall, 2012). This conceptual shift in itself opens up an important space to counter dominant conceptions of disability and childhood. This is important, as there have been problematic strands within childhood studies that have reinforced the notion that disabled children are burdens, and have further medicalized the understanding of disabled childhood experiences. For example:

> disabled children's childhoods are largely invisible in historical accounts of childhood, and where disabled children are present they are visible primarily in deficit terms with a focus on individualised, medicalised and tragic children and childhoods associated with welfare institutions. These practices assume vulnerability and, paradoxically, take attention away from the experiences and concerns of disabled children and their families themselves. (Curran & Runswick-Cole, 2014, pp. 1618–1619)

Calls within childhood studies for a social constructionist understanding of childhood are thus important as they provide alternative conceptualizations of childhood (Tisdall, 2012). Additionally, "the **marginalization**, institutionalization and familialisation of children and disabled people have had certain historical and current similarities" (Tisdall, 2012, p. 183) that provide valuable insight in moving forward with more layered and respectful understandings of disability and childhood. Similar to ways that disability studies have countered the medical model, medical and developmental theories of childhood within childhood studies have also been critiqued (Davis, 2006). Calls to understand childhood as socially constructed, and to include disability in such theorizing, are valuable and provide a foundation for merging critical disability studies and childhood studies. This has the potential to create new spaces that would counter many of the misconceptions about childhood in families with disabled members and would provide opportunities to centre the narratives of disabled persons, particularly those of children.

Tillie Curran and Katherine Runswick-Cole's scholarship around a "disabled children's childhood studies" resonates with me for a number of reasons. Drawing on traditions within both childhood and disability studies, a disabled children's childhood studies would reflect a distinct form of inquiry (Curran & Runswick-Cole, 2014). Here, a space would be created in which disabled children are understood to be free from the kinds of normative constraints that typically shape how their lives are understood, while at the same time creating opportunities to re-imagine relationships among families and within communities (Curran & Runswick-Cole, 2014). There are a few important elements here that I want to draw out. The first is the critical task of separating disabled individuals from normative frameworks that typically dictate how these bodies and their experiences should be read. Detached from normative frameworks, my brother is no longer a dependent body, but instead an active and contributing agent within the family. In this rethinking I do not assume an identity as "caregiver" at his expense, and our experiences as siblings are given the space and freedom to evolve in ways that reflect the affection, companionship, and interdependence that we experienced. For example, when I reflect on my childhood experiences with my brother I do not mourn a childhood of missed opportunities because of the presence of his disability, but instead I remember funny stories, family vacations, holidays, and all those other valued memories that made up our childhood.

Furthermore, through this framework our experiences are not juxtaposed against those of a "normal childhood" but rather appreciated as a part of the diverse and unique rhythm of individual family lives. As a new form of inquiry, disabled children's childhood studies would begin with very different questions about families (Curran & Runswick-Cole, 2014). Firmly centred within the lived experiences of disabled children, I believe inquiry that begins from this new space would do much to bring visibility to the experiences of disabled children. For example, to return to the vignette at the beginning of this chapter, a disabled children's childhood studies would provide a space to explore how my brother experienced these professional interventions and how their intrusive presence shaped his experience of childhood, rather than focusing on how his disability impacted my identity as a sibling or my experience of childhood.

As "disabled children's childhood studies are written by disabled children and young people, disabled scholars and activists reflecting on their childhoods, as well as parents/carers of disabled children, allies and academics listening directly to disabled children and young people's voices" (Curran & Runswick-Cole, 2014, p. 1618), there are opportunities for these narratives to share the important and valued parts of our relationships that remain overlooked in much of the literature. Thus, unlike much of care literature, which tends to focus almost exclusively on nondisabled bodies, or disability studies, which tends to focus almost exclusively on disabled adults, there are promising pieces within existing scholarship that can be integrated within a disabled children's childhood studies framework to allow for the exploration of the interdependent relationships and the sometimes complex and contradictory elements of our experiences. Furthermore, centring this scholarship on disabled voices and including youth voices would help detach understandings of childhood from normative frameworks or expectations, as it would provide a space for disabled bodies to share narratives outside of the caregiving framework.

CONCLUSION

In 2001 while studying for my MA, I took a class with Dr. Kathryn Church at the Ontario Institute for Studies in Education. The class, entitled "**Doing** Disability," illustrated the important mark left by our experiences as siblings. In our first class, after discovering that most of the students were also siblings of disabled people, Kathryn noted that historically her class had attracted a high number of siblings. None of us were there because we felt we had lost our childhood; none of us felt the need to discuss what others perceived as the "burden" of our care. We were there because we were passionate about disability rights. If anything, we were damaged not from extra responsibility, but rather from the things that our brothers and sisters had experienced, including various forms of incarceration, invasive and abusive "therapies," segregation, and verbal and physical assaults. We all understood what was wrong with our experiences, and it had nothing to do with any care or support that we, as siblings, provided.

In this chapter I have argued that aspects of care, disability, childhood, and my role as a sibling have been obscured or erased through dominant social constructions that reinforce narratives of dependency, burden, and lost childhoods. Within much of the current literature related to our childhood, disabled bodies are read as passive recipients of care, my brother's capacities and contributions as a disabled body are ignored, and our childhood is seen through a lens of pity and resentment. Many threads within care literature, particularly earlier ones, frame disabled bodies as a burden and thus many policy interventions in the lives of disabled persons have focused on exclusion in an effort to preserve a "normal" family life. More recent literature around care has moved away from the dependent/independent dichotomy and instead sought to understand how various forms of interdependence better capture our experiences as families. While disability studies has challenged care theorists and refocused the debate around a lack of disability supports, the exclusion of disabled children in disability studies has served as yet another means by which their experiences tend to be rendered invisible. Within childhood studies, calls to acknowledge the social construction of childhood have problematized assumptions about a universal and normal childhood, yet here, too, the exclusion of disabled children's voices has left serious gaps. Taken together, advancements within theories of care, disability studies, and childhood studies have provided opportunities to develop and construct new forms of scholarship that I believe are more inclusive and respectful of our childhoods. A disabled children's childhood studies, which also promotes the inclusion of disabled bodies, would provide a comprehensive paradigm that promotes variations in lived experience and places value on bodies that have historically been ignored and misrepresented. These are positive developments that I believe create new spaces for our experiences to be explored in more layered and honest ways. Through this lens, my childhood experiences as a sibling and my brother's experiences as a disabled body are not read as competing interests or deviations from the norm, but rather are reflective of shared and valued experiences.

CHAPTER SUMMARY

Together, in this chapter, we

- Learned that disability, care, sibling relationships, and related childhoods have been socially constructed in problematic ways. Where disability is present, negative assumptions are often made about the impact of a disabled child on the family.
- Gained insight into how we have idealized and framed "normal childhoods" in ways that exclude the presence of disability. Yet childhood experiences are diverse, and diversity within these experiences should be explored and valued.
- Discussed how notions of dependence and independence are often presented as a dichotomy—for example, individuals are often understood as either independent or dependent actors. Individuals are in fact interdependent actors who both give and receive care and affection.
- Explored how situating disabled children as interdependent allows for a space in which their value and contributions within the family can be seen.
- Considered how critical disability studies and a disabled children's childhood studies can play a role in creating a new space for exploring the experiences of disabled children in childhood studies.

STUDY QUESTIONS

1. Calls for a disabled children's childhood studies seek to include disabled children's voices in real and meaningful ways. How can a disabled children's childhood studies push back against dominant social constructions of disabled children?

2. Interdependence, as a concept, is useful in understanding how each individual can contribute in unique ways. How might reframing disabled children as interdependent actors challenge problematic notions about disabled children and their place within the family unit?

3. This chapter problematized notions of an ideal or universal childhood. Reflecting back on your own childhood, what aspects of your own experiences challenge the notion of a universal and "normal" childhood? Why are these experiences important to those exploring childhood?

4. A number of different fields are interested in the experiences of disabled children and family dynamics (social work, education, etc.). How can other disciplines or fields of practice integrate the importance of interdependence and the value of disabled children's experiences in their work? Why is this important?

5. Moving forward, how can we explore family and sibling narratives in ways that recognize disabled children's agency and do not decentre the experience of disability and/or render these experiences and contributions invisible?

SUGGESTED RESEARCH ASSIGNMENT

Dominant discourse about disability and childhood is not only shaped within academic literature and policy, but is also reproduced in popular cultural representations of disability. Identify three examples of disability and childhood representation in popular culture (film, television, books, etc.). Discuss how each representation perpetuates negative stereotypes about disability and childhood.

SUGGESTED FILMS/VIDEO CLIPS

LIBERTAD—Downeate—Mismas Realidades
www.youtube.com/watch?v=8uJAEI2Afao
A clip that explores the living experiences of a young man with Down syndrome who decides to break from his routine and live one day differently, doing what he wants.

Things People with Down syndrome are Tired of Hearing
www.youtube.com/watch?v=AAPmGW-GDHA
From BBC Three, people with Down syndrome and their friends and family push back against stereotypes about their abilities and capacities.

People with Down Syndrome Speak Out

www.youtube.com/watch?v=ILgLmChIxNg

People with Down syndrome, of various ages, and their family members speak out about their lives.

SUGGESTED WEBSITES

Disability Visibility Project

disabilityvisibilityproject.com/

An online community dedicated to collecting, sharing, and amplifying disability stories and culture.

Sibling Leadership Network

siblingleadership.org/

Network that provides siblings of individuals with disabilities information, tools, and support to advocate and support their disabled siblings.

NOTE

1.   Throughout this chapter, as I explore care and childhood studies literature, I reflect on these debates based on my own experiences of childhood. While there may be parallels to experiences other siblings have had, where I use "our" throughout this chapter, I am primarily reflecting on my own and my brother's childhood experiences and how, when taken into consideration, these complicate dominant discourses around disability, caregiving, sibling relationships, and childhood.

REFERENCES

Beckett, C. (2007). Women, disability, care: Good neighbours or uneasy bedfellows? *Critical Social Policy, 27*(3), 360–380.

Castles, K. (2004). "Nice, average Americans": Postwar parents' groups and the defense of the normal family. In S. Noll & J. Trent (Eds.), *Mental retardation in America* (pp. 351–370). New York: New York University Press.

Connors, C., & Stalker, K. (2007). Children's experiences of disability: Pointers to a social model of childhood disability. *Disability & Society, 22*(1), 19–33.

Curran, T., & Runswick-Cole, K. (2014). Disabled children's childhood studies: A distinct approach? *Disability & Society, 29*(10), 1617–1630.

Davis, J. (2006). Disability, childhood studies and the construction of medical discourses. Questioning attention deficit hyperactivity disorder: A theoretical perspective. In G. Lloyd, J. Stead, & D. Cohen (Eds.), *Critical new perspectives on ADHD* (pp. 45–65). London: Routledge.

Doucet, A. (2013). A "choreography of becoming": Fathering, embodied care, and new materialisms. *Canadian Review of Sociology/Revue Canadienne De Sociologie, 50*(3), 284–305.

Graham, H. (1983). Caring: A labour of love. In J. Finch & D. Groves (Eds.), *A labour of love: Women, work and caring* (13–30). London: Routledge & K. Paul.

James, A., & Prout, A. (Eds.). (2015). *Constructing and reconstructing childhood: Contemporary issues in the sociological study of childhood*. Abingdon & New York: Routledge.

Keith, L., & Morris, J. (1995). Easy targets: Disability rights perspective on "the children as carers" debate. *Critical Social Policy, 15*, 36–57.

Morris, J. (1991). "Us" and "them"? Feminist research, community care and disability. *Critical Social Policy, 11*(22), 22–39.

Morris, J. (1994). Community care or independent living? *Critical Social Policy, 14*(24), 24–45.

Morris, J. (1997). A response to Aldridge & Becker—disability rights and the denial of young carers: The dangers of zero-sum arguments. *Critical Social Policy, 17*, 133–135.

O'Dell, L., Crafter, S., de Abreu, G., & Cline, T. (2010). Constructing "normal childhood": Young people talk about young carers. *Disability & Society, 25*(6), 643–655.

Olsen, R., & Parker, G. (1997). A response to Aldridge and Becker—"Disability rights and the denial of young carers: The dangers of zero-sum arguments." *Critical Social Policy, 17*, 125–133.

Pinto, P. (2008). Re-constituting care: A rights-based approach to disability, motherhood, and dilemmas of care. *Journal of Motherhood Initiative for Research and Community Involvement, 10*(1), 119–130.

Robinson, F. (2011). *The ethics of care: A feminist approach to human security*. Philadelphia: Temple University Press.

Thomas, C. (1993). De-constructing concepts of care. *Sociology, 27*(4), 649–669.

Tisdall, E. K. M. (2012). The challenge and challenging of childhood studies? Learning from disability studies and research with disabled children. *Children & Society, 26*(3), 181–191.

7 Studying Friendship among Children at School from a Sociological Approach to Childhood

Nathalie Bélanger

LEARNING OBJECTIVES

- To understand the importance of children's voices to childhood studies
- To locate research about children's friendship in the contexts of childhood studies and studies of friendship in general
- To be able to see the difference between psychological and sociological approaches to friendship
- To hear children's views on what friendship means to them in the specific context of school
- To consider advantages of examining children's friendship for researching children's lives

---

Children [are] "human beings" rather than "human becomings" and [childhood is analysed] as one among other structural forms, which continuously "interact" with other structural forms in society.

—Qvortrup, 1994, p. 4

INTRODUCTION

Friendship is without any doubt an issue of interest to children. It is not uncommon to hear children saying they like going to school because of the friends they encounter or those they hope to make. Friendship is therefore an important component of the school experience, and one that structures it in many ways. Very little, however, has been written on this topic from a sociological perspective; most of the work published to date on friendship comes from the field of psychology. Consequently, friendship is mainly analyzed with regard to what it brings to individuals, focusing on self-esteem and emotional security, for example, or, conversely, on the pain and distress experienced when one is deprived of friendship. The way friendship structures relationships and the role it plays in societies, and most specifically in schools, is still under-examined. The purpose of this chapter is to remedy this situation in several ways. First, it discusses the **sociology of childhood** and the social theories that finally made it possible to hear children's voices and to seriously consider their social and political positions in societies. Second, friendship among children is specifically and sociologically examined as one component of the larger field of social theories and sociology of childhood. Finally, childhood friendship is explored in the context of school. Due to the fact that frequenting a school is inevitable for most children, it is relevant to examine the relationships that are forged in this context and not just what children learn academically. French-language regional schools, where we conducted our research, are a minority in Ontario. Their catchment areas are necessarily much wider than those of English-language schools. As such, examining the issue of friendship was doubly interesting because children develop and maintain different friendships in these schools than those in their own neighbourhoods. In the conclusion, we raise questions to further the discussion of friendship from a sociological perspective.

SOCIAL THEORIES AND THE SOCIOLOGY OF CHILDHOOD

As a relatively recent field in sociology, social theories and sociology of childhood bring children's voices to the foreground and include them in the study of social processes and inequalities in society, including those in the educational system (Sirota, 2006). Albanese (2016) points out that the displacement of dominant 1960s developmental discourses by critical and identity-based **discourses** encouraged a growing interest in understanding children's contributions to society, which coincided with the emergence and expansion of children's rights discourses in the 1980s. These fields created a space for children's voices to be heard. This was quite a novel change, as even in the recent past, it seemed impossible to give voice to children. The controversy surrounding Harper Lee's Pulitzer-winning novel *To Kill a Mockingbird*, published in 1960, is an illustration of this. As noted by commentator Isabelle Hausser (2005), at its release, the novel was regarded as simple "hammock reading" because it was not commonly believed that a little girl could express herself and narrate her own life as Scout did in this novel.

Social theories and the sociology of childhood have progressively created an area of research that allows children's social and political positions and voices to be heard and taken seriously. Sirota (2006) noted that children are no longer considered small, vulnerable, "strange objects" (*petits objets insolites*) (p. 31), but rather a force and fundamental part of every society (Mayall, 2002; Mannheim, 1928/1990). Yet childhood is often still positioned in relation to the adult world. Children are generally presented as under development (Woodhead, 2008), and are therefore considered subjects or spectators of their own socialization (Parsons, 1973), or they are cast as the uncivilized, irresponsible, and immature "Other" (James & Prout, 1990; Delalande, 2001).

Taking children's voices into account involves disrupting existing categories. For instance, Qvortrup, Bardy, Sgritta, and Wintersberger (1994) question the categorization and opposition of childhood and adulthood, which typically considers the former an unfinished state of being. These authors avoid characterizing children in terms of ascriptive variables, like age, nor do they regard them as immature or incompetent subjects in comparison to adults.

More recent studies about childhood have returned to children the same legitimacy and **agency** granted to adult actors in society (Montandon, 1997). They have also shown the informed point of view held by children who are engaged in relationships with their peers and adults. Sirota (1998, 2006) has situated this research trend within a general sociological movement returning to agency, and to a new sociology of education that no longer restricts itself to statistical analyses of disembodied students whose success or failure depends on their parents' social class. In the same vein, James and Prout (1990) have problematized more rigid established understandings of this particular stage of life, emphasizing the fact that childhood is a social construction—one that is based not on a single, universal model, but rather on a plurality of childhoods (see also Qvortrup, 1991). What this means, more specifically, is that "the immaturity of children is a biological fact of life but the ways in which this immaturity is understood and made meaningful is a fact of culture" (James & Prout, 1990, p. 7). Among other significant characteristics, these authors see children as active in the construction of their own social lives and in the societies in which they live. Consequently, they argue, children's social relationships and cultures are worthy of study in their own right (see pp. 7–8).

Whether enacted in the context of schools, youth clubs, or neighbourhoods, relationships and social relations between peers have to be taken seriously if children's autonomy and participation in society are to be adequately considered, and these have increasingly become a topic of interest (James, Jenks, & Prout, 1998). This chapter addresses this particular component of the social construction paradigm of childhood by looking at friendship and child-to-child socialization to see how these were understood in the past, how our understanding has evolved over the years, and how children's relationships and social relations have been analyzed in recent literature. It also asks how children, themselves, in specific school settings, conceive of friendship. Studying friendships is a means to better understand, from the standpoint of children, social changes and processes of inclusion and exclusion in our societies and in diversified schools.

FRIENDSHIP AND SOCIAL RELATIONSHIPS BETWEEN CHILDREN

While friendship is usually viewed, from a psychological perspective, as a personal, voluntary, and private reciprocal bond between individuals, from a sociological standpoint, it involves a **relational** phenomenon inherently structured by social components (Allan, 1979, 1989). As such, friendships are a product of time and place: they are developed through different networks and can take different forms, evolving fluidly over time, and are either sustained or abandoned over the years (Allan, 1989; Bell & Coleman, 1999; Pahl, 2000).

Sociologists like Allan (1989) and Spencer and Pahl (2006) therefore suggest moving away from research that presumes an idealized definition of friendship—studies that focus essentially on someone's "best friends" or that count the number of friends someone has through surveys—towards approaches that seek to **qualitatively** understand friendships in specific sociocultural contexts. Spencer and Pahl (2006) want to know what friendship really means for individuals, to inquire about and describe real "flesh-and-blood relationships."

Sociologists, in general, have taken a long time to become interested in friendship due to the fact that it has not been purposefully recognized by or incorporated into social institutions. Rather, friendship is an informal and more diffuse phenomenon (Allan, 1989). Sociological inquiry into friendship has largely been absent from modern thought because it was considered a private matter by even the most renowned sociological theorists, like Durkheim. This belief held strong despite arguments to the contrary made by other theorists, like Tocqueville and Arendt, that "political friendship" operates in modern societies (Mallory, 2012). Similarly, sociology of education has long been more preoccupied with institutional settings, schooling, and the study of inequalities than by informal contexts of interrelationships like friendship. Moreover, methods of inquiry usually put forward by sociologists, such as questionnaires or interviews focusing on individual responses, cannot grasp the complex interactional ties and patterns of friendship that can be accessed using direct observational methods stemming from the field of anthropology (Allan, 1989).

While scholars like Allan (1989) eventually tried to highlight the relevance of a sociology of friendship, his research mainly concerns friendship among adults. Only a small portion of his work specifically relates to children's friendship. Meanwhile, in the context of **childhood studies,** friendship is still mostly examined in relation to early education, play, arts, leisure, school, and family institutions, and much less in terms of informal socialization between children, or friendship, *per se*. Following Sirota's (2012) validation of children's power in society, research interests in childhood studies have varied regionally and nationally. In Scandinavia, for instance, the main preoccupations to date have been with the place of children in the city and in the preservation of a folklore. In Britain, children's place and voice have been prominent in the literature, whereas educational requirements for new generations, in the context of reunification, have been the main focus of studies in Germany. In Italy, early childhood, desinstitutionalization, and city policy have dominated discussions by researchers, and French studies have been concerned with equal opportunities in the context of republican ideology (Sirota, 2012). In Canada, poverty, **Indigenous** children, **citizenship**, and the history of childhood have been well documented (Albanese, 2016; Chen, 2005; Gleason, 1999). One commonality among these varied social studies of childhood is that the topic of friendship has only recently appeared to be worthy of interest.

Let us, here, revisit the theoretical steps that finally led to the increased sociological examination of child-to-child relationships and friendship. James et al. (1998) observe that the **child peer group** is generally perceived as the benchmark against which children measure themselves and each other. Although adults encourage friendships between children, the child peer group, as a particular culture, has historically been perceived as problematic (not beneficial for the child) in the eyes of adults in some parts of the world. This concern about or negation of the value of the peer group left little room for the recognition of potential socialization among children, or "child-to-child socialization" (p. 94). Furthermore, there has been little conceptualization or consideration of child-to-child interactions in studies of socialization. Traditional socialization theory, based on psychological approaches to child development, "assumes a unidirectional flow of cultural information from competent adult to incompetent and passive child" (p. 94). Within this framework, as far back as the 1920s, child peer groups have been viewed by some theorists as having a potentially negative influence on individual children. Rather paradoxically, adult anxiety also arose about children who were deprived of such peer groups (James et al., 1998). It should be noted, though, that in contrast to these theorists' views, in everyday life, adults have consistently encouraged some mentoring between children, as when older children take responsibility for disciplining or even caring for younger ones. In non-Western countries, mentoring between children was and still is an important component of their daily life. When, in the 1970s, peer groups finally came to be seen more broadly by (Western) scholars as a context for socialization, as James et al. point out, the predominant research theme was deviancy. Little consideration was given to ordinary child-to-child interaction, as is still the case.

Similarly, the study of children's friendships first focused on psychological child development theory and followed more or less the same evolution as the socialization theories briefly described above. It was first assumed that children grasp the concept of friendship by progressing through a series of stages that teach them the adult definition or social representations of friendship (see James et al., 1998, p. 94). James (1993), however, shows that the meaning of friendship is quite different for adults and children; whereas "having friends" is initially more important to children than "being friends" in the long run, the latter is more meaningful for adults. Lately, more research has focused on how children experience friendship. This is reflected in the "new social studies of childhood" that combine interests in socialization and friendship (James et al., 1998). These new studies take children's agency and characteristics into consideration, and show that peer groups contribute more positively to children's socialization. Children are also now believed to contribute to processes of social production and reproduction in societies. For Albanese (2016), children "carry out important social activities that make and remake their relationships and daily lives. As such, children are seen and treated as active reproducers of meanings … and contribute to cultural reproduction and change" (p. 34).

Literature reviews on peer groups, socialization, and friendship show, however, that while this area of research has become significant over the years, the first social studies were principally concerned with early childhood rather than with school-aged children (Corsaro, 1985; Gayet, 2006; Javeau, 2000), and others mostly or specifically investigated the playground (Delalande, 2001; Rayou, 2000). Sirota (1998, 2006) was intrigued by the rituals of children expressed through play, such as invitations to birthday parties or other events, describing them as a means of building social connections. These rituals are part of what Corsaro and Miller (1992) call "interpretive reproduction," in which children occupy a dynamic position as active actors in their own socialization. Children participate in the child and adult worlds by affirming, reaffirming, and negotiating their identities within both worlds. This fact became obvious to Corsaro while he was studying the rituals and routines that lead young children to create abstract concepts and question authority or manage conflict through role-playing (Corsaro, 2005/2015). He also demonstrates that the concept of friendship is not only understood by children old enough to likely understand the idea of **reciprocity** (at roughly age 11), but it is also understood by younger children, who experience it in the present moment (Corsaro, 2003). Children produce friendships and participate in friendship groups by sharing and by controlling situations of inclusion and exclusion among themselves, for instance, when they set up informal clubs for which they manage how membership is offered to other children (Corsaro, 2005/2015). This point of view is also developed by James, cited above (1993). Through such appropriations of social situations, children reproduce the adult world while contributing to changing it (James & James, 2004). According to Mayall (2002), although children may represent a minority, they are, at the same time, a permanent and influential group in society. Indeed, while specific children grow up and change over time, children are present at every point in history and they contribute, in different contexts, to the production of the social order. Researchers who take children seriously are thus better able to better understand the society in which we live.

FRIENDSHIPS AT SCHOOL

The examples below show how research on children's school experiences has attempted to "grasp the manner in which students construct their experience and build the relationships, strategies and meaning through which they construct themselves" (Dubet & Martuccelli, 1996, p. 14). Based on the accounts of 80 10- and 11-year-old children, Montandon, Dominicé, and Bottinger's (2000) study aimed to understand how those children appropriated the world around them and constructed their social networks. In particular, children's statements about solidarity, friendship, and conflict were analyzed. It turned out that three elements—cohesion, **power**, and regulation—contributed most to the development of children's social skills and to their position in the classroom, especially in terms of who is friends with whom and how these relationships affect their school trajectories.

Pasquier (2005) examined sociability practices among students by analyzing secondary school students' peer cultures in three French *lycées*. Recently, parent/child relationships have profoundly changed in France, becoming more egalitarian, and young people are now staying in school longer and entering the job market later. Pasquier found that within this new context, peer culture had become more important than social categorization, specifically family socioeconomic status, in defining who hangs out with whom. Peer culture, Pasquier (2005) writes, can also help students move outside the social capital transmitted by their parents and overcome the social reproduction that occurs through schooling (as first identified by Bourdieu & Passeron [1964/1985]). School alone no longer defines and controls the normative horizon. Rather, a mediatized youth culture imposes its own codes and norms, which have an impact on the possibilities of friendship. Pasquier (2005) shows how relationships are re/organized between the *lycéens* through the use of new media. Inspired by Hannah Arendt, she argues that this peer culture can, however, be crueler than it was before, in terms of exclusion. Whereas some intellectuals fear the new digital culture, which young people are so much a part of, thinking the ties of friendships and solidarity disintegrate in modern society, things appear more complicated to Pasquier and others, like Spencer and Pahl (2006). They show how friendships and relationships among peers have been largely underestimated by researchers who cling to a nostalgic conception of friendship.

Although sociologists of childhood have enabled us, over the years, to explore child agency and childhood culture *per se*, according to Lignier and Pagis (2014), they seem to have lost interest in or minimized the usual sociological reasoning that aims to understand the genesis of "rankings and social judgments" (p. 36). Focusing on friendship and especially on "unfriendships," these authors wish to reintroduce social categorization into analysis. Looking particularly at networking between children aged 6 to 11 years, Lignier and Pagis analyzed the reasons why children do not want to make friends with others. Not surprisingly, their results show that children's social networks are gendered and divided in terms of social belonging. More interestingly, the authors point out how academic grades have an impact on who is friends, and how "domestic patterns of judgment" learned in the family (p. 54) and reinforced at school operate in friendship. Bodily hygiene and appearance were also found to affect how children chose friends.

Winkler-Reid (2015), who studied girls' friendships and the formation of person-hood, spent 14 months in a London secondary school observing how friendships were constituted according to specific categorizations. Although it is usually taken for grant-ed that friendship falls within the private sphere, as recalled above, Winkler-Reid ex-plained how it is actually "public and governed by social conventions" (p. 167). This was especially evident when the girls, who were interacting at different levels of intimacy, discussed their tastes and opinions, what music they listened to, or what people wore (p. 171). These criteria for inclusion and exclusion, which are gendered and sometimes ra-cially coded, delineated how friendships were re/composed. Thus, making and breaking friendships are "performative acts" (p. 179) that produce and reproduce the criteria by which girls judge and are judged by others.

In summary, socialization and friendships, as the starting point of children's agency, are at the heart of the social construction paradigm of childhood, and are of particular significance for understanding children's school experiences. As the research reported below shows, an approach that takes this into account might help improve interventions in schools, thereby limiting processes of exclusion and reducing the perpetuation of inequalities between children and different social groups.

METHODOLOGY

In an attempt to understand children's representations of friendships and child-to-child socialization, I drew on data gathered in the context of a larger research project[1] con-ducted in French-language schools in Ontario,[2] which specifically aimed to comprehend how children, themselves, defined an inclusive school. Using an ethnographic approach, I intended to understand how the Ontario Ministry of Education's (Ministère de l'Éd-ucation de l'Ontario, 2009) broad strategy of inclusion—promoting acceptance and inclusion for all students and delineating prohibited grounds for discrimination—was actually put forward and experienced by children and young people.

School Observation and Data Collection with Child Participants

Three different urban French-language schools in Ontario were visited, and young re-search participants who were at the end of their elementary education were invited to join the research project, as shown in table 7.1.

These three schools were among the lowest ranked group of schools in Ontario in terms of standardized test results, and were located in mixed socioeconomic neighbour-hoods with low-income housing. In light of the increasing competitiveness found be-tween schools in Ontario, I believe it is worthwhile to examine children's representations of friendship and child-to-child socialization within the particular school contexts of the study because the general atmosphere of competitiveness may negatively affect such schools. For instance, if one school appears more attractive than another to some parents with regard to test results, for instance, the social and school integration or inclusion processes might be slowed to the disadvantage of the children in some schools (Bélanger, 2011; Bélanger, Audet, & Plante, 2014). Studying lower-ranking schools is also a way to learn more about inequalities at school, and to grasp the valuable points of view of the children who are central actors in these specific contexts.

Specific data collection methods were developed and used with the children in order to understand their experiences of and perspectives on inclusion. They consisted of questionnaires, drawings, interviews, and classroom and playground observations (as shown in table 7.2), all of which are methods best suited for research conducted with children; a more conventional adult-centred methodological approach would have rendered it difficult to grasp children's representations and interactions. Since children are social actors involved in production and reproduction practices, it was relevant to carefully analyze the discursive and social practices of children as legitimate actors and producers of culture (Delalande, 2001).

Table 7.1: Number of Students Participating versus Total Pupils by School

Du Sentier School	De la Passerelle School	Du Plateau School
Grade 5 classroom: 8/26 students	Grade 5 classroom: 10/30 students	Grade 5 classroom: 7/20 students
	Grade 6 classroom: 5/28 students	Grade 6 classroom: 14/28 students
Source: Nathalie Bélanger, SSHRC research project Representations of Pupils and Inclusion in French-Speaking Schools in Ontario, 2007–2010.		

Table 7.2: Use of Three Survey Methods and Related Data

School/Data Collection Method	Du Sentier School	De la Passerelle School	Du Plateau School
Social constellation (sociometric questions, drawings)	8	15	19
Open interviews with children (transcripts)	8	14	19
Classroom and playground observations (reports)	16	26	28
Source: Nathalie Bélanger, SSHRC research project Representations of Pupils and Inclusion in French-Speaking Schools in Ontario, 2007–2010.			

Using an approach inspired by Christensen and James (2008), among others, participating children were also invited to build a "social constellation" in which they drew and answered short questions about their friends, their daily or weekly schedule, and their school experiences (see also Kirby, 1999, 2004; Clarke, 2005; Hart & Rajbhandary, 2003). This social constellation activity established the foundation for the interviews that followed. Close attention was paid to the challenges and obstacles the children had faced throughout their schooling experience. Consequently, the focus was on the way problems are formulated and solved between children, especially between small groups and friends.

SOCIAL RELATIONSHIPS AND FRIENDSHIPS IN SCHOOLS

As briefly mentioned in the introduction, children attending regional French-language schools in Ontario build friendships that extend beyond their neighbourhoods because the catchment areas of these minority schools are larger than those of their neighbourhoods' English-language schools. Children consequently develop friendships in school that are complementary to those they have already established in their neighborhoods, communities, and recreational centres.

Friendship represents a form of capital that children can count on in their journey toward social recognition (Honneth, 2000). In general, we found that friendship greatly influences the school experience and facilitates the organization of school life. This was especially evident at the first school I visited, briefly described below, where friendship facilitated the settling and welcoming processes of families in the area, as well as the integration or inclusion of their children in the school. I have elsewhere documented how children in such schools represented their school experience and indicated, in accordance with Mayall (2002), how friendship is an intrinsic motivation for going to school, while more distant rewards such as future employment prospects or bilingualism appeared to be extrinsic or remote motivations (Bélanger & Kayitesi, 2010). Leroy-Audouin and Piquée (2004) similarly asked children living in Burgundy (France) about their favourite things about going to school. Although the most common answer was "learning new things," the presence of "buddies" was mentioned second most often, either positively or negatively. This exemplifies how friendship is central for children in school.

The school environment (including school norms and organization, teacher culture, and so on) has a significant impact on children's schooling experiences and on their friendship-making practices. In turn, children also influence the school environment. The "**school effect**" (*l'effet établissement*) has already been documented by authors Arum (2000), Charlot (1994), and Cousin (1993), who explain that each school can be viewed as an organization with a specific set of social relations and resources of its own. When an organization is less rigid, expressions of friendships are made possible in everyday life at school. Lastly, in terms of friendship, we noticed a significant divide between boys and girls, especially in the third school visited, as discussed below.

At the first school we visited, referred to here as École de la Passerelle, the high proportion of students from families who had newly immigrated to Canada or who had arrived partway during the school year, including **refugees**, was striking. Within this context, children expressed an interest in issues related to respect and security and improving their knowledge of the school system and the language spoken at school, as well as making friends. For instance, although making friends was a central concern for Jessica, who had recently arrived from the Democratic Republic of the Congo and did not yet feel completely at ease in school, having "lots of things to improve" and "speaking with the right accent" also represented priority goals for her. It should be noted that concerns about speaking the language used at school is a factor in the development of school friendships. Jessica's responses revealed her expectations about school, since she wished that the school would "give us good things, teach us well, do nice activities with us, like going to the gym or playing music." Taking into account these kinds of desires and recognizing the context of the diversity of languages spoken in the school's families and the surrounding community, the principal and teachers took time to familiarize students and their families with what they believed to be the culture of the school.

Since the common language at school was French, code-switching between French and heritage languages occurred and contributed to a certain complicity between children. Code-switching means alternating between two or more languages or language varieties in the context of a single conversation. For example, during a math class about the various types of angles, the students expressed interest and interacted among themselves; when Djamila was called to the front to answer a question, one of her comrades sitting in front whispered a few words that made her laugh. The teacher asked what she had said. Djamila replied that she had said a word in Somali. The teacher added, "Are you allowed to speak Somali at school? You get a blue ticket."

This excerpt demonstrates the difference the school creates or attempts to create between the language spoken at home with the family and with some friends, and the public language encouraged by the school. It also reveals the complicity of the children in their attempt to play with or even circumvent the school's operational norms and influence the organization of the class. They try to participate in producing and reproducing parts of the nondominant school organization into which they integrate themselves and interact. This example demonstrates the kind of agency children can exercise through friendship. The fact that the incident ended with the children being regulated and disciplined by the teacher for not speaking French in class also shows the constraints placed on children's agency in school settings. Yet children's agency could be better taken into account in classroom management, or even in curriculum delivery and knowledge organization, which are usually underpinned by specific, adult-centred, dominant norms—in this case, linguistic norms and modes of organization.

Indeed, in a previous study with a less rigid school organization, we demonstrated how children position themselves in their social relations at school and analytically use and critique binary categories, especially in terms of linguistic duality (Bélanger & Farmer, 2010). Children's processes of appropriation at school correspond with the way they make sense of their school experience by incorporating social and out-of-school aspects of their life, including friendships developed in their own neighbourhoods. From their answers and the life experiences they asserted and reflected on, it was clear that children contribute to shaping and transforming their schools through this social production process. Their positions jostle the dominant categories usually at work in schools and in educational policies. Children know how to make decisions about the major issues that affect them and interact with each other, even at the risk of criticizing the school's operational methods (Bélanger & Farmer, 2010).

The second school we visited, École du Sentier, was also highly diversified, but its immigrant population had been established earlier. It now educated more second-generation Canadian students, although some students identified primarily with the culture of their parents' country of origin, such as Julie-Anne, who defined herself first and foremost as Haitian, despite having been born in Canada.

One situation observed in this school illustrates the relational and variable character of friendship, as well as how it can be gendered and ethnocentric. As previously discussed in Bélanger (2016), Ghada, Johanie, and Maria, three girls from the same class, presented themselves as friends. During their interviews and when they completed their questionnaires, each acknowledged the others as friends. Ghada is the daughter of **immigrants**. She wears the veil and attends an Arabic school on Saturdays to learn the language. Johanie is the daughter of mixed parents (English mother and French father) who have always lived in Canada. Maria also comes from linguistically mixed parents. In spite of the obvious friendship between the three girls, it was possible to observe that Ghada is sometimes at a disadvantage in a power relationship with her two companions. For example, when completing the questionnaires, we observed collaboration between Johanie and Maria, while Ghada tried to get closer to her friends and validate her own answers by taking a look at those her friends had written down. This shows the fluidity of friendship and the inherently timely and spatial nature of its development.

In the third school, École du Plateau, which also had a highly diverse student population that included many new Canadian families, the children's activities and friendships were notably more divided by gender than at the other schools. This school was well-known for its excellence in sports and seemed to especially attract male students who, according to the principal, chose to attend it because of their interest in sports. Although team sports were played more on the playground by the boys, girls sometimes participated, such as Ayan, Délirose, and Stacey, a group of friends. Team captains stood out from the other children. When we asked, one child, Charles, gave a long explanation of how the sports teams were made up during recess. "The

1. Montre-moi ce que tu fais dans une semaine :

Figure 7.1: My Week Schedule (Example of a Question Completed by a Student Co-participant in the Project)

Source: Nathalie Bélanger, SSHRC research project Representations of Pupils and Inclusion in French-Speaking Schools in Ontario, 2007–2010.

captains—the most popular kids—choose the strongest, 'coolest' kids, and then everyone else is left." Boys who were less interested in sports appeared to be excluded from this dynamic, which structured the activities in this sports-focused school. Once again, we noticed how the children's participation in the school's culture, in this case centred around sports and a specific representation of masculinity, echoed Winkler-Reid's (2015) and Pasquier's (2005) fieldwork results: peer groupings and friendships appear to be gendered.

The young people we interviewed had many thoughts to share on these topics. For instance, according to their teachers, many of the female students from immigrant and religious families were raised from a young age to value modesty, but were nevertheless vocal about denouncing what they saw as inequalities between boys and girls. A discussion about inequality led the girls to talk about gender and the gendered roles they each played at school. During a period of free time, a group of girlfriends complained that they "have to do everything, cleaning and food" during school parties. Indeed, during a lunchtime celebration marking the end of a student teacher's placement, we noted in our observation journal "that it was the girls (Sabina, and a group of her friends, among others) who helped to set the table, serve the food, clean up, etc. They volunteered right away. During this time, the boys played with the ball." Again, a clear gender division appeared between peer groups. This observation echoes Barrie Thorne's work on gender and play at school. She argues that school sets the ground for gendered division that students embrace and reproduce (1993). Based on her ethnographic fieldwork, she identified gendered separation among children and in friendship and relationship patterns on the playground. She also examined how cross-gender affiliations sometimes form in neighbourhood contexts, and how children delicately manage these relationships, choosing whether or not to display them at school—the fear of being teased was always prioritized!

Friendship appeared especially structured by gender at École du Plateau, far more than at the other two schools we studied, and further divisions existed within gender categories. For example, among boys, friendships tended to be structured around who played basketball and presented themselves as strong, and who did not. Nevertheless, friendships change over time; they changed even during the short period of the time we spent observing children. What remains consistent is the central importance of friendship to students. In the above drawing, we see that for one female student at École du Plateau, friends had a central role, and were as important as learning in terms of her motivations for attending school.

Friendship is also structured by social categorizations like religious affiliation. One of the students at École du Plateau who had previously lived in Lebanon answered our question about what unites her with her friends by saying, "most of my friends actually are Sunni, that's what I am." This example shows how simplistic it would be to only consider psychological characteristics when studying friendship. It is clearly a relational phenomenon that is inherently socially structured. In this case, processes of exclusion operated in relationships based on religious categorizations.

What stood out most acutely in our research and conversations with children at this school was their denunciation of acts of disrespect, including bullying. Teachers sometimes had to help resolve student conflicts that arose from the school's highly gender-divided culture, overemphasis on sports, and narrow ideal of masculinity. They taught in a paradoxical context, forced to juggle the contrasting educational values at work in the system: inclusiveness and competition. Teachers could count, however, on some more vocal students to attempt to disrupt some of the values and norms of the school. For instance, although competition is emphasized through standardized testing and sport activities at École du Plateau, one student, Charles, raised to the idea of a more welcoming school environment. He said that everyone has "the right" to participate in sports activities, whether they are "stronger and more popular, or not as strong." It is interesting to note how, within this context, children developed and vocalized aspirations for a more democratic school setting and organization; this again demonstrates their agency and interest in the production of norms and practices at school.

CONCLUSION

Social theories and the sociology of childhood have created a space where we can finally listen to children's voices and take their perspectives and representations into consideration when studying social processes and inequalities, including those enacted in the educational system. This fascinating and growing field of study has grown out of the many critical discourses (from women's and civil rights studies, for instance) that displaced dominant developmental and psychological approaches to childhood. It also coincides with the emergence and expansion of children's rights discourses. As such, children are no longer regarded as adults-in-development or simple subjects or objects of research, but are, rather, seen as a permanent force in society that contributes to maintaining and changing our society. More specifically, James and Prout (1990) proposed a new paradigm whereby childhood is a social construction based on a plurality of childhoods, not on a universal model. Significant components of this paradigm relate to relationships between peers, and serious consideration must, therefore, be given to children's friendships and to the research methodologies we devise to understand children. It is important to find approaches and tools that are meaningful and useful for the study of children and childhood friendship. This chapter situates the study of friendship as a theme emerging from broader social studies of childhood, and reviews current findings in the field.

The research described here relies on data derived from interviews with children and from classroom and playground observations, and developed with the children, in three different urban French-language schools in Ontario. This work stems from a larger project that seeks to understand how the provincial strategy for inclusion in schools is actually put forward and how it is experienced by children and young people. I specifically focused, in this chapter, on the data related to friendship and children's socialization. The results and ensuing discussion shed light on how friendships are constituted in schools. They also provide information about the particular challenges children face on a daily basis and allow us to better understand processes of inequality as they unfold in children's daily lives.

Moreover, this study shows how when groups of friends and children interact with each other, they play with the rules, discuss school norms, and even circumvent the dominant school culture, thereby influencing, resisting, and sometimes changing classroom organization. The children in our study were empowered through the research process to express themselves and to participate in exploring issues that directly affect them. Some of the excerpts discussed above show how these students conceptualize the role of friendship as a counterpoint to the inequality and exclusion resulting from their schools' norms and organization. For other children, friendship was an individualized strategy for children from immigrant-background families, for example, to seek integration into the school's social culture. Gender was found to be an important and inescapable factor in the creation of friendships among children at each school. It was particularly influential at the third school we studied, where the emphasis on sports and the promotion of a particular definition of masculinity predominantly shaped this microcosm, and significantly affected the children's interactions and peer groupings.

CHAPTER SUMMARY

Together, in this chapter, we

- Discussed the importance of children's voices in research on childhood and, consequently, the impetus for research on friendship among children.
- Examined the status of sociological studies on children's friendship in childhood studies and studies of friendship in general.
- Examined why and how friendship has more often been studied from a psychological perspective.
- Learned what friendship means to children and how they practise friendship in their everyday lives at school.
- Discovered that how schools are organized has an impact on experiences of friendship among children.
- Identified the advantages of studying friendship among children.

STUDY QUESTIONS

1. Following what you have learned in this chapter, how would you explain the way friendship among children has become a field or theme of research?
2. Why is it important and relevant to consider friendship from a sociological perspective? And how is it different from a psychological perspective?
3. How would you describe the friendships you experienced when you were younger? How different are friendships experienced in school from those in less-structured social settings?
4. What benefits can studies of children's friendship bring to teachers and children in school?
5. How can research on friendship among children help us to understand and ultimately avoid perpetuating inequalities between groups in society, particularly minority students, whether they are from a linguistic or religious group, from First Nations, Inuit, or Métis families, or from families that have recently immigrated to Canada?

SUGGESTED RESEARCH ASSIGNMENT

From the specific studies of friendship among children summarized in this chapter, describe and discuss what you would say are the main sociological findings about friendship among children. Watch one or more of the films/video clips listed below, and discuss what connections you may be able to make between them and the sociological findings about children's friendship.

SUGGESTED FILMS/VIDEO CLIPS

Friendship—Gorseland Primary School
vimeo.com/30720555
This video shows what the word *friend* means for children from a particular school. Also, very interestingly, children were involved in the production of the video.

Friendship Soup Video Lesson
www.teachertube.com/video/friendship-soup-video-lesson-305061
This video gives a voice to children who explain what friendship is. It is a useful tool for teachers who want to discuss this theme with their students.

Comptines
www.onf.ca/film/comptines/
This video shows little girls in 1970s Montreal interacting with each other. Children make connections with each other through informal play in ways that are obviously much less structured than in school. This video also makes us think about how children's play and games are different today from those in the past.

SUGGESTED WEBSITES

Naître et grandir
naitreetgrandir.com/fr/etape/5-8-ans/ecole/fiche.aspx?doc=amitie-enfant
This webpage is mostly for parents, explaining how important it is for children to make friends, what to do in cases of conflict, etc. While this is valuable information, friendship is mostly defined here in terms of what it brings to the child individually, a limitation that is addressed in this chapter.

Life Education
www.lifeeducation.org.au/parents/item/526-children-and-the-benefits-of-friendship
This website is for parents and caregivers based in Australia. Interestingly, it addresses

the issue of building and navigating friendship. It takes into account that friendships are made of ups and downs, and that friendship is not a linear process.

NOTES

1. I acknowledge that the results discussed here come from a larger research project funded by SSHRC. I would also like to thank the students who worked with me as research assistants on this project. Many thanks to the children and to the school personnel who opened their door to us.

2. In Ontario, four school systems are publicly funded: the French public system, the French Catholic system, the English public system, and the English Catholic system. Of the 72 school boards in Ontario, 12 are French-language, with over 425 elementary and secondary French-language schools. In these schools, the curriculum is taught exclusively in French, with the exception of English class. French-language schools in Ontario have a mandate to protect, enhance, and transmit the French language and culture. These schools serve students whose parents are considered rights-holders according to Section 23 of the *Canadian Charter of Rights and Freedoms*. Rights-holders are therein defined as Canadian citizens whose first language (learned and still understood) is French, Canadian citizens who have received their elementary school instruction in Canada in French, or any Canadian citizens of whom any child has received or is receiving elementary or secondary school instruction in French in Canada. French-language schools can also admit children of non–rights-holding parents through admission committees, particularly children from French-speaking immigrant families that do not qualify as holders of French-language education rights under the Charter, or immigrant children whose parents' mother tongue is neither French nor English (allophone) (Policy/Program Memorandum number 148, Ontario Ministry of Education [www.edu.gov.on.ca/extra/eng/ppm/148.html]). These dispositions described in the Memorandum take into account the changing profile of the French-speaking community in Ontario resulting, for example, from increased immigration. Within the context of English-language predominance in Ontario and in the world, they recognize a need to protect and enhance minority languages.

REFERENCES

Albanese, P. (2016). *Children in Canada today*. Don Mills, ON: Oxford University Press.

Allan, G. A. (1979). *A sociology of friendship and kinship*. London: George Allen and Unwin.

Allan, G. A. (1989). *Friendship: Developing a sociological perspective*. London: Westview Press.

Arum, R. (2000). Schools and communities: Ecological and Institutional Dimensions. *Annual Review of Sociology, 26*, 395–418.

Bélanger, N. (2011). Le choix de l'école secondaire de langue française en Ontario par les parents. *Lien social et Politiques, 66*, 197–224.

Bélanger, N. (2016). Reconnaissance à l'école de langue française en Ontario: Une entrée par l'amitié. In Y. Lenoir, A. Froelich, & V. Zuniga (Eds.), *La reconnaissance à l'école: Perspectives internationales* (pp. 159–188). Quebec: Presses de l'Université Laval.

Bélanger, N., Audet, A., & Plante, J. (2014). Dynamiques compétitives et collaboratives entre des écoles secondaires de langue française en Ontario. *International Journal of Canadian Studies/Revue internationale d'études canadiennes, 50*(50), 329–346.

Bélanger, N., & Farmer, D. (2010). Expérience scolaire et appropriation de l'école de langue française en Ontario par les enfants. In N. Bélanger, N. Garant, P. Dalley, & T. Desabrais (Eds.), *Produire et reproduire la francophonie en la nommant* (pp. 201–230). Sudbury: Éditions Prise de parole.

Bélanger, N., & Kayitesi, B. (2010). Mise en œuvre de la Convention internationale des droits de l'enfant: Prendre au sérieux la participation de l'enfant à l'école de langue française en Ontario. In S. Bennett & M. Paré (Eds.), *20e anniversaire de la Convention internationale des droits de l'enfant* (pp. 144–158). Ottawa: PUO Presses de l'Université.

Bell, S., & Coleman, S. (Eds.). (1999). *The anthropology of friendship*. London: Berg.

Bourdieu, P., & Passeron, J.-C. (1985). *Les héritiers. Les étudiants et la culture*. Paris: les Éditions de Minuit. (Original work published 1964)

Charlot, B. (1994). *L'école et le territoire: nouveaux espaces, nouveaux enjeux*. Paris: Armand Colin.

Chen, X. (2005). *Tending the gardens of citizenship: Child saving in Toronto, 1880s–1920s*. Toronto: University of Toronto Press.

Christensen, P., & James, A. (2008). Childhood diversity and commonality: Some methodological insights. In P. Christensen & A. James (Eds.), *Research with children: Perspectives and practices* (pp. 156–172). New York: Routledge.

Clarke, A. (2005). Ways of seeing: Using the Mosaic approach to listen to young children's perspectives. In A. Clarke, A. Trine Kjorhold, & P. Moss (Eds.), *Beyond listening: Children's perspectives on early childhood services* (pp. 29–49.) Bristol: Policy Press.

Corsaro, W. (1985). *Friendship and peer culture in the early years*. Norwood, NJ: Ablex.

Corsaro, W.A. (2003). *We're friends? Right? Inside kids's culture*. Washington: Joseph Henry Press.

Corsaro, W. A. (2015). *The sociology of childhood*. Thousand Oaks: Pine Forges Press. (Second and fourth editions). (Original work published 2005)

Corsaro, W. A., & Miller, P. (1992). *Interpretative approaches to children's socialization*. San Francisco: Jossey-Bass.

Cousin, O. (1993). L'effet établissement. Construction d'une problématique. *Revue francaise de sociologie, 34*(3), 395–419.

Delalande, J. (2001). *La cour de récréation: Contribution à une anthropologie de l'enfance*. Rennes: Presses universitaires de Rennes.

Dubet, F., & Martuccelli, D. (1996). *À l'école, sociologie de l'expérience scolaire*. Paris: Seuil.

Gayet, D. (2006). L'univers social des petits. *Les sciences de l'éducation pour l'ère nouvelle, 39*(2), 53–67.

Gleason, M. (1999). *Normalizing the ideal: Psychology, schooling, and the family in postwar Canada*. Toronto: University of Toronto Press.

Hart, R., & Rajbhandary, J. (2003). Using participatory methods to further the democratic goals of children's organizations. In Kim Sabo (Ed.), *Youth participatory evaluation: A field in the making* (pp. 61–75). Champagne, IL: Jossey-Bass.

Hausser, I. (2005). Postface. In H. Lee, *Ne tirez pas sur l'oiseau moqueur* [*To kill a mockingbird*]. Paris: Le livre de poche.

Honneth, A. (2000). *La lutte pour la reconnaissance*. Paris: Cerf.

James, A. (1993). *Childhood identities: Self and social relationships in the experience of the child*. Edinburgh: Edinburgh University press.

James, A., & James, A. (2004). *Constructing childhood: Theory, policy and social practice*. London: Palgrave.

James, A., Jenks, C., & Prout, A. (Eds.). (1998). *Theorizing childhood*. Cambridge: Polity Press.

James, A., & Prout, A. (Eds.). (1990). *Constructing and reconstructing childhood*. London: Falmer Press.

Javeau, C. (2000). Enfant, enfances, enfants: Quel objet pour une science sociale du jeune âge. In D. Saadi-Mokrane (Ed.), *Sociétés et cultures enfantines*. Lille: Éditions du Conseil scientifique de l'Université Charles-de-Gaulle Lille 3.

Kirby, P. (1999). *Involving young researchers: How to enable young people to design and conduct research*. York: Joseph Rowntree Foundation.

Kirby, P. (2004). *A guide to actively involving young people in research: For researchers, research commissioners and managers*. Hampshire: Involve.

Leroy-Audouin, C., & Piquée, C. (2004). Ce que déclare les élèves de l'école élémentaire et pourquoi. *Éducation et Sociétés*, *13*, 209–226.

Lignier, W., & Pagis, J. (2014). Inimitiés enfantines. L'expression précoce des distances sociales. *Genèses*, *3*(96), 35–61.

Mallory, P. (2012). Political friendship in the era of "the social": Theorizing personal relations with Alexis de Tocqueville. *Journal of Classical Sociology*, *12*(1), 22–42.

Mannheim, K. (1990). *Le problème des générations*. Paris: Nathan. (Original work published 1928)

Mayall, B. (2002). *Towards a sociology for childhood: Thinking from children's lives*. Buckingham: Open University Press.

Ministère de l'Éducation de l'Ontario (MÉO). (2009). *Stratégie ontarienne d'équité et d'éducation inclusive*. Toronto: Imprimeur de la Reine pour l'Ontario.

Montandon, C. (1997). *L'éducation du point de vue des enfants*. Paris: L'Harmattan.

Montandon, C., Dominicé, L., & Bottinger, A. M. (2000). L'expérience du lien social du point de vue des enfants: La place des conduites discutables. *Apprentissage et socialisation*, *20*(2), 143–160.

Pahl, R. (2000). *On friendship*. Cambridge: Polity.

Parsons, T. (1973). *Le système des sociétés modernes*. Paris: Dunod.

Pasquier, D. (2005). *Cultures lycéennes*. Paris: Autrement.

Qvortrup, J. (1991). *Childhood as a social phenomenon: An introduction to a series of national reports* (2nd ed.). Eurosocial Report 36. Vienna: European Centre for Social Welfare Policy and Research.

Qvortrup, J. (1994). Childhood matters: An introduction. In J. Qvortrup, M. Bardy, G. Sgritta, & H. Wintersberger (Eds.), *Childhood matters* (pp. 1–24). Aldershot: Avebury.

Qvortrup, J., Bardy, M., Sgritta, G., & Wintersberger, H. (Eds). (1994). *Childhood matters*. Aldershot: Avebury.

Rayou, P. (2000). Une société de cour. Les compétences politiques à l'épreuve de la récréation. In D. Saadi-Mokrane (Ed.), *Sociétés et cultures enfantines* (pp. 145–150). Lille: Éditions du Conseil scientifique de l'Université Charles-de-Gaulle Lille 3.

Sirota, R. (1998). L'émergence d'une sociologie de l'enfance. Evolution de l'objet, évolution du regard. *Education et Sociétés, 2*, 9–34.

Sirota, R. (2006). *Éléments pour une sociologie de l'enfance.* Rennes: Presses universitaires de Rennes.

Sirota, R. (2012). L'enfance au regard des sciences sociales. *AnthropoChildren, 1*, 1–20. Retrieved from pop-ups.ulg.ac.be/AnthropoChildren/document.php?id=921

Spencer, L., & Pahl, R. (2006). *Rethinking friendship: Hidden solidarities today.* Princeton: Princeton University Press.

Thorne, B. (1993). *Gender play. Girls and boys in school.* New Brunswick, NJ: Rutgers University Press.

Winkler-Reid, S. (2015). Friendship, bitching, and the making of ethical selves: What it means to be a good friend among girls in a London school. *Journal of the Royal Anthropological Institute, 22*, 166–182.

Woodhead, M. (2008). Le développement du jeune enfant: Une affaire de droits. In G. Brougères & M. Vandenbroeck. (Eds.), *Repenser l'éducation du jeune enfant* (pp. 139–161). Brussels: PIE Peter Lang.

8 Pedagogy and Propriety: A Gendered Analysis of Children's Fairy Tales

Nicole Andrejek

LEARNING OBJECTIVES

- To think critically about children's fairy tales
- To consider the social implications of using fairy tales as educational tools
- To understand the social construction of childhood through a gendered perspective
- To compare changes in fairy tales at two historical time periods to explore the ways that gender norms are reworked and/or reproduced

Children, especially attractive, well bred young ladies, should never talk to strangers, for if they should do so, they may well provide dinner for a wolf. I say "wolf," but there are various kinds of wolves. There are also those who are charming to a young woman at home and in the streets. And unfortunately, it is these gentle wolves who are the most dangerous ones of all.

—Perrault, 1697 (cited in Tatar, 1999b, p. 42)

INTRODUCTION

I open this chapter with the moral that French fairytale writer Charles Perrault provides at the end of his version of "Little Red Riding Hood." This lesson reminds young girls about the troubles they will face when they travel off the proper path and interact with strangers. In Canada and beyond, current anxieties about "stranger danger," sexual predators, and the fear that "wolves" can lure young girls under false pretenses over the Internet show that, although the social landscape has changed, the fears and morals projected in early children's fairy tales continue to echo today. Therefore, an analysis of fairy tales has the capacity to reveal how children's stories can mirror real life fears about the dangers that children might face.

Like the other contributors of this section, this chapter explores the social construction of childhood by analyzing the morals and lessons for children in early fairy tales from the late seventeenth century and early nineteenth century. Xiaobei Chen's chapter (9) in this collection explores the making of multicultural subjects in children's literature. In this chapter, I will explore how children's literature plays an important role in teaching children gendered lessons about how young girls should behave and how girls can evade being the victims of dangerous men. As was described in the preface to this section, the social constructionist perspective aims to analyze how social forces, such as patriarchal dominance, regulation of sexuality, and class-based norms, influence the social meaning of childhood. In this chapter I will demonstrate how those forces that influence the social meaning of childhood are gender-specific. In order to illustrate how the social construction of childhood is also a gendered one, I will examine the **discourses** of girlhood in literary artifacts from the late seventeenth century and the early nineteenth century in Europe.

Social and literary theorists have investigated the implications of how lessons on morality and **social norms** of a given historical context are communicated to children through children's stories (Baker-Sperry, 2007; Lotherington & Chow, 2006; Shavit, 1999; Weinreich, 2008). Specifically, research has analyzed how dominant conceptions on sexual morality and gender norms are illustrated in the fairytale genre (Marshall, 2004; Robinson, 2007; Weingart & Jorgensen, 2013). In this chapter I will expand on this literature by focusing on how mass published fairy tales emerged in the late 1600s and became common throughout Europe in the nineteenth century. These stories were used as a pedagogical tool for parents and educators to teach "proper" decorum to middle- and upper-class children.

MORALITY IN CHILDREN'S FAIRY TALES

Scholars of the **sociology of childhood** have illustrated how common notions of childhood are socially constructed and reflect the dominant norms, morals, and accepted forms of knowledge of their respective historical and geographical context (Margolis,

2014; Shavit, 1999; Tilly & Scott, 2014). Analyzing the social construction of childhood illuminates the taken-for-granted ways that we perceive what children are capable of and what they should know. According to Philippe Aries (1962), in Europe, the concepts of the child and childhood as distinctly separate from adulthood emerged during the seventeenth century. Alongside this development, children's literature became a mode to spread dominant perspectives of what *should* constitute childhood (Shavit, 1999).

The use of formally written fairy tales as a means of teaching morals and proper ways of behaving became common after the publication of Perrault's collection of stories in France in the late seventeenth century and again into the early nineteenth century through the prominence of works by Wilhem and Jacob Grimm, otherwise known as the Brothers Grimm, in Germany (Tatar, 1999a). The tradition of using fairy tales as a means of teaching normative behaviours to children continued to gain popularity as new storytellers emerged throughout Europe, Australia, and North America. Lessons from older fairy tales were adapted or translated to meet the social norms of their respective time and place, and were thought to be effective ways to educate children and produce good, moral subjects. For instance, Weinreich (2008) illustrates that Danish children's fairy tales, by authors like Hans Christian Andersen in the mid-nineteenth century, were used to teach children how they should behave. In the nineteenth century, Danish fairy tales that did not include social and moral lessons were viewed as immoral, improper, and useless to children's development (Weinreich, 2008).

Furthermore, historical research has illustrated that social purity discourses that aimed to control childhood sexuality in the mid-nineteenth to early twentieth century were the focus of children's literature in the United States, England, and Australia at that time (Egan & Hawkes, 2007). These stories reflected the dominant social norms and knowledge during this period regarding the conception of childhood. During this time, children were perceived as innocent and naïve subjects who needed to be protected from the hardships and immorality of the day. This focus on **childhood innocence** became increasingly emphasized between Perrault's publication in 1697 and the twentieth-century renditions (Egan & Hawkes, 2007). Thus, the tradition of moral lessons in fairy tales from Perrault into the early twentieth century further demonstrates how early versions of written fairy tales were being appropriated and slightly altered by new authors to fit their respective cultural context.

A growing body of research has applied content analysis, discourse analysis, and media analysis to past fictional and educational texts to gain insights into how children may have been taught the social norms of their given societies and what those lessons were (Davidson, Woodill, & Bredberg, 1994; Laqueur, 2003; Matthews, 2010; Robinson, 2007; Weingart & Jorgensen, 2013). For example, some research on children's literature in Victorian England has identified themes around "sexual pathologies" and "perversions" like masturbation, the risk of children's sexualization, and racial constructions of the social "other" (Davidson et al., 1994; Egan & Hawkes, 2008a; Egan & Hawkes, 2008b; Hall, 2004; Laqueur, 2003; Matthews, 2010). This recent sociological and literary research on children's stories has provided insights regarding how the conceptualization of childhood sexuality has changed over time, why there is a heightened concern regarding the **sexualization of children** in modern society, and the evolving ways that the child's body has been illustrated and reflected upon in both classic fairy tales and in their subsequent renditions (Davidson et al., 1994; Egan & Hawkes, 2008c; Hawkes, Dune, & Egan, 2013; Sutherland, 2011).

The regulation of girls' bodies, in particular—where they should go with their bodies, how to move in their bodies, how their bodies should look, how to protect their bodies—has been a central focus of many early European fairy tales (Baker-Sperry & Grauerholz, 2003; for recent examples of the attempted regulation of girls' bodies and girls' resistance to this, see Raby and Pomerantz, chapter 15 in this collection). Weingart and Jorgensen's (2013) content analysis of over 200 European fairy tales demonstrates that children's bodies were frequently referenced, particularly girls' bodies. Marshall (2004) applied a feminist framework to an analysis of three versions of "Little Red Riding Hood," examining the differences in the girls' bodily actions prior to being eaten, with a particular focus on whether or not the little girl removes her clothing for the wolf and whether "stripping for the wolf" has an indication as to whether or not she survives. Researchers have also noted that Western fairy tales often focused on teaching young girls how to navigate risky situations, particularly physical or sexual violence against their bodies (Marshall & Gilmore, 2015).

Although there is a considerable amount of research that has been conducted on children's literature written between 1600 and 1900, there have been very few attempts by sociologists to explore early children's fairy tales. Nonetheless, these popular and rare literary artifacts are valuable in helping sociologists understand how childhood has been historically and socially constructed. A sociological analysis of these texts presents an opportunity to further our knowledge on how gendered lessons have been taught to children through children's literature. An examination of early children's literature, in this case children's fairy tales, can help illuminate what gender and sexual norms have been passed down and altered over time.

THE STUDY

This chapter presents findings from a small-scale case study in which I explore what lessons about girls' social and sexual propriety were embedded within classic children's fairy tales. I was interested in uncovering the implicit or explicit moral and social lessons regarding gender and sexuality in a sample of the earliest written fairy tales by Charles Perrault in France, 1697, and the Brothers Grimm in Germany, 1819. I specifically looked at how the intersections of childhood, gender, and sexuality were represented in classic children's fairy tales in relation to **power** and **agency**, and what might be the broader social implications of these representations. My work demonstrates how the emphasis on **risk** and the body in these fairy tales has the capacity to reproduce the normalization of male violence against female bodies and **victim blaming** discourses that maintain patriarchal power relations. It is my hope that exploring these issues will help raise questions about the impact that the lessons and representations in children's fairy tales might have on the conception of childhood and gender relations in Canada today.

For this project I analyzed literary artifacts of the Osborne Collection located at the Toronto Public Library. The collection includes children's literature from the fourteenth century to 1910. Two fairy tales were chosen to serve as a small-scale case study: the stories of Bluebeard and Little Red Riding Hood. Charles Perrault published the first known written versions of both, in France in 1697 (Tatar, 1999b; Tatar, 1999c). These two fairy tales were then rewritten and published in 1819 in Germany by Jacob and Wilhelm Grimm, popularly known as the Brothers Grimm, in their large book of fairy tales, *Kinder- und Hausmärchen*. Although many works within the Osborne Collection would be worthy of analysis, I chose these stories because Perrault was the first author to publish fairy tales written specifically for children, making him an important figure within the genre, and thus an ideal starting point (Zipes, 1983; Shavit, 1999). I also chose them because these fairy tales from Perrault's collection, "The Blue Beard" and "Little Red Riding Hood," were translated from French to German by the Brothers Grimm and retitled "Fitcher's Bird" and "Little Red Cap," making them an ideal pair to look for changes and comparisons over time and across cultures. Finally, both stories specifically focus on a female protagonist and involve the communication of morals for young girls, which will allow me to explore how discourses about gendered norms and morality change as a particular tale gets rewritten for a new audience.

Figure 8.1: Images from Charles Perrault's *Les Contes Des Fees*, 1697

Source: Charles Perrault's *Les Contes Des Fees*, 1697

This project situates itself within the sociology of knowledge approach to discourse (SKAD), developed by Keller (2011). This approach connects a social constructionist perspective to the work of Michel Foucault, which emphasizes how power is reproduced over time and how taken-for-granted social norms shift based on their cultural and historical context (Keller, 2011). A Foucauldian discourse analysis tracks the changes and shifts in discourses over time to map out how power is developed and employed to produce knowledge, truth, and meaning (Grbich, 2011, pp. 146–147). Through a Foucauldian perspective, it is relevant to track the historical changes in gendered discourses within children's literature. This approach allows researchers to explore what knowledge was being produced and extrapolated through educational literature meant for children. Further, by using a social constructionist framework in combination with a Foucauldian discourse analysis, Keller's (2011) SKAD method links data to its particular social context, where the construction of social reality of the given time in which the data was produced must be at the forefront of the researcher's considerations. This project aims to contribute to the growing sociological literature that has examined the intersections of childhood, gender, and sexuality by analyzing the relationship between femininity and representations of how the body is treated in these specific fairy tales.

AND THE MORAL OF THE STORY IS …

Qualitative coding techniques were used to track the shifts in discourses between Perrault's "Little Red Riding Hood" and "The Blue Beard" to the Brothers Grimm's versions "Little Red Cap" and "Fitcher's Bird." This process identified changes and continuities in the stories, with a particular focus on gendered discourses. Through this process, three major themes emerged. The first is how spatial boundaries were articulated in the narrative of each story. The stories illustrate where the girls in the story were supposed to go and the consequences of not doing what they are told. The second theme is the focus on girls' sexual morality. The lessons on sexual and marital morality articulate how girls are vulnerable to the wills and power of others, particularly in relation to protecting their bodies. I show that sexual morality in these stories is also connected to a class-based conception of childhood. The final theme illustrates how victim blaming discourses are features of each tale. I will show how the objectification of girls' bodies and the normalization of the **male gaze** are not problematized in the stories. Rather, the fault of the girls' victimization is consistently placed on their flawed choices.

Defining Spatial Boundaries for Girls

Perrault's and the Brothers Grimm's versions of both fairy tales have a spatial thematic element where a young woman has left home and finds herself alone with a strange (and unassumingly dangerous) male character. Each version of both stories also has an added element of a young woman going where she "ought not." In the case of "Little Red Riding Hood," and "Little Red Cap," the "prettiest young girl you can imagine" (Tatar, 1999b) leaves home and is walking through the woods. Instead of going directly to her grandmother's house she diverges from her path and naïvely speaks to the wolf, unknowing of his villainous intentions.

In Perrault's story "The Blue Beard," a group of sisters are brought with their mother to the elaborately decorated home of a blue-bearded man in his hopes to convince one of them to be his wife. Despite fearing Bluebeard because of his unusual appearance and the unexplained disappearances of his previous wives, one sister is seduced by the luxurious home and marries him. She is given the keys to every chamber, but is forbidden by Bluebeard to go into one particular room. Her curiosity gets the best of her, and in the chamber she discovers his dead and mutilated ex-wives. She is sentenced to death by Bluebeard but is saved at the last minute by her brothers.

Similarly, in "Fitcher's Bird" a sorcerer dresses as a poor man, and when helped by a young maiden he abducts her to his home to be his wife. There, she is seduced by the sorcerer, and, similar to the wife in "The Blue Beard," is told not to enter one chamber in the house. When she inevitably does and witnesses the sorcerer's dead wives, she is murdered and dismembered by him. He then abducts her sister and the pattern is replicated. He subsequently abducts a third sister, who discovers her two sisters' dead bodies and puts their dismantled bodies back together, which magically revives them. The third sister cleverly devises a plan to inform their brothers of the sorcerer's location and the brothers eventually come to save the young maidens, maintaining the motif of the male saviour and female victim.

The plot and consequences outlined in the texts illustrate how the authors articulate the ways in which spatial boundaries were to be understood for women. "The Blue Beard" and "Fitcher's Bird" present horrifying results for women whose curiosity leads them to disobey the rules of a patriarch by entering a space where they are not permitted. In the case of "Little Red Riding Hood" and "Little Red Cap," there is a set path through an unknown territory that a young girl must navigate, and once Little Red Riding Hood leaves the path she is meant to follow, danger befalls her. Implicitly, when considering the historical time period of both Perrault and the Brothers Grimm, this thematic element could metaphorically reflect the maturation process where young girls begin to physically develop and are pursued by seducers and suitors with both good and bad intentions. They must therefore be wary of the metaphorical path they take in order to fulfill social standards of "appropriate" femininity.

The narratives give a clear indication that girls are powerless against the wills of wolves and blue-bearded men, and become vulnerable when they disobey orders and do not stay within predefined spatial confines. The lesson to *do what you are told, or there will be grave consequences,* runs through both versions of each fairy tale. The emphasis on spatial confines, staying on the path to grandmother's house or out of the forbidden chamber, suggests that a lesson for girls was to accept the lack of personal agency in their lives for fear of punishment. Further, the young girls' powerlessness against assailants of their bodies is emphasized in the narratives of each story—the focus of the next section.

Sexual and Marital Morality: Lessons for Little Girls to Protect Their Bodies

When comparing how the plot differed structurally between authors, one finds that Perrault's texts are shorter in length and have an explicitly written "moral of the story" in their conclusion. Alternatively, the morals of the Brothers Grimm's stories are not *directly* stated, but rather are implied. The moral of "Little Red Riding Hood" that prefaces this chapter demonstrates how it is dangerous to disregard your mother's warnings and talk to strangers. Perrault tells his reader that this is particularly true for "children, especially attractive, well bred young ladies" (Tatar, 1999b, p. 42). In Perrault's version, "Little Red Riding Hood took off her clothes and climbed into the bed" and this impropriety leads her to be eaten by the wolf (Tatar, 1999b).

Perrault's fairy tale intended to teach "well bred" young girls to beware of the consequences of men's attentions and to not get undressed and into bed with wolves. The emphasis on "well bred" children demonstrates how Perrault's conception of childhood is a classed one. There is a growing field of literary theorists who have explored the themes, motives, narratives, and rhetoric in Perrault and the Brothers Grimm fairy tales (Hurlimann, 1959; Hanks & Hanks, 1978; Luthi, 1970; Zipes, 1983). Jack Zipes (1983), a prominent critical theorist of children's literature, noted that through his fairy tales, Perrault sought to educate children about the social norms of the day, particularly the norms of the upper class in France—*the Haute Bourgeoisie*—that Perrault himself belonged to.

Perrault has been critiqued for making no attempt to subvert the "status quo" and intending instead to "civilize" children based on the upper-class social norms of the time (Zipes, 1983, p. 17). Zipes has argued that Perrault uses his fairy tales to attempt to ideologically indoctrinate children to conform to dominant social standards. Drawing on Norbert Elias's sociohistorical study of the civilizing process, Zipes demonstrates that Perrault's fairy tales sought to "civilize" children, from his upper-class perspective, through "literary socialization" (1983, pp. 18–20). Although teaching children to be aware of risks is not inherently problematic, it is important to see that the texts promote narrow and limited gender norms for girls. Perrault's fairy tale of an aristocratic gentleman and his curious new wife in "The Blue Beard" directly promotes young upper-class girls' propriety.

> *Moral*: Curiosity, in spite of its appeal, often leads to deep regret. To the displeasure of many a maiden, its enjoyment is short lived. Once satisfied, it ceases to exist, and always costs dearly. (Tatar, 1999c, pp. 61–62)

Specifically, Perrault's pedagogical pursuit in his fairy tales is the transmission of good manners and morals for women (Zipes, 1983, p. 22). Perrault reproduced social standards for girls, with severe consequences for young women who did not follow bourgeois feminine propriety of the time. Despite having written their version of each tale decades later, the Brothers Grimm followed in this tradition, focusing the stories' lessons on the maintenance of innocence, manners, appropriate dress, and consistent reminders of the defencelessness of girls against dangerous men. This reveals the tenacity of moral standards for women and the pervasiveness of dominant discourses about feminine traits and the female body.

The stories give the impression that women of the day were thought to be vulnerable to the uncontrollable sexual desires of men (Zipes, 1983, p. 22). "Little Red Riding Hood" and "Little Red Cap" as well as "The Blue Beard" and "Fitcher's Bird" contain lessons within the narrative of the story that reveal concern for young women's relationships with men. In both "Little Red Riding Hood" and "Little Red Cap," there are clear sexual undertones, which are closely tied to the larger context of lessons for women, though there are some relevant differences between the versions. In "Little Red Riding Hood," Perrault's moral, at the end of the tale, explicitly states that the wolf is a metaphor for dangerous men. Part of his overall message to young, upper-class female children, as they grow into young (upper-class) women, was to be on alert for handsome and charming men. Another sexual message comes in the form of the wolf eating the girl, which some have argued represents her rape and subsequent murder (Marshall, 2004).

From a less sinister interpretation, the metaphor could also be pointing towards the ease with which some women are seduced when they find themselves off the proper path. In this interpretation, engaging in nonmarital sexual acts results in their social death—the exclusion from polite society—after they lose their innocence and virtue to a wolf. In other words, Perrault's version of "Little Red Riding Hood" centres on an erotic metaphor that ends tragically (Hanks & Hanks, 1978, p. 68). The wolf is the only man present in Perrault's version of the story and Perrault's moral that young women should keep to themselves is reinforced by the tragic end where the young girl is seduced out of her clothes and into bed with the wolf, only to be eaten (Hanks & Hanks, 1978, p. 73).

The Brothers Grimm's stories have been critiqued for their "sexist and racist attitudes and … a socialization process which placed great emphasis on passivity, industry, and self sacrifice for girls" (Zipes, 1983, p. 46). In the Brothers Grimm story of "Little Red Cap" the sexual metaphors are not as explicit as they are with Perrault. Maria Tatar's (1999d) critical analysis of the Brothers Grimm fairy tales asserts that the gender representations in their stories generally highlighted the dangers of girls' childhood abuse and assault. In the Brothers Grimm version, Little Red Cap does not get into bed; rather, upon entering her grandmother's house she becomes suddenly hesitant and afraid. She cautiously questions the wolf dressed in her grandmother's clothes from outside of the bed, but is unable to escape the wolf, who jumps out of bed on top of her and, like in the Perrault version, eats her up. In the Brothers Grimm version, a huntsman, who cuts Little Red Cap and her grandmother out of the wolf's stomach, ultimately saves her from the belly of the wolf. This moment acts as a sort of educational rebirth where she is pulled—still fully clothed—from inside the wolf, who manages to sleep through the entire ordeal.

The story does not end there in the Brothers Grimm version. The tale moves forward, and Little Red Cap is confronted by a second wolf. This time she finds herself aware of the dangers that come from speaking to strange wolves. She has learned her lesson and remains on the proper path. The Brothers Grimm give her the opportunity to learn from her mistakes—something that does not happen in Perrault's version (Marshall, 2004, p. 264). Although this revised ending gives Little Red Cap a chance to learn from her mistakes, both versions of the story reproduce the knowledge that men have the capacity of deception and violence and that women's bodies are easily subject to men's desires and aggression. Further, because these texts are written specifically for children, it is implied that the authors believed these are lessons that young girls should learn early in life.

In contrast, an unexpected finding in the two Bluebeard stories was an absence of specifically sexual lessons and morals. The closest moral that might be associated with sexuality is in the seduction of the protagonists to stay and marry the blue-bearded man. In Perrault's version the female protagonist is seduced by her suitor's generosity and wealth. The sisters in the Brothers Grimm version were abducted simply by being "touched" by the sorcerer. In Perrault's text there is, however, a lesson regarding the need for young women to be cautious in both choosing a husband and in indulging in unfettered curiosity. What this might suggest about the type of knowledge reproduced in Perrault's text regarding feminine gender roles is that young women must learn to be patient and obedient, to avoid being meddlesome, and that impropriety comes with consequences. The lessons of what constitutes "appropriate femininity" reproduce dominant discourses that femininity should be equated with being unquestioning and passive, and the subversion of these qualities is what gets the wife in "The Blue Beard" and "Fitcher's Bird" into trouble—she was curious and questioning of her husband's demands. This said, in the cunning plan of the third sister in "Fitcher's Bird," there is a subversive quality about gender norms that suggests that women are capable of being clever.

Sexual Violence and Victim Blaming in the Enchanted Forest and Beyond

In both versions of the Red Riding Hood story there is an element of victim blaming; both renditions suggest that it was Red Riding Hood's fault that she was eaten because of the choices she made in deviating from her path and speaking to a stranger. The objectification of Red Riding Hood by the wolf, where her body becomes an object of the wolf's gaze and then an object to be consumed, fits within the feminist contemporary critiques about victim blaming of women that continues to be reproduced today (Cahill,

2000). Some gender scholars have addressed how women's bodies are often aligned with victimization and weakness (Cahill, 2000). This connection between women's vulnerable bodies and lessons for young girls is easily translatable today. For example, girls are taught to not walk alone and to fear strange men, and girls' dress codes in school are said to be in place to prevent men's sexual gaze and girls' bodies distracting men and boys—and all of these examples place emphasis on the actions of the girl. Women's victimization is often attached to the choices that they make rather than the wrongdoing of the perpetrator (Cahill, 2000). Therefore, there is a clear connection between lessons that girls received centuries past and concerns for girls today.

Raby and Pomerantz's chapter in this collection demonstrates the agency and resistance of girls today. Although the third sister in "Fitcher's Bird" showed agency in her cleverness, we cannot know if there were cases of resistance and agency by girls in real life during the historical context of Perrault or the Brothers Grimm based on their fairy tales. Nonetheless, the fear-based lessons that both authors articulated in their versions of Little Red Riding Hood, popular stories to this day, have potentially contributed to the ways in which young girls have learned to be in a subject position to men. The tales of young, attractive, innocent, and sweet girls being hunted by the wolf reproduce discourses of women as the object of the male gaze and the subject of gendered violence.

Although the third sister in "Fitcher's Bird" demonstrates cleverness, the female character cannot fully save herself and is not the hero at the end of her story. The young women in all four texts fall victim to a devious and dangerous male character. Yet in three of the four tales, other male characters ultimately save the young female victims from having their bodies devoured or mutilated. In the Brothers Grimm's "Little Red Cap" a huntsman finds the wolf and cuts him open, releasing Little Red Cap and her grandmother. In Perrault's "The Blue Beard," the young bride's brothers save her at the last moment before she meets her death. Although the plan to escape is conceived by the third sister in "Fitcher's Bird," it is her brothers who ultimately save the sisters from the manipulative sorcerer.

Given Perrault's and the Brothers Grimm's time period, "The Blue Beard" and "Fitcher's Bird" might reflect the girls' worries about marriage. Women often married at a young age, and in some cases were subject to isolation, abuse, sex with a strange man, and the possibility of death in childbirth—all likely causing fear and anxiety among young women (Tatar, 1999c). The protection of the wife, in both versions by a family member, emphasizes that family—and male family members in particular— will be there to save you. Again, the physical violence against the girls can only be stopped when they are rescued by a male character. These elements of the texts reproduce the dominant discourse in both cultures of the damsel in distress who needs to be saved by a man after making a flawed decision. What is interesting is that the man who saves them, in the three texts that this occurs, is not a potential lover. Rather, the huntsman and the brother(s) are patriarchal figures who save the young girls from the perils of their faulty choices.

The closest anyone comes to being a female hero in the four texts is the third sister in "Fitcher's Bird." She finds her two murdered and dismembered sisters in the forbidden chamber and uses cunning to devise a plan for her brothers to come rescue her. This gives the impression that in the Brothers Grimm tales, few women have the cunning to come to their own rescue. What these interpretations of this sample of fairy tales by the Brothers Grimm might suggest is that, although there are some aspects of the fairy tales that subvert gender norms in the Brothers Grimm's time period, their stories tend to reproduce patriarchal notions about femininity to their readers, quite similarly to Perrault's stories. They also demonstrate the persistence of fear culture and rape culture in two European contexts, a pattern that continues to this day in most parts of the world. Thus, although there are subtle differences between Perrault's stories and the Brothers Grimm's versions, the similarities demonstrate the pervasiveness of gender discourses that paint the female body as vulnerable, and girls as victims of their own foolishness and disobedience.

IN CONCLUSION, THEY ALL LIVED HAPPILY EVER AFTER ...

This study reveals that children's fairy tales, rewritten and retold centuries later, in different cultural contexts, have the capacity to reflect and reproduce tenacious, patriarchal morals and social norms through the guise of an entertaining story. This chapter presented the findings of a small-scale discourse analysis based on Keller's (2011) SKAD model. I aimed to explore how femininity and morals relating to women's sexuality are represented in two of the earliest written versions of the Little Red Riding Hood and Bluebeard tales.

This research was able to capture only some of the dominant discourses that have been reproduced through the fairytale genre, as they have been translated over time and in different parts of the world. According to a Foucauldian methodological framework, a discourse analysis should track the development of discourses over time to fully capture and identify the social, economic, and political power relations that exist underneath the surface of language (Grbich, 2011, p. 150). Further research should thus more deeply trace and analyze how Perrault's fairy tales shift over time in the hands of the Brothers Grimm, Hans Christian Andersen, Disney, and many others, to further explore how children's stories reproduce or have the capacity to subvert heteronormative gender roles and norms. The lessons in these sample fairy tales remind young girls about the troubles they will face when they travel off the proper path and interact with strangers. As I have stated, in Canada and beyond, current anxieties about "stranger danger" and concerns for young girls' safety in early children's fairy tales continue to echo today. Therefore, an analysis of fairy tales has the capacity to reveal how children's stories reflect real-life fears about the dangers that girls might face in their youth.

In this chapter I have addressed how children's fairy tales reflect the dominant moral norms of their time and that they might mirror concerns about the dangers that children might face. As I have suggested, many of the worries in the sample of fairy tales analyzed in this chapter regarding young girls' innocence and safety continue to be concerns for parents and educators today. This leads me to assert that a continuation of this research, expanding from Perrault to modern writers, could yield important findings that could illuminate the ways in which knowledge about gender and sexual morality has reproduced and changed, and how these norms are potentially being challenged on a larger scale in the modern Canadian context and internationally.

CHAPTER SUMMARY

Together, in this chapter, we

- Developed critical thinking around children's fairy tales.
- Explored how fairy tales have been used as educational mediums to teach children social norms and morals.
- Sought to understand the social construction of childhood through a gendered perspective, with particular emphasis on how norms for girls and women were constructed in early fairy tales.
- Explored the ways that fairy tales changed or remained the same, demonstrating the pervasiveness of gendered discourses and anxieties about girls' safety.

STUDY QUESTIONS

1. Consider how young girls are represented in the classic fairy tales reviewed in this chapter. How are girls expected to behave? What do you think these lessons for children suggest about the different roles and expectations of boys and men compared to girls and women?

2. What might fairy tales tell us about how the concept of childhood (and more specifically girlhood) was constructed in the late 1600s and the early 1800s in Europe? In thinking about recent children's stories or films, has our understanding of childhood and girlhood changed?

3. What kinds of lessons do you recall getting from books and movies you read or watched during your childhood and youth? In what ways did they relate to or formulate your own sense of what it means to be a boy or a girl?

4. You have been asked by a school board to edit the story of Little Red Riding Hood to be read to children in Canadian elementary schools. With consideration to the potential capacity of fairy tales to influence how children learn social norms and morals, what changes would you make to the story?

5. Imagine that you have decided to compare contemporary children's stories or films, like those by Disney or Pixar. Consider how and why fairy tales have changed (or remained the same) over time by extending your analysis to how children's films and stories deal with issues of gender as well as race and class.

SUGGESTED RESEARCH ASSIGNMENT

Choose three books from a specific genre, like sci-fi or fantasy. Consider the characters and lessons from each story and identify the ways that gender norms are explicitly or implicitly reflected upon and represented. Be sure to consider how gender is constructed through language choices, character descriptions, and the main plot points of male or female characters in the book.

SUGGESTED FILMS/VIDEO CLIPS

Myths and Legends Podcast
www.mythpodcast.com/
This podcast discusses myths, legends, and folklore. Jason Weiser tells common stories, including classic stories like Pocahontas, Aladdin, and the Little Mermaid, using historical data. The podcast shows how these stories have unexpected origins.

The Big Bad Wolf Reconsidered
www.youtube.com/watch?v=mTTT9Gc5WdU
This lecture by Maria Tatar analyzes the dynamic evolution of the story of Little Red Riding Hood, paying close attention to the role of the wolf.

How Fairy Tales Failed Me
www.youtube.com/watch?v=xQd45LQKPJE
In this TED talk, psychologist Anne Kieran discusses the heteronormative messages in fairy tales, focusing on representations of intimate relationships, romance, and sexuality.

SUGGESTED WEBSITES

Room to Read
www.roomtoread.org/page.aspx?pid=284
Room to Read focuses on educating children around the world, focusing the ways that literacy and education can improve gender equality and address poverty. The organization collaborates with communities and local governments across Asia and Africa. They

teach girls literacy skills and encourage girls to complete secondary school and to gain a passion for reading.

The Horror and the Beauty
harvardmagazine.com/2007/11/the-horror-and-the-beaut.html

Harvard Magazine published an interview by Craig Lamberton with Maria Tatar, a professor of Germanic languages and literatures who studies the dark side of children's fairy tales. She provides enlightening perspectives on violence, abuse, and sexism in children's fairy tales. She also addresses the ways in which the construction of childhood has changed in recent years.

United Nations Girls' Education Initiative
www.ungei.org/

United Nations Girls' Education Initiative is a partnership of organizations whose aim is to narrow the gender gap in primary and secondary education. Their goal is to ensure that all boys and girls go to school to take steps to improve gender equality.

HISTORY
www.history.com/news/the-dark-side-of-the-grimm-fairy-tales

HISTORY discusses the dark side of Grimm's fairy tales, outlining some of the surprising elements of anti-Semitism, incest, child abuse, and wicked stepmothers in the classic children's stories.

REFERENCES

Aries, P. (1962). *Centuries of childhood: A social history of family life.* New York: Vintage Books.

Baker-Sperry, L. (2007). The production of meaning through peer interaction: Children and Walt Disney's Cinderella. *Sex Roles, 56*(11/12), 717–727.

Baker-Sperry, L., & Grauerholz, L. (2003). The pervasiveness and persistence of the feminine beauty ideal in children's fairy tales. *Gender and Society, 17*(5), 711–726.

Cahill, A. (2000). Foucault, rape and the construction of the feminine body. *Hypatia, 15*(1), 43–63.

Davidson, I., Woodill, G., & Bredberg, E. (1994). Images of disability in 19th-century British children's literature. *Disability & Society, 9*(1), 33–46.

Egan, R. D., & Hawkes, G. (2007). Producing the prurient through the pedagogy of purity: Childhood sexuality and the social purity movement. *Journal of Historical Sociology, 20*(4), 443–461.

Egan, R. D., & Hawkes, G. (2008a). Endangered girls and incendiary objects: Unpacking the discourse on sexualization. *Sexuality & Culture, 12*(4), 291–312.

Egan, R. D., & Hawkes, G. (2008b). Imperiled and perilous: Exploring the history of childhood sexuality. *Journal of Historical Sociology, 21*(4), 355–367.

Egan, R. D., & Hawkes, G. L. (2008c). Developing the sexual child. *Journal of Historical Sociology, 21*(4), 443–465.

Grbich, C. (2011). Discourse analysis. In *Qualitative data analysis: An introduction* (pp. 146–154). London: Sage.

Hall, L. (2004). Hauling down the double standard: Feminism, social purity and sexual science in late nineteenth century Britain. *Gender & History, 16*(1), 36–56.

Hanks, C., & Hanks, D. T. (1978). Perrault's "Little Red Riding Hood": Victim of the revisers (Vol. 7). In F. Butler & L. Mendelsohn (Eds.), *Children's Literature* (pp. 68–77). Storrs Mansfield, CT: Parousia Press.

Hawkes, G., Dune, T., & Egan, D. (2013). Introduction: Narratives of the sexual child: Shared themes and shared challenges. *Sexualities, 16*(5/6), 622–634.

Hurlimann, B. (1959). *Three centuries of children's books in Europe.* Cleveland & New York: The Word Publishing Company.

Keller, R. (2011). The sociology of knowledge approach to discourse (SKAD). *Human Studies, 34*(1), 43–65.

Laqueur, T. W. (2003). *Solitary sex: A cultural history of masturbation.* New York: Zone Books.

Lotherington, H., & Chow, S. (2006). Rewriting "Goldilocks" in the urban, multicultural elementary school. *The Reading Teacher, 60*(3), 242.

Luthi, M. (1970). *Once upon a time: On the nature of fairy tales.* New York: Frederick Ungar Publishing.

Margolis, M. L. (2014). Putting mothers on the pedestal. In B. Fox (Ed.), *Family patterns, gender relations* (3rd ed.) (pp. 118–135). Don Mills, ON: Oxford University Press.

Marshall, E. (2004). Stripping for the wolf: Rethinking representations of gender in children's literature. *Reading Research Quarterly, 39*(3), 256–270.

Marshall, E., & Gilmore, L. (2015). Girlhood in the gutter: Feminist graphic knowledge and the visualization of sexual precarity. *Women's Studies Quarterly, 43*(1), 95–114.

Matthews, J. (2010). Back where they belong: Gypsies, kidnapping and assimilation in Victorian children's literature. *Romani Studies, 20*(2), 137–159.

Robinson, O. (2007). Does sex breed gender? Pronomial reference in the Grimms' fairy tales. *Marvels & Tales, 21*(1), 107–123.

Shavit, Z. (1999). The concept of childhood and children's folktales: Test case—"Little Red Riding Hood." In M. Tatar (Ed.), *The classic fairy tales: Texts, criticisms* (pp. 309–332). New York & London: W. W. Norton & Company.

Sutherland, J. (2011). *Language, gender and children's fiction.* London & New York: Continuum International Publishing Group.

Tatar, M. (1999a). Introduction. In M. Tatar (Ed.), *The classic fairy tales: Texts, criticisms* (pp. ix–xviii). New York & London: W. W. Norton & Company.

Tatar, M. (1999b). Little Red Riding Hood. In M. Tatar (Ed.), *The classic fairy tales: Texts, criticisms* (pp. 3–10). New York & London: W. W. Norton & Company.

Tatar, M. (1999c). Bluebeard. In M. Tatar (Ed.), *The classic fairy tales: Texts, criticisms* (pp. 138–144). New York & London: W. W. Norton & Company.

Tatar, M. (1999d). Sex and violence: The hard core of fairy tales. In M. Tatar (Ed.), *The classic fairy tales: Texts, criticisms* (pp. 364–373). New York & London: W. W. Norton & Company.

Tilly, L. A., & Scott, J. W. (2014). The family economy in pre-industrial England and France. In B. Fox (Ed.), *Family patterns, gender relations* (3rd ed.) (pp. 56–83). Don Mills, ON: Oxford University Press.

Weingart, S., & Jorgensen, J. (2013). Computational analysis of the body in European fairy tales. *Literary and Linguistic Computing, 28*(3), 404–416.

Weinreich, T. (2008). Between art and pedagogy: The history of Danish children's literature. *Bookbird, 46*(3), 5.

Zipes, J. (1983). *Fairy tales and the art of subversion*. London: Heinemann.

9 Racism, Culture, and Power in Children's Books[1]

Xiaobei Chen

LEARNING OBJECTIVES

- To identify characteristics of multicultural children's books available in Canada from the 1960s to the present, their proportion to all children's books published, representations of minority and majority characters, and ideological themes
- To be able to explain, drawing on scholarship discussed here, why it is important to be critically reflective about children's literature and its potential in reproducing or challenging racist ideology
- To understand and engage with concepts such as the white norm, Eurocentrism, multicultural governmentality, and cultural racism
- To identify main patterns of problematic messages about racism, culture, and difference in children's books
- To assess and apply the lines of inquiry and arguments developed in the chapter in order to identify teachable moments around a children's book

INTRODUCTION

In the spring of 2015, a series of well-publicized events hosted by the Truth and Reconciliation Commission of Canada forced the nation to face its mistreatment of **Indigenous** children at Indian Residential Schools as well as broader colonial devastations. How it felt to be an Indigenous child suffering the brunt of colonialism can be gleaned in the voluminous documentation of witnesses' statements throughout the report:

> It can start with a knock on the door one morning. It is the local Indian agent, or the parish priest, or, perhaps, a Mounted Police Officer. The bus for residential

school leaves that morning. It is a day that parents have long been dreading. Even if the children have been warned in advance, the morning's events are still a shock. The officials have arrived and the children must go.

For tens of thousands of Aboriginal children for over a century, this was the beginning of their residential schooling. They were torn from their parents, who often surrendered them only under threat of prosecution. Then, they were hurled into a strange and frightening place, one in which their parents and culture would be demeaned and oppressed.

...

Taken from their homes, stripped of their belongings, and separated from their siblings, residential school children lived in a world dominated by fear, loneliness, and lack of affection. (Truth and Reconciliation Commission of Canada, 2015, pp. 37–41)

In his speech prior to the release of the report, the chair of the Commission, Justice Murray Sinclair, stated that the secret to reconciliation lies in how we, as parents and teachers, educate our children to make sure they have a proper understanding of Canada's colonial past (Cobb, 2015). I was about to give a presentation on children's literature and racism when I read his words in the newspaper. My immediate thought was, how might children's books, even picture books, educate our young people about Indian Residential Schools—their role as instruments of colonial oppression and their legacy of harm and injustice? Indeed, how many children's books are there on the topic of Indian Residential Schools and the colonization of Indigenous people in general? What do children learn about Canada's colonial history and its continued impact when they read? These questions reflect the kind of concerns that I address here.

This chapter is an initial step in a project that explores the promises and illusions of multicultural **citizenship** in Canada through a critical examination of children's literature. My interest in children's books arose in part from my previous research on international adoptions from China to Canada. I quickly found that children's literature was seen as an important tool for adoptive parents to ensure that they did the right thing with regard to fostering their children's cultural identities. While I was impressed by parents' efforts in using recommended books, I often found those books' contents to be unsatisfying. Not only did these books include many culturally essentialist and stereotypical representations of Chinese culture and people in their texts and illustrations, but, most troubling of all, they also tended to sidestep discussions of racism and the historical and social meanings of being Chinese in North America (Chen, 2015). This compelled me to study how issues of racism, multiculturalism, and social justice are addressed by mainstream children's literature in Canada, with the goal of contributing a critical sociological understanding of what messages a growing body of children's literature is sending out about issues of racism, culture, colonial history, identity, and belonging within the Canadian nation.

This chapter explores some themes that have emerged from a textual analysis of a sample of 27 children's picture books suggested to me by staff members at a school in Ottawa, Canada, as potential resources on diversity. With a focus on identifying the overarching message about diversity and inequality that exists among the books, I make use of selected texts that are examples of dominant ideological stances and messages about racism, colonialism, cultural differences, and social justice. I begin by briefly discussing critical scholarship on racism and children's literature. Then, I explain the theoretical tools that inform my research: **multicultural governmentality** and **cultural racism**. The subsequent sections elaborate on two analytical themes that I highlight in this chapter: (1) **power** and justice; and (2) the objectification of culture. The chapter concludes with a discussion of a few directions for your critical reflection on children, politics of culture, and ethics of recognition. I should caution that, in identifying the problematic messages in children's books, the point is not to attribute them to individual writers, as other factors such as readers' expectations and the publishing industry's marketing concerns are as, if not more, important in shaping the books we have. As a sociologist, I understand these prominent messages in books as manifestations of structural conditions and of dominant discourses about race, culture, and identity. Another important point to note is that children's books may never be perfect, but educators, parents, and others, as critical readers, can elicit many teachable moments around a book. In other words, how we use children's books is also crucial. As Brown, Souto-Manning, and Tropp Laman point out, books may not create "interruptive space," but the conversations around the books may (Brown et al., 2010, p. 527).

CHILDREN'S LITERATURE AND RACIST IDEOLOGY

American scholar Nancy Larrick's 1965 article "The All-White World of Children's Books" is widely considered a landmark in the critical examination of racism in children's literature. Larrick criticized the lack of diversity in children's literature and the impact of this on not only **racialized** children, but also on white children. In the decades that followed—since the late 1970s—diversity in children's books started to be emphasized by educators, writers, and publishers (Edwards & Saltman, 2010) in response to a broader shift in the politics of differences, as "norms of integration and assimilation [were giving] way to concerns with identity and difference on the left" (Brown, 2006, p. 2; Nicholson, 1996). The emergence of identity politics was a central issue foregrounding the exploration of minority identities and fostering pride in minority cultures in order to promote the psychological well-being of oppressed people, and to enable them to escape self-contempt (Chin, 1974).[2] In children's literature, we have seen more minority characters appear, and categories such as "multicultural books," "Aboriginal books," "Black History Month books," and so on, have become themes used by librarians to classify books (see e.g. Canadian Children's Book Centre, n.d.). While these are welcome changes from Larrick's (1965/1991) "all-white world of children's books," some serious issues remain.

One recurrent theme in critical scholarship on children's literature is the still persistently low number of children's books on the topics of multiculturalism, racism, and colonialism. To be sure, since the 1980s, the proportion of children's books including nonwhite characters has been expanding; however, not to the degree one would expect. In the US, the Cooperative Children's Book Center at the University of Wisconsin-Madison reported that out of about 5,000 books published in 2014, approximately 396 (or less than 8 percent) are written from the perspective of people of colour or address their experiences. An "apartheid of literature" is how Christopher Myers, a renowned illustrator and writer of children's books, characterizes the status quo, pointing to the disturbingly low number of children's books on people of colour, but also to a pattern whereby characters of colour are limited to "occasional historical books" and "are never given a pass card to traverse the lands of adventure, curiosity, imagination or personal growth" (C. Myers, 2014). While comparable statistics are not available for Canada (Communication with Library and Archives Canada, June 12, 2015), my initial research suggests that Canadian public libraries and schools make frequent use of American publications, and that Canadian books about people of colour are not likely to be more numerous.

How minority characters are represented when they do appear in children's literature has been at the centre of much critical scholarship. Characters conforming to negative stereotypes, as objects of ridicule and denigration, were prevalent in children's literature prior to the American civil rights movement and other antiracism movements it spawned (Deane, 1989; Kyle, 1978; Larrick, 1965/1991). Many agree that since the 1970s and 1980s, in general, such starkly discriminatory portrayals of minorities have become less common in children's literature (Deane, 1989). Nonetheless, Varga and Zuk (2013) remind us that some blatant stereotypes, such as the racialized golliwog character, still find their way into children's books. Scholars have also increasingly turned their attention to **structural racism** in children's literature. They ask how, despite more numerous and "nicer characters of colour," children's books still tend to reproduce implicit and nuanced structural racism (van Belle, 2010, p. 14) and gently endorse racialized dominance (Ching, 2005).

One concept that has been important to scholars in developing such analyses is that of the **white norm**: the idea that arose with European colonialism and US expansionism and holds Western economy, religion, philosophy, and polity as the standard, marking higher development. The white norm is an often invisible but very real form of white privilege, meaning the various advantages accorded to people with light-coloured skin as a result of dominant white-supremacist racism (Dyer, 1997; Frankenberg, 1993). One manifestation of the white norm is the description of nonwhites as primarily cultural subjects, but whites as universal subjects. Similarly, ideas and practices of Western origin tend to be universalized as the unmarked centre of all culture. For example, "ethnic dance" is commonly understood as referring to dances from places other than the West, whereas people do not commonly describe ballet as an ethnic dance, even though it also originated from a particular cultural context.

In children's books, racialized minority characters often appear in predictable, troubling ways at the periphery of the white norm. Larrick (1965/1991) vividly captured this pattern of people of colour being relegated to the background: "In books of science experiments, it is usually a white hand that holds the thermometer, a white arm reaching for a test tube, white children feeding animals" (p. 7). Unfortunately, decades later, the practice of featuring white protagonists alongside racialized background characters as helpers, companions, or followers is still prevalent. Fondrie's (2001) reflection that "if the author does not specifically identify race, I automatically assume that the main characters are white" (p. 9) draws our attention to the continuity of this pattern of white as the norm. In her research on American grade 3 basal readers, van Belle (2010) lends supports to this conclusion, powerfully critiquing the readers' representation of white characters' connections to economic, cultural, and symbolic capitals, concepts developed by French sociologist Pierre Bourdieu. She reveals that, for example, while these textbooks present whites as mathematically literate, financially savvy, and successful as business owners and employers, Black children—and not adults—are only sometimes presented as mathematically literate, financially savvy, or successful in running their own businesses (which employ themselves and not others), among other notable differences in racialized representations (p. 148).

In tandem with the implicit white norm, assimilation is an ideological theme that scholars such as Yoon, Simpson, and Hagg (2010) have identified in multicultural children's books. Through a glorification of the dominant culture and the mapping of a path leading to cultural "blending," some of these texts communicate the message that it is best for immigrant children to accept the dominant culture and to embrace the expectation that they should blend in. They say nothing about the value of a child's minority cultural backgrounds and, in contrast, only praise the dominant culture (Yoon et al., 2010, p. 115). Even when other themes, such as racial discrimination, are present in the text, assimilation ideology often appears to be the overriding theme (Yoon et al., 2010, p. 115; see also Ghiso & Campano, 2013). To resist assimilation, "sustaining identities" has often been proposed as a key strategy. For example, Yoon et al. (2010) suggested that questions teachers use in selecting multicultural books should include, "Do the central characters maintain their identity in the native culture? Does the text support the native culture at the end of story?" (p. 116).

I have outlined above some key themes in critical scholarship on children's literature and racism. My chapter builds on these, bringing in the additional concepts of multicultural governmentality (Chen, 2015, in press) and cultural racism to further problematize **discourses** of culture and identity in children's literature. Following French philosopher Michel Foucault's governmentality approach, I conceptualize official multiculturalism in Canada as a particular mode of governmentality affecting our social world, including children's books. A number of other authors have also contributed analyses inspired by this Foucauldian notion (see Ang, 2010; Beauregard, 2008; Brown, 2006; Hage, 1998; Ong, 1996; Shome, 2012). Multicultural governmentality refers to considered, rational activities that seek to shape the mental, emotional, social, and even political conduct of racialized multicultural Others—officially known as "visible minorities" in Canada—as well as the conduct of unmarked, seemingly cultureless dominant groups (Chen, in press). As a form of governmentality, official multiculturalism is analyzed for its mobilization of a range of accepted truths, strategies, and techniques to achieve white-centred nation-building ends. One key logic of multicultural governmentality is what French scholar Balibar termed "cultural racism" (1991). Since the 1950s, the word "race"[3] has gradually almost disappeared in everyday discourses, either because people have been convinced by the scientists who have made strong statements disputing the validity of the notion of race, or, more likely, because people are afraid of being accused of being racist if they talk about race (Goldberg, 2008). At the same time, other words, specifically *ethnicity* and *culture*, have started to be used more frequently to basically refer to those peoples who were previously described as being of nonwhite races. This "cultural turn," or "ethnic turn" is a complex story in itself (Chen, 2015). For our purpose here, it suffices to note that Balibar argues that what we have now is a new kind of racism that does not mention the word *race*, but operates instead around the notion of culture. In this neo-racist ideology, culture is treated as nature, as if it were biologically embedded in each member of a group regardless of the impact of social processes such as migration and adaptation, and as if each culture were an insular package defined by an immutable essence. The concept also envisions fundamental differences between cultures such that, perhaps, one could learn to tolerate, but never to mix with, another culture. Samuel Huntington's infamous "clashes of civilizations" thesis (1996) is a typical right-wing formulation of cultural racism that reduces geopolitics to incommensurate cultures. As I mentioned earlier, cultural racism often expresses Euro-centrism and the white norm through the practice of describing nonwhites primarily as cultural subjects, and whites as universal. Drawing on the concepts of multicultural governmentality and cultural racism, I will elaborate on a number of critical observations about current children's literature that showcase different cultural practices, norms, and languages.

A QUESTION OF CULTURAL DIFFERENCES OR POWER INEQUALITIES?

In this section, I argue that multicultural children's books tend to reflect the ways that multicultural governmentality encourages a depoliticized, culturalized understanding of social ills. As such, these books convey to their audiences that divisions and conflicts in society are due to cultural differences and that respect for cultural diversity is the solution to these issues. While this may be a positive value, we need more than that to address long-entrenched inequalities and to achieve substantial social justice. In order to teach children about social justice, we need to first teach them about injustices in the past and present that have shaped our society and the lives of people in it.

While it is generally accepted that children's books have an important role to play in teaching diversity, tolerance, and respect, it is rare that they equip the reader with a critical awareness of injustices, inequalities, domination, and resistance. Two prize-winning picture books, one American and one Canadian—both well-known and often used, as I was informed—are good examples of texts that are valuable for broadening children's awareness of cultural diversity, but that fail to discuss issues of social justice: *Henry and the Kite Dragon* and *Yetsa's Sweater*. The prize-winning *Henry and the Kite Dragon*, by Bruce Edward Hall (2004), a prolific writer and fourth-generation Chinese-American who published a number of books about life in Chinatown, is a story about conflict between some boys from Chinatown and others from Little Italy. Henry loved to fly kites over Chinatown and the park, but Tony and his friends kept throwing rocks at the beautiful kites. As Henry later found out, this was because the kites scared Tony's pigeons. Although the story portrays cultural practices in two ethnic communities—making kites and raising pigeons—as positive and fun, thereby teaching mutual understanding, respect, and the lesson that people often have more in common than they realize, it does not explain why, at the time, Italian and Chinese **immigrants** lived in adjacent, poor, and crowded neighbourhoods. Without such information, the story communicates a depoliticized understanding of reality—the boys' conflict becomes mere ethnic strife resolved through individual acts.

Likewise, *Yetsa's Sweater*, a bestseller in British Columbia, by Sylvia Olsen (2013), a prize-winning writer and speaker who is non-Native but has lived in an Indigenous community, represents a missed opportunity to provide a more complete picture of the life of Cowichan people and colonialism in Canada. It tells the story of Yetsa learning to make Cowichan sweaters from her mother and grandmother. The reader learns about all the steps involved, from preparing the sheep fleeces to designing and knitting. Both the

Box 9.1: How to Break from Cultural Racism?

One book that avoids the problem of cultural racism is American writer James Rumford's *Silent Music: A Story of Baghdad* (2008), about a boy, Ali, who, like many children around the world, loves playing soccer and listening to "parent-rattling" music. What fascinates Ali most is traditional Arabic calligraphy, like the art of Yakut, a thirteenth-century calligrapher. The beauty of calligraphy brings him consolation and peace as he copes with the wartime devastation around him. This story celebrates the uniqueness of the Arabic language and its meaningfulness to Ali, without reducing his life to history or shying away from how his life is shaped as much by his cultural heritage as by contemporary geopolitical events. It is important for children's books to have content that conveys some understanding of the spatial and historical specificities of cultural practices, and to avoid reductionist, binary, and hierarchical understandings of cultures (www.youtube.com/watch?v=GOoYs5jZyDg).

book and the accompanying Teacher's Guide (Sono Nis Press, n.d.) focus on craft-making and family tradition. The story might have addressed issues of power and justice by discussing colonialism and its devastating effects on Indigenous peoples, or culture as a process of hybridizing—in this case the creation of a unique art form by innovatively combining Salish and European textile techniques—and human resilience and creativity in adverse conditions.

RESPECT OF WHAT, BY WHOM, AND TO WHAT END?

Under multicultural governmentality, social ills are understood to have primarily been caused by a lack of respect and recognition for a nondominant culture, and to be addressed through extending respect and recognition. This leaves the central issue of power unaddressed. Nicholson (1996) points out that liberal discussions often focus too much on the legitimacy of the nonwhite Others demanding recognition and the ritual of the dominant majority bestowing recognition, and too little on the "people or institutions in a position to recognize" and their practices of recognition (Nicholson, 1996, p. 7). In other words, the typical official multiculturalist argument for greater sensitivity to and accommodation of cultural difference fails to question how power is exercised, and by whom, in deciding what, precisely, to recognize and respect. Thus, multicultural governmentality conceals the persistence of structural, Euro-centric racism and its role in producing hegemonic assumptions about culture and ethnicity as neat packages of practices and meanings that are "easily distinguishable and opposable to each other" (Cowan, Dembour, & Wilson, 2001, p. 8; Muehlmann, 2009). After centuries of colonialism and imperialism, and in the context of present-day cultural globalization, this understanding of culture is a fantasy (Cowan et al., 2001, p. 18) that reproduces Euro-centric stereotypes about the Other. In this fashion, multicultural governmentality produces what Brown (2006) characterizes as the paradox of legitimizing and simultaneously subordinating the nonwhite Other.

The objectification of culture as a persistent set of practices and meanings, detached from their histories, that can transcend time, national borders, regional boundaries, and class hierarchies is common in children's literature. In many ways, the turn to diversity in children's literature since the 1980s is a welcome step forward, making books that highlight different languages, art forms, values, food and eating customs, and traditional apparel available. The majority of multicultural books I examined, however, inform children about differences in ways whereby a culture is objectified and believed to be too fundamentally and innately different to have any connection to another culture in the past, present, or future. Some supposedly progressive children's books actually inculcate an essentialist understanding of culture—in other words, a belief in culture having "fixed" properties and a "true" core. *Ruby's Wish*, by Chinese-American writer Shirin Yim Bridges (2002), which tells the story of a grandmother who persuaded her family to support her education when she was a little girl in China, is a case in point. While the text mentions that it was unusual for girls in China to learn to read or write in the grandmother's time, it fails to explain to the reader that the education of girls in the West was also unusual in the early twentieth century. Without adding this perspective, the book imparts the culturally racist message that, in opposition to the West, China is where discrimination against girls exists. Moreover, the book's use of present tense (e.g., "If you walk down a certain road in a certain city in China") and its illustrations of characters—even contemporary ones—dressed in clothing rarely seen in everyday life, convey an impression that Chinese culture is unchanging and static.

CHILDREN, POLITICS OF CULTURE, AND ETHICS OF RECOGNITION

What are the implications of these observations of children's books in terms of racism and multicultural governmentality? In this last section, I identify a few directions for your critical reflection on children, politics of culture, and ethics of recognition. The first concerns the construct of **childhood innocence** and how it plays a role in the avoidance of discussions about racism and power with children. While children's developmental characteristics do distinguish them from youth and adults in their experiences, perceptions, and approaches, the notion of childhood innocence is far from simply describing a natural aspect of childhood. In fact, scholars have examined historical shifts in Western beliefs about children's innocence and its connection to capitalist modes of production and the rise of bourgeois ideals (see e.g. Duschinsky, 2013; Robinson & Davies, 2008). Childhood innocence is seen as a universal natural state of ignorance and carefree-ness about topics such as sex, money, racism, and colonialism. Tatum's (1997, p. xvi) work shows that most parents and adults, regardless of racialization and ethnicity, feel uncomfortable talking with children about racism, often because they assume that children are "colourblind," and they worry that discussing these topics may cause children to lose their innocence. This, however, denies the reality that children's lives are affected from birth by both material and **symbolic inequalities** and that they are affected by racism from a young age, similar to the impact of poverty (see Albanese, chapter 11, this volume). Like van Belle (2010), I believe this notion of childhood innocence needs to be questioned and that even children in the lower grades of elementary schools possess sufficient life experiences, reasoning skills, and emotional maturity to engage in some discussions about racism, inequalities, and power.

Second, you might reflect on how children's books do not just passively depict lives; we need to ask what social relations are enacted and reproduced through them (Varga & Zuk, 2013). The depoliticizing form of recognizing cultural diversity in children's books, mirroring the liberal mode of cultural celebration in the broader society, produces normative white subjects as unmarked, universal subjects who grant respect to cultural

Others. Young white readers are guided to cultivate and express normative responses—respect, tolerance, and empathy towards acceptable elements of other cultures—that denote a nonracist positioning. They are positioned as generous in accepting and even loving other cultures and cultural Others, all, apparently, outside of the power relations that reproduce and circulate dominant perceptions of cultures. Young white readers are also guided to take a superior spectator's stance towards elements of other cultures that are unacceptable within the current dominant cultural context, such as patriarchal, oppressive practices, as if these are restricted only to other cultures. As Oh and Banjo (2012) have argued, this privileged positioning is a mode through which multiculturalism strengthens the white centre of society by "constructing a positive self in relief against the negative other" (p. 462).

Third, one axiom of Canadian multicultural governmentality is what I have termed *the cultural identity imperative*, defined as the depoliticized preoccupation with essentialized cultural identities for the racialized nonwhite populations—in other words, the making of ethnicized citizens in the existing hierarchy of belonging (Chen, 2015). Multicultural governmentality foregrounds ethnicity as the primary means of identification (Mahtani, 2002; Shome, 2012) of its racialized minority citizenry; it assumes and seeks to produce a normative nonwhite subject that yearns to maintain their minority culture (but without pushing for social change) and participates in society as an ethnicized, complementary citizen (Chen, in press). Butler (2005) proposes an ethics of recognition that "recognises the subjecthood of the Other, but does so without restricting the terms of this subjecthood or turning this recognition into yet another occasion for our own self-recognition" (Youdell, 2011, p. 152). In other words, to truly recognize the Other is to disrupt the power of being in a position to assume that we already know the Other. This alternative would engage a politics concerned with "letting the other live," in the sense of letting the Other exercise **agency** in defining and redefining their subjecthood, their selves, and their identifications. We need to critically examine the role of culture, as portrayed in children's books, in constituting persons, the Others, and the nation itself (Ang & Stratton, 1994; Cowan et al., 2001). To what extent do our children's books about cultural diversity validate children's experiences with a complex cultural reality that is charged with power, but is also interactive and negotiable (Gilroy, 2000; Handa, 2003)? Do they let children recognize themselves in their stories, validate their existence as human beings, and acknowledge children's value (W. D. Myers, 2014)?

A fourth point to consider is that it has been noted by scholars that racialized minority adults seldom appear in children's books (Kyle, 1978), and if they do, they are often less competent or less acceptable than the minority children who appear in the same text. For example, van Belle (2010, p. 148), as I argued earlier, has shown that Blacks, as a group, are represented in grade 3 basal readers as less mathematically and financially literate; in instances where Black characters are literate or are successful in running their own businesses (typically employing only themselves), these characters are children. This narrative pattern raises questions about how and why children of colour are imagined to be more desirable, acceptable subjects than their parents and similar adults around them in a society characterized by intersections of racialization, culture, age, and belonging. Is this a disturbing way of imagining minority children as better citizens than minority adults? What notions about minority adults are implicit in this message?

CONCLUSION

This paper is part of a larger project that develops a critical understanding of how children's books have challenged or reproduced modes of nationalist, ethnic absolutist, and culturalist discourses that are organized by logics of racial and cultural purity, exclusivity, incompatibility, and hierarchy. I have highlighted two problematic patterns in contemporary children's literature in Canada: (1) the avoidance of exploring power, exclusion, and injustice in children's books, which masks realities and closes off opportunities for nurturing a critical awareness in children; and (2) the tendency to portray cultures in an essentialist manner and in implicit contrast to the West, thereby entrenching a binary, hierarchical understanding of humanity that ultimately subordinates Othered cultures. Renowned writer Walter Dean Myers explained the social and psychological effect of his books featuring inner-city youth on young people: "They have been struck by the recognition of themselves in the story, a validation of their existence as human beings, an acknowledgment of their value by someone who understands who they are" (W. D. Myers, 2014). The challenge still faces us: how to write books that validate children's experiences and acknowledge their value as they confront racism and colonial mentality, as they navigate ambivalent recognition politics that naturalize identity while reducing stigma, and as they construct identities through discursive practices "within the play of specific modalities of power" (Hall, 1996, p. 4)?

CHAPTER SUMMARY

Together, in this chapter, we

- Reviewed some main characteristics of children's books on topics of multiculturalism, racism, and colonialism: their persistently low number and the implicit dominance of white characters and ideas and practices of Western origin.
- Explored critical scholarship on children's literature that together argue that the above characteristics of children's literature impact on not only racialized children, but also on white children. This plays an important role in reproducing or challenging racist ideology.
- Learned about concepts such as the white norm, Euro-centrism, multicultural governmentality, and cultural racism.

- Were presented with analyses that argue that children's literature tends to practise depoliticized celebration of diversity that excludes a critical awareness of injustices and inequalities, and that non-Western cultures are often represented as static and the binary Other of the West.
- Considered that children's books may not ever be perfect. However, we as critical readers can elicit many teachable moments around a book and guide conversations to foster awareness about social justice, power, and resistance.

STUDY QUESTIONS

1. What are some of the problems with children's books that merely inform children about cultural diversity but do not help them understand issues of social justice, experiences of racism, and power?

2. Consider the concept of multicultural governmentality or the concept of cultural racism. Explain how it raises different questions about racism and how it helps us have a critical and nuanced understanding about books that may appear good, especially in contrast to prevalent and blatant racist stereotypes in children's books before the 1970s.

3. Think about some multicultural children's books that you read when you were younger. Were issues of racism and social injustice addressed in those books? If not, were they brought up by the teacher, your parents, or others for discussion?

4. Do you think children in elementary schools should learn something about the colonization of Indigenous peoples in Canada and how it connects to inequalities in education, health, and economic prosperity that Indigenous people face today, including some of the consequences of colonialism, like high rates of homelessness?

5. What might be some key messages you would convey to young people if you were to write a children's book on Canada's Indian Residential Schools?

SUGGESTED RESEARCH ASSIGNMENT

Go to your local library and ask the librarian to suggest ten pictures books on multiculturalism and/or racism. Study these books carefully, both their texts and illustrations. Explore some or all of the following analytical themes: How are cultures discussed in these books? Do the books try to situate the cultures discussed in historical and social contexts? Are commonalities, similarities, interactions, or mingling between these and the West explored, or is there an assumed dichotomy and hierarchy between the West and the Rest? Do the books provide age-appropriate openings for fostering some awareness about inequality, exclusion, and power in children? Try to engage with concepts presented in the chapter to develop your analysis.

SUGGESTED FILMS/VIDEO CLIPS

10 Children's Books You Didn't Know Were Racist
www.youtube.com/watch?v=GCdBmddPa1Q
This video highlights problematic racist representations in ten celebrated children's books, from *The Secret Garden* (1910) to *The Chronicles of Narnia* (1950), that are well-known to children even today. These are examples of blatant racist portrayals prior to the 1970s.

Meet the Author: Arlene Chan
www.youtube.com/watch?v=VTuGWkpGaEE
In this video produced by the Canadian Children's Book Centre, Arlene Chan explains why she is passionate about writing books about Chinese-Canadian history.

Author Walter Dean Myers: "Reading Is Not Optional" for Kids
www.youtube.com/watch?v=nUJ37nrfNV4
Walter Dean Myers, cited in the chapter, tells us about his important work depicting young Black men's lives in the US.

US Minorities Underrepresented in Children's Books
www.bbc.com/news/magazine-24216082
As referred to in the chapter, the Cooperative Children's Book Center in Wisconsin has found that racialized minorities continue to be underrepresented in children's books. In this video, we hear from staff at the Center, a parent, youth, an author, and a publisher explaining the importance of children's books that reflect their lived reality.

SUGGESTED WEBSITES

Canadian Children's Book Centre
www.bookcentre.ca
This is a Canadian organization for supporting and promoting the production of Canadian books for young readers. Check out their useful resources such as Themed Book Lists.

Cooperative Children's Book Center
ccbc.education.wisc.edu
This is an American children's book resource centre. It features important research, such as "Publishing Statistics on Children's Books about People of Color and First/Native Nations and by People of Color and First/Native Nations Authors and Illustrators."

sarahpark.com | Musings on Korean Diaspora, Children's Literature, and Adoption
readingspark.wordpress.com

You will enjoy exploring this website—it is fun and full of insights about children's literature, racism, mobility, and politics of authorship.

Chimamanda Ngozi Adichie: The Danger of a Single Story
www.ted.com/talks/chimamanda_adichie_the_danger_of_a_single_story?
 language=en
This is one of my favourite talks. An accomplished writer and eloquent speaker, Adichie urges us to move beyond a single story about another person, culture, or country, which could be repeated on different sites, including, for our purpose here, children's books.

NOTES

1. I would like to express my respect and gratitude to the school staff who generously shared with me some of their teaching resources on diversity. Together we have explored, and continue to explore, "interruptive space" through conversations about children's books (Brown et al., 2010, p. 527). My sincere thanks to Yu Shen and Melissa Conte for their helpful research assistance and to Elizabeth Paradis for her editorial help with an earlier draft.

2. As I have discussed elsewhere (Chen, 2015), this shift took place within the context of oppressed people grappling with the disillusioning elusiveness of equality and the intellectual influence of anticolonial movements around the world, especially those seeking to understand the social and psychological dimensions of oppression.

3. In the rest of the paper I do not put quotation marks around the term "race" to denote its constructed nature; however, it is important to clarify that race is understood not as a biological fact, but as an ideological construct with material and nonmaterial consequences.

REFERENCES

Ang, I. (2010). Between nationalism and transnationalism: Multiculturalism in a globalising world. *Centre for Cultural Research Occasional Paper Series, 1*(1), 1–14.

Ang, I., & Stratton, J. (1994). Multicultural imagined communities: Cultural difference and national identity in Australia and the USA. *Continuum: Australian Journal of Media and Culture, 9*(2), 124–158.

Balibar, E. (1991). Is there a "neo-racism"? In E. Balibar & I. M. Wallerstein, *Race, nation, class: Ambiguous identities* (pp. 19–28). London: Verso.

Beauregard, G. (2008). Asian Canadian studies: Unfinished projects. *Canadian Literature, 199*, 6–27.

Bridges, S. Y. (2002). *Ruby's wish.* San Francisco: Chronicle Books.

Brown, S., Souto-Manning, M., & Tropp Laman, T. (2010). Seeing the strange in the familiar: Unpacking racialized practices in early childhood settings. *Race, Ethnicity and Education, 13*(4), 513–532. doi:10.1080/13613324.2010.519957

Brown, W. (2006). *Regulating aversion: Tolerance in the age of identity and empire.* Princeton, NJ: Princeton University Press.

Butler, J. (2005). *Giving an account of oneself.* New York: Fordham University Press.

Canadian Children's Book Centre. (n.d.). Retrieved from www.bookcentre.ca/resources_librarians

Chen, X. (2015). Not ethnic enough: The cultural identity imperative in international adoptions from China to Canada. *Children and Society, 29*(6), 626–636.

Chen, X. (in press). Governing cultures, making multicultural subjects. In D. Brock (Ed.), *Re-making normal: Governing the social in neoliberal times.*

Chin, F. (Ed.). (1974). *Aiiieeeee! An anthology of Asian American writers.* Washington, DC: Howard University Press.

Ching, S. H. D. (2005). Multicultural children's literature as an instrument of power. *Language Arts, 83*(2), 128.

Cobb, C. (2015, May 31). Education a first step in "long journey" to Aboriginal reconciliation, commission chairman says. *Ottawa Citizen.* Retrieved from ottawacitizen.com/news/local-news/long-journey-to-aboriginal-reconciliation-starts-sunday

Cooperative Children's Book Center. (2015). *Children's books by and about people of color published in the United States.* Retrieved from ccbc.education.wisc.edu

Cowan, J. K., Dembour, M., & Wilson, R. (2001). *Culture and rights: Anthropological perspectives.* New York: Cambridge University Press.

Deane, P. (1989). Black characters in children's fiction series since 1968. *The Journal of Negro Education, 58*(2), 153–162.

Duschinsky, R. (2013). Childhood innocence: Essence, education, and performativity. *Textual Practice, 27*(5), 763–781. doi:10.1080/0950236X.2012.751441

Dyer, R. (1997). *White.* New York & London: Routledge.

Edwards, G., & Saltman, J. (2010). *Picturing Canada: A history of Canadian children's illustrated books and publishing.* Toronto: University of Toronto Press.

Fondrie, S. (2001). "Gentle doses of racism": Whiteness and children's literature. *Journal of Children's Literature, 27*(2), 9–13.

Frankenberg, R. (1993). *White women, race matters: The social construction of whiteness.* Minneapolis: University of Minnesota Press.

Ghiso, M. P., & Campano, G. (2013). Ideologies of language and identity in U.S. children's literature. *Bookbird: A Journal of International Children's Literature, 51*(3), 47–55.

Gilroy, P. (2000). *Against race: Imagining political culture beyond the color line.* Cambridge, MA: Belknap Press of Harvard University Press.

Goldberg, D. T. (2008). Buried, alive. In *The threat of race* (pp. 1–31). Oxford: Wiley-Blackwell.

Hage, G. (1998). *White nation: Fantasies of white supremacy in a multicultural society.* Annandale, Australia: Pluto Press.

Hall, B. E. (2004). *Henry and the kite dragon.* New York: Philomel Books.

Hall, S. (1996). Introduction: Who needs "identity"? In S. Hall & P. Du Gay (Eds.), *Questions of cultural identity* (pp. 1–17). London & Thousand Oaks, CA: Sage.

Handa, A. (2003). *Of silk saris and mini-skirts: South-Asian girls walk the tight-rope of culture.* Toronto: Women's Press.

Huntington, S. P. (1996). *The clash of civilizations and the remaking of world order.* New York: Simon & Schuster.

Kyle, D. W. (1978). Changes in basal reader content: Has anyone been listening? *The Elementary School Journal, 78*(5), 304–312.

Larrick, N. (1991). The all-white world of children's books. *Journal of African Children's & Youth Literature, 3,* 1–10. (Original work published 1965)

Mahtani, M. (2002). Interrogating the hyphen-nation: Canadian multicultural policy and "mixed race" identities. *Social Identities, 8*(1), 67–90.

Muehlmann, S. (2009). How do real Indians fish? Neoliberal multiculturalism and contested indigeneities in the Colorado Delta. *American Anthropologist, 111*(4), 468–479.

Myers, C. (2014, March 15). The Apartheid of children's literature. *The New York Times.* Retrieved from www.nytimes.com/2014/03/16/opinion/sunday/the-apartheid-of-childrens-literature.html

Myers, W. D. (2014, March 15). Where are the people of color in children's books? *The New York Times.* Retrieved from www.nytimes.com/2014/03/16/opinion/sunday/where-are-the-people-of-color-in-childrens-books.html

Nicholson, L. (1996). To be or not to be: Charles Taylor and the politics of recognition. *Constellations, 3*(1), 1–16.

Oh, D. C., & Banjo, O. O. (2012). Outsourcing postracialism: Voicing neoliberal multiculturalism in *Outsourced. Communication Theory, 22*(4), 449–470. doi:10.1111/j.1468-2885.2012.01414.x

Olsen, S. (2013). *Yetsa's sweater.* Winlow, BC: Sono Nis Press.

Ong, A. (1996). Cultural citizenship as subject making: Immigrants negotiate racial and cultural boundaries in the United States. *Current Anthropology, 37*(5), 737–762.

Robinson, K. H., & Davies, C. (2008). "SHE'S KICKIN' ASS, THAT'S WHAT SHE'S DOING!" Deconstructing childhood "innocence" in media representations. *Australian Feminist Studies, 23*(57), 343–358. doi:10.1080/08164640802233294

Rumford, J. (2008). *Silent music: A story of Baghdad.* New York: Roaring Brook Press.

Shome, R. (2012). Mapping the limits of multiculturalism in the context of globalization. *International Journal of Communication, 6,* 144–165.

Sono Nis Press. (n.d.). *Teacher's guide (Yetsa's sweater).* Retrieved from www.sononis.com/tg126.pdf

Tatum, B. D. (1997). *Why are all the black kids sitting together in the cafeteria? and other conversations about race.* New York: Basic Books.

Truth and Reconciliation Commission of Canada. (2015). *Honouring the truth, reconciling for the future: Summary of the final report of the truth and reconciliation commission of Canada.* Winnipeg: Truth and Reconciliation Commission of Canada.

van Belle, L. A. (2010). *"Gentle doses of racism": Racist discourses in the construction of scientific literacy, mathematical literacy, and print-based literacies in children's basal readers.* PhD dissertation, ProQuest, UMI Dissertations Publishing.

Varga, D., & Zuk, R. (2013). Golliwogs and teddy bears: Embodied racism in children's popular culture. *The Journal of Popular Culture, 46*(3), 647–671.

Yoon, B., Simpson, A., & Haag, C. (2010). Assimilation ideology: Critically examining underlying messages in multicultural literature. *Journal of Adolescent & Adult Literacy, 54*(2), 109–118.

Youdell, D. (2011). Fabricating "Pacific Islander": Pedagogies of expropriation, return and resistance and other lessons from a "multicultural day." *Race, Ethnicity and Education, 15*(2), 141–155.

10 From Babies to Teens: Children Are a Marketer's Dream

Cheryl Williams and Natalie Coulter

LEARNING OBJECTIVES

- To understand how youth is categorized, defined, and shaped by consumer culture
- To see how these categories are designed to meet the needs of consumer culture and not to reflect the needs of young people
- To appreciate the historical shifts in how children are constructed as markets
- To consider how young people actively engage with consumer culture
- To think about how consumer culture provides resources for subjectivity for young people

INTRODUCTION

We both remember playing Lego as kids. There were always a few sets of the multico-loured bricks tucked in shoeboxes in our rec rooms. It seemed like every Canadian child, girls and boys alike, had one of these shoeboxes. We would dump the box out on the carpet to build houses, trucks, towers, and spaceships—whatever we could imagine. Our parents would curse at the scattered pieces of Lego they would inevitably step on and we would curse when our siblings inevitably destroyed our prized creations to scavenge pieces for their own constructions.

Lego was founded in 1932 when Danish carpenter Ole Kirk Kristiansen began building wooden pull toys from the scraps in his shop. In 1958 the company designed the ubiquitous interlocking Lego brick that has become a mainstay of many people's youth, and in 1961 the Lego System of Play became available in North America.

Now that we are both parents, it is our children who play with Lego, but today's Lego is radically different than the Lego of our youth. No longer are there simple buckets of coloured bricks; today there are endless Lego "themes," all tailored to a child's age, gender, and interests, one for every stage of childhood: Lego Duplo for ages 18 months to 5 years, Lego Juniors for ages 4 to 7—with sets such as the garbage truck marketed to boys and the princess play castle marketed to girls—and classic Lego sets for ages 7 and up. The Lego Friends theme, designed specifically for girls, features pink, purple, and teal blocks in sets like Pop Star Dressing Room and City Park Café, while for boys there is Lego City, Speed Champions, and Legends of Chima. Because no one is ever too old for Lego, the company offers an architecture series geared to teens and adults who are up for the challenge of building the Louvre or the Statue of Liberty. While the Lego bricks of yesteryear could be assembled into virtually anything imaginable, today's Lego sets are predesigned to mimic popular characters and scenes from leading media franchises, including Marvel Superheroes and Disney Princesses for younger children, while Minecraft, Doctor Who, and The Lord of the Rings sets are designed to appeal to tweens and teens.

The marketing strategy for Lego has also radically changed. Lego has developed into a massive **transmedia** franchise with a number of successful television series, including *Hero Factory* (2010–present) and *Lego Ninjago: Masters of Spinjitzu* (2011–present), plus dozens of TV movies airing on kids' specialty cable channels. Lego is producing original series exclusively for Netflix beginning with *Lego Bionicle: The Journey of One* (2016–present) and *Lego Friends: The Power of Friendship* (2016–present) to bolster the selection of Lego TV shows and specials already available on the streaming site. Lego has even conquered the big screen with the 2014 hit *The Lego Movie*, accompanied by the hit theme song "Everything Is Awesome." Today Lego offers an array of digital media in the form of advergames, video, online galleries, and digital downloads. At the time of writing, the Lego website lists almost 100 Web games, 20 console video games, a Lego social network, and the Lego Minifigures and Lego Chima MMOGs (massively multiplayer online games), while Apple's App Store lists 34 Lego apps available for smartphones and tablets. These digital games are complemented by an array of trailers, webisodes, bloopers, mini-movies, and character videos, all available in an extensive online video gallery.

Lego's rise from a carpenter's workshop to one of the world's largest toy companies exemplifies a shift in children's **consumer culture**. Today, the LEGO Group is a conglomerate of global divisions and has infiltrated leisure, education, and media culture with products targeted to every age and stage of life. The story of Lego is part of a broader history of capitalism's compartmentalization of young people into discrete marketing niches. Turning young people into consumer markets has been essential for the continuation of consumer culture and capitalism (Ewen, 1976) as children are at the "epicentre" of consumer culture (Schor, 2004, p. 9) and have made "capitalism hum" (Cook, 2001).

Children have been central to the development of the capitalist economy and capitalism has been one of the key institutions to define categories of young people. The toddler in the 1930s (Cook, 2004), the teenager in the 1950s (Schrum, 2004), and the tween in 1980s (Coulter, 2014) are all segmented categories of young people with origins in consumer culture, as media, manufacturers, retailers, and advertisers segment and interpellate these categories of childhood. Throughout the twentieth century, and continuing into the twenty-first century, marketers have shifted from grouping young people together in large, unwieldy categories to dividing them into smaller and more specific market segments, all of which offer more unique and intense marketing opportunities. As the Lego example illustrates, not only are children positioned as consumer markets, their culture has become more gendered, more licensed, and more technological. The purpose of this chapter is to illustrate how children and childhood are constructed according to the political and economic structures of consumer capitalism. First, we will examine how notions of the child consumer developed over the course of the nineteenth and twentieth centuries, then we will discuss the role of the consumer marketplace in defining categories of childhood and youth today.

Box 10.1: What Do Children Say about Lego?

I like how you can be creative and create anything you want and also provide a challenge for yourself. Like challenge yourself to build something or get a challenging Lego set.... I have a ton of just loose Lego for building stuff with. And a bunch of Lego sets, most are from Star Wars sets, some are from Marvel and a few are from Lego City. My favourite set I have is probably Millennium Falcon. It's a ship from Star Wars, it's one of the main ships.... We watched the Lego Movie and umm we watch a few Lego shows, like *The Freemaker Adventures*, we watched Lego Stories *Droid Tales*. And me and my Dad we play a few Lego Xbox games, like Lego Star Wars, Lego Marvel, and Lego DC. Oh and we play Harry Potter sometimes. My favourite Lego project, that I've made from scratch, is probably the prison castle with me and my Dad, with instructions it is probably the Millennium Falcon. (Luke, age 10; Favourite: Lego Death Star)

Boys' Lego is like they have lots of different types of people. Sometimes it is based off of a movie and they have guns and stuff. (Kira, age 9; Favourite: Lego Friends)

Lego is blocks you build and you can build anything. You can watch a TV Lego show. When you watch it then you can build lots of things like trees and houses and windows and leaves and a pool and your brother and Yoda. (Joey, age 6; Favourite: Lego Pokémon [Doesn't exist])

I usually, like, play with Lego cars and Lego people, and sometimes race them. Well we watch that *Freemaker Adventures* and not that much else. I like how, it's like, if you put a piece down really hard you need like a thing that pulls it up to get it off. My favourite thing to make is cars.... I just build stuff and then I play with it after. I usually play by myself.... I would like the Lego Death Star. Half of it is the Death Star on the outside and it has like a laser that can destroy an entire planet. It's from Star Wars and the Dark Side uses it and they can destroy the rebels. I like that it has so many pieces, it probably has about 3,000 pieces. If I got it I would probably have my Dad and my brother help me, then I would display it.... My favourite part is like building characters and making what they are going to be wearing, and like choosing their pants. (Gus, age 7; Favourite: No favourite Lego, just making stuff with bright colours)

I'm too old for Lego but I still play with it ... in general, it's just embarrassing. [If people at school found out] I would have to lie and say that I don't play with it. If they saw it in my room I would just say it's my brother's and I was playing with him. It's a very simple excuse for me. (Nate, age 14; Favourite: Anything but Lego Friends)

Lego can help you if you want to be an engineer when you are older ... Lego Friends is for girls. It's just too easy to build and some of the stuff doesn't make sense like there aren't any car seats [in the cars].... After I saw the Lego movie I liked Lego more 'cause it's cool how they built all the stuff in it and there's a LOT of stuff. And it's all made out of Lego. (Jaiden, age 10; Favourite: Lego Star Wars)

I play with Lego a lot. I play with my sister and little brother. I play a few times a week. I like to build houses and stuff. I don't really watch Lego shows. I watched the movie when it was out in theatres. (Tess, age 11; Favourite: Lego Friends)

I like that you can build a ton of stuff. I like to build houses and that's about it. I play with my sister. It's one of my favourite toys. I like little Lego, the boys Lego things. I want the rainforest with the slide and the animals. (Payton, age 7; Favourite: Lego Friends)

I play with Lego at my friend Lilah's house. She has lots of Lego, she has the rainforest, the adventures, she also has one more that I forgot. I watched the TV show with my other friend. (Cambie, age 7; Favourite: Lego Friends Rainforest)

But, as James, Jenks, and Prout (2004) have stated, children are not passive. They are active agents in the construction of their own social lives. Thus, the chapter will conclude with a discussion on how young people engage with, negotiate, and resist these constructions as the constructions provide resources of subjectivity.

PART I—HISTORY OF CHILDREN AS A MARKET SEGMENT

It is difficult to envision today, but until the mid-nineteenth century there were very few products geared specifically for children and advertisers rarely spoke directly to the child consumer. What little attention children received treated them as homogenous groups of boys and girls, with hardly any age distinction. It was the newspaper industry that first began to recognize a specific youth audience. Publishers of periodical magazines such as *Youth's Companion* (1827–1927), *Robert Merry's Museum* (1841–1872), *Our Young Folks* (1865–1873), and *St. Nicholas* (1873–1905) recognized that children had distinct interests from the general newspaper readership and editors began to select content designed specifically to attract young readers. Unlike children's magazines, the contents of these periodicals were designed to mould children into the respectable ladies and gentlemen of tomorrow, as opposed to selling directly to youth (Cross, 1997; Kelly, 1974). Instead the audience were mostly mothers who may have read the magazines with their children. Speaking to mothers must have been an effective vehicle, as by 1880 there were more than 200 children's periodicals in print.

In these periodicals, the children were directly addressed as "boys" and "girls," terms that described youth roughly between the ages of 5 and 18 years old and, aside from gender differences, the media approached this age range as a relatively uniform group. For example, the same selection of goods that was offered for 6-year-old boys was also offered for 14-year-old boys. The function of children's periodicals and consumer goods was to prepare youngsters for their eventual role in the adult world, and the marketplace provided the necessary goods to facilitate this transition to adulthood. Thus, the nineteenth-century marketplace did not construct children as consumers in their own right, but rather as "adults-in-training" and part of the family.

Twentieth-Century Developments in Children's Consumer Culture

In the early 1900s advertisers continued to view young people as part of the family market (Cook, 2004). The family was viewed as an economic unit, and manufacturers and retailers of children's goods targeted the mother, who was seen as the gatekeeper, for family purchases (Schor, 2004, p. 17). Advertisements informed her that it was up to her to purchase the proper selection of products for her children to ensure their future success in life. Children were mainly ignored as a direct market because it was thought that they had little money, and any money they did have was spent on candy, comic books, or toys. Beyond these industries, the youth market did not warrant serious consideration and, for the most part, it was seen as a bit vulgar for business to pursue a typical "business/consumer relation" with children (McNeal, 1987, p. 134).

Things began to change in the 1930s with the emergence of aged-based distinctions in the consumer marketplace. Daniel Cook's (2004) history of the children's clothing industry outlines the institutionalization of a new category of childhood: the toddler. Today accepted as a legitimate biological and social stage of childhood, the toddler was actually an invention of the retail and manufacturing industry that designed and sold clothes tailored specifically for a toddler's body by accommodating diapers and the swayback of a young child learning to walk. Once the toddler was defined as different from an infant or child by the clothing industry, other industries followed suit and took up this distinction as well, further legitimizing the category.

By the mid-1950s, with the proliferation of television, more companies began to realize the value of speaking directly to children and youth. Walt Disney, for example, recognized the potential of the children's market and exploited it in 1954 with the launch of *Disneyland* (1954–1959), an hour-long melange of animation and action dramas. Building on this early success, Disney saw an opportunity in the programming schedule to reach young consumers by scheduling their programs for the late afternoon, when mothers were busy making dinner and fathers had not yet returned home from work. Disney's *Mickey Mouse Club* (1955–1959) was the first network show to air consistently five times a week during the after-school time slot, when children were at home and in control of the television set. Disney's success with a child audience signalled to advertisers and marketers the potential gains in communicating directly with children. This was a lucrative proposition, both due to the large growth in the child population with the birth of the Baby Boomers and because the consumer population was eager to overcome the scarcity of the war and depression eras. The 1950s and 1960s saw further growth in television shows—for example, the development of Saturday morning cartoons—that segmented children from the adult market and allowed marketers to effectively speak directly to children as consumers, often when their parents were not with them.

The Invention of the Teenager

At the same time that Disney was speaking directly to children, advertisers, the media, and manufacturers were waking up to the potential of a new demographic that eventually became known as "teenagers." During the affluence of the postwar era, many middle-class youth did not need to work full time to contribute to the family economy. Instead, teenagers stayed in school and used their discretionary income to cultivate a distinct youth market and culture with particular patterns of consumption and tastes—think Elvis Presley, poodle skirts, and black leather jackets (Schrum, 2004).

The teenager began to emerge as a distinct **market segment** with its own youth culture in the late 1940s when marketing research companies, such as the newly formed Youth Marketing Co., hired surveyors to interview teenagers about their tastes and spending habits. By the 1950s, the teenage consumer was solidified in the social imagination of the North American psyche as a separate and discrete segment of the population and many companies began to cater specifically to them. In doing so, these industries started to play an active role in shaping and disseminating the tastes, styles, and attitudes of teenage America (Palladino, 1996).

By the late 1950s, the teen had become a powerful force in the marketplace. Teen tastes and styles began to drive trends and consumer products. The iconography of the youth market sold the idioms of "youth as fun" and promoted a new consumer value system that prioritized commodity consumption and immediate gratification. Teens were given the responsibility of encouraging and celebrating the prosperity that was promised in the postwar era (Adams, 1997; Osgerby, 2002; Palladino, 1996).

1980s "Mediatization" of Children's Culture

In the 1980s, there was an explosion of children's consumer culture as the mediascape changed drastically in North America. The rise of cable television meant entire channels could be dedicated to the tastes and desires of niched audience segments. Teenagers watched MTV in the United States and MuchMusic in Canada, while their younger siblings watched Nickelodeon in the US and YTV and the Family Channel here in Canada.

At the same time, governments in both the US and Canada (with the exception of Quebec) began to deregulate children's media by removing policy protections that were designed to shelter children from crass commercialism, as it was previously thought that children were too young to comprehend the persuasive tactics of advertising. Media corporations argued that governmental agencies such as the Federal Communications Commission (FCC) in the US and the Canadian Radio-television and Telecommunications Commission (CRTC) did not have the authority to operate as "national nannies." Instead, they suggested it should be left up to parents to police their children's media consumption (Kline, 1993, p. 215; Quart, 2003, p. 57).

Such deregulation signalled a drastic shift in the conceptualization of the child as a consumer. Prior to deregulation, the child was viewed as vulnerable to the pressures of the marketplace, and it was thought that children under 12 should be protected from the strong influence of commercial messages. Removing these protective policies legitimized children as competent consumers who could be directly addressed by advertisers as market savvy. There was no sense that children needed to be protected or shielded from the marketplace; instead children were positioned as consumers in their own right with access to a disposable income in the billions (Pecora, 2004, p. 25), leading *Marketing Magazine* to proclaim in 1990 that the child was the "dream consumer" (Marney, 1990, p. 15).

One of the key policies under regulation was that children's television shows had to be distinctly separate from advertised products. However, with deregulation, this was no longer the case. Shows and products could be integrated, meaning that the promotion of products could now occur within the content of a television show. This radical shift altered both children's media and how children were positioned and understood as consumers. Television shows featuring Transformers, My Little Pony, and Smurfs became, in effect, 22-minute commercials for the toys of the show, along with a slew of licensed products such as clothing, bed sheets, umbrellas, lunchboxes, breakfast cereals, board games, and stickers (Englehardt, 1986).

This dramatically changed the commercial viability of children's media, and simultaneously transformed both the children's entertainment and toy industries. Instead of vying for a large audience that it could sell to advertisers as the basis of success (as Disney had done in the 1950s), media companies relied on merchandise for the bulk of their profits. Toy companies adopted similar strategies by developing toys first and then producing cartoons, films, and video games to promote them. In addition to selling a higher volume of merchandise, this strategy also sped up the product lifecycle, as such characters quickly fell out of style and lost their appeal as children latched on to the newest media-generated trend.

The Discovery of the Tween

Deregulation in the 1980s also meant that the girl audience now had value. Prior to this, most shows were geared to boys, since it was thought that girls would watch shows geared to boys but boys were averse to "girls' shows." But with deregulation, shows such as Strawberry Shortcake began to cater to girl audiences to entice them to buy (and even better, collect) character-based merchandise. The fact that the value in a TV show was in the audience's merchandise-buying power, and not in the size of an audience that could be sold to advertisers, led to the dramatic gendering of children's media culture (Seiter, 1993).

It was during the 1980s that the tween was "discovered" as a specific market demographic. The tween, roughly between the ages of 8 and 12, has become a media construction of a youth who is not quite a teenager but is no longer a child. The tween, like the teen in the 1950s, was framed and defined as a specific market segment according to the logics of the marketplace as advertisers, and the media responded to a confluence of demographic shifts happening in the 1980s. Families were raising fewer children, and grandparents were living longer; meanwhile, participation of middle-class women in the labour force was increasing. These factors meant that more economic resources were funnelled to each child; working mothers and fewer children and grandchildren meant that each child had access to more of the family resources (Coulter, 2014). At the same time, advertisers were losing their ability to connect with teenagers who were at the mall or the video arcade, and instead realized that it was easier to talk to their younger siblings who were still at home watching TV (Coulter, 2014). It was in this socioeconomic space that advertising and the media began to talk directly to eight- to twelve-year-old girls as tweens, allowing tweenhood to become a space of subjectivity, meaning that young girls defined themselves as tweens. By the 1990s, tweens were a fully implemented market niche with their own media (*You Can't Do That On Television*, *Saved by the Bell*, and later the *High School Musical* franchise), their own stores (Justice), and their own stars (Miley Cyrus, Hilary Duff, and Mary-Kate and Ashley Olsen). The tween became an accepted category of youth and, like the teen of the 1950s, became an established part of the social imagination and an accepted category of youth well beyond consumer marketplace (Coulter, 2014).

PART II—CHILDREN'S CONSUMER CULTURE TODAY

Explosive advances in hardware and Internet technologies since the turn of the twenty-first century are transforming youth culture and facilitating more targeted and complex relationships between young people and the consumer marketplace. Historically, television had been the primary vehicle for communicating brand messages to children, but, as the most recent *Young Canadians in a Wired World* study indicates, young people are now getting more of their media from the Internet than from television (Steeves, 2014a, 2014b). The children's media landscape has changed significantly, as three quarters of Canadian students in grades 4 to 11 maintain a social media profile or a blog, 91 percent have played online games, 75 percent list YouTube as their favourite website, and 39 percent actually sleep with their cell phones (Steeves, 2014a, 2014b). Much of young people's leisure time is spent streaming video and music, playing mobile games, posting to social media, and communicating via chat, text, and video services, among others. Children's brands are shifting their advertising efforts towards digital spaces with webisodes, chat stickers and emojis, iTunes soundtracks, and branded mobile apps becoming standard components of marketing plans. Games researcher Sara Grimes (2015) points out that advertising is integrated into digital play itself as consumer priorities shape video game design and children's play experiences.

Data Mining and the Prosumer

Unlike television, digital channels provide a continuous flow of data that tracks what children interact with online. Of the top 50 websites visited by Canadian young people, all but one employ data trackers (Steeves, 2014b). Trackers allow site owners to determine which content generates the most clicks, likes, and shares and, more importantly, which of these interactions lead to sales, downloads, and upgrades. This data is often linked to robust demographic profiles detailing age, gender, location, likes, friends, and online activities that can be "mined" for market research and behavioural advertising.

When young people use Web platforms and services, they become participants in a more sophisticated digital marketplace driven by complex algorithms that trigger behavioural advertising and ad retargeting. For example, when tweens watch YouTube videos, they are presented with ads targeting their specific location and demographic profile. As they continue to watch, like, and comment on more and more videos, tweens provide even more specific data about their interests and interactions that can be mined to produce even more targeted behaviour-based ads. In addition, children's online games and virtual worlds such as *Neopets*, *Club Penguin*, *Moshi Monsters*, and *Animal Jam*, to name a few, generate massive amounts of data on the tastes and preferences of young people that can be packaged and sold as detailed market-research reports. In some cases, players are rewarded with bonus points in the game as an incentive to complete surveys (Grimes & Shade, 2005, p. 183).

Unlike broadcasting, digital media enable audiences to *speak back* to message producers in the form of comments, ratings, and reviews, and otherwise posting texts, images, and videos. User-generated content (UGC) allows consumers to have a voice, which means that they not only consume products, but also produce product-related content and information. Consumers who also produce content are known as **"prosumers"** (Ritzer & Jurgenson, 2010) and young people in particular produce volumes of UGC in the form of YouTube videos, app ratings, fan art, blog posts, snaps, and more (see Williams, in press). When "real" people post about products online, it is viewed as more authentic and believable than standard marketing jargon. Eager for the trust of consumers, corporate brands are creating tools specifically to enlist the help of young people in boosting the visibility and authenticity of their brands (Pybus, 2011). When a shoe brand wants to appear "cool" to teen skateboarders, it no longer advertises on MTV. Instead, it reaches out to a cool teen video blogger who will generate buzz and stimulate comments, likes, and other UGC promoting the brand. When children engage in prosumer activity they are no longer passive recipients of consumer culture but they are actually active in the production of it. Their likes and comments boost search engine rankings, generate online sales, and add authenticity to the brand, which helps that company more effectively reach and "speak to" other young people as potential customers.

Babies and Toddlers

The age at which today's tech-saturated children stop playing with toys is being pushed younger and younger in favour of video games and digital play. Toy companies are not just competing with each other for children's attention, but they also must compete with Apple, Google, and online games like *Candy Crush* and *Angry Birds*. Now, smartphones, tablets, iPods, and gaming consoles top the wish lists of children as young as 4 or 5 years old. The answer, it seems, is for traditional children's brands to reach the potential market as early as possible. Brands make use of touchscreens and mobile devices that can be propped up on baby bouncers, laid on the floor, or inserted into toys to facilitate new opportunities for marketing to infants and toddlers. Today, marketing has reorientated from targeting parents for baby-based consumption to targeting the baby herself. An *Adweek* article from 2011 labels infants to three-year-olds "The Next Great American Consumer" and explains that "by getting their logos and iconic characters in front of babies—even those with still-blurry eyesight—[companies] hope to establish brand-name preference before she or he has uttered a word" (Braiker, 2011).

Despite the fact that the American Academy of Pediatrics and the Canadian Paediatric Society recommend zero screen time for children under age two, 38 percent of children age zero to one have used a mobile device such as a smartphone or tablet and 6 percent use mobile devices every day (Common Sense Media, 2013). Recognizing this trend, industry giants such as Playskool, Fisher-Price, Pampers, and Disney have developed hundreds of "educational" mobile apps that claim to stimulate learning in children as young as six months old. But these apps also generate demand for branded products and train toddlers to recognize logos and to bond early with in-app brand characters. This allows very young children to point to particular brands on store shelves, thus indicating purchase preferences to parents even before they develop verbal communication. Infants and toddlers are much more aware of corporate brands than one would think. One study found that by the age of six months, babies begin to form mental images of corporate logos and mascots (McNeal & Yeh, 1993), and more recently, the marketing industry has found that toddlers are requesting brands as soon as they can speak (Linn, 2005, p. 42).

Today we often refer to the younger generation as "digital natives" because they have been exposed to digital technologies practically from birth. This term implies that children are naturally gifted at using technology, and many adults defer to children as the experts whenever a screen is involved. However, digital natives are not born digital (Selwyn, 2009). These skills are acquired and developed the same way as any other life skill. Similarly, when advertising and consumerism pervade infants' daily lives, this constructs the child consumer as "natural" and "just the way kids are these days." But consumerism is also learned, and the marketplace is a key educator. When the consumer marketplace begins to act on children from birth, it constructs the child as an innately sophisticated consumer with distinguished tastes and brand preferences, which further legitimates consumption as a natural component of human behaviour.

Children in the Global Marketplace

As with the children's magazine industry in the nineteenth century, the segmentation of young people over the last century has taken place within a rigid set of **discourses** that have failed to address a wide range of demographics. Age and gender are privileged above other subjectivities in the division of the children's market, while distinctions in class, race, and sexuality are overlooked. The child consumer is most often assumed to be white, middle class, heterosexual, and able-bodied. When there are occasional integrations of broader demographics, the characters are usually peripheral, and their representations often clichéd.

Today's global marketplace has opened the door for multinational corporations like Lego (as well as others such as Disney, Nickelodeon, and Toys "R" Us to name a few) to access hundreds of millions of young people in local markets around the world. This phenomenon has concerning influences on the positioning of children. Western corporations don't generally conduct local research and development to inform product design and marketing campaigns. Instead, they export pre-existing products (designed for the Western marketplace) and use recognizable (Western) media characters to promote them to young people in new markets. This meets the needs of global capitalism as companies can efficiently access global youth markets without having to produce content tailored to specific individual regions (Wise, 2008). However, this form of globalization imposes predominantly Western values, ideologies, and subjectivities onto regional populations, erasing local culture and values in the process. By privileging the universalizing aspects of childhood (age and gender), the racial, ethnic, sexual, and cultural diversities of young people across and between transnational spaces are erased. Troublingly, this marks the emergence of a globalized youth culture in which global capitalism homogenizes young people through a Western lens, as gendered and aged consuming subjects, to the exclusion of collective, regional subjective experiences (Buckingham, 2011; Wise, 2008).

PART III—AGENCY AND THE YOUNG CONSUMER

Framing children and youth as consumers plays an ideological role in constructing young people's subjectivity. Some outspoken activists promote an image in which children are depicted as malleable and gullible, in need of protection from corporate pressures. Adults in this equation are immune to this influence, but the young, with their seemingly "tender minds," are at risk of manipulation. Marketers, on the other hand, promote an ideal in which young people of any age (even infants) are sovereign, savvy consumers who are productively engaged with the marketplace. These two polarized understandings of young consumers remain at the heart of much of the concern over young people's exposure to media and advertising.

In his critical work *The Material Child* (2011), childhood scholar David Buckingham rejects this "exploited versus empowered" debate. Children, he argues, are not incompetent vulnerable consumers. Nor do they express unfettered **power** and autonomy through consumption. These absolutes oversimplify the issue and obscure the reality in which the consumer marketplace is a site of *both* constraint and control, and choice and creativity. Up to this point we have explored the ways in which the marketplace constructs children primarily as consumers. However, as Buckingham has pointed out, this is far from the whole picture. Despite the undeniable power of the consumer marketplace, children and youth also act back upon the marketplace by actively engaging in producing their own social and cultural meanings. In fact, as soon as the marketplace identified the teen market, teenagers pushed back by resisting stereotypes and defying cultural expectations. Media historian Thiel-Stern (2014) describes the 1950s Elvis craze that left parents, child experts, and law enforcement scrambling to quash Elvis's raucous and rebellious, hypersexual, "hillbilly" rock and roll music, which threatened white, middle-class America. Despite parental panic, teenagers saved their allowances for albums and concert tickets, demanded his appearances on television shows, adopted sideburns and ducktail haircuts, donned blue jeans, and even wore dog tags in protest of his recruitment into the army. Thirty years later, in the 1980s, young "punks" resisted the dominant "yuppie" culture by using safety pins, piercings, spikes, and shaved heads to reject **social norms** and institutionalized forms of control. The final section of this chapter will explore just a few of the myriad ways today's young consumers are exercising **agency** and "speaking back" to corporations through entrepreneurship, activism, technology, creativity, and localization.

Consumer Activism

Today, child activists and entrepreneurs are using consumer culture itself as a site to redefine the same narrow definitions of childhood it creates. At just 13, McKenna Pope noticed her four-year-old brother cooking with her Easy-Bake Oven and successfully lobbied Hasbro to produce a black and silver gender-neutral oven to make it more acceptable for boys to bake too. Frustrated by the limited options in the boys' clothing industry, Moziah Bridges began sewing his own bowties out of his grandmother's scrap fabrics. The nine-year-old founded his company Mo's Bows and just four years later was supplying Neiman Marcus and Cole Haan with ethnic- and vintage-patterned bowties. And Jazz Jennings, who founded the TransKids Purple Rainbow Foundation with her parents at age six, leverages her appearances in Clean & Clear's "See the Real Me" advertising campaign and the TLC reality show *I Am Jazz* to further her advocacy for awareness and acceptance of **transgender** children. Or consider the SPARK Movement of girl activists, ranging in age from 13 to 22, who work together to challenge sexism. The SPARK Movement's most notable actions include petitioning Lego to include more positive representations of girls in the Lego Friends theme and also challenging *Seventeen* magazine to reduce photoshopping in photo editorials.

New Media and Fanworks

New media technologies create unprecedented opportunities for young people to contribute to cultural discourse and otherwise exercise their personal agency. Canadians in grades 4 to 11 primarily use the Internet for entertainment and communication but a surprising one-third have posted comments on news sites, 50 percent have shared links to news items and current events, and about one-third have joined or supported activist groups online (Steeves, 2014a). In her study of girls' use of Facebook, Thiel-Stern observes that the "ability to create their own media online affords girls a larger arsenal than ever to fight mass culture's stereotypical constructions of commercialized femininity and sexuality, and many do just that" (2014, p. 151). Body-positive Instagrams with hashtags such as #HonorMyCurves and the 687,000+ uses of #EffYourBeautyStandards defy the typical photoshopped image of girlhood advanced by consumer culture. The Canadian-based eGirls Project (Bailey & Steeves, 2015) probes the ways teens and young women are using digital technology to participate in political activism and civic discourse. Shade's (2015) chapter describes the student-led "Stop the Meter" campaign, which used a comedic YouTube video to speak out against a proposition that would allow usage-based billing for Internet service. Rosenblatt and Tushnet's (2015) chapter relates how young producers of fan art and fan fiction use digital platforms to advance interests that fall outside of traditional commercial culture, to add representations that may be overlooked in mainstream media, to experiment with alternate sexualities and gender roles, and to otherwise "talk back to mass culture" (p. 389).

Globalization

Globalization of consumer culture has undoubtedly impacted childhood in much of the world, but children also play a role in defining the nature of globalization (Stearns, 2005). For instance, Japanese children's "otaku" culture has contributed significantly to the globalization of Japanese toys and media. Otaku involves reworking and remixing manga, anime, video, and gaming to produce new cultural forms, and this practice, primarily enacted by children, has spawned global media and merchandising phenomena such as Pokémon and Yu-Gi-Oh (Ito, 2008). The global influence of Japanese, and more often American, media has been critiqued for its homogenizing effect that erases traditional ethnic, cultural, and religious differences. But children and youth actively repurpose and reinterpret global consumer symbols to adapt to the local culture. Children around the world localize Pokémon cards by playing with them in ways the Japanese creators never intended. Israeli children have integrated narratives of fighting and peace in their Pokémon play, French children used the cards to play traditional French card games, and Aboriginal Australian children left out the competitive aspects of the game altogether (de Block & Buckingham, 2007). Similarly, Estonian and Russian youth have used Western clothing brands to construct an identity that demarcates and preserves ethnic differences that can be interpreted as a "courageous, even resistant, re-processing of global references" (Vihalemm & Keller, 2011, p. 307).

Like the Canadian teeny-boppers and Elvis fans who defied their parents in the 1950s, global consumer culture has strengthened young people's agency within the family, as Asian youth use fast food restaurants, music, and blue jeans to subvert parental control and defy traditional religious and cultural practices (Stearns, 2012). These diverse examples of consumer agency throughout history and across geographies illustrate that while consumer culture shapes children and childhood, it is not a one-way relationship. Young people think and act freely, participate and effect change, and, whether through remarkable ingenuity or the simple practices of everyday life, play a part in defining and reshaping consumer culture.

CONCLUSION—WAYS OF "KNOWING"

Recently, a representative for Canadian-based Spin Master toys spoke to the press about the company's successful bid to become the "master toy partner" for the film *The Secret Life of Pets*. He enthusiastically explained, "With such a variety of fun pet characters, each with their own unique personality, there's a pet that will resonate with every consumer" (Langsworthy, 2016). Not only does this statement betray that the film's characters are designed specifically to resonate with toy purchasers, but it also reveals that the toy company conceives of the film's audience not as "viewers," "fans," or even "children," but as "consumers."

Childhood studies tell us that categories of young people are socially, culturally, politically, and economically constituted within particular historical moments and spaces (see James et al., 2004; Jenkins, 1998; Zelizer, 1985). These constitutions serve the needs of adult-centred social, cultural, political, and economic systems. This brief overview of the dramatic growth of children's consumer culture illustrates how young people have been framed according to the logics and needs of consumer culture. In 1900, the marketplace approached children as one homogenous group, but as the twentieth century progressed, marketers realized that segmenting children into narrower niches offered more intense marketing opportunities, forging such categories as the toddler, the teen, and the tween. These categories are not random divisions or reflections of psychosocial stages of development. Instead they are defined, understood, and organized according to the needs of manufacturers and advertisers.

Child market segments such as the toddler, the teen, and the tween are not replications of real children. Instead, they are imagined constructs of gendered and aged subjectivities. These categories are "figment(s) of the commercial imagination" (Cook, 2004, p. 7), produced to meet the needs of the cultural industries of children (advertising, marketing, media, retail, and technology) as they research, target, and trade their knowledge of children and youth and vie for their attention in the marketplace. In his later work, Cook calls these the "commercial epistemologies of children's consumption" (2011, p. 258). He describes a commercial epistemology as a way of "knowing" about children and youth that serves the interests and needs of the "knower," as in the case of the Spin Master executive quoted above, who only sees the child as a consumer.

As we have shown, data tracking and market research is focused on knowing children as potential customers and audiences in order to understand them as consumers, as opposed to understanding young people in ways to empower them as citizens. The market research conducted on children is interested in youth only as a pattern of consumption and not as a social demographic or as citizens (Davies, Buckingham, & Kelley, 2000; Danesi, 1994). The problem with this is that in segmenting youth into categories constructed purely in market terms, young people are often reduced to objects and are "commodified and marketed back to themselves, stripped of any history, individual identity or power" (Giroux, cited in Brooks, 2003, p. 13). While this may be true, it is also an oversimplification. Young people are not merely passive victims of consumer culture. By looking into the lived experiences of young people in the marketplace, online, and around the world we have offered several examples of young people exercising their agency to shape their own identity and cultural meanings within the framework of consumer culture.

CHAPTER SUMMARY

Together, in this chapter, we

- Traced the example of Lego to show how simple children's toys have evolved into transmedia franchises.
- Outlined the changing ways that children are defined by consumer culture, in particular how they are niched into smaller, tighter market segments such as the toddler, tween, and teen.
- Explored some of the ways that young people have repurposed, negotiated, or resisted the ways that consumer culture frames youth.
- Thought about the ways that consumer culture shapes children's play.
- Have begun to question how young people and young people's consumer culture are central to the evolutions of capitalism.

STUDY QUESTIONS

1. Look at the children's TV shows, films, and toys that are currently available—how do you think that these shape our understandings of gendered childhoods?
2. As the Lego example shows, children have been segmented and niched into smaller and tighter age and gender categories over the course of the past 100 years. Why do you think this has happened? What role do you think consumer culture plays in defining the categories of youth? Engage with the concept of social construction.

3.   Despite the delineation of young people into smaller and smaller marketing niches, which categories of youth are generally underrepresented or missing altogether? Share an example of this exclusion with your class.

4.   Is it ethical for large corporations to track children online, sell their data, or use the content young people produce to promote their brands? What if the privacy policy is clear that young people are engaging in these practices?

5.   What are the ways young people resist the tropes of consumer culture and media culture to push back on how corporations define what it means to be a child? How would you organize children to push back? What would you push back on? What types of actions would you take? How would you incorporate children's own views in these actions?

SUGGESTED RESEARCH ASSIGNMENTS

1.   Identify a children's transmedia franchise and do background research on the franchise; find out who owns the parts of the franchise, what the relationships are between the media companies, where it is promoted, what its history is, how the text has changed over time, who its target audience is, etc. Do you think the franchise uses transmedia to make more money? How does it position children as consumers? Does the transmedia franchise lend itself easily to merchandising? How does it merchandise its product? You may wish to consult Henry Jenkins's blog for more critical analysis of transmedia texts (henryjenkins.org/2007/03/transmedia_storytelling_101.html). Jenkins is the most prominent scholar on transmedia texts.

2.   Find an elder in your community or in your family and conduct an oral history interview of their childhood. Ask them questions about their youth in terms of their consumption and engagement with media. What kinds of things did they have? What did they play with? What items did they desire? Did they go shopping? What was that like? How many things did they own (clothes, toys, etc.). What did they think of these things? What did types of things did other people have? Did they have access to money that they could spend? Ask them questions about advertising. Do they remember ads? What were they like? Where were the ads? What kinds of products do they remember being advertised? Ask questions about the media in terms of how it treated them as an audience. What kind of media did they consume? What kind of stories did the media tell? How did they engage with this media?

SUGGESTED FILMS/VIDEO CLIPS

Consuming Kids

shop.mediaed.org/consuming-kids-p80.aspx

This film, produced by the Media Education Foundation, sheds light on the massive marketing machine that tries to sell a huge array of products to both children and their parents. It incorporates the viewpoints of both industry insiders and critics from a wide range of professions, including the health care industry.

Mickey Mouse Monopoly

shop.mediaed.org/mickey-mouse-monopoly-p112.aspx

This Media Education Foundation film explores how the Walt Disney Company has grown into a global transmedia franchise with unprecedented influence on children's culture over the last century. It deconstructs the ideological biases throughout the Disney franchise, with particular focus on race, gender, and the commercialization of children's culture.

The High Price of Materialism

www.newdream.org/resources/high-price-of-materialism

A short film on consumer culture and how it distracts us from happiness, health, and overall well-being. The film was created for the New American Dream.

The Story of Stuff

storyofstuff.org

A 20-minute online film about the cycle of consumer culture. It details the way we make goods and throw goods away. It also highlights the media and advertising's role in this cycle. While the film doesn't specifically reference children, it is an excellent critical overview on the workings of consumer culture. The website also offers ways to engage with activism on this topic.

SUGGESTED WEBSITES

Campaign for a Commercial-Free Childhood

www.commercialfreechildhood.org

The CCFC was founded in 2000. It is an American organization with the mission to encourage healthy childhoods by limiting commercial access to children.

MediaSmarts

mediasmarts.ca

MediaSmarts is a Canadian organization to help children and youth develop digital and media literacies. The organization has resources for teachers, parents, and young people. There are also research reports on young people's experiences with digital media.

SPARK

www.sparkmovement.org/

SPARK started in 2010 in response to an APA report on the sexualization of girls. SPARK has over 30 partners and its goal is to challenge the negative impacts of the sexualization of girls.

Companies Committed to Kids

cck-eee.ca/en

Formerly the Concerned Children's Advertisers, CCK is a group of companies in Canada such as Google, Mattel, Bell Media, and McDonald's. CCK produces both public service announcements as well teaching materials for children in K–8, as well as resources for parents and caregivers.

The Centre for a New American Dream

www.newdream.org

A website designed to inspire us to find new ways to consume and to reinvent the American dream. Started by Juliet Schor, the idea is to forge a new dream that is based in community, ecological sustainability, and the celebration of nonmaterial values.

REFERENCES

Adams, M. L. (1997). *The trouble with normal: Postwar youth and the making of heterosexuality.* Toronto: University of Toronto Press.

Bailey, J., & Steeves, V. (Eds.). (2015). *eGirls, eCitizens: Putting technology, theory and policy into dialogue with girls' and young women's voices.* Ottawa: University of Ottawa Press.

Braiker, B. (2011, September 26). The next great American consumer. *AdWeek.* Retrieved from www.adweek.com/news/advertising-branding/next-great-american-consumer-135207

Brooks, K. (2003). Nothing sells like teen spirit: The commodification of youth culture. In K. Mallan & S. Pearce (Eds.), *Youth cultures: Texts, images and identities* (pp. 1–16). Westport, CT: Praeger.

Buckingham, D. (2011). *The material child.* Cambridge: Polity.

Common Sense Media. (2013). Zero to eight: Children's media use in America 2013. *Common Sense Media.* Retrieved from www.commonsensemedia.org/research/zero-to-eight-childrens-media-use-in-america-2013

Cook, D. T. (2001, August 20). Lunchbox hegemony? Kids and the marketplace, then and now. *LiP Magazine.* Retrieved from www.alternet.org/story/11370/lunchbox_hegemony_kids_%26_the_marketplace%2C_then_%26_now

Cook, D. T. (2004). *The commodification of childhood: The children's clothing industry and the rise of the child consumer.* Durham: Duke University Press.

Cook, D. T. (2011). Commercial epistemologies of childhood: "Fun" and the leveraging of children's subjectivities and desires. In D. Zwick & J. Cayla (Eds.), *Inside marketing.* Oxford: Oxford University Press.

Coulter, N. (2014). *Tweening the girl: The crystallization of the tween market.* New York: Peter Lang.

Cross, G. (1997). *Kids' stuff: Toys and the changing world of American childhood.* Cambridge, MA: Harvard University Press.

Danesi, M. (1994). *Cool: The signs and meanings of adolescence.* Toronto: University of Toronto Press.

Davies, H., Buckingham, D., & Kelley, P. (2000). In the worst possible taste: Children, television and cultural value. *European Journal of Cultural Studies, 3*(1), 5–25.

De Block, L., & Buckingham, D. (2007). *Global children, global media: Migration, media and childhood.* Basingstoke & New York: Palgrave Macmillan.

Englehardt, T. (1986). The shortcake strategy. In T. Gitlin (Ed.), *Watching television: A Pantheon guide to popular culture* (pp. 68–110). New York: Pantheon.

Ewen, S. (1976). *Captains of consciousness: Advertising and the social roots of the consumer culture.* New York: McGraw-Hill.

Grimes, S. M. (2015). Playing by the market rules: Promotional priorities and commercialization in children's virtual worlds. *Journal of Consumer Culture, 15*(1), 110–134.

Grimes, S. M., & Shade, L. R. (2005). Neopian economics of play. Children's cyberpets and online communities as immersive advertising in NeoPets.com. *International Journal of Media and Cultural Politics, 1*(2), 181.

Ito, M. (2008). Mobilizing the imagination in everyday play: The case of Japanese media mixes. In K. Drotner (Ed.), *International handbook of children, media and culture* (pp. 397–412). Los Angeles: SAGE.

James, A., Jenks, C., & Prout, A. (2004). *Theorizing childhood.* Cambridge: Polity Press.

Jenkins, H. (1998). *The children's culture reader.* New York: NYU Press.

Kelly, R. G. (1974). *Mother was a lady: Self and society in selected American children's periodicals, 1865–1890.* Westport, CT: Greenwood.

Kline, S. (1993). *Out of the garden: Toys, TV, and children's culture in the age of marketing.* New York: Verso.

Langsworthy, B. (2016, March 23). Spin Master confident of Secret Life of Pets success. *Toy News.*

Linn, S. (2005). *Consuming kids: Protecting our children from the onslaught of marketing and advertising.* New York: Random House.

Marney, J. (1990, January 29). Children: The powerful new consumers. *Marketing Magazine,* p. 15.

McNeal, J. U. (1987). *Children as consumers.* Lanham, MD: Lexington Books.

McNeal, J. U., & Yeh, C. H. (1993). Born to shop. *American Demographics, 15*(6), 34.

Osgerby, B. (2002). A caste, a culture, a market: Youth, marketing and lifestyle in postwar America. In R. Strickland (Ed.), *Growing up postmodern* (pp. 15–33). New York: Roman and Littlefield.

Palladino, G. (1996). *Teenagers: An American history.* New York: Basic Books.

Pecora, N. (2004). Nickelodeon grows up: The economic evolution of a network. In H. Hendershot (Ed.), *Nickelodeon nation: The history, politics, and economics of America's only TV channel for kids* (pp. 15–44). New York: NYU Press.

Pybus, J. (2011). The subjective architects: When tweens learn to immaterial labor. *Journal of Communication Inquiry, 35*(4), 403–409.

Quart, A. (2003). *Branded: The buying and selling of teenagers.* London: Arrow.

Ritzer, G., & Jurgenson, N. (2010). Production, consumption, prosumption. *Journal of Consumer Culture, 10*(1), 13–36.

Rosenblatt, B., & Tushnet, R. (2015). Transformative works: Young women's voices on fandom and fair use. In J. Bailey & V. Steeves (Eds.), *eGirls, eCitizens: Putting technology, theory and policy into dialogue with girls' and young women's voices.* Ottawa: University of Ottawa Press.

Schor, J. (2004). *Born to buy: The commercialized child and the new consumer culture.* New York: Scribner.

Schrum, K. (2004). *Some wore bobby sox: The emergence of teenage girls' culture, 1920–1945.* New York: Palgrave Macmillan.

Seiter, E. (1993). *Sold separately: Children and parents in consumer culture.* New Brunswick, NJ: Rutgers University Press.

Selwyn, N. (2009). The digital native—myth and reality. *Aslib Proceedings, 61*(4), 364–379.

Shade, L. R. (2015). I want my Internet! Young women on the politics of usage-based billing. In J. Bailey & V. Steeves (Eds.), *eGirls, eCitizens: Putting technology, theory and policy into dialogue with girls' and young women's voices.* Ottawa: University of Ottawa Press.

Stearns, P. (2012). Globalization and childhoods. In H. Morrison (Ed.), *The global history of childhood reader* (pp. 235–244). Abingdon & New York: Routledge.

Stearns, P. N. (2005). Preface: Globalization and childhood. *Journal of Social History, 38*(4), 845–848.

Steeves, V. (2014a). *Young Canadians in a wired world, phase III: Life online.* Ottawa: MediaSmarts.

Steeves, V. (2014b). *Young Canadians in a wired world, phase III: Trends and recommendations.* Ottawa: MediaSmarts.

Thiel-Stern, S. (2014). *From the dance hall to Facebook: Teen girls, mass media, and moral panic in the United States, 1905–2010.* Boston: University of Massachusetts Press.

Vihalemm, T., & Keller, M. (2011). Looking Russian or Estonian: Young consumers constructing the ethnic "self" and "other." *Consumption, Markets & Culture, 14*(3), 293–309.

Williams, C. (in press). The work of playing: Girls' immaterial labor, smart toys, and the digital economy. In M. Forman-Brunell & D. Anselmo-Sequeira (Eds.), *Girls' economies.* Chicago: University of Illinois Press.

Wise, M. (2008). *Cultural globalization: A user's guide.* Carlton: Blackwell.

Zelizer, V. A. R. (1985). *Pricing the priceless child: the changing social value of children.* New York: Basic Books.

SECTION III

INEQUALITIES AND INTERSECTIONS IN EXPERIENCES OF CHILDHOOD AND YOUTH

In chapter 4, Marnina Gonick introduced us to Amerah, a thoughtful 13-year-old Palestinian immigrant girl from Saudi Arabia who lives in Halifax and chooses to wear the hijab. Her narrative begins with a photograph of a drawing that she made with the words "So Think about It," followed by Internet photos of a woman in a head scarf, the Canadian and Saudi Arabian flags, a view of the Halifax skyline, and an image of a line of people staring wide-eyed, suspicious, and curious. She shares a number of questions that she is constantly bombarded with: Are you bald? Are you forced to wear it? Will they kill you if you take it off? As powerful as these images and words are, her response to them is even more powerful: "I explain that it is because of my religion and that I want to wear it. Canada is freedom. Here I can go out shopping if I want. In Saudi Arabia I only stay inside; I can't go anywhere. So why are they telling me in Canada? ... Everyone should be able to wear what they want ... All people are different. I've thought about it. I'd like others to think about it. So please think about it."

Despite popular beliefs to the contrary, inequalities are structurally embedded in Canadian society. These inequalities often take subtle but enduring forms, as they are reproduced through discourses and institutions that touch the lives of children and youth. As we saw vividly captured in this example, and again in other chapters throughout this collection, children and youth in Canada are deeply affected by material and symbolic inequalities arising from significant, intersecting social divisions like gender, race, class, sexuality, disability, age, and generation. Attention to such intersections is fundamental to a sociological analysis. In this section, as in the example above, we present chapters that explore how inequalities on the basis of class, race, ethnicity, culture, immigration status, Indigeneity, gender, sexuality, and ability play out in the lives of young people in this country. We also see in this collection that children and youth are, or can be, important and invested players in disrupting and chiselling away at barriers created by some of these inequalities. The chapters in this section document some of these key aspects of inequality in the lives of young people. They also advocate ways to address these inequalities, with frequent consideration of young people's voice and participation.

One of the most persistent structural dimensions of inequality is economic, which is why we have opened this section with Patrizia Albanese's chapter 11, "By the Year 2000? Child Poverty in Canada." Albanese takes a close look at enduring rates of poverty in Canada, and their impact on the lives of diverse groups of children. As part of this discussion, Albanese illustrates what poverty means to young people themselves. Through her chapter, readers also get a sense of how things could be done differently in terms of policy to address poverty in Canada.

Historical and enduring inequalities associated with the treatment of Indigenous people in Canada are also crucial to address. In chapter 12, "Settler Colonialism, Biopolitics, and Indigenous Children in Canada," Dale Spencer and Raven Sinclair focus their attention on child protection services. Spencer and Sinclair outline past and current patterns of racism and consequent discrimination to contextualize the severe overrepresentation of Indigenous children and youth at every stage of child protection intervention across Canada. Specifically, they examine the practice of child removal—from the Indian Residential School system, to the so-called Sixties Scoop, to ongoing effects of racism and settler colonialism—in the context of settler colonialism and biopolitics.

A portion of chapter 13, "Giving Voice: Prioritizing Youth Agency in Criminal Justice Diversion" by Marinos, Innocente, and Goodwin-DeFaria, also points to how the erosion of Indigenous culture, through the implementation of the Indian Act and the imposition of residential schools, is at the root of much of the poverty and challenges faced by Indigenous youth who find themselves in the youth criminal justice system. Chapter 13 is concerned with inequalities embedded in the youth criminal justice system and identifies spaces, like youth mental health courts and Aboriginal Youth Courts, where attempts are being made to do things differently, with the hope of overcoming systemic barriers. Seeking ways to mediate the criminalization of marginalized youth, chapter 13 explores how we can prioritize diverse young people's voices and interests through diversionary tactics as well, including extrajudicial measures.

Another group of young people facing high rates of poverty, discrimination, underrepresentation, and silencing are immigrant and refugee children and youth, yet they too play an active role in voicing their concerns and needs. It is well-known that Canada receives tens of thousands of immigrants and refugees annually, but their experiences once in Canada—both positive and negative—are considerably less well documented, and this is especially the case among immigrant children and youth. In chapter 14, "Making Friends, Negotiating Belonging," Erwin Dimitri Selimos shares research done with young people who are fairly recent migrants to Canada—coming either as immigrants or refugees—and explores how they claim a sense of belonging here, particularly with peers. In this way, Selimos focuses on friendship to conceptualize young people as actively involved in negotiating their lives and relationships in Canada to remind us that these processes are firmly linked to context, with inequality, racism, and consequent exclusion shaping the conditions within which their peer negotiations take place.

Gender and sexuality are also key categories of social inequality, and are pivotal to young people's experiences. Gender and gender inequalities significantly shape the expectations and experiences of young people within families, schools, workplaces, extracurricular activities, and beyond (Kimmel, 2016). Andrejek's chapter in section II discussed gender inequality as it is embedded in historic and enduring fairy tales. In this section, we share a chapter that focuses on one concrete example of gender inequality within the school system, and how young people have sought to address it. In chapter 15, "Dress Codes as Gender Politics: Feminist Action in Canadian High Schools," Rebecca Raby and Shauna Pomerantz review reported cases of young people's challenges to their high school dress codes. They highlight how this activism increased dramatically in 2014 and 2015 and how it was newly and notably feminist, drawing attention to students' experiences of gender inequality in the regulation of school dress codes. They also highlight the role of social media in this recent activism.

Schools also figure prominently in research on LGBTQ+ youth. While there are certainly more supports available today for LGBTQ+ youth than in the past, many face bullying, isolation, and rejection from peers and parents, and face a broader society that assumes that everyone is and should be heterosexual. It is frequently in schools that this discrimination can be most intense, and it is in schools where we have seen recent interventions to better support gender and sexual diversity. In chapter 16, "Queer and Trans at School: Gay-Straight Alliances and the Politics of Inclusion," Greensmith and Davies document the gendered and sexual oppressions that some young people can face in their schools, and outline students' work fighting for and building Gay–Straight Alliances (GSAs) as a way to challenge these oppressions, build supportive communities, and foster youth activism. Greensmith and Davies do not present GSAs as a panacea. They recognize that schools need to do far more to be fully inclusive of gender and sexual diversity, and that not all LGBTQ+ youth are comfortable in GSAs, as they can reproduce other forms of inequality, including racism.

Taken together, the chapters in this third section remind us that across young people's lives, including in families, support services, schools, and court systems, we need to better understand how young people variously experience and tackle oppressions and privileges when they are located at different cross-points of social divisions and social inequalities. A starting point is to try to understand children's and youth's perspectives on what inequality, inclusion, and justice mean to them, and then to recognize and value their attempts to change things. The importance of young people's voice and participation, and how we understand these in relation to citizenship, will be the focus of the final section of our collection.

REFERENCE

Kimmel, M. (2016). *The gendered society* (6th ed.). New York: Oxford University Press.

11 By the Year 2000? Child Poverty in Canada

Patrizia Albanese

LEARNING OBJECTIVES

- To identify recent rates and trends in child poverty in Canada
- To see how Canadian numbers and social policies compare to those in other Western nations
- To understand the impact of poverty on children
- To hear from children in terms of what poverty means to them
- To consider some examples of children's engagement and agency, on what can and should be done to overcome poverty

INTRODUCTION—CHILD POVERTY RATES AND TRENDS

I blinked repeatedly at a Facebook post, not believing my eyes. I was looking at recent photos of products on grocery store shelves: a cabbage with a price tag of $28.54; a tub of peanut butter, $17.99; a roll of Pillsbury dough in the store refrigerator, $15.77. These were examples of the cost of food in northern communities in Canada. It is no wonder then that when grade 4 and 5 students in North Bay, Ontario, were asked, "What is poverty?" one child answered by saying: "pretending that you forgot your lunch" (Canadian Teachers' Federation, 2009, p. 3). Across Canada, in both urban and rural communities, far too many Canadian children go to school hungry because of the high cost of food, parental underemployment, low minimum wages, and a shortage of government policies that could help prevent families from falling into poverty in the first place.

There is no doubt that when we talk about child poverty, we are actually, in most cases, referring to family poverty. Most children and youth are poor because their parent(s) is/are poor. In this chapter, I limit the discussion to child poverty because in some cases, youth are poor or street-involved as a result of other factors affecting their home environments, at times unrelated to economic disadvantages (for example, in the case of domestic abuse or fear of coming "out" to parents). That said, understanding poverty, and the social policies that frame it, is fundamentally important within child and youth studies because of the exceptionally profound and far-reaching consequences of poverty on young people's lives today. Understanding child poverty not only showcases a range of class-based inequalities and their impact on and relationship to children, but also clearly demonstrates the compounded impact of a plurality of intersecting inequalities based on social class, race, immigration status, **Indigeneity**, and the realities of living with a disability.

In this chapter you will read about some of the persistent inequalities and high rates of child poverty in this country and across social groups of children. We will see how Canadian numbers compare to those in other Western nations. The chapter will then present research on the impact of poverty on children. While important and insightful, this research often fails to include input from children themselves. Paternalistic approaches to understanding this important issue have led many to avoid asking children what it means to be poor. Thankfully, a small number of studies have done so. This chapter looks at some striking similarities across a handful of research projects that collected insightful views from children living on three distinct continents. Their thoughts on poverty *should* be enough to stun policy makers into attention and action. Unfortunately, this is not the case, as we will also see that Canadian social policies fall far short of politicians' publicly stated goals of eradicating child poverty. The chapter ends with reflections and examples of children's engagement and **agency**, as they and concerned adults challenge leaders to finally fulfill the (seemingly empty) political promises made to them.

Since the late 1980s Canadian political leaders have made a number of national and international commitments to eradicate child poverty in this country. Most notably, in 1989, in an all-party resolution, the Canadian Parliament unanimously pledged to eradicate child poverty by the year 2000. Yet in the year 2000, child poverty rates were actually *higher* than they had been in 1989 (Campaign 2000, 2015), and on the twenty-fifth anniversary of that pledge—and approximately 15 years after that missed deadline—some 19 percent of children in Canada were living in poverty (Campaign 2000, 2014; 2015). Even more disturbing is that 40 percent of Canada's **Indigenous** children live in poverty (Campaign 2000, 2015; for more on the historical legacy of colonial policies affecting Indigenous children, see chapter 12 in this collection). Between one-quarter and one-third of all recent immigrant children (33 percent), **racialized** children (26 percent), and children raised in single-parent families (26.6 percent) live in poverty (National Council of Welfare, 2009). Children with disabilities are also disproportionately likely to be living in poverty (Campaign 2000, 2015).

In recent years, child poverty rates have surpassed the 1989 rates in Prince Edward Island, Nova Scotia, New Brunswick, Ontario, Manitoba, Saskatchewan, and British Columbia, and hover at about 33 percent in Nunavut, a territory that did not exist in 1989 (Campaign 2000, 2014). In most of these provinces, increases in poverty rates are the result of recent economic downturns that negatively impacted the manufacturing and resources sectors of provincial economies. This has resulted in parental job losses in what were once relatively secure and well-paid occupations. Many recent **immigrants** to Canada find themselves landing in these uncertain economic circumstances alongside their Canadian counterparts, while at the same time having their foreign credentials questioned or outright disregarded (see e.g. Li & Li, 2008).

Children living in poverty are now disproportionately likely to be living with a parent or parents who work one or more part-time jobs that offer low wages, poor job security, and few or no benefits, often in the **service sector** of the Canadian economy (see Galarneau & Fecteau, 2014). According to a Statistics Canada survey conducted in 2013, the average hourly wage of (full-time) employees who were paid by the hour was $22.27 (this, for example, was the average for those employed in the shrinking manufacturing sector [Galarneau & Fecteau, 2014]). The growing number of those earning the minimum wage, on average, earned 46 percent of the average hourly earnings of other Canadians. While a large number of those earning the minimum wage were younger Canadians, the proportion of all paid employees (including adults/parents) earning the minimum wage was 17 percent among those in retail trade (the largest employer of Canadians) and 27 percent in accommodation and food services industries. Statistics Canada revealed that these two industries alone accounted for over 60 percent of all employees earning the minimum wage in 2013 (Galarneau & Fecteau, 2014). As a result of low wages and other profound economic inequalities, a growing proportion of Canadian families with children rely on the use of food banks to meet their daily needs (Food Banks Canada, 2015). More than one-third of the more than 850,000 people who access food banks each month in this country are children (Food Banks Canada, 2015). It is important to note that many of their parents earn the bulk of their income through (low) paid work. In the current economic climate, many parents are forced to work (multiple) part-time and low-waged jobs.[1]

HOW DO WE COMPARE?

Despite the relatively low value of the Canadian dollar, high cost of living (and especially housing), and fluctuating oil prices that have in recent years negatively affected western Canada, it is widely noted that Canada was not as devastatingly hard-hit as the United States and many European nations by the global economic crisis of 2008 (see UNICEF, 2014). That said, UNICEF's Report Card on Child Poverty (UNICEF, 2014) revealed that despite slight improvements since 2008, some 20 percent of Canada's children lived in poverty in 2012. This placed Canada in the middle of the pack of the 41 nations that were compared; it placed below Australia, Czech Republic, France, Germany, Japan, Korea, Poland, Slovakia, and Slovenia, and very far below Scandinavian countries that are consistently far better in their policies' treatment of children and families (UNICEF, 2014).

A recent report from the Organisation for Economic Co-operation and Development (OECD) similarly revealed that Canada placed in about the middle of the 34 economically "advanced" nations that were compared (OECD, 2014). OECD (2014) reports put Canadian child poverty rates at just above the average among the OECD counties compared, making Canada one of the wealthiest countries in the world, with one of the higher rates of child poverty. Clearly many other nations, equally negatively affected by the global economic crisis, are doing things differently from Canada when it comes to implementing policies and programs that help keep children, youth, and families out of poverty.

PARENTAL INCOMES AND SELECT CHILD OUTCOMES

What does this level of poverty mean for Canada's children? Canadian and international research reveals that parental incomes affect child outcomes into adolescence and adulthood. Without question, poverty and inadequate housing negatively affect children's health and contribute to childhood obesity, high rates of diabetes, lead poisoning, respiratory infections, and a wide range of other chronic health problems (Kakinami et al., 2014; Kovesi, 2012; Raphael, 2011; Séguin, Qian, Potvin, Zunzunegui, & Frohlich, 2003). What is at times less obvious is that on top of the troubling health outcomes of poverty, children's academic success and school engagement have been negatively affected; so too has children's self-esteem (for more on school engagement, see Bélanger in this collection). This in turn has made an already invisible group of young people even more **marginalized** and silenced.

The achievement gap—the difference between the learning (i.e. achievement) of students living in poverty and their peers—has been well documented in research coming out of the US (Kennedy, 2010; McGee, 2004; Morgan, 2012). While our Canadian social safety net is intended to shelter children and families from such a gap, we continue to see comparable inequity in outcomes in Canada as well (Burton, Phipps, & Zhang, 2014). Thus, while the specific statistics may vary (Levin, 2007), the actual impact of this inequality does not (Davies & Aurini, 2013). American research revealed that on the 2001 third-grade Illinois Standards Achievement Test (ISAT), for example, 40 percent of low-income students met state reading standards, compared to 75 percent of their peers (McGee, 2004). Comparable differences were found among math scores, across different age groups, and across jurisdictions (Gazeley, 2010; Kennedy, 2010; McGee, 2004; Morgan, 2012). To further mark such inequities, Canadian research by Davies and Aurini (2013) found that socioeconomic disparities in learning tended to widen over the summer months, when children from affluent families actually gained literacy, while those from poorer families lost it. It goes without saying, then, that if some children do not have the family or community resources to help them develop their reading skills to the same level as their peers, they will face a disproportionate number of barriers as they progress through the school system.

There are many reasons why children living in low-income families achieve lower scores, and most have to do with not having access to the same resources as other children, as was implied by Davies and Aurini's (2013) research on the widening gaps in literacy across socioeconomic groups over the summer months. A British study, too, examined the key barriers to learning among pupils from low-income backgrounds (Demie & Lewis, 2011). The study's findings suggest that one of the main reasons for pupil underachievement identified in their case study of schools and in focus groups is **social deprivation**—a vaguely defined term commonly used in the UK to refer to a combination of structural factors that prevent people from having access to diverse aspects of their culture and society. The social deprivation experienced by students living in economically strained families was found to be perpetuated by factors such as feelings of marginalization within the community, a lack of community and school engagement (due to lack of funds for diverse activities), low levels of parental engagement (because of the demands of work, or parental alienation from the school system), and lack of targeted support to break the cycle of poverty and disadvantage (Demie & Lewis, 2011). Some Canadian teachers have helped to concretize the presence of some of these factors in the lived realities that accompany the class bias, stigma, **power** differences, and economic inequalities experienced by some of their students. The Canadian Teachers' Federation (2009), for example, quoted some of their members, teachers in Ontario, who shared their observations in the classroom. Teachers wrote about students who move and change schools frequently during the school year because their families don't have enough money to pay the rent, inevitably contributing to feelings of marginalization. Other teachers described students' feelings of alienation, and "students who shrink from shame or lash out from anger and who feel the stigma of poverty" (Canadian Teachers' Federation, 2009, p. 3).

The effect of poverty and income disparity on the psychological well-being of children and youth has been well documented (Ho, Li, & Chan, 2015). Educational achievement is influenced by a myriad of complex and interrelated processes and some have argued that improving educational achievement for students must incorporate strategies aimed at fostering positive self-esteem, while reducing stigma, marginalization, and feelings of social exclusion (Smith, 2004). Many have argued that school engagement matters (see Bélanger in this collection). In fact, motivation and engagement have long been highlighted as key factors in children's academic development (Kennedy, 2010).

Children need to be given opportunities to participate and become more actively involved in school activities. When parents cannot afford school trips or special school activities or school lunches, children are stigmatized. This in turn affects children's effort, concentration, persistence, and contributions in class (Kennedy, 2010). Social engagement in school is important for children's emotional well-being, which in turn affects their ability and openness to learn (Kennedy, 2010). Children themselves are well aware of this.

CHILDREN'S VIEWS ON POVERTY

A small number of researchers around the world have taken the time to ask children about their views on and understanding of poverty. Horgan (2009), on behalf of Save the Children, for example, spoke to children in Northern Ireland who lived in disadvantaged neighbourhoods. Horgan (2009) found that children who were seven years of age and older had a clear sense of what it was like to live in relative poverty. Despite living under very different social, economic, and political circumstances, Saidov (n.d.), for UNICEF, had similar findings for children in Tajikistan. The responses of children in Northern Ireland and in Tajikistan to the question "What does it mean to be poor?" were not dissimilar to those of children in Canada (Canadian Teachers' Federation, 2008).

Despite significant variations within and across countries, a few things were evident in children's responses to the question "What does it mean to be poor?" First, children of almost all ages could easily recognize poverty when they saw it. Children in Tajikistan, like those in Canada and Northern Ireland, noted that poor people dressed differently, had less access to good food, and were less able to purchase school supplies or participate in school activities like other children. For example, Saidov quoted Radjabali, age 12, from Khamadoni, Tajikistan, as saying the following:

> Poor people are different from the rich. They buy cheap food and goods. Children from poor families wear slippers or galoshes. They carry textbooks and notebooks in plastic bags because they have no school bags. They go to school in the same clothes they wear at home. Their parents cannot afford school uniforms. (Saidov, n.d., p. 26)

Saidov also quoted Chasurbek, a 10-year-old child from Sabo village in Shahrinav, Tajikistan, as saying, "children suffer most from poverty because they want to wear clothes and shoes as well as those of children from well-to-do families. Parents of such children cannot pay for school [or] buy all the supplies necessary for their children to study" (Saidov, n.d., p. 33).

The Canadian Teachers' Federation (2008, p. 3) uncovered similar responses from grade 4 and 5 students in North Bay, Ontario, who said that poverty is "Not buying books at the book fair" or "Not getting to go on school trips."

The responses of children in Northern Ireland echoed these. For example, Horgan (2009) presented the views of a 15-year-old girl and 16-year-old boy, who together said of poor children that "they don't have the things everyone else has like trainers, a nice school bag ... it starts towards the end of primary school and the start of secondary school, and it doesn't end" (Horgan, 2009, p. 9). A nine-year-old girl said, "They can't go on trips from schools;" a nine-year-old boy shared that "they aren't able to go places and do stuff, like Funderland [an amusement park];" and a seven-year-old girl contributed that "you might not get so much treats" (Horgan, 2009, p. 4).

When reviewing quotes from the children interviewed in these three very diverse locations, it became obvious that children were well aware of the stigma and feelings of shame associated with poverty. They clearly articulated, in ways that some adults (including some politicians and policy makers who can make a difference) are not willing or able to do, that poverty in childhood often amounts to social exclusion.

Saidov (n.d) for example, cited Saida, a student from Khodjent, Tajikistan, as saying, "A poor person keeps his head low, he is always thinking of where and how to earn his living; he is ashamed of his clothes and he does not say much" (Saidov, n.d., pp. 26–27). On social stigma, a grade 4/5 student in North Bay, Ontario, mentioned that poverty is "feeling ashamed when my dad can't get a job" (Canadian Teachers' Federation, 2008, p. 3). Not far off, children in Northern Ireland spoke about how poverty contributed to children being left out. For example, a nine-year-old girl living in a rural area said, "They can't go to parties … because they might not have enough money to buy a present for the kid and they might not have enough money to buy a car to take them there (Horgan, 2009, p. 9); and an eight-year-old explained that "they might be picked on or something. Or they might be left alone rather than brought into lots of games" (Horgan, 2009, p. 9).

Often, parents do their best to try to protect their children from the realities of poverty, but children are perceptive. Despite living under very different circumstances, children in these various locations recognized the difficulties parents faced when they could not pull their children out of poverty. Children across these locations were well aware of how worrying about money negatively affected parents' well-being. For example, ten-year-old Mavzuna from Khodjent, Tajikistan, said, "They want their children to be raised in good conditions and comfort. They are always upset and miserable thinking about it" (Saidov, n.d., p. 27). Similarly, a child from Northern Ireland said, "it can be kinda depressing, you know, knowing that they (parents) are depressed about bills and things" (Horgan, 2009, p. 8).

As a nine-year-old girl from Northern Ireland revealed, children demonstrated an acute awareness of the demands on their parents. She noted that "mummies and daddies have to pay … in our school there was letters going out and they have to pay like £2 for … the Peter Pan Adventure wee thing, and then there was £2 for a trip and there's £2 and £2 and there's lots of different things (Horgan, 2009, p. 8). Recognizing the pressure on parents, a child in North Bay, Ontario, similarly noted that poverty meant "being afraid to tell your Mom you need gym shoes" (Canadian Teachers' Federation, 2008, p. 3).

The causes of poverty around the world are many and varied, as are the consequences and outcomes. That said, the eerily similar insights provided by children in distinct parts of the world reminds us of the importance of asking for and listening to input from children. Children's insight into what poverty is and does reveals that children see and understand it, and that too many, unfortunately, feel it firsthand. Acting as if poverty does not exist when we are in the presence of children (in the same way that Chen, in this collection, notes is happening with racism in children's books) is not only pointless, as we saw from the quotes above, it is irresponsible. We delude ourselves by claiming

Box 11.1: Children as Agents of Change

Instead of shielding the perceptive eyes of young people from the realities of poverty, some projects have engaged young people in their efforts to bring and keep the issue of poverty on the political agenda and in the public eye, and one focuses on schools. The Canadian Teachers' Federation (2014), for example, on top of issuing a discussion booklet entitled *Poverty, What Is It?* for students in grades 5 to 8, brought together 55 students and 30 teachers from around the country, in Ottawa, for two days in November 2014, to support Keep the Promise, an anti-poverty campaign (Théoret, 2015). This event followed months of students' preparatory work in their respective classrooms, back in their home communities. In November 2014, students and teachers came together to share their ideas on how to best tackle poverty on a local and national level. On this brief trip, students met with Members of Parliament, Senators, and community-based organizations that work with people living in poverty (Théoret, 2015). Students also voiced their concerns and shared their insights via a public town hall on November 18, 2014, that was livestreamed and posted on YouTube (www.youtube.com/watch?v=ml5Gyw3l9Zl&list=PLsaWW-2mRW4PkBQjZvdBnYg3tV2KWTE4; for a similar initiative in the UK, see www.appgpoverty.org.uk/childrens-voices/).

This initiative was part of the Canadian Teachers' Federation's social justice program, Imagineaction, which offers educational resources and tools to help teachers facilitate class discussions and local initiatives related to key social justice issues in children's communities (see www.imagine-action.ca). Among other things, this initiative has helped teachers and students develop school-based community social action projects that address the issue of poverty in their communities. To facilitate students' community-based social action, Imagineaction offers online resources and support, along with small school subsidies to offset project expenses. Similar initiatives have been tried by other organizations, in other jurisdictions, and in other countries (for example, see one in the UK, as noted above).

to be "protecting" children from poverty by remaining silent about it in their presence. Only vigorous efforts to eradicate poverty can "protect" children and their parents from it, and Canadian social policies currently fall far short of this. There are numerous examples of how things can be done differently, including examples where children themselves are agents of change (see box 11.1).

DOING THINGS DIFFERENTLY

Years ago, the North Central Regional Education Laboratory (NCREL) published a study of high-performing, high-poverty schools in Wisconsin (McGee, 2004). They found the schools that performed the best had common characteristics, including purposeful and proactive administrative leadership, a strong sense of community, student-centred programs and services designed around individual needs, staff-initiated professional-development opportunities, peer coaching, project-based instruction, strong parent and community involvement, small class sizes, and a range of alternative support programs (McGee, 2004).

These initiatives reveal a recognition of the importance of heightened efforts to improve student engagement and teacher awareness through strong leadership and children's involvement in community work and activism. Lawson and Lawson (2013) underscore that student engagement, particularly among students challenged by poverty, social exclusion, and isolation, is an important and emerging area of research and policy. Clearly more can and should be done at both the local level and when it comes to national policy.

NATIONAL POLICY AND SOCIAL (IN)ACTION

Howe and Covell (2003) remind us that by ratifying the UN Convention on the Rights of the Child (CRC) in 1991, Canada is obligated to advance the basic economic security rights of children. Instead, policies and services targeting children and youth in economic need remain underfunded or marginalized (Gharabaghi & Stuart, 2010). Reports by international organizations measuring Canada's formal commitments to children, and particularly to those living in poverty, have been scathing. For example, the Committee on the Rights of the Child (2012), an international body put in place to measure national adherence to the CRC, noted that Canada's action on poverty reduction has been poor.

In their concluding observations following the third and fourth periodic review of Canada, on the standard of living of Canada's children, the Committee stated that "while the Committee appreciates that the basic needs of the majority of children in the State party are met, it is concerned that income inequality is widespread and growing and that no national strategy has been developed to comprehensively address child poverty despite a commitment by Parliament to end child poverty by 2000" (UNICEF Canada, 2013, p. 15).

The Committee was especially concerned about the inequitable distribution of tax benefits and social transfers for children in need, and about the limited provision of welfare services to Indigenous children (UNICEF Canada, 2013). This point was recently underscored by a January 26, 2016, landmark ruling that the Canadian government is racially discriminating against over 160,000 Indigenous children and their families by providing inequitable child welfare services (see First Nations Child and Family Caring Society of Canada, 2016). The Committee therefore recommended that the Canadian state

a.   Develop and implement a national, coordinated strategy to eliminate child poverty as part of the broader national poverty reduction strategy, which should include annual targets to reduce child poverty;

b.   Assess the impact of tax benefits and social transfers and ensure that they give priority to children in the most vulnerable and disadvantaged situations;

c.   Ensure that funding and other support, including welfare services, provided to Aboriginal, African-Canadian, and other minority children, including welfare services, is comparable in quality and accessibility to services provided to other children in the State party and is adequate to meet their needs. (UNICEF Canada, 2013, p. 16)

Improving Canada's reputation and international standing when it comes to child poverty involves commitment by many, and on many levels. Improving the lives of all of Canada's children involves more than simply putting more money into existing programs—though that may be a short-term solution. Instead, real change and real improvement can only come from national, provincial, and local commitments to do things differently and better. This calls for a reorientation in our thinking. While there are challenges and limitations to being a federation with a decentralized governance structure, steps can still be taken towards building a more **social democratic** approach to social policy, as was the case at the provincial level in Quebec and at the national level in Sweden, and among numerous other countries and jurisdictions that have less wealth than Canada as a whole, but lower child poverty rates.

Quebec, for example, has been one of the most progressive provinces in the country when it comes to taking action on poverty, as it was the first province to introduce a legislated poverty reduction strategy, in 2002. Following broad-based discussions among a coalition of individuals and organizations across the province and widespread public consultations, the Government of Quebec, in 2002, unanimously passed an Act to Combat Poverty and Social Exclusion. Two years later, in 2004, the Government released its first five-year action plan on poverty (it released its second in May 2010). It also rolled out an array of policies and programs, including improved parental leave benefits and universal $5 per day child care, aimed at improving parental employment options and reducing unemployment rates (Albanese, 2011).

While far from perfect, Quebec's policies have yielded some significant changes. Quebec has gone from having among the lowest rates of female labour-force participation and dual-earning families to among the highest. For example, according to Statistics Canada, in 2014, only Saskatchewan (at 74 percent) had a higher proportion than Quebec (at 73 percent) of dual-earning families among couple families with children. In 1976, the corresponding proportion for Quebec was among the lowest, at 29 percent of couple families with children (Uppal, 2015). At the same time, Quebec had the lowest proportion of families with a stay-at-home parent in 2014, at 13 percent. This was a significant change from 1976, when Quebec had the highest proportion (59 percent) of such families (Uppal, 2015). The proportion of families with a stay-at-home parent declined faster in Quebec than in other regions of the country (Uppal, 2015). This is not to say that having a stay-at-home parent does not benefit children (if the family is economically able to support this); however, for the average Canadian child, the economic benefits of having more than one parent in the labour force are undeniable.

The lessons from Quebec and from social democratic nations like Sweden and Finland are clear. Tackling child poverty requires a national strategy and a legislated, unified, and holistic plan that integrates a range of ministries (education, employment, social services, etc.) and branches of government. It requires a commitment to providing universal programs and services that prevent individuals and families from falling into strained economic circumstances in the first place. It requires, among other things, a (progressive) taxation system that is more equitable; a national housing strategy committed to providing more affordable housing; higher minimum wages; improved short-term parental leaves that reach beyond the first year of their child's life; affordable postsecondary education; a recognition of foreign credentials, where applicable; and more and better apprenticeship and training (and retraining) programs. Only when policies and programs are understood to be interrelated, and planned in tandem, can we begin to build a better, more just society. This country desperately needs a national family policy, a national anti-poverty strategy, a national housing policy, and a firm commitment to a national children's agenda (with teeth). All the while, such policies should be sensitive and responsive to the diverse needs of children residing in different regions of Canada (urban/rural/remote; provinces/territories; north/south), raised in diverse family forms, who may be living with a disability, under different social circumstances, and from different cultural backgrounds. A one-size-fits-all solution would not receive provincial approval, nor would it be effective. Instead, policies that have their roots in a commitment to cultivating a more just society for all of Canada's children might stand a chance. As we begin to consider our options, Canadian adults need to recognize, acknowledge, include, foster, and amplify the voices and rights of children in this country. Because, after all, whatever we do to improve the lives of children can only stand to benefit our country as a whole.

CHAPTER SUMMARY

Together, in this chapter, we

- Reviewed recent rates and trends when it comes to child poverty and considered who is most vulnerable and why.
- Sought to understand the impact of poverty on children, with a focus on the impact related to children's education and learning.
- Read about and mapped similarities and differences in children's responses to the question of what poverty means to them.
- Reviewed types of social policy responses to poverty to see how Canada's policies compare to those in other Western nations.

- Saw examples of children's engagement as they considered what can and should be done to overcome poverty.

STUDY QUESTIONS

1. Looking around your community, what would you say are the most evident structural factors (as identified in the chapter) contributing to child poverty?
2. Why do you believe that we continue to use the concept of "child poverty" when we know that most children are poor because their parents are poor? Why not simply refer to it as "poverty" or "family poverty"?
3. Have you or any of the people around you been touched by poverty? How has it affected your approach to studying this issue?
4. You have been asked to advise the federal government on the most effective measures to tackle child poverty in this country. What would you tell the prime minister? How might you engage children in your efforts?
5. Imagine that you decide to do research on child poverty that includes input from children. What might that research look like? What do you anticipate would be your biggest challenges? How would you propose to overcome them?

SUGGESTED RESEARCH ASSIGNMENT

Identify three countries with significantly different child poverty rates. Doing background research, identify what you believe accounts for the differing rates. Be sure to consider social policies, government funding of social services/programs, economic factors, etc. that may be contributing to the differences.

SUGGESTED FILMS/VIDEO CLIPS

Child Poverty in Canada: Why are 10 percent of kids poor?
www.youtube.com/watch?v=qt6s1maEMtw
This TVO clip outlines trends in child poverty in Canada since the 1989 resolution to end child poverty by the year 2000. Panelists Peter Clutterbuck, Theresa Schrader, Brigitte Kitchen, and Nance Ackerman discuss why so many children are poor in a rich nation.

Just Eat It—A Food Waste Story
www.foodwastemovie.com/
In *Just Eat It*, filmmakers Grant Baldwin and Jen Rustemeyer go dumpster diving to teach families about the shocking amount of food we waste.

Listen to This

listentothisdocumentary.com/

This documentary tells the story of pianist Thompson Egbo-Egbo, who created a music program for children living in an economically disadvantaged community in the Jane and Finch area of Toronto.

People of a Feather

www.peopleofafeather.com/

In this documentary, Joel Heath and the community of Sanikiluaq teach children about Indigenous communities and about life in changing regions of northern Canada.

Poor No More

www.youtube.com/watch?v=GIWrol1wymg

Poor No More is a documentary about average Canadians who are worrying about how to make ends meet.

SUGGESTED WEBSITES

Campaign 2000

campaign2000.ca/

Campaign 2000, created in 1991, is a vibrant network of national, regional, and local partner organizations that have come together with a commitment to working to end child and family poverty in Canada

National Child Benefit

www.nationalchildbenefit.ca/eng/home.shtml

The National Child Benefit (NCB) is a joint initiative of Canada's federal, provincial, and territorial governments. The initiative combines two key elements: federal monthly payments to low-income families with children, and benefits and services designed and delivered by the provinces, territories, and First Nations to meet the needs of low-income families with children.

Social Planning Network of Ontario

www.spno.ca/

The Social Planning Network of Ontario has existed since 1991. It is a coalition of social planning councils, community development councils, resource centres, and planning committees from across Ontario. They are connected in the cause of effecting change on social policies, conditions, and issues.

UNICEF, *The State of the World's Children*

www.unicef.org/sowc/

UNICEF's *The State of the World's Children* is their flagship publication, which closely examines a key issue affecting children each year. The report includes supporting data and statistics on the status of children around the world.

NOTE

1. Part-time and low-waged work used to be seen as jobs held by youth (entry-level or after-school, weekend, and summer work). Now part-time work has become a norm among employers looking to cut labour costs (and benefits). With more people competing for part-time work, youth unemployment rates remain high (Campaign 2000, 2014), even in parts of the country where the economy has "bounced back" from a recent recession and the global economic crisis.

REFERENCES

Albanese, P. (2011). Addressing the interlocking complexity of paid work and care: Lessons from changing family policy in Quebec. In C. Krull & J. Sempruch (Eds.), *A life in balance? Reopening the family-work debate* (pp. 130–143). Vancouver: UBC Press.

Burton, P., Phipps, S., & Zhang, L. (2014). The prince and the pauper: Movement of children up and down the Canadian income distribution. *Canadian Public Policy, 40*(2), 111–125.

Campaign 2000. (2014). *2014 report card on child and family poverty, 25 years later: We can fix this.* Toronto: Campaign 2000. Retrieved from www.campaign2000.ca/anniversaryreport/CanadaRC2014EN.pdf

Campaign 2000. (2015). *2015 report card on child and family poverty: Let's do this, let's end child poverty for good.* Toronto: Campaign 2000. Retrieved from www.campaign2000.ca/reportCards/2015RepCards/NationalReportCardEn2015.pdf

Canadian Teachers' Federation. (2008). *Child poverty and schools.* Brief Presented to the Senate Committee on Social Affairs, Science and Technology. Retrieved from www.ctf-fce.ca/Research-Library/Brief-reChildPovertyandSchools-eng.pdf

Canadian Teachers' Federation. (2009). *Supporting education ... building Canada. Child poverty and schools.* Background Material for Parliamentarians and Staff. CTF Hill Day 2009. Ottawa: Canadian Teachers Federation. Retrieved from www.ctf-fce.ca/Research-Library/FINAL_Hilldayleavebehind_eng.pdf

Canadian Teachers' Federation. (2014). *Poverty, what is it? A discussion booklet for students in Grades 5 to 8.* Ottawa: Canadian Teacher's Federation. Retrieved from www.imagine-action.ca/Documents/KTP/Poverty-Discussion-Booklet.pdf

Committee on the Rights of the Child. (2012). Concluding observations on the combined third and fourth periodic report of Canada, adopted by the Committee at its sixty-first session (17 September–5 October 2012). CRC/C/CAN/CO/3-4. United Nations. Retrieved from tbinternet.ohchr.org/_layouts/treaty-bodyexternal/Download.aspx?symbolno=CRC/C/CAN/CO/3-4&Lang=En

Davies, S., & Aurini, J. (2013). Summer learning inequality in Ontario. *Canadian Public Policy, 39*(2), 287–307.

Demie, F., & Lewis, K. (2011). White working class achievement: An ethnographic study of barriers to learning in schools. *Educational Studies, 37*(3), 245–264.

First Nations Child and Family Caring Society of Canada. (2016). *I am a witness: Human rights tribunal hearing*. Ottawa: First Nations Child and Family Caring Society of Canada. Retrieved from fncaringsociety.com/i-am-witness

Food Banks Canada. (2015). *HungerCount 2015*. Toronto: Food Banks Canada. Retrieved from www.foodbankscanada.ca/getmedia/01e662ba-f1d7-419d-b40c-bcc71a9f943c/HungerCount2015_singles.pdf.aspx

Galarneau, D., & Fecteau, E. (2014). The ups and downs of minimum wage. *Insights on Canadian Society*. Catalogue no. 75-006-X. Ottawa: Statistics Canada. Retrieved from www.statcan.gc.ca/pub/75-006-x/2014001/article/14035-eng.pdf

Gazeley, L. (2010). The role of school exclusion processes in the re-production of social and educational disadvantage. *British Journal of Educational Studies, 58*(3), 293–309.

Gharabaghi, K., & Stuart, C. (2010). Voices from the periphery: Prospects and challenges for the homeless youth service sector. *Children & Youth Services Review, 32*(12), 1683–1689.

Ho, K. Y., Li, W., & Chan, S. (2015). The effect of poverty and income disparity on the psychological well-being of Hong Kong children. *Public Health Nursing, 32*(3), 212–221.

Horgan, G. (2009). *Speaking out against poverty*. Retrieved from www.savethechildren.org.uk/sites/default/files/docs/SOAP_Booklet_1.pdf

Howe, B., & Covell, K. (2003). Child poverty in Canada and the rights of the child. *Human Rights Quarterly, 25*(4), 1067–1087.

Kakinami, L., Saguin, L., Lambert, M., Gauvin, L., Nikiema, B., & Paradis, G. (2014). Poverty's latent effect on adiposity during childhood: Evidence from a Québec birth cohort. *Journal of Epidemiology & Community Health, 68*(3), 239–245.

Kennedy, E. (2010). Narrowing the achievement gap: Motivation, engagement, and self-efficacy matter. *Journal of Education, 190*(3), 1–11.

Kovesi, T. (2012). Respiratory disease in Canadian First Nations and Inuit children/Les maladies respiratoires chez les enfants inuits et des Premières nations du Canada. *Paediatrics & Child Health, 17*(7), 376–380.

Lawson, M. A., & Lawson, H. A. (2013). New conceptual frameworks for student engagement research, policy, and practice. *Review of Educational Research, 83*(3), 432–479.

Levin, B. (2007). Schools, poverty, and the achievement gap. *Phi Delta Kappan, 89*(1), 75–76.

Li, P., & Li, E. X. (2008). University-educated immigrants from China to Canada: Rising number and discounted value. *Canadian Ethnic Studies, 40*(3), 1–16.

McGee, G. W. (2004). Closing the achievement gap: Lessons from Illinois' golden spike high-poverty high-performing schools. *Journal of Education for Students Placed at Risk, 9*(2), 97–125.

Morgan, H. (2012). Poverty-stricken schools: What we can learn from the rest of the world and from successful schools in economically disadvantaged areas in the US. *Education, 133*(2), 291–297.

National Council of Welfare. (2009). *Poverty Profile 2007. (Report #3)*. Retrieved from www.cwp-csp.ca/wp-content/uploads/2011/07/2009-A-Snapshot-of-Children-Living-in-Poverty-NCW1.pdf

Organisation for Economic Co-operation and Development (OECD). (2014). CO2.2: Child poverty. *OECD Family Database*. OECD: Social Policy Division: Directorate of Employment, Labour and Social Affairs. Retrieved from www.oecd.org/els/soc/CO_2_2_Child_Poverty.pdf

Raphael, D. (2011). Poverty in childhood and adverse health outcomes in adulthood. *Maturitas, 69*(1), 22–26.

Saidov, F. (n.d.). Children's voices: A qualitative study of poverty in Tajikistan. UNICEF. Retrieved from www.unicef.org/ceecis/070501-Taj-ChildrensVoices.pdf

Séguin, L., Qian, X., Potvin, L., Zunzunegui, M.-V., & Frohlich, K. (2003). Effects of low income on infant health. *CMAJ: Canadian Medical Association Journal, 168*(12), 1533–1538.

Smith, V. G. (2004). Strategies for educators: A six-step program. *Challenge, 11*(1), 17–32.

Théoret, P. (2015). Canadian students raise their voices about child poverty. *Perspectives, 16*. Retrieved from perspectives.ctf-fce.ca/en/article/3066/

UNICEF. (2014). Innocenti Report Card 12: Children in the Developed World. *Children of the Recession: The impact of the economic crisis on child well-being in rich countries*. Florence: UNICEF. Retrieved from www.unicef.ca/sites/default/files/imce_uploads/images/reports/unicef_report_card_12_children_of_the_recession.pdf

UNICEF Canada. (2013). *Recommendations for Canada from the UN Committee on the Rights of the Child*. The Office of the Provincial advocate for children and Youth, Ontario. Retrieved from cwrp.ca/sites/default/files/publications/en/UNICEF_concluding_observations_in_youth_friendly_language_EN_1.pdf

Uppal, S. (2015). Employment patterns of families with children. *Insights on Canadian Society*. Catalogue no. 75-006-X. Ottawa: Statistics Canada. Retrieved from www.statcan.gc.ca/pub/75-006-x/2015001/article/14202-eng.pdf

12

Settler Colonialism, Biopolitics, and Indigenous Children in Canada

Dale C. Spencer and Raven Sinclair

LEARNING OBJECTIVES

- To understand how settler colonialism has affected and affects the lives of Indigenous children
- To understand how biopolitics links with the removal of Indigenous children in Canada
- To consider how white European conceptions of the child have particular effects on nonwhite children
- To understand how the Canadian government and related settler agents utilized assimilationist techniques to try to eliminate the prior Indigenous population in Canada
- To understand how the residential school system and forced Indigenous adoption has affected the Indigenous population in Canada

---

INTRODUCTION

Indigenous children and youth are severely overrepresented at every stage of child protection intervention across Canada, a manifestation of structural inequalities faced by Indigenous communities in Canada. As indicated by Canada's Truth and Reconciliation Commission (2015), the contemporary removal of children and youth from Indigenous families and communities happens within an historical framework of the Canadian Government's removal of Indigenous children from their families during the Indian Residential School system; the forced removal of children from Indigenous families to foster or adoptive homes, often termed the Sixties Scoop; other practices of cultural genocide; and ongoing systems of racism and **settler colonialism**. Drawing from the literature on settler colonialism and **biopolitics** (a Foucauldian notion, explored in more detail below, where a population is treated as a political problem), this chapter offers a theoretical perspective on Indigenous child removal in Canada. Specifically, this chapter situates the figure of the Indigenous child and the practice of child removal within systems of settler colonialism and biopolitical forms of state racism.

This chapter contributes to critical understandings of Indigenous child removal and settler colonialism. While biopolitics has been considered in relation to settler colonialism (Morgensen, 2011), heretofore scholars have not focused on the Indigenous child, specifically, as the central focus of biopolitical intervention. This chapter considers how the Indigenous child fails to fit into white, European, middle-class visions of the child and childhood and how this failure serves as the historic basis of and the justification for the oft-violent assimilationist techniques used against Indigenous children. Here we consider the better-known residential school system and the lesser-known, but equally destructive, period of Indigenous child removal and forced Indigenous adoption, the "Sixties Scoop" (Sinclair, 2007a, 2007b) or the "Canada Scoop" (see Spencer, 2016a).[1]

This chapter is structured in three main sections. In the first section, we provide an overview of settler colonialism and biopolitics. In the second, we offer a discussion of the Western conception of the child and childhood and how that relates to the justification for the mass removal of Indigenous children from their families starting in the late nineteenth century. In the final section, we analyze two modalities of child removal, specifically the Indian Residential School system and forced Indigenous adoption.

SETTLER COLONIALISM AND BIOPOLITICS

Settler colonialism occurs when foreign peoples from a metropole, or a centre of imperial **power,** move en masse to a region and displace people indigenous to the land through genocide, expulsion, or segregation. The settlers take over lands, impose laws, and attempt to terminate or subordinate the Indigenous population (Monchalin, 2016). It should be understood that settler colonialism exists both in the past and present (Cavanagh, 2012). It is often rationalized by rhetoric whereby the Indigenous population is represented as belonging to an ancient past and is thus incommensurate with the modern nation and its promise of progress and civilization. This temporal dissonance provides the justification for negation of the prior Indigenous inhabitants (Povinelli, 2011). Settler colonialism works to marginalize, dominate, and even eliminate the prior Indigenous inhabitants through a variety of *techniques,* which include more direct forms of genocide and eugenics (Pegoraro, 2015; Woolford, 2013, 2015a; Woolford, Benvenuto, & Hinton, 2014), and more insidious approaches such as the normalization and enculturation of Indigenous peoples into the dominant settler ways of life (McGillivray, 1997).

For Patrick Wolfe (2006), a well-known settler colonialism scholar, settler colonialism follows a logic of elimination. That is, it is an entrenched system that is dedicated to the termination of the Indigenous population. But, as he demonstrates, settler colonialism is inherently eliminatory but not invariably genocidal. Unlike **genocide**, as a phenomenon, settler colonialism does not rely on the presence or absence of the formal apparatus of the state. At its foundation, settler colonialism involves contests over land and, as such, life. Wolfe explains that the primary motive for elimination of the native population is not discrimination based on race (or religion, ethnicity, grade of civilization, etc.), but access to territory. He sums it up, saying, "Settler colonialism destroys to replace" (Wolfe, 2006, p. 388). The effect is the establishment of a social structure that, according to Wolfe, has both productive and destructive dimensions. On the destructive side, it involves the termination of the native population. On the productive side, settlers establish a new colonial society on the expropriated land base. In this way, they come to stay, as "invasion is a structure not an event" (Wolfe, 2006, p. 388). Elimination becomes an organizing principle of settler-colonial societies rather than a singular occurrence. In terms of outcomes, the logic of elimination can involve "officially encouraged miscegenation, the breaking down of native title to alienable individual freeholds, native citizenship, child abduction, religious conversion, resocialization in total institutions such as missions or boarding schools, and a whole range of cognate biocultural assimilations" (Wolfe, 2006, p. 388).

In other ways, settler colonialism, as put forth by Audra Simpson (2016, p. 3), serves as an "analytic, as a social formation, as an attitude, as an imaginary, as something that names and helps others to name what happened and is still happening in spaces seized away from people in ongoing projects to mask that seizure while attending to capital accumulation under another name." This is to say that settler colonialism is a disposition towards the Indigenous population that involves ways of thinking that support removing the Indigenous population for the purposes of financial gain. Settler colonialism is undergirded by liberalism's protection of rights of person and private property that attaches these rights to bodies that live and move in settler societies. By moving the Indigenous population off land, be it through assimilation or forced removal, these rights provide the protection of possessed land and, as such, the context for capital accumulation and personal protections for those who are deemed worthy. The language of liberalism sanctifies individualism and the free market (Povinelli, 2011; Simpson, 2016) and as such, ensures the acquisition of land. According to Michael Yellow Bird, there is, among other forms, an "internal" form of settler colonialism (see Monchalin, 2016). He defines internal colonialism as the biopolitical management of people. In relation to the Indigenous peoples, this is the biopolitical management of their land, territory, vegetation, and wildlife within the imperial settler nation. So what is biopolitics and how does it relate to settler colonialism?

Michel Foucault (1990) was one of the first to identify the emergence of biopolitics and its contribution to the development of capitalism. Foucault highlights how, in the premodern period, the king maintained the right to defend his own survival. Sovereign power rested in the right to decide life and death. He explains that this power over life and death was "in reality the right to *take* life or *let* live" (emphasis in original, 1990, p. 136). With the rise of the modern state form, the seventeenth century saw a transformation in mechanisms of power. According to Foucault, sovereign power came to be overshadowed by biopower. In opposition to sovereign power, which is fixated on impeding forces, making them submit, and destroying them, biopower is concerned with generating forces, making them grow, and ordering them in strategic ways (Foucault, 1990, p. 136). Whereas the limit of sovereign power is at the death of the accused, biopower is productive and oriented to the exigencies of the administration of life. In *The History of Sexuality*, Foucault goes so far as to suggest that the ancient right to take life or let live has been substituted with the power to foster life or disallow it to the point of death.

Biopolitics, then, is focused on governmental investment in bodies with the mechanics of life and concern with the biological processes—indicators such as births and mortality, life expectancy and longevity, and health—and the circumstances that cause these to fluctuate. Interventions and regulatory controls make up the biopolitics of the population. Complemented by a *disciplinary apparatus* concerned with optimization of bodies' capabilities, the docility of bodies, and utility of forces (Foucault, 1995), biopower brings life and its mechanisms into the realm of explicit calculations and makes knowledge-power an agent of transformation of human life. Biopolitics deals with the whole population as a simultaneously political and biological problem (Foucault, 2003). For example, through the accumulation of health indicators or birth rates regarding a population, governments can make decisions regarding what types of life to foster and what types of life to let die. In some instances, this can be articulated into forms of state racism whereby some groups, such as Europeans, are allowed to enter Canada and thrive and live, while other groups, such as recent **immigrants** and **refugees**, are rejected and excluded, in the name of the well-being of Canadian population (Chen, 2008). Similarly, Indigenous populations are let die, and even proactively eliminated. The problems of the biological life of the population are aleatory and specific to historical periods.

Biopolitics is concurrently consumed with the preservation of certain forms of life and with the definition and classification of forms of life not worth living. In the face of recalcitrant populations, these forms of life deemed not worth living are exposed to death. Achille Mbembe (2013) introduces the concept of "necropolitics" to denote the ways in the contemporary period that the political, under the guise of war, resistance, or the fight against terror, makes the murder of the enemy its primary and absolute objective. He is specifically concerned with such figures, however embodied, "whose central project is not the struggle for autonomy but the *generalized instrumentalization of human existence and the material destruction of human bodies and populations*" (emphasis in original, Mbembe, 2013, p. 163). His contention is that such figures of sovereignty are by no means the exception, due to temporary social breakdown for instance, but remain with us and "constitute the *nomos* of the political space in which we still live" (Mbembe, 2013, p. 163). The normative basis of the right to kill those deemed as surplus populations (Li, 2009) presupposes a relation of enmity to a given population or persons. In the event of the biopolitical claim of a state of siege of one group against another or the state against a defined group, war is deployed as a means of maintaining and fostering certain forms of life while negating others (see also Butler, 2009). This manifests into death worlds, where individuals can be killed with relative impunity.

In relation to the settler/Indigenous relationship, the biopolitical interventions into the Indigenous population begin, especially within the British colonies, with a position of enmity towards the population. The primary biopolitical aim has been to convert Indigenous forms of life into settler forms of life and, through various strategies, to inculcate colonial norms and morality. The former involves investments in "healthy" practices and dispositions of the colonizers (Gregory, 2004), including wide-ranging assimilationist practices, such as permanent, stationary housing, and the imposition of food production and consumption patterns. Those recalcitrant elements of the Indigenous populations—those that resist assimilation—are refigured as enemies and objects to be negated and subject to death worlds.

THE CIVILIZED AND UNCIVILIZED CHILD

The "child" and "childhood" are understood in different ways in different societies across time and geographical spaces. The work of social historians has shown that the category of the child and childhood did not exist in the medieval period, and as a category, the child is a relatively recent convention (Aries, 1965, 2012). Childhood was and remains an abstraction that refers to a particular stage of life, rather than a group of persons implied by the term *children* (Heywood, 2001). In addition, the "healthy" as well as the "neglected" and "uncivilized" child are cultural inventions and products of our historical epoch. This is to say that ideas about what are healthy or uncivilized childhood practices have much to do with social, economic, and political structures and contestations of any given era and cultural context. One longstanding constant across time and place, however, is the investment in children as hope (Kraftl, 2008; te Riele, 2010). This involves an investment, through children, in hope for the future, be it under the trope of "children are our future" or in more abstract terms, interweaving children with the health of the nation. The health and education of the child, then, is a hopeful investment in not only the life of children, but also the population, and remains a primary site of biopolitical intervention.

The historical invention of the division between the properly parented, healthy child and the neglected, unhealthy child was discursively constructed in the eighteenth and nineteenth centuries, with the emergence of experts on the child and childhood in both Europe and North America. In the mid-eighteenth century, there was a profusion of literature on the preservation and education of children in Europe. The aim of this movement was to "save" children from all sorts of maladies through proper child-rearing, education, and medical care, regardless of class background (Donzelot, 1979). The social became oriented toward the health of the family and medical **discourses** expounded in this period on the profound repercussions of poor health on child development. The family and the school became two of the primary loci of intervention and correction (Donzelot, 1979; Foucault, 1995). For example, the government of the family became oriented to the biopolitical ends of hygiene, specifically of treatment and prevention to produce a healthy industrial workforce. In both the United States and Canada, this was particularly the case with the emergence of child-oriented medical regimes aimed at producing healthy outcomes (Apple, 1995; Warsh & Strong-Boag, 2005). Similarly, concerns about young people's morality and prospects as "future-citizens" or burdens on the society forcefully drove the institutionalization of education and child protection (Chen, 2005; Gleason, 2001; Osborne, 2000).

Along with the expert-driven, biopolitical understanding of childhood connecting children's lives to the well-being of the population and the vitality of the nation, the more popular child-saving movement emerged in the US, Canada, and elsewhere in the late nineteenth century. Led by middle-class social reformers, this movement was dedicated to controlling the "immoral" behaviour of lower-class families and immigrants that were interpreted as posing a threat to the values and economic interests of the ostensibly more respectable middle class. Influenced by **social Darwinism**, this moral crusade intervened in the families of the lower classes and utilized often medicalized discourses of pathology, infection, immunization, and treatment to address the moral defects of lower-class children and prevent them from moving on to lives of assumed crime and immoral behaviour (Platt, 1977; Rothman, 2002). Underpinned by racist and classist notions of social Darwinism, comparable movements in Canada sought to correct immoral and uncivilized young people through interventions via the juvenile justice system and various other state agencies (Doob & Cesaroni, 2004; Haig-Brown, 2003).

The Indigenous child within the European, white framework figured, and continues to figure, as that which is both unhealthy and uncivilized. In the social Darwinian hierarchy, the Indigenous child is seen to be embedded in an uncivilized family and must be saved from his or her "degenerate" surroundings. Alongside the settler-colonial logic of elimination, the assimilation of the child has served as the primary modality to systematically remove the prior Indigenous population. The Indigenous child, then, becomes an investment for settler hopes in a future without the Indigenous prior, where biopolitical intervention and attendant discipline through school and family are the techniques of elimination. As Norbert Elias (2000) avers, the means of *civilizing* is a matter of inculcating certain habits of thought and manners. Following this logic, in the Canadian context, the Indigenous child must be removed from their families and inculcated with the ways of being of the settler. In the following section, we analyze two such techniques of assimilation—the residential school system and forced Indigenous adoption—utilized by the Canadian nation state and affiliated settler stakeholders.

TWO CHILD-FOCUSED COLONIAL TECHNIQUES OF ASSIMILATION

When the Europeans began to colonize what is now known as Canada, they brought with them theological, philosophical, and legal rulings that assured their "superiority" and right to seize land from Indigenous populations, who were perceived as inferior and uncivilized. European colonizers relied on a cluster of papal and self-serving legal documents known as "the doctrine of discovery" to gain authority over lands. Providing the rationalization for settler authority and presence, this doctrine served as the principal justification for expansion of European settlement in Canada for almost 500 years. The concept of *terra nullius* means "territory without people." This concept served as the basis for asserting that Indigenous lands were not occupied in the European sense of private ownership, while the doctrine of discovery provided the settlers with the right to claim underlying title to the land on behalf of the monarch. Where these notions were not invoked, other strategies, such as treaties, were used throughout the course of European conquest. Treaties were arranged between the colonizers (Britain and France, primarily) and various First Nations, to extinguish Indigenous people's title to the land so as to make colonial settlement legal. Negotiated in circumstances of duress for Indigenous peoples, these treaties were drastically unfavourable to them, and then often broken, annulled, or interpreted by the government in extremely narrow and limiting ways. Still today, many Canadians live on vast areas that are unceded territories.

In the case of Canada, settler colonialism was and is fundamentally aimed at normalizing and enculturing Indigenous people into settler-colonial ways of life. This aim is exemplified in the statement made to the Canadian Parliament by the then head of the Department of Indian Affairs, Duncan Campbell Scott, in 1920: "Our objective is to continue until there is not a single Indian in Canada that has not been absorbed into the body politic and there is no Indian question, and no Indian Department, that is the whole object of this Bill." More broadly, Elizabeth Povinelli (2011) avers that in the governance of the prior Indigenous population, especially in the British Americas, the priority of the prior was acknowledged and then annulled through treaty, land seizure, and genocide (see also Kulchyski, 2013). The Canadian Indigenous populations were first depleted through wars between the colonizers, and then through epidemics of infectious diseases in the eighteenth and nineteenth centuries. Then, in relation to genocide (Powell, 2011), they were subjected to assimilation strategies aimed at swallowing the Indigenous population into the body politic. Initially assimilation was to be achieved through education and the inculcation of "civilized" ways of living (Woolford, 2015a). The most insidious but devastating techniques of assimilation and civilization that were aimed at Indigenous children are the residential school system and forced Indigenous adoption.

The Residential School System, Biopolitics, and the "Missing" Child

Although the French in New France in the seventeenth and eighteenth centuries had established boarding schools to educate Indigenous children, it was not until the early nineteenth century that various religious groups (Protestants, Catholics, and Methodists) initiated Canada's residential school system. These residential schools were attended by Indigenous students and included industrial schools, boarding schools, homes for students, and various combinations of these educational delivery systems. The primary aim of these schools was to give the children a Christian education and to protect them from their "backward" parents' influence. The children were not allowed to speak their own language and they had to adopt patriarchal family values and skills oriented to participation in the industrial capitalist economy.

The Canadian state put this assimilation strategy into policy and funded the system of residential schools. Recognizing the importance of this domestic education and religious instruction in assimilating Aboriginal peoples into "civilized" settler society, the Canadian government passed the Gradual Civilization Act in 1857, which enfranchised Aboriginal peoples and recognized them not as Aboriginal but as British subjects. As early as 1874 the Canadian government shifted from day schools for educating Indigenous children to the development and administration of the Indian Residential School system (Morse, 2008). Empowered by the Indian Act, the central aim of residential schools was to reform Native people from their presumably uncivilized nomadic hunting and fishing lifestyle to the ostensibly civilized ways of white settlers (Blackstock, 2009; Furniss, 1995). By 1920, the government had made attendance at

Figure 12.1: Students of the Shingwauk Indian Residential School

Source: Ontario Museum Association, www.museumsontario.ca/sites/default/files/styles/featured-photo-full/public/images/2011-6_001_052_0.jpg?itok=PthzG951

residential schools mandatory for all Aboriginal children between 7 and 15 years of age. As a result of this law, priests, Indian agents, and police officers forcibly took children from their families. By 1931 there were 80 residential schools operating in Canada; in 1948, there were 72 schools with 9,368 students. The residential school system served as a *technique* for assimilation or, in other words, colonial genocide.

With rising public concern over the treatment of Indigenous populations in Canada and a major revision to the Indian Act in 1951, the federal government began to phase out the residential school system, with the last school closing in 1996. By that time, over 100,000 Indigenous children had been forcibly removed from their homes and placed in residential schools (Corntassel, Chaw-win-is, & T'lakwadzi, 2009).

Stories abound of the physical, psychological, sexual, and emotional abuse experienced by children within residential schools at the hands of "educators" (Fontaine, 2010; Furniss, 1995; Loyie, Brissenden, & Spear, 2014; Woolford, 2015b). Violence was the norm and was used by priests and nuns as a means of inculcating Western "civilized" habits and thinking. This included martial forms of rigid discipline aimed at a "loss of all emblems of cultural identity upon entry into the school, prohibitions against the use of Indigenous languages, a regimented timetable with days split between education (often religious and including debasements of Indigenous cultures) and manual labour, and severe punishments for perceived indiscretions" (Woolford, 2015a, p. 142). Through education the children were inculcated with values that debased Indigenous culture and elevated European ways of living and goals.

In addition to the more disciplinary techniques, Indigenous children were subject to a number of biopolitical interventions. For example, Ian Mosby's (2015) work shows how between 1942 and 1952 an unprecedented series of nutritional studies was conducted on Aboriginal communities and residential schools. He indicates that while the best known of these was the 1947–1948 James Bay Survey of the Attawapiskat and Rupert's House Cree First Nations, there were two separate, less well-known, long-term studies that included controlled experiments conducted, apparently without the subjects' **informed consent** or knowledge, on malnourished Indigenous populations in Northern Manitoba and, later, in six Indian Residential Schools. As a biopolitical strategy, nutritional studies promote the life of settler bodies, while, at best, putting Indigenous people's lives in peril, and at worst, exposing them to death. In the name of the nation's health, the bodies of children in residential schools served as the site for experimentation, much like the experimentation by Josef Mengele in Germany and like Japanese Unit 731's human experimentation in China during World War II (see Spencer, 2016b).

Indian Residential Schools also operated as death worlds. The Truth and Reconciliation Commission identified 3,200 deaths, including both named and unnamed residential school students. For just under one-third of these deaths, the schools and the government failed to record the name of the child who died (Truth and Reconciliation Commission, 2015). The reality that many students who went to residential school never returned to their families points to the fact that these "schools" operated in such a way that children died or were killed with little consequence. These death worlds qua residential schools were guided by enmity towards the Indigenous children they sought to assimilate.

Even among the survivors, the legacy of the residential school system left its deep mark. Fournier and Crey (1998) show that while the homecomings of Aboriginal children may have ended the abuse, it presented new problems. They discuss that that survivors were embarrassed by their Indigenous heritage, lacked language and cultural knowledge, and therefore many found it difficult to readjust to life on the reserve. Fournier and Crey state that many returning students were unable to trust other community members and thus remained silent about the abuse they had experienced and/or witnessed. They also note that many who returned home from a childhood of harsh discipline and abuse experienced symptoms related to post-traumatic stress disorder. Symptoms of this disorder include panic attacks, anger, alcohol and drug use, sexual inadequacy or addiction, the inability to form relationships, and eating disorders. Assimilation, in this sense, exacts manifold forms of violence against Indigenous children and their families, both at macro and micro levels.

Forced Indigenous Adoption as Biopolitical Intervention

Since the *ancien regime*—the social and political system instituted in the Kingdom of France in the fifteenth century—the family has been the continuous site for inculcating the values of Western liberalism (Donzelot, 1979). The family is the crucible in which the liberal child is produced and geared towards private property and individual autonomy. This process includes the inscription of the moral values of liberalism and capitalism deep within the fibre and details of the family (Deleuze & Guattari, 1983). The white settler family, then, is a particularly apposite site for producing children with Western "civilized" habits and ways of thinking. It is no surprise, then, that Indigenous child removals "into care" followed the residential school system. Procured with federal-provincial transfers through the Canada Assistance Plan (1966), the child welfare system emerged swiftly, staffed with a newly trained cadre of social workers (a new profession), and quickly began removing massive levels of Indigenous children from their homes for adoption and foster care. In fact, the number of Indigenous children taken into "care" grew exponentially from the late 1950s. This trend has continued today. Despite Indigenous people representing, on average, 4 percent of the population, Indigenous children represented up to 80 percent of all the children in the care of the child welfare system in 2006, and this level has continued. Here biopolitics and settler-colonial analyses can help us understand this drastic disparity. The child welfare system presents a positive façade; after all, who does not want children protected? But in reality, it has become a site for the continued elimination of Indigenous people through assimilation and "identity pulverization" of the children, all under the auspices of child-saving rhetoric.

Unbeknown to Indigenous families in North America and Australia, in the 1960s and 1970s the removal of Indigenous children reached epidemic proportions. According to Margaret Jacobs (2014), "Indigenous child removal had grown to be so naturalized in these three nations that it became a matter of common sense, a *habit* that was rarely challenged by state authorities, concern of non-Indigenous citizens, or even, initially Indigenous people who experienced child removal" (p. 190). Jacobs has labelled this as the "habit of elimination," playing off of Wolfe's "logic of elimination" of settler colonialism. The "culture of removal" of Indigenous children in Canada is in line with Jacob's argument in the US and Australian contexts. The child welfare system in Canada, built upon imperialistic and racist foundations, has failed to adequately account for the elimination-based perspectives and methods that it perpetuates.

For example, in 1985 the Manitoba government review committee on Indian and Métis adoptions and placements published a final report, entitled "No Quiet Place," otherwise known as the Kimelman Report. In reviewing the adoptions and placements of Indigenous children in Manitoba, Justice Edwin Kimelman stated "unequivocally that cultural genocide has been taking place in a systematic, routine manner" (cited in Barkwell, Longclaws, & Chartrand, 1984), and he subsequently placed a moratorium on Indigenous transracial adoption. Indigenous children had been routinely sent to homes outside of Manitoba, to other provinces, other countries, and other continents. Placed in non-Indigenous homes, their cultural background was not valued or fostered. We now know that over 20,000 Indigenous children were subjected to this adoption program (Fournier & Crey, 1998; Sinclair, 2007b) and it is probable that the totals are higher. While this moratorium was only officially mandated in Manitoba, other provinces followed suit, and in the immediate aftermath of the inquiry, adoption numbers dropped drastically while foster and institutional care numbers increased (Sinclair, 2007b). In Manitoba, despite the provincial child welfare system's negotiated agreements with bands, requiring regulated consultation and consent, this process also deteriorated. Now the system has evolved in such a way that children are still being removed at vastly disproportionate rates relative to white children, and child welfare agency policies and legislation have emerged as the source of authority for continued Indigenous child removals.

Such recent developments suggest a lack of understanding about the connection between colonial wrongs and Indigenous child removals, and the need to stop such removals. In 2004, Saskatchewan Justice Ryan-Froslie in *Re R.T.* (2004) ruled that it was a violation of Indigenous children's rights to be deemed ineligible for adoption, arguing that every child has a right to a family. This case buttressed a 1983 Supreme Court case (*Racine v. Woods*) wherein Justice Bertha Wilson concluded that when Indigenous children are in foster care for a period of time, and those foster parents wish to acquire permanency over the children, the "best interest" of the Indigenous child was to prioritize the child's bonding with the foster family because, she argued, the significance of culture abates over time. Her findings fly in the face of adoption research as well as research on notions of bonding and attachment (Sinclair, 2017). Currently, there is a preponderance of cases in which foster families have sought permanency over children; when birth family and kin fight for their children and such cases go to court, the almost inevitable result is that the child is awarded to the non-Indigenous family. In these contexts, critiques of settler colonialism and the biopolitics of child welfare help us to see that the white family is always determined as the one that meets the Euro-Canadian legal test of the best interests of the child.

Against the backdrop of United Nations Convention of the Rights of the Child (United Nations, 2012), the Canadian government's right to remove Indigenous children from their homes has and continues to supersede the rights of Indigenous children. In the contemporary period, the assumption underlying legal rulings on adoption is that adoptive Indigenous children are "better off" once removed from their Indigenous communities and placed in non-Indigenous homes. The non-Indigenous family, consequently, becomes the site of inscribing civilized ways of living into the Indigenous child (see Spencer, 2016a). There is ample evidence from Indigenous children of the Sixties Scoop, or Canada Scoop, that in the broad context of settler colonialism and associated assimilationism, the non-Indigenous settler family can be a space of violence for Indigenous children (see Spencer, 2016a). For example, Marlene Orgeron, a Manitoba adoptee, states that she "grew up wanting to die, wanting the pain to end.... I spent 20 years putting myself back together" (Puxley, 2015). This statement is emblematic of the broader experiences of forced assimilation through adoption, as evidenced in the well-attended healing ceremonies and rallies orchestrated by Indigenous adoptees in Ontario and Manitoba (Pelley, 2015; Russell, 2016). As a form of biopolitical intervention, then, the process of civilization is experienced as a violent upending of adoptees' lives and a perpetual sense of loss of identity (see Sinclair, 2007a).

CHAPTER SUMMARY

Together, in this chapter, we

- Reviewed approaches to, and understandings of, settler colonialism and biopolitics.
- Analyzed the place of the Indigenous child in white European conceptions of the child and childhood.
- Read about the Indigenous residential school system and the period of Indigenous transracial adoption that followed.
- Sought to understand the relationship between settler colonialism and biopolitics in relation to assimilationist practices of forced Indigenous child removal.

STUDY QUESTIONS

1. How do settler colonialism and biopolitics relate to Indigenous child removal?
2. How do the doctrines of discovery and *terra nullius* affect contemporary social, political, and economic systems and ways of thinking?
3. How and when did you first hear about residential schools? What is your experience with how friends, colleagues, and family understand or discuss residential schools?
4. If you were a high school teacher and you wanted students to understand the impact of settler colonialism on Indigenous people in Canada, how would you present this history? What props, pictures, or videos would you use and why?
5. Why is it important to consider historical contexts when discussing Indigenous child removal?

SUGGESTED RESEARCH ASSIGNMENT

Identify/locate historical and contemporary writings regarding, or images of, Indigenous children, produced by non-Indigenous people. In relation to historical materials, How are Indigenous children represented or framed? What types of phrases or visual representations are used? In relation to contemporary writings or representations, How are Indigenous children depicted? How much has changed when you compare the historical materials with contemporary ones?

SUGGESTED FILMS/VIDEO CLIPS

We Were Children
www.nfb.ca/film/we_were_children/trailer/we_were_children_trailer/
In this film, the story of the Indian Residential School system is conveyed through the eyes of two children who survived terrible hardships in the schools. Lyna Hart and Glen Anaquod describe their experiences of physical, sexual, and emotional abuse in residential schools and the long-lasting effects that continue into their adult lives.

Dispatch: The Hidden Colonial Legacy: The 60s Scoop
www.cbc.ca/8thfire/2012/01/hidden-colonial-legacy-the-60s-scoop.html
In this film, Colleen Rajotte documents two Cree men, Jeff and Sydney Dion, returning home to Manitoba after 39 years away, and a young boy who benefited from new strategies in adoption aimed at ensuring that Aboriginal kids stay within their communities.

Unrepentant: Canada's Residential Schools Documentary
www.youtube.com/watch?v=0brD50Dlv5Q

This controversial documentary reveals Canada's Indian Residential Schools and the theft of Indigenous land under the guise of religion. It focuses on the story of former minister Kevin Annett, who blew the whistle on his own church after he learned of thousands of murders in its Indian Residential Schools.

SUGGESTED WEBSITES

The 60s Scoop: A Hidden Generation, Facebook page
www.facebook.com/AHiddenGeneration?fref=ts
This is the official Facebook page for the forthcoming documentary on the Sixties Scoop. It provides useful resources on the Sixties Scoop and forced Indigenous adoption.

Indigenous Foundations: The Sixties Scoop and Aboriginal Child Welfare
indigenousfoundations.arts.ubc.ca/home/government-policy/sixties-scoop.html
This University of British Columbia website is an excellent resource for information regarding residential schools and the Sixties Scoop.

Residential Schools Settlement
www.residentialschoolsettlement.ca/english_index.html
This is the official court website for the settlement of the Residential Schools Class Action Litigation.

NOTE

1.   As the horrors of the Indian Residential School system were increasingly exposed to Canadian Indigenous communities in the 1960s and 1970s, the federal and provincial governments shifted to forced adoption as their primary assimilation modality. All the while, residential schools operated alongside forced adoption, with the last residential school closing in 1996.

REFERENCES

Apple, R. D. (1995). Constructing mothers: Scientific motherhood in the nineteenth and twentieth centuries. *Social History of Medicine, 8*(2), 161–178.

Aries, P. (1965). *Centuries of childhood: A social history of family life*. New York: Vintage.

Aries, P. (2012). The discovery of childhood. In H. Morrison (Ed.), *The global history of childhood reader* (pp. 9–20). London and New York: Routledge.

Barkwell, L., Longclaws, L., & Chartrand, D. (1984). *Report of the Review Committee on Indian and Métis Adoptions and Placements* (pp. 33–53). Winnipeg, Manitoba.

Blackstock, C. (2009). The occasional evil of angels: Learning from the experiences of Aboriginal peoples and social work. *First Peoples Child & Family Review, 4*(1), 28–37.

Butler, J. (2009). *Frames of war: When is life grievable?* London: Verso.

Cavanagh, E. (2012). History, time and the indigenist critique. *Arena Journal, 37/38*, 16, 39.

Chen, X. (2005). *Tending the gardens of citizenship: Child saving in Toronto, 1880s–1920s.* Toronto: University of Toronto Press.

Chen, X. (2008). The child citizen. In *Recasting the social in citizenship* (pp. 162–186). Toronto: University of Toronto Press.

Corntassel, J., Chaw win is, & T'lakwadzi. (2009). Indigenous storytelling, truth-telling, and community approaches to reconciliation. *English Studies in Canada, 35*(1), 137–159.

Deleuze, G., & Guattari, F. (1983). *Anti-Oedipus: Capitalism and schizophrenia.* Minneapolis: University of Minnesota Press.

Donzelot, J. (1979). *The policing of families.* Baltimore: Pantheon Books.

Doob, A. N., & Cesaroni, C. (2004). *Responding to youth crime in Canada.* Toronto: University of Toronto Press.

Elias, N. (2000). *The civilizing process: Sociogenetic and psychogenetic investigations* (2nd ed.). Oxford, UK & Malden, MA: Wiley-Blackwell.

Fontaine, T. (2010). *Broken circle: The dark legacy of Indian Residential Schools: A memoir.* Victoria: Heritage House Publishing.

Foucault, M. (1990). *The history of sexuality: An introduction.* New York: Vintage.

Foucault, M. (1995). *Discipline & punish: The birth of the prison* (2nd ed.). New York: Vintage.

Foucault, M. (2003). *"Society must be defended": Lectures at the Collège de France, 1975–1976.* (D. Macey, Trans.) (Reprint ed.). New York: Picador.

Fournier, S., & Crey, E. (1998). *Stolen from our embrace.* Vancouver: Douglas & Mcintyre.

Furniss, E. (1995). *Victims of benevolence: The dark legacy of the Williams Lake Residential School.* Vancouver: Arsenal Pulp Press.

Gleason, M. (2001). Disciplining the student body: Schooling and the construction of Canadian children's bodies, 1930–1960. *History of Education Quarterly, 41*(2), 189–215.

Gregory, D. (2004). *The colonial present: Afghanistan, Palestine, Iraq.* Malden, MA: Wiley-Blackwell.

Haig-Brown, R. (2003). Problems of modern life and young offenders. In *Histories of Canadian children and youth* (pp. 207–210). New York: Oxford University Press.

Heywood, C. (2001). *A history of childhood: Children and childhood in the West from medieval to modern times.* Cambridge, UK & Malden, MA: Polity.

Jacobs, M. D. (2014). The habit of elimination: Indigenous child removal in settler colonial nations in the twentieth century. In *Colonial genocide in Indigenous North America* (pp. 189–207). Durham, NC: Duke University Press.

Kraftl, P. (2008). Young people, hope and childhood-hope. *Space and Culture, 11*(2), 81–92.

Kulchyski, P. (2013). *Aboriginal rights are not human rights.* Winnipeg: ARP Books. Retrieved from arp-books.org/books/detail/aboriginal-rights-are-not-human-rights

Li, T. (2009). To make live or let die? Rural dispossession and the protection of surplus populations. *Antipode, 14*(6), 1208–1235.

Loyie, L., Brissenden, C., & Spear, W. (2014). *Residential schools with the words and images of survivors.* Brantford: Indigenous Education Press.

Mbembe, A. (2013). Necropolitics. In *Biopolitics: A reader* (pp. 161–192). Durham, NC: Duke University Press.

McGillivray, A. (1997). Therapies of freedom: The colonization of Aboriginal childhood. In A. McGillivray (Ed.), *Governing childhood* (pp. 135–200). Aldershot: Dartmouth.

Monchalin, L. (2016). *The colonial problem: An Indigenous perspective on crime and injustice in Canada.* Toronto: University of Toronto Press.

Morgensen, S. L. (2011). The biopolitics of settler colonialism: Right here, right now. *Settler Colonial Studies, 1*(1), 52–76. doi:10.1080/2201473X.2011.10648801

Morse, B. (2008). Indigenous peoples of Canada and their efforts to achieve true reparations. In F. Lenzerini (Ed.), *Reparations for Indigenous peoples: International and comparative perspectives.* Oxford: Oxford University Press.

Mosby, I. (2015). Administering colonial science: Nutrition research and human biomedical experimentation in Aboriginal communities and residential schools, 1942–1952. *Histoire sociale/Social History, 46*(91). Retrieved from hssh.journals.yorku.ca/index.php/hssh/article/view/40239

Osborne, K. (2000). Public schooling and citizenship education in Canada. *Canadian Ethnic Studies, 32*(1), 8–37.

Pegoraro, L. (2015). Second-rate victims: The forced sterilization of Indigenous peoples in the USA and Canada. *Settler Colonial Studies, 5*(2), 161–173. doi:10.1080/2201473X.2014.955947

Pelley, L. (2015, November 2). Indigenous children removed from homes in the 1960s begin to heal. *Toronto Star.* Retrieved from www.thestar.com/news/canada/2015/11/02/indigenous-children-removed-from-homes-in-the-1960s-just-now-beginning-to-heal.html

Platt, A. M. (1977). *The child savers: The invention of delinquency.* Chicago: University of Chicago Press.

Povinelli, E. A. (2011). *Economies of abandonment: Social belonging and endurance in late liberalism.* Durham NC: Duke University Press.

Powell, C. (2011). *Barbaric civilization: A critical sociology of genocide.* Montreal & Kingston: McGill-Queen's University Press.

Puxley, C. (2015, June 18). Manitoba says sorry for taking Aboriginal children from homes. *Toronto Star.* Retrieved from www.thestar.com/news/canada/2015/06/18/manitoba-says-sorry-for-taking-aboriginal-children-from-homes.html

Rothman, D. J. (2002). *Conscience and convenience: The asylum and its alternatives in progressive America.* Piscataway, NJ: Transaction Publishers.

Russell, A. (2016, August 23). What was the "60s Scoop"? Aboriginal children taken from homes a dark chapter in Canada's history. *Globalnews.ca.* Retrieved from globalnews.ca/news/2898190/what-was-the-60s-scoop-aboriginal-children-taken-from-homes-a-dark-chapter-in-canadas-history/

Simpson, A. (2016). Whither settler colonialism? *Settler Colonial Studies, 6*(4), 438–445. doi:10.1080/2201473X.2015.1124427

Sinclair, R. (2007a). *All my relations ~ Native transracial adoption: A critical case study of cultural identity.* PhD dissertation. University of Calgary, Canada. Retrieved from search.proquest.com/docview/304898656/abstract/DFC892F20EA44BA5PQ/1?accountid=9894

Sinclair, R. (2007b). Identity lost and found: Lessons from the sixties scoop. *First Peoples Child & Family Review, 3*(1), 65–82.

Sinclair, R. (2017). Indigenous transracial adoption in Canada. In J. D. Ned & C. J. Frost (Eds.), *Contemporary issues in child welfare: American Indian and Canadian Aboriginal contexts.* (pp. 157–178). Vernon: J Charlton Publishing.

Spencer, D. C. (2016a). Extraction and pulverization: A narrative analysis of Canada scoop survivors. *Settler Colonial Studies, 7*(1), 57–71. doi:10.1080/2201473X.2016.1152651

Spencer, D. (2016b). Ethics as witnessing: "Science," research ethics and victimization. In *Engaging in ethics in international criminological research* (pp. 106 122). New York: Routledge.

te Riele, K. (2010). Philosophy of hope: Concepts and applications for working with marginalized youth. *Journal of Youth Studies, 13*(1), 35–46. doi:10.1080/13676260903173496

Truth and Reconciliation Commission. (2015). *The final report of the Truth and Reconciliation Commission of Canada: Volume 4, Canada's residential schools: Missing children and unmarked burials.* Montreal & Kingston: McGill-Queen's University Press.

United Nations. (2012). The UN Convention on the Rights of the Child. In H. Morrison (Ed.), *The global history of childhood reader* (pp. 341–358). London & New York: Routledge.

Warsh, C. K., & Strong-Boag, V. (2005). *Children's health issues in historical perspective.* Waterloo, ON: Wilfrid Laurier University Press.

Wolfe, P. (2006). Settler colonialism and the elimination of the native. *Journal of Genocide Research, 8*(4), 387–409.

Woolford, A. (2013). Nodal repair and networks of destruction: Residential schools, colonial genocide, and redress in Canada. *Settler Colonial Studies, 3*(1), 65–81. doi:10.1080/18380743.2013.761936

Woolford, A. (2015a). *This benevolent experiment.* Lincoln: University of Nebraska Press.

Woolford, A. (2015b). *This benevolent experiment: Indigenous boarding schools, genocide, and redress in Canada and the United States.* Lincoln: University of Nebraska Press.

Woolford, A., Benvenuto, J., & Hinton, A. L., (Eds.). (2014). *Colonial genocide in Indigenous North America.* Durham: Duke University Press.

CASES CITED

Racine v. Woods [1983] 2SCR 173. P. 187.

Re. R.T. (2004), [2005] 248 D.L.R. (4th) 303, I.C.N.L.R., 289 (Sask. Q.B. Family Division).

13 Giving Voice: Prioritizing Youth Agency in Criminal Justice Diversion

Voula Marinos, Nathan Innocente, and Christine Goodwin-DeFaria

---

LEARNING OBJECTIVES

- To consider how prioritizing youth voice and youth agency assists in our understanding of diversion
- To understand what it means to divert youth away from the formal justice system
- To capture the experience of diversion from justice-involved youth in three distinct diversionary contexts in Ontario
- To understand both the limitations of youth diversion and areas of promise
- To highlight youth voice as an embedded component within the structure of diversion

---

They do all these things that they think are best for us, but they don't know a damn thing about what is best for us. Only we do. (*Male, 19 years, participant in Aboriginal Youth Court, Toronto*)

INTRODUCTION

The voices of justice-involved youth have traditionally been overlooked, forgotten, and unexamined within academic, policy, and professional contexts, and, for the most part, within literature about children and youth. The quote above is from a young person participating in Aboriginal Youth Court in Toronto. At the most fundamental level, the quote reinforces the importance of giving youth space to express their views. As a particularly vulnerable population, youth who are justice-involved often feel too unworthy and intimidated to provide their views and experiences about the very processes that subjugate them. On another level, the quote from the young person captures the critical insight and valuable feedback that participants in the justice system can provide.

Youth within the criminal justice system reflect, most often, social inequities based upon poverty, race, gender, and, of course, age. These categories often intersect, and therefore can have compounding effects when a young person "fits into" multiple **marginalized** positions. The **Youth Criminal Justice Act** has attempted to address the lives and needs of youth in conflict with the law and their lived experiences. More broadly, the act is representative of the **United Nations Convention on the Rights of the Child**, which outlines the rights of youth to make decisions and have their voice heard in judicial proceedings. The legislative principles underlining youth as having **agency** are consistent with a growing body of literature within child, childhood, and youth studies (Cotnam-Kappel, 2014; Prout & James, 1997). As Prout and James (1997) argue, children and youth ought to be thought about as being active agents in constructing their own lives. This chapter thus examines youth agency and voice within the context of **diversion** under the Youth Criminal Justice Act.

This chapter showcases the voices of youth involved in the youth criminal justice system that have had experience with diversion. Agency, in the context of this chapter, is conceived as young people having the capacity to think about and reflect on their experiences and make decisions in their best interests, as they see them. Diversion covers a broad spectrum of responses outside of traditional judicial proceedings—encompassing **extrajudicial measures** (EJM), **extrajudicial sanctions** (EJS), and specialized diversionary courts. The Youth Criminal Justice Act (YCJA) emphasizes the use of EJM and EJS as the first consideration for police and Crown attorneys (sections 4–12, YCJA). These responses are imposed for a large proportion of youth, and therefore they make up an important segment of the youth justice system. The use of EJM and EJS is cited as one among many factors responsible for the relative decline in completed youth court cases since 2003/2004, and the lowest number since 1991/1992 (see Alam, 2015). Additionally, as youth needs are emphasized within the YCJA (Declaration of Principle), we see the development of specialized diversionary courts for those struggling with mental health problems or Indigenous youth who self-identify. Scholars have identified several problems with diversion at all levels of the youth criminal justice system; however, little is known about how youth themselves interpret, experience, or negotiate the diversion process. Giving voice to youth and exploring youth agency in the diversion process is valuable in itself, but can also help us to understand the nuances of the nature, scope, and structure of diversionary practices.

In this chapter we present evidence of youth voices from within three different diversionary contexts in Ontario—extrajudicial measures, a youth mental health court, and an Aboriginal Youth Court. In "giving voice" to youth we underscore two fundamental elements of research on youth, agency, and criminal justice. First, in championing Hogeveen and Minaker's (2009) call to incorporate youth voices as research and broaden strategies for responding to youth crime, we use interview data with youth to give voice to their experiences in the criminal justice system. We reinforce the view of justice-involved youth, who are often marginalized, as valuable informants of criminal justice practices. But youth provide us with an understanding of the processes and effectiveness of diversion from their positions. Second, through diversionary court observations and interview data, we see how youth and agency are *embedded* within the very structure of diversion processes, allowing space for youth to express their voice and be heard by justice officials. Taken together, we begin to develop an understanding of how youth agency informs the diversion process and its effectiveness, and how youth agency is encouraged through the structure and process of diversion. These themes are explored through contemporary and ongoing research conducted by the authors in three diversionary contexts: interview data from pre- and post-charge diversions to community agencies, court observations of a youth mental health diversion court, and interviews and observations at an Aboriginal Youth Court. Overall, the chapter illustrates that when we listen to or ask for their perspectives, youth give us a different and meaningful picture of diversion, one that is critical of diversion but reflects some promise. We end with critical questions to think about for future research.

This chapter begins by providing the legislative context for youth diversion, followed by an analysis of how youth are conceptualized under the YCJA. We then provide an examination of youth voices in three diversion contexts, and the summative and concluding statements.

DIVERSION AND THE YOUTH CRIMINAL JUSTICE ACT (YCJA)

Diversion involves redirecting youth away from the justice system in order to avoid the stigmatizing effects of justice involvement and provide opportunities for youth committing minor offences to address their wrongdoings without recourse to formal justice sanctions (Doob & Cesaroni, 2004). As some have argued, the development of a separate youth justice system itself represents a central diversion policy for youth (Greene, 2011). Indeed, the YCJA promotes diversion though the emphasis on key principles of rehabilitation and reintegration, accountability, and meaningful consequences. Diversionary responses—including EJM, EJS, and specialized courts—are shaped to serve the diverse needs of the offence and the young person. It is acknowledged within the act that responses should be tailored to the individual needs of youth within the context of other legal factors such as the offence and offence history. Section 3(1)(c)(iv) states that within the limits of proportionality, measures should "respect gender, ethnic, cultural and linguistic differences and respond to the needs of aboriginal young persons and of young persons with special requirements."

Extrajudicial Measures

The principles of EJM are set out in section 4 of the YCJA, which specifies that they are often the most appropriate response, they allow for effective intervention, they are presumed adequate to hold youth accountable for nonviolent offences, and they should be used if they are determined to be sufficient to hold youth accountable. Diversion under the YCJA is discretionary. EJM in Ontario (sections 6, 7, and 8) represent pre-charge diversions by police that can include a warning, a caution, a referral to a program or agency in the community, or simply taking no further action. If a young person cannot be adequately dealt with through an EJM and is formally charged, then the young person may be offered EJS by the Crown (section 10). A young person must consent to diversion. When an EJS is offered, the young person must accept responsibility for his or her offending behaviour (not a plea of guilty) (section 10(2)(e)).

EJS can take many forms, and the youth may be required to complete one or more of the following: present a written or verbal apology; write an essay; make a poster; complete community service; attend counselling; attend an education/information session; attend a specialized program; make a charitable donation; accept a referral to a specialized crime prevention program; or attend peer mediation (Harris, Weagant, Cole, & Weinper, 2004). For example, two youths charged with the same offence of shoplifting may benefit from completely different diversionary responses based on their needs, personal life stories, and reasons for breaking the law. Front-line professionals such as police, Crown attorneys, or diversion coordinators are tasked with developing the appropriate response based on an assessment about what is appropriate, sometimes—but not always—in consultation with the young person.

Diversionary Courts

The model of specialized or **problem-solving courts** is premised on the idea that youth with specific needs underlying a criminal offence, such as mental health and/or addiction issues, should have those needs addressed. Youth with mental health problems, and other corresponding issues such as addictions, are more likely than other youth to be involved in the justice system (Peterson-Badali et al., 2015). Specialized courts attempt to address underlying problems through the law in a transformative way and within a therapeutic environment (Winick & Wexler, 2003).

Mental health courts are expected to be qualitatively different from the adversarial process by emphasizing diversion, team approaches by professionals, a less formal atmosphere, the active voices of accused persons, and the positive and therapeutic possibilities of the legal structure (Fritzler, 2003). Within the court is an assigned "specialized" judge, lawyers, mental health workers from local organizations, probation officers, and sometimes representatives from local school districts and parents/guardians. Accused persons are encouraged to be active participants in their proceedings as part of the justice process (Fritzler, 2003; Marinos & Gregory, 2012). Youth who have been offered diversion by way of EJS are eligible, in some jurisdictions, to be heard in the mental health court. Typically, charges are withdrawn and criminal records expunged upon completion of treatment (Weagant, 2015).

The first and only Aboriginal Youth Court (AYC), located in Toronto, Ontario, is structured around provisions in the YCJA that attempt to address the needs of Aboriginal youth (Declaration of Principle), and to consider sanctions other than custody, with particular attention to the circumstances of Aboriginal youth (section 38(2)(d)) (Clark, 2016). Such provisions are meant to address the significant overrepresentation of Indigenous youth in the criminal justice system attributed to the history and continued legacy of colonialism (Clark, 2016; LaPrairie, 2002; Royal Commission on Aboriginal Peoples, 1996; Rudin, 2007; Truth and Reconciliation Commission of Canada, 2015). The AYC is less formal than traditional courts in both the structure, which is aligned in a "circle," and in the format, where support persons are welcome to join the circle. Those participating in the circle are invited to speak (Clark, 2016). The AYC resolves most matters by referring youth to alternative programs, primarily to those offered by **Aboriginal Legal Services** (ALS)—an organization dedicated to the provision of legal services and culturally based justice alternatives. The court itself accepts diversion and, in most cases, charges are withdrawn as a result of the youth accepting his/her restorative/rehabilitative plan (Clark, 2016).

CONCEPTUALIZING YOUTH AGENCY IN YOUTH CRIMINAL JUSTICE

That the act places such a focus on diversion, broadly speaking, is a testament to the ways in which young people have been conceptualized. Under the YCJA, young people are conceptualized as rational, responsible, and invested with legal rights. Compared to adults, they are assumed to have diminished capacity to understand their actions and consequences (see section 3(1)(b)), and are in a process of development towards maturity (see section (3(1)(b)(ii)). However, at least two important shifts occurred with the crafting of the YCJA, compared to previous youth justice legislation,[1] in how youth were thought about in relation to the justice system. First, the principle of proportionality (section 3(1)(b)(ii)) was introduced, restricting the use of lengthy or onerous sentences, particularly in cases where the courts wish to emphasize rehabilitative treatment (see section 3(i)(c)). While youth needs are important, the justice system's response must always be roughly equivalent to the severity of the offence.

Second, under the YCJA young people are assumed to have agency, capable of making decisions in their own interests (section 3(1)(d)(i)). The YCJA allows for special considerations in proceedings against young persons and, as noted in the act,

> [Y]oung persons have rights and freedoms in their own right, such as a right to be heard in the course of and to participate in the processes, other than the decision to prosecute, that lead to decisions that affect them, and young persons have special guarantees of their rights and freedoms.

More broadly, the United Nations Convention on the Rights of the Child (CRC) is specifically mentioned in the preamble to the YCJA. This represents the commitment of Parliament to ensure that all rights outlined in the CRC, including those pertaining to youth in conflict with the law, are adhered to. The CRC outlines the rights of youth to make decisions and to have their voice heard in judicial proceedings:

> State Parties shall assure to the child who is capable of forming his or her own views the right to express those views freely in all matters affecting the child, the views of the child being given weight in accordance with the age and maturity of the child. (Article 12.1)
>
> For this purpose, the child shall in particular be provided the opportunity to be heard in any judicial and administrative proceeding affecting the child, either directly, or through a representative or appropriate body, in a manner consistent with the procedural rules of national law. (Article 12.2)

The legislative principles underlining youth as having agency are consistent with a growing body of literature within child, childhood, and youth studies (Cotnam-Kappel, 2014; Prout & James, 1997). As Prout and James (1997) argue, children and youth are not merely the products and objects of social structures and institutions, but are active agents in constructing their own lives. As a result, the social relationships and cultures of children are deserving of study, independent of the control of adults. Tilleczek (2011) notes that "youth studies cannot be separated from the lived experiences, social organization, and reproduction of age, ethnicity, social class, race, religion, sexualities, gender, and their intersections" (p. 143). "Youth" as a status intersects with these various statuses, and such intersectionality can compound disadvantage when compared to similarly situated adults (Cote, 2014). Incorporating youth voice in research assists in understanding the complexity of young people's lives. The ways in which youth actively construct their social lives, and not just how adults have constructed life for them, is critical to the field of youth studies (Tilleczek, 2011).

A similar call to incorporate the voices of youth is paralleled in the criminal justice literature. Hogeveen and Minaker (2009) state,

> Possibilities for meaningful change are apparent when youth are respected—that is, recognized as valuable, contributing members of society, and not merely seen as a "problem" that adult society must manage.... Not only does listening to youth represent a departure from established academic and youth justice traditions, but it also broadens the array of strategies for responding to youth and crime. (p. 270)

Before discussing in more detail research on youth experiences with diversion as a broad criminal justice response, we turn to outlining some of the critiques of diversion.

Diversion in Practice

While in theory diversion is laudable, particularly the emphasis on community integration and on avoiding the stigmatizing effects of criminal justice system involvement, diversion has not been without its critiques, including a relative absence of knowledge about the diversion process, variation and arbitrariness in the treatment of youth, **net-widening**, and restrictions on due process. Authors have long cautioned that little is known about the diversion process, its effectiveness, or whether diversion achieves the objectives set out in the legislation (Bala, 2005; Greene, 2011). While the gaps remain significant, research has demonstrated significant variation in the treatment of diverted youth across regions (Bala, 2005; Harris et al., 2004). The ample latitude to interpret policy by those administering youth justice (Maclure, Campbell, & Dufresne, 2003), variations in diversion procedures across provinces and eligibility criteria directing Crown discretion[2] (Milligan, 2010), and the widely discrepant availability of community programs and resources (Alvi, 2014; Bala, 2005; Carrington & Schulenberg, 2005; McNaught, 1998; Moyer & Basic, 2005; Nuffield, 2003) contribute to this significant variation across regions.

Moreover, authors have long feared that the lack of formal policy structuring diversion may lead to net-widening (Greene, 2011; McNaught, 1998; O'Brien, 1984; Sprott, Doob, & Greene, 2004). Through diversion programs, youth who may have previously received a simple police warning for a minor offence are being required, informally, to submit to some form of bureaucratically managed supervision and control. Evidence shows many youth are persuaded into admitting their guilt to facilitate their participation. Thus, although diversion provides an alternative to the formal court process, it can be interpreted as a veiled form of coercion and control. Indeed, some have argued that the referral process itself may undermine due process (Harris et al., 2004; McNaught, 1998; O'Brien, 1984), particularly when youth are compelled to accept responsibility for an offence in order to receive a more lenient option when the evidence of their guilt has not been substantiated in a court of law. Similarly, while there is increasing literature on the mental health court model and its benefits for some offences and offenders

(Behnken, Arrendondo, & Packman, 2009; Skowyra & Cocozza, 2006), some literature has been critical, highlighting the coercive nature of providing participants with "choice" of treatment, in exchange for withdrawal of charges (see Moore, 2007). While the critiques of diversion are significant, there is a lack of understanding of the programs and court processes for youth *by* youth.

EXPLORING YOUTH VOICE AND PARTICIPATION IN DIVERSION

This section explores youth voice at three points of diversion. First, we present research highlighting the insights of youth who participated in a pre-charge diversion program offered by police (EJM) and a post-charge diversion program (EJS) offered by Crown prosecutors in Ontario. Second, we offer examples of youth voice, largely from a study involving observations within a youth mental health court in Ontario. The third and final section reflects the experiences of youth in an Aboriginal court. Each of these diverse contexts reveals how youth agency informs the diversion process and its effectiveness, and how youth agency is encouraged through the structure and process of diversion.[3]

Extrajudicial Measures

Community agency representatives are often responsible for speaking with youth and arranging appropriate EJM (when a police officer has offered the youth a referral to a community program). In an ongoing study of all community agencies offering EJM programs in five diverse regions in Ontario, diversion program representatives were asked about the diversion process and the role of youth in this process. While in some cases the response of the agency is predicated on the nature of the offence rather than the needs of youth, in many other cases the agency representatives speak extensively with youth during intake, giving youth an opportunity to provide an account for their behaviour and to participate actively in shaping the diversion. One agency representative from a **Youth Justice Committee** notes the following:

> A lot of young people that I deal with are absolutely terrified to go to court, so in that sense they would rather come here. And I explain to the young person that the judge isn't going to care about problems at home or the circumstances around the offence that we're asking you now to tell us about so we can be fair to you and give you something meaningful.

When youth are asked about their experiences with diversion offered by police (EJM) and Crown attorneys (EJS), they are thoughtful in providing a critical analysis of their position vis-à-vis the criminal justice apparatus. In Greene's (2011) study of youth diversion programs in Ontario, a significant majority (around 90 percent) of a sample of 157 youth participating in diversion believed that the use of diversion in their case was fair, and that the police made the correct decision in recommending them to diversion. As mentioned earlier, youth have the choice to engage in diversion and must consent to a response or program. Youth reported, however, that the "choice" to accept diversion was made under duress. They felt that accepting the diversion was the only way for them to avoid a more severe criminal justice sanction, including a criminal record. As Greene (2011) observes,

> The vast majority of youth from both programs believed that if they refused to participate, the police would have taken them to court while others felt that they would be taken right to detention. Youth sent to court by the police also believed refusal to take part in EJS would result in a more severe penalty. Understood from this perspective, it becomes clear why these young people "chose" diversion. Those youths who "chose" diversion did so because it was the only way, from their perspective, to avoid much more severe consequences such as court, jail, and a criminal record. This also explains, in part, why most diverted youth felt that referral to diversion was exactly what the police (or court) should have done. (pp. 191–192)

They are also articulate in pointing to what is valuable to them and less so about the diversionary programs. In a small **qualitative** study of 20 young people offered EJS in one courthouse in Ontario,[4] young people were asked questions about the extent to which the EJS process was expected to meet, and met for them, the goals of accountability, proportionality, and meaningful consequences as articulated under the YCJA (Hyde, Marinos, & Innocente, 2016). Youth were aware and critical of the differences between what is considered a meaningful consequence for a youth, as interpreted by an adult (justice professional) deciding on the diversion program, compared to asking a youth. For example, many youths mentioned that there were components of programs that were not meaningful to them, such as writing an essay about why their behaviour was a criminal offence and morally wrong. As one youth noted, "I just wrote it to get it done" (Participant 20).

Youth articulated that some aspects of sanction programs are more valuable than others. On the whole, youth were more likely to appreciate elements of a program that repaired family relationships that were meaningful to them. Yet only two participants reported any involvement from their parents in the program because most program activities, such as essay writing, newspaper assignments, and letters of apology, were focused on the individual youth. Other participants discussed the value of counselling, because it went beyond learning that the offence is wrong, and was connected to their lives and important relationships to them. For one youth, counselling taught her "respect, and how to treat people and like how to influence by actions, like how my mind works" (Participant 17).

Some youth reported that the process of coming to court to formally accept an EJS offer, was, in itself, a meaningful consequence, and held them accountable for their offence (Hyde et al., 2016). One youth reflected on her experience:

> [Y]eah, even this process, I would never do it again … it's scary, to learn that oh this is the same courtroom that a killer would come into, it's like scary … like you don't know what to say, like you stand up front … it's just, they all just look you in your eye … it's not cool. (Participant 8)

The research presented here illustrates that giving youth voice is informative in understanding what is or is not effective from their standpoints and their needs. While the scope of this study is limited, these youth perspectives both reinforce the critique of "lack of choice" by youth, and offer us positive elements of diversion that connect with what they define as their underlying needs.

Youth Mental Health Court

Relatively little is known about young people's experiences within diversionary courts in Ontario (see Weagant, 2015). In Ontario, a number of youth mental health courts have been developed in various jurisdictions. The model of the specialized or problem-solving court involves, quite often, the young person completing a program, monitored by the court and specialists, after which the charge(s) is withdrawn. While some evaluations have been conducted of a youth mental health court in Toronto (Davis, Peterson-Badali, Weagant, & Skilling, 2015) with respect to outcomes, less attention has been directed towards exploring the experiences and voices of youth.

Marinos and Gregory (2012), in contrast, were especially interested in documenting the voices of young people while they were observed in a diversionary court process, compared to a traditional, guilty plea court.[5] Their small observational study (37 youth cases; 15 in guilty plea court and 17 in mental health court) was conducted to understand the extent to which a youth mental health court was distinct from a youth guilty plea court with respect to the active participation of the accused. A traditional criminal court is structured by the adversarial system. Under the adversarial model, lawyers have the "recipe" or expert knowledge (Ericson & Baranek, 1982) and speak on behalf of accused persons. With respect to young people, Bala and Anand (2009) explain two possible reasons for the lack of youth input in the traditional youth court:

> Judges should ask the youth and parents if they have anything to say before sentence is imposed. Typically, the parents and youth feel intimidated by the court setting and are likely to say little or nothing. Further, defence counsel will sometimes advise the youth not to say anything for fear that the youth may make statements that could indicate a lack of remorse or an anti-social attitude.… There is some

controversy about how actively the judges should attempt to engage the young person in the court process, especially at the sentencing stage. (p. 506)

Compared to the traditional youth court, youth in the mental health court were more likely to speak openly within the court when asked by the judge, and without being addressed by the judge. Youth were observed to ask questions about clarifications on various topics such as living arrangements/locations, as well as placement location(s) to receive services. Some youth asked, for example, whether or not they could continue their placement within certain organizations. Others asked if they could be kept in certain environments in order to feel more comfortable, or to help them refrain from future offending.

The youth mental health court environment reflected **power** dimensions between the judge and the accused that was less hierarchical than the traditional guilty plea court. For example, the lawyers and judge often made statements such as "congratulations," "job well done," "[first name of youth], you've done exceptionally well." The environment was more personalized, intimate, and supportive of youth to complete treatment and achieve "success."

This environment facilitated young people expressing themselves in open court. When one youth was asked about the program he was enrolled in, he said, "I want to stay in [name of program]." The judge then asked, "what do you want to do once you are out of the program?" The youth said, "I want to build army tanks." The lawyers, judge, and youth had a conversation about how he could pursue his interests. In contrast, when youth spoke openly in the guilty plea court, they were focused on past behaviour: "I feel awful for assaulting a staff. I will abide by the conditions of the court" (Case 1).

The active participation of youth in mental health diversionary court seemed to be the result of the court providing a more open and accepting environment. Youth were encouraged to ask questions, while being supported by their lawyer. While it is likely that these young people were being encouraged and supported to speak by their lawyers, they seemed to feel comfortable, nevertheless, to do so. In contrast, the adversarial model is much more lawyer-driven, with youth voice being expressed through counsel.

Youth with mental health needs are typically treated as a vulnerable and marginalized population. The court was structured in a less formalized and hierarchical way to facilitate, among other things, all participants of the court working together. That the youth spoke more frequently and openly in the specialized court, compared to a traditional court, is testament to one effective component of this diversionary process.

The Voices of Indigenous Youth

Typically, when youth are diverted to the Community Council at Aboriginal Legal Services (ALS), they meet with a restorative circle of Indigenous volunteers who talk with the youth about "why" the offence occurred, as opposed to the offence itself. With significant input from youth, the Council creates a rehabilitative program for him/her. Thus, young peoples' voices are given space within the very structure of this process. They are encouraged to give their input on how they want to make amends for offences and what type of programming would be best for them (Clark, 2016).

Semi-structured interviews were conducted with 10 youth who were processed in the court and diverted to the Community Council. The findings revealed that nearly all respondents expressed a pride in being Indigenous and explained that their culture is very important to them. They understood that as Indigenous youth, they face inequalities and differential treatment in their everyday lives, as well as in the justice system. As a result, youth were clear that a separate court for Indigenous youth and culturally specific programming is needed. Additionally, youth expressed that they liked participating in the circle, and the informal setting made them feel more at ease. They described how they felt cared about, as opposed to just being a "number." This idea is explained by a 17-year-old male, who stated the following:

> The judge, she was a pretty happy lady so that made me more comfortable. And they remembered you every time you went in. It was a friendly environment because everyone sits around the table. It was a lot better than the normal court where you are just basically a piece of paper that goes on your file.

When asked if completing their diversion would have any impact on their future choices, most youth said yes because their diversion requirements were (1) something they wanted to do; (2) something they perceived as being "good" for them (i.e. going to school); and (3) something that connected them to their culture.

While youth's experiences at the Aboriginal Youth Court were generally positive, a few youth were critical of aspects of the court, and of diversion in general. In terms of diversion requirements at ALS, an 18-year-old male also stated that culture should be further incorporated:

> Get the Native youth out there for cultural programs. If it's run by Native people then it feels more natural to the Native community and to Native youth. The Native kids in Toronto, and the old people ... we don't belong on concrete. The more we stay on concrete, the more we go crazy. We lose ourselves in a land where people don't understand us, and we don't understand them.

One youth was critical of the youth justice system in general. A 19-year-old male who participated in the AYC study framed his concerns about the youth justice system within the wider context of colonialism and overrepresentation:

> They do all these things that they think are best for us, but they don't know a damn thing about what is best for us. Only we do.... It is a very big step for our

people, to say that we are being acknowledged in the court. But … they also need to understand why our people are in jail. They need to change the fact that Natives are in jail.

These comments are significant because they refer to marginalization and the vast overrepresentation of Indigenous people, including youth, in the criminal justice system. Although the AYC is still relatively new and developing, it shows great promise, a conclusion generally expressed by the Indigenous youth who were interviewed. By acknowledging the **systemic discrimination** and historical factors Indigenous peoples face, the AYC benefited some of the youth that were interviewed. More broadly, this study suggests that more effective justice responses for *all* youth may be achieved by being more youth-focused, and by accounting for the experiences of marginalized youth.

CONCLUSIONS: FUTURE RESEARCH ON YOUTH VOICE AND DIVERSIONARY RESPONSES

This chapter takes up the call by scholars to present the voices of justice-involved youth. The chapter highlights the voices of youth in three distinct diversionary contexts in Ontario: extrajudicial measure programs, youth mental health courts, and Aboriginal Youth Courts. The research herein prioritizes the voices of youth. We "give voice" to youth experiences in the criminal justice system, providing us with an understanding of the processes and effectiveness of diversion from their positions. By exploring these three contexts, we begin to develop an understanding of how youth agency informs the diversion process and its effectiveness, and how youth agency is encouraged through the structure and process of diversion. We also highlight where youth voice is "given," as an embedded component within the very structure of the diversion process. When we listen to, or ask for, their perspective, youth give us a different and meaningful picture of diversion, one that is critical of diversion but reflects some promise from and for them.

The research agenda of "giving voice" to youth experiences in diversion is relatively absent from the literature. Considering that youth justice policies and diversions are designed for youth, it is important that the diverse realities of their lives are recognized and that they are given space to articulate their experiences and views. Age intersects with class, gender, ethnicity, and race, leading to compounding effects for young people. Youth who are justice-involved are, most often, marginalized and vulnerable. While statistics and scholarly critical analysis are important, it is from asking youth about their experiences in diversion that we can learn a great deal. The subjective experiences of young people in the justice system offer a way of understanding youth as subjects within evolving youth justice processes, rather than as objects of study (Drake, Fergusson, & Briggs, 2014; James, 1993). In order to more fully understand diversion's workings and bridge existing gaps between theory and practice, research must account for the voices of youth who actually experience these programs firsthand. After all, if social research is used to inform youth policy, young people have a right to be heard as part of that research (Grover, 2004).

CHAPTER SUMMARY

Together, in this chapter, we

- Gained insight into how youth voice and youth agency can enhance our knowledge of the process and effectiveness of youth diversion.
- Learned about diversionary responses under the Youth Criminal Justice Act, including extrajudicial measures and extrajudicial sanctions.
- Sought to understand youth diversion in three contexts, including an extrajudicial sanctions program, a mental health court, and an Aboriginal Youth Court.
- Reviewed the benefits and limitations of youth diversion through considering current literature and by listening to the voices of youth.
- Highlighted how youth and agency are embedded within the structure of the diversion process, allowing space for youth to express their voices and be heard by justice officials.

STUDY QUESTIONS

1. Why is it important to investigate "youth voice" and agency in criminal justice?
2. What are some of the ways in which youth have been conceptualized in relation to diversion in Canada?
3. Think about a time when you were required to participate in an activity about which you had views and beliefs, but were not given an opportunity to express them. How did this situation make you feel?
4. How does giving "youth voice" assist other fields in which youth are involved, such as education, child welfare, employment, and mental health?
5. How do the lived experiences of young people and intersections of age, gender, class, race, and ethnicity impact their experiences of diversion?

SUGGESTED RESEARCH ASSIGNMENT

Using primary research, explore the ways in which extrajudicial measures and extrajudicial sanctions are administered in your community. Using background research in diversion, explain why measures and sanctions are administered this way, taking into consideration agency funding, community networks, police structure, and other factors that may be relevant to the local community.

SUGGESTED FILMS/VIDEO CLIPS

Youth Criminal Justice Act—Extrajudicial Measures & Sanctions
www.youtube.com/watch?v=N1AlNgZVvxg
This short piece, created by the Department of Justice Canada, explains the various options available to police and Crown prosecutors in offering youth an extrajudicial measure or extrajudicial sanction. There are appearances by criminal justice professionals and youth, outlining their experiences with various responses.

Claiming Space: Voices of Urban Aboriginal Youth
www.youtube.com/watch?v=2bb2c240sQE
This very important yet short piece from the Museum of Anthropology is an excellent example of how Indigenous youth can voice their beliefs and experiences using the media.

Rethinking the Impact of Traditional Justice: Natalie DeFreitas at TEDxVancouver
www.youtube.com/watch?v=Jx4ExrPT8Wg
An excellent, captivating TED Talk on the importance of thinking beyond traditional judicial proceedings. Restorative justice represents a paradigm shift in how we think about how to deal with youth and adult crime outside of traditional court proceedings and sentences.

The Gladue Report.mov
www.youtube.com/watch?v=7lyPJsNHdQw
This short clip by BearPaw Legal Education & Resource Centre provides an excellent explanation of the needs and purposes of Gladue courts for Aboriginal youth and adults.

SUGGESTED WEBSITES

Aboriginal Legal Services
www.aboriginallegal.ca
Established in 1990, Aboriginal Legal Services emerged from an assessment by the Native Canadian Centre of Toronto signalling a need for a dedicated organization for legal programs. Aboriginal Legal Services was formed to strengthen the capacity of the Aboriginal community through the provision of legal services and culturally based justice alternatives.

Justice for Children and Youth

jfcy.org/en/

A nonprofit legal aid clinic representing low-income children and youth. Segments of their website focus on youth rights, particularly youth rights in the court process and for post-charge diversion.

Mental Health Commission of Canada

www.mentalhealthcommission.ca/English/

The MHCC, through community partnerships, projects, and recommendations, seeks to improve the mental health system and to change attitudes and behaviours around mental health in Canada. Of particular importance is the MHCC's focus on the justice system and on early intervention with children and youth.

NOTES

1. Canada's first youth justice legislation was the Juvenile Delinquents Act (1908), following by the Young Offenders Act (1984). For an in-depth history see Bala and Anand, 2009.

2. The Crown prosecution review in the provinces is a provincial responsibility, while in the three territories it is the responsibility of the federal Department of Justice.

3. The research findings on youth agency, voice, and diversion presented here are at different stages and in different forms, including either current, or ongoing, or published research. The research on Aboriginal Youth Court is part of Christine Goodwin-DeFaria's current PhD research at Ryerson University.

4. There were 20 youth who were interviewed before they began their EJS program, and there were follow-up interviews with 13 of the youth.

5. These findings were part of a larger study conducted by Marinos and Gregory; the manuscript is currently under preparation. The location of the court is confidential by design.

REFERENCES

Alam, S. (2015). Youth court statistics in Canada, 2013/2014. *Canadian Centre for Justice Statistics*. Retrieved from www.statcan.gc.ca/pub/85-002-x/2015001/article/14224-eng.htm

Alvi, S. (2014). Recognizing new realities: A left realist perspective on the YCJA. *Canadian Criminal Law Review, 18*(3), 341–358.

Bala, N. (2005). Community-based responses to youth crime: Cautioning, conferencing, and extrajudicial measures. In K. Campbell (Ed.), *Understanding youth justice in Canada* (pp. 176–197). Toronto: Pearson Education Canada.

Bala, N., & Anand, S. (2009). *Youth justice criminal law* (2nd ed.). Toronto: Irwin Law.

Behnken, M. P., Arrendondo, D. E., & Packman, W. L. (2009). Reduction in recidivism in a juvenile mental health court: A pre-and post-treatment outcome study. *Juvenile and Family Court Journal, 60*(3), 23–44.

Carrington, P. J., & Schulenberg, J. L. (2005). *The impact of the youth criminal justice act on police charging practices with young persons: A preliminary statistical assessment.* Ottawa: Department of Justice Canada.

Clark, S. (2016). Evaluation of the Aboriginal Youth Court, Toronto. *Aboriginal Legal Services.* Retrieved from www.aboriginallegal.ca/assets/ayc-evaluation-final.pdf

Cote, J. (2014). *Youth studies: Fundamental issues and debates.* New York: Palgrave Macmillan.

Cotnam-Kappel, M. (2014). Tensions in creating possibilities for youth voice in school choice: An ethnographer's reflexive story of research. *Canadian Journal of Education, 37*(1), 140–162.

Davis, K. M., Peterson-Badali, M., Weagant, B., & Skilling, T. A. (2015). A process evaluation of Toronto's first youth mental health court. *Canadian Journal of Criminology and Criminal Justice, 57*(2), 159–187.

Department of Justice Canada. (2002). *Youth Criminal Justice Act.* Retrieved from www.laws-lois.justice. gc.ca/PDF/Y-1.5.pdf

Department of Justice Canada. (2005). *The impact of the Youth Criminal Justice Act on police charging practices with young persons: A preliminary statistical assessment.* Retrieved from www.justice.gc.ca/eng/rp-pr/cj-jp/yj-jj/pdf/prelimin.pdf

Department of Justice Canada. (2011). *The Youth Criminal Justice Act: Summary and background.* Ottawa, Canada. Retrieved from www.justice.gc.ca/eng/pi/yj-jj/ycja-lsjpa/back-hist.html

Doob, A., & Cesaroni, C. (2004). *Responding to youth crime in Canada.* Toronto: University of Toronto Press.

Drake, D., Fergusson, R., & Briggs, D. (2014). Hearing new voices: Reviewing youth justice policy through practitioners' relationships with young people. *Youth Justice, 14*(1), 22–39.

Ericson, R. V., & Baranek, P. M. (1982). *The ordering of justice: A study of accused persons as dependants in the criminal process.* Toronto: University of Toronto Press.

Fritzler, R. B. (2003). 10 key components of a criminal mental health court. In B. J. Winick & D. B. Wexler (Eds.), *Judging in a therapeutic key: Therapeutic jurisprudence and the courts* (pp. 118–123). Durham, NC: Carolina Academic Press.

Greene, C. T. (2011). *Creating consensus: An exploration of two pre-charge diversion programs in Canada.* PhD dissertation, Centre of Criminology and Sociolegal Studies, University of Toronto.

Grover, S. (2004). Why won't they listen to us? On giving power and voice to children participating in social research. *Childhood, 11*(1), 81–93.

Harris, P., Weagant, B., Cole, D., & Weinper, F. (2004). Working "in the trenches" with the YCJA. *Canadian Journal of Criminology and Criminal Justice, 46*(3), 367–390.

Hogeveen, B., & Minaker, J. (2009). *Youth, crime, and society: Issues of power and justice.* Toronto: Pearson Education Canada.

Human Rights Department of Canada Heritage. (1991). *Convention on the Rights of the Child.* Hull, QC: Minister of Supply and Services.

Hyde, C., Marinos, V., & Innocente, N. (2016). What do meaningful consequences and fair and proportionate accountability mean to youth offered extrajudicial sanctions in Ontario? *Canadian Journal of Criminology and Criminal Justice, 58*(2), 194–220.

James, A. (1993). *Childhood identities: Self and social relationships in the experience of the child*. Edinburgh: Edinburgh University Press.

LaPrairie, C. (2002). Aboriginal over-representation in the criminal justice system: A tale of nine cities. *Canadian Journal of Criminology*, *44*(2), 181–208.

Maclure R., Campbell, K., & Dufresne, M. (2003). Young offender diversion in Canada: Tensions and contradictions of social policy appropriation. *Policy Studies*, *24*(1), 135–150.

Marinos, V., & Gregory, D. (2012). *Balancing multiple objectives of youth justice: The tale of a guilty plea court & a youth therapeutic court in Ontario, Canada*. Paper presented at the Law & Society Conference, Honolulu, Hawaii, Tuesday, June 5, 2012.

McNaught, A. (1998). *Alternative measures programs in Ontario*. Ontario Legislative Library: Legislative Research Services, Backgrounder 24, ISSN 1206-1514.

Milligan, S. (2010). Youth court statistics, 2008/2009. *Juristat*, *30*(2). Statistics Canada Catalogue no. 85-002-X. Ottawa: Statistics Canada. Retrieved from www.statcan.gc.ca/pub/85-002-x/2010002/article/11294-eng.pdf

Moore, D. (2007). Translating justice and therapy: The drug treatment court networks. *British Journal of Criminology*, *47*(1), 42–60.

Moyer, S., & Basic, M. (2005). *Crown decision making under the Youth Criminal Justice Act*. Ottawa: Department of Justice Canada. Retrieved from www.justice.gc.ca/eng/rp-pr/cj-jp/yj-jj/moyer_basic/decision/p1.html

Nuffield, J. (2003). *The challenges of youth justice in rural and isolated areas in Canada*. Ottawa: Research and Statistics Division, Department of Justice Canada. RR03YJ-5e.

O'Brien, D. (1984). Juvenile diversion: An issues perspective from the Atlantic Provinces. *Canadian Journal of Criminology*, *26*(2), 217–230.

Peterson-Badali, M., McCormick, S., Vitopoulos, N., Davis, K., Haqanee, Z., & Skilling, T. A. (2015). Mental health in the context of Canada's youth justice system. *Canadian Criminal Law Review*, *19*(1), 5–20.

Prout, A., & James, A. (1997). A new paradigm for the sociology of childhood? Provenance, promise and problems. In A. James & A. Prout (Eds.), *Constructing and reconstructing childhood: Contemporary issues in the sociological study of childhood* (2nd ed.) (pp. 7–33). London: Falmer Press.

Royal Commission on Aboriginal Peoples. (1996). *Bridging the cultural divide: A report on Aboriginal people and criminal justice in Canada*. Ottawa: Minister of Supply and Services Canada.

Rudin, J. (2007). *Aboriginal peoples and the criminal justice system*. Report prepared for the Ipperwash Inquiry (Ontario). Retrieved from www.archives.gov.on.ca/en/e_records/ipperwash/policy_part/research/pdf/Rudin.pdf

Skowyra, K. R., & Cocozza, J. J. (2006). *Blueprint for change: A comprehensive model for the identification and treatment of youth with mental health needs in contact with the juvenile justice system*. Delmar, NY: The National Center for Mental Health and Juvenile Justice Policy Research Associates.

Sprott, J., Doob, A. N., & Greene, C. (2004). *An examination of the Toronto police service youth referral program*. Ottawa: Department of Justice Canada. Retrieved from www.justice.gc.ca/eng/rp-pr/cj-jp/yj-jj/exam/p1.html

Tilleczek, K. (2011). *Approaching youth studies: Being, becoming and belonging.* Toronto: Oxford University Press.

Truth and Reconciliation Commission of Canada. (2015). *Honouring the truth, reconciling the future: Summary of the final report of the truth and reconciliation commission of Canada.* Retrieved from www.trc.ca/websites/trcinstitution/File/2015/Findings/Exec_Summary_2015_05_31_web_o.pdf

United Nations, Human Rights Office of the High Commissioner (OHCCHR). (1989). *Convention on the Rights of the Child.* Geneva: Office of the United Nations High Commissioner for Human Rights (OHCHR). Retrieved from www.ohchr.org/Documents/ProfessionalInterest/crc.pdf

Weagant, B. (2015). A perspective on Toronto's community youth court. *Canadian Criminal Law Review, 19*(1), 41–46.

Winick, B. J., & Wexler, D. B. (2003). *Judging in a therapeutic key: Therapeutic Jurisprudence and the courts.* Durham, NC: Carolina Academic Press.

14

Making Friends, Negotiating Belonging: How Immigrant and Refugee Youth Negotiate Peer Relations to Claim Belonging

Erwin Dimitri Selimos

LEARNING OBJECTIVES

- To better understand the lived experience of migration, settlement, and social inclusion of young immigrants and refugees in Canada
- To consider examples of young immigrants' and refugees' agency and creative capacities
- To consider the complex social factors that shape how and with whom young immigrants and refugees make friends
- To recognize how racism, xenophobia, and social exclusion personally affect young immigrants and refugees

INTRODUCTION

In this chapter I aim to analyze how **immigrant** and **refugee** youth negotiate peer relationships in their new "home" country. This chapter is based on the insight that making friends and building social networks among peers constitutes a key component of immigrant and refugee youth's **settlement** experience (Devine, 2011; Hebert, Lee, Sun, & Berti, 2008; Teja & Schonert-Reichl, 2013). This chapter is guided by the following questions: What meanings do immigrant and refugee youth give to **friendship**? How do they make friends? With whom do they become friends? Why these people and not others? What consequences, if any, does this have on their sense of belonging in Canada? In order to explore these questions, I focus on the lives of three young people: Wahid, Moti, and Joseph. Through a micro-analysis of their friendship experiences, I demonstrate how they actively build their "social beings" in Canada through their negotiation of peer relationships.

Although immigrant and refugee youth make up a significant proportion of Canada's population, research has—relatively speaking—focused predominantly on the concerns of immigrant adults (Anisef & Murphy Kilbride, 2003). This is not to say that Canadian scholarship has neglected immigrant and refugee youth. A cross-disciplinary body of scholarship focuses on various aspects of immigrant and refugee youth settlement experiences.[1] There is a tendency in this literature, however, to depict immigrant and refugee youth as passive "objects of concern," "problems of adaptation," "**at-risk**," or "in need of services" in ways that neglect their active participation in their own lives. Furthermore, many of these studies are concerned with issues of immigrant and refugee youth's integration in society, where society is often conceived of as a static entity (Rathzel, 2010). Scholars advocate moving beyond unilinear metaphors of integration to explore young migrants' **agency** and everyday practices, the **relational** and contextual aspects of identity, and the cultural complexity that mark their lives. In doing so, these scholars reject definitive conceptualizations of identity, being Canadian, being an immigrant, integration, social inclusion, or home (Chirkov, 2009; Gérin-Lajoie, 2008; Rathzel, 2010; Shahsiah, 2006; Colombo & Rebughini, 2012).

I believe that it remains important to appreciate the creative capacities of how young people of migrant backgrounds work to build lives for themselves in their new country of residence. Thus, in line with the central themes outlined in the introductory statement of this section, I offer a person-centred approach (Smart, 2007) to youth migration that highlights young people's everyday practices, their agency, and their active participation in unique peer cultures (Corsaro, 2014). The life narratives of Wahid, Moti, and Joseph were chosen for several reasons. First, all three are male, have lived in Canada for nearly the same amount of time, and came to Canada around the same age. These similarities provide an opportunity to compare their differing experiences of peer relations and consider the implications these experiences have on their sense of belonging in Canada. Second, Wahid, Moti, and Joseph were exceptionally articulate in explaining their lives and actions—especially with respect to their friendship practices—which made an analysis of their interviews especially productive. I recognize that these case studies are not statistically representative and I do not seek to make statistical generalizations. Rather, as exemplars (Flyvbjerg, 2001) these cases offer insights into the social-psychological dynamics of migration and settlement, providing important opportunities for further analytical exploration (Becker, 2014; Flyvbjerg, 2001).

Overall, through the presentation of these cases I demonstrate that **newcomer immigrant** and refugee youth's migration experiences provide an interpretive frame from which they make sense of and invest meaning into their migration to and settlement in Canada. These meanings inform how they view friendship and what type of friends they may want. However, these meanings mix with various factors including personal dispositions, language abilities, the social organization of schooling, the perceived "openness" of friendship groups among their peers, and societal **discourses** of racism, xenophobia, and Islamophobia to shape the type of friendships possible. The result is highly complex and differential experiences of belonging. Before presenting and discussing the stories of Wahid, Moti, and Joseph, I first provide a brief explanation of the context of the study from which these cases are taken.

ABOUT THE STUDY

The narratives explored in this chapter were taken from a larger dissertation research project that examined the migration and settlement experiences of immigrant and refugee youth living in a deindustrializing, immigrant-receiving city in Ontario, Canada. Between January 2014 and March 2015, I conducted 14 months of fieldwork that included interviews with teachers and settlement workers (n = 18) who work closely with immigrant youth, as well as focus groups (n = 35) and in-depth interviews (n = 30) with young people themselves. There were 13 male and 17 female participants in the in-depth interviews. The study did not focus on specific ethnic groups. Instead, it aimed to capture the "horizons of meaning" (Holstein & Gubrium, 1995) of what it meant to be young, to settle, and to come of age in this Canadian city.

Young people were recruited through local settlement agencies and a local high school. They ranged from 16 to 22 years of age. At the time of the interviews, most participants had lived in Canada for more than one but less than five years. Some participants came to Canada with their families while others came alone; about two-thirds came as refugees, either alone or accompanied by family members. Their countries of origin were also diverse: Iraq, the Democratic Republic of Congo, Somalia, Ethiopia, Albania, Guinea, Haiti, Eritrea, and China. The category of country of origin hides the religious, racial, ethnic, and linguistic diversity of participants. Many lived in multiple countries before coming to Canada, as well as in other Canadian cities.

All interviews were active interviews (Holstein & Gubrium, 1995). In line with social interactionism, active interviews are understood to be social occasions through which the interviewer and interviewee interpret and produce meaning together (Holstein & Gubrium, 1995). A researcher's own social positions shape the type of thoughts, feelings, stories, and perceptions evoked during an interview. My own statuses as an adult, second-generation, white male researcher undoubtedly influenced the types of insights and stories expressed by participants. In order to create an interview environment in which my participants would feel comfortable exploring a range of experiences, I purposely framed our meetings as opportunities for me to learn about their lives. Such a framing placed me in a position of ignorance and the participants in positions of expertise of their own lives. I also attempted to create a comfortable and open atmosphere by framing our meetings as informal conversations about their experiences in Canada. Participants were asked about various aspects of their migration and settlement experience, their everyday lives in the city, their families, their schools, their neighbourhoods, and their goals and aspirations for the future. Interviews were conducted in English and analyzed according to themes that produced insights into these young people's migration and settlement experiences.

Considerable variation existed in the size and composition of participants' families in Canada. They were variously living here without parents, with relatives, in one-parent households, or in large families with many siblings. Some had parents who were highly educated professionals or who came from, as one participant remarked, "distinguished families," in their country of origin. Others had parents with limited university education who worked in nonprofessionalized occupations, such as farmers, bakers, or stonemasons, before coming to Canada. Still others had parents who were small business owners in their home country. Many of the participants' parents were attending English courses and were either unemployed or underemployed. Some young people I interviewed had part-time employment to help support their families.

When newcomer youth first arrive in the city, local schools assess their academic history and language abilities. Based on the results of this assessment, they are placed in specific academic programs. Two schools in the city typically receive immigrant newcomer students, mostly because these schools have developed robust English-language learning programs. Ninety percent of those I spoke with were attending or had attended one of these schools. These two schools are socially and culturally diverse, including a mix of newcomer immigrants, youth who immigrated to Canada before their early teens, and Canadian-born youth of various racial, ethnic, and religious backgrounds. According to publicly available school demographic data, about one-fifth of each school's student body was identified as newcomer immigrant (having arrived in Canada within the last three years); about half of the students' first languages were not English, and approximately one-quarter of the students were classified as low-income. Participants recognized these schools as a critical site for their social inclusion and settlement: the key places where they learned English, learned about the community, and—important to this chapter—met their friends. Some participants also regularly attended youth groups organized by local settlement agencies, a secondary, yet important, site where immigrant youth forged friendships.

When many young immigrants and refugees talked about "building a life" in Canada, finding the "right" friends represented a critical feature of their narratives. They sought friends who shared similar life goals and values. A good friend was one whom they could trust, who offered respect and support. Most participants liked having or wanted diverse friendship groups. "Mixing" offered the possibility to learn about other places, practise and refine their developing English skills, and gain access to knowledge and social resources advantageous to settlement and making a life in Canada.

The daily structure of school and after-school life meant that many developed friendships with other newcomer immigrant peers, often across different cultural or linguistic backgrounds, bonding over "shared tastes" (Harris, 2013, pp. 42–45)—common interests in school, music, film, sport, or fashion—and their common experience of migration and settlement. However, participants did note that "immigrants that are from the same culture, they stay together." Recent immigrants were more likely to "hang out" with their own ethnocultural groups or with students who shared similar cultural, religious, or regional affiliations. Limited English language abilities also encouraged people to interact more closely with those who could speak their language. Some identified strong social pressure to hang out with peers from their ethnocultural background, relaying stories of being criticized when they sought to make friends with other peers. Others explicitly said that they distanced themselves from people of their own cultural or linguistic background, actively seeking friendships with those who did not share their cultural background. They found their co-ethnic peers "gossipy," judgmental, and jealous.

Close friendships between newcomer immigrants and Canadian-born or long-term resident youth were relatively uncommon, and participants highlighted the lack of opportunities to interact with Canadian-born or long-term residents. This makes sense considering that most of their school time was spent in English development and English-language learning courses. It was only after they successfully transferred out of these courses into the "regular" stream that they had more opportunities to interact and build new friendships. Yet lack of English abilities and a lack of confidence in their communication skills discouraged some from approaching "Canadian" students. They worried about being teased or criticized for linguistic errors. Canadian students also belonged to already established, close-knit groups that often stretched back to elementary school. These groups formed identities, interests, and norms and were not necessarily open to new members. Immigrant youth described these friendship groups as difficult to break into.

Some did not want to befriend certain Canadian-born or long-term resident youth because they felt that they shared few interests or tastes. A few were wary of getting too close to certain Canadian youth, including those who shared a similar ethnic or racial background, disliking certain ways they thought other peers behaved: being disrespectful to teachers, doing drugs, drinking alcohol, swearing, or being sexually active or open about their sexual exploits. These behaviours went against their moral sentiments and values. Some also spoke of racist slurs or xenophobic comments made by Canadian youth toward them that qualified their sense of acceptance in Canada.

Several participants did form friendships with Canadian-born youth. In many cases, this was a result of a Canadian peer reaching out and introducing themselves, and typically this friendship formed after several years of living in Canada. Male participants were more likely to comment that they formed friendships with Canadian-born youth through participation in extracurricular or leisure activities, especially sports teams. Some remarked that being good at sports was a key reason they became friends with Canadian-born males. This was less common for female participants, many of whom had no history of sport participation and therefore could not use physical aptitude as a means of forming friendships. Females were also more likely to speak about restrictions placed on them by their parents, regarding when and where they could hang out with friends. This meant that peer socializing happened either at school or in formally structured extracurricular activities.

Overall, these general findings corroborate previous sociological research that demonstrates how social environments shape the choices individuals can make about their personal relationships. Davies (2011), drawing on the work of Bottero (2005), argues that we all have very complex networks of relations to a range of different people. But social characteristics such as class, gender, race, and migration status are systematically embedded in these social networks. The people closest to us also tend to be socially similar along the various dimensions of difference and inequality. The tendency towards **homophily** (the fact that people tend to associate with people socially similar to them) is caused by many factors including geographic location, our membership in organizations, family, and informal roles.

Although illuminating patterns of everyday peer relations, the presentation of tendencies across my interview sample hides the active work young people do as they attempt to "make friends." In fact, what was striking to me as I listened to young people's reflections on their life in Canada was the everyday effort they put into negotiating peer relations. I now turn to an examination of these everyday practices through a micro-analysis of how Wahid, Moti, and Joseph actively build their "social being" in Canada through their negotiation of peer relationships.

WAHID: "THEY REALLY TEND TO TRUST YOU MORE WHEN THEY SEE YOU'RE HANGING OUT WITH CANADIANS"

When I met Wahid, he was entering his second year of university. Eight years before we spoke, his family had left Iraq in search of a "better future." Together with his mother, father, and brother, he had lived in Ukraine for five years, moving to Canada about three-and-a-half years ago. Wahid understood Ukraine as a transitional place away from war and instability, where his family could arrange their Canadian immigration application. He describes Ukraine as the best five years of his life: "All I cared about was just having fun, playing soccer, going out with my friends, eating ... I didn't have any responsibilities back then.... My parents had to do all the worrying." At the time of the interview, Wahid spoke of paying little attention to the situation in Iraq, but remained connected to Ukraine, maintaining contact with friends and often listening to Ukrainian pop music.

When they received word that they were accepted to Canada under the skilled workers program (both his parents were highly educated professionals), Wahid was very happy. He saw Canada as "professional place," where you "want to have your family ... want to study ... want to work in. It's something that you feel proud to be part of." When discussing his immigration to Canada, his parents' sacrifices were not lost on him: "They faced everything. They gave their jobs up just for us." His words expressed a feeling of finally being in a place where a better life could be built, of being in a stable place permanently. His words also expressed an understanding that he had to work hard to make a life in Canada; his future success would be repayment of his parents' sacrifices. Perhaps these feelings animated his drive to achieve and make something of his life in Canada.

Even though he had nearly graduated high school in Ukraine, when Wahid arrived in Canada, he was placed in grade 9, mostly due to his limited English abilities. He learned English quickly, finishing four years of high school in three years. He committed himself to speaking English, meeting new people—especially Canadians—and trying hard not to be, in his opinion, like other newcomers who he thought tended to stay "in their own circle." He actively extended his social networks considerably by joining sports teams, getting involved in extracurricular activities, and volunteering extensively in the community. As Wahid explained,

> I don't want to say I am a different case, but my teachers have always told me that I'm different.... I was always outside my circle. I would talk to Canadian friends.... I valued the Canadian morals more than other newcomers, like helping the community, being part of the sports team, not being afraid of English—always talking English in class.

His Iraqi peers criticized him for "mixing" and only speaking English in school. They accused him of showing off in front of the teacher and not wanting to be an Arab. But, "it's not that I don't want to be an Arab.... I just tend to distance myself from Arab people lots of the time." The complexity of this "distancing" was revealed in the following narrative:

> It's most likely [the] reputation that is around Arabs. You know how they say "there is trouble wherever an Arab is?" ... So that's why most likely I actually started distancing myself from Arabs. [It] even started when I was in Ukraine, when I started developing Ukrainian friends.... But I just want to explain something to you about talking only English. I really think that talking only in English—this thing of kind [of] distancing myself from Arab groups—is also what made me close to a lot of teachers. This is because I don't want to say they look bad at students, because they don't. All the teachers are great.... [But] they really tend to trust you more when they see you're hanging out with Canadians.... That's why lots of them trust me. And I'm really proud of this thing and I don't regret it at all. It's the image that people have of [Arabs].... It's more like a stereotype rather than as an actual thing.... Again I did not fully distance myself from them.... I distance myself, but I also picked who I wanted to be with.

After living in Canada for three and a half years, Wahid has developed deeply intercultural friendship groups, which he divided into his Canadian friends and his Arab friends. He described his Canadian friends as culturally diverse in the sense that they had different ethnic heritages but were all born in Canada. Wahid told me that "there is no mix" between these two friendship groups, hanging out with his Canadian friends and then separately with Iraqis.

Bolstered by his view that Canada was a "professional place" and his desire to establish a life there, Wahid saw "mixing" and developing intercultural friendships, especially with Canadian-born peers, as a strategy to showcase his desire to become Canadian. In some ways, we can say that accumulating Canadian friends was a means for Wahid to accumulate "Canadian-ness." Wahid strategically decided to only "go with one or two" Iraqis. He understood that social discourses framed Arabs as bad, violent, dangerous—even "integration failures." He learned this while living in Ukraine, but these notions followed him to Canada. He feared that being seen to have too many Arab friends would be detrimental to his social advancement, cause "trouble," and interfere with his acceptance as a Canadian. Being seen to "mix" differentiated him from other immigrants in ways that garnered the praise of teachers who labelled him as a unique case of "successful integration"—a distinction of "belonging" that he took much pride in.

MOTI: "TO RESPECT MY REPUTATION ... I GET AWAY FROM PEOPLE WHO ARE NOT FROM MY RACE OR MY RELIGION"

When I met Moti he had been living in Canada for about two years. He was in his final year of high school, but had recently decided to return to school for one more year to upgrade some of his courses. When he was young, Moti left Ethiopia, the country of his birth, with his father, mother, and seven siblings after his father was targeted by government officials. After abandoning their properties in Ethiopia, they fled to Kenya where his father was jobless and all nine members of the family lived in a one-room apartment. In time, however, Moti and his family had established a life. His father, a doctor, found work, and Moti "started getting used to the people," making many friends in school. However, life was still marked by a sense of fear, uncertainty, and insecurity: "They [were] hunting down my father.... They crossed the border even after seven years. We moved six or seven times, like from different apartments, because of that." Then, all of a sudden, "we got a call from the Canadian embassy."

The move happened quickly, with only a short period of time to say good-bye to friends and family. Moti remembered his experience of leaving with mixed emotions. While they were leaving friends and family they loved, Canada represented a release from the insecurities and fears his family faced: "It was the most peaceful time for [my father] ... because [he could] put all that behind him." Canada was also a place from which they could support their family remaining in Africa. "Now it is our responsibility," he told me, reflecting on moving to Canada, "to take care of ... all of those [relatives] in Ethiopia."

Similar to Wahid, the sense of opportunity, responsibility, and obligation motivated Moti to work hard in school. Since being in Canada for a little over two years, he has learned English, garnered the respect of his teachers, and developed close friendships with two other immigrants—one originally from Sudan and the other from Ethiopia. These two young men are his only "good friends" who he can look to for advice and support, and who share similar values and life goals. He contrasted these friends—the trust and security he feels with them—to other peers, both immigrant and Canadian-born, in his school: "You have to stay away from them because they are on drugs and they don't pay attention in school. I know that they will pull me back.... I'll just say 'Hi. How are you?'"

Moti spoke of the intercultural peer network he has developed by living in a neighbourhood and attending a school with peers from various places around the world. But he also told me that he does not really have "white" or "Canadian" friends, terms he often conflated when talking about his peers. In fact, he avoided getting too friendly with Canadians or "white" people. As he explained,

> Some people are just saying bad stuff about refugees [and] immigrants coming to Canada.... Anybody who's Black and has an accent: "They come from the bush, a jungle." That's how they consider you.... Even though they seem nice, [if] something happens, they'll put it on us for sure.... It makes me feel like if I have a friend who is Canadian, what will happen if something happens? Who are they going to blame? Probably me because I'm from a different country. That's how everything is turning out now.... I think because of ISIS. I think because of that kind of stuff.... Before I went to the University and I went to the washroom, opened the door, I close the door and I see, "ALL MUSLIMS GO KILL YOURSELVES. WE DON'T LIKE YOU. WE DON'T LIKE YOU IN OUR COUNTRY." This is at a university! How could this happen?

Moti responded to this social hostility by not forging too close of a relationship with white people: "To respect my reputation, it is better for me to just be quiet about it. I get away from people who are not from my race or my religion. It is not that I hate them. It's for their safety, so they can feel better." But Moti did not want to leave our conversation on such a note. Near the end of our conversation, he told me that there was one more "important thing" he would like to say. "I'm actually glad that I'm here ... I want to say thank you to Canada [for] taking us refugees.... I hope I can do something really good to give back."

To Moti, then, Canada was a place of opportunity and a place from which to support his family, both in Canada and abroad. Motivated by a sense of duty, he was very concerned with staying out of trouble and on the straight path. With this in mind, he made friends with peers who would support him and who shared similar values, actively steering clear of others who he believed were "on drugs" or did not care about

> **Box 14.1: The Canadian Council for Refugees, the Youth Network, and Youth Advocacy**
>
> Young immigrants and refugees take a leading role in raising awareness of the issues and social concerns they face, and many local and national nonprofit organizations offer important spaces for these young people to do this work. For example, the Canadian Council for Refugees (CCR) is a national nonprofit organization that focuses on the rights and protection of refugees and vulnerable migrants in Canada. Given that young people constitute an important component of immigrants and refugees in Canada, the CCR has supported the young people through the creation of the CCR Youth Network. According to their webpage, the "Youth Network gives youth and youth allies a voice to address challenges faced by newcomer youth and a space to share ideas on how to meet these challenges" (Canadian Council for Refugees, n.d.). The Youth Network engages in youth-led initiatives that aim to address challenges faced by newcomer youth, advocate for the social inclusion of young people, and promote newcomer youth representation (Canadian Council for Refugees, n.d.). Their website has a link to issues directly impacting immigrant and refugee children and youth in Canada, as well as links to various initiatives and campaigns advocating for their rights and protections. For more information, please visit their website at ccrweb.ca/en/youth/youth-voices.

school. He formed close friendships with two immigrant peers who shared common experiences of being **racialized** and being newcomers to Canada. Unlike Wahid, he avoided making friends with Canadians or "white people." Even though they may appear "nice," he felt that at any moment new global events like the rise of ISIS could cause people to turn on him, blame him, or target him. In order to maintain dignity in the face of xenophobia and Islamophobia, he purposely distanced himself from "white" peers, searching for existential safety in other immigrant youth. He framed this distancing as a polite act of accommodation for Canadians—"so they can feel better"—revealing an attitude that as a racialized Muslim immigrant, he must keep his head low and avoid attention, perhaps in an attempt to show respect to the country that accepted him.

JOSEPH: "I JUST FEEL LIFE DOESN'T MOVE"

Joseph was 19 years old and a senior in high school at the time I met him. Throughout the interview, he spoke slowly, often pausing for quite some time before answering my questions. Joseph told me that when he was 10 years old, a conflict broke out near his village in the Democratic Republic of Congo, which forced his family to flee for safety in neighbouring Uganda. Separated from his parents and other siblings, Joseph and his brother lived with relatives in Uganda for six years. Uganda "wasn't that good, because of the insecurity" and because "it was not easy to get a good job there." So, after six years, with the help of family members, he was accepted to Canada, and was sent with his younger brother to live with an uncle. Today, they no longer live with their uncle; he and his brother rent two rooms in a small house, living off the limited amount of money they receive from social services.

Like Wahid and Moti, Joseph described Canada as a place that offered stability and opportunity—firm ground upon which to build a life. Informed by a sense of hope and opportunity, he committed himself to academic success. Although he is fluent in French and had the opportunity to attend a French high school in the city, Joseph decided to study in English, believing that "with English you're going to get more opportunities to get jobs." He was placed in an English-language learning stream, and after three years of studying has learned to speak English fluently, achieving honours several times.

Joseph described school as the central site of his social life, and the central node of connection to the city. This was where he learned English, met friends, and participated in leisure activities. He spoke highly of his school, and the support he received as an immigrant, describing it "like a family" where students and teachers are nice and welcoming. When it came to choosing friends, what was important to Joseph was finding people who shared the same morals, and who were supportive: "What matters to me is just a moral. You were nice to me. You respect yourself.... That's it. Then we are good."

He told me that most of his "mates" were Arab, the largest ethnolinguistic group in his school. He got to know them through class or participation in extracurricular sports activities. He qualified these friendships when he told me that he does not "hang out a lot with friends," either in school or outside of it, and admitted to difficulties making good or close friends. He related this to his estimation that only about 2 percent of the school population were immigrants from the Democratic Republic of Congo and that "many kids want to hang out with their own kind [because] they feel more comfortable when they speak to each other in their language.... There is not this huge connection [among] the different kids from another culture."

This sense of being locked out of the various cultural/linguistic-based friendship groups seemed connected to a negative experience he had dating an immigrant peer. Her parents "were not okay" with her dating a "Black guy" and forbade the relationship. This event generated significant negative gossip. Insults were hurled and the experience made him feel "very bad." Her parents never asked to meet him or learn about him as a person. Joseph also expressed difficulties breaking into friendship groups composed of his Canadian-born peers or peers who had lived in Canada long enough to form relatively cohesive friendship networks. He described these peer groups as racially and culturally diverse, but closed off, unhelpful, or unwilling to open their arms to new members:

It's very difficult to get new friends whom you've never grew up with. Most Canadians they want to hang out people they went [to] the grade school [with]. Sometimes we try to get close to them. But man they are not that much friendly. I feel so tired and I feel kind [of] awkward every time I have to come to [you] when I want to talk to you.... Some of the Black kids who have been here for so many years, they [have] Canadian friends and they hang out with Canadian friends.... We just don't hang out a lot because we don't know each other that much.

At the time of the interview, Joseph was very close to graduating and many of his concerns centred on finishing high school and getting a job in order to raise money for college and alleviate the pressures of supporting himself and his brother on a small allowance. Similar to his experiences of making friends, he felt locked out of the job market, having applied for various low-wage employment opportunities with no success. He saw his peers getting jobs through family connections, and recognized that he lacked these personal connections. At the time of the interview, he was considering changing his last name to sound less "African" and more "Canadian," having heard from his peers that employers screen out immigrant-sounding names. "It's like life is stuck somewhere," he tells me; "I just feel life doesn't move, I am just somewhere.... Right now I don't have so many friends, so it is really hard. What should I say? We're going to try our best, man. We're going to try our best [for] the future."

Similar to Wahid, Joseph worked hard to mix, seeing diverse friendships as important sources of support and access to knowledge and resources. Despite these efforts, at the time of the interview, he had been unable to develop close friendships with Canadian-born or immigrant peers. As a minority among minorities, he was unable to break into established friendship groups among either his immigrant peers or among Canadian-born or long-term residents. His negative cross-cultural dating experience heightened his sense of isolation, and represented one of his first explicit experiences of racism. This sense of exclusion was further heightened by his inability to access the labour force, something that he was beginning to attribute to the dual status of being an immigrant and a racialized young person.

CONCLUDING REMARKS

In this chapter I aimed to analyze how young people with migrant backgrounds negotiate peer relationships in their new "home" country. Primarily through a micro-analysis of three immigrant and refugee male youths, I considered the meanings they attributed to friendship, and how they attempted to make friends and with whom. I illustrated that making friends is a complex endeavour influenced by many factors and contingencies. This chapter underscores several important points. First, immigrant and refugee youth's migration experiences provide an interpretive frame through which they invest meaning into their settlement in Canada. These meanings shape many aspects of their lives, including their views of friendship and what type of friends they want. However, these meanings mix with various factors including personal dispositions, language abilities, the perceived "openness" of friendship groups among their peers, the social organization of schooling and everyday routines, and societal discourses of racism, xenophobia, and Islamophobia to shape the type of friendships possible. The result is highly complex and differential experiences of belonging.

Second, the lives of these three young men remind us to appreciate the everyday "work" young people of migrant backgrounds do as they actively negotiate "on the ground" the deep complexities and ambivalences of their lives. Analysts must attend to their agency-in-context and the complex strategies they employ as they try to address the problems and pressures they face (c.f. Shahsiah, 2006). However, these personal stories reveal that processes of belonging in socially and culturally complex contexts are multidimensional and multivalent (Malsbary, 2012), always evolving (May, 2011), and the result of the "coalescence of factors that condition people's lives" (Vertovec, 2007, p. 1045). The social context into which immigrants are incorporated shape how they come to belong (Malsbary, 2012). When immigrant and refugee youth come to live in a new country, they bring a particular biographical history, but live in a particular place, surrounded by particular people, and shaped by particular social arrangements (George, Selimos, & Ku, 2015). This demands approaches to studying immigrant and refugee youth belonging that pay attention to how local realities are nested in larger societal discourse, social arrangements, and dynamics of social exclusion that shape the types of social connections possible.

Migration and settlement is "work" intensive. Immigrant and refugee youth work hard to find a place for themselves in their new society and employ multiple strategies to negotiate belonging. Through this work, they forge complex identifications and ambivalent feelings of belonging. The lives of these three young people reveal "personal troubles" (Mills, 1959/2000) that foreground complex and multidimensional factors that shape how youth of migrant backgrounds live their life and with whom. Through the narratives of these three young men, I hope to have gained some degree of "sympathetic penetration" (Waller, 1934, p. 288) into the complexities, ambivalences, pressures, and puzzles that mark their lives.

CHAPTER SUMMARY

Together, in this chapter, we

- Analyzed how young people with migrant backgrounds negotiate peer relationships in their new "home" country.
- Considered the meanings immigrant and refugee youth attribute to friendship, how they attempt to make friends, and with whom.

- Explored the various social factors that shape how and with whom young immigrants and refugees make friends.
- Demonstrated some of the personal effects of racism, xenophobia, and social exclusion as they relate to the friendship practices and identities of young immigrants and refugees.

STUDY QUESTIONS

1. Identify and explain the social factors that shaped the friendship formation practices of Wahid, Moti, and Joseph.
2. Homophily refers to the fact that we often make friends with those who have similar social characteristics to ourselves. Who are your friends? Why are they your friends? To what extent does the principle of homophily apply to your own life? What social factors can you identify that shaped why these people became your friends and not others?
3. How would you describe the system of peer relations among peers of your former high school? What role did the social organization of school play in shaping who became friends with whom? Furthermore, how did race, class, gender, migration status, etc., shape peer relations?
4. Design an initiative to encourage social connections and friendships between immigrant and refugee youth and their long-term resident or Canadian-born peers.
5. You have been asked by a local nonprofit to conduct a qualitative interview research study that explores the migration, settlement, and social inclusion experiences of immigrant and refugee youth living in your city. They want to use these findings to help design programs and initiatives to support young immigrants in the city. Create seven to ten questions you would ask immigrant and refugee youth about their migration and settlement experiences.

SUGGESTED RESEARCH ASSIGNMENT

There is growing interest in understanding intercultural relations among young people living in socially and culturally diverse settings, and scholars are increasingly interested in the types of peer relations that develop among young people living in these settings. Conduct a preliminary literature review on the topic of youth peer relations in socially and culturally diverse settings. What major themes and findings are emerging in this area of research?

SUGGESTED FILMS/VIDEO CLIPS

Everybody's Children
www.nfb.ca/film/everybodys_children/
This documentary explores a year in the life of two teenage refugees, Joyce and Sallieu, who attempt to make a new life in Ontario. Joyce, 17, left the Democratic Republic of Congo to avoid being forced into prostitution by her family. Sallieu, 16, had witnessed the murder of his mother as a young boy in war-torn Sierra Leone. Both youths must deal with the pressures of being young and going through the refugee application process.

In My Own Voice: A Visual Diary of Newcomer Youth
www.youtube.com/watch?v=TX8OL7rESFQ&list=PL8654912443830BED
This video was created by a group of young people and organized by Ottawa Community Immigrant Services Organization's Youth Program (YOCISO). It features the lived experiences of immigrant newcomer youth to Canada and highlights some of the challenges they faced during their initial settlement in Canada. The video was made possible by a grant provided by the Canadian Council for Refugees.

The Immigrant Story Bank
www.youtube.com/user/uwosocialscience
This YouTube playlist was created jointly by Pathways to Prosperity Partnership and the Western Centre for Research on Migration and Ethnic Relations initiative. The Pathways to Prosperity Partnership (P2P) is an alliance of researchers and practitioners that aims to foster welcoming communities for immigrants that promote the economic, social, and civic integration of migrants and minorities in Canada. The Western Centre for Research on Migration and Ethnic Relations conducts research to improve the well-being of immigrants and ethnic minorities in Canada and internationally. The playlist features the personal stories of immigrants and refugees to Canada.

SUGGESTED WEBSITES

Canadian Council for Refugees
ccrweb.ca
The Canadian Council for Refugees is a national nonprofit organization that focuses on the rights and protection of refugees and vulnerable migrants in Canada, as well as the settlement of refugees and immigrants in Canada. Their website has a link to issues directly impacting immigrant and refugee children and youth in Canada, as well as links to various initiatives and campaigns advocating for these individuals' rights and protection.

Ontario Council of Agencies Serving Immigrants
www.ocasi.org/

Formed in 1978, the Ontario Council of Agencies Serving Immigrants (OCASI) acts as a collective voice for immigrant-serving agencies in Ontario. It conducts research and advocates for the shared needs and concerns of immigrants in Ontario, Canada.

UNICEF, Children on the Move
www.unicef.org/emergencies/childrenonthemove/

This UNICEF website provides general information about the topic of children and migration from a global perspective. The website has links to various reports and policy briefs, as well as to information about ongoing initiatives aimed at improving the quality of life of migrant children and youth.

NOTE

1. Topics include, but are not limited to, the challenges of language acquisition (Anisef & Murphy Kilbride, 2003); access to services and resources (Rossiter & Rossiter, 2009; Walsh, Este, Krieg, & Giurgiu, 2011); acculturation processes (Berry, Phinney, Sam, & Vedder, 2006; Poteet & Simmons, 2015); peer group relations (de Finney, 2010; Teja & Schonert-Reichl, 2013); experiences of discrimination (Shahsiah, 2006; Tomic, 2013); changing family dynamics and intergenerational relationships (Merali & Violato, 2002; Tyyska, 2008); schooling and education (Hebert, Sun, & Kowch, 2004; Krahn & Taylor, 2005; Stermac, Elgie, Clarke, & Dunlap, 2012; Sweet, Anisef, & Walters, 2010; Taylor & Krahn, 2013); transitions to adulthood (Mondain & Lardoux, 2012); labour market participation (Lauer, Wilkinson, Yan, Sin, & Tsang, 2012; Taylor & Krahn, 2013; Wilkinson, Yan, Tsang, Sin, & Lauer, 2011); and mental health, especially of refugee youth (Guruge & Butt, 2015; Yohani & Larsen, 2009).

REFERENCES

Anisef, P., & Murphy Kilbride, K. (Eds.). (2003). *Managing two worlds: The experiences and concerns of immigrant youth in Ontario.* Toronto: Canadian Scholars' Press.

Becker, H. (2014). *What about Mozart? What about murder? Reasoning from cases.* Chicago: Chicago University Press.

Berry, J. W., Phinney, J. S., Sam, D. L., & Vedder, P. (2006). Immigrant youth: Acculturation, identity, and adaptation. *Applied Psychology, 55*(3), 303–332.

Bottero, W. (2005). *Stratification: Social division and inequality.* London: Routledge.

Canadian Council for Refugees. (n.d.). Retrieved from ccrweb.ca

Chirkov, V. (2009). Critical psychology of acculturation: What do we study and how do we study it, when we investigate acculturation? *International Journal of Intercultural Relations, 33*, 94–105.

Colombo, E., & Rebughini, P. (2012). *Children of immigrants in a globalized world: A generational experience.* London: Palgrave Macmillan.

Corsaro, W. (2014). *The Sociology of childhood.* Thousand Oaks, CA: Sage.

Davies, K. (2011). Friendship and personal life. In V. May (Ed.), *Sociology of personal life* (pp. 72–84). London: Palgrave Macmillan.

de Finney, S. (2010). "We just don't know each other": Racialised girls negotiate mediated multiculturalism in a less diverse Canadian city. *Journal of Intercultural Studies, 31*(5), 471–487.

Devine, D. (2011). *Immigration and schooling in the Republic of Ireland.* Manchester, UK: Manchester University Press.

Flyvbjerg, B. (2001). *Making social science matter: Why social inquiry fails and how it can succeed again.* Cambridge, UK: Cambridge University Press.

George, G., Selimos, E. D., & Ku, J. (2015). Welcoming initiatives and immigrant attachment: The case of Windsor. *Journal of International Migration and Integration, 18*(1), 29–45. doi:10.1007/s12134-015-0463-8

Gérin-Lajoie, D. (2008). *Educators' discourses on student diversity in Canada: Context, policy, and practice.* Toronto: Canadian Scholars' Press.

Guruge, S., & Butt, H. (2015). A scoping review of mental health issues and concerns among immigrant and refugee youth in Canada: Looking back, moving forward. *Canadian Journal of Public health, 106*(2), 72–78.

Harris, A. (2013). *Young people and everyday multiculturalism.* New York: Routledge.

Hebert, Y., Lee, J. W.-S., Sun, S. X., & Berti, C. (2008). Relational citizenship as social networks: Immigrant youth's maps of their friendships. *Encounters on Education, 4*, 83–106.

Hebert, Y., Sun, X. S., & Kowch, E. (2004). Focusing on children and youth: The role of social capital in educational outcomes in the context of immigration and diversity. *Journal of International Migration and Integration, 5*(2), 229–249.

Holstein, J., & Gubrium, J. F. (1995). *The active interview.* Thousand Oaks, CA: Sage.

Krahn, H., & Taylor, A. (2005). Resilient teenagers: Explaining the high educational aspirations of visible-minority youth in Canada. *Journal of International Migration and Integration, 6*(3/4), 405–434.

Lauer, S., Wilkinson, L., Yan, M. C., Sin, R., & Tsang, A. K. T. (2012). Immigrant youth and employment: Lessons learned from the analysis of LSIC and 82 lived stories. *Journal of International Migration and Integration, 13*, 1–19.

Malsbary, C. B. (2012). "Assimilation, but to what mainstream?" Immigrant youth in a super-diverse high school. *Journal of Phenomenology and Education, 1*, 89–112.

May, V. (2011). Self, belonging, and social change. *Sociology, 45*(3), 363–378.

Merali, N., & Violato, C. (2002). Relationships between demographic variables and immigrant parents' perceptions of assimilative adolescent behaviors. *Journal for International Migration and Integration, 3*(1), 65–81.

Mills, C. W. (2000). *The sociological imagination.* New York: Oxford University Press. (Original work published 1959)

Mondain, N., & Lardoux, S. (2012). Transitions to adulthood among first generation sub-Saharan African immigrant adolescents Canada: Evidence from a qualitative study in Montréal. *Journal of International Migration and Integration, 14*, 307–326.

Poteet, M., & Simmons, A. (2015). Not boxed in: Acculturation and ethno-social identities of Central American male youth in Toronto. *International Journal of Migration and Integration, 17*(3), 867–885. doi: 10.1007/s12134-015-0442-0

Rathzel, N. (2010). The injuries of the margins and the restorative power of the political: How young people with migrant backgrounds create their capacity to act. *Journal of Intercultural Studies, 31*(5), 541–555.

Rossiter, M. J., & Rossiter, K. R. (2009). Diamonds in the rough: Bridging gaps in support for at-risk immigrant and refugee youth. *Journal of International Migration and Integration, 10*, 409–429.

Shahsiah, S. (2006). Identity, identification, and racialisation: Immigrant youth in the Canadian context. Retrieved from ceris.ca/virtual-library-search/#vlsearch

Smart, C. (2007). *Personal life: New directions in sociological thinking.* Cambridge, UK: Polity Press.

Stermac, L., Elgie, S., Clarke, A., & Dunlap, H. (2012). Academic experiences of war zone students in Canada. *Journal of Youth Studies, 15*(3), 311–328.

Sweet, R., Anisef, P., & Walters, D. (2010). Immigrant parents' investments in their children's post-secondary education. *Canadian Journal of Higher Education, 40*(3), 50–80.

Taylor, A., & Krahn, H. (2013). Living through our children: Exploring the educational and career "choices" of racialized immigrant youth in Canada. *Journal of Youth Studies, 16*(8), 1000–1021.

Teja, Z., & Schonert-Reichl, K. A. (2013). Peer relations of Chinese adolescent newcomers: Relations of peer group integration and friendship quality to psychosocial and school adjustments. *Journal of International Migration and Integration, 14*, 535–556.

Tomic, P. (2013). The color of language: Accent, devaluation and resistance in Latin American immigrant lives in Canada. *Canadian Ethnic Studies, 43*(1/2), 1–21.

Tyyska, V. (2008). Parents and teens in immigrant families: Cultural influences and material pressures. *Canadian Diversity/Diversité Canadienne, 6*(2). Retrieved from canada.metropolis.net/pdfs/Pgs_can_diversity_parents_spring08_e.pdf

Vertovec, S. (2007). Super-diversity and its implications. *Ethnic and Racial Studies, 30*(6), 1024–1054.

Waller, W. (1934). Insight and the scientific method. *American Journal of Sociology, 40*(3), 285–297.

Walsh, C. A., Este, D., Krieg, B., & Giurgiu, B. (2011). Needs of refugee children in Canada: What can Roma refugee families tell us? *Journal of Comparative Family Studies, 42*(4), 599–613.

Wilkinson, L., Yan, M. C., Tsang, A. K. T., Sin, R., & Lauer, S. (2011). The school-to-work transitions of newcomer youth in Canada. *Canadian Ethnic Studies, 44*(3), 29–44.

Yohani, S. C., & Larsen, D. J. (2009). Hope lives in the heart: Refugee and immigrant children's perceptions of hope and hope engendering sources during the early years of adjustment. *Canadian Journal of Counseling, 43*(4), 246–264.

15 Dress Codes as Gender Politics: Feminist Action in Canadian High Schools

Rebecca Raby and Shauna Pomerantz

LEARNING OBJECTIVES

- To learn about a social issue that has been brought to the public's attention through the activism of young people
- To identify shifts over time in how young people have responded to school rules
- To recognize young activists' specific concerns that dress codes and their enforcement are linked to gender inequality, sexism, and rape culture
- To recognize the role of both the established media and social media in shaping a social issue

---

INTRODUCTION

"Your school district contributes to **rape culture**" (Youth Feminists, 2014). This is how a group of girls in Fredericton, New Brunswick, opened their 2014 Change.org petition calling for their school district to "abolish the dress code and create a sexual assault policy" (Youth Feminists, 2014). Their petition included a video of girls speaking out against dress codes for sexualizing young women. They raised concerns about the policing of girls' dress within a broader rape culture, where women are sexually assaulted but few rapists end up in prison. They spoke forcefully about an injustice—that their school dress code sexualized and blamed young women, while their school district did not even have a sexual assault policy. These girls and other supporting students then held a walkout at their school, garnering attention from local and national news outlets. The three girls were then suspended. Feelings of frustration were high, as the girls felt that their attempts to address a serious concern in their school had been ignored, and now they were being punished. This story has a somewhat happy ending, however. In part due to the skills of a mediating teacher, three months later, the young women were working with school administrators to draft a sexual assault policy for the district, although the dress code remained (Poitras, 2015).

This protest was far from an isolated incident. In 2014 and 2015 there was a surge in actions against dress codes in Canada, the United States, and overseas. Led by girls, in Canada these protests included putting up posters around school, turning to social and traditional media, and inviting other students to resist dress codes in solidarity. This explosion of student activism, a particularly active and engaged form of participation expressly focused on making social change, gained significant media attention and commentary. Some celebrated the students' commitment to addressing their concerns and drawing attention to a legitimate social issue ("Check Dress Codes," 2015; Pomerantz & Raby, 2015; Strapagiel, 2015), while others suggested that the protesters were spoiled attention-seekers who unfairly played the "equal rights card" over a hollow goal, instead of addressing more significant social issues (Blizzard, 2015; Culic, 2015; Wente, 2015).

As researchers who have been studying dress codes for over a decade and speaking out frequently on dress codes in the press, we have seen a shift in the kinds of protests taking place and in the ways young people are framing their concerns about these school rules. We argue that these more recent actions are important instances of young people's activism that mark a groundswell of student engagement with concerns about sexism. Dress code protests are certainly not new (e.g. see Schrum, 2004). Yet, as we illustrate through a review of news articles about actions challenging dress codes across Canada since 2000, the number and style of actions, and the language used in them, are powerful examples of young feminist activism. Rather than dismissing challenges against dress codes as a hollow battleground, we begin from the position that such actions are political and valuable instances of young people's participation—in both the democratic life of their school and in addressing the everyday sexism and objectification to which girls are subject.

YOUNG ACTIVISM AND FEMINISM IN CANADA

A popular belief about young people today is that they are disengaged from civic involvement (e.g. see Kennelly, 2011a). For instance, it has been repeatedly reported that in Western countries, young people are less likely than adults to join political parties or other established organizations that are interested in working towards social change; and among those who are old enough, young people are less likely to vote (Barnes & Virgint, 2010; Henn, Weinstein, & Wring, 2002; Putnam, 2000). Researchers also suggest that young people have become more individualized and private in their activities, and disconnected from community (Furlong & Cartmel, 2007). In response, various governments have instituted mandatory civics education that tends to emphasize a narrow, conservative conceptualization of **citizenship** (Kennelly, 2011b). Yet others have countered that **youth civic engagement** is not dead—it is simply oriented in different directions than towards more traditionally established organizations and venues (Gauthier, 2003; O'Neill, 2007; Skelton & Valentine, 2003). Instead, young people are involved in extensive volunteer work, joining movements that are short-term and issue-based, and often participating in politics online (Buckingham, 2000; Keller, 2015; Kellner & Kim, 2010; O'Neill, 2007; Rheingold, 2008).

In the last 20 years, concerns have arisen within feminist circles that there has been a similar decline in feminist activism (e.g. Bellafante, 1998; Budgeon, 2015; see also Pomerantz, Currie, & Kelly, 2004, for discussion). Young women, especially, have been seen as increasingly unwilling to identify themselves as feminists, often premised on the opinion that we now live in an era of **neoliberalism** and **post-feminism**, where gender equality has been achieved (Currie, Kelly, & Pomerantz, 2009; McRobbie, 2009; Pomerantz, Raby, & Stefanik, 2013; Scharff, 2011). Examples of such denunciations of **feminism** continue. For example, daily we see young women posting to the Women Against Feminism Tumblr, denying gender inequality and speaking out against the victim-status that they presume feminism to require (Women Against Feminism, n.d.). Others counter that while young women may not identify as feminists, their concerns with gender inequality take forms that look different from more traditional feminist resistance—for example, a focus on bodily freedoms, fluidity of identity, playful engagement with popular culture, and/or recognition of multiple identities including those based on intersections of race and sexuality (Harris, 2008). Some are, in turn, critical of what is seen as a new expression of "choice feminism," with a problematic and depoliticized focus on individualism over collective, equality-seeking feminist politics (Budgeon, 2015; McRobbie, 2009; see also Ringrose, 2013, for discussion). When looking more specifically at dress, young women have been criticized for embracing an understanding of feminism that seems to simply celebrate dressing in sexualized clothing (e.g. Wente, 2015; Levy, 2005), or wearing provocative dress in order to challenge slut-shaming (see Church, 2011).

In this chapter, we start from the premise that young people are embedded in material conditions, social structures, and **discourses** that shape how they come to see themselves, how others see them, and what is considered possible. For example, as we are looking at young people challenging school rules, we need to first recognize that students are embedded in the school as a physical, bureaucratic, and hierarchical institution charged with containing and educating large numbers of students. Schools, and young people's experiences within them, are also shaped by broader dominant discourses, including powerful neoliberal and post-feminist emphases on the centrality of the individual over the collective, and denial of gender and other inequalities (see Gill & Scharff, 2011). Further, young people are embedded in dominant constructions of what it means to be a teenager, including pervasive assumptions that they are immature, irresponsible, incomplete, potential trouble, and **at risk** (Lesko, 2001; Raby, 2002; Raby & Raddon, 2015).

Young people are not automatons within these structures and discourses, however. Rival experiences, including those emerging through structural inequalities (e.g. see Ferguson, 2001), related dispositions (Bourdieu, 1983/2001), and exposure to competing discourses, such as those found in media outlets and peer groups (e.g. see Dickar, 2008), can clash with the dominant structures and belief systems of schools, and these shape how young people think about themselves, their schools, and broader social issues. Young people are not simply moulded by these forces; they play a part in both reproducing and challenging them. In other words, young people are participants in the production of their social worlds (Harris, 2008; James, 2009; Keller, 2015; Wyness, 2006). This participation is embedded in mundane, day-to-day life; it can also be more dramatic, forceful, and resistant, as we see with student actions against dress codes.

Through schools, young Canadians are often involved in charitable enterprises, community-based volunteering, and sometimes more political activism work, such as social justice and environmental clubs. Interestingly, however, points of confrontation within the school most commonly arise around codes of conduct, which cover rules from banning drugs and alcohol to determining where students can go during the day and what they can wear (Raby, 2012). While students may take issue with various rules in their school, the frequent "hot" issue is dress. Dress codes outline what kind of student the school considers respectable, appropriate, or normal. This hidden curriculum (Glossary of Education Reform, 2016) often includes narrow ideals of gender, race, class, and sexuality (Schrum, 2004; Pomerantz, 2007; Raby 2005, 2012). For example, dress codes can be productive of certain preferred citizens—such as those who are compliant and oriented towards working in an office—but also preferred presentations of gender and sexuality. School staff attempt to enforce these ideals among diverse student bodies with differing cultural backgrounds, classes, and personal tastes (Morris, 2005; Pomerantz, 2008; Raby, 2012), and among students who frequently consider the logic behind etiquette rules, such as those about dress, to be unconvincing (Thornberg, 2008).

METHODOLOGY

To examine recent changes in young people's confrontations with their school dress codes, we conducted a textual analysis of Canadian student actions and protests against dress codes since 2000. While a smattering of protests and other actions around dress codes occurred in the 1990s and 2000s, there was a significant surge in action, conflict, and commentary in 2014 and 2015. We conducted widespread online searches to find articles on dress code protests in Canada in order to explore the explosion in actions during a particular time period. We focused on changes in the form of the conflicts and the commentary about them. We specifically looked for articles addressing moments when students went public against their school's dress code and/or its enforcement, through things like speaking to the press, walking out of class, making a video, or putting up posters.

After a general online search for newspaper articles between 2000 and 2015, using the terms *Canada*, *school*, and *dress code protest*, and the creation of a Google timeline on Canadian school dress code protests, we focused our searches on more specific topics. For example, if the initial search yielded an article on a "crop top" protest, then a Google search was done on this topic and related links to find additional articles. Next, the Canadian Business and Current Affairs (CBCA) Database was used to search for Canad* AND "dress code" AND school OR education AND protest OR challeng* between 2000 and 2015 to find articles that may not have been uncovered via the Google search. The Canadian Newsstand Database was then used to search for articles related to *school*, *education*, *dress code*, and *protest* between 2000 and 2015 to uncover remaining articles that may have still escaped us. The Ontario Community Newspapers database was used to search for *school dress code* between 2000 and 2015 as well. Finally, the Canadian Periodical Index Quarterly (CPIQ) database was used to search for Canad* AND "dress code" AND school OR education AND protest OR challeng* between 2000 and 2015. While our searches will have missed unreported actions and those not picked up by our search words, these extensive searches yielded a total of 63 articles, covering 27 protests, with the bulk of the protests occurring in 2014 or 2015 (see table 15.1).

The news articles were analyzed for key themes. The articles were first organized by which part of the dress code was being challenged and how (e.g. "crop top" protest), the date of the protest, key words, and the reporting of specific comments from students and administrators. The articles were then reviewed a second time with a particular focus on dress code protests that concentrated on girls' dress, coupled with patterns among the comments in older and newer news articles. In examining these articles, we were particularly interested in exploring quotations from student participants when they provided reasons for their actions, as well as the official school response (e.g. from principals), in order to note whether and how arguments shifted over time. Of course, when students or administrators speak to journalists, they do not get to choose what parts of their conversations will be quoted or how—we are thus working with a selective part of the wider conversations students and administrators had around dress code actions.

Table 15.1: Summary of Findings

2001 (2 protests/actions, 2 news articles)	*April 13, Hamilton, ON: Students organized a knee-high day when their school banned knee-high socks. * May 2, Abbotsford, BC: Students protested against the introduction of a new dress code.
2002 (1 protest/action, 1 news article)	* April 20, Markham, ON: Grade 11 student, Shae Ayerhart, organized a protest against the introduction of a dress code.
2003 (2 protests/actions, 2 news articles)	* September 21, Edmonton, AB: Students protested against the introduction of a dress code. * October 27, Red Deer, AB: Students responded to a school crackdown on "extremes" in clothing.

Continued

2004 (1 protest/action, 2 news articles)	* April 3, Winnipeg, MB: Students went to the press after their school banned pyjama pants.
2007 (1 protest/action, 1 news article)	* September 6, Halifax, NS: A school retreated from an attempt to ban hoodies after student-and-parent protest.
2009 (1 protest/action, 1 news article)	* January 6, Moncton, NB: Students started a Facebook group in response to their school banning sweatpants.
2011 (1 protest/action, 1 news article)	* November 30, Barrhaven, ON: Students reacted to school banning yoga pants unless worn with a long T-shirt.
2012 (3 protests/actions, 3 news articles)	* April 23, Halifax, NS: A number of girls showed up in yoga pants and leggings to protest their school's ban on these items of clothing. * March 23, Pickering, ON: Students protested when their school banned shorts on dress-down day. * June 30, Abbotsford, BC: Girls circulated petitions against their dress code.
2014 (5 protests/actions, 22 news articles)	* May 13, Montreal, QC: Lindsey Stocker was singled out in a school-wide dress code sweep. She faced suspension after she then put posters up around her school critical of the fact that girls were being shamed for their bodies. * May 14, Truro, NS: Makayla King and other girls were disciplined for wearing shorts that were too short. Her mother started an online petition and a boy staged a protest by wearing girls' shorts to school. * May 27, Ottawa, ON: Tallie Doyle wore a spaghetti-strap top to school to challenge her school's dress code. * May 29, Menihek, NL: Over 20 girls and 2 boys were sent home from their school for wearing tank tops. * November 17, Fredericton, NB: The Fredericton Youth Feminists developed a video advocating an end to their school's dress code.
2015 (10 protests/actions,[1] 28 news articles)	* May 1, Trenton, ON: Cynthia Hazelwood was suspended for 24 hours for wearing a sundress that revealed her shoulders. * May 12, Moncton, NB: Lauren Wiggins received a detention for wearing a halter dress and was suspended for complaining to the vice-principal. * May 15, Guelph, ON: Students put up posters and planned a protest in response to a principal announcing that students should dress "cool and not skanky."

* May 26, London, ON: Laura Anderson was sent home for wearing ripped jeans and a tank top. This led to an on-line petition, the Twitter hashtag #MyBodyMyBusiness, and other students dressing in solidarity.

* May 26, Etobicoke, ON: A "crop top" protest against the dress code.

* May 26, North York, ON: A "crop top" protest against the dress code.

* May 29, Mississauga, ON: Catholic high school students attempted a sit in after they heard that girls would not be able to wear shorts on dress-down day. The school explained that there was a misunderstanding.

* June 9, St. Stephen, NB: A mother and 12-year-old daughter took to social media after the daughter was publicly asked to change because her tank top was showing.

* June 15, Montreal, QC: A "crop top" protest against the dress code.

* September 10, Toronto, ON: Project Slut, led by three girls, sought to end dress codes in their school and school board. These girls also sought to include the voices of students of colour, queer students, trans students, and students with larger bodies.

* September 16, Ottawa, ON: A Catholic school tweaked a new rule banning ripped jeans after student protest.

Note: 1. Additionally, there were three incidents of parents complaining to the press about how the dress code was used to discipline their elementary-school–aged children.

Source: Rebecca Raby and Shauna Pomerantz, research project, Dress Code Activism.

THE BEGINNING OF THE TWENTY-FIRST CENTURY

Actions around dress codes during the first decade of the twenty-first century that gained media attention were limited and largely in response to schools either introducing new codes, strengthening existing ones, or more rigorously enforcing those already on the books, all of which were part of a "moral panic" around girls' styles at the time (Pomerantz, 2007). As the superintendent of Red Deer Public School District, Don Falk, noted, "there has been a liberalization in clothing trends and schools have an obligation to tighten rules" ("Red Deer," 2003). Students responded to these changes in a range of ways and for a variety of cited reasons. In Abbotsford, British Columbia, in 2001, students wore alternative outfits to school, including one made of sticky notes, because they felt that their new dress code was vague and undermined their individuality. In Markham, Ontario, in 2002, students skipped class to protest their dress code, saying that a wider range of clothing should be acceptable for comfort, especially when the school's air conditioner was broken. And later, in Moncton, New Brunswick, students created a Facebook group against a new ban on sweatpants in school, arguing that they should be comfortable and focused on learning rather than worrying about dressing up ("No Sweats," 2009). Students in Winnipeg, Manitoba, cited comfort in their desire to wear pyjama pants as well.

Schools countered student protests with the familiar argument that schools are like businesses (Raby, 2005, 2012). For example, in response to the protest against the new dress code in Abbotsford, the principal explained that the school is a place to learn, "not a place where you lounge in beachwear" (Proctor, 2001). Similarly, the administration in Moncton, defending its ban on sweatpants, argued that students should come to school dressed as they would for a part-time job ("No Sweats," 2009). Administrators also emphasized the importance of rules, and the need for schools to withstand the negative influences of media trends such as MTV and Britney Spears.

Only two protests stood out for specifically addressing girls' dress during this time frame. In Hamilton, Ontario, in 2001, students held a "Knee-High Day" in response to their school's new ban on knee-high socks. The principal was concerned that the decreasing length of kilts affected the morality of the school and tarnished the school's image, as people could see girls' underwear when the girls bent over. Students felt that the rule was unfair because it was only a small group of girls who wore their skirts short, and knee high socks were more comfortable (and cheaper) than tights. In the second instance, a new dress code was introduced in Edmonton, Alberta, in 2003, banning any kind of revealing dress, including crop tops and low-riding pants. In protest, boys came to school wearing crop tops and showing their boxers. One grade 12 female student, Dana Coombes, said, "now, all of a sudden, we have to change just because a little bit of our stomach is showing. We should be able to wear whatever we want" (Sinnema, 2003). Another newspaper article that was not about a specific protest, but was published in 2002, suggested that girls were disproportionately sent home from school for breaking dress codes, raised concerns that larger-breasted girls were being unfairly targeted, and argued that it is men's reactions to how girls dress, and not the dress itself, that is the issue (Page, 2002). Though few in number, these articles exhibit the emergence of a feminist argument.

MORE RECENT PROTESTS

Our survey of news articles illustrates a change in the frequency and content of actions in Canada starting in 2011, and then a significant surge in 2014 and 2015, particularly in terms of actions articulated around gender discrimination. Near the end of 2011, at a school in Barrhaven, Ontario, students pushed back when their school's administration banned them from wearing yoga pants unless accompanied by a long T-shirt. The next year a similar incident arose in Halifax, Nova Scotia. Also in 2012, students at a Catholic school in Pickering, Ontario, were told that they were not allowed to wear shorts on their dress-down days, but boys and girls showed up in shorts anyway, resulting in 63 students being sent home to change. And at a middle school in Abbotsford, British Columbia, girls circulated two petitions requesting that their school administration amend what they saw as an overly restrictive and unrealistic dress code, given the summer weather and what was available in stores.

In May 2014 the issue of dress codes hit centre stage. In Montreal, Quebec, student Lindsey Stocker was singled out as part of a school-wide sweep for dress code violations. After being told to change because her shorts were too short, she put posters up around her school that said, "Don't humiliate her because she is wearing shorts. It's hot outside. Instead of shaming girls for their bodies, teach boys that girls are not sexual objects" (Kelly, 2014). These actions earned her a one-day suspension. The next day, in Truro, Nova Scotia, Makayla King and her mother started an online petition when Makayla and other girls were disciplined for wearing short shorts (O'Connor, 2014). Later in May, Tallie Doyle, a grade 8 student in Ottawa, Ontario, intentionally challenged her school's dress code by wearing a spaghetti-strap top to school, and in Labrador City, Newfoundland and Labrador, students went to the press when more than twenty girls and two boys were sent home from their school for wearing tank tops. This was the same year that the Fredericton Youth Feminist group, introduced at the beginning of this chapter, posted its Change.org petition.

In 2015, even more actions emerged. In London, Ontario, when grade 12 student Laura Anderson was sent home for wearing ripped jeans and a tank top, students started an online petition, introduced the hashtag #MyBodyMyBusiness, and showed up to school in similar clothes in solidarity. Students went to the press after getting in trouble for their outfits in Moncton, New Brunswick; St. Stephen, New Brunswick; and Trenton, Ontario. In Toronto, Ontario, and Montreal, Quebec, students held "crop top" days to protest their dress codes, while another group of students held a demonstration when their Catholic school discussed banning shorts on dress-down days. At about the same time, students in Guelph planned a protest in response to a principal's comments that students should be dressing "cool and not skanky" (Seto, 2015). A school board in Ottawa also eventually tweaked a new rule banning ripped jeans after a school protest. Finally, in 2015, three Toronto girls started a group called Project Slut, which petitioned their school and school board to end dress codes. The girls called for activism and commentary around dress code injustices to include the voices of students of colour, **queer** students, **trans** students, and students with larger bodies, all of whom might feel less comfortable speaking up.

Additional incidents involved parents complaining to the press about how the dress code was used to discipline their elementary-school–aged children. One case in New Brunswick involved a 10-year-old girl who was told her shirt was inappropriate because it rode up while she was skipping. In Regina, Saskatchewan, students as young as grade 4 were not allowed to wear tank tops, and in Mississauga, Ontario, a grade 7 student's mother went to the press after her daughter was sent home three days in a row for breaking the dress code.

PATTERNS IN THE PROTESTS

These more recent protests generally arose during the warmer months, and almost all occurred in response to schools enforcing their dress codes with girls. In many of the newspaper articles in which specific girls were challenging the rules, their mothers, and sometimes their fathers, were cited as supporting their daughters. Most notably, the language of the later protests was also significantly different from earlier protests. While some of the actions still emphasized the importance of individual choice and comfort, most drew attention to gender inequalities. Five dominant concerns arose.

First, there were frequent comments suggesting that the process of being singled out was, in essence, shaming. As Lindsey Stocker explained after she was called out for her dress, "It was in front of my entire class … I felt attacked, it was humiliating" (Kelly, 2014). Naomi Scott felt similarly embarrassed for being singled out (Gowan, 2015), while Laura Anderson more generally suggested that schools "pick and choose who gets shamed for what they are wearing" ("Dress Code in Question," 2015). In a climate where girls must carefully negotiate the line between being comfortable and attractive, but not too revealing, being publicly singled out and told that they are dressing too provocatively stood out for many of the girls as a form of slut-shaming and sexism.

Second, many noted that girls were more likely than boys to be singled out for dress code infractions. While administrators often emphasize that the school rules are gender-neutral, sometimes the codes themselves betray an emphasis on girls' bodies and dress, and the policing of the dress codes tends to focus on girls (Raby, 2010, 2012). As Alexi Halket said, after being sent home for wearing a crop top to school, there is an unfair double standard at play when "there are males in gym class and on the back field running around shirtless" (Russell, 2015). After some twenty-eight girls and two boys were sent home for dress code infractions at Menihek High School, various students spoke to the press, saying that while the policy may seem neutral, the focus is really on girls. This impression was reinforced by school announcements that if girls wore revealing shirts, it would be a problem for boys. As Danielle Matias said, girls are told that if they wear certain shirts, "male students will take it the wrong way" ("Menihek High," 2014).

This last observation links to the third pattern, which is that girls were frequently told that their dress was specifically distracting to boys. When grade 8 student Makayla King was sent to the principal's office due to the length of her shorts, the vice-principal reportedly said her shorts "were a distraction to the male population of the school" (O'Connor, 2014), which she objected to. In another example, a petition that was started in support of Laura Anderson noted that the school should reconsider the line in their school's dress code stating, "clothing must not be inappropriately revealing" ("London Student," 2015). Of the incident, Laura Anderson said, "If it's distracting, it's distracting because we're over-sexualizing other people's bodies" (Dubinski, 2015) and a boy added, "We are not savages [sic] or brutes who see a girl and have to look down her shirt" (Dubinski, 2015).

Fourth, girls felt that the tone of the dress code enforcement suggested that girls and women are held responsible for their own sexual harassment, and that instead, boys and men should be taught not to harass girls. As one student in Mississauga, Ontario, put it, "Men should be taught not to rape instead of teaching women not to get raped" ("Mississauga Students," 2015). This was a key position behind the Youth Feminists of Fredericton's petition when they asked why there was a dress code policy but not a sexual harassment policy at their school.

Finally, and most dominantly, the students frequently and critically noted that schools were communicating that girls are viewed as sexual objects. This was a central concern for Alexi Halket, who organized the "crop top" protest in Toronto and felt that women should be respected regardless of their dress, rather than being "objectified and sexualized" (Stern, 2015). Ashlyn Nicolle, in London, Ontario, similarly argued that "The **sexualization** of a teenage girl's body is not her problem, it is the problem of those who choose to sexualize a 17-year-old's body" ("London Student," 2015). These comments reflect an overall pattern of commentary from girls, and some boys: dress codes disproportionately and problematically regulate girls' bodies. As 16-year-old Montreal student Raphaelle Lalonde argued, "We find that the way the dress code is enforced is sexist, and it promotes the message that girls should be punished for their bodies and we don't think that's ok" ("Montreal High School," 2015). Lindsey Stoker's view was that schools are contributing to a pervasive rape culture without even realizing it (Kelly, 2014). These were strong, unambiguous statements criticizing a culture of gender discrimination.

In contrast, with some notable exceptions, the explanations given by most school administrators did not change much over time. Schools and school board personnel continued to iterate the need to treat the school like a workplace, even though this argument is often unconvincing to high school students (Raby, 2012). Others echoed the Ottawa District School Board's position that "This student dress policy is based on the expectation that schools shall be safe and respectful learning environments" (McKay, 2015). Another argument used by school personnel was that students should simply obey any school rule, and follow the "proper" channels for raising concerns, rather than engaging in protests, although such avenues are frequently unclear and largely unarticulated to students (Raby, 2012). In fact, students were frequently disciplined for simply speaking out against the school's dress code enforcement.

A few administrators took a somewhat different tack, suggesting that it is acceptable and even valuable for students to critically engage with the rules. For example, in response to the crop top protest in Etobicoke, Ontario, Principal Rob McKinnon invited students to discuss the issues and told the press that critical thinking is important (Casey, 2015). He still affirmed that "It's about appropriate dress for this setting, not sexualizing students or objectifying them, but what's OK in school" (Russell, 2015), but he welcomed the discussion. His statement was echoed by the school board's spokesperson who said that "when they delve into the professional world, students will quickly find that it is not appropriate to show up in a sports bra or a crop top. [However], we encourage kids to think critically and speak their minds" (Deschamps, 2015).

FEMINIST ACTIVISM

Through this examination of student actions against dress codes and their enforcement in Canadian schools, we see a significant increase in 2014 and 2015, largely fuelled by student concerns about gender discrimination and the sexual objectification of girls and women. Counter to the argument that young people are politically unengaged, these actions illustrate young people standing up for an issue that concerns them. While to some, dress code protests may seem focused on a trivial matter—dress—and teen rebels posturing for the media (e.g. Blizzard, 2015; Wente, 2015), we argue that the statements being made by these young people are examples of political, collective, and feminist action. As Alexi Halket, who organized the crop top protest in Etobicoke, Ontario, stated, "'I'm definitely not a bratty teenager, or someone being disrespectful…. This whole thing was about women's freedom, rights, and the fact that our bodies are objectified and sexualized'" (Stern, 2015).

The young women initiating dress code protests had grown up in a so-called post-feminist milieu, where gender equality had supposedly been accomplished (Budgeon, 2015; Currie et al., 2009; McRobbie, 2009; Scharff, 2011), and yet they were also seeing prominent and more personal examples of sexual harassment and sexism, which proved otherwise. Cases of campus sexual assaults in the United States were circulating through the news in 2014 and 2015, and early in May 2015 a scandal erupted at Dalhousie University when it was found that 13 dentistry students had been involved in sexually harassing female classmates on Facebook (see e.g. Taylor, 2015). During 2014 and 2015, a number of women came forward to report that they had been sexually assaulted at the hands of the prominent CBC radio host Jian Ghomeshi (Donovan, 2014) and in 2015 much media attention focused on allegations of sexual assault against actor Bill Cosby (O'Connor, 2015). It was also in the spring of 2015 that frequent news articles critically reported on female journalists across Canada being interrupted by young men shouting FHRITP, or "fuck her right in the pussy" ("FHRITP Phenomenon," 2015). In May of 2014, Canadians heard disturbing news of a young man shooting a group of young women sitting outside a sorority in California after saying, "I don't know why you girls aren't attracted to me, but I will punish you all for it" (Boniello, Li, Italiano, & Massarella, 2014). This incident was even cited by a girl involved in one of the dress code protests as an example of ongoing sexism that was a concern to her (Kelly, 2014). In 2013, the suicide of Cole Harbour District High School student Rehtaeh Parsons, after the online distribution of photos of her alleged gang rape, drew attention to sexual assault and cyber-bullying ("Rape, Bullying," 2013), especially as it was right on the heels of the suicide of Amanda Todd the year before, who had been blackmailed after showing her breasts to a man via webcam ("Weeks After," 2012). These incidents all occurred against a broader backdrop of ongoing concerns about gender inequality, including sexual harassment in high schools (e.g. Safe Schools Action Team, 2008) and ongoing concern about unequal pay for men and women (Zamon, 2015). In such a climate, girls' anger and activism make sense. As Lauren Wiggins, a teen sent home for exposing her shoulders, said, "I'm tired of the unjust standards that we as women are held up to. I'm tired of the discrimination against our bodies, and I'm absolutely fed up with comments that make us feel like we can't be comfortable without being provocative" ("Lauren Wiggins, Moncton Teen," 2015).

Dress code actions also arose in the context of media and Internet *responses* to these kinds of events, many problematizing the sexism underlying all of these incidents. Most notable was the advent of SlutWalk, which emerged in 2011 as a large-scale protest after a police officer at York University said that "women should avoid dressing like sluts in order not to be victimized" (Millar, 2011). The ensuing feminist response involved people taking to the streets wearing "provocative" clothing and carrying placards that were loud and clear—women should be able to wear what they want without fear of sexual assault. SlutWalk spread around the world, as women and men protested against clothing as an excuse for rape.

Recent student actions have been facilitated by new Internet applications and trends. Stories of gender inequality, and of political responses to that inequality, circulate quickly through platforms such as Facebook, Twitter, Snapchat, and Instagram. And responsive actions, such as protests, can be similarly shared and communicated through these multimedia platforms. Experiences at one school can thus quickly be shared with students at another. Rather than being an example of what some have disparagingly termed the "slacktivism" of the current online generation (Gilmore, 2014), these dress code actions indicate how young people understand social media as a powerful platform for protest, and also how online and "on the ground" are brought together to make social change (see e.g. Kearney, 2006).

One thing that has been less likely to come up in these dress code protests is acknowledgment of intersectional issues that work alongside gender, the kinds of issues that Project Slut points to (Strapagiel, 2015). Terms like *skanky* are not just gendered, for example, but are also about class-based judgments about dress, and school references to students' future workplaces presuppose middle-class work environments (Raby, 2012). Similarly, race-based inequalities in meting out school discipline have been documented in both the United States and Canada (Morris, 2005; Ferguson, 2001; see also Raby, 2012), and there is evidence in the United States that Black students are more likely to be disciplined for dress code violations (Tsai, 2013). It has also been observed that American schools with large numbers of minority students are more likely to have a rigid, "zero-tolerance" approach towards the rules (Verdugo, 2002) and that dress codes themselves sometimes specifically discriminate against groups of students by banning culturally significant dress (Dickar, 2008). Such intersections of class and race are in need of further attention.

In their actions against dress codes, many young people pushed back, including by intentionally breaking their dress codes. To some, these actions might look like "choice feminism" (Budgeon, 2015), where dress codes are being challenged because of an individualized focus on personal choice and a misdirected desire to embrace a sexualized form of femininity that is far from liberating (Wente, 2015). But when we listen to what girls are saying, these protests are replete with feminist politics: they are about addressing a broader culture of gender inequality that scrutinizes what girls and women wear, negatively judges women who are seen to be "too sexual," and fails to address issues of sexual harassment where they lie—in the actions of perpetrators. In this light, we must ask why media pundits, and many people commenting online in response to articles about these recent student actions, have been so hostile towards young people for speaking out. Young people, and specifically young feminists, are criticized for failing to be political, and yet are criticized, and sometimes even punished, for engaging in political activity. This reaction speaks to an ongoing dismissal of young people in our culture, who are not taken seriously when they speak out (Raby & Raddon, 2015), or are expected to simply obey (Raby, 2012). Unfortunately, while girls and some boys may be engaging in feminist activism vis-à-vis dress code protests, they remain largely ineffectual if adults, such as principals, parents, teachers, journalists, and academics, dismiss them. Rather, we argue that young people have legitimate concerns and they need adults' support. To provide this support, we need to better listen to what they are saying, and expand our ideas of what constitutes politics, activism, and feminism.

CHAPTER SUMMARY

Together, in this chapter, we

- Highlighted an explosion of young people's activism around dress codes and their enforcement in Canadian schools.
- Discussed a social issue that has been brought to the public's attention by young people, specifically their concerns about dress codes and their enforcement.
- Reviewed shifts in Canadian students' activism around dress codes, and the coverage of this activism in the media.
- Heard young people's arguments while also analyzing the pattern of their arguments through a feminist lens.
- Drew on students' comments in the press to recognize that their concerns have recently focused on gender inequality, sexism, and rape culture.
- Noted the role of social media in both informing and facilitating young people's activism.

STUDY QUESTIONS

1. What are the key issues highlighted by the protestors in relation to dress codes? How do schools often respond?
2. The girls argued that the application of dress codes perpetuates rape culture. What examples do they point to when they make this argument? Do you agree with them?
3. Were you ever involved in a protest at your high school? If so, what was the protest about and did you feel that the protest was successful? If not, are there any issues you wish you had protested as a high school student?
4. If you were a school principal, would you invite students to participate in creating a school dress code? What are the pros and cons of such student involvement? What are the pros and cons of having a dress code at all?
5. Do you think that dress code protests are feminist? Have the authors made a convincing argument?

SUGGESTED RESEARCH ASSIGNMENT

Interview classmates about their opinions about dress codes, then look to see where there are patterns in their comments and where there are disagreements. Draw on these interviews to write a mock newspaper article about what university students think about dress codes today.

SUGGESTED FILMS/VIDEO CLIPS

Project Slut Brings Attention to Discriminatory School Dress Code
www.thestar.com/opinion/2015/09/15/project-slut-brings-attention-to-discriminatory-school-dress-code.html
Project Slut activist Andrea Villanueva shares a spoken-word poem, about being slut-shamed, in a Toronto subway station.

Moncton Takes Stand against School Dress Code
www.cbc.ca/news/canada/new-brunswick/lauren-wiggins-moncton-teen-takes-stand-against-unjust-school-dress-code-1.3071203
CBC reports on the case of Lauren Wiggins, who was sent home for wearing a halter dress. This clip includes a response from the school administrator and also reviews other dress code protests.

SlutWalks and Modern Feminism
www.youtube.com/watch?v=ol-ND8oQREc

An engaging debate about SlutWalk from *The Agenda* with Steve Paikin, including Susannah Breslin (freelance journalist and blogger), Jaclyn Friedman (Executive Director of Women, Action and the Media), Gail Dines (Professor of Sociology and Women's Studies and author of *Pornland*), Heather Jarvis (co-founder of SlutWalk), and Kate McPherson (Professor of History and Women's Studies at York University).

SUGGESTED WEBSITES

Abolish the Dress Code and Create a Sexual Assault Policy
www.change.org/p/anglophone-west-school-district-abolish-the-dress-code-and-
 create-a-sexual-assault-policy
This link to the Change.org online petition started by the Young Feminists group in Fredericton, New Brunswick, in 2014 includes the petition and a video that they made, explaining why they wanted to launch the petition.

These Teens Are Trying to End "Oppressive" Dress Codes in Toronto
www.buzzfeed.com/laurenstrapagiel/a-group-of-teens-are-trying-to-end-oppressive-
 dress-codes-in
This article focuses on how Project Slut highlights the white, middle-class, and heterosexist nature of current dress code media coverage.

12 Times Badass Women Fought Ridiculously Sexist Dress Codes in 2015
www.buzzfeed.com/norawhelan/girls-who-fought-against-school-dress-codes-in-2015
An overview of some headline cases of dress code enforcement in the United States and Canada in 2015.

REFERENCES

Barnes, A., & Virgint, E. (2010). *Youth voter turnout in Canada: 1. Trends and issues.* Ottawa: Legal and Legislative Affairs Division. Parliamentary Information and Research Service. Publication No. 2010-19-E. 7 April 2010. Retrieved from www.parl.gc.ca/Content/LOP/ResearchPublications/2010-19-e.pdf

Bellafante, G. (1998, June 29). Feminism: It's all about me! *Time International, 26,* 54–60.

Blizzard, C. (2015, May 26). School dress codes are part of life. *Toronto Sun.* Retrieved from www.torontosun.com/2015/05/26/school-dress-codes-are-part-of-life

Boniello, K., Li, D. K., Italiano, L., & Massarella, L. (2014, May 25). Gunman vowed to "punish" sorority before shooting. *New York Post.* Retrieved from nypost.com/2014/05/25/virgin-gunman-vowed-sorority-sluts-must-die-before-rampage/

Bourdieu, P. (2001). The forms of capital. In M. Granovetter & R. Swedberg (Eds.), *The sociology of economic life* (2nd ed.) (pp. 96–111). Boulder, CO: Westview Press. (Original work published 1983)

Buckingham, D. (2000). *The making of citizens: Young people, news and politics.* London: Routledge.

Budgeon, S. (2015). Individualized femininity and feminist politics of choice. *European Journal of Women's Studies, 22*(3), 303–318.

Casey, L. (2015, May 28). "They were sexualizing my outfit": Toronto students wear crop tops to school after teen told to cover up. *National Post.* Retrieved from news.nationalpost.com/toronto/they-were-sexu-alizing-my-outfit-toronto-students-wear-midriff-baring-crop-tops-to-school-to-protest-cover-up-order

Check dress codes for sexist attitudes: Editorial. (2015, May 27). *Toronto Star.* Retrieved from www.thestar.com/opinion/editorials/2015/05/27/check-dress-codes-for-sexist-attitudes-editorial.html

Church, E. (2011, May 10). SlutWalk sparks worldwide protest movement. *Globe and Mail.* Retrieved from www.theglobeandmail.com/news/toronto/slutwalk-sparks-worldwide-protest-movement/article583076/

Culic, J. (2015, June 3). Dress codes something girls (and boys) should get used to. *Niagara This Week.* Retrieved from www.niagarathisweek.com/opinion-story/5658384-dress-codes-something-girls-and-boys-should-get-used-to/

Currie, D. H., Kelly, D. M., & Pomerantz, S. (2009). *"Girl power": Girls reinventing girlhoods.* New York: Peter Lang.

Deschamps, T. (2015, May 26). Toronto students organize "Crop Top Day" to protest dress codes. *Toronto Star.* Retrieved from www.thestar.com/yourtoronto/education/2015/05/26/toronto-students-organize-crop-top-day-to-protest-dress-codes.html

Dickar, M. (2008). *Corridor cultures: Mapping student resistance at an urban high school.* New York: New York University Press.

Donovan, K. (2014, October 26). CBC fires Jian Ghomeshi over sex allegations. *The Toronto Star.* Retrieved from www.thestar.com/news/canada/2014/10/26/cbc_fires_jian_ghomeshi_over_sex_allegations.html

Dress code in question after Lucas student sent home. (2015, May 26). *CTV News London.* Retrieved from london.ctvnews.ca/dress-code-in-question-after-lucas-student-sent-home-1.2392265

Dubinski, K. (2015, May 26). Lucas student who was sent home for her "inappropriate" clothing doesn't want students to be perceived as disrespectful. *Lfpress.com.* Retrieved from www.lfpress.com/2015/05/26/lucas-student-who-was-sent-home-for-her-inappropriate-clothing-doesnt-want-students-to-be-per-ceived-as-disrespectful

Ferguson, A. A. (2001). *Bad boys: Public schools in the making of black masculinity.* Ann Arbor: University of Michigan Press.

FHRITP phenomenon: CBC reporters share "mortifying" experiences. (2015, May 14). *CBC News.* Retrieved from www.cbc.ca/news/canada/fhritp-phenomenon-cbc-journalists-share-mortifying-expe-riences-1.3072191

Furlong, A., & Cartmel, F. (2007). *Young people and social change: New perspectives* (2nd ed.). Berkshire, UK: Open University Press, McGraw-Hill Education.

Gauthier, M. (2003). The inadequacy of concepts: The rise of youth interest in civic participation in Québec. *Journal of Youth Studies, 6*(3), 265–276.

Gill, R., & Scharff, C. (Eds.). (2011). *New femininities: Postfeminism, neoliberalism, and subjectivity.* Basingstoke, UK: Palgrave.

Gilmore, S. (2014, November 11). The problem with #slacktivism. *Maclean's.* Retrieved from www.macleans.ca/society/the-real-problem-with-slacktivism/

Glossary of Education Reform. (2016). *Hidden curriculum*. Retrieved from edglossary.org/hidden-curriculum/

Gowan, D. (2015, June 9). Grade 7 student in St. Stephen told to call home for a change of clothes. *Telegraph-Journal*. Retrieved from www.telegraphjournal.com/daily-gleaner/story/42681840/grade-7-student-from?source=story-related

Harris, A. (Ed.). (2008). *Next wave cultures: Feminism, subcultures, activism*. New York & London: Routledge.

Henn, M., Weinstein, M., & Wring, D. (2002). A generation apart? Youth and political participation in Britain. *British Journal of Politics and International Relations, 4*(2), 167–192.

James, A. (2009). Agency. In J. Qvotrup, W. A. Corsar, & M. Honig (Eds.), *The Palgrave handbook of childhood studies* (pp. 34–45). Hounsmills, Basingstoke: Palgrave-Macmillan.

Kearney, M. C. (2006). *Girls make media*. New York: Routledge.

Keller, J. (2015). *Girls' feminist blogging in a postfeminist age*. New York: Routledge.

Kellner, D., & Kim, G. (2010). YouTube, critical pedagogy, and media activism. *The Review of Education, Pedagogy, and Cultural Studies, 32*, 3–36.

Kelly, A. (2014, May 30). Montreal teen protests high school dress code. *Global News*. Retrieved from globalnews.ca/news/1364959/montreal-teen-protests-high-school-dress-code/

Kennelly, J. (2011a). *Citizen youth: Culture, activism, and agency in a neoliberal era*. New York: Palgrave Macmillan.

Kennelly, J. (2011b). Educating for active compliance: Discursive constructions in citizenship education. *Citizenship Studies, 15*(6/7), 897–914.

Lauren Wiggins, Moncton teen, takes stand against "unjust" school dress code. (2015, May 12). *CBC News*. Retrieved from www.cbc.ca/news/canada/new-brunswick/lauren-wiggins-moncton-teen-takes-stand-against-unjust-school-dress-code-1.3071203

Lesko, N. (2001). *Act your age! A cultural construction of adolescence*. New York: Routledge.

Levy, A. (2005). *Female chauvinist pigs: Women and the rise of raunch culture*. New York: Free Press.

London student in jeans, tank top sent home for breaking dress code. (2015, May 16.) *CBC News*. Retrieved from www.cbc.ca/news/canada/windsor/london-student-in-jeans-tank-top-sent-home-for-breaking-dress-code-1.3088412

McKay, A. (2015, May 1). The hidden dress code message in the school hallways. *Yahoo News*. Retrieved from ca.news.yahoo.com/blogs/dailybrew/the-hidden-dress-code-message-in-school-hallways-210528382.html

McRobbie, A. (2009). *The aftermath of feminism: Gender, culture and social change*. London: Sage.

Menihek High School students' bra straps violate dress code. (2014, May 30). *Huffington Post Canada*. Retrieved from www.huffingtonpost.ca/2014/05/30/bra-strap-dress-code_n_5415064.html

Millar, S. (2011, March 17). Police officer's remarks at York inspire "SlutWalk." *Toronto Star*. Retrieved from www.thestar.com/news/gta/2011/03/17/police_officers_remarks_at_york_inspire_slutwalk.html

Mississauga students protest no-shorts policy during dress-down day. (2015, May 15). *680 News*. www.680news.com/2015/05/29/mississauga-students-protest-no-shorts-policy-during-dress-down-day/

Montreal high school dress code forbidding crop tops "sexist," students say: High school students at FACE in Montreal say dress code unfairly target girls. (2015, June 5.) *CBC News*. Retrieved from www.cbc.ca/news/canada/montreal/montreal-high-school-dress-code-forbidding-crop-tops-sexist-students-say-1.3102237

Morris, E. (2005). "Tuck in that shirt!" Race, class, gender and discipline in an urban school. *Sociological Perspectives, 48*(1), 25–48.

No sweats allowed at Moncton school. (2009, February 12). *CBC News.* Retrieved from www.cbc.ca/news/canada/new-brunswick/no-sweats-allowed-at-moncton-school-1.831616

O'Connor, J. (2014, May 13). Nova Scotia school says jean shorts "too distracting" for boys, gives girl detention for fashion crime. *National Post.* Retrieved from news.nationalpost.com/news/canada/nova-scotia-school-says-jeans-shorts-too-distracting-for-boys-gives-girl-detention-for-fashion-crime

O'Connor, L. (2015, April 23). 3 women bring new sexual assault allegations against Bill Cosby. *The Huffington Post.* Retrieved from www.huffingtonpost.com/2015/04/23/new-cosby-victims_n_7129458.html

O'Neill, B. (2007). *Indifferent or just different? The political and civic engagement of young people in Canada: Charting the course for youth civic and political participation.* Ottawa: Canadian Policy Research Networks.

Page, S. (2002, April 22). Shame, shame on who? School dress controversy reflects adult fear of girls burgeoning sexuality. *Star-Phoenix,* D1.

Poitras, J. (2015, February 6). FHS dress code fight sees "complete shift," young feminists say. *CBC News.* Retrieved from www.cbc.ca/news/canada/new-brunswick/fhs-dress-code-fight-sees-complete-shift-young-feminists-say-1.2948046

Pomerantz, S. (2007). Cleavage in a tank top: Bodily prohibition and the discourses of school dress codes. *Alberta Journal of Educational Research, 53*(4), 373–386.

Pomerantz, S. (2008). *Girls, style, and school identities: Dressing the part.* New York: Palgrave MacMillan.

Pomerantz, S., Currie, D., & Kelly, D. (2004). Sk8er girls: Skateboarders, girlhood and feminism in motion. *Women's Studies International Forum, 27,* 447–557.

Pomerantz, S., & Raby, R. (2015, June 1). Taking on school dress codes: Teen rebels with a cause. *Globe and Mail.* Retrieved from www.theglobeandmail.com/globe-debate/taking-on-school-dress-codesteen-rebels-with-a-cause/article24704035/

Pomerantz, S., Raby, R., & Stefanik, A. (2013). Girls run the world? Caught between sexism and post-feminism in the school. *Gender and Society, 27*(2), 185–207.

Proctor, J. (2001, May 2). Kids protest dress code: If it's not too tight and not too loose it will be just right. *The Province,* A6.

Putnam, R. D. (2000). *Bowling alone: The collapse and revival of American community.* New York: Simon & Schuster.

Raby, R. (2002). A tangle of discourses: Girls negotiating adolescence. *Journal of Youth Studies, 5*(4), 425–448.

Raby, R. (2005). Polite, well-dressed and on time: Secondary school conduct codes and the production of docile citizens. *Canadian Review of Sociology and Anthropology, 42*(1), 71–92.

Raby, R. (2010). "Tank tops should be ok but I don't want to see her thong": Girls, dress codes and the regulation of femininity. *Youth and Society, 41*(3), 333–356.

Raby, R. (2012). *School rules: Obedience, discipline and elusive democracy.* Toronto: University of Toronto Press.

Raby, R., & Raddon, M. B. (2015). Is she a pawn, prodigy or person with a message? Public responses to a child's political speech. *Canadian Journal of Sociology, 40*(2), 163–188.

Rape, bullying led to N.S. teen's death, says mom. (2013, April 9). *CBC News.* Retrieved from www.cbc.ca/news/canada/nova-scotia/rape-bullying-led-to-n-s-teen-s-death-says-mom-1.1370780

Red Deer high school bans students from wearing spikes, face paint. (2003, October 27). *Canadian Press Newswire*.

Rheingold, H. (2008). Using participatory media and public voice to encourage civic engagement. In W. L. Bennett (Ed.), *Civic life online: Learning how digital media can engage youth* (pp. 97–118). Cambridge, MA: The MIT Press.

Ringrose, J. (2013). *Postfeminist education? Girls and the sexual politics of schooling*. London: Routledge.

Russell, A. (2015, May 26). Toronto student organizes "crop top day" to protest school dress code. *Global News*. Retrieved from globalnews.ca/news/2018351/toronto-students-wear-crop-tops-to-school-in-dress-code-protest/

Safe Schools Action Team. (2008). *Shaping a culture of respect in our schools: Promoting safe and healthy relationships*. Ministry of Education, Ontario. Toronto: Queen's Printer for Ontario.

Scharff, C. (2011). *Repudiating feminism: Young women in a neoliberal world*. Aldershot, UK: Ashgate.

Schrum, K. (2004). *Some wore bobby sox: The emergence of teenage girls' culture, 1920–1945*. New York: Palgrave Macmillan.

Seto, C. (2015, May 12). "Skanky" comment ignites slut-shaming debate at Guelph high school. *Guelph Mercury*. Retrieved from www.guelphmercury.com/news-story/5614570--skanky-comment-ignites-slut-shaming-debate-at-guelph-high-school/

Sinnema, J. (2003, September 21). Coverup underway at schools with bans on skimpy clothing. *Edmonton Journal*, A1 Front.

Skelton, T., & Valentine, G. (2003). Political participation, political action and political identities: Young D/deaf People's perspectives. *Space and Polity*, 7(2), 117–134.

Stern, C. (2015, May 27). Student, 18, organizes campaign against her school's "sexist" dress code by asking girls to wear midriff-baring crop tops in protest against the "sexualization of women." *Daily Mail*. Retrieved from www.dailymail.co.uk/femail/article-3099681/Student-18-organizes-campaign-against-school-s-sexist-dress-code-asking-girls-wear-midriff-baring-crop-tops-protest-against-sexualization-women.html

Strapagiel, L. (2015, June 8). These teens are trying to end "oppressive" dress codes in Toronto. *Buzzfeed*. Retrieved from www.buzzfeed.com/laurenstrapagiel/a-group-of-teens-are-trying-to-end-oppressive-dress-codes-in#.kl8NK8Zml

Taylor, S. (2015, January 5). Dalhousie University suspends 13 dentistry students from clinical activities over Facebook posts. *Toronto Metro News*. Retrieved from www.metronews.ca/news/canada/2015/01/05/dalhousie-university-suspends-13-students-from-clinical-activities-over-dentistry-scandal.html

Thornberg, R. (2008). School children's reasoning about school rules. *Research Papers in Education*, 23(1), 37–52.

Tsai, T. (2013). Black students more likely to be disciplined at school than whites. *Population Reference Bureau*. Retrieved from www.prb.org/Publications/Articles/2013/race-school-discipline.aspx

Verdugo, R. (2002). Race-ethnicity, social class, and zero-tolerance policies: The cultural and structural wars. *Education and Urban Society*, 35(1), 50–75.

Weeks after posting haunting YouTube video on her years of torment at classmates' hands, 15-year-old B.C. girl commits suicide. (2012, October 12). *National Post*. Retrieved from news.nationalpost.com/news/canada/amanda-todd-suicide-2012

Wente, M. (2015, June 9). Are school dress codes sexist and oppressive. *The Globe and Mail.* Retrieved from www.theglobeandmail.com/globe-debate/are-school-dress-codes-sexist-and-oppressive/article24864430/

Women Against Feminism. (n.d). Retrieved from womenagainstfeminism.com

Wyness, M. (2006). *Childhood and society: An introduction to the sociology of childhood.* Basingstoke & New York: Palgrave Macmillan.

Youth Feminists. (2014). *Abolish the dress code and create a sexual assault policy.* Change.org petition. Retrieved from www.change.org/p/anglophone-west-school-district-abolish-the-dress-code-and-create-a-sexual-assault-policy

Zamon, R. (2015, May 6). The gender pay gap in Canada is twice the global average. *Huffington Post Canada.* Retrieved from wwww.huffingtonpost.ca/2015/05/06/gender-pay-gap-canada_n_7223508.html

16 Queer and Trans at School: Gay-Straight Alliances and the Politics of Inclusion

Cameron Greensmith and Adam Davies

LEARNING OBJECTIVES

- To understand what Gay-Straight Alliances (GSAs) are—their possibilities and potentials
- To identify and explain the differences between cissexism and heterosexism
- To understand how the larger structure of schooling can contribute to the oppression of questioning, queer, and trans youth
- To examine how questioning, queer, and trans youth resist oppression and engage in action/activism
- To address some of the tensions that exist within GSAs and among GSA members

---

GSAs alone are not likely to change the heterosexist discourses that pervade schools.

—Young, 2010, p. 466

INTRODUCTION

For many lesbian, gay, bisexual, **trans**, **queer**, **questioning**, two-spirited, and intersex (LGBTQ2SI) youth, school can feel incredibly isolating and unsafe (Taylor & Peter, 2011).[1] Experiences of oppression for **LGBTQ2SI** youth typically result from a schooling environment (e.g., teacher/student relations, peer cultures, curriculum design, classroom practice, and policy) that continually normalizes and reproduces **heterosexism** and **cissexism** (Toomey, 2016). Gay-Straight Alliances (GSAs) provide all young people with the capacity and agency to challenge heterosexism and cissexism within their school environments. **Agency**, an important element of youth activism, can be understood as "assuming strategic perspectives and/or taking strategic actions towards goals that matter" (O'Meara, 2013, p. 2). For the purposes of this chapter, heterosexism is defined as the cultural logic that presumes heterosexuality to be normal, natural, and superior to that of other sexualities (Alden & Parker, 2005; Herek, 2004; Smith, Oades, & McCarthy, 2012). For example, within the biology classroom, youth will learn through their curriculum content that heterosexuality is the only *natural* way of existing in the world (Bazzul & Sykes, 2011). Cissexism can be defined as the privileging and normalization of cisgender experience through the constant regulation and devaluation of trans people and their experiences (Enke, 2012; Serano, 2007; Taylor, 2010). For example, cissexism is entrenched within schooling environments by the usage of gendered washrooms, which reinforces and limits youth's gendered possibilities to a male/female imaginary (Ingrey, 2012).

While we highlight the gendered and sexual oppression that LGBTQ2SI youth experience, within this chapter we specifically home in on and speak to the experiences and lived realities of questioning, queer, and trans youth at school (refer to the glossary for a more comprehensive explanation of these terms). Thus, we utilize questioning, queer, and trans as an umbrella category, with the understanding that two-spirited youth and intersex youth experience their **marginalization** differently, and often with a greater degree of silencing than other identities in the LGBTQ2SI acronym. We argue that it would be inappropriate to merely include two-spirited and intersex youth within this chapter, given its scope and the particular contexts in which these youth live. Therefore, for questioning, queer, and trans youth, we ask, How can questioning, queer, and trans youth work towards fostering more inclusive spaces in their schools, thus advocating for themselves and challenging systemic forms of inequality and oppression? And how might they work against oppressive structures to ensure that their identities and experiences are celebrated rather than erased or denigrated?

Although questioning, queer, and trans youth still experience clear forms of heterosexism and cissexism in schools today (Taylor & Peter, 2011), such challenges are often downplayed by narratives of progress and inclusion. Oppression can be overlooked due to dominant "post-gay" **discourses** that produce the realities of heterosexism and cissexism as things of the past (Lapointe, 2016; Nash, 2013). The term *post-gay* was first coined by British journalist Paul Burston in 1994 (Collard, 1998). *Post-gay* can refer to a shift in LGBTQ2SI communities and politics, whereby sexual and gendered differences are framed—both individually and within the larger culture—as no longer impacting or impeding upon their day-to-day interactions with the heterosexual majority.

Notably, in Canada, gays and lesbians have achieved same-sex marriage, adoption rights, and access to military enlistment (Tremblay & Paternotte, 2015). Furthermore, in 2016, gender identity was included in the Canadian Human Rights Act, allowing trans people to have rights and legally address any discrimination they face (Haig, 2016). While the above are all important and crucial interventions into the Canadian landscape for gay, lesbian, and, increasingly, trans people, the challenging lived realities of questioning, queer, and trans youth remain a constant. Questioning, queer, and trans youth still experience strife and innumerable obstacles, such as homelessness (Abramovich, 2013; Ferguson & Maccio, 2015; Whitbeck, 2009), physical and emotional abuse (Peter, Taylor, & Edkins, 2016), bullying and harassment at school (GLSEN & Harris Interactive, 2008), and societal discrimination (Unks, 2003). While intervention is necessary for *all* questioning, queer, and trans youth, it is imperative that we acknowledge the multiple systems of oppression that questioning, queer, and trans youth of colour; disabled questioning, queer, and trans youth; poor questioning, queer, and trans youth; gender nonconforming questioning, queer, and trans youth; and otherwise marginalized questioning, queer, and trans youth experience.

In an effort to combat the pervasive oppression questioning, queer, and trans youth face, Dan Savage (2010) launched the It Gets Better Project, in the US, which has had international success as an intervention to interrupt homophobic bullying, in light of the suicides of many gay and lesbian youth. Numerous public figures, including Ellen DeGeneres, Adam Lambert, and Barack Obama, have created YouTube videos urging youth to deal with the conditions of schooling and to encourage them that life will in fact *get better*. Rick Mercer (2011), a prominent Canadian public figure and comedian, urged the public to consider the immediacy of queer youth suicides and suggested that "it's no longer okay to tell kids that it is going to get better, we need to make it better now."

This immediacy can be addressed through the implementation of GSAs in private and public elementary and secondary schools. GSAs are typically understood as school clubs where straight, questioning, queer, and trans youth can connect, form alliances, educate one another and the larger schooling community, and take action to end heterosexism and cissexism. As such, GSAs provide necessary spaces for questioning, queer, and trans youth to connect over similar lived experiences, while simultaneously being supported by the administration and teachers at school (Lapointe & Kassen, 2013).

In order to address the potentials and possibilities of GSAs, this chapter provides an overview into the heterosexist and cissexist climate of schooling. First, we provide the theoretical framework through which we engage with GSAs, and then situate GSAs within the contemporary school environment. Next, we contextualize GSAs as sites where questioning, queer, and trans youth can engage in action and activism. We conclude by asking some critical questions of GSAs, including how the heterosexist and cissexist realities of schooling might be ruptured. In its entirety, this chapter works to centralize questioning, queer, and trans youth within and beyond schools, so that when we envision queer and trans politics and activism in Canada, we do not erase the pressing needs of children and youth and their advocacy efforts.

THEORETICAL FRAMEWORK

Within this chapter, theories and concepts are derived from the sociology of education, schooling, and peer cultures scholarship. The fields of critical sociology, the **sociology of childhood** and youth, and interdisciplinary social sciences pose questions about how individuals make meaning within their social world and look to how histories, cultures, and geographies can directly shape identity and our relationships with one another. More specifically, the sociology of education considers how meaning is made within the institution of schooling by analyzing the various "structures, processes, and practices" (Saha, 2011, p. 300) at play, and the multiple actors (e.g. teachers, youth, administrators) that make up and exist within schools. Sociological theories and paradigms are utilized here to understand the links between education and the larger culture in which schooling is produced on individual, discursive, and structural levels. In conjunction with sociological literatures, we employ queer theory as our theoretical framework in order to disrupt and critique the entrenched gendered and sexual binaries that are produced, reproduced, and maintained (Butler, 1990; Foucault, 1979) within schools.

Queer theory provides the necessary theoretical lens to examine the various and complex ways GSAs are enacted within schools and the identities youth produce within them. While we acknowledge and strive to work against the normalizing tendencies of queer theory (Duggan, 2003) as it is deeply seated in whiteness (Morgensen, 2011; Puar, 2007), we nonetheless find the theoretical premise useful as one way to deconstruct and disrupt the ways heterosexism and cissexism continue to be normalized in the lives of questioning, queer, and trans youth. We evoke Helen Hok-Sze Leung (2008), who suggests that a queer theoretical perspective "theorize[s] what escapes, exceeds, and resists normative formations" (p. 3), and Kath Browne and Catherine Nash (2010), who argue that queer "can and should be redeployed, fucked with and used in resistant and transgressive ways" (p. 9). Our utilization of queer theory, as a disruption of the normative, provides an opportunity to consider how and under what conditions GSAs work to challenge structures of oppression in schools, and address the divergent ways young questioning, queer, and trans people are working against hetero- and cis-normalcy in their lives, schools, and communities.

In order to address such normalizing tendencies, we ground our analysis of GSAs within the contemporary climate of schooling. Schools are sites of surveillance, where youth learn that heterosexuality and a two-gender binary system are normal and natural. For example, in chapter 15, Raby and Pomerantz note that girls' sexuality is continually scrutinized and policed through the implementation of school dress code policies. Such theorizations of youth's experiences of surveillance can be drawn from the seminal work of French philosopher Michel Foucault (1979). Foucault's theorization of the panopticon engaged with the particular architectural design of British philosopher Jeremy Bentham's Panopticon prison, which allowed for a single prison guard in the centre of a prison to watch and surveil all of the prisoners. Consequently, prisoners would regulate themselves even when the guard was not present; in this sense, the guard was *always* watching. Foucault's work on surveillance can be applied to the context of schooling, where youth will regulate themselves and one another, as they fear they are always being watched (Taylor, 2013).

Thus, within schools, the gendered and sexual cultures of youth are policed not only by adults, but also within their peer cultures (Renold, 2005; Warrington & Younger, 2011). Through the act of policing and surveillance, youth, in turn, monitor their peers' gendered and sexual behaviours as one way to reify and naturalize heterosexuality. If contemporary schooling reproduces the normativity of heterosexism and cissexism, and youth self-surveil due to *potential* ridicule or punishment, then GSAs, as sites of resistance, become ever so important. Below, we examine the ways heterosexism and cissexism are maintained within contemporary schooling, and how these are experienced in the lives of questioning, queer, and trans youth.

GAY-STRAIGHT ALLIANCES: RESISTING THE NORMATIVE LOGICS OF HETEROSEXISM AND CISSEXISM

Recent research on questioning, queer, and trans youth has shown that GSAs can disrupt the pervasiveness of oppression within their school environments. It has been well documented that children and youth experience extraordinary amounts of oppression just by virtue of their age (Wall, 2013). In conjunction with youth's experiences of childism, or oppression based on being a child or youth (Young-Bruehl, 2013), many questioning, queer, and trans youth experience oppression, discrimination, and prejudice at school through verbal and physical harassment and bullying of all forms (Grace & Wells, 2015; Taylor & Peter, 2011).

Within the recent study *Every Class in Every School*, Equality for Gays and Lesbians Everyday (Egale) found that 70 percent of all students who participated in their study—regardless of their sexual or gender identity—had overheard blatantly homophobic and transphobic comments at school, with 10 percent stating that they had heard such comments from educators and administrators at school (Taylor & Peter, 2011). Homophobia and transphobia are made possible within broader school climates of heterosexism and cissexism, where all youth are routinely assumed to be straight and cisgender. Consequently, we must interrogate the ways heterosexism and cissexism are normalized and maintained within schools, and the ways that youth in GSAs are working against these issues and related oppressive structures. GSAs provide a venue for youth to actively challenge homophobia and transphobia, and to disrupt heterosexism and cissexism in their school communities, while encouraging them to become active leaders and activists at school and in their communities at large (Lapointe, 2015).

GSAs have proliferated throughout Canada and the United States as a means of disrupting homophobia and heterosexism within school climates since the late twentieth and early twenty-first centuries (Collin, 2013; Wells, 2006). The first GSA was founded in an American high school in 1988 in Concord, Massachusetts (Collin, 2013), and the first Canadian GSA was founded in 2000 in Coquitlam, British Columbia (Wells, 2006). While GSAs are becoming increasingly common in Canada, especially with the advent of Ontario's 2012 Accepting Schools Act (Bill 13), various groups, including religious leaders, school administrators, parents, and teachers, still oppose GSAs in school settings (Clarke & MacDougall, 2012). In Ontario, despite some backlash, the Accepting Schools Act maintains that *all* students are guaranteed the right to formulate a GSA in any publicly funded school (Broten, 2012), so long as there exists both student desire and teacher supervision. Alberta (Jansen, 2015) and Manitoba (Allen, 2013) have similar legislation that ensures that youth who wish to form a GSA are provided with the resources (e.g. space, administrative support) to do so. Such legal measures are enacted to produce schools that are safe and supporting of questioning, queer, and trans youth, and are one attempt to work against the normalization of heterosexism and cissexism in schools.

While individual school climates may not be as supportive of GSAs as one would hope, the activism of young GSA participants is a testament to what can be done when youth's identities and experiences are affirmed. Questioning, queer, and trans youth, alongside straight members[2] of GSAs, are resisting normativity that contributes to their oppression by (1) challenging the ways homophobia and transphobia are perpetuated in schools; and (2) generating spaces where diversity around gender and sexuality can be celebrated. To evoke Michel Foucault (1979) once more, youth regulate themselves within the school setting on an everyday basis, whether it is in terms of the clothes that they wear, the music and media that they engage with, or the peer groups they belong to. For example, Meyer and Stader's (2009) research shows that questioning, queer, and trans youth often feel as though they need to act straight due to the pervasiveness of heterosexism and cissexism in school. Thus, GSAs provide a space where questioning, queer, and trans youth are able to break gendered and sexual norms by fostering a sense of overall well-being and community. Within GSAs, youth are able to break the panoptic gaze of school hallways, classrooms, bathrooms, and change rooms in a safe environment that supports their sense of self and community development.

QUEER AND TRANS YOUTH RESISTANCE

Youth activism within schools plays an integral part in the formation of safe school climates and the development and integration of social justice in the lives of youth (Noguera, Cammarota, & Ginwright, 2006). In 2002, Azmi Jubran, who was subjected to years of homophobic bullying, won a harassment complaint against his school board in British Columbia. This case puts emphasis on the ways youth can advocate for themselves and work against the oppressive conditions (e.g. homophobic bullying) of schooling (Meyer & Stader, 2009). Within GSAs, questioning, queer, and trans youth can develop and hone their advocacy skills while working with straight youth to create school communities that are more engaged with and informed about queer and trans topics and lived experiences (Lapointe, 2015; Young, 2010). Moreover, in Calgary, Alberta, young GSA members, particularly trans youth, have successfully petitioned their school administration to include a gender-inclusive bathroom for trans, genderqueer, and gender nonconforming youth—this despite parental backlash (CBC News, 2015). Questioning, queer, and trans youth are speaking back and working against oppression by seeking to employ inclusive initiatives addressing inequities through gender-neutral bathrooms, LGBTQ2SI-specific Valentine's Day greeting cards, and even queer proms.

Through the kinds of youth activism highlighted within "Snakes and Ladders," GSAs provide youth with a space for self-advocacy, which highlights both their agency and visibility within their school communities. Through GSAs, youth are able to exert their agency as activists while resisting ingrained heterosexism, cissexism, homophobia, and transphobia within their schools (Marx & Kettrey, 2016; Poteat, Calzo, & Yoshikawa, 2016; Walls, Kane, & Wisneski, 2010). In addition to explicitly taking action against the oppression that youth experience, GSAs can foster individual and collective empowerment within schools. This empowerment is fuelled by a sense of belonging as straight, questioning, queer, and trans youth co-construct a space to share experiences, create meaningful change in their communities and peer groups, and affect policy making (Mayberry, 2012). In other words, participation in GSAs (which become woven into the everyday fabric of the schooling structure) provides questioning, queer, and trans youth with a sense of collectivity and pride in their identities (Flanagan, 2004).

While heterosexuality is overtly naturalized, (re)produced, and reified within school curricula, youth's peer cultures, and interactions with teachers, GSAs can provide a subversive space for questioning, queer, and trans youth to *queer* and unsettle heterosexism (Pascoe, 2007) and cissexism. Alicia Lapointe's (2015) writings on GSAs articulate how GSAs can encourage student bonding, a sense of safety, and youth activism, but that GSAs also formulate "pedagogic sites for interrupting heteronormativity" (p. 150). Thus, GSAs not only benefit questioning, queer, and trans youth, but also cultivate positive environments for the whole school. Ultimately, GSAs, which emerge out of the activism of questioning, queer, and trans youth, unsettle the normalization and omnipresence of heterosexism and cissexism, while opening up new possibilities and imaginings for *all* youth.

Box 16.1: Snakes and Ladders: A Performed Ethnography

Questioning, queer, and trans youth can congregate together to formulate collective activist groups, such as GSAs, as a means of exerting their agency. By joining together, straight, questioning, queer, and trans youth can use their **power** to address inequities within their school climate (Mayo, 2009; Lapointe, 2015). This kind of activism is exemplified in Tara Goldstein's (2010) performed **ethnography** "Snakes and Ladders." Below is a dramatized exchange among GSA members and their teacher-supervisor on what kinds of activist initiatives GSAs might take on during an event called "Gay Pride Day."

Anne [Teacher]: Mr. Rodriguez, why don't you tell us the ideas you and Ms. Davis have come up with for Gay Pride Day....

Roberto [Rodriguez (Student)]: Okay. We talked about inviting a group called T.E.A.C.H. to come and do an anti-homophobia workshop with us. T.E.A.C.H. stands for Teens Educating and Confronting Homophobia. The members of T.E.A.C.H. identify as LGBTQ [lesbian, gay, bisexual, trans, and queer] and straight.

Helen [Student]: Are they all white?

Roberto: No. The group is mixed. And as part of the workshop they tell their coming-out stories, of when they first knew they might not be or weren't heterosexual....

Chris [Student]: What about a queer talent night? And a drag contest?

Diane [Student]: What's drag?

Helen: It's when guys dress up like girls and girls dress up like guys.

Chris: Or maybe we could put on an "Ask Dr. Ruth" show with questions and answers about queer sex. (Goldstein, 2010, pp. 90–91)

Although a dramatization, this exchange outlines the possibilities that GSAs hold for questioning, queer, and trans youth. Roberto's comment on T.E.A.C.H. being racially diverse addresses the realities of questioning, queer, and trans youth of colour who are seeking out mentors and looking to see themselves represented in queer and trans activism. This conversation between some GSA participants highlights the strength and determination of questioning, queer, and trans youth, especially with regard to the kinds of queerness they *need* within such spaces like GSAs and "Gay Pride Day." Moreover, here youth's activism emerges from their *own* lived experiences to sketch out a space where they can feel *safer* and that they truly belong. Simultaneously, Goldstein's excerpt highlights how questioning, queer, and trans youth are seeking out *experts* who may have more experience or knowledge in the area of anti-homophobic education. Seeking out knowledgeable figures, for some questioning, queer, and trans youth, can alleviate some pressure to be experts regarding their own respective identities, especially in school climates that are unsupportive.

ARE GAY-STRAIGHT ALLIANCES ENOUGH?

This chapter has attempted to provide a comprehensive review of the everyday realities of heterosexism and cissexism in school for questioning, queer, and trans youth. Drawing from the sociological literatures on education and adolescence, we demonstrate how questioning, queer, and trans youth experience strife, everyday violence, and erasure. We illustrate how GSAs provide an opportunity for questioning, queer, and trans youth to engage in activism as one way to challenge the pervasiveness of heterosexism, cissexism, homophobia, and transphobia within and beyond schools. As such, GSAs provide a means to disrupt the heterosexist and cissexist school climates (and the larger culture) for youth while fostering and uplifting their agency and activism—developing an accepting, *safer*, and open environment for their overall well-being. Moreover, GSAs encourage questioning, queer, and trans youth to engage in activism—although through the guidance of an adult figure and anti-oppressive school policy—to develop a sense of self-advocacy and awareness of social justice issues.

While GSAs are beneficial for youth in attendance, it is worth posing the question, *Which* youth, in particular, benefit from GSAs? Mollie Blackburn and Lance McCready (2009) have questioned the nature and benefits of GSAs for questioning, queer, and trans youth of colour as GSAs can easily reproduce and normalize particular versions of queerness while rejecting others entirely. David, a Black gay youth, called the GSA group in his school "a select group of White girls … just teatime for a few lesbians and their friends … I went two consecutive weeks and then I stopped going because it wasn't doing anything for me. There's nothing there for me" (Blackburn & McCready, 2009, p. 227).[3] GSAs can indeed reflect the larger culture of queer communities in Canada by placing whiteness at the centre and limiting dialogue surrounding other intersecting identities and multiple experiences of race, class, disability, and nation, among others. For example, returning to Goldstein's (2010) "Snakes and Ladders," the kinds of queer and trans activism that questioning, queer, and trans youth imagine can reproduce normative articulations of queer politics such as a "Gay Pride Day" that might be exclusionary. Or questioning, queer, and trans youth might mimic representations of queer and trans youth in the media, such as in *Out Magazine*, which typically consolidates queer and trans representation into images of wealthy white gay men who typically embody hegemonic masculinities.

Moreover, Giwa and Greensmith (2012) explain how the seemingly imagined Toronto LGBTQ community frames its narrative in whiteness, and how events, such as Pride Toronto, that focus on cohesiveness and inclusion function through exclusion. The imagined cohesive community attempts to assimilate all questioning, queer, and trans individuals under a "colourblind" approach that fails to recognize racial marginalization and upholds white supremacy. In this example, we can see how LGBTQ2SI activism—within and outside of schools—can normalize the whiteness of queerness, leaving **racialized** youth further "Othered" and excluded (Blackburn & McCready, 2009).

Gendered oppression is another means through which questioning, queer, and trans youth can experience oppression, even within their respective inclusive communities. For example, effeminate men can experience femmephobia within gay men's communities (Bergling, 2002) and transwomen have lamented the gender discrimination they experience as women (Serano, 2007). Therefore, it is important for GSAs to embrace the tenets of intersectionality. Intersectionality, a concept that emerged out of the writing and activism of Black feminists, examines individuals' multiple intersecting and overlapping social identities, such as race, class, and gender. Intersectionality can be utilized within GSAs to acknowledge and value the various identities and experiences that make up questioning, queer, and trans youth's lives.

Additionally, to push conversations beyond race, gender, and whiteness, how might our Western conceptions of queerness hold negative ramifications for **Indigenous** peoples (Morgensen, 2011)? For example, Pride festivals sometimes appropriate the cultures of Indigenous peoples—through costumes, for instance—which can produce overt forms of racism and sexism within these seemingly inclusive spaces (Greensmith & Giwa, 2013). Similarly, the initiatives that GSAs take on might mimic a normative queer politics that perpetuates and sustains the exclusion and erasure of Indigenous peoples who are questioning, queer, trans, and two-spirited. Thus, while it is important to highlight the productive possibility of GSAs for questioning, queer, and trans youth, it is necessary to consider who is left out and, more importantly, why.

Another concern is that GSAs alone are not enough to challenge the pervasiveness of heterosexism and cissexism in schools. Thus, we firmly believe that GSAs must be utilized in a way that extends dialogue and action surrounding the heterosexist and cissexist realities of schooling for *all* youth. As C. J. Pascoe (2007) writes, "'Making our schools safe for sissies' (quoted from Rofes, 1995, p. 79) can make them safer places for all students: masculine girls, feminine boys, and all those in between" (p. 174). Yet, within our contemporary schooling climate, GSAs are typically offered as Band-Aid solutions, filling the gap where questioning, queer, and trans content is absent from schooling curricula and where there is little systemic change happening within schools as a whole. Further, if GSAs are produced as a site of queer and trans inclusion alone, there is potential for the reinforcement of the very binaries that GSAs are trying to resist and work at dismantling. For example, the title *Gay-Straight Alliance* can easily obscure the diversity within queer and trans communities. Some youth within their local communities are thus changing the name of GSAs to *Queer-Straight Alliances* or *Genders & Sexualities Alliances* to signal inclusivity (Genders & Sexualities Alliance Network, n.d.). Thus, in accordance with Deborah Britzman (1998), if GSAs are only imagined as relevant at certain times, and for certain people, instead of being embedded into everyday learning, heterosexism and cissexism in schooling will not be altered.

Beyond the name, and beyond the everyday workings of heterosexism in schools, we must consider the spaces and places where GSAs are enacted. Within smaller towns or rural communities, many questioning, queer, and trans youth feel heightened degrees of isolation, as they often experience heterosexist and cissexist forms of oppression along-side fewer supports than in urban areas (Brown, 2012; St. John et al., 2014). While we speak to the importance of GSAs, especially for questioning, queer, and trans youth, it is equally important to consider the importance of GSAs within particular geograph-ical contexts (Fetner & Kush, 2008). We do so within the particular national context, whereby most provinces in Canada do not have GSA supportive legislation.

To conclude, we want to highlight the resilience, activism, and agency of ques-tioning, queer, and trans youth. Their work, through GSAs and beyond, can prevent negative peer and self-surveillance in schools and can help shift heterosexist, cissexist, homophobic, and transphobic school climates. We want to challenge the cookie-cutter model of queer activism—within and outside of GSAs—by asking difficult questions, so that we can support and encourage youth in their work against heterosexism and cis-sexism, but also to see the relevance of understanding and addressing other intersecting forms of oppression in the lives of questioning, queer, and trans youth. Thus, we offer some final thoughts: What promises do GSAs offer in terms of dismantling structures of oppression beyond heterosexism and cissexism? And in what ways might GSAs (and the activism of youth) further normalize and naturalize some queer and trans identities and experiences, while making the others into "Others"?

CHAPTER SUMMARY:

Together, in this chapter, we

- Saw that while many questioning, queer, and trans youth can experience gen-dered and sexual oppression within their school environments, youth experi-ence such oppressions differently based on their multiple identities, experiences at school, peer groups, families, and work, among other contexts.
- Explored how GSAs provide an opportunity to subvert oppressive school cli-mates to formulate a safer school for questioning, queer, and trans youth.
- Investigated, through a lens that employs the sociology of education, child-hood, and queer theory, how GSAs can be sites that disrupt heterosexism and cissexism.
- Learned that school climates can engender negative self-surveillance and peer monitoring as youth regulate themselves to fit the heteronormative and cisnor-mative codes ingrained within schools.
- Learned that GSAs are spaces where youth can develop into activists while building bridges between questioning, queer, and trans youth, teachers, and straight youth.
- Explored how youth's activism in GSAs transpires from their own lived expe-riences and the sense of safety and acceptance they feel *within* GSAs.

- Acknowledged that GSAs still need to be expanded to provide safe climates for *all* questioning, queer, and trans youth.

STUDY QUESTIONS

1. Outline how questioning, queer, and trans youth are resisting oppression.
2. Describe the differences between heterosexism and cissexism.
3. Were there GSAs at your school? If so, did you participate? Why? If not, why didn't you participate?
4. In what ways can adults (e.g. teachers, child and youth workers) better support questioning, queer, and trans youth so that their identities are affirmed?
5. What are the limits of GSAs in their capacity to challenge heterosexism and cissexism? How can schools as a whole address these limits in conjunction with GSAs?

SUGGESTED RESEARCH ASSIGNMENT

In order to understand the complexities of genders and sexualities in the lives of children and youth, go to a local marketplace (e.g. bookstore, toy store) that children and youth attend. Pay attention to your surroundings and make sure you take notes: What do you see? How are children and youth being asked to participate in sexual and gendered cultures? What is normalized (e.g. colour, dress, body size)? Write a reflective piece on the ways youth are gendered and sexualized within the marketplace you have chosen. The goal of this assignment is to engage with the ever-growing marketplace that questioning, queer, and trans youth participate in and to address the ways heterosexism and cissexism are being naturalized, subverted, and/or challenged.

SUGGESTED FILMS/VIDEO CLIPS

But I'm a Cheerleader (1999)
www.imdb.com/title/tt0179116/
Megan (Natasha Lyvonne), a high school cheerleader, is beginning to explore her sexual attraction to other women as she realizes that she is not attracted to her boyfriend. After suspecting her to be a lesbian, Megan's family and friends provide her with an intervention, and send her to True Directions, a conversion therapy camp. While at the camp, Megan wrestles with her desire to appease her friends and family by conforming to heterosexual standards and her burgeoning love for Graham (Clea DuVall). Directed by Jamie Babbit.

C.R.A.Z.Y. **(2005)**

www.imdb.com/title/tt0401085/

Zac (Michel Côté), the youngest son in a devout Roman Catholic family in Québec in the 1970s, experiences internal turmoil over his nonmasculine behaviours throughout his adolescence as his father struggles to accept him as gay. After having his same-sex desires discovered by his father, Zac is sent to conversion therapy to discuss his sexual desires. Following this, Zac embarks on a journey towards self-acceptance. Directed by Jean-Marc Vallée.

Fire Song **(2015)**

www.imdb.com/title/tt4123506/

Shane (Andrew Martin), a gay Anishinaabe teenager, is left with a challenging decision as his sister commits suicide weeks before he is scheduled to leave his hometown to attend university. While trying to cope with the aftermath of his sister's death and piecing his family back together, Shane is left to decide between supporting his family or his own future plans. Directed by Adam Garnet Jones.

The Kids Are All Right **(2010)**

www.imdb.com/title/tt0842926/

Nic (Annette Bening) and Jules (Julianne Moore), a married lesbian couple in Los Angeles who have had two children through artificial insemination, are forced to confront their son's (Josh Hutcherson) questions regarding his donor father's identity. Upon finding the donor father, Paul (Mark Ruffolo), Nic and Jules welcome Paul into their family's life and begin a journey of self-discovery getting to know him while growing as a family. Directed by Lisa Cholodenko.

SUGGESTED WEBSITES

Egale

egale.ca

Egale Canada, or Equality for Gays and Lesbians Everywhere, was founded in 1986 as an organization to advocate for equality for LGBTQ2SI communities across Canada. Egale has advocated for equality causes within Canada, such as same-sex marriage, and continues to educate workplaces and educational institutions on LGBTQ2SI issues and advocacy.

GSA Network

gsanetwork.org

GSA Network is an American organization founded by Carolyn Laub in the San Francisco area in 1998. GSA Network started as Gay-Straight Alliance Network and was renamed to Genders and Sexualities Alliance Network in 2016 to reflect the increasing diversity in representation of genders and sexualities in North America.

LGBT Youth Line

www.youthline.ca

LGBT Youth Line is an Ontario-based Canadian organization founded in 1993 in Toronto to provide a means for queer, questioning, and trans youth in Ontario to be able to access phone counselling and guidance. The peer-based format of the phone line is utilized to decrease the loneliness that queer, questioning, and trans youth often face.

MyGSA.ca

www.mygsa.ca

MyGSA.ca is an initiative run by Egale Canada to provide youth, educators, parents, and community members with information regarding GSAs and their importance in formulating safer school climates. MyGSA.ca provides educators and community members with detailed lesson plans, resources for starting a GSA, as well as community for queer, questioning, and trans youth.

Native Youth Sexual Health Network

nativeyouthsexualhealth.com

The Native Youth Sexual Health Network (NYSHN) is a North American–based organization that advocates for justice regarding sexual and reproductive health, specifically for Indigenous youth. This organization is run by Indigenous youth 30 years and under and works with Indigenous youth to ensure that they are provided with a sexuality education that is accessible for them.

NOTES

1. Cameron and Adam would both like to thank all of the queer, trans, and questioning youth who have survived despite all of the odds against them. We especially want to thank Tara Goldstein, Rebecca Raby, and Shauna Pomerantz for inspiring us to think about and with young people, and to engage with young people's everyday encounters with homophobia and transphobia as activism.

2. As Sara Lewis-Bernstein Young (2010) illustrates, straight youth's participation in GSAs helps to challenge the pervasive heterosexism experienced by questioning, queer, and trans youth in schools. Thus, the presence of straight youth within GSAs can allow for questioning, queer, and trans youth to join GSAs without the necessity of coming out.

3. While we find David's narrative productive in highlighting the exclusion he faced within the particular local GSA he tried attending, we nonetheless find his illustration deeply sexist for those "lesbians and their friends." Despite the tensions that exist, we wanted to highlight David's

experience to showcase a very real representation of oppression many questioning, queer, and trans youth of colour may experience within queer spaces like GSAs. Highlighting David's narrative also brings awareness to the messy contradictions that arise within inclusive initiatives, by showcasing the ways horizontal violence is normalized among youth who *all* experience forms of gendered and sexual oppression.

REFERENCES

Abramovich, A. I. (2013). No fixed address: Young, queer, and restless. In S. Gaetz, B. O'Grady, K. Buccieri, J. Karabanow, & A. Marsolais (Eds.), *Youth homelessness in Canada: Implications for policy and practice* (pp. 387–403). Toronto: Canadian Homelessness Research Network Press.

Alden, H. L., & Parker, K. F. (2005). Gender role ideology, homophobia and hate crime: Linking attitudes to macro-level anti-gay and lesbian hate crimes. *Deviant behavior, 26*(4), 321–343.

Allen, N. (2013). *Bill 18, The Public Schools Amendment Act (Safe and Inclusive Schools)*. Winnipeg, Manitoba, Canada: Legislative Assembly of Manitoba.

Bazzul, J., & Sykes, H. (2011). The secret identity of a biology textbook: Straight and naturally sexed. *Cultural Studies of Science Education, 6*(2), 265–286.

Bergling, T. (2002). *Sissyphobia: Gay men and effeminate behavior.* Philadelphia: Haworth Press.

Blackburn, M. V., & McCready, L. (2009). Voices of queer youth in urban schools: Possibilities and limitations. *Theory into Practice, 48*(3), 222–230.

Britzman, D. (1998). *Lost subjects, contested objects: Towards a psychoanalytic inquiry of learning.* New York: State University of New York Press.

Broten, L. (2012). *Bill 13 (Chapter 5), Statutes of Ontario, 2012: An act to amend the Education Act with respect to bullying and other matters.* Toronto, Ontario, Canada: Legislative Assembly of Ontario.

Brown, G. (2012). Homonormativity: A metropolitan concept that denigrates "ordinary" gay lives. *Journal of Homosexuality, 59*(7), 1065–1072.

Browne, K., & Nash, C. J. (2010). *Queer methods and methodologies: Intersecting queer theories and social science research.* Surrey, UK: Ashgate Publishing.

Butler, J. (1990). *Gender trouble: Feminism and the subversion of identity.* New York: Routledge.

CBC News. (2015, February 6). Gender-neutral washrooms part of CBE's plan for new schools. *CBC News.* Retrieved from www.cbc.ca/news/canada/calgary/gender-neutral-washrooms-part-of-cbe-s-plan-for-new-schools-1.2949037

Clarke, P., & MacDougall, B. (2012). The case for gay–straight alliances (GSAs) in Canada's public schools: An educational perspective. *Education Law Journal, 21*(2), 143–165.

Collard, J. (1998, August). Leaving the gay ghetto. *Newsweek, 132*(7), 53.

Collin, R. (2013). Making space: A gay–straight alliance's fight to build inclusive environments. *Teachers College Record, 115*(8), 1–26.

Duggan, L. (2003). *The twilight of equality? Neoliberalism, cultural politics, and the attack on democracy.* Boston: Beacon.

Enke, A. (2012). Note on terms and concepts. In A. Enke (Ed.), *Transfeminist perspectives in and beyond transgender and gender studies* (pp. 16–22). Philadelphia: Temple University Press.

Ferguson, K. M., & Maccio, E. M. (2015). Promising programs for lesbian, gay, bisexual, transgender, and queer/questioning runaway and homeless youth. *Journal of Social Service Research, 41*(5), 659–683.

Fetner, T., & Kush, K. (2008). Gay–straight alliances in high schools: Social predictors of early adoption. *Youth & Society, 40*(1), 114–130.

Flanagan, C. A. (2004). Volunteerism, leadership, political socialization, and civic engagement. In R. M. Lerner & L. Steinberg (Eds.), *Handbook of adolescent psychology* (2nd ed.) (pp. 721–745). Hoboken, NJ: Wiley.

Foucault, M. (1979). *Discipline and punish: The birth of the prison.* New York: Vintage Books.

Genders & Sexualities Alliance Network. (n.d.). *Gay-Straight Alliance Network is now Genders & Sexualities Alliance Network.* Retrieved from gsanetwork.org/NameFAQ

Giwa, S., & Greensmith, C. (2012). Race relations and racism in the LGBTQ community of Toronto: Perceptions of gay and queer social service providers of color. *Journal of Homosexuality, 59*(2), 149–185.

GLSEN, & Harris Interactive. (2008). *The principal's perspective: School safety, bullying and harassment, a survey of public school principals.* New York: GLSEN.

Goldstein, T. (2010). Snakes and ladders: A performed ethnography. *The International Journal of Critical Pedagogy, 3*(1), 68.

Grace, A. P., & Wells, K. (2015). *Growing into resilience: Sexual and gender minority youth in Canada.* Toronto: University of Toronto Press.

Greensmith, C., & Giwa, S. (2013). Challenging settler colonialism in contemporary queer politics: Settler homonationalism, Pride Toronto, and two-spirit subjectivities. *American Indian Culture and Research Journal, 37*(2), 129–148.

Haig, T. (2016, May 17). Canada moves forward with legislation to guarantee the rights of transgender people across the country. *Radio Canada International.* Retrieved from www.rcinet.ca/en/2016/05/17/canada-moves-forward-with-legislation-to-guarantee-the-rights-of-transgender-people-across-the-country/

Herek, G. M. (2004). Beyond "homophobia": Thinking about sexual prejudice and stigma in the twenty-first century. *Sexuality Research & Social Policy, 1*(2), 6–24.

Ingrey, J. C. (2012). The public school washroom as analytic space for troubling gender: investigating the spatiality of gender through students' self-knowledge. *Gender and Education, 24*(7), 799–817.

Jansen, S. (2015). *Bill 10: An act to amend the Alberta Bill of Rights to protect our children.* Edmonton, Alberta, Canada: Legislative Assembly of Alberta.

Lapointe, A. (2015). Standing "straight" up to homophobia: Straight allies' involvement in GSAs. *Journal of LGBT Youth, 12*(2), 144–169.

Lapointe, A. (2016). Postgay. In E. Brockenbrough, J. Ingrey, W. Martino, & N. M Rodriguez (Eds.), *Critical concepts in queer studies and education: An international guide for the twenty-first century* (pp. 205–218). New York: Palgrave Macmillian.

Lapointe, A., & Kassen, J. (2013). After the happily ever after: One year post-Bill 13, are Ontario Catholic schools supporting gay-straight alliance development? *Education Canada, 53*(4), 12–17.

Leung, H. H. (2008). *Undercurrents: Queer culture and postcolonial Hong Kong.* Vancouver: UBC Press.

Marx, R. A., & Kettrey, H. H. (2016). Gay-Straight Alliances are associated with lower levels of school-based victimization of LGBTQ+ youth: A systematic review and meta-analysis. *Journal of Youth and Adolescence, 45*(7), 1–14.

Mayberry, M. (2012). Gay-straight alliances: Youth empowerment and working toward reducing stigma of LGBT youth. *Humanity and Society, 37*(1), 35–54.

Mayo, J. B., Jr. (2009). Critical pedagogy enacted in the Gay-Straight Alliance: New possibilities for a third space in teacher development. *Educational Researcher, 42*(5), 266–275.

Mercer, R. (2011). *Rick Mercer Report: Rant: Teen suicide.* Canadian Broadcasting Corporation. Retrieved from www.youtube.com/watch?v=J1OvtBa2FK8

Meyer, E. J., & Stader, D. (2009). Queer youth and the culture wars: From classroom to courtroom in Australia, Canada and the United States. *Journal of LGBT Youth, 6*(2/3), 135–154.

Morgensen, S. L. (2011). *The spaces between us: Queer settler colonialism and Indigenous decolonization.* Minneapolis: University of Minnesota Press.

Nash, C. J. (2013). The age of the "post-mo"? Toronto's gay village and a new generation. *Geoforum, 49,* 243–252.

Noguera, P., Cammarota, J., & Ginwright, S. (Eds.). (2006). *Beyond resistance! Youth activism and community change: New democratic possibilities for practice and policy for America's youth.* New York: Routledge.

O'Meara, K. (2013). Advancing graduate student agency. *Higher Education in Review, 10,* 1–10.

Pascoe, C. J. (2007). *Dude, you're a fag: Masculinity and sexuality in high school.* Oakland, CA: University of California Press.

Peter, T., Taylor, C., & Edkins, T. (2016). Are the kids all right? The impact of school climate among students with LGBT parents. *Canadian Journal of Education, 39*(1), 1–25.

Poteat, V. P., Calzo, J. P., & Yoshikawa, H. (2016). Promoting youth agency through dimensions of Gay–Straight Alliance involvement and conditions that maximize associations. *Journal of Youth and Adolescence,* 1–14.

Puar, J. K. (2007). *Terrorist assemblages: Homonationalism in queer times.* Durham, NC & London, UK: Duke University Press.

Renold, E. (2005). *Girls, boys, and junior sexualities.* New York: RoutledgeFalmer.

Rofes, E. E. (1995). Making our schools safe for sissies. In G. Unks (Ed.), *The gay teen: Educational practice and theory for lesbian, gay and bisexual adolescents.* (pp. 109–24). New York: Routledge.

Saha, L. J. (2011). Sociology of education. In T. L. Good (Ed.), *21st century education: A reference handbook* (pp. 299–307). Thousand Oaks, CA: Sage.

Savage, D. (2010). It gets better project. *It Gets Better Project.* Retrieved from www.youtube.com/watch?v=7IcVyvg2Qlo

Serano, J. (2007). *Whipping girl: A transsexual woman on sexism and the scapegoating of femininity.* Berkeley, CA: Seal Press.

Smith, I. P., Oades, L., & McCarthy, G. (2012). Homophobia to heterosexism: Constructs in need of re-visitation. *Gay and Lesbian Issues and Psychology Review, 8*(1), 34–44.

St. John, A., Travers, R., Munro, L., Liboro, R., Schneider, M., & Greig, C. L. (2014). The success of gay–straight alliances in Waterloo Region, Ontario: A confluence of political and social factors. *Journal of LGBT Youth, 11*(2), 150–170.

Taylor, C., & Peter, T. (2011). *Every class in every school: The first national climate survey on homophobia, biphobia, and transphobia in Canadian schools. Final report.* Toronto: Egale Canada Human Rights Trust.

Taylor, E. (2010). Cisgender privilege: On the privileges of performing normative gender. In K. Bornstein & B. S. Bergman (Eds.), *Gender outlaws: The next generation* (pp. 268–272). Berkeley, CA: Seal Press.

Taylor, E. (2013) *Surveillance schools: security, discipline and control in contemporary education.* Basingstoke, UK: Palgrave Macmillan.

Toomey, R. B. (2016). School climate. In A. E. Goldberg (Ed.), *The SAGE encyclopedia of LGBTQ studies.* Thousand Oaks, CA: Sage.

Tremblay, M., & Paternotte, D. (Eds.). (2015). *The Ashgate Research companion to lesbian and gay activism.* Burlington, VT: Ashgate Publishing.

Unks, G. (2003). Thinking about the gay teen. In A. Darder, M. Baltodano, & R. D. Torres (Eds.), *The critical pedagogy reader* (pp. 322–330). New York: RoutledgeFalmer.

Wall, J. (2013). All the world's a stage: Childhood and the play of being. In W. R. Ryall, & M. MacLean (Eds.), *The philosophy of play* (pp. 32–43). New York: Routledge.

Walls, N. E., Kane, S. B., & Wisneski, H. (2010). Gay-straight alliances and the school experiences of sexual minority youth. *Youth & Society, 41,* 307–332.

Warrington, M., & Younger, M. (2011). "Life is a tightrope": Reflections on peer group inclusion and exclusion amongst adolescent girls and boys. *Gender and education, 23*(2), 153–168.

Wells, K. (2006). *Gay–straight student alliances in Alberta schools: A guide for teachers.* Edmonton: Alberta Teachers' Association.

Whitbeck, L. B. (2009). *Mental health and emerging adulthood among homeless young people.* New York: Psychology Press.

Young, S. L. B. (2010). "Rocking the boat": Developing a shared discourse of resistance. *Equity & Excellence in Education, 43*(4), 463–477.

Young-Bruehl, C. (2013). *Childism: Confronting prejudice against children.* New Haven, CT: Yale University Press.

SECTION IV

CITIZENSHIP, RIGHTS, AND SOCIAL ENGAGEMENT

In the spring of March 2013, a group of six Cree youths and a guide trekked over 1,600 kilometres, from Whapmagoostui, Quebec, the most northern Cree community in Quebec, to Canada's capital city, Ottawa, Ontario. The walkers called it the "Journey of the Nishiyuu," or the "Journey of the People," and they walked for over two months through remote, snowy wilderness, towing their supplies (see nishiyuujourney.ca/). These young people were walking to support the Idle No More movement, seeking to bring attention to Indigenous rights and well-being, for their own personal growth, and to champion the welfare of the land. They started out as a group of seven but then as they went, other walkers joined them, including many children and youth. As they approached Ottawa, they were a group of 400 walkers ("Cree Walkers," 2013). At the end of the walk, 17-year-old David Kawapit Jr. explained that "This is to show the youth have a voice. It's time for them to be shown the way to lead. Let them lead the way." ("Nishiyuu Walkers," 2013)

In this book we address many forms of inequality. We have explored ways childhood and youth are constructed categories that produce certain ways of thinking about young people and shape how they experience their lives. These conceptualizations of childhood and youth are often adultist in that they focus on vulnerability, incompetence, and incompleteness compared to an adult ideal. These conceptualizations prevent adults from recognizing young people as able to speak up and act for themselves, in research or in decision-making, as examples in previous sections of this book have shown us. Age can thus be considered one form of inequality, but we have also discussed many others that are deeply relevant to the lives of children and youth who are growing up at the intersections of class, race, gender, sexuality, and disability. In the "Journey of the Nishiyuu" we see how young Indigenous people make a deep and visceral statement about themselves, their culture, and the inequalities experienced by Indigenous people.

In this section, we present chapters that explore more deeply what it means to think about children's rights, participation, and agency, and to recognize the many ways that young people are socially engaged. This participation can be seen in the micro-settings of family relationships and the negotiations of friendships, in young people's everyday involvement in schools, the community, and online, and in larger political involvements and advocacy, such as the Journey of the Nishiyuu. Rather than simply being receptacles of socialization, children and youth are involved in shaping the society that they are growing up in, both in everyday mundane activities and in quite exceptional ways.

We open this section with Noah Kenneally's chapter 17, "Doing Children's Rights: Moving beyond Entitlements and into Relationships in Canadian Contexts." Kenneally provides a generous overview of children's rights both globally and in Canada, noting how such rights have been framed through a legal lens and how we might want to think about them more in terms of relationships, highlighting children's rights as actions that are embedded in interactions with those around them, including adults. Rather than seeing rights as something bestowed on children, or seeing children and adults as holding opposing rights, Kenneally seeks to shift our understanding of rights to better recognize children as ongoing participants with others.

Cornelia Schneider's chapter 18, "Between Children's Rights and Disability Rights: Inclusion and Participation of Children and Youth with Disabilities," provides a concrete example of how children's participatory rights must be considered for all young people, with a concentrated focus on children and youth with disabilities. Drawing on research she has conducted on inclusive classrooms, peer relationships, and transitions into adulthood in France, Germany, and Canada, Schneider draws attention to places where children's rights—particularly rights to protection and rights to participation—may clash. She illustrates how children and youth with disabilities experience inclusion or exclusion, as well as social participation, in diverse ways, arguing that teachers, families, employers, and other stakeholders must better understand and enact the rights of children and youth with disabilities, particularly their participatory rights.

Various commentators have worried that young people are withdrawing from civic politics as they are less likely to vote than older Canadians and also less likely to become involved in political parties. As previous chapters illustrate, many young people are interested in social change, however. In chapter 19, "The Civic and Political Engagement of Canadian Youth," L. Alison Molina-Girón discusses the specific issue of civic engagement and explores the extent of young people's participation in the public, more formal political realm. She notes that young people are indeed involved in Canada's civic and political life, but in less traditional ways than voting. She also pays particular attention to which young people are more and less likely to be involved, as this kind of participation is significantly shaped by race, ethnicity, class, and level of education.

Molina-Girón asks us to consider more diverse ways that young people are involved in civic politics. Our concluding chapter returns to these more conceptual questions with a focus on participation and citizenship. Sriskandarajah, in chapter 20, "Negotiating Youth Citizenship and Belonging in a Toronto 'Priority' Neighbourhood," explores how particular spaces, specifically marginalized neighbourhoods, shape feelings and practices of belonging and citizenship among racialized youth. Sriskandarajah argues that it is through these neighbourhoods that young people cultivate alternative understandings of citizenship that are more about practice than status.

REFERENCES

Cree walkers meet minister at end of Idle No More trek. (2013, March 25). *CBC News*. Retrieved from www.cbc.ca/news/canada/ottawa/cree-walkers-meet-minister-at-end-of-idle-no-more-trek-1.1392239

"Nishiyuu Walkers" complete 1,600 km trek to Ottawa. (2013, March 25). *CTV News*. Retrieved from www.ctvnews.ca/canada/nishiyuu-walkers-complete-1-600-km-trek-to-ottawa-1.1209929

17 Doing Children's Rights: Moving beyond Entitlements and into Relationships in Canadian Contexts

Noah Kenneally

LEARNING OBJECTIVES

- To describe the development and history of the Convention on the Rights of the Child and Canada's relationship to children's rights, and identify the core principles of children's rights
- To contrast the dominant legal approach to children's rights with a relational approach
- To discuss and analyze how the perspective of the sociology of childhood supports a relational approach to children's rights
- To make connections between concepts of children/childhood and underlying philosophical assumptions
- To effectively critique children's rights from a variety of perspectives

INTRODUCTION

In this chapter, I join an ongoing conversation about children's **rights** that challenges dominant legal discussions. The most common approaches to children's rights conceive of them as being in the realm of law and international relations. As mentioned in chapter 1, this legal approach has taken important steps to ameliorating the circumstances of children worldwide. However, it is also removed from children's actual lived experiences. In this chapter, I investigate how seeing children as agentive social actors can make children's rights more concrete, especially for children themselves. I propose that we reconceptualize children's rights as *doing*—actions and interactions that directly involve children—rather than things that are *done to* or *for* children. In the spirit of this collection, I explore how the **sociology of childhood** can help relocate children's rights to a more concrete, observable, and enactable space—by reframing children's rights as **relational** practices, as elements of children's everyday relationships and interactions, and as tools children can use to participate in the shaping of culture and the production of our social worlds.

First, I will outline the history of children's rights, how they are understood and implemented, and Canada's relationship to them. I will then discuss some of the conceptual tools of the sociology of childhood, and discuss how they can help to reorganize our perceptions of children's rights. Finally, I will use those tools to describe some of the ways that children's rights can be understood as aspects of relationships, and provide examples that demonstrate ways of *doing* children's rights, both from an adult's perspective and from a child's perspective.

WHAT ARE CHILDREN'S RIGHTS?

Chapter 1 of this volume briefly outlined the **UN Convention on the Rights of the Child** (CRC); described provision, protection, and participation rights; and pointed to some of the impacts that the CRC and children's rights thinking has had on issues such as **citizenship** and social engagement. In the three and a half decades since it was created, the CRC as a framework for thinking about children's rights has been central to many positive changes addressing children's experiences around the world. The CRC exists to guide governments in forming laws that would universally ensure the necessary conditions for all children, in all cultures and parts of the world, to have the "best possible childhood." However, it has also become an object of criticism. The CRC came into existence at a particular time in history, and was drafted within a particular philosophical framework. It has become increasingly clear that what the CRC means by "best possible childhood" is profoundly informed by history and the philosophical framework that it was developed in. Some of the common sense assumptions embedded in the CRC about what it means to be a child or what the "best possible childhood" is reveal normative standards that do not match the majority of children's lived experiences, either in the Western or minority world,[1] such as here in Canada, or around the world. We will discuss these later in the chapter.

A SHORT HISTORY OF CHILDREN'S RIGHTS AND THE CRC—GLOBALLY AND IN CANADA

Decades of social change around the world—anti-colonial movements against Euro-American domination in the majority world; the civil rights movements of marginalized groups in the Western or minority world; and the growing presence of media and communication technologies linking all parts of the world—made it increasingly apparent that although existing human rights texts proposed general principles that acknowledged children's rights, a specific document that could be converted into enforceable laws would make children's rights more achievable. Therefore, an international convention—a document that could be adopted by member states of the United Nations and translated into legislation by their governments—was seen as a necessary next step. This international convention was the Convention on the Rights of the Child.

UNICEF declared 1979 as the International Year of the Child, kicking off a decade of effort developing the CRC. Delegations from many UN member nations, intergovernmental organizations (IGOs), and nongovernmental organizations (NGOs) formed an international Committee on the Rights of the Child (UNCRC) that undertook drafting the Convention (Johnson, 1992). Marshall (2013) gives a detailed account of Canada's participation. She notes that Canadian delegates were members of committees that developed the League of Nations' Declaration of the Rights of the Child in 1924, and the United Nations Declaration of the Rights of the Child in 1959. Canadians of that era were supportive of these treaties, as the political climate was focused on building a more socially responsible society. This provided a foundation for Canadian participation in the development of the CRC.

The United Nations General Assembly unanimously adopted the CRC in 1989, and it became the most ratified, and most *quickly* ratified, international human rights treaty (Alderson, 2008; Human Rights Watch, 2014; Freeman, 2010). Countries that ratify the CRC commit to integrating its principles into their policies and laws. They also commit to submitting periodic reports to the UNCRC describing their progress in implementing children's rights. The Committee responds to these reports with recommendations to assist with further implementation (OHCHR, 2016b). The UN and the OHCHR do not have the capacity to enforce the CRC—there are no children's rights police. Instead, it is hoped that public opinion, international relations, and international standing are enough impetus for nations to implement the CRC and actualize children's rights.

Both the pace by which nations ratified the CRC and the high number that did so are "further testimony to the importance now attached internationally to promoting children's rights" (Lansdown, 1996, p. 57). As of this writing, the United States of America is the only UN member state, out of 197, that has yet to ratify the CRC (OHCHR, 2016c). Since the CRC was drafted, three optional protocols have been added to address domains of particular concern (OHCHR, 2016a). Optional protocols are additional agreements that address a portion of that treaty in greater depth. They are optional because they are even more demanding in their obligations than the original treaty, and nations decide independently whether it is possible to adhere to them or not. The Optional Protocol to the Convention on the Rights of the Child on the Sale of Children, Child Prostitution and Child Pornography (OPSC) addresses child exploitation, slavery, and trafficking. The Optional Protocol to the Convention on the Rights of the Child on the Involvement of Children in Armed Conflict (OPAC) addresses children involved in armed conflict. Both were adopted by the General Assembly in

2000 and entered into force in 2002. A third optional protocol, the Optional Protocol on a Communications Procedure (OP3 CRC), allows individual children to challenge rights violations committed by states. OP3 CRC was approved in 2011 and went into force in 2014. Together, the CRC and the three optional protocols are the primary texts of international children's rights (OHCHR, 2016a).

The Canadian government signed the CRC in 1990 and ratified it in 1991; it then ratified the first two optional protocols in 2002 but has yet to adopt the third. By ratifying the CRC, the Canadian government indicated that it was committed to the "fundamental obligations with respect to protecting and promoting the rights of children throughout the country" (Pearson & Collins, 2009, p. 57). Ratification, however, is merely the first step. Implementation—the translation of the CRC into laws and policies, to make them happen—is a complex process that demands ongoing effort from all levels of government, civil society organizations, and the Canadian populace. The Canadian Human Rights Commission is responsible for submitting the required reports to the UNCRC for Canada and for assessing its progress. According to an analysis by the Canadian Coalition for the Rights of Children (CCRC), the Canadian governments' implementation of the CRC over the past two and half decades has been sporadic at best (Canadian Coalition for the Rights of Children, 2011).

Canada could substantially improve the circumstances of all Canadian children by implementing the general measures of the CRC (Canadian Coalition for the Rights of Children, 2011). General measures are considered the basic tools of implementation and consist of the following elements: Law reform is necessary to incorporate the principles of best interest and child participation into all levels of government and domains of the law. Monitoring mechanisms—including data collection on children in Canada, impact assessments of policy and practices, and reporting procedures to the UNCRC—need to be put in place so a clearer understanding of children's circumstances across the country can be determined. Children's rights programs need to be evaluated, to ensure that they are meeting their goals. Clear children's budgets from all levels of government need to be developed, so that expenditures can be committed to, accurately tracked, and assessed. Finally, mechanisms and governmental offices that specifically champion children's rights need to be put in place to make them a priority in Canadian politics. The Canadian Coalition for the Rights of Children (2011) notes that if the Canadian government takes action on these general measures, children's rights in Canada will be substantially improved.

Even though Canada is a Western or minority world nation, and the population in general has substantial access to economic, social, and cultural resources when compared to other nations around the world, children continue to experience circumstances that have negative effects on their well-being, both on a personal and structural level (Canadian Coalition for the Rights of Children, 2011; Pearson & Collins, 2009). Canada ranks 72nd on the 2016 KidsRights Index, a worldwide ranking of how well countries care for children and promote children's rights in proportion to their wealth (KidsRights Index, 2016). Canada falls behind other industrialized countries in similar social and economic circumstances, especially in the areas of children's health, well-being, and development. The following outlines some of the situations faced by children in Canada:

- Canada ranks 26th out of the 35 wealthiest countries in the world when contrasting rates of child poverty (UNICEF Canada, 2016). Fourteen percent of Canada's children live in circumstances of poverty. There is a strong connection between access to resources and access to rights, and poverty is a clear violation of the human rights of children (Vandenhole, 2014). (See Albanese, chapter 11 in this collection, for more detail regarding child poverty in Canada.)

- Although the CRC addresses the rights of children with disabilities, and Canada ratified the **UN Convention on the Rights of Persons with Disabilities** in 2010, Canadian children with disabilities and their families still face significant barriers in accessing services, assistance, and support (Canadian Human Rights Commission, 2015; Statistics Canada, 2013). It is particularly difficult for school-aged children with disabilities to find a school with the adequate resources, equipment, and training to meet their needs, and this affects their future achievement. (See chapter 6 by Abbas and chapter 18 by Schneider for more information regarding children with disabilities in Canada.)

- Inuit and First Nations children are the fastest-growing young population in the country—46 percent of the Canadian **Indigenous** population is under 25 years. Indigenous children are subject to multiple forms of injustice at the same time, often referred to as intersectionality. They experience race-based discrimination; have higher rates of living in poverty; face barriers to accessing resources; are overrepresented in the child-welfare system; and live with the legacy of Indian Residential Schools, displacement, and cultural **genocide**, which can affect their well-being and development (Aboriginal Children in Care Working Group, 2015). Canadian Indigenous children would particularly benefit if children's rights were addressed more concretely. (See the introductory chapter of this text as well as chapter 12, by Spencer and Sinclair, for a more detailed discussion of the issues faced by Indigenous children in Canada.)

- Almost 20 percent of new permanent residents to Canada are children when they arrive. **Newcomer** children to Canada face challenges while integrating into a new context, and **refugee** children and children with precarious citizenship status (undocumented children, unaccompanied child migrants, etc.) experience even more **marginalization** (Bernhard, 2012). Children's rights in particular have taken a central role in the response to the ongoing conflict in Syria. The world was galvanized into action by media images of the drowning of Alan (Aylan) and Ghalib Kurdi, two Syrian Kurdish refugee boys who, along with their mother, died attempting to reach Greece from Turkey in an effort to join family and resettle in Canada (Smith, 2015). Significantly, 34 percent of refugees who arrived in Canada from Syria in 2014 alone were under the age of 15, and an additional 15 percent were 15 to 24 years of age (Citizenship and Immigration Canada, 2015).

A more concerted effort to realize children's rights in Canada would benefit these different groups, and all children in the country, in significant ways. Children's circumstances in Canada are changing all the time, and some important changes occurred at the time of this writing. In 2016, a landmark case was brought before the Canadian Human Rights Tribunal by the First Nations Child and Family Caring Society and the Assembly of First Nations regarding the overrepresentation of Indigenous children in the child welfare system. It cited **systemic discrimination** on the basis of First Nations ancestry. The Tribunal found that the formula used by the federal government to allocate funds to child and family services for First Nations children on reserves was inadequate and discriminatory. The Tribunal referred to the CRC in its decision-making process, and ordered the federal government to cease these discriminatory practices and take measures to redress and prevent them (First Nations Child and Family Caring Society of Canada, 2016). However, the federal government has yet to comply and commit to providing funds to address the disparity in health services for children living on reserve.

In another promising turn of events, the newly elected Liberal government committed to welcoming 25,000 Syrian refugees shortly after it came into power in 2015. Children, women, and families were prioritized, By February 2016, this goal was achieved, and Canada continues to assist and resettle Syrian refugees across the country (Citizenship and Immigration Canada, 2016). Finally, a restructuring of federal support for families with children was introduced in 2016 with the new Canada Child Benefit. This benefit provides funding to families based on how many children they have and is geared to the family's net income—families with less income will receive more support—as one way of addressing child poverty (Canadian Coalition for the Rights of Children, 2016; Canada Revenue Agency, 2016). All of these shifts in Canada's approach to children's rights signal an increased sensitivity and political awareness of their importance. In the next section, we'll take a closer look at how children's rights are understood and put into practice.

UNDERSTANDING AND IMPLEMENTING CHILDREN'S RIGHTS

Children's Rights under the CRC

Children's rights can be understood in many ways. Two primary understandings of children's rights are commonly referred to as the Three Ps and the Four Guiding Principles. In the Three Ps framework, provision, protection, and participation rights are intertwined. The ideal proposed by the CRC is that one type of right cannot supersede another type of right—they are of equal value and all three should be worked towards simultaneously in every aspect of children's lives. However, in practice it is difficult to balance them evenly, and the different types of rights can often seem at odds with each other. Common ways of understanding children frame them primarily as vulnerable, needing the protection of adults, and incapable of understanding the world around them or of forming an opinion. This is one of the reasons that a sociological approach to children and childhood can support children's rights, as the sociology of childhood recognizes children's capacities and sees them as social actors. For children's rights to flourish, children must have what they need to survive and thrive, be protected from harm, and be considered legitimate and active parts of society.

The Four Guiding Principles run like connecting threads throughout the entire CRC, and provide a solid base on which children's rights can be developed and assessed. Each is considered a core concept of the CRC itself, and while all 54 articles fall under one or more guiding principle, each principle is primarily represented by an article in particular:

- Article 2: Nondiscrimination
- Article 3: **Best interests of the child**
- Article 6: Life, survival, and development
- Article 12: Respect for the views of the child

When taken together, the Three Ps and the Four Guiding Principles provide a powerful conceptual framework that can be used to describe and evaluate the status of children's rights and the implementation of the CRC.

In human rights treaties, nations are referred to as *state parties*, and much of the language of the CRC is geared towards the governments of state parties. The CRC invests governments with the responsibilities to ensure children's rights are respected and upheld. Therefore, legal systems and structures are considered the primary mechanisms for making children's rights happen, and laws and legislation are understood as the arenas where children's rights are enacted (and enactable). Children's rights are seen as things that children are entitled to, just by being alive, and the primary approach to implementing them is a legal approach (Alderson, 2008; Freeman, 1983, 2007, 2011; Jones, 2011; Jones & Welch, 2010).

For children's entitlements to be recognized by legal systems, national governments are expected to translate them into laws—the rules that control the behaviours and decisions of a nation's population. Entitlements are also closely linked to obligations—you are owed something, and I am obliged, either by law or by social convention, to provide you with it. Given that children are rarely considered power-holders in society, their rights are most often framed as obligations expected to be actualized by those who have authority over them, such as their parents, their families, other adults acting on their behalf, and the institutions of governments (Alderson, 2008; Freeman, 1983, 2000,

2007; Jones & Welch, 2010). Since children are dependent on adults in many ways, this perspective of obligation and entitlement is seen as particularly meaningful. You are a child, and we have to take care of our children, so we will give you these rights. From this perspective, rights can be seen as a type of exchange that is almost economic: adults and governments are obliged to take care of children and ensure their well-being, and so pay them in a currency of things they are entitled to—children's rights.

CRITICISMS OF THE CRC

Although the CRC was signed and ratified almost unanimously, it has been met with reservations from the international community and with critique from children's rights scholars and activists. According to O'Neill and Zinga (2008), "the number of declarations, reservations and objections to the Convention show that the world does not accept it as a monolithic code" (p. 5). Some governments are concerned that they lack the resources to actualize children's rights in their countries. Others have reservations about the underlying ideologies that underpin the Convention, feeling as though the universalizing claims made in the CRC about the "best possible childhood" go against traditional or cultural values (Cowan, Dembour, & Wilson, 2001; Johnson, 1992; Stephens, 1995). Canada itself has declared reservations to the CRC, including a reservation regarding Article 21 on adoption being in the child's best interest, as a way to acknowledge that among Indigenous peoples in Canada there are other customs of care for children, and a reservation regarding Article 37 on the detention of children separate from adults in situations where this is not feasible (Canadian Children's Rights Council, 2015).

Other critics of the CRC contend that the high levels of its ratification are primarily symbolic—that countries signed on to the treaty to appear to be doing something to address children's rights without having to do very much in practice—and that without a system of enforcement the Convention does little to improve the lives of children (Brown, 2004; MacIntyre; 2007; Mutua, 2002). Similarly, others feel that the rights accorded to children in the CRC, particularly participation rights, exist only on paper, or that states treat them in tokenistic ways, honouring the word of the CRC but not the spirit. Although there were reports of a collegial climate during the drafting of the CRC, many developing or majority nations did not feel included in the process at the time, and feel underrepresented by the document itself (Johnson, 1992; Van Bueren, 2011; Viljoen, 1998). Some regions have responded by developing their own children's rights documents for particular contexts—for example, the African Charter on the Rights and Welfare of the Child (Adu-Gyamfi & Keating, 2013; Chirwa, 2002; Njungwe, 2009).

The open-endedness of the CRC, which according to Johnson (1992) and Van Bueren (1995, 2011) was included in order to provide flexibility so that children's rights could be enacted differently in different countries and contexts, also causes problems. Critics feel that by making the CRC so open to interpretation, its impact is diluted. In many countries that have signed and ratified the CRC, children are still unable to access the basic necessities of life, let alone the varied elements they might need to achieve their full potential or enjoy that elusive "best possible childhood." Finally, and particularly central to this discussion, the CRC is biased towards Western or minority world conceptualizations of childhood, which make the Convention's claims to universality troubling (Reynaert, Bouverne-de-Bie, & Vandevelde, 2012; Wells, 2015).

The Normative Ideas in the CRC

As mentioned above, the time at which the CRC was developed and the philosophical framework upon which it is based profoundly shaped taken-for-granted ideas in the CRC: what it means to be a child, what the ideal child is, and what sort of childhood is considered the "best possible childhood." These normative ideas set a standard for how children and childhood should be. The philosophical framework at the core of the CRC and the dominant approaches to children's rights are shaped by the ethics of liberal theory. Liberal theory has been one of the dominant theories underpinning contemporary politics and philosophy in the Western or minority world since the Enlightenment (Skott-Myhre & Tarulli, 2008; Tisdall & Punch, 2012; Wall, 2008; Wells, 2015). Liberal ethics conceptualize humans as independent, rational subjects who are free to make autonomous choices. This way of imagining human beings infuses almost every element of Western or minority world political life, which dominates global politics in the twenty-first century. It follows that it has tremendous influence on how we understand children's rights and what we think it means to be a child. To quote Wells (2015), "International children's rights law, news reporting on children and how NGOs frame their work with children are each inscribed with these same ethical premises that the child is a universal subject who should everywhere be enabled to be a free, autonomous, choosing and rational individual" (p. 203).

Liberal ethics are at the foundation of children's rights, and as Wells outlines above, they portray children as free, autonomous, choosing, and rational individuals, all assumptions which can be deconstructed.

- Free—means being independent, being a distinct and unconstrained person. Few children would be considered free, as most are held accountable to the adults in their lives, and to social structures over which they have little control. However, similarly few adults have access to enough resources—social, material, or economic—to be considered unconstrained. From a sociological point of view, everyone is constrained by rules, conventions, and values that organize our social worlds.
- Autonomous—means being self-sufficient and capable of taking care of yourself. Again, given contemporary ideas about children, and the reality that the majority of children are dependent on adults for their basic needs, few children around

the world are autonomous. In fact, few adults could be considered autonomous. Generally, everyone today is dependent on social institutions like the family, economy, government, and so on to secure the necessities of life. At another level, we also all share the same water sources, breathe the same air from the same atmosphere, and depend on healthy ecosystems to provide our food. We are far more *interdependent* than liberal ethics would lead us to believe.

- Choosing—means making decisions about how you spend your time, where you put your efforts, and how you spend your resources. For the most part, decisions are made *for* children, and young people are rarely invited to give input regarding their day-to-day activities. Again, this applies to all people, regardless of age, as everyone is constrained by the social and economic factors at a personal and societal level. Many adults' choices are controlled by what they can afford to do, where they are positioned in society, their family and cultural background, what they look like, and other aspects of our social worlds.

- Rational—means using logic to think your way through decisions and situations. Children are rarely considered to be capable of rational thought, and are more often thought of as being in the process of developing the capacities to do so. The same could be said for many adults—few grown-ups operate logically in the world at all times, and it seems as though human nature includes irrational, emotional aspects that also define who we are.

Following this argument, from a sociological perspective it becomes increasingly difficult to find the type of subject idealized by the CRC. All children do not enjoy the same privileges and resources—some have more, many have a lot less. In addition to economic access, gender, race, and cultural factors also influence how much choice, freedom, and autonomy a young person has. The term *individuals* may even be misleading. The idea of an independent and self-sufficient individual is also part of liberal theory, and demonstrates a bias towards the Western or minority world's systems of social organization (Wells, 2015). In other societies, for example Indigenous communities, the emphasis may be more on the collective and community than on the individual. In addition, given the intense physical and social interdependence of humanity, and the fact that we rely on many other organisms and species for our survival, health, and well-being, it might be more useful to understand our social worlds by focusing on relationships, and what happens when subjects and structures interact.

After taking this closer look, we begin to see the divergence at the heart of liberal thinking about children's rights. On the one hand, it understands children as free, autonomous, choosing, and rational individuals—investing them with a lot of **power**, independence, and capabilities. On the other hand, the majority of articles of the CRC are preoccupied with children's protection and their development, highlighting children's vulnerabilities. Understanding and working towards achieving children's rights, as well as translating the guidelines of the CRC into law and policy, becomes a very complicated process. What happens, then, if we shift the arena of children's rights away from the dominant legal approach and into the realm of relationships, and how might the sociology of childhood help to do this?

THE SOCIOLOGY OF CHILDHOOD AND A RELATIONAL PERSPECTIVE OF CHILDREN'S RIGHTS

According to Donati and Archer (2015), relational sociology examines the social world by paying attention to human relationships. It frames relationships not as transactions between fluid forces, but as interactions between beings that are imbued with care, emotions, and meaning. My exploration of a relational approach to children's rights is inspired in part by former Canadian Senator Landon Pearson, who has been a child advocate for decades. In a lecture in 2012, Pearson stated the following:

> First of all I have learned that while there are a number of ways that we can frame issues that are related to children and youth, the human rights perspective is a particularly constructive one. Using it pushes you to engage directly with young people and of course with the voices of women, and to let them help you find solutions to their problems that are likely to work. Secondly, human rights properly understood, are about relationships, rather than about entitlements. They are about the relationships between individuals in society and between individuals—either alone or in groups—and the state. (Pearson, 2012)

Scholars committed to exploring a relational approach to children's rights push beyond the legal framework. For instance, Priscilla Alderson emphasizes the personhood of children and sees children's rights as a viable frame to acknowledge their **agency** and involve them in social life. She calls on adult power-holders to reconsider their assumptions about children and to investigate how those preconceptions may interfere with or impede children's rights. She also recommends that adults use children's rights frameworks to restructure the interactions they have with children in ways that value children's views and experiences (Alderson, 1999, 2008). Similarly, Phil Jones and Sue Welch call on adult service providers to investigate how rights-informed approaches to relating to children can transform the ways that they and their child clients interact. They contend that doing so can shift service provision for children to more collaborative approaches that respect children in ways that reinforce their rights within their relationships (Jones & Welch, 2010). To further support our point, many philosophers argue that rights must be seen within their cultural, economic, and social contexts and are subjective rather than universal (MacIntyre, 2007). The sociology of childhood can really help us see rights in this light.

The sociology of childhood emerged as an interdisciplinary approach to studying children and childhood at roughly the same time as the children's rights framework. It offers several conceptual tools that support rethinking children's rights as being about, or even located in, children's relationships.

First, the sociology of childhood investigates *children's social lives* (Corsaro, 2011; James, 2010; James & James, 2004; Mayall, 2002, 2013). Sociology looks both at large-scale populations, trends, and themes—or childhood as a social category—as well as childhood as children's specific lived experiences (James, 2010; Qvortrup, 1994, 2008, 2009). Children's lives and experiences are perceived as worthy of study and as important sources of information that are unavailable through any other means. If children's lived experiences are the best terrain to explore childhood, looking at children's relationships as potential sites for *doing* children's rights makes sense.

Second, the sociology of childhood perceives *children as social actors* (James & James, 2004; Mayall, 2002). That children have an influence on their social worlds is well documented by sociology of childhood research. Understanding children as actors whose choices and actions have concrete effects in their social worlds supports our exploration of children's practices within their relationships as a way for children's rights to take place.

Third, the sociology of childhood pays attention to the *context of childhoods* (Corsaro, 2011; James, 2010; James, Jenks, & Prout, 1998; Mayall, 2002, 2013). The idea that childhood manifests differently according to historical and cultural context has spurred a wealth of research into the childhoods of different contexts (see e.g. Liebel, 2012; Punch, 2003; Twum-Danso, 2009). This approach situates particular beliefs about what it means to be a child, and what a "good" or "bad" childhood might be within a particular nexus of time, place, and culture. Context is seen as a major influence regarding the possible types of relationships and forms of interaction. Paying attention to the context of these social processes can shed light on the ways that children's rights can be aspects of different relationships.

Finally, the sociology of childhood *pushes against the ideas of universal norms and standards* for children and childhood (Gabriel, 2014; James & James, 2004; Prout, 2011; Ruffolo, 2009; Smith, 2010). If we understand childhood as contextual then the idea of childhood being the same everywhere for all children does not make sense. Even general patterns of development are influenced by context and do not manifest in the same ways for all children in all places (Burman, 2008). There can be no "normal" childhood, as the standards by which we might measure are themselves based in time, place, and culture. The sociology of childhood helps us by relocating the patterns of childhood within specific social worlds.

RELATIONSHIPS OF RECIPROCITY

I have found the work of the following scholars helpful in thinking about children's rights as relational actions instead of entitlements. Wall (2006, 2008) reframes children's rights as tools to be used in interpersonal relationships for the respectful response to others' differences. He proposes that children's rights be seen as a framework used to build respectful and responsive interactions. These interactions involve intentionally opening to children's "otherness" by careful listening, and weaving our own perspectives into our understanding of theirs. Similarly, Skott-Myhre and Tarulli (2008) locate children's rights in the living bodies and experiences of children themselves. They see rights as being produced by the actions of people, and so children's rights happen in children's lives rather than the realm of law. Building on their work, we can conceptualize the relationships of children as their realms of action—spaces where dialogues that value difference can flourish, and children's rights can be re-imagined as creative processes of interaction.

However, Tisdall and Punch (2012) call our attention to some potential dangers of focusing on a relational approach to children's rights. First, they state that if we see rights as a part of a relational ethics of care, we acknowledge that children are important elements of social networks. Yet in doing so we run the risk of obscuring the fact that children are not simply members of family units, but are also their own distinctive selves. Similarly, a relational approach also runs the risk of shifting the focus off the social category of children as a separate group with particular needs. Finally, they draw our attention to seeing children's rights as responsibilities, a perspective that recognizes that children make real contributions to their worlds (although others note that in recognizing responsibility, we may be producing the expectation of a "responsible" child wherein any child who doesn't act "responsibly" becomes deviant).

Tisdall and Punch (2012) suggest an alternative—a narrative of **reciprocity**. Reciprocity can be understood from a neoliberal or capitalist perspective as payback, or an exchange of equal value. Inspired by Tisdall and Punch, I prefer a definition that "can respect the dignity of all contributors" (2012, p. 258) and acknowledges our interdependence as social creatures embedded in social worlds. From this perspective, reciprocity is a collaborative interaction that mutually benefits those involved. The following two examples illustrate possibilities for children's rights at work in a relational context of reciprocity. The first is from recent news and the second is from my own work and research with children.

Kipling Acres is a long-term care facility for seniors that also houses an early childhood centre, Kipling Early Learning and Child Care Centre. Elderly residents and children interact regularly and have developed reciprocal relationships (Monsebraaten, 2016). Both groups experience segregation in Canadian society—young children are often secluded in the family home or in daycare, and our aging population is increasingly sidelined by our youth-fixated society. Health benefits and social effects for both groups have been documented in a growing body of research (Gigliotti, Morris, Smock, Jarrott, & Graham, 2005; Holmes, 2009; Isaki & Towle Harmon, 2015; Kaplan & Larkin, 2004; Lee, Camp, & Malone, 2007).

Looking through a lens of the sociology of childhood, the relationships between the children and seniors can be seen as reciprocal and rights-based. The way Kipling Acres is organized emphasizes that both children and seniors are actively involved in social life. Working against prevalent segregation by integrating children and seniors in everyday interactions, such as meeting in the hall and having regular visits, allows for the possibility of enacting a fundamental principle of rights: Article 2—non-discrimination. Monsebraaten (2016) reports that families describe positive effects for their children's social understanding and interactions emerging from their daily encounters with the elderly. Similarly, the seniors report feeling enlivened by their interactions with the children. The integrated social engagement crosses normalized boundaries in contemporary Canadian society, where young and old people are siloed from the rest of the world. From a relational rights perspective, the interactions between the seniors and young children become immediate, intimate sites where children can practise respecting others and being respected by doing both in the context of concrete, lived relationships.

My second example emerged during my own work as a student teacher/researcher at an alternative elementary school in Toronto. I conducted a project with a grade 2 class, visualizing the articles of the CRC after exploring children's rights through a variety of activities, picture books, and reflective discussions.

Figure 17.1 is a photograph of one of the students' drawings—Article 12: Respect for the views of the child. When I asked Isa to explain what it meant, she described Article 12 as a demonstration of children's rights as a creative, relational, interactive process. She explained that the drawing depicted a family, two adults and three children, and that the parents listened to their children. *Doing* this created a lot of love in

Figure 17.1: "Article 12"

Source: Isa Blackstock-Berinstein, participant in research project Grade 2 Exploration of Children's Rights, 2012.

the family, represented by the many hearts. One of the parents is drawn with a speech bubble that reads "I respect my children." The student had written on her drawing "You have the right to give your opinion and for adults to listen to it seriously."

While this is a visual representation of Article 12 of the CRC, it also depicts a relationship that *does* other components of children's rights as well—for example, Article 5, parental guidance, by affirming the relationship between parents and children; Article 13, children's freedom of expression, in the way that it recognizes children's rights to share information and express their opinions; and Article 14, freedom of thought, conscience, and religion, by acknowledging that children have the right to believe and think what they want as long as they are not stopping others from enjoying their own rights. From the perspective of the sociology of childhood, this example values children's social lives and perspectives as important sources of information that are unobtainable any other way. Isa makes connections between listening, respect, and family that shed invaluable light on where she sees children's rights as being possible—in her explanation of her drawing it becomes clear that she could see children's rights happening, with adults listening and respecting children in living and dynamic interactions as an everyday part of their social lives.

CONCLUSION

It is possible to interpret children's rights as relational processes instead of as dynamics of law, in the two examples I discuss above. By grounding our perspective in the sociology of childhood, and looking at children's social lives as the spaces where children's rights can take place, it is also possible to make children's rights more tangible and concrete. This has far-reaching implications for professionals working with children, in helping children themselves learn and make sense of children's rights, and regarding attitudes towards children's rights in general.

First, relational approaches to children's rights can be useful to professionals in creating relationships of respect, where power imbalances between adults and children can be grappled with. Educators and school officials are presented with an opportunity to rethink classroom and school dynamics to include children more in design and decision-making processes, and in that way making education more relevant to young people and grounded in their lived experiences. Alternatively, health care professionals in Canada already have a foundation for forging rights-based relationships with the children in their care, foremost by framing children as deserving of dignity and the best possible care available. The Canadian Paediatric Society encourages medical practitioners to take the position that "decision-making for children and adolescents should be interdisciplinary and collaborative, and should actively involve the family and, when appropriate, the child or adolescent" (Harrison & Canadian Paediatric Society, 2004, p. 99). These are the types of collaborative relationships in which children's rights become an active, engaged *doing* by all parties involved. Professionals in social work or providing other forms of direct care can benefit from relational approaches to children's rights as well. Similar to medical relationships, involving children in ways that respect their views and productively include their input can lead to designing programs of care that take children's preferences into consideration. This may even make young peoples' participation more likely.

Second, a relational approach to children's rights could make it easier for children to learn about and understand their rights. The dominant legal framework uses technical jargon and abstract concepts that makes learning about rights opaque for many adults, let alone children developing their language and conceptual capacities. Grounding children's rights in aspects of their social lives has the potential to make them easier to understand. Examples of the principles at the core of children's rights—respect, listening to and taking others' views seriously, protection from harm, nondiscrimination, and so on—presented in an experiential way through interactions with other children and adults can make those principles more visible and meaningful. Additionally, sociology and social psychology research has shown that collaborative prosocial behaviours are learned through practice (Alderson, 2008; Callero, 1986; Brownell, Svetlova, Anderson, Nichols, & Drummond, 2013). Practising children's rights by *doing* them in relationships could be an excellent approach to take in children's rights education (Howe & Covell, 2007b).

Finally, a relational approach to children's rights may have a positive impact on attitudes towards children's rights in general. As mentioned in chapter 1, children's rights and the CRC are not a part of the common **discourse** of everyday life for the populace of many nations, Canada included (Howe & Covell, 2007a). In fact, some groups are actively opposed to them. Most notable of these are parental rights groups, whose primary concern is that children's rights might undermine the role of parents in decision-making processes by involving state sanction or control. However, reframing children's rights as mutually beneficial aspects of relationships in which power is shared in collaborative interactions rather than undermining one individual's or party's power in favour of another's may shift resistant or ambivalent attitudes towards children's rights in general.

In closing, the sociology of childhood offers conceptual tools that make it possible to see children's rights as aspects of children's social lives. This relational approach has the potential to reframe children's rights as social actions that take place in the relationships children have with other children or adults. Given Canada's diverse cultural and geographical contexts, with so many different perspectives regarding children and childhood, and so many different *experiences* of being children and having a childhood, seeing children's rights as being situated in lived social worlds presents a sensitive approach that can account for those differences. *Doing* children's rights has the potential to make them more concrete—we can see and feel our interactions with others—and make children's rights something that everyone can be involved in and relate to.

CHAPTER SUMMARY

Together, in this chapter, we

- Described the development of the Convention on the Rights of the Child (CRC), the central document of children's rights in the world. Canada signed the CRC in 1990, and ratified it in 1991, committing to adopt the principles of children's rights into law and practice.
- Distinguished between a *legal approach* and a *relational approach* to children's rights. In the first, children's rights happen in the domain of legal systems and policies. In a relational approach, children's rights happen as part of children's relationships.
- Investigated some of the conceptual tools offered by the sociology of childhood to help us see how children's rights can be aspects of children's relationships. These tools are (1) the investigation of the social lives of children; (2) the perspective of children as social actors; (3) understanding context as a central aspect of childhood; and (4) the deconstruction of universal norms or standards of childhoods.
- Saw how children's rights relationships are reciprocal—everyone involved in these relationships benefit from them. *Doing* children's rights in relationships has the potential to make them visible, concrete, immediate, and understandable.

STUDY QUESTIONS

1. In what ways does the sociology of childhood help to reframe children's rights as relational processes?
2. Identify some of the ways that the legal approach to children's rights has made children's circumstances around the world better. How has the legal approach created challenges to achieving children's rights? How might a relational approach to children's rights move through those challenges?
3. Have you ever had an experience of children's rights in your own life from (a) a legal perspective or (b) a relational perspective?
4. What are some of the stumbling blocks in your profession or discipline that stand in the way of engaging with children in relational ways that acknowledge and respect their rights?
5. From a sociological perspective, what needs to happen in Canada to encourage children's rights to be enacted and realized?

SUGGESTED RESEARCH ASSIGNMENT

Explore other examples of relational approaches to children's rights in Canada, focusing on the groups of children that the chapter highlighted as particularly marginalized by intersecting forms of oppression. Consider the following contexts as potential sites for relational approaches to children's rights:

- Schools
- Extracurricular activities
- Children's services
- Media

How might these different contexts treat a relational approach to children's rights in different ways?

SUGGESTED FILMS/VIDEO CLIPS

Your Right to Speak
www.youtube.com/watch?v=ZbvIpleO4fU&feature=y
This is a short commercial promoting UNICEF and children's rights.

Alan Kurdi: Friends and Family Fill in Gaps behind Harrowing Images
www.theguardian.com/world/2015/sep/03/refugee-crisis-friends-and-family-fill-in-
 gaps-behind-harrowing-images
This article and video clip outline the story behind how the images of Alan Kurdi galvanized world attention regarding the Syrian crisis.

*From Strength to Strength: The Intersection of Children's and Women's Rights over the
 Life Cycle*
www.youtube.com/watch?v=TgHGOo7yvwQ
In this lecutre, former Canadian Senator Landon Pearson reflects on her work in children's rights, and how they intersect with feminism.

Magic Abounds When Daycare, Seniors Home Share Roof
www.thestar.com/news/gta/2016/02/09/magic-abounds-when-daycare-seniors-home-
 share-roof.html
This article and video clip outline how elderly residents and young children at Kipling Acres/Kipling Early Learning and Child Care Centre interact.

SUGGESTED WEBSITES

Canadian Coalition for the Rights of Children
rightsofchildren.ca
The CCRC is a network of organizations and individuals in Canada involved in promoting children's rights in Canada.

Landon Pearson Resource Centre for the Study of Childhood and Children's Rights
www.landonpearson.ca
The LPRC has a wealth of resources and information regarding children's rights and childhood, both here in Canada and around the world.

UNICEF: Convention on the Rights of the Child
www.unicef.org/crc/
The UNICEF CRC pages provide information regarding children's rights from the perspective of the United Nations and the UNCRC.

UNICEF Office of Research—Innocenti
www.unicef-irc.org
Innocenti is the UNICEF Office of Research. You can access many publications and resources from their website on the topics of children, childhoods, and children's rights in a wide variety of contexts.

UNICEF Canada
www.unicef.ca
Canada's UNICEF office offers information regarding children's rights in Canada and beyond.

NOTE

1.   In this chapter, I use the terms *minority world* and *majority world* instead of *developed/developing*, *Western/Eastern*, and *Global North/Global South*. Following Shallwani (2015), I feel that the language of minority/majority world reflects the global context with more geographic and demographic accuracy, countering the dominant West-centric narrative of civilization and development.

REFERENCES

Aboriginal Children in Care Working Group. (2015). *Aboriginal children in care: Report to Canada's premiers.* Retrieved from canadaspremiers.ca/phocadownload/publications/aboriginal_children_in_care_report_july2015.pdf

Alderson, P. (1999). Human rights and democracy in schools: Do they mean more than "picking up litter and not killing whales?" *International Journal of Children's Rights, 7*(2), 185–205.

Alderson. P. (2008). *Young children's rights: Exploring beliefs, principles and practice* (2nd ed.). Philadelphia: Jessica Kingsley.

Adu-Gyamfi, J., & Keating, F. (2013). Convergence and divergence between the UN Convention on the Rights of the Child, and the African Charter on the Rights and Welfare of the Child. *Sacha Journal of Human Rights, 3*(1), 47–58.

Bernhard, J. K. (2012). *Stand together or fall apart: Professionals working with immigrant families.* Black Point, NS: Fernwood Publications.

Brown, W. (2004). "The most we can hope for …": Human rights and the politics of fatalism. *The South Atlantic Quarterly, 103*(2), 451–463.

Brownell, C. A., Svetlova, M., Anderson, R., Nichols, S. R., & Drummond, J. (2013). Socialization of early prosocial behaviour: Parents' talk about emotions is associated with sharing and helping in toddlers. *Infancy, 18*(1), 91–119.

Burman, E. (2008). *Deconstructing developmental psychology.* Hove, UK: Routledge.

Callero, P. L. (1986). Putting the social in prosocial behaviour: An interactionist approach to altruism. *Humboldt Journal of Social Relations, 13*(1/2), 15–32.

Canada Revenue Agency. (2016). *Do you have children? The new Canada child benefit may affect your family.* Retrieved from www.cra-arc.gc.ca/nwsrm/txtps/2016/tt160525-eng.html

Canadian Children's Rights Council. (2015). *Canada's Declarations and Reservations to the Convention on the Rights of the Child.* Retrieved from canadiancrc.com/UN_CRC/UN_Canada_Declarations_Reservations_Convention_Rights_Child.aspx

Canadian Coalition for the Rights of Children. (2011). *Right in principle, right in practice.* Retrieved from rightsofchildren.ca/resources/childrens-rights-monitoring/

Canadian Coalition for the Rights of Children. (2016, March 23). *Children and budget 2016.* Retrieved from rightsofchildren.ca/newsroom/page/2/

Canadian Human Rights Commission. (2015). *The rights of persons with disabilities to equality and non-discrimination.* Retrieved from www.chrc-ccdp.gc.ca/sites/default/files/chrc_un_crpd_report_eng.pdf

Chirwa, D. M. (2002). The merits and demerits of the African Charter on the Rights and Welfare of the Child. *International Journal of Children's Rights, 10*(2), 157–177.

Citizenship and Immigration Canada. (2015). *Population profile: Syrian refugees.* Retrieved from www.cpa.ca/docs/File/Cultural/EN%20Syrian%20Population%20Profile.pdf

Citizenship and Immigration Canada. (2016). *Syria—by the numbers.* Retrieved from www.cic.gc.ca/english/refugees/welcome/commitment.asp

Corsaro, W. A. (2011). *The sociology of childhood* (3rd ed.). Thousand Oaks, CA: Pine Forge.

Cowan, J. K., Dembour, M., & Wilson, R. (2001). *Culture and rights: Anthropological perspectives*. New York: Cambridge University Press.

Donati, P., & Archer, M. S. (2015). *The relational subject*. Cambridge, UK: Cambridge University Press.

First Nations Child and Family Caring Society of Canada. (2016). *Information sheet: Victory for First Nations children*. Retrieved from fncaringsociety.com/sites/default/files/Information%20Sheet%20re%20 CHRT%20Decision.pdf

Freeman, M. D. A. (1983). *The rights and the wrongs of children*. London: Frances Pinter.

Freeman, M. D. A. (2000). The future of children's rights. *Children & Society, 14*(4), 277–293.

Freeman, M. D. A. (2007). Why it remains important to take children's rights seriously. *International Journal of Children's Rights, 15*(1), 5–23.

Freeman, M. D. A. (2010). The human rights of children. *Current Legal Problems, 63*(1), 1–44.

Freeman, M. D. A. (2011). *Human rights* (2nd ed.). Cambridge, UK: Polity Press.

Gabriel, N. (2014). Growing up beside you: A relational sociology of early childhood. *History of the Human Sciences, 27*(3), 116–135.

Gigliotti, C., Morris, M., Smock, S., Jarrott, S. E., & Graham, B. (2005). An intergenerational summer program involving persons with dementia and preschool children. *Educational Gerontology, 31*, 425–441.

Harrison, C., & Canadian Paediatric Society. (2004). Position statement: Treatment decisions regarding infants, children and adolescents. *Paediatric Child Health, 9*(2), 99–103.

Holmes, C. L. (2009). An intergenerational program with benefits. *Early Childhood Education Journal, 37*(2), 113–119.

Howe, R. B., & Covell, K. (Eds). (2007a). *A question of commitment: Children's rights in Canada*. Waterloo, ON: Wilfrid Laurier University Press.

Howe, R. B., & Covell, K. (2007b). *Empowering children: Children's rights education as a pathway to citizenship*. Toronto: University of Toronto Press.

Human Rights Watch. (2014, November 17). *25th anniversary of the Convention on the Rights of the Child*. Retrieved from www.hrw.org/news/2014/11/17/25th-anniversary-convention-rights-child

Isaki, E., & Towle Harmon, M. (2015). Children and adults reading interactively: The social benefits of an exploratory intergenerational program. *Communication Disorders Quarterly, 36*(2), 90–101.

James, A., & James, A.L. (2004). *Constructing childhood: Theory, policy and practice*. Hampshire, UK: Palgrave Macmillan.

James, A., Jenks, C., & Prout, A. (1998). *Theorizing childhood*. Cambridge, UK: Polity Press.

James, A. L. (2010). Competition or integration? The next step in childhood studies? *Childhood, 17*(4), 485–499.

Johnson, D. (1992). Cultural and regional pluralism in the drafting of the UN Convention on the Rights of the Child. In M. D. A. Freeman & P. Veerman (Eds.), *The ideologies of children's rights* (pp. 95–114). Dordrecht, NL: Martinus Nijhoff.

Jones, P. (2011). What are children's rights? Contemporary developments and debates. In P. Jones & G. Walker (Eds.), *Children's rights in practice* (pp. 3–16). Thousand Oaks, CA: Sage.

Jones, P., & Welch, S. (2010). *Rethinking children's rights: Attitudes in contemporary society*. London: Continuum.

Kaplan, M., & Larkin, E. (2004). Launching intergenerational programs in early childhood settings: A comparison of explicit intervention with an emergent approach. *Early Childhood Education Journal, 31*(3), 157–163.

KidsRights Index. (2016). *The KidsRights Index 2016*. Retrieved from www.kidsrightsindex.org/Portals/5/ The%20KidsRights%20Index%202016%20-%20Research%20Report.pdf?ver=2016-05-12-160259-830

Lansdown, G. (1996). Implementation of the UN convention on the rights of the child in the UK. In M. John (Ed.), *Children in our charge: The child's right to resources* (pp. 57–72). London: Jessica Kingsley.

Lee, M. M., Camp, C. J., & Malone, M. L. (2007). Effects of inter-generational Montessori-based activities programming on engagement of nursing home resident with dementia. *Clinical Interventions of Aging, 2*, 477–483.

Liebel, M. (Ed.). (2012). *Children's rights from below*. New York: Palgrave Macmillan.

MacIntyre, A. (2007). *After virtue: A study in moral theory* (3rd ed.). Notre Dame, IN: University of Notre Dame Press.

Marshall, D. (2013). Children's rights from below: Canadian and transnational actions, beliefs and discourses, 1900–1989. In D. Goutor and S. Heathorn (Eds.), *Taking liberties: A history of human rights in Canada* (pp. 190–212). Don Mills, ON: Oxford University Press.

Mayall, B. (2002). *Towards a sociology for childhood: Thinking from children's lives*. London: Open University Press.

Mayall, B. (2013). *A history of the sociology of childhood*. London: Open University Press.

Monsebraaten, L. (2016, February 9). Magic abounds when daycare, seniors home share roof. *Toronto Star*. Retrieved from www.thestar.com/news/gta/2016/02/09/magic-abounds-when-daycare-seniors-home-share-roof.html

Mutua, M. (2002). *Human rights: A political and cultural critique*. Philadelphia: University of Pennsylvania Press.

Njungwe, E. N. (2009). International protection of children's rights: An analysis of African attributes in the African Charter on the Rights and Welfare of the Child. *Cameroon Journal on Democracy and Human Rights, 3*(1), 4–25.

Office of the High Commissioner for Human Rights (OHCHR). (2016a). *Committee on the Rights of the Child*. Retrieved from www.ohchr.org/EN/HRBodies/CRC/Pages/CRCIndex.aspx

Office of the High Commissioner for Human Rights (OHCHR). (2016b). *Committee on the Rights of the Child—Monitoring children's rights*. Retrieved from www.ohchr.org/EN/HRBodies/CRC/Pages/CRCIntro.aspx

Office of the High Commissioner for Human Rights (OHCHR). (2016c). *Ratification status for CRC—Convention on the Rights of the Child*. Retrieved from tbinternet.ohchr.org/_layouts/TreatyBodyExternal/Treaty.aspx?Treaty=CRC&Lang=en

O'Neill, T., & Zinga, D. (2008). Introduction. In T. O'Neill & D. Zinga (Eds.), *Children's rights: Multidisciplinary approaches to participation and protection* (pp. 3–18). Toronto: University of Toronto Press.

Pearson, L. (2012, April 26). *From strength to strength: The intersection of children's and women's rights over the life cycle*. Florence Bird Lecture, March 8 [video file]. Retrieved from www.youtube.com/watch?v=TgHGOo7yvwQ

Pearson L., & Collins, T. (2009). *Not there yet: Canada's implementation of the general measures of the Convention on the Rights of the Child.* Florence, IT: UNICEF/Innocenti Research Centre.

Prout. A. (2011). Taking a step away from modernity: Reconsidering the new sociology of childhood. *Global Studies of Childhood, 1*(1), 4–14.

Punch, S. (2003). Childhoods in the majority world: Miniature adults or tribal children? *Sociology, 37*(2), 277–295.

Qvortrup, J. (1994). Childhood matters: An introduction. In J. Qvortrup, M. Bardy, G. Sgritta, & H. Wintersberger (Eds.), *Childhood matters: Social theory, practice and politics* (pp. 1–24). Aldershot: Avebury.

Qvortrup, J. (2008, July). *Diversity's temptation—and hazards.* Paper presented at Re-presenting Childhood and Youth, University of Sheffield Centre for the Study of Childhood and Youth, Sheffield, UK.

Qvortrup, J. (2009). Childhood as a structural form. In J. Qvortrup, W. Corsaro, & M. S. Honig (Eds.), *Palgrave handbook of childhood studies* (pp. 21–33). London: Palgrave MacMillan.

Reynaert, D., Bouverne-de Bie, M., & Vandevelde, S. (2012). Between "believers" and "opponents": Critical discussions on children's rights. *International Journal of Children's Rights, 20*(1), 155–168.

Ruffolo, D. V. (2009). Queering child/hood policies: Canadian examples and perspectives. *Contemporary Issues in Early Childhood, 10*(3), 291–308.

Shallwani, S. (2015, August 4). Why I use the term "majority world" instead of "developing countries" or "third world" [Blog post]. Retrieved from sadafshallwani.net/2015/08/04/majority-world/

Skott-Myhre, H., & Tarulli, D. (2008). Becoming-child: Ontology, immanence, and the production of child and youth rights. In T. O'Neill & D. Zinga (Eds.), *Children's rights: Multidisciplinary approaches to participation and protection* (pp. 69–84). Toronto: University of Toronto Press.

Smith, H. (2015, September 3). Alan Kurdi: Friends and family fill in gaps behind harrowing images. *Guardian.* Retrieved from www.theguardian.com/world/2015/sep/03/refugee-crisis-friends-and-family-fill-in-gaps-behind-harrowing-images

Smith, R. (2010). *A universal child?* Hampshire, UK: Palgrave Macmillan.

Statistics Canada. (2013). *Disability in Canada: A 2006 profile.* Retrieved from www.esdc.gc.ca/eng/disability/arc/disability_2006.shtml

Stephens, S. (1995). *Children and the politics of culture.* Princeton, NJ: Princeton University Press.

Tisdall, E. K., & Punch, S. (2012). Not so "new"? Looking critically at childhood studies. *Children's Geographies, 10*(3), 249–264.

Twum-Danso, A. (2009). Reciprocity, respect and responsibility: The 3Rs underlying parent-child relationships in Ghana and the implications for children's rights. *International Journal of Children's Rights, 17*(3), 415–432.

UNICEF Canada. (2016). *UNICEF report card 13: Fairness for children.* Retrieved from www.unicef.ca/en/unicef-report-card-13-fairness-for-children

Van Bueren, G. (1995). *The international law on the rights of the child.* Dordrecht, NL: Martinus Nijhoff Publishers.

Van Bueren, G. (2011). Multigenerational citizenship: The importance of recognizing children as national and international citizens. *The Annals of the American Academy of Political and Social Science, 633*(1), 30–51.

Vandenhole, W. (2014). Child poverty and children's rights: An uneasy fit? *Michigan State International Law Review, 22*(2), 609–636.

Viljoen, F. (1998). Supra-national human rights instruments for the protection of children in Africa: The Convention on the Rights of the Child and the African Charter on the Rights and Welfare of the Child. *The Comparative and International Law Journal of Southern Africa, 31*(2), 199–212.

Wall, J. (2006). Childhood studies, hermeneutics, and theological ethics. *The Journal of Religion, 86*(4), 523–548.

Wall, J. (2008). Human rights in light of childhood. *The International Journal of children's rights, 16*(4), 523–543.

Wells, K. (2015). *Childhood in a global perspective* (2nd ed.). Cambridge, UK: Polity Press.

18 Between Children's Rights and Disability Rights: Inclusion and Participation of Children and Youth with Disabilities

Cornelia Schneider

LEARNING OBJECTIVES

- To learn about the rights of children with disabilities
- To reflect on the issue of protection rights versus participation rights
- To recognize the agency of children with disabilities
- To assess how to improve the recognition of the rights of children with disabilities

If you want support me, you can learn about all the things I like and don't like, like toilets and hand driers. You can be quiet and cuddly. You must listen to me and get down to my level if you want to talk to me. Don't talk for too long and sometimes you might need to explain things to me a bit more. You need to tell me what is going to happen and prepare me for new things, showing me a picture can help. And don't forget my biscuit at bedtime!

So, to remind you of the things that are important to me and for me:

- My mum, my dad and my sister
- My friends and people at school
- That you know about things that I like and don't like
- That you are calm, quiet and kind to me
- That you listen to me
- That you help me to do the things I enjoy.

(Stevie, 5 years old, in Tyrie, Tyrie, Tyrie, & Tyrie, 2013, p. 7)

INTRODUCTION

Stevie, a five-year-old girl with cerebral palsy tells us in no uncertain terms about the people and objects in her life that matter to her and that she needs. Her words are a story of belonging and participating, and the things that she needs her allies to recognize. Reading those simple words, one can see how Stevie claims human rights that have been so long disrespected for children and youth with disabilities. With this, she positions herself as a social actor claiming participation in the decisions that are made around her.

The Universal Declaration of Human Rights was adopted by the United Nations in Paris at the Palais Chaillot on December 10, 1948. As a consequence of the atrocities of war and the German Nazi regime, the United Nations had set it as their goal to give more protection to humanity, especially to oppressed minority groups, by expressing the entitlement to human rights for any human being. Almost 70 years have passed since the Universal Declaration of Human Rights was adopted, and over the course of those years, there have been additional declarations with the goal to guarantee the rights of more specific groups suffering from oppression and human rights violations across the world. Examples of these include the Convention on the Prevention and Punishment of the Crime of Genocide (1948), the Convention on the Elimination of All Forms of Discrimination against Women (1979), and the Declaration on the Rights of Indigenous Peoples (2007).

In 2006, the **UN Convention on the Rights of Persons with Disabilities** was adopted by the UN General Assembly in New York, and was lauded as another step in furthering the recognition of the rights of people with disabilities. The convention was written, with the support of many international disability rights groups, to include the goal of giving the right and opportunities for full participation in society. Children with disabilities are obviously included in the declaration; however, their specific rights *as children* were already mentioned in the earlier **UN Convention on the Rights of the Child** in 1990. The rights set out in these two documents, elaborated in an international context connected with the United Nations organization, find their resonance in national politics, policies, and charters. Canada has recognized and ratified those texts, and given itself the obligation of recognizing and implementing these rights.

However, the Canadian Coalition for the Rights of Children (n.d., pp. 1–2), in a working paper citing the Participation and Activity Limitation Survey of 2006, enumerates a number of issues in Canada when it comes to children with disabilities, which demonstrates that the rights of children with disabilities are clearly undermined, especially in terms of finances and the provision of services:

- Children with disabilities are twice as likely as other children to live in households that rely on social assistance as a main source of income.
- Nearly one in five (19.1 percent of) children with disabilities live in households that fall below the Low Income Cut-Off, compared to 13.4 percent of children without disabilities.

- Children with disabilities are overrepresented in provincial/territorial child welfare systems.
- Children with disabilities are two or more times as vulnerable to violence and abuse.
- Almost 55 percent of children with disabilities who need aids and devices do not have access to them. Cost is cited as the most common reason for unmet needs.
- 40 percent of children with disabilities experience daily difficulties in participating in everyday life.
- Of the many parents who report needing additional help, nearly three-quarters (73.5 percent) cite cost as the barrier.
- Over one-third of parents report having out-of-pocket costs for getting the assistance they need.
- 21.5 percent of families report that child care services or programs had refused to provide care for their child.
- Due to their child's disability, parents report the following:
  - Having to work fewer hours (38.4 percent) or change their work hours (36.5 percent)
  - Having not taken a job (26.4 percent)
  - Having to quit work (21.6 percent)
  - Turning down a promotion (19.7 percent)
- Mothers are most commonly the main person to be impacted (64.1 percent)

The question of children's rights, and more specifically the rights of children with disabilities, has been addressed at this point mainly by activist or political organizations in Canada, such as the Canadian Coalition for Children's Rights or UNICEF. There are a few Canadian researchers that have been addressing these issues in their work, such as Owen et al. (2008) and, with a focus on "psychiatrised children," Brenda LeFrançois (2007; LeFrançois & Coppock, 2014). Relevant research has also been carried out by the Cape Breton Children's Rights Centre, led by Dr. Katherine Covell and Dr. Brian Howe, whose goals are to monitor the general implementation of the CRC and to educate the broader public about these issues.[1] In this chapter, I will rely on some of this research and my own international research to construct my argument for supporting the recognition and implementation of the rights of children with disabilities.

This chapter is organized into several parts: first, I will address the rights of children with disabilities at the intersection of the different UN human rights conventions, and examine possible contradictions between them stemming from the use of different models of disability. I will then illustrate the complex issues arising when implementing the rights perspective, using examples from my own research with children and youth with disabilities. Finally, I will examine how a relationship perspective on rights can solve the issue of competing rights occurring in these conventions, also considering what teachers and other stakeholders need to know about the recognition and implementation of the rights of children and youth with disabilities in schools and in the workplace, especially in a Canadian context.

BETWEEN THE CONVENTION ON THE RIGHTS OF THE CHILD AND THE CONVENTION ON THE RIGHTS OF PERSONS WITH DISABILITIES

When it comes to the human rights of children with disabilities, there are three main conventions that cover the field: the Universal Declaration of Human Rights of 1948 (UDHR), the Convention on the Rights of the Child of 1990 (CRC), and, as the latest document adopted in 2006, the Convention on the Rights of Persons with Disabilities (CRPD). Obviously, the time span between these documents is enormous, which means that one needs to consider the context of each declaration and when it was drafted and subsequently adopted. The UDHR came on the heels of the surrender of the Nazi regime in Germany, and was also a reaction to the discovery of concentration camps, forced labour, medical experimentation, and **genocide** of Jewish people and many other groups of people who did not fit into the fascist parameters, such as people with nonheterosexual orientations, travelling people, people with differing political beliefs, as well as people with disabilities.

As a consequence, the United Nations adopted this document in the spirit of protecting future generations from anything like this ever happening again. It recognizes a breadth of rights for any human being, and thus recognizes all those rights for people with disabilities.

> The CRPD and the UDHR call for similar rights for "all persons with disabilities" (CRPD) and "for all peoples and all nations" (UDHR). These documents provide the right to family, work, rest and leisure, a standard of living, education and participation in the community for all family members. (Muir & Goldblatt, 2011, p. 631)

In a similar spirit, in the late 1980s, the Convention on the Rights of the Child (CRC) stood for a major shift in the perception of children. Historically, children have not been recognized as full members of society; they have been seen as "adults to become," "immature," or "incompetent" (see e.g. Corsaro, 2014; James & Prout, 2002). According to Howe and Covell (2010), children were generally seen as being the property of and/or being under the tutelage of their parents. One of the major advances of the CRC is that it positions the child as a subject and as an actor instead. (For more on the CRC, see chapter 17 by Noah Kenneally, in this collection.) In a more specific way, the CRC mentions the rights of children with disabilities, but under a focus on **care** (Covell & Howe, 2001):

The Convention on the Rights of the Child 1989 (CRC) does refer to "mentally and physically disabled" children in Article 23. This Article sets out a range of obligations designed to ensure that children with disability receive "special care" in relation to their "special needs" with a view to them "achieving the fullest possible social integration and individual development." (Kayess & French, 2008, p. 12)

The focus on special care and special needs for children with disabilities endorses a particular perspective on disabilities, as I will elaborate on in the following section.

BETWEEN THE SOCIAL AND THE MEDICAL MODELS OF DISABILITY

The rights addressed both in the CRC and the CRPD each cover three types of rights. For the CRC, they are named the 3Ps: provision, protection, and participation (see Covell & Howe, 2001); the CRPD is similarly organized into rights of protection, of special services, and of full participation. However, even though it appears that the conventions are providing similar sets of rights to children and to people with disabilities, there are differences that need to be observed, which could ultimately lead to a "competing set of rights."

The CRC clearly addresses the rights of children with disabilities under a protective lens, with an emphasis on "special needs," which highlights the CRC's orientation towards the **medical model of disability**. The medical model of disability (see also Barnes & Mercer 2010; Davis, Watson, & Cunningham-Burley, 2008; Shakespeare, 2013) considers an individual's disability as an issue stemming from the person's condition that needs to be treated or fixed with specialized care. It also means that the disability lies uniquely within the individual, and not in the environment. While the CRPD has not abandoned the medical model completely, it has moved closer towards the **social model of disability**, which analyzes a person's environment and situates the issue of disability within the restricted accessibility and barriers to full participation of society (see Barnes & Mercer, 2010). This model asks for reducing/abolishing disabling barriers to participation in society and in the person's environment, as opposed to the medical model, which only situates disability within the individual. As Mckenzie and Macleod (2012) point out, the CRPD contains "three disparate discourses relating to rights—namely, rights to full participation, rights to special services and rights to protection—draw[n] off different supposedly oppositional models of disability—namely, the social, medical and protective models" (p. 16). The protective model assumes the person with a disability to be inherently vulnerable and in need of protection from potential harm.

Working with two models, the medical and the social (I contend that the protective and medical models are very similar, as they have an assumption of an impairment, a weakness, or a vulnerability inherent to the person with disability at the core), when it comes to the rights of people with disabilities, means that situations might arise where those rights are competing, as the two models pursue fundamentally different goals. The medical model is much more interested in "fixing" the person with disabilities, and is aimed directly at the person's condition, while the social model's goal is social change for the living conditions of the person with disabilities. Ideally, those rights should be complementary; however, they can become competing, especially if the idea of providing services collides with the idea of participation. For example, the question of where a child with disabilities receives their education can be in contradiction with the right to special services, as the special services might not be available in a mainstream setting. We will see a bit further in this chapter how this contradiction can play out to the detriment of a child or youth when it comes to the right to participation in research, in general education, and in the transition into the workplace.

RECOGNIZING THE PARTICIPATION RIGHTS OF CHILDREN WITH DISABILITIES

Despite the fact that the CRC has been in place for almost three decades, the recognition of children's rights is not achieved, as reports from many countries in both the Global North and South show. On an even bigger scale, the recognition of the rights of children with disabilities lags severely behind (e.g. UNICEF, 2009; Canadian Coalition for the Rights of Children, n.d.). More than other children, those with disabilities are seen as "incompetent." As Davis, Watson, and Cunningham-Burley (2008) note, medical and psychological notions of disability can "pathologize children who do not achieve universally standardized developmental targets, seeing the disability as a consequence of impairment. [There is] little awareness of the possibility that disability and a lack of ability to meet targets associated with developmental stages may have social and cultural roots" (p. 222). It is also crucial to address the **power** differential between children with disabilities and the adults surrounding them (e.g. teachers, caretakers, psychologists). Davis and Watson (2000) critique the misrecognition of children's rights, especially when it comes to school settings, which might "allow children's opinions to be overlooked on the grounds of 'safety' (when it is thought that inclusion in decision making processes could harm the child) or 'competency' (when the child is not thought capable of understanding the process)" (p. 212). Davis and Watson (2000) have been examining how "adults actually judge competency in everyday settings" (p. 212). Their findings show that adults are at risk of having their judgment clouded with their personal and professional perspectives. One might hear in a current discussion this kind of argument: "Yes, I am respecting the rights of children with disabilities, but...."

In what follows, I draw on my own research over the past decade to illustrate how research can help unearth moments when rights and participation of children and youth with disabilities have not been respected, as well as to demonstrate the often dismissed competency of children and youth with disabilities. I use examples drawn from data from a comparative research study on peer relationships in inclusive classrooms (grades 1 to 5) in France and Germany (Schneider, 2007, 2009, 2011); an ethnographic study of youth aged 17 to 25 transitioning into the workplace in a Canadian program (Schneider, 2010); and a mixed-methods (surveys, focus groups, and interviews) study of the alumni of this program, with youth between the ages of 19 and 30 (Schneider, 2015).

As Davis and Watson (2000) underscore, my examples support the position that participation is not about an entirely autonomous child, but rather about "the need for co-operation between adult and child" (p. 226). Children's **agency** does not exist in a vacuum, but instead is lived in the interactions and relationships that they have with the people around them (see e.g. Corsaro's Orb Web Model, which shows how children's agency is embedded in a web of relationships with their environment; Corsaro, 2014). There are many things that adults and adult experts can learn from these kinds of examples and by challenging their own assumptions about the competency of children and youth with disabilities. Participation, as shown in both UN conventions, is a basic human right; however, participation rights are the most challenging to implement. In the following, I will demonstrate this by using examples of children's participation in research, participation in education, and participation in the labour market.

Research: Between Participation Rights and Protective Rights

The first obstacle that can be encountered when it comes to doing research on this topic is the requirements set up by research ethics bodies—for example, in Canada, the 2010 Tri-Council Policy Statement: Ethical Conduct for Research Involving Humans (TCPS 2). Children and people with disabilities are part of a group that traditionally has been considered to be vulnerable. Even if the language around vulnerability has been slightly modified, and those groups are now labelled as "requiring special care," the obstacles to participating in research remain at times problematic. The TCPS 2 states a rather restricted view on research with children, making research with adults the "default option" over children's participation: "Participation of children in research is justifiable when the research objective cannot be achieved with adult participants only" (Canadian Institutes of Health Research, Natural Sciences and Engineering Research Council of Canada, & Social Sciences and Humanities Research Council of Canada, 2010, art. 4.4). It does not acknowledge automatically the value of doing research with children and youth (with disabilities) in their own right. Furthermore, the TCPS 2 systematically requires the consent of an authorized third party for a young person with intellectual disabilities to participate in a research project. Initially conceived to protect vulnerable populations from exploitation through research projects, now such rules can occasionally also impede a person's participation in a project.

In one of my projects, a Canadian youth with a disability, who was over the age of 18 and under the tutelage of his mother, wanted to participate in one of my research projects, but did not receive the consent of his mother. He resented her decision and was disappointed to not be able to participate in the study. As we were required to have both parental consent and **assent** from the actual participant, we could not allow him to participate in the study. This example demonstrates the issue of competing rights between the rights of the family and the rights of the young adult with disabilities, who was very excited to have an opportunity to participate in a study. In the spirit of Howe's argument (2001), parental rights trumped the rights of the youth with disabilities. We must question whether research ethics boards or the Tri-Council Policy Statement on Research Ethics are giving too much decision-making power to families/caretakers, at the expense of possible child/youth participants. Skelton (2008) points out the following:

> It leaves children locked within the authority of parents/guardians and unable to make a decision for themselves about their own involvement in research which specifically pertains to an aspect of their own lived experience. What if the child really wants to participate but the parent says no? Legally, we would probably have to side with the parental decision but ethically we would probably want to go with the child's choice. (p. 27)

Furthermore, Skelton (2008) also stresses that articles 12 and 13 of the CRC enshrine the child's freedom of expression, and therefore contradict the priority of parental consent over the child's consent. She calls for an adequate integration of the CRC framework into the research ethics frameworks. Additionally, the CRPD should equally be included into those debates.

Education: Between Participation Rights and Special Provision Rights

Howe and Covell (2010) stress that, in the CRC, there has been a lot of emphasis put on rights related to education:

> Education is of special importance in the Convention.... Children's education rights can be divided along three tracks. First, children have the right to education. Under article 28, children have the right to free primary education and to accessible secondary and higher education. Under article 23, children with disabilities have the right to special assistance and care in education as well as in other areas. Second, children have rights in education. Under article 2, they have the right to nondiscrimination. Under article 12, they have the right to participate in educational decisions that affect them. And under articles 13, 14 and 15, they have the rights to freedom of expression, freedom of thought and religion, and freedom of association and peaceful assembly, subject to reasonable limits. (p. 93)

Similarly, article 24 in the CRPD recognizes the right to access full **inclusive education** at all levels of education. Equally, both conventions are highlighting participation rights, especially for young people to partake in decisions concerning their own lives. As Kayess and French (2008) point out, this is one of the points where the rights of the family can collide with the rights of the child with a disability, and the question remains largely

Box 18.1: What School to Go To?

The question of which school a child should go to can be a crucial one, especially when the child is in a system that allows for options between specialized and mainstream (inclusive) schooling. In my studies, I interviewed children who were not consulted when the choice needed to be made about which secondary school to attend. One example is Prisca (Schneider 2007, 2009), a girl with a learning disability who had been attending inclusive school in Germany, but had been oriented towards a special secondary school for the following year. She wished to remain in class with the rest of her classmates from elementary school, but teachers told her it would not be possible. She was not happy about this, as she expressed in her interview. One of her friends also told me that they were trying to find a strategy to make it possible for Prisca to go to Main School with her friends:

> Verena will go to Main School and Prisca … how do they call it? Special school. But I thought that it would have been better if she waited another year, in order to go to Main School, too. That would have been better. (Annemarie)

Annemarie knows that Prisca was unhappy about this decision and she tried to comfort her in her grief:

> She said, I think this is totally unfair, and so I said, Prisca, maybe your mother can tell Mrs. F that you should wait for one more year so that you can be able to go to Main School. (Annemarie)

In the end, nothing changed, and Prisca, after having been learning successfully in an inclusive setting, had to leave and attend a special school instead. Parents and experts decided on her behalf what was in "her best interest." It is important to also note here the larger implications of children's participation in the decision-making process. The reason for sending her to a special school was that the mainstream school would not be able to accommodate her needs, indicating that her right to attend an inclusive school is undermined by the current lack of pedagogical accessibility in Germany. Instead of improving accessibility, Prisca was excluded from the mainstream school, and as such was not able to exercise her rights. This also shows the political implication of children's voices, and the possibility of social change if their agency and decision-making abilities are taken seriously.

unsolved as to whom to give priority in this debate if there is a disagreement. Assumptions of vulnerability and incapacity often trump the recognition of the abilities of the child to participate in decision-making processes concerning their life. Often, families are following the advice of adult experts who might have misrecognized the capacities of the child. Howe (2001) has elaborated that parents have the right and the duty to interpret what their children's best interest is, and that they have "fundamental rights" as parents, but this does not mean that they have absolute rights. The following two examples of Prisca and Sébastien will show how children's agency concerning access to and choice in education gets easily dismissed or overlooked at the benefit of parents/families or other adult experts.

Another example of implementing participation rights is the importance of consulting children when it comes to the use of assistive devices or technology in the classroom. In one of the French elementary school classes I did a research project in (Schneider, 2007, 2009), I did several interviews with Sébastien, a little boy who, according to the teachers, needed a laptop in class to support his writing. Over the time that I spent in the classroom, I found out that Sébastien felt stigmatized by the laptop and had not been consulted about whether he wanted to use it or not. At that time, he was the only child in the classroom using a laptop, which he felt set him apart from his peers. Thus, he developed strategies to memorize the things the teacher said, so that he did not need to use the laptop as much. Sébastien should have been more involved in the decision about how to use assistive technology in the classroom, as he was clearly not comfortable with the way this was handled. He felt it exposed him in the classroom in a way he deemed to be negative. Recognizing his participation rights in this case would have meant listening to his concerns about the implementation of the assistive technology, and how he experienced stigma when using it. Including his viewpoints on the matter, the classroom teacher might have found other ways to use this piece of equipment in the classroom that would not have made him feel stigmatized and singled out.

Transition to Work: Impeding Participation Rights of Youth with Disabilities

A further example of how participation rights of youth disabilities can be impeded stems from two studies with youth with disabilities transitioning to work in Canada. From the observations of research participants who were part of my project studying transitions into adulthood for people with disabilities, one could observe the immense vulnerability that persons with disabilities can be placed in when it comes to the workplace. For example, George shared his experience with the research team about how he lost his employment at the fast food restaurant where he had been working, once the supervisor had changed (Schneider, Chahine, & Hattie, 2014).

> *Investigator:* Yeah, you liked that. What about, and the supervisor you had before the one that came in and didn't like you, what was that person like?

George: Kind of cranky at me, they weren't giving me any hours, cut back my hours.

Investigator: Oh, even the one before—

George: No, the one that came in that didn't like me. The one before that was super nice, she knew how people with disabilities are like and wanted to give me a chance.

Other participants found themselves with reduced work hours when their supervisors changed, too. We know that underemployment of people with disabilities is a worldwide issue, and the labour rights protection of workers with disabilities who are employed is not very strong. Unions are often not involved in precarious workplaces such as the fast food industry. There is a lack of oversight to enforce the rights of people with disabilities in labour market participation and protection of workers' rights. In our studies, if participants experienced continued protection in their workplace, it was because of their own very active and protective parents who intervened when necessary. It also needs to be pointed out that those parents had a higher socioeconomic background and higher educational levels than parents of our other participants (see also Trainor, 2008, 2010). The fact that the parents of young people with disabilities are still the ones negotiating these young people's experiences at work is an example of how they are further denied their rights to a full and equal voice.

RIGHTS OF CHILDREN WITH DISABILITIES? "YES! BUT ..."

The examples in this chapter demonstrate that the advancement of the rights of children and youth with disabilities remains a complex issue. Children and youth with disabilities continue to experience discrimination and misrecognition of their rights, even if now ascribed in the different UN conventions. As I have shown above, the competing models of disability are contributing to those issues. As long as disability is primarily viewed as a medical or developmental phenomenon, societies will continue to discount the viewpoints of children and youth with disabilities as "immature" or "incompetent." We can clearly see that disability continues to be perceived as a medical issue that excludes children and youth with disabilities from being taken seriously or being allowed more participation in making decisions involving their lives. This is the case for several of the children that I had the privilege to interview during my different research projects. Once they felt they were taken seriously, they opened up and spoke about their personal strategies of navigating the system, even though or because their voices were not taken into account.

The **sociology of childhood** and the field of **childhood studies** have helped to recognize children's agency and their rights. Pioneers Prout and James (1997) have called for a double engagement for researchers: to have children contribute to research, as well as to be supporters to children's causes. They explained that "to proclaim a new paradigm of childhood sociology is also to engage in and respond to the process of reconstructing childhood in society" (Prout & James, 1997, p. 8). Research with children with disabilities gives a testimony to children's agency, their perceptions of the world, and their strategies to deal with the nonrecognition of their agency and rights by adults and adult experts (see also Davis et al., 2008). But even under the different models of disability, we can see that the rights to education and to work, and also to participate in research, are still being undermined—by, for example, a lack of labour rights and/or a lack of enforcement and implementation of those rights—ultimately impacting negatively on the right to labour market participation. This is the case in Canada, but even more so in other places in the world, for example the Global South, where the right to education and work suffers in addition from a lack of financial means (e.g. Miles & Singal, 2010; UN, 2015). The implementation and enforcement of those rights needs financial and structural support. If children's rights to education are generally not implemented in those countries due to a lack of schools and teachers, it becomes obvious that children who are learning and accessing knowledge in less traditional ways are at a high risk of falling through the cracks.

I argue that our current approach to the rights of children and youth with disabilities is best described as the "Yes! But ..." attitude. In principle, we are willing to recognize the rights, but are quick to dodge those rights if economics tell us that there is no funding to support those rights, or if our personal and professional biases about persons with disabilities get in the way. Similarly, when rights seem to be competing between what we see as provision or protection and participation, we are quick to decide on the side of protection, thereby impeding the children's rights to participation.

Nedelsky (2008, p. 141) offers another way of thinking about the issue of competing rights, by addressing them under the imperative of relationships. We need to examine the competing interpretations of those rights and determine the underlying values we wish to achieve (e.g. increased participation of the child with a disability). Once we determine which values are at stake, we can work on establishing relationships with the child and their environment to foster them. Nedelsky's approach shows the importance of the contribution of research involving children and youth with disabilities to help resolve some of those contradictions elaborated on in this chapter: it builds on relationships to uncover the agency of those children and to help facilitate their participation in decision-making processes, as well as to challenge conventional ways of assessing children's agency (Davis et al., 2008). Researchers, professionals in the field, and families need to challenge themselves to build relationships that reach beyond preconceived medical notions of disability, vulnerability, incompetence, and helplessness, and fulfill the disabled person's desire for and right to recognition.

Honneth's work "The Struggle for Recognition" (1995) highlights the importance of different levels of recognition. Honneth demonstrates that recognition arises from these different levels: love/personal relationships, rights, and solidarity. According to Honneth, the recognition of rights is a central element. However, it needs to be fostered on the level of personal relationships as well as on the level of overall societal solidarity in order to achieve full recognition of an oppressed social group (see also Kenneally, chapter 17). We cannot give recognition to children and youth with disabilities if we neither engage on a personal level with them, nor express general solidarity at a higher societal level. If we embed these levels into our actions, we can establish relationships that help us to improve the participation and inclusion of our fellow citizens regardless of their age and abilities. We can better recognize children's and youth's ability to participate if we know them well, and if we are open to listening to their viewpoints and experiences, and are ready to include them in our cultures, policies, and practices. Our response to the recognition of the rights of children and youth with disabilities needs to evolve from paying lip service to co-constructing with children with disabilities rights-respecting contexts and environments.

IMPLEMENTING THE RIGHTS OF CHILDREN WITH DISABILITIES IN SCHOOLS AND IN THE WORKPLACE

Evidently, many issues concerning the rights of children with disabilities stem from the general societal lack of recognition due to misconceptions and stereotypical assumptions about persons with disabilities, often based on a very medicalized and deficiency-based perspective on disabilities. In addition, children's rights in general have not been implemented in a satisfactory way, especially when it comes to education and schooling. Given that typically children spend about 12 years in schools and classrooms, it is natural to think of this place as one of the major locations to implement and teach children's rights in general, and the rights of children with disabilities specifically. Canadian research has shown very positive outcomes when schools consciously become rights-respecting schools (Covell & Howe, 2008). Children's participation in their own learning and learning environment has proven to increase tremendously when a rights-based curriculum is implemented. This shows that such improvements are a positive starting point that could then be expanded on to include the more specific rights of children with disabilities.

One of the key components is education, of both the children and youth with disabilities and the adult stakeholders. As often occurs, the knowledge around children's rights or disability rights is quite limited, and fraught with assumptions; for example, adult stakeholders might dismiss children's rights or disability rights because they might oppose their own agenda. Rights education can help provide educators, families, or employers with a more nuanced picture about children's rights and disability rights, as well as help implement them in their everyday work in schools and in the workplace. Firstly, educators and employers need to know the relevant human rights conventions in detail and fully understand what they imply for their work in schools and the workplace. Secondly, it is essential to create greater awareness and knowledge of the agency of children and youth with disabilities. Research outcomes from the field of sociology of childhood, childhood studies, and disability studies can make an enormous contribution to teacher education and professional development. As I have shown in this chapter, listening to and building relationships with children and youth with disabilities, and finding ways to include their opinions, experiences, and expertise on their own lives are central to respecting the rights of children and youth with disabilities. Only when we have done this can we grow towards becoming a society where participation of all its members is considered to be truly inclusive.

CHAPTER SUMMARY

Together, in this chapter, we

- Learned about the necessity of recognizing the rights of children and youth with disabilities.
- Sought to understand the different models of disability and how they affect the perspectives on the rights of children and youth with disabilities.
- Reviewed examples of children and youth whose rights have not been respected.
- Reviewed the importance of relationship-building when it comes to implementing the rights of children with disabilities.
- Recognized the importance of rights education for teachers and employers to improve the situation of children and youth with disabilities.

STUDY QUESTIONS

1. What are the different types of rights addressed in the CRC and the CRPD (as identified in the chapter), and how can they come to contradict each other?
2. What does the social model of disability mean for the participation rights of children and youth with disabilities?
3. How could you personally support a child or youth with disabilities in improving access and participation?
4. Discuss ways of improving participation rights of children and youth with disabilities in schools or in the workplace.
5. Why is the recognition of the rights of children and youth with disabilities so important to their education and participation in social life?

SUGGESTED RESEARCH ASSIGNMENT

Imagine you are a consultant hired by the government and you have to write a report with recommendations on improving the situation of children and youth with disabilities. Research the facts about the situation of children with disabilities, and elaborate on recommendations for action from your findings.

SUGGESTED FILMS/VIDEO CLIPS

On the Way to School

www.youtube.com/watch?v=vZsEvLaua4w

A documentary of children around the world on their way to school. One of them is a little boy in India, Samuel, who uses a wheelchair and who goes to school with the help of his two brothers. The video exemplifies the importance of access to education for children with disabilities.

Me Too! Yo Tambien!

www.youtube.com/watch?v=rDIlPQNrLU8

Spanish movie about a young man who is the first university graduate with Down syndrome and his struggles to find recognition.

Listen up! Children with Disabilities Speak Out

www.youtube.com/watch?v=FjhF-pdlJ8M

Clip by Plan International about the importance of respecting the rights of children and youth with disabilities around the globe.

SUGGESTED WEBSITES

UN Declaration on the Rights of Persons with Disabilities

www.un.org/development/desa/disabilities/convention-on-the-rights-of-persons-with-
   disabilities.html

Provides an overview, the text of the declaration, and additional information.

Promoting the Rights of Children with Disabilities

www.un.org/esa/socdev/unyin/documents/children_disability_rights.pdf

A resource provided by UNICEF Council of Canadians with Disabilities (CCD); additional resources and information related to the general situation of people with disabilities in Canada available at www.ccdonline.ca/en/.

NOTE

1.   See also their website: childrensrightseducation.com/cbu-childrens-rights-centre.html.

REFERENCES

Barnes, C., & Mercer, G. (2010). *Exploring disability: A sociological Introduction* (2nd ed.). Cambridge, UK: Polity Press.

Canadian Coalition for the Rights of Children. (n.d.). *Realizing the rights of children with disabilities in Canada. Working document.* Retrieved from rightsofchildren.ca/resources/childrens-rights-monitoring/

Canadian Institutes of Health Research, Natural Sciences and Engineering Research Council of Canada, & Social Sciences and Humanities Research Council of Canada. (2010). *Tri-Council policy statement: Ethical conduct of research involving humans.* Retrieved from www.pre.ethics.gc.ca/pdf/eng/tcps2/TCPS_2_FINAL_Web.pdf

Corsaro, W. A. (2014). *The sociology of childhood* (4th ed.). Thousand Oaks, CA: Sage.

Covell, K., & Howe, R. B. (2001). The challenge of children's rights for Canada. Waterloo, ON: Wilfried Laurier University Press.

Covell, K., & Howe, R. B. (2008). Rights, respect and responsibility: Final report on the County of Hampshire Rights Education Initiative September 2008. Retrieved from www.cbu.ca/sites/cbu.ca/files/pdfs/crc-pub-rights-respect-responsibility-2008.pdf

Davis, J., & Watson, N. (2000). Disabled children's rights in everyday life: Problematising notions of competency and promoting self-empowerment. *The International Journal of Children's Rights, 8*(3), 211–228. doi:0.1163/15718180020494622

Davis, J., Watson, N., & Cunningham-Burley, S. (2008). Disabled children, ethnography and unspoken understandings: The collaborative construction of diverse identities. In P. Christensen & A. James (Eds.), *Research with children: perspectives and practices* (pp. 220–238). Hoboken, NY: Taylor & Francis.

Honneth, A. (1995). *The struggle for recognition: The moral grammar of social conflicts.* Cambridge, UK: Polity Press.

Howe, R. B. (2001). Do parents have fundamental rights? *Journal of Canadian Studies, 36*(3), 61.

Howe, R. B., & Covell, K. (2010). Miseducating children about their rights. *Education, Citizenship and Social Justice, 5,* 91–102. doi:10.1177/1746197910370724

James, A., & Prout, J. (Eds.). (2002). *Constructing and reconstructing childhood: Contemporary issues in the sociological study of childhood.* London: Routledge Falmer.

Kayess, R., & French, P. (2008). Out of darkness into light? Introducing the Convention on the Rights of Persons with Disabilities. *Human Rights Law Review, 8*(1), 1–34. doi:10.1093/hrlr/ngm044

LeFrançois, B. A. (2007). Children's participation rights: Voicing opinions in inpatient care. *Child & Adolescent Mental Health, 12*(2), 94–97. doi:10.1111/j.1475-3588.2007.00439.x

LeFrançois, B. A., & Coppock, V. (2014). Psychiatrised children and their rights: Starting the conversation. *Children & Society, 28*(3), 165–171. doi:10.1111/chso.12082

Mckenzie, J. A., & Macleod, C. I. (2012). Rights discourses in relation to education of people with intellectual disability: Towards an ethics of care that enables participation. *Disability & Society, 27*(1), 15–29. doi:10.1080/09687599.2012.631795

Miles, S., & Singal, N. (2010). The education for all and inclusive education debate: Conflict, contradiction or opportunity? *International Journal of Inclusive Education, 14*(1), 1–15.

Muir, J., & Goldblatt, B. (2011). Complementing or conflicting human rights conventions? Realising an inclusive approach to families with a young person with a disability and challenging behaviour. *Disability & Society, 26*(5), 629–642. doi:10.1080/09687599.2011.589195

Nedelsky, J. (2008). Reconceiving rights and constitutionalism. *Journal of Human Rights, 7*(2), 139–173. doi:10.1080/14754830802071950

Owen, F., Tardif-Williams, C., Tarulli, D., McQueen-Fuentes, G., Feldman, M., Sales, C., ... Griffiths, D. (2008). Human rights for children and youth with developmental disabilities. In D. Zinga & T. O'Neill (Eds.), *Children's rights: Multidisciplinary approaches to participation and protection* (pp. 163–194). Toronto: University of Toronto Press.

Prout, A., & James A. (1997). A new paradigm for the sociology of childhood? Provenance, promise and problems. In A. James & A. Prout (Eds.), *Constructing and reconstructing childhood. Contemporary issues in the sociological study of childhood* (pp. 7–33). London: RoutledgeFalmer.

Schneider, C. (2007). Être intégré, être en marge, être reconnu? L'enfant en situation de handicap et son statut social dans une classe ordinaire. *Education et Sociétés, 20*(2), 149–166.

Schneider, C. (2009). Equal is not enough—Current issues in inclusive education in the eyes of children. *International Journal of Education, 1*(1), E1. Retrieved from www.macrothink.org/journal/index.php/ije/article/ view/101

Schneider, C. (2010). "Ready for work": Feeling rules, emotion work and emotional labour for people with disabilities. *Interactions, 4*. Retrieved from www.ctnerhi.com.fr/images/revue_interactions/schneider_en.pdf

Schneider, C. (2011). *Une étude comparative de l'éducation inclusive des enfants avec besoins particuliers en France et en Allemange: Recherches dans onze salles de classe* [A comparative study of the inclusion of children with special needs in mainstream schools in France and Germany: Case studies of eleven classrooms]. Lewiston, NY: Edwin Mellen Press.

Schneider, C. (2015). Social participation of children and youth with disabilities in Canada, France and Germany. *International Journal of Inclusive Education, 19*(10), 1068–1079. doi:10.1080/13603116.2015.1037867

Schneider, C., Chahine, S., & Hattie, B. (2014). Trajectoires et transitions de vie de jeunes adultes en situation de handicap. Une étude des anciens bénéficiaires d'un programme d'insertion professionnelle. *La Nouvelle Revue de L'adaptation et de la Scolarisation, 68*, 209–225.

Shakespeare, T. (2013). *Disability rights and wrongs revisited* (2nd ed.). London: Routledge.

Skelton, T. (2008). Research with children and young people: Exploring the tensions between ethics, competence and participation. *Children's Geographies, 6*(1), 21–36. doi:10.1080/14733280701791876

Trainor, A. A. (2008). Using social and cultural capital to improve postsecondary outcomes and expand transition models for youth with disabilities. *Journal of Special Education, 42*, 148–162.

Trainor, A. A. (2010). Re-examining the promise of parent participation in special education: An analysis of cultural and social capital. *Anthropology and Education Quarterly, 41*, 245–263.

Tyrie, S., Tyrie, C., Tyrie, C., & Tyrie, B. (2013). My story. In T. Curran & K. Runswick-Cole (Eds.), *Disabled children's childhood studies: Critical approaches in a global context* (pp. 3–9) Basingstoke: Palgrave Macmillan.

UNICEF. (2009). *Not there yet. Canada's implementation of the general measures of the Convention on the Rights of the Child.* Retrieved from www.unicef-irc.org/publications/pdf/canada_nty.pdf

United Nations (UN). (2015). *The Millennium Development Report goals 2015.* New York: United Nations.

19 The Civic and Political Engagement of Canadian Youth

L. Alison Molina-Girón

LEARNING OBJECTIVES

- To understand what youth civic engagement is
- To discuss the various participatory practices (e.g. institutionalized and non-institutionalized) youth employ to engage in the democratic process
- To explain the importance to a strong democracy of youth participation in public life
- To identify determinant factors that both contribute to and deter active youth engagement in civic and political life
- To outline key issues to equal participation among majority and minority youth in Canada

---

INTRODUCTION

What elements are essential to creating and maintaining a strong democracy? It is often thought that the health and stability of a democracy depends on its political institutions (e.g. the three branches of government, the political party system). While these are fundamental, there is another critical condition: the conscious participation of citizens. There is no doubt that the active and reflective participation of all citizens, youth included, in the governing process is vital to a strong democracy. Yet, do young Canadians participate in civic and political life? This is the question this chapter explores; it is an issue that has garnered increased attention since the 1990s. This renewed interest stems from a concern with reported low levels of youth engagement in the electoral process in Canada and elsewhere (Blais & Loewen, 2011; O'Neill, 2007; Turcotte, 2015a). *Disengaged, apathetic, alienated,* and *indifferent* are some of the qualifying words used to describe youth interest and engagement in political life. Notably, though there is evidence showing a decline in voting and participation in other forms of institutionalized political participation, the opposite is also true: Youth *do* engage in civic and political life. Idle No More and the 2012 Quebec student protests, as well as the Arab Spring and the Occupy movement are examples of recent national and overseas grassroots movements where young citizens have played leading roles (see Stolle, Harell, Pedersen, & Dufour, 2013; Hoffman & Jamal, 2012; Reimer, 2012; Tupper, 2014).

This chapter examines the engagement of Canadian youth aged 15 to 24 in the nation's civic and political life. In this work, youth are conceived of as active, interested, involved, opinionated, concerned, and invested citizens whose **agency** is central to shaping the future of their societies. To what extent are Canadian youth engaged in the democratic process? What actions and behaviours do they perform in the public sphere as engaged citizens? Do they vote, discuss civic and political issues, and protest? Do youth write/blog about social problems? Do they join political groups or volunteer? Social and cultural diversity is a distinctive feature of Canada's democratic society. As such, this chapter also explores the civic engagement of minority youth and asks, in a multicultural society like Canada, is participation equal across majority and minority youth? Before continuing to read, I invite you to answer these questions so you can assess what you know now and what you learn by reading this chapter.

To a great extent, civic engagement is a lived experience influenced by one's civic identity and social positioning. Citizen participation is often navigated within particular structural and discursive conditions. As we will see, one's race, ethnicity, class, and level of education are factors that affect whether and to what extent young people participate in public life. This chapter begins by presenting a profile of salient sociodemographic characteristics of Canadian youth to contextualize youth (dis)engagement from civic and political life. I then discuss what civic engagement is, including the **self-actualizing citizen** as a model of youth engagement, as well as the realms of youth public participation—civic, political, and digital. Next, I review the literature focusing on the actual civic and political engagement of young Canadians aged 15 to 24 and the factors likely to contribute, or not, to such engagement. The review does not aim to be exhaustive; rather it is indicative of the state of the field as suggested by the most recent literature on Canadian **youth civic engagement**.

A SOCIODEMOGRAPHIC PROFILE OF CANADA'S YOUTH[1]

To set the stage, what follows is a very brief description of today's Canadian youth. According to the most recent 2011 census data, the population aged 15 to 24 comprised 4,324,585 people, or 13 percent of the total population (Galarneau, Morissette, & Usalcas, 2013; Public Health Agency of Canada [PHAC], 2014).[2] The majority lives in urban areas. However, the North (Yukon, the Northwest Territories, and Nunavut) has the youngest population. In 2011, about one-quarter of the population living in the North were aged 15 and under, compared to 5.8 percent who were 65 or older (PHAC, 2014). In Nunavut alone, 28.6 percent of the population was 10 to 24 years old—the highest percentage in Canada (PHAC, 2014).

How is Canada's youth population different from previous generations? Most pertinent to this discussion, young Canadians are more educated and ethnically diverse than their predecessors. In 2006, over 86 percent of Canada's youth aged 20 to 24 had earned a high school diploma and over 28 percent had had some postsecondary education (Blais & Loewen, 2011; PHAC, 2014). Particularly of note is the fact that 68 percent of the 25- to 29-year-old demographic holds a postsecondary degree or diploma (Galarneau et al., 2013). In addition, 58 percent of those aged 18 to 24 were full-time students in 2012, compared to 39 percent in 1981 (Galarneau et al., 2013).

With regards to employment, younger Canadians experience relatively high unemployment rates and lower wages. In 2012, the unemployment rate among 15- to 24-year-olds was 14.3 percent, double that of the national average (7.2%) (Galarneau et al., 2013). Aboriginal, **immigrant**, and visible minority youth face the highest unemployment rates.[3] In addition, they are more likely to be paid the minimum wage and earn $30,000 or less. In 2013, 50 percent of employees aged 15 to 19 and 13 percent of those aged 20 to 24 were paid the minimum wage (Galarneau & Fecteau, 2014). Increasingly, younger Canadians report living at home, having no religious affiliation, and not being married (Bilodeau & Turgeon, 2015; Blais & Loewen, 2011).

Canada's ethnocultural composition has been shaped by its history of European colonization of Indigenous peoples and by immigration. In 2011, Canada's foreign-born population was 6,775,800, accounting for 20.6 percent of the total population—the highest among the G8 countries (Statistics Canada, 2013a). A greater proportion of Canada's youth have been born abroad or are the children of immigrants. By 2011, recent **newcomers** aged 15 to 24 made up 14.5 percent of all immigrants arriving within five years of the census (Statistics Canada, 2013a). There is also an important growing second-generation, visible minority Canadian population. In 1971, for example, 75 percent of Canadians were Canadian-born from Canadian-born parents: by 2011 this was the case for 66 percent of young Canadians, and by 2031 it is predicted that this proportion may decrease to 54 percent (Galarneau et al., 2013). In the 2011 census, the top self-reported ethnic origin for visible minority youth was South Asian (23.2%), followed closely by Chinese (21.5%) and Black (16.4%) (PHAC, 2014).

Canada's Indigenous peoples also make up a significant—and the fastest-growing—segment of the Canadian population. In Canada there are 254,515 Indigenous youth aged 15 to 24, representing 18.2 percent of the total Indigenous population and 5.9 percent of all Canadian youth (Statistics Canada, 2013b). Between 2006 and 2011, the Indigenous population increased by 20.1 percent (Statistics Canada, 2013b). The Indigenous youth population aged 15 to 24 grew by 19.5 percent, from 212,910 in 2006 to 254,515 in 2011 (Statistics Canada, 2013b). This trend is expected to continue.

Population projections for Canada's Indigenous youth present four different scenarios: 2.2 percent, 15.9 percent, 26 percent, and 38.9 percent growth rates. Note that in three of these scenarios the Indigenous youth population is expected to grow by at least 15 percent by the year 2031 (Morency, Caron-Malenfant, Coulombe, & Langlois, 2015).

YOUTH CIVIC ENGAGEMENT: WHAT IS IT?

Youth civic engagement, a relatively new field, is primarily concerned with research, practice, and the development of programs that promote young people's active participation in civic and political life (Checkoway, 2011; Levine, 2011; Sherrod, Torney-Purta, & Flanagan, 2010). Although consensus has yet to be reached on a single overarching definition of civic engagement, for our purposes here it refers to individual and collective actions aimed at addressing an issue of public concern or contributing to the betterment of the community and society (Checkoway, 2011; Levine, 2011; Sherrod et al., 2010). Civic engagement can take a variety of forms including working in a soup kitchen, serving on a neighbourhood association, writing a letter to an elected official, voting, or protesting.

To this day, the field of youth civic engagement has accrued a significant body of knowledge and developed theoretical frameworks, approaches, and practices to promote the informed and active participation of youth. In addition, research shows that youth participation benefits the individual and society at large. Young people acquire critical knowledge and relevant skills, build positive self-esteem, and strengthen their sense of social responsibility (Checkoway, 2011; Head, 2011). Society at large also benefits, as democracy is strengthened by the active involvement of its citizenry all the while providing real opportunities to develop capabilities for effective **citizenship** (Barber, 2003; Held, 2006).

Youth participation is also a right ratified by the **UN Convention on the Rights of the Child** (Checkoway, 2011; Head, 2011). However, as identified in the literature, an important challenge remains: recognizing and overcoming the limitations imposed by a developmental child rights framework that stresses child welfare over participation. A focus on the protection of children's participation rights has been the dominant approach to children and youth citizenship (Earls, 2011; Head, 2011; Rehfeld, 2011). While protection is important, a less prominent view is that of children as democratic citizens with developing capabilities to participate in the governing process (Checkoway, 2011; Rehfeld, 2011). To illustrate, think about the oft-used phrase describing children in government and education policy: "The children of today are the citizens of tomorrow." This phrase captures a prevalent developmental understanding of children's citizenship: children become citizens at age 18 when they acquire the right to vote and are then expected to assume the roles and duties of adulthood, including acting as informed and participatory citizens (Sherrod et al., 2010). Unfortunately, youth are often seen as citizens-in-waiting, with limited **agency**, and their actual democratic engagement is barely taken into account

(Kennelly, 2009; Molina-Girón, 2013). When civic engagement is narrowly viewed as participation in electoral politics, for instance—like voting and party membership—age can become an "artificial barrier" to meaningful citizenship (Earls, 2011, p. 11).

The Realms of Youth Civic Engagement

Being engaged necessarily involves some form of participation in the public realm. In general, there are two types of engagement depending on the area of participation: civic and political. Civic participation consists of "non-remunerative, publicly spirited action that is not motivated by the desire to affect public policy" (Campbell, 2006, p. 30). Citizen engagement, through this model, is framed mainly as a commitment to the immediate welfare of others and the community. Proponents of civic participation contend that undertaking "good" actions can help develop desirable civic attitudes such as trust and empathy, and can encourage public participation, since being involved awakens young people's interest in issues that demand government attention (Dalton, 2008; Levine, 2011; O'Neill, 2007).

This altruistic framework to civic engagement is the dominant approach being taken to revitalize youth civic engagement in Canada and abroad (Kennelly, 2009; Levine, 2011; Westheimer & Kahne, 2004). Citizenship education programs across Canada often include community service requirements whereby students are asked to do positive, often charitable, acts to help others or better the community. Twenty-two-year-old community organizer Brigette DePape explains the problem with this approach: "We are trapped in a structure that bars us from meaningful engagement.... We are encouraged to do charity or development work ... to 'help the poor'. The mainstream celebrates these philanthropic efforts" (DePape & Shaker, 2012, pp. 19–20). To her, the problem is clear: by championing an altruistic approach to civic engagement "society is failing to show us how to be agents for social change" (DePape & Shaker, 2012, p. 19). There is disagreement on whether this kind of participation enhances participation in public affairs. Youth civic participation research in Canada and elsewhere has found that engagement that stresses doing "good actions" like visiting the elderly and cleaning public parks—as desirable as they are—may limit youth engagement towards social change (Kennelly 2009; Molina-Girón, 2013; Westheimer & Kahne, 2004).

By contrast, political participation includes "all activities by individual citizens intended to influence either directly or indirectly political choices at various levels of the political system" (Milbrath & La Goel, 1979, p. 2). Democracy requires, and is strengthened by, citizens' direct and continual involvement in public decision-making. For many pundits, this kind of engagement is critical to developing effective citizens—citizens concerned with the governing process and collective problems, and having a strong sense of political efficacy (Barber, 2003; Held, 2006).

Research indicates that in Canada, as in other Western democracies, young people have turned away from electoral and other political forms of **institutionalized participation** like contacting elected officials and party membership, towards more direct, individualized, and informal modes of participation including demonstrating, online activism, consumerism politics, volunteering, and membership in civil associations (Cohen, Kahne, Bowyer, Middaugh, & Rogowski, 2012; O'Neill, 2007; Stolle et al., 2013). While some scholars warn that a decline in political participation can lead to a democratic deficit, others contend that the changing forms of participation may represent a new model of youth engagement—that of the "self-actualizing citizen" (Bennett, Wells, & Rank, 2009, p. 105; Bennett, 2012). As such, youth public engagement seems to stem more from a personal expression than from a sense of civic duty—which negatively impacts voting, but not volunteering. Being engaged, then, is something that is seen as personal and meaningful to the individual (Bennett, 2012; Bennett et al., 2009; Cohen et al., 2012). The civic engagement of the self-actualizing citizen is interest-driven and "not guided by deference to elites or formal institutions" and it favours interactive, nonhierarchical, peer-to-peer activities to achieve desired goals (Cohen et al., 2012, p. 4; Bennett et al., 2009). Twenty-five-year-old Canadian activist Trace Kaleigh captures the essence of the self-actualizing citizen: "I think," she asserts, "that the voting system is pretty alienating and disenchanting.... Rather than being apathetic, youth are being very creative and invigorating the ways [we can engage in the democratic process]" (cited in DePape & Shaker, 2012, p. 24).

Indeed, recent research suggests that new media—including Facebook, Twitter, and blogs—deeply affect whether and how youth engage with public issues, and that there is greater overlap between civic and political participation than was previously thought (Cohen et al., 2012; Kligler-Vilenchik & Shresthova, 2014; Rundle, Weinstein, Gardner, & James, 2015). Online engagement provides a space and gives voice to youth to act on issues affecting their lives (Caron, Raby, Mitchell, Théwissen-LeBlanc, & Prioletta, 2016; Kligler-Vilenchik & Shresthova, 2014; Rundle et al., 2015). Social media seems to increase youth offline participation in political activities, such as voting and working for a political party (Cohen et al., 2012; Kahne, Lee, & Feezell, 2012). Digital participation appears to reduce the participatory gap across racially and ethnically diverse youth groups as well. For example, Rogowski and Cohen (2015) found that Black youth is the group most engaged in online politically oriented activity in the United States, a group that up until the 2008 presidential election had had the lowest levels of political participation.

DO YOUNG CANADIANS PARTICIPATE IN CIVIC AND POLITICAL LIFE?

There are many activities that youth undertake to shape the future of the communities in which they live. However, there is growing concern with decreasing levels of youth democratic engagement in electoral politics. It is important to note here that youth civic participation research in Canada and elsewhere has primarily employed large-scale studies that focus on electoral political behaviour, such as voting and political knowledge and interest (Griffin, 2005). Thus, further research is needed to better understand other forms of **noninstitutionalized participation** youth employ to engage in the democratic process. Youth participation research seems to indicate that as a group, young Canadians have the lowest voter turnout rate, lowest affiliation in political parties, and lowest levels of political interest (Bilodeau & Turgeon, 2015; Blais & Loewen, 2011; Gélineau, 2013; Turcotte, 2015a). In the 2015 federal election, the participation of voters aged 18 to 24 increased by 18.3 percent. However, when compared to other age cohort groups, youth aged 18 to 24 have consistently had the lowest voting rates[4] in the last three federal elections: 57.1 percent in 2015, 38.8 percent in 2011, and 37.4 percent in 2008 (Elections Canada, 2012, 2016). Further, recent research indicates that youth are more likely to be **habitual non-voters**, or to systematically abstain from voting at every election (Bilodeau & Turgeon, 2015, p. 4). While only 10 percent of Canadians 35 and older report not having voted in elections, this proportion increases to 31 percent for those aged 25 to 34 and to 47 percent for those 18 to 24 years old (Bilodeau & Turgeon, 2015).

In addition, young voters in Canada and in other Western democracies like the United States and the United Kingdom have become less likely to identify with and become members of political parties (Martin 2012; Young & Cross, 2007). In 2000, only 3 percent of party members of registered political parties were aged 25 or younger; those who joined were "unusually privileged ... in their exposure to politics and in their socio-economic background" (Young & Cross, 2007, p. 1). Similarly, only 25 percent of those aged 15 to 35 have contacted elected officials compared to 33 percent who are 35 and older (Samara, 2013).

Though participation of youth aged 15 to 24 in institutionalized forms of political participation is low, this group does, however, participate in other noninstitutionalized political activities at rates higher than older Canadians (Bastedo, Dougherty, LeDuc, Rudny, & Sommers, 2012; Stolle et al., 2013; Turcotte, 2015a). The 2013 General Social Survey (GSS) revealed that in the previous 12 months, 26 percent of youth aged 15 to 19 and 35 percent of youth aged 20 to 24 had signed a petition, compared with 22 percent of those aged 65 to 74 and 14 percent among those aged 75 and over (Turcotte, 2015a). In addition, they were twice as likely as older cohorts to support causes of public concern by wearing a badge or T-shirt and/or having held a sign at a rally or assembly (Turcotte, 2015a). Nine percent of youth aged 15 to 24 had participated in a demonstration or a march—twice the percentage of any other cohort group (Turcotte, 2015b). Paradoxically, while youth clearly did engage in substantial political activities, they were less likely to report that they intended to vote in the next federal election (Turcotte, 2015a).

Young Canadians engage in individual and collective online and offline actions to address social issues like racism, poverty, and environmental degradation. Their civic actions range from creating videos (Caron et al., 2016), to leading grassroots organizations (DePape & Shaker, 2012), to protesting, to acts of civil disobedience (Kennelly, 2009). While these kinds of activism are legitimate in a democratic society, when they are perceived as being too radical, youth activists can face government and police repression (see Kennelly, 2009).

Youth also display greater levels of volunteerism and membership in civic groups and organizations than older people. Between 2003 and 2013, the participation of youth aged 15 to 24 in voluntary associations rose from 64 percent to 69 percent (Turcotte, 2015a). The highest increase was seen among those aged 15 to 19, with their participation rising from 68 percent to 74 percent (Turcotte, 2015a). According to the GSS, in 2013 66 percent of youth aged 15 to 19 and 64 percent of youth aged 20 to 24 volunteered in an organization or association—the highest volunteering rates of all age cohorts in Canada (Turcotte, 2015a). The types of groups that young Canadians were most likely to participate in were sports and recreational organizations, followed by cultural, educational, or hobby organizations (e.g. theatre groups), school groups, or neighbourhood associations (Turcotte, 2015b). Forty five percent of youth aged 15 to 19 and 30 percent of those aged 20 to 24 who volunteer regularly also participate in planned association meetings and activities (Turcotte, 2015a). However, it is important to note that it is citizens with higher incomes and higher levels of education who are more likely to be members of civic-oriented organizations—regardless of the type (Turcotte, 2015a).

What do we know of the public engagement of Canadian minority youth? A striking and enduring finding is that in Canada, youth institutionalized political participation is highly unequal: higher-income, better-educated youth are much more likely to participate compared with lower-income, less-educated youth (Bilodeau & Turgeon, 2015; Blais & Loewen, 2011; Gélineau, 2013; Turcotte, 2015a). Box 19.1 discusses current trends of the electoral participation of majority and minority Canadian youth. It is important to note that besides voting, very little is known of the public involvement of Canadian minority youth.

Box 19.1: The Electoral Participation of Majority and Minority Youth in Canada

Indigenous, new immigrant, and visible minority youth vote in alarmingly lower numbers compared with majority youth (Bilodeau & Turgeon, 2015; Ladner & McCrossan, 2007; Tossutti, 2007). Gélineau (2013), for example, found a 20-percentage-point voting gap between Indigenous and non-Indigenous youth. In addition, new research reveals that Canadian-born youth vote more often than those who are born abroad, with a voting gap ranging from 6 (Gélineau, 2013) to 12 percentage points (Blais & Loewen, 2011). "The effect for being a recent immigrant is substantial," affirmed Bilodeau and Turgeon (2015, p. 26). Bilodeau and Turgeon (2015) estimated that the probability of having voted in the 2011 federal election for those aged 18 to 24 was 64 percent for Canadian-born youth, compared to 17 percent for recent immigrant youth—a 47-point gap. Further, it is immigrant youth who are most likely to be habitual non-voters: Bilodeau and Turgeon's study predicts that 23 percent of Canadian-born youth aged 18 to 24 would be habitual non-voters compared with 90 percent of recent immigrant youth (2015).

DETERMINANT FACTORS OF YOUTH ENGAGEMENT

What seems to encourage youth participation in civic and political life? What may explain low levels of youth participation, especially in electoral politics? Certain socioeconomic characteristics and political attitudes have been identified as determinant factors with regard to youth public engagement. In the next section, I focus on the factors most often cited in the Canadian-based civic engagement literature.[5]

Socioeconomic Characteristics

Education and place of birth are among the two most significant sociodemographic predictors of higher voter turnout and overall higher civic and political participation (Bilodeau & Turgeon, 2015; Blais & Loewen, 2011; Gélineau, 2013; Turcotte, 2015a). Since the impact of place of birth on civic engagement was addressed in the previous section, I will focus here on education and other sociodemographic factors. Blais and Loewen estimated that citizens with higher levels of education "have odds of voting 52% higher than those who do not have post-secondary education" (2011, p. 10). Similarly, Gélineau (2013) concluded that there is an almost 30-percentage-point gap in youth voter turnout between those who have had postsecondary education compared with those who have not. In fact, active students have a 7-percentage-point higher turnout rate than those who are not (Gélineau, 2013). Turcotte's study further confirmed these findings (2015a): he found that for all age groups, having higher levels of education is positively correlated with increased participation in all types of civic and political activities.

Other important factors affecting youth civic and/or political involvement are age and income. Associated with age is the life-cycle effect: people are more likely to vote as they get older (Blais & Loewen, 2011; Gélineau, 2013). However, this pattern does not follow a linear trend: first-time voters (i.e. 18- and 19-year-olds) vote more often than those who were eligible to vote in the previous election (i.e. 20- to 24-year-olds) (Gélineau, 2013). With regards to income, there is a 6-point voter turnout gap between youth aged 18 to 24 with a household income below $40,000 and those above, and an 11-point gap between those aged 25 to 30 (Blais & Loewen, 2011). In contrast, Bilodeau and Turgeon (2015) found a 14-point voting gap between the poorest and wealthiest Canadians in the 25 to 35 age cohort, but no such relationship was observed among the 18 to 24 age cohort. A counterintuitive relationship was found by Bilodeau and Turgeon (2015): among those aged 18 to 24, being unemployed is positively associated with voting.

Socioeconomic status can also impact youth participation in noninstitutionalized forms of political activity, but evidence is somewhat mixed. In a study of young activists, over three-quarters were from a middle-class background, highlighting the role that socioeconomic status plays in youth decisions to protest to affect public policy (Kennelly, 2009). In contrast, Stolle and colleagues (2013) found that it was youth with lower socioeconomic resources—e.g. those who felt they could not pay tuition increases, who worked while studying, and who had student loans—who had participated more in the 2012 Quebec student protests compared to their more affluent counterparts.

As illustrated, there are diverse forms of civic and political engagement, although voting has been the most measured indicator to investigate youth political participation (Turcotte, 2015a). Even a focus on this relatively easy to measure indicator suggests that there is great disparity among those who actually participate in the democratic process. In Canada, there is an engagement gap along the lines of race and social class. This disparity in public engagement has tremendous impact especially on government policy as the voices of the "have-nots" are barely heard.

Political Attitudes of Younger Voters

Political knowledge, political interest, and belief that voting is a civic duty are strong predictors of voting (Bilodeau & Turgeon, 2015; Blais & Loewen, 2011; Gélineau, 2013; Turcotte, 2015a). Blais and Loewen (2011) found that youth aged 18 to 24 with high levels of political knowledge vote at a rate of 23 percentage points higher than those with little political knowledge. Similarly, Gélineau (2013) reported a 35-point voting gap between the two groups.

Unsurprisingly, youth who are interested in politics are more likely to vote, but youth political interest remains low compared to other age cohorts. In a 2013 survey, only 51 percent of youth aged 15 to 19 and 53 percent of youth aged 20 to 24 reported being somewhat or very interested in politics, compared to 61 percent of those aged 35 to 44 and 75 percent of seniors aged 65 to 74 (Turcotte, 2015a). Gélineau (2013) reported that over 50 percent of youth who were interested in the 2011 election voted, compared with only 10.5 percent who voted yet were uninterested in the election. In addition, voting participation rates among youth aged 15 to 24 who follow the news and are informed about politics is 16 (Blais & Loewen, 2011) to 25 (Gélineau, 2013) percentage points higher than among those who were not informed.

Recent research reveals a concerning trend for many pundits: youth are less likely to consider voting as a civic duty (Bilodeau & Turgeon, 2015; Turcotte, 2015a). For example, 48 percent of those aged 18 to 24 would feel guilty if they did not vote compared with 55 percent of those aged 25 to 34, and 74 percent of those over 35 (Bilodeau & Turgeon, 2015). Bilodeau and Turgeon (2015) found a 52-point voting gap between Canadians aged 18 to 24 who strongly agree that they would feel guilty if they did not vote (83%) compared with those who admitted they would not experience guilt (31%). Similarly, the propensity to be a habitual non-voter decreases by seven points if a young Canadian feels guilty when not exercising the right to vote (Bilodeau & Turgeon, 2015). Paradoxically, it is a sense of civic duty that motivates youth to volunteer and get engaged (Bastedo et al., 2012).

Having a connection to a political party is also likely to increase the propensity to vote (Bilodeau & Turgeon, 2015; Gélineau, 2013), as is engaging in other forms of political participation such as protesting or signing petitions (Blais & Loewen, 2011; Gélineau, 2013), or believing that one's vote has the potential to make a difference (Bilodeau & Turgeon, 2015; Turcotte, 2015a).

CONCLUSION

This chapter has provided an overview of youth civic engagement in Canada and the avenues young people aged 15 to 24 use to participate in civic and political life. Increasingly, youth favour noninstitutionalized forms of participation, suggesting a new model of youth civic engagement: that of the self-actualizing citizen. While some scholars have warned that this shift can lead to a democratic deficit, others contend that what is needed is a renewed understanding of youth civic engagement that moves beyond traditional markers of engagement such as voting and party membership. Twenty-year-old Canadian artist and student activist Elise Graham clearly expresses this view: "[Youth] I know [are] involved ... working with artist-run centres ... or local food issues, which people do not see as political, but [they] definitely [are]" (cited in DePape & Shaker, 2012, pp. 25–26). Youth's changing patterns of democratic engagement compel us to further reflect on what should count towards youth democratic engagement.

In addition, youth participation in public life is alarmingly unequal. It is higher-income, better-educated, Canadian-born youth who are more politically involved. Unequal participation among a nation's citizenry has significant implications: it erodes a nation's social fabric by excluding those in already **marginalized** positions. In Canada, it is poor minority youth who become excluded. In addition, this heavily influences who has the **power** to affect public decision-making and, therefore, who is more likely to benefit from public policies. Full civic participation across social and cultural groups is essential to building a more equal and democratic society.

CHAPTER SUMMARY

Together, in this chapter, we

- Sought to understand what youth civic engagement is and the arenas for public participation including civic, political, and digital.
- Reviewed institutionalized and noninstitutionalized participatory practices youth employ to engage in the democratic process.
- Explored the self-actualizing citizen as a new model of youth civic engagement.
- Identified some key factors and issues hindering youth democratic engagement especially for minority youth.

STUDY QUESTIONS

1.   Review your answers to the questions posed in the introduction to the chapter. What have you learned that you did not know before?

2.   It is argued that youth favour more direct, individualized, and informal modes of civic participation over institutionalized ones like voting and party membership. In what ways does this shift potentially affect youth's active participation in the nation's civic and political life?

3.   How politically active and civically engaged do you think you are? What motivates you to be engaged? What deters you from actively engaging in the democratic process?

4.   You have been invited to be part of a group designing a federal initiative to strengthen youth civic engagement. What strategies would you suggest? What environments would you target? What civic qualities and capacities would the program stress? Why?

5.   What are some of the potential negative consequences of low youth engagement in public life on an otherwise strong democratic society?

6.   The active participation in public life is an important aspect of a positive integration of immigrant citizens into Canada's society. What barriers might immigrants face that deter them from participating in civic and political life? How does unequal participation across groups affect our building a more just and democratic Canadian society?

SUGGESTED RESEARCH ASSIGNMENT

Research five online and offline practices that can encourage youth, especially underprivileged and ethnic minority youth, to become civically and politically engaged. Explain the potential and most likely drawbacks that the practices can have to encourage youth civic engagement.

SUGGESTED FILMS/VIDEO CLIPS

The Antidote to Apathy
www.ted.com/talks/dave_meslin_the_antidote_to_apathy?language=en
Are we becoming less interested in politics? Toronto-based community activist Dave Meslin contends that people do care, but there are real barriers preventing citizens from public participation. He proposes ways to overcome such barriers.

Youth Engagement in Politics: Indifferent or Just Different?
www.youtube.com/watch?v=vdDFLzyk94k
Youth activist Jacob Helliwell challenges the commonly held view that youth are apathetic. He argues that today's youth are finding new and innovative ways to be engaged beyond the ballot box.

Envisioning Democracy: Participatory Filmmaking with Homeless Youth

carleton.ca/socanth/research-blog/envisioning-democracy-participatory-filmmaking-
  with-homeless-youth/

Challenges of Somali Youth

memuslim.rcinet.ca/mobile/video/index_mobile.php?watch=13

11 Facts about the Gap between First Nations and the Rest of Canada

www.youtube.com/watch?v=pWK6ChJw8hs

In these three videos, low-income and ethnic minority youth describe the challenges
they face in Canadian society, such as discrimination and police violence. In their view,
building a strong democratic nation requires fighting existing inequality.

The Impact of Digital Media on Youth Political Participation

www.civicsurvey.org/content/joseph-kahne-mills-college-professor-education-
  discusses-impact-digital-media-youth-0

Youth participation researcher Joseph Kahne underscores the importance of digital
media to youth public participation. Contrary to conventional wisdom, youth interest in nonpolitical online groups can be a catalyst to youth active civic and political
engagement.

SUGGESTED WEBSITES

Samara

www.samaracanada.com

Samara Canada is a nongovernmental, nonprofit advocacy organization for citizen engagement and participation. It conducts research on the state of Canada's democratic
institutions and citizen democratic engagement.

Inspire Democracy

inspirerlademocratie-inspiredemocracy.ca/index-eng.asp

An Elections Canada initiative, Inspire Democracy is a repository of current and recent
research on civic education and youth democratic participation. It also provides tools and
resources to strengthen youth public engagement.

The Centre for e-Democracy

www.centreforedemocracy.com/about-us/

The Centre for e-Democracy is a charitable organization dedicated to initiating, translating, and disseminating research and knowledge on the impact of digital technologies
on politics and democracy.

The Center for Information and Research on Civic Learning and Engagement (CIRCLE)

civicyouth.org/

The Center for Information and Research on Civic Learning and Engagement (CIRCLE) focuses on the civic and political engagement of youth in the United States, paying close attention to marginalized and disadvantaged youth populations. CIRCLE's scholarly research aims to inform policy and programs to strengthen citizenship education and participatory democracy.

NOTES

1. This chapter focuses on youth aged 15 to 24; however, often a different age range is used. This is due to the distinct age variations used in youth research.

2. Canada's youth population is declining. In 1971, 19 percent of Canadians were aged 15 to 24. By 2011, this proportion had decreased to 13 percent, and by 2031, Statistics Canada population projections estimate that this proportion could fall to 11 percent (Galarneau et al., 2013).

3. For a complete review on youth employment across various Canadian youth groups (Aboriginal, immigrants, visible minorities, and youth with disabilities), see the report of the House of Commons Standing Committee on Finance (2014).

4. Since the federal election of 1980, youth 18 to 24 have consistently had the lowest voting rates—with the exception of the 1997 federal election (Barners & Virgint, 2013).

5. The majority of the youth civic engagement research in Canada comes from large-scale surveys that investigate voter turnout. Further research is needed to better understand determinant factors for other types of civic and political engagement among youth.

REFERENCES

Barber, B. (2003). *Strong democracy: Participatory politics for a new age* (2nd ed.). Berkeley, CA: University of California Press.

Barners, A., & Virgint, E. (2013). *Youth voter turnout in Canada: Trends and issues.* Retrieved from www.lop.parl.gc.ca/content/lop/researchpublications/2010-19-e.htm#txtib

Bastedo, H., Dougherty, I., LeDuc, L., Rudny, B., & Sommers, R. (2012). *Youth, democracy and civic engagement: The "apathy is boring" surveys.* Retrieved from www.cpsa-acsp.ca/papers-2012/Leduc.pdf

Bennett, W. L. (2012). The personalization of politics: Political identity, social media, and changing patterns of participation. *The Annals of the American Academy of Political and Social Science, 644*(1), 20–38.

Bennett, W. L., Wells, C., & Rank, A. (2009). Young citizens and civic learning: Two paradigms of citizenship in the digital age. *Citizenship Studies, 13*(2), 105–120.

Bilodeau, A., & Turgeon, L. (2015). *Voter turnout among younger Canadians and visible minority Canadians: Evidence from the provincial diversity project.* Retrieved from inspirerlademocratie-inspiredemocracy.ca/rsch/yth/vot/index-eng.asp

Blais, A., & Loewen, P. (2011). *Youth electoral engagement in Canada*. Elections Canada. Retrieved from www.elections.ca/res/rec/part/youeng/yeefr-2011-eng.pdf

Campbell, D. E. (2006). What is education's impact on civic and social engagement? In R. Desjardins & T. Schuller (Eds.), *Measuring the effects of education on health and civic engagement: Proceedings of the Copenhagen Symposium* (pp. 25–126). Retrieved from www.oecd.org/education/innovation-education/37437718.pdf

Caron, C., Raby, R., Mitchell, C., Théwissen-LeBlanc, S., & Prioletta, J. (2016). From concept to data: Sleuthing social change-oriented youth voices on YouTube. *Journal of Youth Studies, 20*(1), 47–62.

Checkoway, B. (2011). What is youth participation? *Children and Youth Services Review, 33*(2), 340–345.

Cohen, C., Kahne, J., Bowyer, B., Middaugh, E., & Rogowski, J. (2012). *Participatory politics: New media and youth political action*. YPP Research Network. Retrieved from ypp.dmlcentral.net/sites/default/files/publications/Participatory_Politics_Report.pdf

Dalton, R. (2008). Citizenship norms and the expansion of political participation. *Political Studies, 56*(1), 76–98.

DePape, B., & Shaker, E. (2012). *Power of youth: Youth and community-led activism in Canada*. Ottawa: Canadian Centre for Policy Alternatives.

Earls, F. (2011). Children: From rights to citizenship. *The Annals of the American Academy of Political and Social Science, 633*(1), 6–16.

Elections Canada. (2012). *Estimation of voter turnout by age group and gender at the 2011 federal general election*. Retrieved from www.elections.ca/content.aspx?section=res&dir=rec/part/estim/41ge&document=index&lang=e

Elections Canada. (2016). *Voter turnout by age group*. Retrieved from www.elections.ca/content.aspx?section=res&dir=rec/eval/pes2015/vtsa&document=table1&lang=e

Galarneau, D., & Fecteau, E. (2014). *The ups and downs of minimum wage*. Retrieved from www.statcan.gc.ca/pub/75-006-x/2014001/article/14035-eng.htm#a7

Galarneau, D., Morissette, R., & Usalcas, J. (2013). *What has changed for young people in Canada?* Retrieved from www.statcan.gc.ca/pub/75-006-x/2013001/article/11847-eng.htm

Gélineau, F. (2013). *Who participates? A closer look at the results of the national youth survey*. Retrieved from inspirerlademocratie-inspiredemocracy.ca/rsch/yth/wpa/wpa-e.pdf

Griffin, C. (2005). Challenging assumptions about youth political participation: Critical insights from Great Britain. In J. Forbrig (Ed.), *Revisiting youth political participation: Challenges for research and democratic practice in Europe* (pp. 145–153). Strasbourg: Council of Europe.

Head, B. (2011). Why not ask them? Mapping and promoting youth participation. *Children and Youth Services Review, 33*(4), 541–547.

Held, D. (2006). *Models of democracy* (3rd ed.). Stanford, CA: Stanford University Press.

Hoffman, M., & Jamal, A. (2012). The youth and the Arab spring: Cohort differences and similarities. *Middle East Law and Governance, 4*(1), 168–188.

House of Commons Standing Committee on Finance. (2014). *Youth employment in Canada: Challenges and potential solutions: Report of the Standing Committee on Finance*. Retrieved from www.parl.gc.ca/content/hoc/Committee/412/FINA/Reports/RP6658485/finarp06/finarp06-e.pdf

Kahne, J., Lee, N., & Feezell, J. (2012). Digital media literacy education and online civic and political participation. *International Journal of Communication, 6*, 1–24.

Kennelly, J. (2009). Good citizen/bad activist: The cultural role of the state in youth activism. *Review of Education, Pedagogy, and Cultural Studies, 31*(2/3), 127–149.

Kligler-Vilenchik, N., & Shresthova, S. (2014). "Feel that you are doing something:" Participatory culture civics. *Conjunctions: Transdisciplinary Journal of Cultural Participation, 1*(1), 3–25.

Ladner, K., & McCrossan, M. (2007). *The electoral participation of Aboriginal people*. Retrieved from elections.ca/res/rec/part/paper/aboriginal/aboriginal_e.pdf

Levine, P. (2011). What do we know about civic engagement? *Liberal Education, 97*(2), 12–19.

Martin, A. (2012). *Young people and politics: Political engagement in the Anglo-American democracies*. London: Routledge.

Milbrath. L. W., & La Goel, M. (1979). *Political participation: How and why people get involved in politics*. Chicago: Rand McNally.

Molina-Girón, L. A. (2013). Educating active citizens: What roles are students expected to play in public life? In L. E. Bass, S. K. Nenga, & J. K. Taft (Eds.), *Sociological studies of children and youth: Vol. 16. Youth engagement: The civic-political lives of children and youth* (pp. 47–72). Bingley, UK: Emerald.

Morency, J., Caron-Malenfant, E., Coulombe, S., & Langlois, S. (2015). *Projections of the Aboriginal population and households in Canada, 2011 to 2031*. Retrieved from www.statcan.gc.ca/pub/91-552-x/91-552-x2015001-eng.htm

O'Neill, B. (2007). *Indifferent or just different? The political and civic engagement of young people in Canada: Charting the course of youth civic and political participation*. Ottawa: Canadian Policy Research Networks.

Public Health Agency of Canada [PHAC]. (2014). *Population-specific status report—HIV/AIDS and other sexually transmitted and blood born infections among youth in Canada*. Retrieved from www.phac-aspc.gc.ca/aids-sida/publication/ps-pd/youth-jeunes/assets/pdf/youth-jeunes-eng.pdf

Rehfeld, A. (2011). The child as democratic citizen. *The Annals of the American Academy of Political and Social Science, 633*(1), 141–166.

Reimer, M. (2012). "It's the kids who made this happen": The occupy movement as youth movement. *Jeunesse: Young People, Texts, Cultures, 4*(1), 1–14.

Rogowski, J., & Cohen, C. (2015). *Black millennials in America: Documenting the experiences, voices and political future of young Black Americans*. YPP Research Network. Retrieved from ypp.dmlcentral.net/publications/252

Rundle, M., Weinstein, E., Gardner, H., & James, C. (2015). *Doing civics in the digital age: Casual, purposeful, and strategic approaches to participatory politics*. YPP Research Network. Retrieved from ypp.dmlcentral.net/publications/238

Samara. (2013). *Lightweights? Political participation beyond the ballot box*. Retrieved from www.samaracanada.com/research/active-citizenship/lightweights

Sherrod, L., Torney-Purta, J., & Flanagan, C. (Eds.). (2010). *Handbook of research on civic engagement in youth*. Hoboken, NJ: Wiley.

Statistics Canada. (2013a). *Immigration and ethnocultural diversity in Canada: The National Household Survey, 2011*. Retrieved from www12.statcan.gc.ca/nhs-enm/2011/as-sa/99-010-x/99-010-x2011001-eng.cfm

Statistics Canada. (2013b). *Aboriginal peoples in Canada: First Nations people, Métis and Inuit. The National Household Survey, 2011*. Retrieved from www12.statcan.gc.ca/nhs-enm/2011/as-sa/99-011-x/99-011-x2011001-eng.cfm

Stolle, D., Harell, A., Pedersen, E. F., & Dufour, P. (2013). Maple spring up close: The role of self-interest and socio-economic resources for youth protest. Retrieved from profs-polisci.mcgill.ca/stolle/publications.html

Tossutti, L. (2007). *The electoral participation of ethnocultural communities*. Elections Canada. Retrieved from www.publications.gc.ca/site/eng/460014/publication.html

Tupper, J. (2014). Social media and the idle no more movement: Citizenship, activism and dissent in Canada. *Journal of Social Science Education, 13*(4), 87–94.

Turcotte, M. (2015a). *Political participation and civic engagement of youth*. Statistics Canada. Retrieved from www.statcan.gc.ca/pub/75-006-x/2015001/article/14232-eng.pdf

Turcotte, M. (2015b). *Civic engagement and political participation in Canada*. Statistics Canada. Retrieved from www.statcan.gc.ca/access_acces/alternative_alternatif.action?l=eng&loc=/pub/89-652-x/89-652-x2015006-eng.pdf

Westheimer, J., & Kahne, J. (2004). What kind of citizen? The politics of educating for democracy. *American Educational Research Journal, 41*(2), 237–269.

Young, L., & Cross, W. (2007). *A group apart: Young party members in Canada*. Ottawa: Canadian Policy Research Networks.

20 Negotiating Youth Citizenship and Belonging in a Toronto "Priority" Neighbourhood

Anuppiriya Sriskandarajah

LEARNING OBJECTIVES

- To understand the impact of socio-spatial marginalization on youth
- To hear from youth on what belonging and citizenship mean to them
- To consider some examples of how racialized young people engage in their neighbourhoods
- To understand citizenship as practice, as opposed to simply status

---

I remember going to school, my teacher in high school was like where do you live Hajda? And I then I am like I live in Chester Le, and then they used to be like, I used to teach one of the gangsters there. It is like what?! There is good people there, not everyone is a gangster.... You are stigmatized. You are, you are judged by where you live to be honest and how you look like especially where I lived in Scarborough [east-end suburb in the City of Toronto], especially there. (*Hadja, second-generation Somali female youth*)

INTRODUCTION

In line with the themes of this section this chapter centres on the importance of looking at both the material and **symbolic inequalities** that young people contend with in their everyday life. This chapter looks at how social divisions of age, race, and class, as well as spatial location intersect and inform belonging and **citizenship**. The purpose of this chapter is to foreground space as an analytic tool, as opposed to simply a backdrop, in order to look at how spatial positions inform youth citizenship practices and sense of belonging. The significance of civic incorporation to youth is what makes this research question important. The central argument of this paper is that socio-spatial inequalities in **marginalized** neighbourhoods inform a particular sense of belonging and citizenship. This paper lays out how marginalized realities cultivate particular neighbourhood identities and ways of being that inform young people's sense of civic engagement in the city: many disengage, while others engage in alternative ways. I also suggest that civic participation can possibly be increased if we widen the scope of what we consider engagement. This chapter begins with an overview of the youth citizenship literature, expands conceptualizations of citizenship from formal status to practice, examines young people's neighbourhood attachments, interrogates neighbourhood identities and ways of being that are cultivated in these spaces, and lastly looks at how these socio-spatial negotiations inform young people's citizenship practices and sense of belonging in the city.

This chapter is based on ethnographic research collected for a larger research project. The research was conducted at community centres that cater to youth from two "priority" neighbourhoods in the east end of Toronto (Scarborough), "Malvern" and "Chester Le." I focused on both youth and youth service providers. The data is a culmination of 16 months of fieldwork consisting of five days a week at the sites. For the purposes of this chapter, I focus on the neighbourhood of Malvern.

In 2014, Toronto was named the most "Youthful City" by the international Youthful Cities initiative ranking 25 global cities from a youth perspective. The news was received with much fanfare from mainstream media applauding Toronto's coveted number one spot. In addition to ranking number one overall, Toronto ranked number one for diversity. It also ranked top-five in 9 of the 16 categories. However, what received much less attention was Toronto's poor ranking for civic participation, coming in at 23 out of 25. This led me to wonder why, despite Toronto ranking high for many things including diversity, there has been a failure to ensure a sense of belonging to the politic and to engender attachment expressed in the form of citizenship. According to Siemiatycki (2011, p. 1220) the incorporation of youth in everyday aspects of "housing, employment, education, religion, media, and popular culture" are all important. However, civic incorporation carries with it the most "symbolic resonance." It is the political realm that defines the rules of society, and how we are responsible to others (Siemiatycki, 2011).

The second issue the ranking brought to the fore was the importance of space. These international rankings often foreground space, assessing which place is better for what.

So we learn on a grand scale that Toronto is a "youth friendly" space, but how does living in a cosmopolitan city actually affect young people's citizenship practices at the everyday level? How are youth differently positioned within the city, and does this influence their sense of belonging and citizenship practices? These large-scale rankings often overlook the internal lived nuances of these spaces; how youth experiences in Toronto are marked by their racial, class, gender, and sexuality positionalities. This led to the main research question I explore in this chapter: how do particular spaces inform **racialized** youth's sense of belonging and citizenship negotiations and practices?

This paper is guided by Pierre Bourdieu's (1984) key concepts of social **field** and **habitus**. I argue that marginalized or "priority" neighbourhoods act as "social fields," the settings where individuals and their social locations are positioned. These settings, or more specifically these "priority" neighbourhoods, create a particular way of being, or what Bourdieu refers to as habitus, the embodiment of dispositions (Wacquant, 2013). Habitus is formed in relation to specific social fields. In this chapter I explore how these neighbourhoods cultivate particular neighbourhood habitus that inform youth citizenship practices. I argue that by living in marginalized neighbourhoods, racialized young people cultivate their own alternative conceptions of engagement.

NEIGHBOURHOODS AND MARGINALIZATION

Omitted from the large-scale international rankings is the fact that Toronto, like all cities, is not a homogenous geographic entity. But what is of particular interest is that Toronto is often described as a "city of neighbourhoods" (Hulchanski, 2010, p. 3). Although most cosmopolitan cities are of course made up of neighbourhoods, the description is intended to indicate the especially distinctive nature of Toronto's neighbourhoods (Hulchanski, 2010, p. 3). Differences are marked along neighbourhood lines. For example, the landmark 2004 report by United Way "Poverty by Postal Code" found that poverty had become concentrated by neighbourhood areas over the last 20 years (United Way & CCSD, 2004). The report led to the creation of a taskforce, and informed the "priority neighbourhood" designation whereby 13 neighbourhoods were identified as being underserviced and resources were set aside to specifically target these neighbourhoods.

J. David Hulchanski's (2010) report a few years later found that Toronto really has three cities within its borders, demarcated by income disparities among Toronto's neighbourhoods. Neighbourhoods where incomes have increased since the 1970s are for the most part found in the city's core, close to the city's subway lines—what he refers to as City #1. City #3 is the low-income areas where neighbourhood incomes have decreased compared to the city average and they are found mostly in the northeast and northwest parts of Toronto, or what is commonly referred to as the "inner suburbs." Lower-income neighbourhoods in Toronto are mostly concentrated in the outer layers of the city, as urban development has sprawled outwards where land and housing are cheaper. White middle-class flight went either out of Toronto or towards the core. City #3 also happens to be where most of the "priority" neighbourhoods are located. The middle-income areas of the city (City #2) have shrunk from 1970 to 2005, while the high-income areas have increased slightly and the low-income areas have dramatically increased. Changes to income can be partly attributed to shifts in the economy, an increase in precarious work, difficulties new immigrants face when they look for work, and changes in government taxes and income transfers. These changes also coincide with Toronto's tremendous growth in diversity in the last few decades; in other words, social inequality in the city has taken an undeniably racial form. In 1971, 5 percent of Toronto's population was non-European, and by 2000 this number had grown to 40 percent. By 2001, 44 percent of Toronto's population was born outside Canada (Gaskell & Levin, 2011). In City #1, the number of foreign-born people declined from 35 percent to 28 percent between 1971 and 2006, whereas in City #3, the number of immigrants almost doubled in that 35-year period, from 31 percent to 61 percent (Hulchanski, 2010, p. 11). The visible minority population increased in poorer neighbourhoods, from 20 percent in 1981 to 29.5 percent in 2001 (United Way & CCSD, 2004, p. 49).

Despite the fact that researchers have found that young people are often more affected by the neighbourhoods where they live than any other demographic group (Kintrea, Bannister, & Pickering, 2010), there is little literature on these kinds of differential spatial realities and their impacts on young people's lives in the Canadian context. Space, for the most part, is taken for granted in sociological research. Researches position space as the backdrop to research, as opposed to interrogating the socio-spatial implications of place on young people. Because young people have fewer freedoms and less money than their adult counterparts, they are more rooted in their local environments (Harris, 2009). Therefore, underscoring the everyday realities that unfold in local spaces bears great sociological importance.

YOUTH CITIZENSHIP

Turner (1997, p. 5) defines "citizenship as a collection of rights and obligations which give individuals a formal legal identity" in relation to the state and each other. The youth citizenship literature can be divided into two strands, the "civic deficit" thesis and the "new engagement thesis" (Harris, Wyn, & Younes, 2007). The "civic deficit" thesis is premised on the belief that young people, due to globalization and economic restructuring, do not experience uninterrupted "structured identities and predictable life trajectories" compared to previous generations and that this in turn influences their limited sense of citizenship (Harris, Wyn, & Younes, 2007, p. 19). Studies show that because of higher feelings of alienation, youth express little interest in civic engagement through conventional political forums (Bang, 2004; Harris, Wyn, & Younes, 2010). For further discussion of youth citizenship, see L. Alison Molina-Girón, chapter 19 of this volume.

One of the reasons the "civic deficit" thesis is popular is because most research on citizenship continues to examine more institutional approaches to citizenship that focus on "political or civic culture" (Miller-Idriss, 2006, p. 543). The institutional focus of citizenship research has led to a concentration on measuring the decline of normative citizenship practices such as voting rates and membership in political parties as opposed to examinations of different ways citizens actually engage in citizenship in their everyday lives (Vromen & Collin, 2010; Lister, Smith, Middleton, & Cox, 2003).

Despite the traditional focus on formal engagement and the "deficit thesis," recently there has been a new emphasis on the "new engagement thesis" (Harris & Wyn, 2009; Harris, Wyn, & Younes, 2010; Vromen & Collin, 2010). This thesis looks at different forms of civic engagement by young people outside formal politics as partly a result of the unique realities that condition contemporary youth engagement. Scholars that subscribe to this thesis argue that the decline in interest of young people in conventional forums is due to an increasingly heightened sense of alienation from these entities. Instead, research shows young people connect with civic life in new ways that are related to their "fragmented and individualized biographies" (Harris, Wyn, & Younes, 2007, p. 19). These practices are less based on collective affiliations and take form more with the use of "information technologies and engagement with recreational and consumer choice as politics" (Harris, Wyn, & Younes, 2007, p. 19). Harris, Wyn, & Younes (2007, p. 25) argue that in light of increased fragmentation and a sense of individualism, and despite new pressures such as a lack of "predictable pathways and social safety nets," youth are not simply apathetic, as they are often presented. Young people's understanding of civic engagement involves more than participation in formal political activities. They are finding alternative ways to participate. Bang (2004) identifies a broader shift away from engagement with the state and formal sites of citizenship activities towards network-building and issues-driven civic action. If we use the same template to examine youth citizenship as is applied to adult citizenship then it is generally thought that youth are not engaged. Instead young people need to be examined in light of their difference in capacity, independence, and access to resources. It is for this reason that Lister (2003) proposes a **differentiated universalism** model to citizenship that accounts for different ways people participate as citizens. This approach requires a move past the understanding of citizenship as simply status and instead to view it as practice.

WIDENING THE SCOPE: CITIZENSHIP AS PRACTICE

To understand citizenship as only a legal status does not capture the different ways young people practise citizenship. When we depart from the conceptualization of citizenship as only a legal idea and instead consider it a social practice we see the importance of looking at social factors to understand how young people practise citizenship (Kurtz & Hankins, 2005). Feminist research on citizenship has helped move the concept of citizenship from the abstract to a lived approach. Ruth Lister (2003) found that focusing only on the formal realm of citizenship often ignores the plight of women. This outcome can lead to erroneous conclusions that women are not active citizens. However, by expanding her scope to look at citizenship as practice outside formal avenues, she found that women's assertions of citizenship were often within arenas of informal politics. Women who might feel excluded from formal avenues and who look for ways to have their voices heard might turn to alternative practices to engage. Practice is composed of both **agency** (capacity to act independently) on the part of actors and structural constraints (the level of restriction placed on options by the social role one occupies, or lack of access to resources due to one's social positionality) that limit women's participation in the formal arena. A practice-focused approach therefore allows us to rethink this relationship between individuals and the state in terms of differentiated universalism, linking a necessary universalism (whereby everyone deserves the same rights bestowed by the concept of citizenship), while accounting for the particular lived experiences of individuals (Lister, 2003). Differentiated universalism captures the tension between the universal and the particular of people's experiences. I would add that an understanding of citizenship that does not factor in local spaces also misses how people in different spaces practise citizenship. This exclusion occurs not only in lived reality but also in how citizenship is studied.

Conceptualizing citizenship as a mutually negotiated network of practices between individuals and the state foregrounds the need to research both structural constraints and agency. To work through the structure/agency dilemma I draw on Bourdieu's concepts of social fields and habitus (see also Kennelly, Stam, & Schick, chapter 5). For Bourdieu, social life is made up of social relations. These relations happen in two forms, fields and habitus. Bourdieu describes the social world as being divided into different arenas or "fields," each with its own rules and forms of capital. Each field has its own positions and practices, and it is in fields that struggles for **power** and social claims take place. For the purpose of this paper, I conceptualize the neighbourhood of Malvern as a social field.

Society is made up of social fields and each field has its particular values and "regulative principles" (Bourdieu & Wacquant, 1991, p. 17). Being from a particular neighbourhood or social field informs one's perspectives and actions. For example, if you grew up in a middle-class neighbourhood you might be more likely than others to know how to navigate university life. You might be better prepared with the skills needed for filling out applications, picking courses, and studying, all of which are required for success at university. However, if you were then displaced into a low-income, crime-ridden neighbourhood, you might not have the necessary set of skills and dispositions that would be useful to survive on the "streets"—in other words, your middle-class field would not fit easily within another neighbourhood, or field. The concept of field can help us understand why growing up in marginalized neighbourhoods might shape particular forms of engagement.

Habitus is the embodiment of the habits and dispositions that actors possess (Wacquant, 2013). Habitus can be the way the youth in my study dress, the brands they wear, the music they listen to, their mannerisms, their values, and the way they carry themselves or perform their identities. Our habitus allows us to navigate our surroundings. Habitus is the framework and resources we unconsciously draw on in our everyday lives and practices. For example, an upper-class person might be more inclined to attend an opera because they have been exposed to this form of entertainment and socialized to appreciate it from an early age. Tastes, likes, and dispositions are seen as natural or taken for granted; habitus allows us to see them as culturally informed. The concept of habitus can help us understand how marginalized neighbourhoods construct certain ways of being, interests, and values that lead young people to construct forms of citizenship that move beyond normative understandings of engagement.

YOUTH CITIZENSHIP PRACTICE IN LOCAL SPACES: SETTING THE FIELD

This chapter is based on ethnographic research that evolves throughout the study. Ethnographic research involves empirical work, especially observation with the goal of constructing a nuanced text. It allows for participation in people's daily lives for an extended period of time. Researchers watch, listen, and ask questions; they produce rich, detailed field notes that seek to describe and makes sense of social settings and relationships to produce theoretically informed, contextualized accounts (O'Reilly, 2005). One of the major fields where youth citizenship unfolds is in the youth's neighbourhood. Malvern is a priority neighbourhood with a population of about 40,000. It is made up of mixed housing, including high-rises, townhouses, public housing (also known as TCHC—Toronto Community Housing Corporation—housing), single privately owned homes, and, more recently, new builds in its northern parts. Malvern has two high schools, a secular public and a Catholic public school. It has a large recreational centre in the middle of the community and a mall that acts as a central hub. I conducted my research at a local community centre. It served youth from both nearby high schools. The two main visible minority groups that make up Malvern are South Asian (mostly Tamil) and Caribbean Black, followed by Filipino and Chinese. Visible minorities make up 87 percent of Malvern, higher than the city's average of 49 percent. The low-income rate for the city is 19 percent whereas in Malvern it is 21 percent (City of Toronto, 2014). This is the demographic context within which the local young people navigate belonging and citizenship.

The importance of neighbourhoods for the construction of belonging and citizenship is a common theme that emerged in the accounts of young people and youth service providers in my study. The micro-territories in which young people's everyday lives unfold impact their sense of belonging. First, Parekh (1999) states that in order to belong to a community, a person must feel they are a part of it, see it as their own, feel a sense of commitment to it, and enjoy a special relationship to the community (whether it is at the neighbourhood, city, or national level). Second, for a person to feel they belong to a space they must feel they are entitled to make certain claims to the space and be accepted as a valued member. Belonging involves mutuality and **reciprocity**. A person cannot feel they belong to a community unless they are accepted as valued members by both the state and civil society.

I draw on and reproduce in the chapter large excerpts from my collected data with the explicit intention of allowing marginalized young people to tell their stories through their own words, slang, metaphors, and descriptions. I want their stories to appear as they were told. At times this can read as choppy and does not flow smoothly, but as much as possible I want to stay true to the words of the youth and youth service providers. Often these quotes are fraught with the conflict, ambiguity, and at times contradictions that frame their lives.

MARGINALIZED SPACES AND NEIGHBOURHOOD ATTACHMENT

Young people in the study are aware of the negative framings of their neighbourhoods by outsiders. Youth service providers and youth recognize that their neighbourhoods more often than not fall within two dichotomized framings in dominant **discourses**. Their neighbourhoods—and more specifically the racialized bodies that occupy these spaces—are presented as either agents of violence and/or victims of violence in need of community support. MP, a service provider at the community centre, articulates these sentiments.

> I think [pause] the media creates a synopsis of Malvern based on things that have been in the media. So, um a lot of attention in the media regarding Malvern on two fronts, those form a negative perspective or positive perspective. There isn't a medium or a happy medium in terms of a general approach on how the media news corporations look at Malvern. So it is either they are writing a story about violence or they are writing a story about community support.

Yet these "positive" pieces reiterate ideas of these communities as over-reliant on public support and draw on paternalistic tropes that frame these communities as in need of government "saving." Despite recognition of negative framings by media and outsiders and perhaps in resistance to these framings, most young people contend that their neighbourhood provides a great sense of community, and demonstrate a strong attachment to their community. This position is in contradiction to hegemonic rhetoric of racialized young people as having little attachment to community life, engaging in antisocial behaviour, generally being responsible for the urban decay that plagues their neighbourhoods, and living in self-imposed social isolation. Young people, I found, take great pride in their neighbourhoods and highlight the deep sense of community that is cultivated in these spaces. Tina, a second-generation Latina youth, shared her experiences of life in Malvern and her deep sense of community:

> There is a lot of community and there is a lot of love. If anyone is sick, like everyone goes to the house and is just like do you need anything. Even if you are going to the grocery store they will ask like do you need me to pick something up for you. I feel like there is so many positive in Malvern but you just don't get to see that because of what they portray on the news. It is a nice place.

This is not to romanticize marginalized spaces. While these spaces do provide comfort and safety in familiarity, this does not come without concurrent feelings of ambivalence among many young people. For example, in Malvern the sense of safety is often accompanied by simultaneous feelings of fear that result from living in impoverished conditions. My conversation with a group of Tamil male youth captures this constant, often contradictory, negotiation that is involved in navigating life in marginalized spaces.

> *Abalsh:* I am kind of glad I grew up in Malvern.
> *Anu:* How come?
> *Abalsh:* I don't know.
> *Pragash:* Just the people that you grow up [with].
> *Abalsh:* Also like.
> *Pragash:* Like we got taught, like,
> *Abalsh:* In Malvern we are with our own people [Tamils], if we go somewhere else you would be an outcast. So I rather be here.
> *Anu:* So what do you guys like about your neighbourhood? What do you dislike?
> *Taran:* I dislike that I can't walk around at any time. You can't, you always have to watch out.
> *Abalsh:* Yea.
> *Shanthan:* You can't just freely walk around.
> *Pragash:* There is no ever 100 percent you are safe. There is always that chance that they call you over, any time of the day.
> *Anu:* Who is "they"?
> *Pragash:* Those gangs …
> *Abalsh:* At times it is pretty quiet. I don't know about other areas.
> *Pragash:* I would say the people.
> *Tharan:* The area. The parks. Since there is a lot of Tamil people you feel comfortable with them right.
> *Abalsh:* You feel safe.

Both youth and service providers attributed strong neighbourhood attachment to young people's limited opportunities outside their communities. The blame for limited opportunities was placed directly on systemic racism and lack of social resources. Marginalized young people have fewer spaces to cultivate belonging. A heightened sense of neighbourhood is often a result of lack of opportunities to identify with anything else (see similar findings in Council of Europe, 2007). Angela, a second-generation Ethiopian youth, discussed at length that when youth are marginalized from other spaces they grow deeper attachments to the only space available to them:

> I think what it comes down to is like, like when that is all you have, that is what you identify with. They can't even go out, well they can, but even for them to go out they can't … you don't have nowhere else to connect with, you will make, you connect with where you at. Because you don't have anything else.

MARGINALIZED SPACES AND NEIGHBOURHOOD HABITUS

Isolation from wider society is often found alongside a strong sense of "place attachment" (Kintrea, Bannister, & Pickering, 2010, p. 448). Strong neighbourhood identification informs specific neighbourhood habitus. Space can inform the way people act, speak, dress, the music they listen to, the way they carry themselves, their values, and what they deem is possible for people that live in that space. I found that many young people often reproduce dominant negative discourses. Despite the positive aspects of living in Malvern young people often internalize negative perceptions, experience various forms of marginalization, and engage in certain activities or forms of posturing to belong. This can often have undesirable outcomes, whether it is involvement in gang activities, drugs, violence, or other crimes. Manuela, a second-generation mixed Afro/Latina Caribbean youth, captures this contradiction. She speaks to how lovely it is to live in Malvern but how young people sometimes take on the negative perceptions of wider society, "because maybe we feel we have to live the way we are perceived." Engagement in negative activities such as gang violence and robberies, she says, is reinforced by over-policing of the area. Over-policing of certain spaces leads to overrepresentation of crime in those spaces. Residents of these spaces then become seen as prone to crime, when the higher crime statistics can partially be attributed to over-policing. This reinforces the idea that racialized youth in these marginalized spaces are criminals. When these representations are constantly reinforced, some young people might then see criminal activities as their only viable option. For Manuela, when young people perceive their neighbourhood as "bad," they feel they have to live up that identity:

Malvern is a very exciting community to live in. Malvern is like this big pot of gumbo, jambalaya that tastes so good. Malvern like any other community has its ups and downs. Its pros and cons, its challenges and its beauties and joys. Uh, Malvern is just so vibrant you know. Like it is, I love, I love walking through Malvern in the summer time and just seeing and coming into connect with everybody around the globe and it is beautiful and I love Malvern for that, I really do. Uh, one of the things that pains me about Malvern is obviously the perception of Malvern, and the subsequent police presence in Malvern uh and even us Malvernites taking that on, or embodying that because maybe we feel we have to live the way we are perceived.

Mike, a service provider, spoke to how young people had to "walk the walk" in order to survive in a neighbourhood that puts primacy on a street culture that values toughness:

I think one of the big challenges is that young people in this neighbourhood have to, even when they are good, when I say good I don't mean the kids are bad. When they are law-abiding, they are trying to strive for success they still have to walk the walk of the neighbourhood which means they have to still look like they are tough just to survive.... I think some of them feel a sense of power saying they are from Malvern, you better not mess with me because I am from Malvern. And it is. In the absence of the positive reinforcement then you take things that are left, right?

There is also a sense of power that comes from saying they are from these marginalized spaces. This is particularly important because it bestows a form of local social and cultural capital that these young people are often denied in other social fields. When you have limited access to other spaces you cultivate parallel fields where different understandings of prestige, honour, and recognition exist, or what Bourdieu calls symbolic capital. For example, many youth and service providers spoke about the great weight that was put on youth, especially boys, on appearing "tough" and "street smart," and displaying a particular type of machismo with a strong sense of territoriality. However, this can also mean there is potential for detrimental consequences. Priya, a second-generation Tamil youth, explains:

So if you are from Malvern you would be like I am from Malvern, this is sort of like I felt it was more guys always presenting I am from Malvern. Oh I am from this area so don't mess with me kind of thing.... If you are from the Scarborough neighbourhood you know, if you grew up in Scarborough from when you were little you could tell who is from Malvern and who is not. Sometimes when they say they are from Malvern I just laugh cause I know who is from Malvern and who is not.... You can also tell from their physical appearance, the way they are, you can just tell.

Priya speaks to how neighbourhood habitus is internalized and informs how young people exist in space. She can't quite articulate it in words but, as she states, "you can just tell" from the way the young people act, carry themselves, and look that they are from certain neighbourhoods. Young people recognize that different spaces produce different ways of being. Some of the service providers who work across the city also recognize how different neighbourhoods in Toronto inform different outlooks on life. For example, Esquire discussed different neighbourhoods as social fields that inform neighbourhood habitus differently, depending on which part of the city people were in:

> When you end up going along the, again Church Jarvis area, there is a certain culture you see there. If you walking past Lawrence market than you would see [different things than] when you passing Malvern mall. It is just a different outlook when you getting from that. It is just embracing that uniqueness that really tells a, that really tells an important story ... there is a uniqueness to being from Scarborough that you won't get from being anyone else. It is the same that you get from being from Jane and Finch. That you are a little bit harder, a little bit street smarter. I welcome that.... So there is some pride that comes in that, you know what I mean. That you are not able to get anywhere else. I appreciate that you are able to see a lot more being from Scarborough that you would from being from other parts of the city.

A sense of community facilitates possibilities for change and citizenship (Travis, 2013). Neighbourhoods remain important sites for youth citizenship practices (Dillabough & Kennelly, 2010; Nayak, 2003). Wacquant (2007) argues that people in marginalized areas often try to separate themselves from others in their neighbourhood, saying things like "I want to move out" or "I am not really like others here." He refers to this as "lateral denigration and mutual distanciation" (p. 68). I argue, however, that this is not always the case for racialized young people. Racialized young people take great pride in their neighbourhoods. This is often because they are not able to easily move outside their neighbourhood and have yet to live or work outside their localities. There isn't a sense of shame that is imposed on them from the outside since most of their daily encounters continue to be restricted to their immediate localities. It is when they seek out opportunities like employment that takes them outside their neighbourhood that they face the harsh realities of living in racialized neighbourhoods. Young people's claims to the city are more subject to scrutiny when they leave the confines of their neighbourhoods.

Consequently, some young people are cognizant of the divide between their neighbourhoods and outside spaces, especially the centre of the city and how it affects their dispositions. I had a particularly revealing conversation with Deque, a second-generation Ghanaian youth. Deque, who had recently graduated from high school and was working at a local pizza shop, often spoke about feeling unwelcomed when he leaves Malvern.

Deque, who is also a rapper and civically active in the city—with both roles often taking him out of his neighbourhood—feels the most social distancing when he travels to more well-off areas. This can explain why marginalized youth often do not traverse both physical and imaginary boundaries. Deque recognizes that when he ventures out of his neighbourhood, a different social field operates. There is a different habitus, a different way to exist and even to speak in these spaces. Deque, active in his community, said that he confronts this difference the most when he engages in his advocacy work:

> It is like, it is like these filters that everybody has to go through as soon as they step into a new environment. I feel that everybody should be living in on a common ground…. There is, it goes back to what I was saying about how there is so many different environments so it is like outside of Malvern there is, there is a different way you have to articulate yourself. You have to communicate differently.

Despite their alienation, and partly as a result, young people's neighbourhood habitus propels them to get involved in their communities. In the final section, I turn to how marginalized social fields inform young people's neighbourhood habitus and more specifically its implications for their citizenship practices.

SOCIO-SPATIAL NEGOTIATIONS AND CITIZENSHIP PRACTICES

Despite hegemonic ideas that racialized youth in marginalized spaces engage in destructive behaviours and act as prime catalysts of urban disorder, my time in the field revealed that young people have strong neighbourhood attachments and a desire to make their neighbourhoods better. Randy was one of the tremendously resilient youth whom I had the pleasure of working with during the course of my research. Randy had started an art program in Malvern, which I refer to as SPEAK. This organization had a mandate for civic engagement (this includes feeding the homeless initiatives, youth empowerment workshops at schools, and even endorsing political candidates). SPEAK holds weekly performances once a week in a local community hall with 50 to 100 youth; on special nights there are upwards of 200 youth in attendance from across the city, but mostly from Malvern. A typical night is filled with spoken word, rap, and song performances that speak to issues of social injustice. Through SPEAK, Randy built a grassroots community of like-minded civically engaged youth. When asked about the success of his organization, he attributed it to his neighbourhood and the social inequality he experienced living in this space. He credited his resilience and his desire for change largely to having grown up in Malvern. Randy illustrates how young people use marginalized neighbourhood identities and attachment as catalysts for citizenship practices:

SPEAK came about because, because of Malvern I would have to say. Because of Malvern and because I knew people didn't have space to express themselves, didn't have the space to come together.... I honestly, I feel when people are self-empowered and people can self-motivate themselves they will, be willing to step outside themselves and help out other people.

When citizenship is conceptualized as a particular type of neighbourhood-building, youth are more willing to become involved compared to when citizenship is defined only in relation to formal arenas of citizenship practice. Young people in my study reconceptualized traditional ideas of citizenship from formal avenues and at the level of the nation state to more local level involvement that moved past normative activities such as petitions or organized walks that might be more easily recognized as citizenship. Randy speaks about how the NDP (New Democratic Party) representative for his area was the person to really reshape how he formulated citizenship:

She said something that stood out to me. She said politics is community building and that is what you are doing. How come people don't talk about politics like that? She is the only person, and the first person to introduce it to me like that. She said politics is community building. So how come I don't see that in other politicians. Why do I just see people dress up in suits and talking about themselves?

There are many other stories like the one Randy shared. Racialized young people are engaged in marginalized neighbourhoods. Their citizenship practices often differ from traditional engagements due to socioeconomic deprivation, racism, and other forms of social inequalities. This study showed that socio-spatial marginalization—and its implications for belonging and citizenship practices—needs to be accounted for when examining young people's everyday lives.

CONCLUSION

This chapter examined how the socio-spatial realities of the social inequalities in marginalized neighbourhoods inform subjectivity, sense of belonging, and citizenship. A racialized, criminalized, marginalized existence produces a neighbourhood habitus that informs young people's sense of belonging and engagement in the city. Many disengage while others engage in subversive ways. This paper advocates centring the socio-spatial when studying young people. This is especially important when examining citizenship practices. Racialized young people who are often more restricted to their local environment than adults due to a lack of opportunities outside their community tend to engage more in their local spaces. This has implications for how youth citizenship is studied, as well as for policy initiatives. A better understanding of civic engagement and belonging allows for reform to citizenship education policies. I recommend a move from a national to a more local focus. A local focus can also inform municipal funding schemes, in recognizing which programs youth feel contribute to citizenship practices and which policies stifle these practices. A socio-spatial focus can also lead to wider understandings of how to cultivate conditions that foster a greater sense of belonging and civic engagement for racialized youth in marginalized neighbourhoods.

CHAPTER SUMMARY

Together, in this chapter, we

- Learned the importance of expanding our understanding of citizenship from one that focuses on status to one that focuses on practice.
- Saw the importance of neighbourhood space for young people's conceptions of belonging and civic engagement.
- Learned that the young people in the study often feel marginalized due to racism and a lack of social resources from other spaces in the city.
- Saw alternative ways young people engage in their neighbourhoods.

STUDY QUESTIONS

1. After reading this chapter, what would you say are some of the sociological factors that inform young people's ideas of citizenship?
2. Why do you believe that we continue to use the concept of "citizenship" as formal status, as opposed to a wider conceptualization of "citizenship" as "practice"?
3. Think of the neighbourhood you grew up in as a social field. What are some ways your neighbourhood informed your habitus?
4. You have been asked to advise the Ministry of Education to help revamp the civics education curriculum. What are some of the ways that a socio-spatial analysis of citizenship could shape that curriculum?
5. This chapter did not focus on gender. Taking into consideration socio-spatial realities, what might be some implications for a gendered analysis of youth citizenship? What are some examples?

SUGGESTED RESEARCH ASSIGNMENT

Research some policies and programs that your three levels of government have put in place to get youth involved in the community. Evaluate their strengths and potential weaknesses.

SUGGESTED FILMS/VIDEO CLIPS

Young Voices Reach Out: A Youth-to-Youth Civic Engagement Initiative
www.youtube.com/watch?v=8mfHME3Niu8
This clip looks at how a group of Lebanese youth use art as a means of civic engagement in high-conflict zones. This video shows the potential of alternative forms of citizenship to cultivate sense of belonging and camaraderie even amidst civil unrest.

Youth Civic Engagement through Social Media
www.c-span.org/video/?299457-1/youth-civic-engagement-social-media
In this clip, the Ronald Reagan Presidential Foundation and Library and the Annenberg Presidential Learning Center host a panel discussion with digital media users. The discussion is centred on the ways young people use social media for civic engagement. Topics include activism, politics, and entrepreneurship.

Arab Canadian Youth: Pursuing Responsible Citizenship to Counter Disempowerment
www.youtube.com/watch?v=3m4g_UZGhC4
This clip outlines the intersection of academia and public policy research concerning youth citizenship among Arab Canadian young people. Bessma Momani, a professor from the University of Waterloo, describes her research project and its main goals.

SUGGESTED WEBSITES

Samara Canada
www.samaracanada.com/
Samara Canada is a charity established in 2009 that is dedicated to reconnecting citizens to politics. Its goal is to increase civic engagement and create a more positive public life. The site offers research and educational programming for all segments of society, including youth.

Youthful Cities
www.youthfulcities.com/
Youthful Cities ranks cities from a youth perspective. Their purpose is to build youth networks. The goal is to gather data from a youth perspective in hopes of informing urban social policies.

United Nations Development Programme
www.undp.org/content/undp/en/home/librarypage/results/fast_facts/Fast-Facts-youth-civic-engagement-and-participation.html

The United Nations Secretary-General has made youth a priority and appointed a Special Envoy on Youth. The UN has also developed a United Nations System-wide Action Plan on Youth (Youth-SWAP). The goal is to support policies aimed at empowering youth and deepening engagement. This site illustrates the many ways youth are involved in the global context.

REFERENCES

Bang, H. P. (2004). *Everyday makers and expert citizens: Building political not social capital* (Working Paper). Australian National University. Retrieved from digitalcollections.anu.edu.au/bitstream/1885/42117/2/Henrik.pdf

Bourdieu, P. (1984). *Distinction: A social critique of the judgment of taste.* Cambridge, MA: Harvard University Press.

Bourdieu, P., & Wacquant, L. (1991). *An invitation to reflexive sociology.* Chicago: University of Chicago Press.

City of Toronto. (2014). *Neighbourhood census/NHS profile.* Retrieved from www1.toronto.ca/wps/portal/contentonly?vgnextoid=100c861b9fdb1410VgnVCM10000071d60f89RCRD

Council of Europe. (2007). *Young people from lower-income neighbourhoods: Guide to new approaches to policies.* Strasbourg Cedex, Belgium: Council of Europe Publishing.

Dillabough, J., & Kennelly, J. (2010). *Lost youth in the global city: Class, culture and the urban imaginary.* New York: Routledge.

Gaskell, J., & Levin, B. (2011). The challenges of poverty and urban education in Canada: Lessons from 2 school boards. In C. Raffo, A. Dyson, H. Gunter, D. Hall, L. Jones, & A. Kalambourka (Eds.), *Education and poverty in affluent countries* (pp. 148–160). New York: Routledge.

Harris, A. (2009). Shifting the boundaries of cultural spaces: young people and everyday multiculturalism. *Social Identities, 15*(2), 187–205.

Harris, A., & Wyn, J. (2009). Young people's politics and the micro-territories of the local. *Australian Journal of Political Science, 44*(2), 327–344.

Harris, A., Wyn, J., & Younes, S. (2007). Young people and citizenship: An everyday perspective. *Youth Studies Australia, 26*(3), 19–27.

Harris, A., Wyn, J., & Younes, S. (2010). Beyond apathetic or activist youth: "Ordinary" young people and contemporary forms of participation. *Young: Nordic Journal of Youth Research, 18*(1), 9–32.

Hulchanski, J. D. (2010). *The three cities within Toronto: Income polarization among Toronto's neighbourhoods, 1970–2005.* Toronto: Cities Centre Press.

Kintrea, K., Bannister, J., & Pickering, J. (2010). Territoriality and disadvantage among young people: An exploratory study of six British neighbourhoods. *Journal of Housing and the Built Environment, 25,* 447–465.

Kurtz, H., & Hankins, K. (2005). Guest editorial: Geographies of citizenship. *Space and Polity, 1*(1), 1–8.

Lister, R. (2003). *Citizenship: Feminist perspectives* (2nd ed.). New York: Palgrave Macmillan.

Lister, R., Smith, N., Middleton, S., & Cox, L. (2003). Young people talk about citizenship: Empirical perspectives on theoretical and political debates. *Citizenship Studies, 7*(2), 235–253.

Miller-Idriss, C. (2006). Everyday understandings of citizenship in Germany. *Citizenship Studies, 10*(5), 541–570.

Nayak, A. (2003). *Race, place and globalization: Youth cultures in a changing world.* Oxford: Berg Publishing.

O'Reilly, K. (2005). *Ethnographic methods.* New York: Routledge.

Parekh, B. (1999). Common citizenship in a multicultural society. *Round Table, 351,* 449–460.

Siemiatycki, M. (2011). Governing immigrant city: Immigrant political representation in Toronto. *American Behavioral Scientist, 55*(9), 1214–1234.

Travis, R., Jr. (2013). Rap music and the empowerment of today's youth: Evidence in everyday music listening, music therapy, and commercial rap. *Child and Adolescent Social Work Journal, 30,* 139–167.

Turner, B. S. (1997). Citizenship studies: A general theory. *Citizenship Studies, 1*(1), 5–18.

United Way of Greater Toronto & Canadian Council on Social Development (CCSD). (2004). *Poverty by postal code: The geography of neighbourhood poverty, 1981–2001.* Toronto: United Way of Greater Toronto.

Vromen, A., & Collin, P. (2010). Everyday youth participation? Contrasting views from Australian policymakers and young people. *Young: Nordic Journal of Youth Research, 18*(1), 97–112.

Wacquant, L. (2007). Territorial stigmatization in the age of advanced marginality. *Thesis Eleven, 91*(1), 66–77.

Wacquant, L. (2013). Symbolic power and group-making: On Pierre Bourdieu's reframing of class. *Journal of Classical Sociology, 13*(2), 274–291.

GLOSSARY

Aboriginal Legal Services: A Toronto-based organization dedicated to strengthening the capacity of Indigenous communities through the provision of legal services and more culturally appropriate justice alternatives. (Chapter 13)

Agency: The capacity to act in a given context in order to engage with and shape the world around us, and our subjective awareness of instigating these actions. Agency is often considered to be part of a humanist perspective in which people are understood to be rational, autonomous beings, although advocates in child and youth studies do not see rationality or autonomy as necessary prerequisites to agency; agency has also been explored and understood through post-structural and post-humanist theorizing. (Introduction and most chapters)

Ancien regime: Refers to the monarchic, aristocratic, social, and political system instituted in the Kingdom of France in the fifteenth century and lasting to the eighteenth century. This term is often synonymous with the older social and political system that was replaced by the contemporary, democratic system. (Chapter 12)

Assent: Involves children agreeing to participate in research where (1) the study takes place in a jurisdiction that only requires informed consent of adults or (2) the researchers conducting the study do not consider children capable of providing informed consent but still seek a child's agreement to participate, even if parental consent has already been provided. (Chapters 1 and 18)

Best interests of the child: The rights of the child principle embodied in Article 3 of the UN Convention on the Rights of the Child, which states that in all actions concerning children—whether undertaken by public or private institutions, courts of law, administrative authorities, or legislative bodies—the best interests of the child shall be a primary consideration. This involves evaluating and balancing all necessary elements, in specific situations and contexts, for specific individual children and youth. What exactly constitutes best interests of the child is, however, a subject of significant debate. (Introduction and chapter 17)

Biopolitics: A concept developed by Michel Foucault, biopolitics involves a rationality and technology of power that deals with the population as a political problem. Biopolitics is concerned with such markers as births and deaths, sexuality, well-being, and the composition of populations. It can be subtle in orientation and involves mechanisms like insurance and safety measures; it can also entail suppressive measures that are justified in the name of the vitality of the population. (Chapter 12)

Care: Both an activity and a state, care encompasses a wide range of activities supporting the health, well-being, and protection of someone. Care can be both formal, i.e. involving organized, paid, professional work, and informal, i.e. involving unpaid care between friends or in the home. (Introduction, chapters 6, 17, and 18)

Childhood: A social construct typically used to refer to the first 18 years of the life course, with its specific dimensions, descriptions, and context as fluid and contested depending on the author, context, policy, place, or time period in which it is used. (Introduction)

Childhood innocence: A powerful and contested idea central to the formation of modern, Western society, childhood innocence refers to children's ignorance of, or an absence of experience with, complex and difficult aspects of human existence such as death, sex, racism, colonialism, crime, and money, which are seen as adult topics. It also refers to children's love for and belief in the imaginary, such as fairies, monsters, and legendary figures such as Santa Claus in Christian cultures. Often considered a desirable characteristic of children, innocence is seen as fragile and fleeting because of children's natural growth and threats posed by dangers ranging from traumatic experiences to, for example, too much information on the Internet. The idea of childhood innocence has also been criticized for fostering ignorance and vulnerability in children. (Chapters 8 and 9)

Childhood studies: Studies that are meant to be interdisciplinary and comprehensive of the lives of children and youth aged from birth to approximately 18 years, and have often been inspired by the rights of the child, among other concepts and approaches. The term was coined in the 1990s to introduce a distinction from child psychology and developmental studies initiated at the beginning of the twentieth century. Its main objective is understanding childhood from multiple perspectives and contexts. These studies thus enable a move away from the idea of a universal childhood to instead consider a variety of childhoods. (Chapters 2, 6, 7, 10, and 18)

Cissexism: The cultural logic that essentializes and normalizes the tie between sex (biology) and gender (social and cultural) through the explicit repudiation of trans people. (Chapter 16)

Citizenship: Citizenship denotes membership, including a set of rights and responsibilities, and participation, in a polity. While seeming fixed, citizenship is a social process that regulates subjectivities and social relationships between individuals and states, and between citizens. Citizenship is premised on inclusion and exclusion, and has been frequently used in ways that exclude specific groups of people. (Introduction, chapters 3, 5, 7, 9, 15, 17, 19, and 20)

Consumer culture: An aspect of capitalism that is concerned primarily with the selling of consumer goods. Advertising, marketing, and branding are all critical activities in consumer culture. The media play an important role in consumer culture by delivering audiences to advertisers. (Chapter 10)

Creative visual methods/visual methods: Methods that offer research participants various techniques, such as drawing, photography, dramatic performance, mapping, and collage, to encourage them to express themselves and reflect on their experiences on their own terms. These techniques usually consort with some form of narrative expression. (Chapters 2 and 5)

Critical sociological empathy: Danish social researcher Hanne Warming suggests using this term as a way of trying to see how things might be seen or experienced from the point of view of study participants, in this case a child, based on critical sociological analysis of the child's experiences, as drawn from ethnographic fieldwork. (Chapter 1)

Cultural racism: A term originally coined by French scholar Etienne Balibar to refer to a form of racism that differs from biological racism, which focuses on different "types," and instead operates around an essentialist notion of culture that assumes certain inherent cultural traits. Cultural racism thus sees cultures as fundamentally different from each other. Consequently, it is assumed that we can learn to tolerate each other across cultures, but never to successfully mix. (Chapter 9)

Democratization of education: A means of both resisting the negative aspects of modernism and capitalism as well as creating an ethical platform for the advancement of positive freedom through education. (Chapter 3)

Differentiated universalism: An approach to citizenship that advocates the idea of universalism, whereby everyone deserves the same rights bestowed by citizenship, while also accounting for differences. This concept captures the tension between the universal and the particular of people's experiences. (Chapter 20)

Digital narratives: Also referred to as digital storytelling, digital narratives refers to any short form of digital media production that allows people in everyday life to share aspects of their life stories. These media productions may include video with sound, animation, pictures, audio only, or any of the other forms of electronic media that people use to tell a story or present an idea. (Chapter 4)

Disability supports: Goods and services that enable disabled persons to participate fully in society. These supports help in the removal of barriers that may prevent individuals from accessing the same economic, social, cultural, and political opportunities available to their nondisabled peers. (Chapter 6)

Discourses: Reflecting the work of French philosopher Michel Foucault, we define *discourse* as a set of concepts, statements, and logics about a particular topic that defines what is "true" and shapes how we think about and talk about something. Discourse is embedded in a social, cultural, and historical context and linked to relations of power. A discourse is not simply perpetuated by a group such as the dominant class or an individual, as many participate in producing discourses across different settings. Discourses are shared and therefore recognizable, and in this way they constrain and enable what is allowable, sayable, and doable within a given social context. Researchers and theorists often also discuss both dominant and subjugated discourses. (Introduction and most chapters)

Diversion: In the context of criminal justice, diversion refers to formal or informal intervention strategies that divert youth away from the criminal justice system. (Chapter 13)

Doing: This concept refers to turning a noun, such as rights, into a verb. For example, to describe rights as something that we do is to understand that rights are actions, or that they come into being through action and its effects. (Chapters 2, 6, and 17)

Doxa: Common sense norms associated with a particular social space or field. They are what is thinkable and sayable, basically what is taken for granted, in any given field. For example, when you started university, you had to learn what your professors' expectations were and how much help you could expect from them. Now you take these expectations for granted. (Chapter 5)

Ethnography: A research method used when a holistic approach to understanding a question is sought. It is useful in exploring emerging phenomena in everyday life and in questioning often taken-for-granted beliefs. It also serves as a means to restitute marginalized voices. Prolonged observations, interviews, and document analysis are often used as techniques to document an ethnographic exploration. (Chapters 1, 2, 4, and 16)

Extrajudicial measure: A process by which a youth in conflict with the law can be dealt with outside of the criminal justice system. A youth who admits responsibility for a crime can receive an intervention that is less formal than going to court. Extrajudicial measures typically refer to pre-charge interventions by the police. (Chapter 13)

Extrajudicial sanctions: A more formal diversion program initiated by the Crown prosecutor. (Chapter 13)

Feminism: There are many varieties of feminism, each with distinct characteristics, but overall feminist movements share the goals of gender equality at multiple levels (e.g. in education, the family, the workplace, the law, and media representations) and an end to the oppression of girls and women. Though often overlapping, different groups of feminists vary in their political goals, strategies, and analyses. For example, some feminists seek to dissect language as an avenue for the construction of women as secondary to men while others seek to address the role of institutions, such as law, capitalism, or colonialism in the domination and exploitation of women and girls. Many feminists foreground intersecting inequalities such as racism and homophobia and challenge universalist notions of gender and sexuality. Others seek to dismantle the gender binary altogether. (Chapter 15)

Field: According to Bourdieu, a field is a social space where people interact. A field could be institutions, community groups, or workplaces. For instance, as a student, you are immersed in the field of university or college. Each field has its own rules, positions, practices, values, and regulative principles, and it is in fields that struggles for power and social claims take place. (Chapters 5 and 20)

Friendship: A relationship usually examined from a psychological perspective, and regarded as a personal, voluntary, and private bond between reciprocal individuals. From a sociological approach, it generally involves close relations between nonfamilial individuals that are inherently structured by social forces, and specific time and space. (Chapters 2, 4, 7, and 14)

Gatekeepers/Institutional gatekeepers: In research, the term is used to refer to people who can grant or deny researchers access to the people, places, documents, and so forth that they wish to study. When conducting research with children, researchers may encounter multiple gatekeepers. (Chapters 1, 2, and 5)

Genocide: The intentional extermination of a large group of people, who share a specific ethnicity or nationality, with the goal of eradicating that group, ethnicity, or nationality. (Chapters 12, 17, and 18)

Habitual non-voter: An eligible voter who routinely abstains from voting at elections. (Chapter 19)

Habitus: A concept, with doxa and field, developed by social theorist Pierre Bourdieu to account for the reproduction of inequality in society. Habitus is the embodied set of dispositions, beliefs, and habits that individuals in a given social space come to share. Habitus organizes the ways in which actors perceive the world. Everyone is socialized to behave and think in certain ways; these behaviours and thoughts become second nature, thus forming, in the words of Bourdieu, your habitus: how society is embodied in you. For example, you (generally) don't wear your pyjamas to class. This is because it is a societal expectation that you dress a certain way when leaving your house. Knowing what clothes are appropriate for different situations is a social skill you have learned. When you enter undergrad, you bring distinct resources with you. These can be economic (financial), social (who you know and your network), and cultural (knowing how to behave and what to do in different social contexts). These resources form your habitus, and you have developed them over time through your experiences and your immersion in society and different fields. (Chapters 5 and 20)

Habitus, doxa, and field: Concepts developed by social theorist Pierre Bourdieu to account for the reproduction of inequality in society. The field is the social space in which people interact; the doxa of the field are the common sense norms associated with that social space; and the habitus is the embodied set of dispositions carried by individuals within the social space. (Chapters 5 and 20)

Heterosexism: The cultural logic that presumes that heterosexuality is normal and natural while concurrently producing other sexualities and desires as problematic or inferior. (Chapter 16)

Homophily: The tendency for individuals to form close social bonds with those who share similar social characteristics. (Chapter 14)

Immigrants: Persons born in one country but who have come to settle permanently in another country. (Introduction, chapters 4, 7, 9, 11, 12, 14, and 19)

Inclusive education: Inclusive education means that all students frequent, and are included in, schools in their neighbourhood. All students attend age-appropriate, regular classes and are supported to learn, participate, and contribute in all aspects of the life of the school. (Chapter 18)

Indigeneity/Indigenous: A term that is growing in use, to replace terms such as *Aboriginal* and the especially problematic term *Indian*, when referring to (status and nonstatus)

First Nations, Métis, and Inuit peoples residing in Canada. It is derived from *indigenous*, which refers to peoples and nations that descend from and identify with the original inhabitants of a territory. In other words, they have a historical continuity with precolonial societies that existed on a given territory. (Introduction, chapters 1, 4, 7, 9, 11, 12, 16, and 17)

Informed consent: In research ethics, this term refers to the act of agreeing to participate in a research project, after having evaluated relevant information and having made a decision to participate. In other words, a person must understand what the research (or other activities) will involve in order to make an informed decision to participate. In some jurisdictions, informed consent can only be provided by an adult. (Chapters 1 and 12)

Inquiry-based learning: A form of hands-on, experiential education guided by students' inquiries and involving the co-creation of meaning between students and their teacher. (Chapters 2 and 3)

Institutionalized participation: Refers to citizen public participation through conventional mechanisms to influence the political system in a direct way including voting, contacting elected officials, and being a member of a political party and/or interest group. (Chapter 19)

Interdependence: The ways in which we mutually support each other, as opposed to being either dependent or independent actors. (Chapter 6)

Language portraits: A methodological approach to the study of languages that consists of visually mapping languages in producing various types of drawings. Participants, through a dialogical approach, interpret these drawings and co-construct rich narratives in the context of language biographies. Sociolinguists such as Busch, Krumm, and Castellotti and Moore have developed language portraits in studies on language awareness, and on power and identity. (Chapter 2)

Language portrait as body mapping: Sociolinguist Brigitta Busch used the body silhouette as a metaphor and particular technique of mapping. (Chapter 2)

LGBTQ2SI/ LGBTQ+: Although not exhaustive, and ever changing and evolving, this acronym is intended on being inclusive of the plurality and divergence within queer and trans communities. It refers to lesbian, gay, bisexual, trans (transgender and transsexual), queer, two-spirited, and intersex groups, and is consciously open-ended. (Introduction, chapters 5 and 16)

Male gaze: First used by feminist critic Laura Mulvey in 1975, this term describes the ways in which the world is understood through a masculine point of view that depicts women as objects of men's visual pleasure. (Chapter 8)

Marginalization: Marginalization involves the processes that produce social inequalities and exclusions, and it is often considered a form of structural violence. Individuals and collectivities from certain social groups or categories are ignored or relegated to the sidelines of political debate, social negotiation, and economic bargaining—and kept there. Homelessness, age, gender, language, class, sexuality, race, and religion are some criteria historically used to marginalize. Marginalized groups tend to overlap; groups excluded in one arena, such as political life, tend to be excluded in other arenas, such as economic status. (Chapters 3, 4, 6, 11, 13, 16, 17, 19, and 20)

Market segmentation: A strategy used by marketers and the media to divide populations into smaller, tighter groups that are perceived as having similar attitudes, desires, and needs. This allows advertisers to specifically address smaller, more cohesive groups of consumers. Often the media participate in this division by creating content that will gather the attention of a specific audience so it can be delivered to an advertiser. For example, YTV delivers a youth audience to Canadian advertisers. (Introduction and Chapter 10)

Materiality: The concrete or material components of the world around us that shape our lives and relations; these material components are unequally distributed, reflect ideological notions about society, and produce dramatic effects and consequences in everyday lives. (Introduction)

Medical model of disability: Views disability as inherent in the individual person, and as a condition that needs to be treated. The medical model does not take into account the social, cultural, or environmental circumstances that might disable an individual, but considers the responsibility for the disability to lie entirely with the individual's body. (Chapter 18)

***Métier d'élève* (or the art of "being a student")**: A notion introduced by Swiss-born sociologist Philippe Perrenoud to illustrate the complexities of life in school. It refers to how a student constructs meaning around her/his sense of "being in school" and of scholarly work, the particular learning contexts in which s/he navigates, and the multiple, and often conflicting, pressures within the particular system in which s/he is located. The notion of *métier d'élève* inspired scholars to focus on the interplay between (school) normativity and student agency in analyzing inequalities in education. (Chapter 2)

Multicultural governmentality: Following French philosopher Michel Foucault's governmentality approach, the concept of multicultural governmentality helps us to examine multiculturalism as a particular mode of governmentality, encompassing a certain network of ideas and logic, as well as considered and rational activities, that seek to shape the mental, emotional, social, and even political conduct of racialized minority Others as well as that of the major group. (Chapter 9)

Neoliberalism: A loosely connected body of social, political, and economic ideas that embrace competition, individualism, entrepreneurialism, free enterprise, and limited state involvement in the economic and social lives of citizens. A neoliberal approach often assumes an equal playing field between individuals, thus denying structural inequality. Some recent scholarship points to the technologies of a neoliberal regime of government that free the state from responsibilities while simultaneously increasing its authoritarian control in regard to crime, border, and so on. (Introduction, chapters 4 and 15)

Net-widening: The process by which more individuals are subjected to more intrusive criminal justice sanctions than before. For diversion, this typically refers to diversion sanctions being imposed on youth who would have otherwise been left alone when diversion options were not available. (Chapter 13)

Newcomers/Newcomer immigrants: Persons who come to settle permanently in a country but have lived in the new country for less than five years. (Chapters 4, 14, 17, and 19)

Noninstitutionalized participation: Citizen public participation through more indirect, looser, and less hierarchical forms of political participation than institutionalized participation, such as participation in marches, signing of petitions, and boycotting/buycotting products. (Chapter 19)

Outdoor classroom: An outdoor learning space; often a defined area of a schoolyard, forest, field, or garden. (Chapter 3)

Participatory action research (PAR): An approach to research in and with communities that emphasizes participation *and* action. In other words, PAR seeks to understand and change aspects of life that are under study following collaboration and reflection. PAR emphasizes collective inquiry, with consequences for people's everyday practices. Some proponents of participatory research paradigms stress that besides participation of co-researchers, participatory research involves a joint process of knowledge production. (Chapter 5)

Participatory research: An approach that involves planning and conducting research *with* those whose lives are under study. (Chapter 1)

Post-feminism: The contentious term, first appearing in the 1980s, that conveys the idea that feminism has achieved its goal of gender equality and is thus no longer relevant or necessary. (Chapter 15)

Power: A mainstream understanding of power is the capacity to direct, influence, or change other people, conditions, events, or things. Such power can be held by individuals or groups, but also within systems and institutions. A more Foucauldian framework suggests that power is not something that one can have or hold, but rather a relation that produces effects. A Foucauldian approach to power seeks to identify different modes of power, their corresponding knowledge, and techniques. This approach to power sees it as circulating among all of us, both closing off possibilities for how we think but also producing possibilities. Importantly, power is productive in the sense that it constitutes us as subjects. (Introduction and most chapters)

Practical knowledge: That form of knowledge that individuals carry within them, used often without thinking. Common sense knowledge. (Chapter 5)

Presentation of self: A concept developed by sociologist Erving Goffman to refer to the way in which individuals represent themselves to others through speech, dress, ways of moving, etc. Uses the analogy of a theatre, where individuals act on a stage for a particular audience, and adjust their behaviour accordingly. (Chapter 5)

Problem-solving court: A court, sometimes in the form of diversion from the traditional judicial process, that is focused on addressing the individual's underlying needs that contributed to his or her offending. (Chapter 13)

Prosumer: A person who both produces and consumes media content. This term is used to imply that in the digital mediascape the audience no longer passively consumes content but instead actively engages with the media and produces content. Some celebrate this as a more democratic imperative of the media and some see this as a form of exploitation in which prosumers produce content for companies without compensation. (Chapter 10)

Provocation: Deliberate and thoughtful decisions made by a teacher to extend the ideas of their students and to encourage thinking, planning, and reflection. As provocateurs, teachers provide materials and direction as needed, but the students take the ideas where they want. (Chapter 3)

Qualitative research: An approach to research that starts from and centres around people's accounts of their lives and experiences rather than around preconceived concepts or variables and measurements of such variables. Associated with interpretive epistemology, qualitative research analysis focuses on understanding meanings attributed by participants to their lived experiences (Chapters 1, 3, 5, 7, 8, and 13)

Queer: An umbrella category that is used by some to bring together sexual and gendered differences within LGBTQ2SI communities. Queer is also used as a political referent that attempts to disrupt and deviate from hetero-normalcy and as an identity category used by some to refer to being nonheterosexual. (Introduction, chapters 4, 15, and 16)

Questioning: Refers to people who are questioning or coming to terms with their gender and/or sexual identity. (Chapter 16)

Racialized: Racialization refers to the complex and contested process through which "races" are socially created and treated as real and unequal. In this way, nonwhite groups come to be problematically categorized as inferior "races" in white-dominating societies, and white people come to be categorized as belonging to a superior race. Through these processes, nonwhite groups are subjected to unequal treatment, an injustice that is often invisible or appears natural to those designated as "white," resulting in some people in this category assuming the authority to name and racialize others. (Introduction, chapters 1, 5, 9, 11, 14, 16, and 20)

Rape culture: A social environment that normalizes, perpetuates, and encourages the violence of men against women. It includes the sexual double-standard, slut-shaming, rape jokes, the eroticization of rape, and the general denigration of girls and women. It is often seen to be operating in popular music, film, television, video games, pornography, and online communities. It is also perpetuated within institutions such as schools and the law when sexual harassment and assault are not taken seriously and victims are blamed. (Chapter 15)

Reciprocity: Being mutually beneficial for all people or parties involved; a dynamic that acknowledges human interdependence and interbeing. (Chapters 4, 7, 17, and 20)

Refugee: A legal designation of a person who has been forced to leave their country of origin to escape war, persecution, and/or natural disaster. (Introduction, chapters 4, 7, 12, 14, and 17)

Relational/Relationality: Refers to the idea that childhood, youth, and adulthood are best understood in terms of their interrelatedness, with a focus on how these concepts and their embodiment have been formed hierarchically and in relation to each other, while at the same time examining these constructions' concrete consequences. Can also refer to a focus on relationships as interactions between beings that are imbued with care, emotion, and meaning. (Introduction, chapters 2, 5, 6, 7, 14, and 17)

Research conversations: Mayall (2008, p. 112) employs what she calls "research conversations" where she starts with an open-ended question that children can take where they choose. For example, in one study with five- and six-year-olds, she started the research conversation with a group of children with the question "what do you like about school?" (Chapter 1)

Rights: There are various ways to think about rights. Narrowly, they can be considered legal entitlements. More broadly, they can be considered access to things that people need in order to survive, thrive, and develop to their full potential. Rights can also be understood as ways that people can behave with each other, actions they can take as part of their relationships that promote respect, engagement, and interdependence. (Introduction and most chapters)

(At) Risk: Much more than the nominal definition of the potential of gaining or losing something of value, this term is closely associated with the work of thinkers like Ulrich Beck and Anthony Giddens, who are critical of a society preoccupied with and organized around increased attention to "problems," insecurities, and hazards. In our case, we are referring to the conceptualizing of youth as both a risk to others, or a "problem," and as at-risk in that they are assumed to be living through a time of life that is fraught with uncertainty, danger, and risk-taking. (Introduction, chapters 5, 8, 14, and 15)

School effect: A concept that encapsulates the idea that each school can be viewed as an organization with a specific set of social relations, culture, mobilization capacity of its participants, and resources of its own. (Chapter 7)

Self-actualizing citizenship: This model of citizen engagement stems more from a sense of individual purpose and intent, and less from a sense of civic duty. The civic engagement of the self-actualizing citizen is interest-driven and not guided by deference to elites or formal institutions, and it favours interactive, non-hierarchical peer-to-peer activities to achieve desired goals. (Chapter 19)

Service sector: This is one of the three major economic sectors (the others being the secondary/manufacturing sector and the primary sector that includes agriculture, fishing, and resources extraction/mining). Also known as the tertiary sector of the economy, it includes work in retail, transport, distribution, and food services, as well as other service-dominated businesses. (Chapter 11)

Settlement: The long-term process through which immigrants achieve full participation in various domains of social life within their society of permanent residence. (Chapter 14)

Settler colonialism: This is a type of colonialism in which foreign peoples from a metropole, or a centre of imperial power, move en masse to a region and displace people indigenous to the land through genocide, expulsion, or segregation. The settlers take over lands, impose laws, and attempt to terminate or subordinate the Indigenous population. (Chapter 12)

Sexualization (of children/childhood): The imposition of adults' conceptualizations of sexuality and their sexual behaviour onto children, whereby children are made aware of adult sexuality, or are sexually objectified in adult ways. (Chapter 15)

Social Darwinism: The application of the biological concepts of natural selection and survival of the fittest to groups of people and societies. Certain groups and societies are viewed as further along the evolutionary scale and are therefore considered more fit. As such, it is considered acceptable that the stronger groups and societies should see their wealth and power increase, while the weaker should see their wealth and power decrease. (Chapter 12)

Social democratic model/approach (Welfare State/Policies): Danish sociologist Gøsta Esping-Andersen classified the most-developed welfare-state systems into three categories: social democratic, conservative, and liberal. The social democratic model encompasses a political, social, and economic ideology that supports economic and social interventions to promote social justice within a capitalist economy. It seeks to create policies that lead to greater democratic, egalitarian, and solidaristic outcomes. (Chapter 11)

Social deprivation: A vaguely defined term referring to a combination of structural factors that prevent people from having access to diverse aspects of their culture and society. (Chapter 11)

Social model of disability: Disability is seen as created in the interaction between individuals and their environments. The main focus of the social model of disability is the analysis of disabling barriers in society and the environment. This model strives for social change in order to improve the living conditions of people with disabilities. (Chapter 18)

Social norms: The written and unwritten rules that designate acceptable behaviours in a particular group, community, society, or culture. Individuals are expected to conform to these norms and there can be negative consequences for those who subvert them. (Chapters 8 and 10)

Social services: The institutional sector concerned with providing care and welfare to individuals in society, including housing, mental health supports, community development, and other areas. Typically either government-funded or run by not-for-profit organizations. (Chapter 5)

Sociology of childhood: A subfield in sociology that prioritizes a focus on children and childhood as valuable topics of study. Within the sociology of childhood, children are seen as subjects of interest, social actors, citizens, and credible members of society to be taken seriously in the context of their daily lives. Children's activities, whether in formal or informal situations, have become a theme of research in this field and are seen to contribute to the production and reproduction of societies. Important and early contributors in this field include British sociologists Allison James and Alan Prout and French sociologist Regine Sirota. (Introduction, chapters 1, 7, 8, 16, 17, and 18)

Structural racism: A concept that focuses on the structural relationship between the white majority and other racialized minority groups, specifically the material and symbolic inequality between the groups. It emphasizes (1) the pervasiveness of racism in society, and (2) the exclusionary effects of collectively reproducing inequality in social institutions, e.g. through systems of child welfare, education, and policing through norms, values, and practices that favour the dominant white group. (Chapter 9)

Structural violence: Structural violence refers to the often invisible systemic patterns of inequality that lead to exclusion and lack of opportunity. These patterns are often composed of ideologies, stigmas, institutional systems or language around gender, race, class, and other markers of social identity. Structural forms of violence are often "normalized" and embedded in the daily reality of people affected by them. Discussions of structural violence are important and complex because they involve accounting for individual experiences while seeking to understand those experiences within the broader social, structural, cultural, and historical contexts in which they occur. (Chapter 4)

Subject formation: The processes through which an individual's sense of self, or subjectivity, is constituted. Structural forces such as discourses and social institutions, as they intersect with people's agency, are important component of these processes. In this way, we must understand our subjectivities to be fluid, shifting, and shaped by relations of power. (Introduction)

Symbolic inequalities: Refers to less tangible types of inequality, like inequalities of status (being more highly valued than others) and power (having control over others). Symbolic inequalities tend to overlap with and reproduce material inequalities. (Introduction, chapters 9 and 20)

Systemic discrimination: Inequitable treatment and outcome(s) that are embedded within the social structure and reinforced by major institutions within society. (Chapters 13 and 17)

Trans: An umbrella category used to bring together people who are transgender, transsexual, genderqueer, gender variant, gender nonconforming, agender, etc. Trans is also used as a political referent that attempts to challenge the way sex is often conflated with gender and an identity category to refer to someone whose gender might not necessarily coincide with their biological sex. (Chapters 10, 15, and 16)

Transgender: One of various terms used to refer to people whose gender expression differs from the gender they were assigned when they were born. This gender expression can be shown in a wide variety of ways. (See **trans**; chapters 10, 15, and 16)

Transmedia franchise: *Transmedia* is the term used to define the strategy of using the elements of one story across multiple media channels, often adding new elements to the story in each platform. For example, the story of Batman has been told in comic book form, as a series of movies, through video games and through at least one television show. A transmedia story becomes a franchise when one company owns the rights to the story (or brand) and uses the story to sell content in other media platforms. An important extension of the transmedia franchise is that the company also licenses the story (brand), creating many opportunities for licensed merchandise—such as Batman toys, Batman clothes, Batman costumes, Batman pillowcases, etc. (Chapter 10)

UN Convention on the Rights of Persons with Disabilities (CRPD): The CRPD is a human rights treaty with the goal of protecting the rights and the dignity of people with disabilities. Adopted in 2006 by the UN General Assembly, it has been signed and ratified by over 160 countries. (Chapters 17 and 18)

UN Convention on the Rights of the Child: A United Nations Convention adopted in 1989, committing countries to recognizing and ensuring the protection, provision, and participation rights of children. To date, all countries have signed the Convention except for the United States. (Introduction, chapters 1, 13, 17, 18, and 19)

Victim blaming: Attitudes or actions of individuals, groups, or institutions that hold the victim of a crime responsible for the crime that was committed against them. This term has been used by feminists to critique the practice of questioning sexual assault victims by implying that they were at fault on the basis of what they were wearing or their actions during and after their assault. (Chapter 8)

White norm: The concept of white norm refers to the ideological belief in the superior position of Western economy, religion, philosophy, and polity, and the social phenomenon of holding these as the universal standard to the disadvantage of non-Western Others. (Chapter 9)

Youth: Like childhood, a social construct typically conceptualized/identified as a period in the life course that has commonly ranged from the chronological age of 13 or even younger, until 18, 24, 35, etc., depending on the context and time period. The concept is contested depending on the author, context, policy, or time period in which it is used. It has been typically used to refer to the (morphing/lengthening) period between childhood and adulthood. (Introduction and most chapters)

Youth civic engagement: A description of young people's involvement in civic and political life and its study through research. Youth civic engagement is recognized and promoted through various programs. (Chapters 5, 15, and 19)

Youth Criminal Justice Act (YCJA): The law governing Canada's youth justice system. It applies to youth between the ages of 12 and 17. (Introduction and chapter 13)

Youth Justice Committee: Empowered under s. 19 of the Youth Criminal Justice Act, a youth justice committee can convene and make recommendations on decisions related to pretrial release, sentence, and any other decision deemed appropriate by the court. (Chapter 13)